*To Thomas Winnett,
Wilderness Press founder, first author and editor,
who has hiked in the Sierra Nevada since 1934,
tersely articulated its splendors, and trained many less-coherent admirers
to ably say what paths they've taken.*

Backpacking
CALIFORNIA

Edited by Paul Backhurst

WILDERNESS PRESS
BERKELEY

FIRST EDITION May 2001
Second printing March 2002

Unless otherwise designated, all photographs placed in a particular trip are by that
trip's author
All maps by Chris Salcedo at Blue Gecko Graphics with the exception of the
locator maps by Jaan Hitt
Book design by Jaan Hitt
Cover design by Jaan Hitt

Front cover photo: Mt. Clarence King–60 Lakes Basin/Kings Canyon National Park,
CA; © 2001 David Muench
Back cover photos: Shadow Creek, CA; © 2001 Ron Felzer
Lily near Lake Ediza, CA; © 2001 Ron Felzer
Frontispiece: Lake Ediza, CA; © 2001 Ron Felzer

Library of Congress Card Catalog Number 2001017896
ISBN 0-89997-286-1

Manufactured in the United States of America

Published by **Wilderness Press**
1200 5th Street
Berkeley, CA 94710
(800) 443-7227; FAX (510) 558-1696
mail@wildernesspress.com

Contact us for a free catalog
Visit our website at **www.wildernesspress.com**

Library of Congress Cataloging-in-Publication Data

Backpacking California /edited by Paul Backhurst.--1st ed.
p. cm.
Includes bibliogaphical references and index.
ISBN 0-89997-286-1
1. Backpacking--California--Guidebooks. 2. Trails--California--Guidebooks.3. California--
Guidebooks. I. Title: California. II. Backhurst, Paul, 1951-

GV199.42.C2 B33 2001
917.9404'54--dc21   2001017896

Contents

Acknowledgments viii

Foreword x

Introduction I

How To Use This Book 4

Bears & Other Hazards 10

Backpacking Tips from the Experts 16

Backpacking Western California: *the Peninsular, Transverse, and Coast Ranges, from South to North*

The Peninsular Ranges 23

  1.   Horsethief Canyon—*Jerry Schad* 27

  2.   Noble Canyon Trail—*Jerry Schad* 31

  3.   San Mateo Canyon—*Jerry Schad* 35

  4.   San Jacinto Peak—*Jerry Schad* 39

  5.   The Great San Jacinto Traverse—*Ben Schifrin* 43

The Transverse Ranges

  6.   San Gorgonio Mountain—*Jerry Schad* 57

  7.   The San Bernardino Mountain Traverse—*Jerry Schad* 62

  8.   The Angeles Crest—Inspiration Point to Cloudburst Summit via the PCT—*Ben Schifrin* 67

  9.   Big Santa Anita Loop (Mt. Zion Loop)—*Jerry Schad* 73

  10. Devils Canyon—*Jerry Schad* 77

  11. East Fork San Gabriel River—*Jerry Schad* 81

The Coast Ranges I: The Ventana Wilderness 84

  12. Chews Ridge—China Camp to Los Padres Dam via Pine Valley—*Jeffrey Van Middlebrook* 87

The Coast Ranges II: Henry W. Coe State Park 93

  13. Poverty Flat & Los Cruzeros or Lost Spring from Coe Park Headquarters—*Jean Rusmore & Betsy Crowder* 95

  14. Redfern Pond from Hunting Hollow — *Jean Rusmore & Betsy Crowder* 103

  15. Long Ridge Open Space Preserve to Portola Redwoods & Big Basin Redwoods State Parks — *Jean Rusmore & Betsy Crowder* 110

  16. Ohlone Wilderness Regional Trail—Sunol to Del Valle —*David Weintraub* 117

  17. Sky & Coast Camps Loop from Bear Valley —*Dorothy Whitnah* 127

**The Coast Ranges III: The Klamath Mountains
& the Lost Coast** 133

18. The Lost Coast Trail, from Orchard Camp
to Usal Camp—*Matt Heid* 137
19. Canyon Creek Lakes & L Lake—*Michael White* 143
20. Tangle Blue Creek & Lake—*Michael White* 151
21. Marble Rim from Lovers Camp
via Sky High Lakes Basin—*Matt Heid* 157

Backpacking Eastern California: the Sierra Nevada
(including Lake Tahoe), Cascade Range, and Warner Mountains, from
South to North

**The Southern Sierra Nevada:
Sequoia-Kings Canyon National Parks** 161

22. Mineral King to Little Five Lakes—*Kathy Morey* 166
23. Crescent Meadow to Whitney Portal
via the High Sierra Trail—*Kathy Morey* 175
24. Lodgepole Campground to Deadman Canyon
—*Kathy Morey* 190
25. Jennie Lakes Wilderness—*Ruby Johnson Jenkins* 201
26. Hockett Meadows & Little Kern River
—*Ruby Johnson Jenkins* 206
27. Cottonwood Lakes to Upper Rock Creek—*Kathy Morey* . .215
28. Horseshoe Meadow to Whitney Portal—*Kathy Morey* 222
29. Onion Valley to Symmes Creek—*Kathy Morey* 228
30. Courtright Reservoir to Rae Lake—*Jason Winnett* 237
31. North Fork Big Pine Creek—*Andy Selters* 243
32. Lake Sabrina to Midnight Lake—*Jason Winnett* 249
33. South Lake to North Lake—*Kathy Morey* 254
34. North Lake to Humphreys Basin—*Kathy Morey* 267
35. Mosquito Flat to Pioneer Basin—*Kathy Morey* 273
36. Lake George to Deer Lakes—*Kathy Morey* 279
37. Agnew Meadows to Thousand Island Lake
—*Kathy Morey* 285
38. Agnew Meadows to Ediza Lake—*Ron Felzer* 291

The Central Sierra Nevada: Yosemite National Park 296

39. Lillian Lake Loop—*Jeffrey P. Schaffer* 299
40. Happy Isles to Merced Lake—*Jeffrey P. Schaffer* 307
41. High Sierra Camps Loop—*Jeffrey P. Schaffer* 316
42. Grand Canyon of the Tuolumne—*Jason Winnett* 329

43. Tuolumne Meadows to Happy Isles
     via John Muir Trail—*Jeffrey P. Schaffer* 340
44. Tuolumne Meadows to Nelson Lake—*Thomas Winnett* 349
45. Tuolumne Meadows to Emeric Lake—*Thomas Winnett* 353
46. Tuolumne Meadows to Agnew Meadows—*Kathy Morey* . . .359
47. 20 Lakes Basin Loop—*Kathy Morey* 369
48. Virginia Lakes to Green Creek—*Kathy Morey* 375
49. Peeler Lake—*Thomas Winnett* 381
50. Kerrick Canyon & Matterhorn Canyon Semi-loop
     via Barney & Peeler Lakes—*Ben Schifrin* 386
51. Burst Rock Trail & Crabtree Trail Loop—*Ben Schifrin* 399

The Northern Sierra Nevada: Lake Tahoe 407
52. Ebbetts Pass to Carson Pass via PCT—*Jeffrey P. Schaffer* . . .412
53. Twin Bridges to the Desolation Valley Basin
     —*Jeffrey P. Schaffer* 421
54. Glen Alpine to Half Moon Lake—*Kathy Morey* 427
55. Bayview Campground to Eagle Falls Picnic Area
     —*Kathy Morey* 431
56. Meeks Bay to Emerald Bay—*Jeffrey P. Schaffer* 439
57. Little Jamison Canyon to Grass, Rock, Jamison, & Wades
     Lakes—*Jeffrey P. Schaffer* 445

*The Cascade Range: Lassen Volcanic National Park
& Mt. Shasta* 451
58. Summit-Twin-Horseshoe-Snag Lakes Loop
     —*Jeffrey P. Schaffer* 455
59. Central Caribou Loop—*Jeffrey P. Schaffer* 463
60. The Mt. Shasta Treeline Circumnavigation
     —*Michael Zanger* 471

The Warner Mountains 476
61. Pine Creek Trail to Patterson Lake—*Jeffrey P. Schaffer* 479
62. The Summit Trail, from Pepperdine Trailhead south
     to Patterson Lake—*Jeffrey P. Schaffer* 485

Appendix 1: The Backpacks—at a Glance 489
Appendix 2: Author Bio & Bib 492
Index 500
Index of Trails 509

Acknowledgments

I want to thank everyone who contributed their favorite backpack trips, maps, photographs, area introductions, wilderness tips, plus substantial helpful criticisms and, above all else, time, to make this project possible.

Before I name specific contributors, I want to acknowledge the terrific support of the management and staff here at Wilderness Press who have shouldered collectively what has seemed at times like a heavy backpack to be borne up one of the John Muir Trail's steeper and longer ascents. Tom and Caroline Winnett championed what promised to be a hefty and time-consuming project. Mike Jones and Jannie Dresser have seen it to completion. Jaan Hitt and Larry Van Dyke have both made valuable contributions to the book's design. A bottle of Visine and many thanks to Jessica Lage for her skillful proofreading.

Most of our authors have been otherwise acknowledged (by name) for the contributions of their trips and photographs. Their photos appear in Appendix 2 with a list of their other titles from Wilderness Press. You will never know the amount of toil involved in their choosing favorite trips (even though most were previously published), updating and tailoring them for our current project, plus offering introductions and tips. I'd be remiss not to spotlight three:

Many thanks to Jerry Schad, whose various endeavors provide models of professionalism for accuracy and quality, and whose responsiveness is an editor's dream—Southern California is his province;

Kathy Morey, who contributed more trips than anyone, was exceedingly generous with her contributions and criticism. She describes her Sierra routes with admirable care and humor (which also figure into her numerous tips)—I wish I had her energy; and

It seems everyone is indebted to Jeff Schaffer, whose precise mapmaking forms the basis for many of the (necessarily) simplified trail maps in this book (see his work in our books that describe The Pacific Crest Trail)—besides his fine backpacks Jeff has supplied many of the area introductions, which offer his insights into California's geology.

Two respected Wilderness Press authors who were unable to participate actively in this project, but whose work laid foundations for many important trail switchbacks and bridges traversed by authors appearing here, are Luther Linkhart and John W. Robinson. Their books, *The Trinity Alps, Trails of the Angeles,* and *San Bernardino Mountain Trails,* have long been stalwart titles in our backlist. Material from John's books, especially, was borrowed for several of the area introductions you will find in this book. We doff our trail caps to you, gentlemen.

Besides Kathy Morey, the "backpacking bug" bit a number of other women, whose fine contributions you'll find in these pages. We are lucky to have the Point Reyes backpack of Dorothy Whitnah, who introduced several generations of hikers to the splendors of the San Francisco Bay Area. Dave

Elliott greatly assisted Dorothy in updating the trail description; here at Wilderness Press, Jannie Dresser coordinated their work and Jessica Lage skillfully edited their words. As we go to press, we mourn the passing of Dorothy Whitnah, valued author and friend, who, though ill for some time, was helpful to this project—always cheerful—until her last day. We also want to acknowledge our deep loss this year of Betsy Crowder, who had been Jean Rusmore's hiking companion and coauthor for many years on many of our popular Bay Area trail guides.

Finally, the book's maps have had a long gestation. We gratefully acknowledge National Geographic, whose TOPO! software program was generously provided to many of our authors, allowing them to accurately render their routes. Thank you, Tom Eckman! Unfortunately, with some backpacks extending 50 miles or more, we realized we couldn't deliver a single, totable volume using this format. However, the TOPO! maps did provide the basic information that Chris Salcedo, at Blue Gecko Graphics, used to design the attractive trail maps that graphically describe what these backpacks offer.

—Paul Backhurst
Berkeley, California

Read This

Hiking in the backcountry entails unavoidable risk that every hiker assumes and must be aware of and respect. The fact that a trail is described in this book is not a representation that it will be safe for you. Trails vary greatly in difficulty and in the degree of conditioning and agility you need to enjoy them safely. On some hikes, routes may have changed or conditions may have deteriorated since the descriptions were written. Also, trail conditions can change from day to day, owing to weather and other factors. A trail that is safe on a dry day or for a highly conditioned, agile, properly equipped hiker may be completely unsafe for someone else or unsafe during adverse weather.

Minimize your risks on the trail by being knowledgeable, prepared, and alert. There are a number of good books and public courses on safety in the mountains, and you should take advantage of them to increase your knowledge. Always be aware of your own limitations and of conditions existing when and where you are hiking. If conditions are dangerous, or if you are not prepared to deal with them safely, choose a different hike! It's better to have wasted a drive than to be the subject of a mountain rescue.

These warnings are not intended to scare you off the trails. Millions of people have safe and enjoyable hikes every year. However, one element of the beauty, freedom, and excitement of the wilderness is the presence of risks that do not confront us at home. When you hike, you assume those risks. They can be met safely, but only if you exercise independent judgment and common sense.

Foreword

Backcountry travelers know the exhilaration of the outdoors in a rich, personal way. Far from the crowds that fill up roadside campgrounds, these wilderness adventurers come to realize the value of solitude, and discover the strength of spirit that derives from a fundamental relationship with the mountains. They come to know the simple satisfaction of deep breaths, strong muscles, and a sound sleep under brilliant stars. But, above all, in renewing their bond with nature they rekindle that cherished spark of childlike innocence that is so easily extinguished by the pressures of city life, pressures that could account for the dramatic increase in popularity of wilderness experiences. California, offering some of the finest and most spectacular wilderness in the United States, has drawn more than its share of outdoor adventurers.

Wilderness Press has published dozens of successful guidebooks to outdoor California, and the Western and Pacific region. *Sierra North* and *Sierra South* have each sold more than one hundred thousand copies in the thirty-plus years since their first printing. Eventually, we felt that our customers would be interested in a volume that contained the best trips selected from all our California backpacking guides—from Jeff Schaffer's Tahoe-area book, from Tom Winnett's High Sierra books, from Jerry Schad's and John Robinson's southern California mountains coverage, from Ben Schifrin's Emigrant Wilderness book, from Kathy Morey's hikes-from-lodgings book, from the multi-author Pacific Crest Trail guidebook, and many more.

Surely you will find in this volume enough trips to fill your backpacking weekends and longer periods for years to come. In a time when some unusual people run the John Muir Trail end to end in four days, your leisurely pace will allow you to store up millions of memories of the finest backcountry in the entire world.

—Tom Winnett
Berkeley, California

Introduction

Although this title is the third in the Wilderness Press Backpacking series covering a state, *Backpacking California* is immediately recognizable as a different sort of book. In 1999 Doug Lorain wrote *Backpacking Oregon* to initiate this series, and followed it in 2000 with *Backpacking Washington*—two strong titles each offering more than 25 trips described in detail from one avid backpacker. By contrast, *Backpacking California* is twice the size of the previous books, and contains 62 trips from 17 different authors, whose responses to California backpacking vary widely.

Backpacking California is different because it covers California, and because we are Wilderness Press. Obviously California is an important state, for its large size and Pacific coastal orientation, crucial economic urban centers and breadbasket Great Central Valley, and for its rapidly expanding diverse population. It is also important for what changes so slowly (if at all) in human terms:

- Backbone mountains of the Sierra Nevada, which, due to their extensive white granite, John Muir called the "Range of Light";
- Enjambed to the north by the south-trending Cascade volcanoes, of which Mt. Shasta for the stream of drivers flowing north on Interstate 5 often looms, surreal, above the clouds;
- Mighty, still-unfettered rivers draining the Klamath Mountains of northwestern California, as well as the harnessed flows from the powerful watersheds of the Sierra;
- More gentle rolling coastal mountains, covered in oak woodlands, virtually unlimited fields of seasonal wildflowers, and coastal scrub, featuring deep relic pockets of tall redwoods;
- Where the Coast Ranges from the north and the Peninsular Ranges from the south intersect the lofty lateral Transverse Ranges, defining the megalopolis, California's ubiquitous fault lines compose a web of stresses that create a unique geology.

For Wilderness Press, California is home turf, where our founder Tom Winnett coauthored a new kind of guidebook geared toward the serious backpacker. Tom launched Wilderness Press with *Sierra North* in 1967 and followed it with the manuscripts of other keen backpackers, which soon became the core of our extensive list. Those younger women and men who approached Tom, perhaps tentatively, with their first manuscripts have grown older, but, in so doing, they have covered thousands of trail miles and gained a wealth of backpacking experience—even life experience, if life can be likened to a long trail.

Short of hiring them to take you to the mountains, this book offers you the most complete repository of what they've learned and the wonders they've seen.

First and foremost, the intent of this book is to offer you the best California backpacking trips, as proposed by our experienced guides and selected, according to tough, winnowing criteria, by Tom Winnett. While a few of the guides are associated closely with one part of the state—like Jerry Schad in Southern California—most have a more indiscriminant wanderlust. Taken together, our authors' trips cover much of California, but certain constellations are discernible. As you might expect, trailheads cluster thickest along the length of the Sierra Nevada; the arcing mountain rim of the southern megalopolis is also well represented; along the central coast and inner Coast Range a scattering of trips offers a sampling of terrain in these often (but not always) more-

Andy Selters

Temple Crag in the Palisades

gentle backpacks. Finally, an arrow of trips north along the Cascades bends a bow from the Lost Coast east to the Warner Mountains.

Besides fully covering the best backpacking in the state, 17 different authors provide a range of response to "guiding." Some provide the trail directions crisply with little patter, leaving you with your own response to the magnificent surroundings. Others, like Jeff Schaffer, offer a wealth of information about the underlying rocks, the soils, and the often dazzling arrays of wildflowers. Some are terse, others are expansive. Delving deeply in this book, you'll discover your favorite guides along with your favorite trips.

While ensuring the overall high standard of this book, we didn't want to crimp our proven authors' styles, for style is a direct reflection of a personality. There are standard things we look for in a guidebook but, ultimately, a response to the glorious, majestic places of the earth is a person's own. When we enter the wilderness—be it any woods or that pristine cirque, whose tarn reflects emerald green due to suspended glacial flour, below sawtooth pinnacles of stone draped with a snowfield—we soon come to recognize our little significance in the scheme of things. But we also come away with an expanded sense of limits—of freedom—borne out in the rich variety of life everywhere apparent. Finally this book is a labor of love, and of many lives respecting, honoring, and safeguarding the birthright we enjoy as Americans. Delve deeply, enjoy, and pass it on.

How To Use This Book

General Organization & Scope

You have a number of "tools" available to gain understanding of and access to the 62 premier backpack trips featured in this book. In the Table of Contents the trips are listed (roughly) south-to-north, first along the western "coastal" ranges from the Peninsular Ranges of San Diego County to the Klamath Mountains, and then from the inland Southern Sierra Nevada to the Cascade Range and the Warner Mountains. Trip numbers found there correspond to the approximate locations of trailheads on the locator map (see page 8). Then Appendix 1 provides a relative overview of what the backpacks offer—and demand of—you. You'll soon have a sense of which trips match your available time, energy, and backpacking expertise.

Short introductions precede each series of trips. These may provide background information on geology, geography, history, managing agencies, or trails of the area covered. Written by some of our best guides, the introductions should prove useful to both neophytes and experienced backpackers.

Because this book assumes you have a basic knowledge and experience of backpacking, you won't find introductory chapters covering basic techniques and what gear to buy. We invite both novices and those seeking specialty "how-to" guidance to consult these books from Wilderness Press authors:

Backpacking Basics by Thomas Winnett with Melanie Findling
Backpacking With Babies & Small Children by Goldie Silverman
Desert Hiking by Dave Ganci
Mountaineering Medicine by Fred T. Darvill, Jr., M.D.
Ticks and What You Can Do About Them by Roger Drummond, Ph.D.
Trail Safe: Averting Threatening Human Behavior in the Outdoors by Michael Bane
Wilderness Cuisine by Carole Latimer

Instead, introductory chapters offer a review of the hazards that you could face backpacking in our wilderness-rich state, plus some tips from our experienced guides. Sprinkled throughout the book are sidebars containing information pertinent to climbing Mt. Whitney, other side trips, and a few author digressions.

What's In the Trips

The Header—For each backpack the header provides standard information at a glance, using icons and short phrases. The following icons are used throughout the book to represent the configuration of your route followed by the number of days in which the average backpacker in good condition should expect to cover it:

Point-to-point route, requiring a car shuttle (two vehicles at two trailheads) or drop-off and pickup by a friend

Out-and-back route

Loop route

Semi-loop route, a substantial loop with an initial out-and-back component, like a balloon on a string

 2 *Overnight*, requiring two days
 3 *Long weekend*, requiring three days
 5–7 *Week*, requiring 5–7 days
 8–14 *Fortnight*, requiring 8–14 days

Next, the header gives you a figure in feet for total elevation gain over the course of the route versus total elevation loss: e.g., 150'/250'. (For his trips Jeff Schaffer also furnishes low and high elevations in feet for each route.) Difficulty ratings assume that you are a fit individual in reasonably good health (if you're not, either make allowances or check with your physician as to a backpack's suitability for you). Ratings are as follows:

 * *Easy*, suitable for both fit beginners or those with limited time
 ** *Moderate*, suitable for all physically fit people
 *** *Moderately Strenuous*, a trip including long length, substantial elevation gain, and/or difficult terrain
 **** *Strenuous*, a long and rugged route in an extremely remote area that may require some orienteering and bushwacking skills—suitable only for experienced backpackers in top physical condition

Next you'll find the total mileage for the entire route, whether round trip or point-to-point, regularly followed by cumulative mileages from the trailhead to specific, recommended campsites.

A list of 7.5-minute USGS quadrangles for each trip appears next, which you will frequently want to refer to on any extended backpacking trip. At a scale of 1:24,000 (2⅝"=1 mile) they provide a wealth of topographical information, which you will be grateful to have if you take the time to read them. Computer technology makes it easy to select and print them on demand at REI and other outfitters. You can also order them over the Web.

The trail map for each backpacking trip is intended to give you a graphic representation of it from trailhead to trailhead, with principal features of the route identified by name or symbol. Regard it as another tool that helps you decide which trip to take. Because of the extreme length of some of these backpacking trips, the scales of the maps vary widely. The trail maps are not intended to replace the topos.

Finally the header includes the recommended season to go, with *"early"* or *"late"* specifying respectively the first six weeks or last six weeks of:

Spring   March through May
Summer   June through August
Fall   September through November
Winter   December through February

The Backpack—The body of each trip is composed of several standard sections plus a couple of optional ones. In "Take this trip!" you can expect a brief description of the main attractions of a hike. The "Trailhead" section describes how to get there as succinctly as possible. If your trip requires a car shuttle, both trailheads are described here. Before the detailed trip description of some backpacks, there's a "Heads Up!" warning to convey quickly any brief information you may need before setting out. All trips will have a "Permits" section near the end to provide essential planning (with managing agency contact) information. Some trips will have a short, self-explanatory "Variations" paragraph following the route description, and many feature unique "Build-up/Wind-down tips," so you can make each classic backpack a fully realized, memorable vacation.

The trip description takes you by hand along your chosen backpacking route from trailhead to trailhead, according to the lights of your particular guide. While you should expect considerable variations both in style and substance with 17 different contributors, you can also expect certain conventions. You will consistently find cumulative mileages from the trailhead to important junctions or campsites appearing in parentheses, without "miles" listed (unless it's needed to avoid confusion). Similarly, elevations in feet are often provided in parentheses like this: (7614). Sometimes you will find mileage and elevation together—e.g., (23.4/7614).

One inconsistency worth noting is how mileage may be provided either in fractions using quarters, thirds, and halves, or in decimals to the tenth of a mile. It turns out that our various guides (some of whom have corrected trails incorrectly shown on the USGS topos) have strong preferences as to which notation to use. Under "Backpacking Tips" Kathy Morey makes the argument for rounding all trail mileage to the nearest quarter. In deference to their strong prefer-ences mileages appear as each author intends.

Unlike many hiking guides, we haven't tried to trim our authors' person-alities with a cookie-cutter guidebook template. In almost every case these Wilderness Press authors bring a wealth of experience to their wild places, and we are very proud of their accomplishments. If you liked a particular back-pack—the terrain encountered or the style in which it's described—see Appendix 2 to learn more about the author and the author's other books avail-able from Wilderness Press.

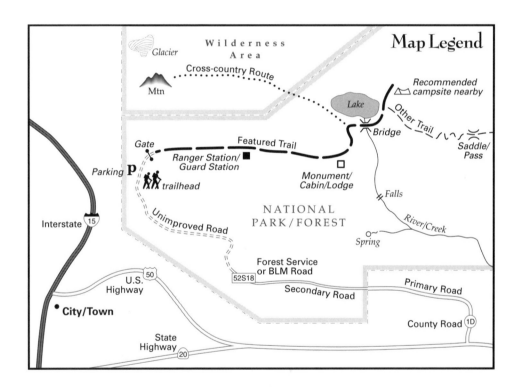

Trip locator map

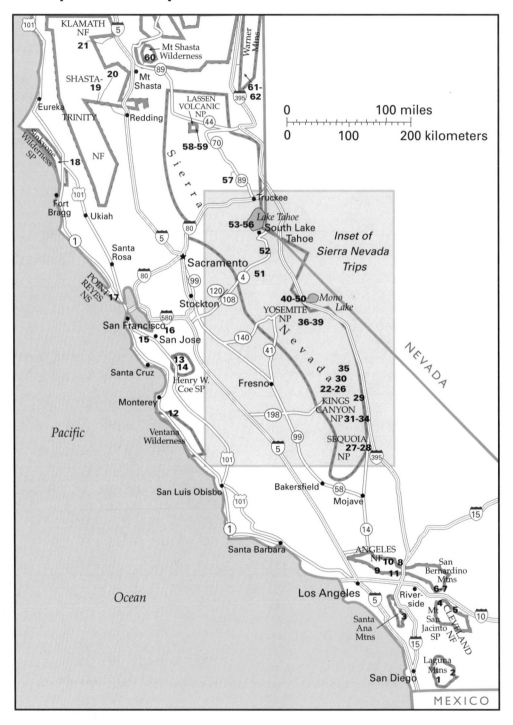

Inset of Sierra Nevada trips

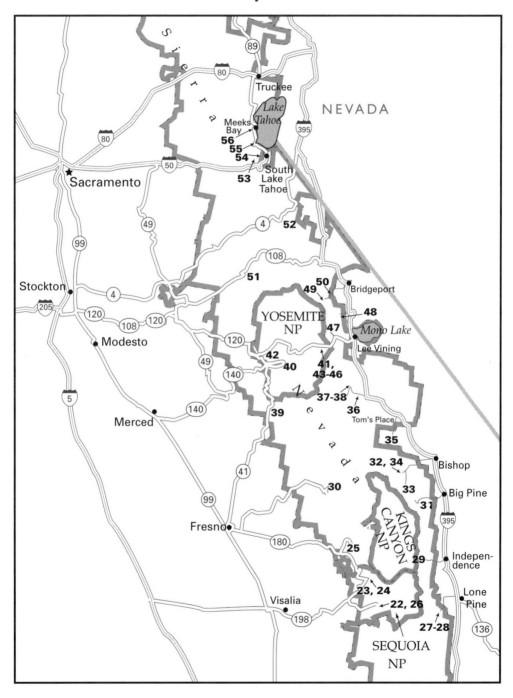

Bears & Other Hazards

This chapter briefly describes the principal hazards you could encounter in the wilderness—hazards posed by other animals, hazards to your health, plus a couple of hazards related to terrain. Recommendations on how to minimize your potential hazard to the wilderness are also made at the end of this chapter.

ANIMAL HAZARDS

American Black Bear

While the more aggressive grizzly bear is extinct in California, American black bears range over many mountain areas of the state. Their coats vary from black to light brown. Relatively unaggressive unless provoked, American black bears run and climb faster than you ever will, are immensely stronger, and are very intelligent. Their normal diet consists largely of plants. However, long ago bears learned to associate humans with easy sources of food. They will try to avoid you whenever possible; but if you do encounter bears, all they want is your food. Consider sighting one a rare privilege, and don't let the possibility of meeting a bear keep you out of the mountains.

Backcountry management policies now hold campers responsible for keeping their food away from bears. Not only can you lose your fuel for the hike, you can be fined. Once you're sure the bear won't be back for seconds, you're responsible for cleaning up the mess. You also have an ethical responsibility in the process that leads to that bear becoming a repeat-problem bear, maybe one destined for execution. Some backcountry areas where bears are a potential problem require specific methods of food protection. To learn what these requirements are, check with the agencies in charge of the areas you plan to visit.

Plan ahead. Since bears have a superb sense of smell, you should avoid taking smelly foods and fragrant toiletries. Consider camping where you can use a bear box or obtain a canister (see the tip on page 17). If you decide to counterbalance your food bags, practice the skill before you need it. (See *Backpacking Basics* for a discussion.) Cook and clean up afterward in a way that doesn't leave food residues to attract bears. Clean any food out of your gear and store it with the rest of your chow; otherwise, you could lose a pack to a bear who went for the granola bar you forgot in a side pocket. Don't take food into your tent or sleeping bag unless you want ursine company. Store your garbage just as carefully as you store your food.

Jean Rusmore

Tarantula in Henry W. Coe Park

Mountain lions (Cougars)

In recent years the mountain lion population of California has apparently burgeoned, and the human population of lion habitats has increased. While it is extremely unlikely that you will see one (because they are shy animals that try to avoid humans), in 1994 a woman runner was killed by a mountain lion in the Sierra Nevada foothills—the first such kill in over 80 years. And there have been other attacks. In case you should encounter a cougar, keep children close to you; stand up straight and try to look as large as possible; act aggressive—yell, wave your arms; do not run, crouch down, or bend over, as the animal interprets all of these as motions of prey.

Rattlesnakes

Rarely seen above 7000 feet, rattlesnakes usually live at lower elevations in a range of habitats throughout California, most commonly near riverbeds and streams. They also like warm sunny spots in the center of backcountry trails or on slabs of open granite. Their bite is rarely fatal to an adult. If you plan a trip below 6000 feet along a watercourse, you may want to carry a snakebite kit of the "Sawyer's extractor" type, which is somewhat effective if used properly within 30 minutes after the bite. Better yet, don't get bitten—watch where you place your hands and feet, and listen for the rattle. If you hear a snake rattle, stand still long enough to determine where it is, then leave in the opposite direction.

Marmots

Marmots live from about 6000 feet to 11,500 feet. Because they are curious and always hungry, and like to sun themselves on rocks in full view, you are likely to see them when hiking at this elevation range. Marmots enjoy many foods you do, including cereal and candy (especially chocolate). They may eat through a pack or tent when other entry is difficult. Marmots cannot climb trees or ropes, so you can protect your food by hanging it.

Ticks

Ticks can sometimes be a scourge of overgrown trails in the sage-scrub and chaparral country, particularly during the first warm spells of the year. If you can't avoid brushing against vegetation along the trail, be sure to check yourself for ticks frequently. Upon finding a host, a tick will usually crawl upward in search of a protected spot, where it will try to attach itself. If you can be aware of the slightest irritations on your body, you'll usually intercept ticks long before they attempt to bite. A potentially serious illness, Lyme disease, can result from the bite of the Western black-legged tick, a one-quarter-inch diameter insect.

Mosquitos

If you have no protection against mosquitoes, they can ruin your trip. Any insect repellent containing *N, N diethylmeta-toluamide* ("DEET") will keep them off. Don't buy one without it.

HEALTH HAZARDS

Altitude sickness

If you normally live at sea level and come to the Sierra to hike, it may take your body several days to acclimate. Deprived of your accustomed level of oxygen, for a few days you may experience shortness of breath even with minimal activity, severe headaches, or nausea. The best solution is to spend time at altitude before you begin your hike, and to plan an easy first day.

Giardia and *Crytosporidium*

Giardiasis can be contracted by drinking untreated water. Symptoms appear 2–3 weeks after exposure. Since giardiasis can be debilitating and difficult to treat, avoid contracting it. First, assume that all open sources of water are contaminated. Second, treat all water you take from open sources, like lakes and streams. Bringing the water to a rolling boil and keeping it there for 1–3 minutes will suffice and is easy to do when cooking. Or use filters. Because a new pest, *Cryptosporidium*, which is several times smaller than *Giardia lamblia*, has been found in the streams of the San Gabriel Mountains and is spreading throughout Southern California, your filter needs to separate at least down to 0.4 microns to be effective. While chemical treatments such as iodine tablets can be effective against *Giardia*, only boiling and filtering prevent both pests.

Hypothermia

Hypothermia refers to subnormal body temperature. More hikers die from hypothermia than from any other single agent. Caused by exposure to cold, often intensified by wet, wind, and weariness, the first symptoms of hypothermia are uncontrollable shivering and imperfect motor coordination. These are rapidly followed by loss of judgment, so that you cannot make the critical decisions to protect your life. To prevent hypothermia, stay warm: carry wind-and rain-protective clothing, and put it on as soon as you feel chilly. Stay dry; carry or wear wool or a suitable synthetic (not cotton) against your skin; bring raingear even for a short hike on an apparently sunny day. If weather conditions threaten and you are inadequately prepared, flee or hunker down. Protect yourself so you remain as warm and dry as possible.

Treat shivering at once—remember, hypothermia acts quickly and destroys judgment. Get the victim out of the wind and wet weather, replace all damp clothes with dry ones, put the victim of hypothermia's onset in a sleeping bag, and provide warm drinks. If the shivering is severe and accompanied by other symptoms, strip him or her and yourself (and a third party if possible), and warm him or her with your own bodies, tightly wrapped in a dry sleeping bag.

Lightning

Although the odds of being struck by lightning are very small, almost everyone who goes to the mountains thinks about it. An afternoon thunderstorm may come rather quickly, but not so fast that you can't get to a safer place if you are exposed. All exposed places are dangerous: a mountain peak, a mountain ridge, an open field, a boat on a lake. But so is the apparent shelter in a small cave or below an overhang.

Your safest refuge is an opening or a clump of small trees in a forest. If you are above treeline, and can get to any pinnacle, do so; take a position no farther from the pinnacle than its height. Lacking any pinnacles, position yourself atop a small boulder that is detached from bedrock. If caught in an open area, get to the lowest place that is not wet.

Wherever you position yourself, the best body stance is one that minimizes the area your body covers. You should drop to your knees and put your hands on your knees. This is because the more area your body covers, the more chance that ground currents will pass through it.

Most people believe that metal as such attracts lightning, but the actual danger from your packframe, tent poles, etc. is due to induced currents. We won't explain them here, but just be sure to get all your metal away from you as fast as you can.

If lightning does strike, there isn't much you can do except pray that someone in your party is adept at CPR—or at least adept at artificial respiration if your breathing has stopped but not your heart. It may take hours for a victim to resume breathing on his or her own. If it's your companions who are victims, attend first to those who are not moving. Those who are rolling around and moaning are at least breathing. Finally, a victim who lives should be evacuated to a hospital, because other problems often develop in lightning victims.

Poison Oak

Poison oak grows profusely throughout California below 5000 feet. It is often found on the banks of streamcourses in the form of a bush or vine, where it prefers semi-shade habitats. Quite often it's seen beside or encroaching on well-used trails. Learn to recognize its distinctive three-leafed structure, and avoid touching it with skin or clothing.

(For a more detailed description of these health hazards, and other less-common ones, please refer to *Mountaineering Medicine*.)

TERRAIN HAZARDS

Stream Crossings

In early season, crossing a river can be the most dangerous part of a back-packing trip. Later, ordinary caution will see you across safely. If a river is running high, you should cross it only if 1) the alternatives to crossing are more dangerous than crossing, 2) you have found a suitable place to ford, and 3) you use a rope. Obviously it's better to turn back than to risk an accident. If you do ford the river, it may take considerable looking around to find a suitable place. If you can find a viewpoint high above the river, you can better check out the river's width, speed and turbulence, any obstructions in it, and the nature of its bottom.

When fording a river you should:

• Wait till morning to cross if the water is at all high (the level will be at its daily low at this time);

• Unfasten the hip belt of your pack, in case you have to jettison it;

• Keep your boots on—they will protect your feet from injury and give your feet more secure placement;

• Never face downstream—the water pushing against the back of your knees could cause them to buckle;

• Move one foot only when the other is firmly placed;

• Never allow your legs to cross—keep them apart; and

• Use a stick as a support on the upstream side.

Snow bridges and Snow Cornices

Stay off them.

THE HUMAN HAZARD

Recent ecological studies confirm what naturalists have long suspected: that our very presence in the wilderness affects the plants and animals that call it home. While many valid arguments support our going there—both to learn about the life around us and for our own renewal—as we enter a new millenium we should consider carefully how to bring an attitude of the greatest respect while leaving the least impact.

Learn to go light. This is largely a matter of acquiring wilderness skills, of learning to be at home in the wilderness rather than in an elaborate camp. The "free spirits" of the mountains are those experts who appear to go anywhere under any conditions with neither encumbrances nor effort but always with complete enjoyment. John Muir, traveling along the crest of the Sierra in the 1870s with little more than his overcoat and his pockets full of biscuits, was the archetype.

Carry *all* your trash out. You packed that foil and those cans and bags when full; you can pack them out empty. Never litter or bury your trash.

Sanitation. Eliminate feces at least 100 feet from lakes, streams, trails, and campsites. Bury feces at least 6 inches deep whenever possible. Intestinal pathogens can survive for years in feces when they're buried, but burial reduces the chances that critters will come in contact with them and carry pathogens into the water. Where burial is not possible due to lack of soil or gravel, as at some places above treeline, leave feces where they will receive maximum exposure to heat, sunlight, etc., to hasten the destruction of pathogens. Help reduce the waste problem in the backcountry by packing out your used toilet paper, facial tissues, tampons, sanitary napkins, diapers, etc. Even if buried, these items may last long enough that they can be unearthed by animals or runoff and be washed into the water. It's easy to carry them out in a heavy-duty, self-sealing bag.

Protect the water from soap and other pollution. While the water is already unsafe to drink due to the likelihood of *Giardia*, don't make yourself responsible for its further degradation.

Pick "hard" campsites, sandy places that can stand the use. Camp at least 100 feet from any stream, lake, or pond, never any closer than 25 feet. Don't make campsite "improvements" like rock walls, bough beds, new firerings, tent ditches, or nails in trees.

Use a backpacking stove. It's convenient and leaves precious downed wood to replenish fragile soils and to shelter small animals. *Always* use a stove when you are above 10,000 feet or in a place where wood is scarce. If you use a stove that requires fuel cartridges, be sure to pack out all the cartridges you bring in.

Never leave any fire unattended. Many disastrous forest fires have begun from unattended campfires and campfires that weren't adequately put out. Fire is part of the natural course of events, but only when it's caused by Nature.

Respect the wildlife. Avoid trampling on nests, burrows, or other homes of animals. Observe all fishing limits. If you come across an animal, just quietly observe it. Above all, don't go near any nesting animals or their young.

Backpacking Tips from the Experts

W hat follows are some useful but by no means comprehensive tips offered by some of the backpacking guides contributing to this book. As with any group of "experts," ours will not in every case agree with each other. Choose the suggestions below that appeal to you, and test them out. Here you'll also find Kathy Morey's Eastern Sierra dining suggestions, for lucky backpackers beginning their treks from trailheads near these towns.

Not Quite Car Camping

If you sleep by your car the night before you hike, you can have all sorts of luxuries there. In addition, in a large clothes bag I put the clothes and boots I will put on in the morning, as well as books, a swimsuit, and other things I may want while I'm with the car. This bag also contains clean clothes to drive home in. While I'm hiking, it contains things that are useless in the wilderness. (TW)

Trailhead Parking Where Bears (or People) Can Be a Problem

If you have a choice, leave your most modest car at the trailhead—treasure those dings, scratches, and bird splats that make it less attractive. Park legally; if in doubt, ask the local authorities. Do your best to make the car secure. If possible, don't leave any odoriferous items (food, toiletries) in the car. Some trailheads offer sheds or bear boxes where you can cache such things while you're away. If you must leave them in the car, wrap them well in odor-containing packaging, and then hope for the best.

Don't leave any valuables in the car, either. Take money, credit cards, etc., with you. Trunks are especially easy to break into; don't imagine your stuff is safer there. If you can disable the car by removing some lightweight, indispensable widget and taking it with you (your mechanic can show you how), do so.

I cover the car's interior from dashboard to back seat or cargo bay with tarps or blankets so that passing bears can't see any tempting outlines, like those of a cooler or grocery bag, and passing thieves can't see whether there's anything worth stealing. Somebody on the other side of the parking lot has probably been dumb enough to take no precautions, thereby drawing critters and thieves to *that* car—not yours or mine. Check two or three times to be sure the car keys are safely stowed in your pack. Then roll up all the windows and lock the car. Check two or three times to be sure all the windows are closed and doors locked. Check again for your car keys.

Then walk away from the car and forget it until you are within a few yards of the trailhead on your return. It's no longer any concern of yours; it's a *trailhead worry*. You have enough to think about on the trail—*trail worries*. It's easy to forget amid the latest wave of horror stories about bears and thieves that the great majority of cars are safe at trailheads. If the worst happens—your car broken into or stolen—calm down: help is probably at hand. Your fellow backpackers, or a nearby pack station's or resort's personnel, will almost certainly help you out. (KM)

Bear Boxes & Bear Canisters

Bear boxes have proven extremely helpful in reducing food loss to bears and encounters between problem bears and people; ultimately, they limit the necessity of destroying rogue bears. Though sites with bear boxes get more heavily used than sites without boxes, you don't have to make camp right next to the bear box! Find a more secluded site a few hundred feet away, and consider the walk a pleasant way to start and end a meal. In the Sierra, only Sequoia and southern Kings Canyon National Parks offer many backcountry bear boxes. Yosemite wants you to carry a bear-resistant canister.

For its three pounds in your pack, the bear canister safeguards several days' worth of food and gives you great freedom of choice in selecting campsites in bear-troubled areas. Following a ranger's suggestion quoted in *Backpacker* magazine, I found that a canister fits best in my internal-frame pack by sitting vertically and centered on top of my sleeping bag, which is at the bottom. Cram clothes and other gear around the canister for best use of the pack space. On an external-frame pack, you have to lash the canister to the outside; the canister manufacturer makes a cover to help you secure the otherwise smooth canister.

Line the canister with a plastic bag to keep its interior cleaner. Pack a canister backward: the lunch you eat on the day you walk out should be on the very bottom, followed by that day's breakfast, followed by the preceding night's dinner, etc. As the ranger also pointed out, you don't need to put the first day's lunch and dinner in the canister, either. Press as much air as possible out of the individual packages in it. For maximum capacity—as you're initially packing—periodically stick a foot in the canister, balance on that leg, and rotate on it to tamp down the contents tightly.

Canisters aren't totally safe from bears. A canister can be lost to you and the bear if the bear rolls it into a lake. A canister rolled off rocks or a cliff may crack open. Stash your canister for the night in a spot where (you hope) the bear will have difficulty rolling it to either of these fates. (KM)

Taking a much needed break beside Sky Blue Lake

Canister/Bear-bagging Alternative

In the Sierra Nevada, where bears are most likely to be a problem, I usually camp near small cliffs, which are quite plentiful. I climb about 15 feet up one and place my food on a ledge. Bears can climb trees but not cliffs. Alternatively, I look for deep cracks and stick my food bag at least 3 feet into it, and then retrieve it with a stick or with my toes the next morning. Bears have only about a 3-foot reach. Rodents *can* be a potential problem, gnawing into your food bag and robbing you of an ounce or two of food. This has happened to me in the North Cascades of Washington, but so far, never in California. (JPS)

Backcountry Travel Classifications

Classes of cross-country/mountain-climbing travel vary principally by their need for handholds and footholds and by the degree of exposure—how easy it is to fall and how badly you'll be hurt if you do fall. Class 1 is, of course, walking on trail. Class 2 travel means there's no trail, and if you fall you're unlikely to be badly hurt. However, Class 2 also includes straightforward boulderhopping, and you can get hurt pretty badly if you fall into a hole between boulders. Class 3 means you'll need occasional handholds and/or footholds, and you'll probably be seriously injured if you fall. What I call Class 2–3 falls between Class 2 and Class 3 and includes what I consider to be some definite Class 3 hiking—particularly, the ascent from Little Five Lakes (see trip 22).

I've adapted these definitions from Steve Roper's classic *The Climber's Guide to the High Sierra* from Sierra Club Books (1976). My only quibble with Roper is that in my experience his ratings are too low: his Class 2 is apt to be my Class 3, etc. There are higher classes of climbs, including those requiring technical aids, but you won't find *me* on them and, consequently, you won't find them described in anything I write. (KM)

Backpacking Photography 1

The best tip I can give for backpacking photography is to use slow, fine-grained film (Fuji Velvia), and wait for great light, usually in the early morning or the late afternoon. For depth of field, you need to brace the camera, use a slow shutter speed, and stop the lens down to f8, f11, or f16. It helps to use a wide-angle lens. (DW)

Backpacking Photography 2

While Fuji Velvia is great for low light and for colors, I wouldn't recommend it for general use; it results in too much contrast with too narrow a latitude, which is especially a problem at high altitudes in the summer, other than at dawn and at sunset. And it is slow. The new Fuji Provia is more than twice as fast, has colors less gaudy but still saturated, and is virtually as sharp as Velvia. The new 100-speed Ektachromes are also better for general use. (AS)

Contact the Managing Agency

When you plan a backpacking trip, first contact the responsible agency for the area to learn current backcountry conditions. The person answering the phone or sitting behind the information desk may tell you which campgrounds have flush toilets, but reaching a more informed person can be difficult. Rather than visiting the ranger station on the fly and taking your chances, phone a few days before your trip, allowing an informed person the opportunity to return your call, if they are unavailable at the time. The best way to obtain the most reliable information when dealing with the US Forest Service or National Park Service is to ask for the recreational officer or a backcountry ranger. (MW)

Assessing Trail Mileage

It's hard to measure trail distances! I go by time on the trail and prefer to give distances to not more than the nearest ¼ mile. Some people count their steps; some use GPS units. Look with skepticism on hiking distances given to tenths of a mile (one decimal place). Even with a GPS unit it is virtually impossible to measure hiking distances that accurately. The error on a GPS x-y datum can be ±100 meters, or about 656 feet, which itself is an error greater than 0.1 mile (528 feet). So why do we use decimal fractions for trail distances? Decimal fractions are easy to typeset, whereas regular fractions (e.g., ½) can be a pain. Don't take tenths of a mile too seriously. (KM)

Hiking Rates and Times

Unless you are counting paces, you won't know—say after 30 minutes—if you've hiked 1.7, 1.8, or 2.2 miles. What's important is your hiking rate. Since every hike has distances between points, the hiker can do simple math to find his or her rate. If a distance to the first junction is 1.5 miles, and you reach it in 30 minutes, you are doing 3 miles per hour. If the trail gradient stays the same, you may continue to do that rate. Of course, you can tire out, and gradients rarely are the same. Plan on 2 miles per hour as an average hiking pace, although many younger hikers may do 3+ m.p.h. If your day's destination is 8 miles away, allow 4 hours. If you like long breaks, throw in an extra hour. (JPS)

Lightness, Comfort, Know-how

It's an open secret that a key to lightness, weather comfort, and versatility is layering. Without skimping on necessary equipment and clothing, bring only essential items to avoid burdening yourself with extra weight. On any off-trail adventure (such as the Mt. Shasta circumnavigation) light gaiters can make a huge difference in comfort on loose and rocky soils; map and compass skills are easy to learn and always useful. (MZ)

Pack Light or Ultralight

If your pack weighs more than 25% of your body weight, you're probably carrying too much. Reconsider what you are bringing along. For hikes up to four days, your loaded pack's initial weight should be no more than 30 pounds (ultralight hikers would say no more than 15 pounds!). (JPS)

Boots That Fit

Make sure your boots fit! A pair of three-year-old, well-broken-in boots, sized 10½, trashed my toes on one trip. Either my boots had shrunk or my feet had gotten longer in the last few years. Despite telltale warnings I wore those boots and suffered the whole time, and how many decades have I been backpacking? I just bought a pair of 11½'s and they feel great! (RF)

Boots or Running Shoes?

For about the first 20 years of my backpacking career, *every* pair of boots I hiked in gave me blisters. Since then I've used running shoes, and have not gotten blisters unless I've exceeded 20 miles a day with thousands of feet of ascent and/or descent (and virtually no reader will want to do this). Running shoes (or breathable hiking shoes), combined with a thin inner pair of socks and a thick outer pair work great. Because they breathe, they'll collect dirt. When you take trail breaks, empty the shoes. I have them loose enough that I can slip them off or on in a second. No need to tie and untie them. Consider wearing boots (with 2–3 pairs of socks) *only* if you have ankle problems or will be carrying a pack that weighs more than 25% of your body weight.

Running shoes are great when crossing streams. Take them off, then your socks. Put your shoes back on, and wade across. Shake them out, put on your socks, then your shoes. Your socks, if the proper kind, will quickly wick away the moisture, so you won't develop blisters. (JPS)

Take Regular Breaks

Whether you feel you need to or not, take a 5-minute break every 2 hours; every hour is better. Also drink; you get dehydrated. If you're wearing running shoes, empty them of whatever dirt may have gotten in them. Your feet enjoy being out of shoes for a few minutes. (Technical rock climbers do this all the time, though their shoes are very tight fitting.) (JPS)

A Fresh Sleeping Bag

On a long backpack, guarding your gear from the stench of body odor can present quite a challenge. There are a couple of ways to protect your sleeping bag from becoming a repository of bad smells. First, using a liner ensures that most of the odor is captured before reaching your bag. After several days the liner could be washed in the field if necessary. Back home, the liner will wash up with much greater ease than a sleeping bag. Second, air out your bag each morning as you attend to camp chores. (MW)

Trekking Poles

Too many hikers buy overpriced trekking poles and then carry them in their hands or else use them ineffectively, tapping the ground in front of them. Poles do nothing to take your pack's weight off your shoulders and precious little in lightening up the load on your feet. Using poles, you are forced to concentrate more on the trail and less on the natural beauty surrounding you. In certain instances using poles, you may be more likely to slip and fall where balancing with pole-free arms would prevent a slip. If you are doing expedition hiking with a 100-pound pack, then poles are a good idea, but there are no such hikes in this book. (JPS)

Shaded Campsites

Camp under trees, not in the open. Under starry skies, temperatures are colder and you can awaken with your sleeping bag saturated with dew. By camping under trees, it will stay much drier. (JPS)

Aunt Kathy's Eastern Sierra Dining Recommendations

I can't pretend to have dined at every beanery in the Eastern Sierra, not by a long shot. However, of those I have tried, here are my picks from Lone Pine on the south to Walker on the north. Note that some resorts and a few places north of Mammoth Lakes have limited hours of operation or are seasonal, usually meaning "the fishing season" from late April to late October. The fact that a restaurant *isn't* listed here means almost nothing (probably only that I haven't tried it).

In **Lone Pine** I enjoy P.J.'s. The food is good, but the real attraction is the view of Mt. Whitney at sunrise over a short stack. P.J.'s is one of the few 24-hour places in the Eastern Sierra. The Pizza Factory is also extremely popular for—what else?

In **Independence**, the Pines Café is okay on most things and has very good coleslaw.

I haven't any picks in **Big Pine** because I haven't tried anything there. Glacier Lodge west of Big Pine used to have a gourmet restaurant, but it went up in flames when the main lodge building burnt down a few years ago. Rebuilding is underway, and that includes the restaurant, so stay tuned.

In **Bishop**, the Western Kitchen offers American food that I haven't tried and Thai food that I have and like a lot. Whiskey Creek is good. Schat's makes great take-out sandwiches; on a nice day, take a Schat's sandwich across the street to Bishop City Park for a picnic. Just off Main Street, kitty-corner from the Bishop library, is the quaint little Country Kitchen, whose food is very good. There's another Pizza Factory here, too.

On the long stretch between Bishop and Mammoth Lakes, the café at Tom's Place Resort is pretty good.

Mammoth Lakes has way too many good restaurants, and I haven't tried them all yet. Among my favorites are Alpenrose (Swiss, Continental), Berger's (American—great burgers, including best veggie burger), Austria Hof (German—very good Wiener schnitzel); Breakfast Club (breakfast plus some lunch items), Café Vermeer in Schat's for lunch, The Chart House (American—killer Boston-style clam chowder), Golden Dragon (Chinese), Giovanni's (very good pizza, spaghetti), Matsu (eclectic Oriental—wonderful potstickers), The Mogul (American), Nevados (American, Continental), Nik 'n' Willie's (best pizza, sandwiches), Roberto's (Mexican), Shogun (Japanese), The Stove (American), and Whiskey Creek (American). Now you know why I gained 25 pounds after moving to Mammoth!

Near Mammoth, you'll enjoy excellent dinners at the Lakefront Restaurant at Tamarack Lodge Resort in the Lakes Basin southwest of town, and at The Restaurant at Convict Lake, associated with Convict Lake Resort on Convict Lake south of Mammoth.

In **June Lake**, Fern Creek Grill is good for lunch. I haven't tried many places in June.

My pick for "Best Burger Right on 395" in the Eastern Sierra is Mono Cone in **Lee Vining**, and they have lots of other good things there, too. The Mono Inn, on 395 just outside Lee Vining and overlooking famous Mono Lake, offers outstanding dining and views.

Just south of **Bridgeport**, Virginia Creek Settlement's café is very good; in town, so is the Bridgeport Inn's restaurant.

The nod for "Best Ribs Right on 395" goes to Mountain View Barbeque in **Walker**; they also have a great chicken sandwich, the "Texas Two-Step." And Walker Burger has very good, battered onion rings and orange freezes. (KM)

The Peninsular Ranges

The Peninsular Ranges geomorphic province consists of a series of discontinuous mountain ranges, several more than 6000 feet high. The ranges are generally parallel to one another, trend northwest-southeast, and are interspersed with high, sometimes narrow valleys. From northern extremities in the 10,000+ foot-high San Jacinto Mountains of Riverside County and in the much lower Santa Ana Mountains bordering Orange County, the Peninsular Ranges encompass the inland portion of San Diego County and stretch south to include the backbone of the entire Baja California peninsula. The Peninsular Ranges resemble the Sierra Nevada to the north in that both ranges are (in rough form) huge, tilted blocks of granitic rock, with steep east escarpments and more gradual west slopes.

The Laguna Mountains

East of the Cuyamaca Mountains—the first great moisture-wringing barrier to Pacific storms within central San Diego County—lies a second and slightly drier range, the Laguna Mountains. Here the storm clouds yield enough precipitation to support a patchwork forest of Jeffrey pines and black oaks. Farther east still, the land falls away abruptly. Below this escarpment lies the desert.

Currently, over 70 miles of hiking trails lace the Laguna Mountains, which lie within Cleveland National Forest. The biggest single share of this mileage is in the form of the Pacific Crest Trail, which passes north-south over the Laguna crest. For several miles the PCT edges close to the spectacular eastern escarpment (the "sunrise" side) of the Lagunas. Nowhere else in San Diego County can you experience so dramatically the interface between mountain and desert.

Pine Creek

The Cleveland National Forest's Pine Creek Wilderness, created in 1984, encompasses more than 13,000 acres of chaparral-covered slopes and riparian woodland south and west of the Laguna Mountains. A 15-mile stretch of Pine Valley Creek (or "Pine Creek" as many people are referring to it now) meanders through the heart of the wilderness, flanked by sloping walls up to 1000 feet high.

San Mateo Canyon

Deep within the Santa Ana Mountains, east of the Orange County metropolis and practically adjacent to the spreading suburbs of southern Riverside County, San Mateo Canyon Wilderness encompasses some 62 square miles of Cleveland National Forest territory. Some 5 million people live within 30 miles of the Wilderness, yet this proximity does not guarantee easy access. Some access roads receive little maintenance and may become impassable in wet weather. Exploring the inner sanctum of the wilderness can be both physically taxing and mentally stimulating; trails may melt into the scenery, and you can lose track of your position. But these difficulties are exactly what shields the area from casual users. If you're willing to put up with them, this is your paradise. (JS)

The San Jacinto Mountains

Of the Peninsular Ranges, only the San Jacintos and the Sierra de San Pedro Martir in Baja California rise above 10,000 feet. San Jacinto Peak is the loftiest summit in the entire 800-mile-long province. The summit country of the San Jacintos, well above the highways and byways that penetrate the lower slopes, is a sky island of delectable alpine wilderness, unsurpassed in Southern California. Under white granite summits and boulder-stacked ridges lie little hanging valleys and tapered benches lush with forest and meadow. A multitude of bubbling springs nourish icy-cold streams that tumble and cascade down the mountain. (JWR)

Jerry Schad

Sugar Pine in the San Jacinto Mountains

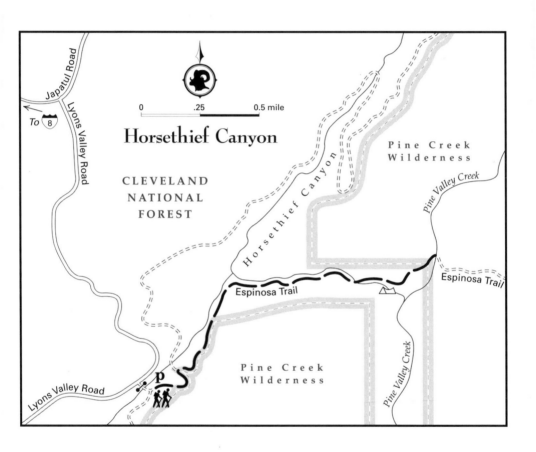

Horsethief Canyon

0   .25   0.5 mile

Japatul Road

Lyons Valley Road

To 8

CLEVELAND
NATIONAL
FOREST

Horsethief Canyon

Pine Creek
Wilderness

Pine Valley Creek

Espinosa Trail

Espinosa Trail

Lyons Valley Road

p

Pine Creek
Wilderness

Pine Valley Creek

Horsethief Canyon

—Jerry Schad

Route	Days	Elev. Gain/Loss	Difficulty	Miles
↲	2	500'/500'	*	3
		(mileage easily extended with dayhikes)		

Campsites: near Pine Valley Creek: 1.5 miles

Map: USGS 7.5-min *Barrett Lake, Viejas Mtn.*

Best season: Late fall, winter, and spring

Take this trip!

The croak of a soaring raven cracked the morning stillness as we sauntered down from our campsite to the placidly flowing creek. A groggy dragonfly flitted through a beam of sunlight. Cool air, slinking down the night-chilled slopes, caressed our faces and set aflutter the papery sycamore leaves overhead. We cupped the clear, cold water in our palms and dashed it across our heads. Ahhh! If you want this kind of escape from the city—and you want it relatively quickly—Horsethief Canyon and Pine Valley Creek, just east of San Diego, is one good place to find it.

Trailhead

Exit Interstate 8 at Tavern Road in Alpine, 25 miles east of San Diego. Go south on Tavern, which after about 3 miles becomes Japatul Road. After a total of 9.5 miles from I-8, turn right on Lyons Valley Road. Go 1.5 miles south to the Pine Creek Wilderness trailhead on the left.

TRIP DESCRIPTION

Heads Up! Operation Gatekeeper, the federal government's attempt to stave off illegal immigration from Mexico into the United States, has resulted in an eastward shift in migration patterns (from the coast to inland) and a significant increase in migrant foot traffic northward through areas such as the Pine Creek Wilderness. Although encounters between traveling migrants and hikers are rare, it's best to travel in groups in any area close to the border, and to carefully hide your camping gear when you are away from camp.

Since this trip is so short, plan to start hiking in the afternoon, and make use of the next morning, when the air is fresh, for dayhikes. From the trailhead parking lot, walk north along a gated dirt road for about 300 yards. Then veer right on the Espinosa Trail, which quickly enters the Pine Creek Wilderness. After a fast, 400-foot elevation loss, Espinosa Trail bends right (east) to follow live-oak- and sycamore-lined Horsethief Canyon. True to its name, this corral-like canyon was used in the late 1800s by horse thieves to stash stolen horses in preparation for their passage across the international border. The canyon bottom is dry about half the year, but always agreeably shaded.

After another mile and not much more descent, you'll cross over to the left side of Horsethief Canyon's little creek, a couple of minutes short of its confluence with the much wetter Pine Valley Creek. Look to your right (south) to spot a broad, grassy bench, densely shaded by coast live oaks. This is one possible wilderness camping spot in the immediate area.

Canyon Live Oaks

In the morning you can try heading a mile or two downstream (south) along the bank of Pine Valley Creek. This involves easy walking and is fine for wildflower watching in the spring season. More adventurously, you can head upstream into the Pine Valley Creek gorge. Beyond a large pool immediately upstream from the Espinosa Trail crossing is a picturesque jumble of car-sized boulders and several mini-waterfalls. Watch your step on the slippery rock, and watch out for poison oak and rattlesnakes. If the water level is too high, don't do this. Beyond the narrowest constriction, the rock-bound canyon widens somewhat and remains scenic for miles ahead.

Permits

A Wilderness Permit for overnight trips into the Pine Creek Wilderness is required. Contact Cleveland National Forest, (619) 445-8341 or (619) 445-6235. Cars parked at trailhead must display a National Forest Adventure Pass, $5 per day or $30 annually.

Cleveland National Forest Web site: **www.r5.fs.fed.us/cleveland/**

To learn about Southern California author Jerry Schad's multifarious activities and accomplishments, and for a list of his titles available from Wilderness Press, see "Author Bio & Bib" on page 492.

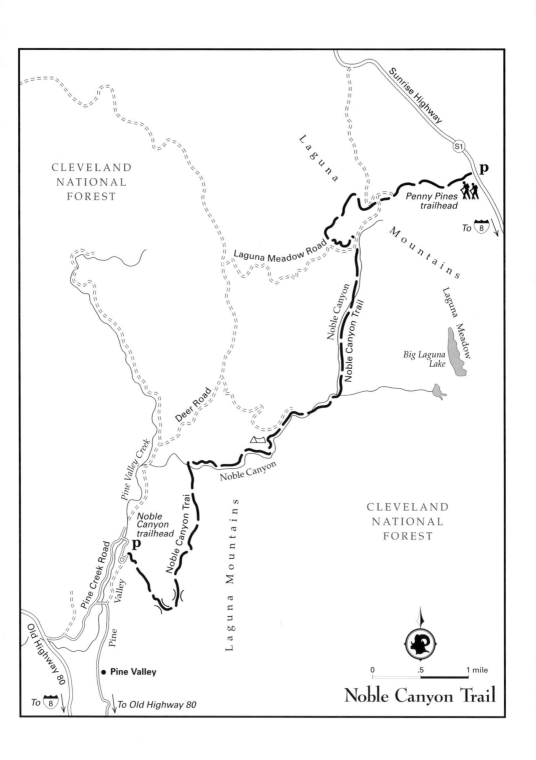

CLEVELAND
NATIONAL
FOREST

Sunrise Highway

S1

p

Penny Pines
trailhead

To 8

L a g u n a

M o u n t a i n s

Laguna Meadow Road

Laguna
Meadow

Big Laguna
Lake

Noble Canyon

Noble Canyon Trail

Deer Road

Pine Valley Creek

Noble Canyon

Noble Canyon Trail

Noble
Canyon
trailhead

p

CLEVELAND
NATIONAL
FOREST

Pine Creek Road

L a g u n a   M o u n t a i n s

Pine Valley

Old Highway 80

● Pine Valley

To 8

To Old Highway 80

0   .5   1 mile

Noble Canyon Trail

Noble Canyon Trail

—Jerry Schad

Route	Days	Elev. Gain/Loss	Difficulty	Miles
↗	2	650'/2400'	*	10

Campsites: near Noble Canyon creek: 5 miles

Map: USGS 7.5-min *Monument Peak, Mt. Laguna, Descanso*

Best season: All year

Take this trip!

Freeway-close for San Diego residents, Noble Canyon in the Laguna Mountains offers an unadulterated look at backcountry Southern California, circa 1920. Today, as suburbia leapfrogs inland from the coast, it's nice to explore an area where the wind sweeps through pine needles, raptors soar overhead, and a crystal-clear brook sings as it tumbles over stone—all with barely any hint of modern civilization. Botanically, this one-way downhill trip takes you from a zone of conifers and oaks into fragrant chaparral.

Trailhead

From San Diego, drive 40 miles east on Interstate 8 to the Sunrise Highway exit just past the Pine Valley exit. To get to the starting point, travel north on Sunrise Highway approximately 14 miles to the Penny Pines trailhead (mile 27.3 according to mile markers on Sunrise Highway). The trip's end point is the Noble Canyon trailhead on Pine Creek Road, 1 mile north of Old Highway 80 in Pine Valley.

TRIP DESCRIPTION

Heads Up! The route, officially known as the Noble Canyon National Recreation Trail, is designed for multiple uses, including mountain biking. Naturally the bikers prefer the downhill direction, and some are likely to be moving excessively fast. Seasonally, Noble Canyon is best in spring and fall. Summer midday temperatures often reach into the 90s, which is fine only if you don't hike during the middle of the day. Snow visits the canyon on several occasions during winter, but it usually melts within a few days. Water flows in the canyon bottom year-round, though it slows to a trickle before the first rains of autumn.

From the Penny Pines trailhead, head west along the marked Noble Canyon Trail. After passing through a parklike setting of Jeffrey pines, you rise a bit along the north slope of a steep hill. From there, the tree-framed view extends to the distant summits of San Jacinto Peak and San Gorgonio Mountain. Next, you descend to cross dirt roads three times, then climb and circle around the chaparral-clad north end of a north-south trending ridge. Three varieties of blooming ceanothus brighten the view in springtime.

Next, you descend into the upper reaches of Noble Canyon, where the grassy hillsides show off springtime blooms of blue-purple beard tongue, scarlet bugler, woolly blue curls, yellow monkey flower, Indian paintbrush, wallflower, white forget-me-not, wild hyacinth, yellow violet, phacelia, golden yarrow, checker, lupine, and blue flax.

The trail sidles up to the creek at about 3.0 miles, and stays beside it for the next 4 miles. Past a canopy of live oaks, black oaks, and Jeffrey pines, you emerge into a steep, sunlit section of canyon. The trail cuts through thick brush on the east wall, while on the west wall only a few hardy, drought-tolerant plants cling to outcrops of schist rock.

Back in the shade of oaks again, you soon cross a tributary creek from the east. This drains the Laguna lakes and Laguna Meadow above. Pause for a while in this shady glen, where the water flows over somber, grayish granitic rock and gathers in languid pools bedecked with sword and bracken fern. Look for nodding yellow Humboldt lilies in the late spring or early summer.

You continue within a riparian area for some distance downstream. Mixed in with the oaks, you'll discover dozens of fine California bay trees and a few scattered incense-cedars. The creek lies mostly hidden by willows and sycamores—and dense thickets of poison oak, squaw bush, wild rose, wild strawberries, and other types of water-loving vegetation. The line of trees shading the trail is narrow enough that light from the sky is freely admitted. Greens and browns—and in fall, yellows and reds—glow intensely. Impromptu campsites for small groups are fairly abundant along this middle portion of the trail, particularly on shady terraces well above the creek.

You'll pass some mining debris—the remains of a flume and the stones of a disassembled *arrastra* (a horse- or mule-drawn machine for crushing ore). This dates from gold-mining activity in the late 1800s. Next, you'll come upon the foundations of two cabins, then two more cabins in disrepair. Someone long ago planted what is now a huge cypress tree in front of the larger cabin.

Crossing to the west side of the creek, you break out of the trees and into an open area with sage scrub and chaparral vegetation. The trail contours to a point about 100 feet above the creek, then maintains this course as it bends around several small tributaries. Yucca, prickly-pear cactus, and even hedgehog cactus—normally a denizen of the desert—make appearances here. There are also excellent vernal displays of beard tongue, scarlet bugler, paintbrush, peony, wild pea, milkweed, wild onion, chia, and larkspur.

At about 7 miles, the trail switches back, crosses the Noble Canyon creek for the last time, and veers up a tributary canyon to the south. The trail joins the bed of an old jeep road, reaches a saddle after about 2 miles from Noble Canyon, then diverges from the road, going right (west) over another saddle. It then descends directly to the Noble Canyon trailhead near Pine Creek Road.

Permits

Noble Canyon does not lie within a wilderness area, nonetheless you must obtain a free remote camping permit for overnight backpacking. For information, call Cleveland National Forest, (619) 445-8341 or (619) 445-6235. Cars parked at either trailhead must display a National Forest Adventure Pass, $5 per day or $30 annually.

Cleveland National Forest Web site: **www.r5.fs.fed.us/cleveland/**

Build-up/Wind-down tips

Sunrise Highway is renowned for the way it chisels across the face of an escarpment overlooking the Anza-Borrego Desert. On the drive up Sunrise Highway toward the upper trailhead, veer off the road at the 23.8-mile mark to visit the Vista Point near Stephenson Peak, one of the better vantage points.

To learn about Southern California author Jerry Schad's multifarious activities and accomplishments, and for a list of his titles available from Wilderness Press, see "Author Bio & Bib" on page 492.

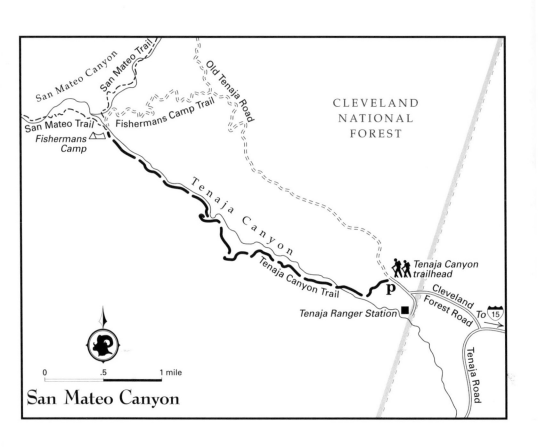

San Mateo Canyon

San Mateo Canyon

San Mateo Trail

Old Tenaja Road

Fishermans Camp Trail

San Mateo Trail

Fishermans
Camp

CLEVELAND
NATIONAL
FOREST

Tenaja Canyon

Tenaja Canyon Trail

Tenaja Canyon
trailhead

p

Cleveland
Forest Road

To 15

Tenaja Ranger Station

Tenaja Road

0   .5   1 mile

San Mateo Canyon

3

San Mateo Canyon

—Jerry Schad

Route	Days	Elev. Gain/Loss	Difficulty	Miles
↗	2	1300'/1300'	*	7.4
		(mileage easily extended with dayhikes)		

Campsites: Fishermans Camp: 3.7 miles

Map: USGS 7.5-min *Wildomar, Sitton Peak*

Best season: Late fall, winter, and spring

Take this trip!

Amid a chorus of droning bees, you hear the soft melody of water sliding over polished rock and your own crackling footsteps on brittle leaves. A fat gopher snake lounging by the creek stiffens at your approach. Tiny fish dart about in the stream eddies, while a pond turtle launches itself from a rock shelf, deftly slicing through the surface of a crystalline pool. You're in the San Mateo Canyon Wilderness—a roadless area almost completely surrounded by the Southern California megalopolis. This is a perfect destination for a cool-season weekend escape, no more than a 2-hour drive from any part of greater Los Angeles or San Diego.

Trailhead

From Interstate 15 in Murrieta, exit at Clinton Keith Road. Go south on Clinton Keith for 5 miles to a sharp rightward curve. Continue west on the road ahead, which is signed Tenaja Road. After 1.7 miles turn right at a marked intersection, staying on Tenaja Road. Continue west for another 4.2 miles, then go right on a narrow paved road signed. Proceed another mile to the Tenaja Canyon trailhead parking area, just north of Tenaja Ranger Station.

TRIP DESCRIPTION

Heads Up! The primary appeal of this trip is the presence of flowing water, so wait until a substantial amount of rain has fallen—December or January in most years. The landscape starts to wither in May, and summers are unpleasantly hot and dry. San Mateo Canyon is prime habitat for rattlesnakes, which are most likely to be seen during the onset of warm weather in April and May. Also, keep an eye out for steelhead trout swimming up San Mateo Canyon's creek to spawn. Recent sightings by people fishing near the mouth of the canyon suggest the revival of a southern subspecies of steelhead formerly thought to be extinct. Please report any such sighting to a ranger.

The backpack to Fishermans Camp is downhill on the way in, uphill on the way out. From the Tenaja Canyon trailhead, start downhill on the trail going west. A few minutes' descent takes you to the shady bowels of V-shaped Tenaja Canyon, where huge coast live oaks and pale-barked sycamores frame a limpid, rock-dimpled stream. Mostly the trail ahead meanders alongside the stream, but for the canyon's middle stretch it carves its way across the chaparral-blanketed south wall, 200–400 feet above the canyon bottom. As you descend, notice Tenaja Canyon's obviously linear alignment. You're following a northwest-trending rift called the Tenaja fault.

After 3.7 miles of general descent, you reach Fishermans Camp, a former drive-in campground once accessible by many miles of bad road. Its name hints of the fishing opportunities afforded by the nearby San Mateo Canyon creek during and after the rainy season. Today the site, distinguished by its parklike setting amid a live-oak grove, serves as a fine, uncrowded wilderness campsite. On quiet winter nights, cold air drains off the nearby slopes, and you may wake up to morning frost.

At Fishermans Camp, three other routes diverge. Fishermans Camp Trail (a remnant of the old road to the camp) travels east uphill to an intersection with the unpaved Old Tenaja Road. The more scenic upper San Mateo Canyon Trail, a narrow footpath, follows the canyon bottom upstream to Old Tenaja Road. In the downstream direction, the superbly scenic lower San Mateo Canyon Trail travels more and more indistinctly for several miles toward the Camp Pendleton marine base (no entry allowed past the east border of the base). By dayhiking 2 or 3 miles downstream, you'll get to enjoy the most agreeable and remote parts of San Mateo Canyon.

Permits

A Wilderness Permit is required for all overnight visits in the San Mateo Canyon Wilderness. Contact Cleveland National Forest's Trabuco Ranger District in Corona, (909) 736-1811. All cars parked at the trailhead must display a National Forest Adventure Pass, $5 daily or $30 annually.

Cleveland National Forest Web site: **www.r5.fs.fed.us/cleveland/**

Build-up/Wind-down tips

In March or April after a wet rainy season, don't miss a visit to the Nature Conservancy's Santa Rosa Plateau Ecological Reserve on your way in or out. The reserve's main entrance is on the east side of Clinton Keith Road, 4 miles south of Interstate 15. A 39-acre vernal pool on the property is one the state's largest, and springtime displays of wildflowers here can be eye-popping.

To learn about Southern California author Jerry Schad's multifarious activities and accomplishments, and for a list of his titles available from Wilderness Press, see "Author Bio & Bib" on page 492.

Rosy Boa

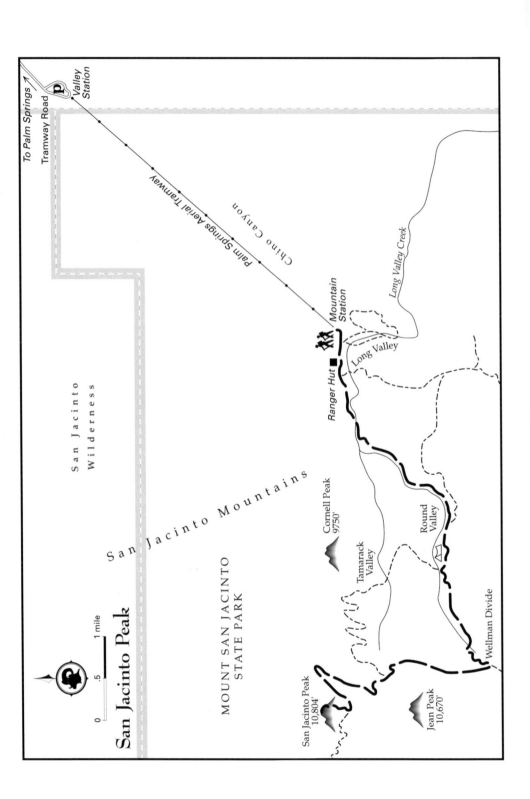

San Jacinto Peak

To Palm Springs
Tramway Road
Valley Station
P

San Jacinto Wilderness

Palm Springs Aerial Tramway

Chino Canyon

Mountain Station
Long Valley
Long Valley Creek

Ranger Hut

San Jacinto Mountains

Cornell Peak
9750'

Tamarack Valley

Round Valley

MOUNT SAN JACINTO STATE PARK

San Jacinto Peak
10,804'

Jean Peak
10,670'

Wellman Divide

0   .5   1 mile

4

San Jacinto Peak

—Jerry Schad

Route	Days	Elev. Gain/Loss	Difficulty	Miles
↰	2	2600'/2600' (to peak and back)	**	12.0

Campsites: Round Valley Camp: 2.0 miles
(see the Trip Description for others)

Map: USGS 7.5-min *San Jacinto Peak*

Best season: Late spring, summer, and fall

Take this trip!

The north face of San Jacinto Peak, at one point soaring 9000 feet up in four horizontal miles, is one of the most imposing escarpments in the United States. Upon witnessing sunrise on the peak a century ago, John Muir exclaimed, "The view from San Jacinto is the most sublime spectacle to be found anywhere on this earth!" Perhaps Muir was exaggerating—especially after seeing so many high places in California—but the emotion and exhilaration behind his statement is easily understood. Today, there's no great hardship involved in reaching the 10,804-foot summit. Simply take the Palm Springs Aerial Tramway to the trailhead just 2300 feet in elevation below the peak, and follow well-graded trails from there.

Trailhead

From Highway 111 just north of Palm Springs, turn west on Tramway Road and continue to the valley station of the Palm Springs Aerial Tramway. Purchase a round-trip ticket there and ride the tram to the mountain station, which includes a restaurant and a gift shop. Start your hike on a paved pathway leading 0.2 mile downhill from the mountain station to the San Jacinto State Wilderness ranger hut in Long Valley. There you must obtain a Wilderness Permit for travel beyond Long Valley.

TRIP DESCRIPTION

Heads Up! There is virtually no time to adjust to the high elevations on this hike. Just before hiking, you ascend on the tramway to 8500 feet elevation in just a few minutes. To acclimatize, consider hiking at some mid-elevation site (5000–8000 feet) a few days prior to your San Jacinto trip. Severe weather can visit the peak, with winter storms bearing down as late as April. By May most or all of the snow is gone.

From the Long Valley ranger hut, follow the wide trail leading toward Round Valley (about 2 miles), where the primary trail-camping sites are located. Additional sites can be found at Tamarack Valley, 0.5 mile north of Round Valley.

On your dayhike to the peak, you climb steeply to Wellman Divide, and then turn north. The leisurely climb ahead takes you through thinning timber to a junction just south of the summit. Veer right, follow the path up along the right (east) side of the summit, pass a stone hut, then scramble from boulder to boulder for a couple of minutes to reach the top. Hopefully the weather will allow you to rest a spell in the warm sun, cupped amid the jumbo-sized rocks, and savor the lightheaded sensation of being on top of the world. The bald, gray (or white if covered by snow) ridge to the north is 11,499-foot San Gorgonio Mountain in the San Bernardino Mountains. The Pacific Ocean can sometimes be seen over many miles of coastal haze to the west. Eastward, where the air is usually most transparent, the tan and brown landscape of the desert rolls interminably toward a horizon near Arizona.

Permits

Call the Palm Springs Aerial Tramway, (619) 325-1391, for information and operating hours. The tramway closes for a period in August for maintenance; otherwise, it normally operates 7 days a week year-round. For information about the necessary Wilderness Permit for hiking and camping, call the Mt. San Jacinto State Wilderness, (909) 659-2607.

San Bernardino National Forest Web site: **www.r5.fs.fed.us/sanbernardino/**

Build-up/Wind-down tips

Perhaps this easy opener to the Southern California high country will whet your appetite for more lengthy routes in the San Jacinto Mountains. Other, more challenging routes to San Jacinto Peak originate near Idyllwild, a piney resort community at about 5000 feet elevation, south of the peak.

Also see this section in trip 5 for more information about the tram, as well as some area recreational suggestions.

To learn about Southern California author Jerry Schad's multifarious activities and accomplishments, and for a list of his titles available from Wilderness Press, see "Author Bio & Bib" on page 492.

Pine snag near San Jacinto Peak

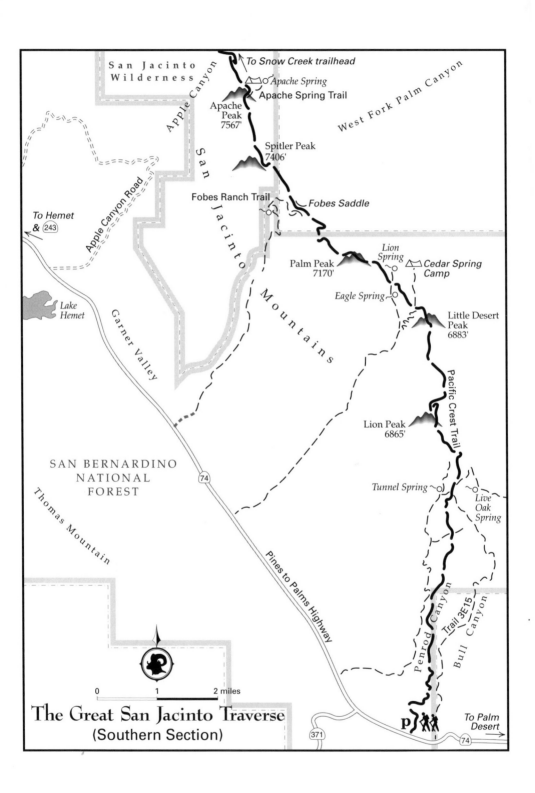

San Jacinto
Wilderness

To Snow Creek trailhead

Apache Spring

Apache Spring Trail

Apache Canyon

West Fork Palm Canyon

Apache
Peak
7567'

Spitler Peak
7406'

Fobes Ranch Trail

Fobes Saddle

San Jacinto Mountains

Palm Peak
7170'

Lion
Spring

Cedar Spring
Camp

Eagle Spring

Little Desert
Peak
6883'

Apple Canyon Road

To Hemet
& 243

Lake
Hemet

Garner Valley

Pacific Crest Trail

Lion Peak
6865'

SAN BERNARDINO
NATIONAL
FOREST

74

Tunnel Spring

Live
Oak
Spring

Thomas Mountain

Pines to Palms Highway

Penrod Canyon

Trail 3E15

Bull Canyon

0   1   2 miles

P

To Palm
Desert

The Great San Jacinto Traverse
(Southern Section)

371

74

The Great San Jacinto Traverse

—Ben Schifrin

Route	Days	Elev. Gain/Loss	Difficulty	Miles
↝	5–7	8240'/12,240'	****	55.9

(add 2⅓-miles, for one-way side trip to San Jacinto Peak)

Campsites: Cedar Spring Camp: 11.7 miles
Apache Spring Camp: 17.3 miles
Little Tahquitz Camp: 24.9 miles
Strawberry Junction Camp: 30.6 miles
Fuller Ridge Camp: 38.5 miles
(see the Trip Description for others)

Map: USGS 7.5-min *Butterfly Peak, Palm View Peak, Idyllwild, Palm Springs, San Jacinto Peak, Whitewater*

Best season: Late spring or early fall (each end of path is exceptionally hot and dry during midsummer)

Take this trip!

This definitive trip in the San Jacintos is a complete south-to-north traverse of the range, culminating in a climb to the viewful 10,804-foot summit of "San Jack." The variety of climates and contrasts of terrain could not be greater. In 50 miles you will traverse every life zone in California, from scorching Sonoran Desert to cool, lofty alpine heights. Our route, on a segment of the famed Pacific Crest Trail, climbs to the jagged granite spine of the aptly named Desert Divide. It then leads north to the rolling, forest-cloaked upland of San Jacinto Wilderness. After traversing the flanks of San Jacinto Peak, the path plummets 7700 feet down the avalanche-raw north slopes of the San Jacintos to end among cacti and desert scrub at San Gorgonio Pass. This strenuous, remote, and demanding route is all the more so, because the presence of very

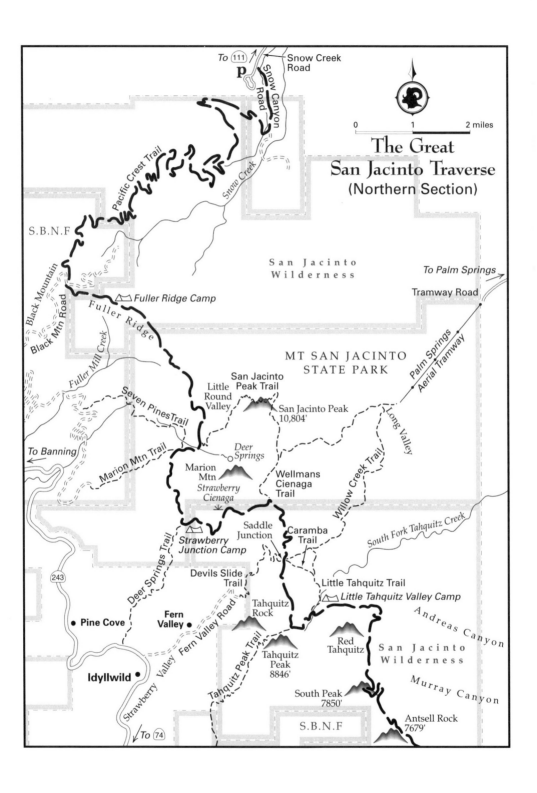

To (111)
p
Snow Creek Road
Snow Canyon Road
Snow Creek

The Great
San Jacinto Traverse
(Northern Section)

0   1   2 miles

Pacific Crest Trail

S.B.N.F

Black Mountain

Black Mtn Road

Fuller Ridge Camp

Fuller Ridge

Fuller Mill Creek

Seven Pines Trail

Marion Mtn Trail

To Banning

San Jacinto Wilderness

To Palm Springs
Tramway Road

MT SAN JACINTO STATE PARK

Palm Springs Aerial Tramway

Little Round Valley

San Jacinto Peak Trail

San Jacinto Peak 10,804'

Deer Springs

Long Valley

Marion Mtn

Strawberry Cienaga

Wellmans Cienaga Trail

Willow Creek Trail

Deer Springs Trail

Strawberry Junction Camp

Saddle Junction

Caramba Trail

South Fork Tahquitz Creek

(243)

Devils Slide Trail

Little Tahquitz Trail

Little Tahquitz Valley Camp

Andreas Canyon

Pine Cove

Fern Valley

Strawberry Valley

Fern Valley Road

Tahquitz Peak Trail

Tahquitz Rock

Red Tahquitz

San Jacinto Wilderness

Idyllwild

Tahquitz Peak 8846'

Murray Canyon

South Peak 7850'

Antsell Rock 7679'

To (74)

S.B.N.F

few springs along the ridgetop route necessitates hikers carrying an extra supply of water.

Trailhead

Your backpack commences at a well-signed Pacific Crest Trail trailhead parking area on the north side of Pines-to-Palms Highway 74, at a point 1 mile east of its junction with Highway 371 and just west of Santa Rosa Summit.

The trail's terminus is at the northern outskirts of the village of Snow Creek. It is reached by paved Snow Creek Road, which heads southwest from Highway 111 a short mile after it branches southeast from Interstate 10 in San Gorgonio Pass. Park on the road shoulder near Falls Creek Road.

Two routes connect the hike terminus with the start: either Highway 111, through Palm Springs and Palm Desert to Highway 74; or Highway 243, which heads south from I-10 at Banning through Idyllwild. I recommend the cooler and much more scenic Highway 243, which allows you to stay at one of the nice campgrounds around Idyllwild or Lake Hemet the night before your trip.

TRIP DESCRIPTION

Leave the trailhead parking area and ascend gently north along the Pacific Crest Trail into a previously burned brushland. Feathery ribbonwood and aromatic chamise are reestablishing themselves as the dominant chaparral species. Just a minute up the trail is a mileage sign and a 6-foot stone monument, which diagrams the PCT route through the San Jacintos and commemorates the death of a trail worker. Beyond it, you walk north to a ridgetop, then switchback once down on its north side. You are soon engaged in a sandy, fitful ascent into and out of numerous small ravines and around picturesque blocky cliffs of crumbling granite. You pass close along the west face of a low ridge, then descend short switchbacks to hop across the usually dry creek that drains Penrod Canyon. Here, about 3.75 miles into the trip, a comfortable but waterless camp could be made under Coulter pines and live oaks. The track winds up-canyon, crossing the streambed twice more before climbing to sunnier chamise and oak chaparral for a traverse of the canyon's eastern slopes.

The PCT eventually intersects Road 6S01A, which ascends from the west to reach an open-pit limestone quarry just above your trail. Proceed directly across the road to resume the now-steeper ascent along Penrod Canyon's east wall. Excellent vistas west over the shoulder of Thomas Mountain and south to Bucksnort Mountain are obtained on this stretch, just before you swing east around a nose to abruptly encounter marble bedrock. Go through a stock gate, then pass southeast-traversing Trail 3E15 to Bull Canyon, which is closed due to its terminus on Santa Rosa Indian Reservation lands. The first leg of the PCT's climb into the San Jacinto Mountains ends 50 yards later, when you top out at a saddle on the Desert Divide. Here are junctions with Live Oak Spring Trail

4EO3 (6.6) right, and the Tunnel Spring Trail left. Be sure to refill your water bottles before continuing north from this saddle!

For the best water and a shady lunch spot, go down to Live Oak Spring. Make the alternative detour to Tunnel Spring (about 0.3-mile distant) for emergency water only—it is much less pleasant. Live Oak Spring is reached by a sunny, 1-mile, well-graded path that descends east from the saddle, eventually reaching two nice campsites under an enormous gold-cup oak and box elders. With much better camping than Tunnel Spring, it has delightfully clean water in a circular concrete trough.

The Tunnel Spring Trail descends southwest from the PCT atop the gap. Steep, rocky tread leads down 0.3 mile to where the trail moderates in a grove of oaks and four, tall Coulter pines, which have scattered huge, clawed cones on the ground. Now look right (north) to a shallow streambed and a faint trail along a black PVC pipe. This goes up a few yards to the metal cattle trough at Tunnel Spring, shaded by box elders. Poor camping is the best that can be found nearby.

Return to the sunny gap. Resuming your northbound trek, turn north along the east face of the Desert Divide. Shady interior live oaks and Coulter pines alternate with xeric chaparral vegetation (look for shaggy Mojave yuccas) as the trail ascends gently across Julian schist, a crumbly striped metamorphic rock, to the east slopes of Lion Peak. Expect to cross a few bulldozed jeep roads on this traverse—the area south of Lion Peak is private property used for cattle range. You'll get sporadic vistas down Oak Canyon to subdivided upper Palm Canyon, and feel the desert's furnace breath wafting from far below. Then, a rough switchback leads to the ridgetop north of Lion Peak. For the next 2 miles the route remains on or near the divide, traversing gneiss, schist, quartzite, and marble bedrock and skirting low chaparral laced with rabbitbrush and cacti. The path leads almost to the summit of Little Desert Peak (6883), which offers panoramas east and north to the Coachella Valley and Palm Springs, and west to conifer-clad Thomas Mountain and pastoral Garner Valley.

Moments later, a short descent ends at a saddle where you meet the Cedar Spring Trail 4E17 (10.7). This well-used path descends left (southwest) to Morris Ranch. More importantly, it extends right, north a short mile to Cedar Spring Camp (6330). Your best choice for a first night's camp, Cedar Spring offers the only permanent water along the southern Desert Divide. The next morning, simply retrace your steps to the PCT. Old trails that once reconnected hikers with the PCT via Lion Spring or Garnet Ridge have fallen into disrepair after brushfires in the 1980s and are not recommended. Carry a full load of water away from Cedar Spring—the day's ridgetop walk is hot, sunny, and entirely dry!

Back on the Desert Divide, the PCT steeply ascends the ridgecrest, and then briefly descends to another saddle with a disused junction. Here a very rough trail that descends steeply south to Morris Ranch passes a polluted cattle trough at Eagle Spring, while an all-but-abandoned trail descends north to often-dry Lion Spring.

Continuing northwest, you soon walk over a low summit, then easily ascend the west shoulder of Palm View Peak. Then, past a 7123-foot summit you descend, often steeply, on a rocky, nebulous tread back into a cooler environment of white firs, which grow at the head of the spectacular West Fork Palm Canyon. Presently the route emerges on brushy Fobes Saddle (about 3.5 miles beyond the Cedar Spring Trail junction) and meets Fobes Ranch Trail 4E02 (14.2). Thirsty hikers may choose to go west down this trail to reach a replenishing spring in about 1 mile (no camping).

The PCT north from this saddle ascends steeply to the upper slopes of Spitler Peak. Here you encounter a charred forest of black oak, white fir, incense-cedar, and Jeffrey pine—all gloomy mementos of a massive 1980 blaze that blackened almost the entire upper West Fork Palm Canyon and Murray and Andreas canyons. You'll find evidence of it all the way to Red Tahquitz. Thankfully, most species have reestablished themselves, but it will be many years before the route will again have useful shade trees. Along your climb you enter San Jacinto Wilderness. Then, beyond some very steep pitches, the PCT levels to wind around north of Spitler Peak. It then descends just east of the rocky spine forming the ridge between Spitler and Apache peaks. Gaining this knife-edge col, we find the Spitler Peak Trail 3E22, which makes a long, waterless excursion west, via rocky switchbacks, to Apple Canyon Road. Beyond the col, the PCT wastes no time in attacking the next objective: Apache Peak. Steep, rocky, and sandy tread leads up its southern slopes to emerge on a black, burned summit plateau. Here you find a sign marking the Apache Spring Trail (16.8), a recommended detour. It descends steeply east ½ mile to poor camps at usually flowing Apache Spring. From your junction too, a short use trail ascends northwest to the viewful, if unappealing, summit of Apache Peak.

North of South Peak, the dynamited trail permits a rocky traverse under precipitous, granitic gendarmes; the ascending hiker can gaze northwest to Tahquitz Peak, north to Red Tahquitz, or east down rugged Murray Canyon. The Desert Divide ascent ends above Andreas Canyon's deep gorge. There, your route turns west to descend gently, over duff and sand, the rolling forested uplands, which characterize the San Jacinto summit massif. Eventually, you cross forested South Fork Tahquitz Creek, and then join, moments later, the Little Tahquitz Trail (24.6). This trail descends north ⅓ mile to good camps and water in Little Tahquitz Valley. It is your best bet for camping north of the Desert Divide. The next morning, you could avoid retracing your steps back to the PCT by continuing to drop north to Tahquitz Meadow, then trace the Caramba Trail briefly northwest to find the PCT at Saddle Junction. But, this would be a mistake—you'd miss terrific vistas from Tahquitz Peak (described below).

From the Little Tahquitz junction, the PCT climbs southwest through dense groves of lodgepole pines and western white pines, which grow on gravelly slopes of decomposed granite. Presently you come to a junction with the Tahquitz Peak Trail 3E08, which offers a side trip ½ mile up to the peak's airy summit lookout. This trip is well worthwhile, for from the 8846-foot summit you can get an idea of how steep canyons, such as Strawberry Valley below, are eroding back into the high, rolling terrain between Red Tahquitz and San Jacinto Peak. Tahquitz Peak commemorates a legendary Cahuilla Indian demon who lived hereabouts, dining on unsuspecting Indian maidens and, when displeased, giving the weather a turn for the worse.

Those who need to press on will turn north and ease down the PCT to Saddle Junction (26.5), the crossroads for an array of trails into the San Jacinto Wilderness. From the saddle, Devils Slide Trail 3E05 descends 2.5 miles west past three springs to Fern Valley Road 5S22, above Idyllwild. Also leaving the saddle are two more trails, including the Willow Creek Trail, branching northeast to Long Valley, and the Caramba Trail, southeast to Tahquitz Valley.

The PCT continues north, soon switchbacking out of the forest to slopes that offer excellent over-the-shoulder vistas toward Tahquitz (Lily) Rock, a magnet for Southern California rock climbers. Almost 1000 feet above Saddle Junction, the PCT levels off, heading left from a junction with the Wellmans Cienaga Trail, just within the confines of Mt. San Jacinto State Park.

From the junction, the PCT immediately leaves the state park and descends on a generally westward bearing above Strawberry Valley's steep headwall to Strawberry Cienaga, a trickling sphagnum-softened freshet that makes a viewful lunch stop. Cienaga is a Spanish word, often seen in Southern California, meaning "swamp" or "marsh." Farther descent leads to a forested junction with Deer Springs Trail 3E17. Just before this junction, Marion Ridge/Strawberry Junction Camp (30.6) is found on a small ridge south of the trail. This makes a very pleasant and viewful, but unfortunately, waterless camp. There may be some trickles of water, until midsummer, in heads of nearby canyons.

Now out of the Federal wilderness and back in Mt. San Jacinto State Park, the PCT turns north to ascend Marion Mountain's pleasant mixed-conifer slopes, and eventually passes two, closely spaced trail junctions. The first trail, the Marion Mountain Trail, descends west-southwest, while the second, the Seven Pines Trail, descends generally northwest. Soon after the second lateral, your trail heads up along a marshy dank creek: the reliable North Fork San Jacinto River (32.7), which you cross below Deer Springs. Once a campsite, it is now closed to allow for revegetation.

A minute beyond the infant San Jacinto River, you climb to a nearby junction with the San Jacinto Peak Trail. This is a "must-do" side trip to the 10,804-foot apex of the San Jacinto Mountains. The top—2⅓ miles away—can be reached in a fast, breathless hour without a pack, but it is best to reserve a half day. Alternatively, you might choose to camp at the designated site in Little Round Valley, an 800-foot climb above the PCT, halfway to the top. It has a constant supply of cool water from the trickling headwaters of North Fork San Jacinto River, and pleasant, shaded camping beside a sloping hillside meadow. Continue above it on sandy tread that leads up to a shoulder just south of the top. Here, wind and ice have reduced the forest to a scattering of gnarled, hunched sentinel pines. Turn left and climb north for ¼ mile, up past a rock-and-masonry shelter, to the slabs of San Jacinto Peak. This is truly one of the greatest Southern California vistas. On a clear day (now rare) one can almost see the Pacific Ocean. More typical days still allow identification of most of the prominent peaks of the southern Coast Ranges. Below, the vertiginous defile of Snow Creek tumbles giddily down to the desert San Gorgonio River.

Before leaving the environs of the San Jacinto River, refill your water bottles and carry extra. The next dependable water along the route is from Snow Creek, barely a mile from the hike's end at the northern base of the San Jacinto Mountains—a punishing 25-mile descent away. In addition, our next night's camp, at Fuller Ridge, is frequently waterless, especially in late summer and autumn.

From the PCT's junction with the San Jacinto Peak Trail, your northbound path continues to traverse the open-forested hillside, then switchbacks down to Fuller Ridge—a rocky, white-fir-covered spine separating the San Jacinto and San Gorgonio river drainages. Here the northbound trekker gets the first good view north of the San Bernardino Mountains' 11,499-foot San Gorgonio Mountain, which is Southern California's highest point. Separating that range from ours is San Gorgonio Pass, 7000 feet below, lying between the Banning fault and other branches of the great San Andreas fault (aka the San Andreas Rift Zone).

The PCT's route along Fuller Ridge is a tortuous one, composed for the most part of miniature switchbacks, alternately descending and climbing, which wind under small gendarmes and around wind-beaten conifers. In a little over 2 miles, though, the route takes to north-facing slopes, and, exchanging state wilderness for a brief stint in the Federal Wilderness, it gently descends to a small dirt-road parking circle at Fuller Ridge Trailhead Remote Campsite (38.5). This pleasant site lies in open stands of ponderosa pine and white fir. Except in springtime and early summer, camping here is usually waterless. Scout for water by walking southwest along the incipient stream at the head of Fuller Mill Creek—if you are desperate, there is usually water to be found, except in late-season, by the time you've dropped to the flats above Black Mountain Group Campground, in about ⅓ mile.

The PCT, marked by a post, resumes on the west side of the road loop, heading due north past a campsite. It rounds northwest above, then drops to cross well-used Black Mountain Road 4SO1. The trail leaves the road on a gentle-to-moderate descent north along a ridge covered with an open stand of mixed conifers. You switchback down three times across the nose of the ridge separating Snow Creek from chaparral-decked Brown Creek.

More open conditions on the west side of the ridge allow for sweeping vistas. Hulking San Gorgonio Mountain looms to the north, above the desert pass that bears its name. Stretching northwest, the San Bernardino and San Gabriel valleys, flanked by the lofty summits of the San Gabriel Mountains, extend toward the Los Angeles basin. On a clear day in winter or spring, snowflecked Mount San Antonio (Mount Baldy) and Mount Wilson are both visible in that range.

Further descent ensues. You reenter San Jacinto Wilderness and presently the sandy, lupine- and penstemon-lined path meets a switchback in a dirt road, which winds eastward into a shallow basin. Marked by large ducks, the trail leaves the northwest side of the open gap containing the road, but soon your route turns south to descend alongside and just below that road. After a bit, your course veers from the road and winds east down dry washes and under the shade of low scrub oaks to a narrow gap in a sawblade ridge of granodiorite needles. Four long switchbacks descend the east face of this prominent ridge, depositing us in noticeably more xeric environs.

Initially, Coulter pines replace other montane conifers, and then, as the way arcs north in continual descent, you enter a true chaparral: yerba santa, buckwheat, holly-leaf cherry, scrub oak, manzanita, and yucca supply the sparse ground cover, while scarlet gilia and yellow blazing star add spring color. Unlike chaparral communities moistened by maritime air, the desert-facing slopes here force these species to contend with much more extreme drought conditions. As a result, many more of these plants are annuals, which avoid drought by lying dormant as seed, while others, such as yerba santa, wilt and drop their soft leaves to prevent water loss during sustained dry periods.

A continued moderate downgrade and another set of long switchbacks soon allow you to inspect the awesome, avalanche-raw, 9600-foot north escarpment of San Jacinto Peak, which rises above the cascades of Snow Creek. To your northeast, the confused alluvial terrain beyond San Gorgonio Pass attests to recent activity along the San Andreas fault. Beyond, suburban Desert Hot Springs shimmers in the Coachella Valley heat, backdropped by the Little San Bernardino Mountains.

Inexorably, your descent continues at a moderate grade, presently switchbacking in broad sweeps across a dry ravine on slopes north of West Fork Snow Creek. After striking a small saddle just west of Knob 3252, the trail, now taking an overly gentle grade, swings north, then northwest down a boulder-studded hillside. You note the small village of Snow Creek lying below you at the mountain's base before the trail makes three small switchbacks and then heads back (southeast) toward Snow Canyon. After winding your way through a veritable forest of 20–30-foot-high orange, granitic boulders, you negotiate a final set of switchbacks before dropping to cross a dry creekbed on the western edge of Snow Canyon. You soon reach narrow, paved Snow Canyon Road, and find another, more welcome vestige of civilization there—a 3-foot-tall concrete water fountain. This is your first certain water since leaving North Fork San Jacinto River. Snow Canyon is both a game refuge and a water supply for Palm Springs, so camping here is not allowed.

In any event, this hike is almost completed. Turn north onto the pavement, and make a moderate descent along narrow Snow Canyon Road, which winds north down Snow Canyon's rubbly alluvial fan, often near a small, usually flowing western branch of Snow Creek. (This stream may be dry by April of drought years.) Eventually, the road simultaneously leaves San Bernardino National Forest and its San Jacinto Wilderness at a Desert Water Agency gate, and then veers northwest across a western stream branch. Just beyond it, your route joins paved Falls Creek Road at the outskirts of the small village of Snow Creek. Now you briefly follow Falls Creek Road northwest to a junction with Snow Creek Road 3S01, to find your waiting car.

Permits

San Bernardino National Forest administers the San Jacinto Wilderness, which you traverse at the start and end of your trip. Get permits from them for the entire walk, including a required separate camping permit if you're using the state park sites at Strawberry Junction and Little Round Valley. They will also have up-to-the-minute reports on water availability along the route. Both ranger stations are just two minutes from each other, in Idyllwild:

San Jacinto Ranger District
Box 518
54270 Pinecrest
Idyllwild, CA 92349
(909) 659-2117

Mount San Jacinto State Park
Box 308
25905 State Highway 243
Idyllwild, CA 92349
(909) 659-2607

Build-up/Wind-down tips

Nomad Ventures, (909) 659-4853, a complete outdoor sports shop, is the place in Idyllwild for last minute items and excellent advice before the trek. If you're spending the night near Idyllwild, have dinner at Restaurant Gastrognome, (909) 659-5055, in the center of town. It offers high-quality, eclectic California cuisine.

After the dusty-dry, knee-pounding descent from the north face of San Jacinto, you'll need three things, and you'll need them quickly, and in the appropriate order: lots of liquid refreshment, a good meal, and a muscular pampering. Head into Palm Springs. Stop anywhere along the downtown strip on South Palm Canyon Drive. Grab a beer at any of the streetside open-air patio bars. Watch tourists and glimpse movie stars. Afterward, amble a bit, either north or south, and cruise the chichi shops. A multihued Hawaiian shirt (perfect for your next desert adventure) is the appropriate trophy.

There are plenty of good meals to be had in Palm Springs, but there is only one fit for conquerors of The Great San Jacinto Traverse: prime rib served at the top of the Palm Springs Aerial Tramway, (888) 515-TRAM. This Swiss-style cable tramway is the second longest in the world: from the desert floor of Chino Canyon, just off Highway 111, it climbs 2.5 miles and almost 5900 feet to Mountain Station, on a cool pine-forested shoulder east of San Jacinto Peak. (See also trip 4, "San Jacinto Peak," which utilizes the tram.) The Alpine Room Restaurant, (760) 325-1449, has an eagle's-aerie dining patio, which overlooks the grand defile of Chino Canyon. Currently, the "Ride'n'Dine" package includes a round-trip tram fare and dinner of prime rib, chicken, ribs, or lasagne for about $25.

After dinner, take your pampering in grand style, as well. A long soak in the 148°F mineral waters of Two Bunch Palms Resort and Spa, is the well-deserved and wickedly decadent finish to your trip. Spend the night in a comfortable room at this funky resort. The next morning, have an excellent breakfast, and spend a few hours of preventative maintenance with more soaks, massage, water shiatsu, hydrotherapy, reflexology, tai chi, or a Native American herbal wrap. The spa is located 12 miles north of Palm Springs:

Two Bunch Palms Resort and Spa
67425 Two Bunch Palms Trail
Desert Hot Springs, CA 92240
(800) 472-4334

Visit their Web site at **www.twobunchpalms.com**.

However self-effacing he might wish to be, Sierra native Ben Schifrin has been a longtime author of, or contributor to, Wilderness Press' most important California backpacking guides (see "Author Bio & Bib" on page 492).

The Transverse Ranges

Geologists place the San Bernardino Mountains, as well as the neighboring San Gabriels, in the Transverse Range province—a system of mountain chains that stretch west to east, athwart the general northwest-southeast structural grain of California. While all the Transverse Ranges were formed by intensive folding and faulting, the generally smooth summit region of the San Bernardinos—in marked contrast to the rough surface of the San Gabriels—reveals that the former were molded in comparatively recent geologic time.

The San Bernardino Mountains

From Cajon Pass and the slanted troughs of the great San Andreas fault, the San Bernardinos rise, rather steeply at first, in chaparral-coated slopes, to the 5000-foot-high summits of Cleghorn and Cajon mountains. Eastward from here, for 30 miles, the crest of the San Bernardinos is remarkably uniform. Undulating ridges and tapered hillocks conceal within their folds forested glens and sparkling blue lakes. This is the Crestline-Lake Arrowhead-Running Springs-Big Bear country, the part of the mountains best known to thousands of Southern Californians. Near Big Bear Lake, the San Bernardinos veer southward, toward the majestic heights of the San Gorgonio Wilderness. Here, under granite spines hammered up against the sky, lodgepole and limber pines grow sturdy and weather-resistant, tumbling streams flow icy cold, and the thin air is crisp with the chill of elevation. Reigning over all is 11,499-foot San Gorgonio Mountain, the rooftop of Southern California.

The San Gabriel Mountains

The San Gabriels extend that great roof over Southern California's coastal lowlands, covering an area stretching north from the edge of the Los Angeles metropolis to the western extremity of the Mojave Desert. This is fault-torn country: the San Gabriels are a conglomeration of rock units of various ages and origins, separated from the surrounding landscape by the San Andreas fault zone on the north, the San Gabriel and Sierra Madre faults on the south, and the Soledad fault on the west.

Throughout most of their length, the San Gabriels are made up of two, roughly parallel ranges. The southern, lower range, about 5000 feet high, rises abruptly from the the city of Pasadena and adjoining communities in the San Gabriel Valley. The northern range—farther inland, longer, and loftier—climaxes near its eastern end at 10,064-foot-high Mt. San Antonio (Old Baldy). Both ranges are incised with deep canyons whose slopes are notoriously steep and easily eroded. Inside many of these canyons, crystalline streams hasten through shady riparian woods, and backpackers find complete escape from the sight and sound of the great suburban metropolis not far away. (JWR&JS)

On the summit, San Gorgonio Mountain

Jerry Schad

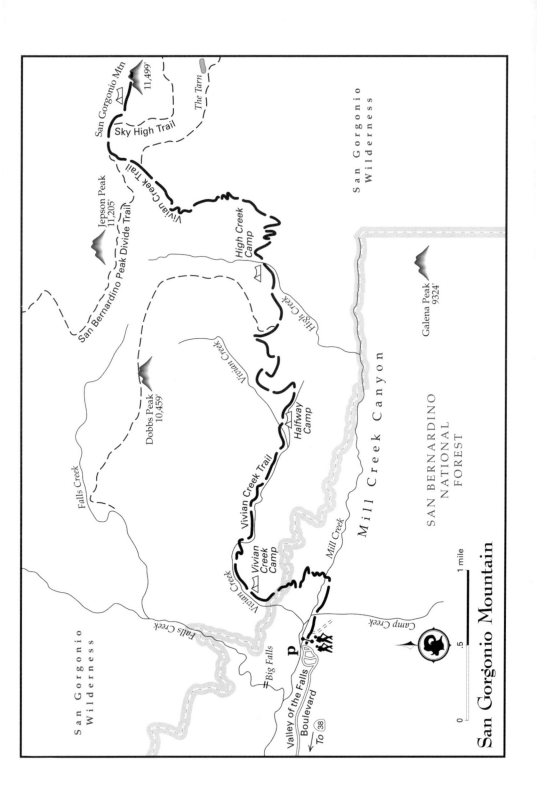

San Gorgonio Mountain

6

San Gorgonio Mountain

—Jerry Schad

Route	Days	Elev. Gain/Loss	Difficulty	Miles
↝	2	5700'/5700'	***	15.6

Campsites: High Creek Camp: 4.8 miles

Map: USGS 7.5-min *Forest Falls, San Gorgonio Mtn.* The US Forest Service *Guide to the San Gorgonio Wilderness* topographic map is an excellent alternative to the USGS maps.

Best season: Late spring, summer, and fall

Take this trip!

The rounded, talus-strewn summit of San Gorgonio Mountain (or "Greyback," as it was called long ago) crowns the San Bernardino Mountains and regally presides over thousands of square miles of varied Southern California terrain. The mountain's 11,499-foot elevation qualifies it as the highest peak in California south of the Tehachapi Mountains. The way up and back down is long and challenging. Even so, no California peak-bagger's long-term itinerary is complete without a visit to the top (see the sidebar below).

Trailhead

From Interstate 10 at Redlands, exit at Orange Avenue (Highway 38), and drive 0.7 mile north to Lugonia Avenue. Turn right (east) staying on Highway 38, and continue 8 miles to the US Forest Service Mill Creek Station (stop here for information and permits). Continue 6.2 miles east on Highway 38 to Valley of the Falls Boulevard (Forest Home Road). Turn right there and continue east for 4.5 miles to the trailhead at the road's end.

TRIP DESCRIPTION

Heads Up! Backpacking Gorgonio and bagging the peak squeezes a lot into a two-day weekend. In November, when the daylight period shortens to less than 11 hours and sunset occurs near 5 P.M., be sure get an early start to ensure enough light during the afternoon. Various three-day intineraries are possible on the route, too. There are three trail camps on the way up, and a fourth camp lies just below the summit. The season for the south-facing Vivian Creek route described here begins in May with the melting of the snow, and ends sometime in November or December with the first heavy snowfall.

The Vivian Creek Trail is the original path to the top of San Gorgonio, built around the turn of the 20th Century. Today, at least seven other routes (or variations on routes) culminate at the summit, but none is shorter and faster.

From the paved parking lot at the trailhead, walk east (uphill) past a vehicle gate and follow a dirt road for 0.6 mile to its end. Go left across the wide, boulder wash of Mill Creek and find the Vivian Creek Trail going sharply up the oak-clothed canyon wall on the far side. The next half mile is excruciatingly steep, but untypical of the route as a whole.

After leveling momentarily, the trail assumes a moderate grade as it sidles alongside Vivian Creek. A sylvan Shangri-La unfolds ahead. Pines, firs, and cedars reach for the sky. Bracken fern smothers the banks of the melodious creek, which dances over boulders and fallen trees. After the first October frost, the bracken turns a flaming yellow, made all the more vivid by warm sunlight pouring out of a fierce blue sky.

Near Halfway Camp (2.5) the trail begins climbing timber-dotted slopes covered intermittently by thickets of manzanita. After several zigs and zags on north-facing slopes, you swing onto a brightly illuminated south-facing slope. Serrated Yucaipa Ridge looms in the south, rising sheer from the depths of Mill Creek Canyon. Soon thereafter, the sound of bubbling water heralds your arrival at High Creek, 4.8 miles, and the trail camp of the same name. If you stay here overnight (your best choice on a one-night trip), be prepared for a chilly night. Cold, nocturnal air flows down along the bottom of this canyon from the 10,000-foot-plus peaks above.

Next morning, with a light load on your back, you plod upward on long switchback segments through lodgepole pines, and attain a saddle on a rocky ridge. The pines thin out and appear more decrepit as you climb crookedly up along this ridge toward treeline. At 7.2 miles (from the trailhead), the San Bernardino Peak Divide Trail intersects from the left. Stay right and keep climbing on a moderate grade across stony slopes dotted with cowering krummholz pines. Soon, nearly all vegetation disappears.

On the right you pass Sky High Trail. Keep straight and keep chugging upward into the thinning air. A final burst of effort puts you on the summit boulder pile, 7.8 miles from your starting point. From this airy vantage, even the soaring north face of San Jacinto Peak to the south appears diminished in stature. With the midmorning sunlight knifing downward from the southeast, your best views are likely to be of the vast Mojave Desert spreading north and east. Under ideal atmospheric conditions, you may be able to spot certain high peaks in the southern Sierra Nevada, plus Telescope Peak—the high point of Death Valley National Monument.

Peak-baggers & Elevation Revisions

Peak-baggers are a touchy lot: the higher the peak, the higher the prestige of having climbed it. Heaven help the scientist who tries to stick a new, lower elevation on that peak. Southern California's highest peak, Mt. San Gorgonio, is officially 11,499' high, a value often rounded off to 11,500'. One day I was hiking with a friend who noted aloud that Mt. San Gorgonio was 11,495' high. "No," I corrected him, having recently bagged it myself, "it's 11,499." And a voice boomed out of nowhere, It's 11,500! For many years, Mt. Whitney's elevation was given as 14,496', and you'll still see that value widely used. However, the official number is now 14,491', thanks to satellite data. "No thanks!" say many peak-baggers. (KM)

Permits

A Wilderness Permit is required for climbing San Gorgonio Mountain. Get one at the Mill Creek Ranger Station (open 7 A.M. weekends), or better yet, obtain one in advance by mail. Call (909) 794-1123 for information. All cars parked at the trailhead must display a National Forest Adventure Pass, $5 daily or $30 annually.

San Bernardino National Forest Web site: **www.r5.fs.fed.us/sanbernardino/**

Build-up/Wind-down tips

Just west of the trailhead for Vivian Creek is a short path leading across Mill Creek Canyon wash and up near the base of Big Falls, one of the highest cascades in Southern California. This is worthwhile spot to visit in the spring, when there's enough runoff from melting snow.

To learn about Southern California author Jerry Schad's multifarious activities and accomplishments, and for a list of his titles available from Wilderness Press, see "Author Bio & Bib" on page 492.

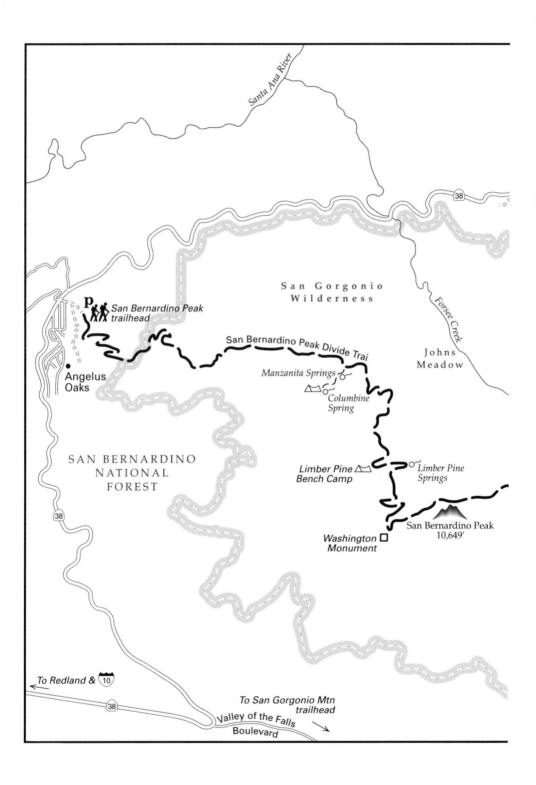

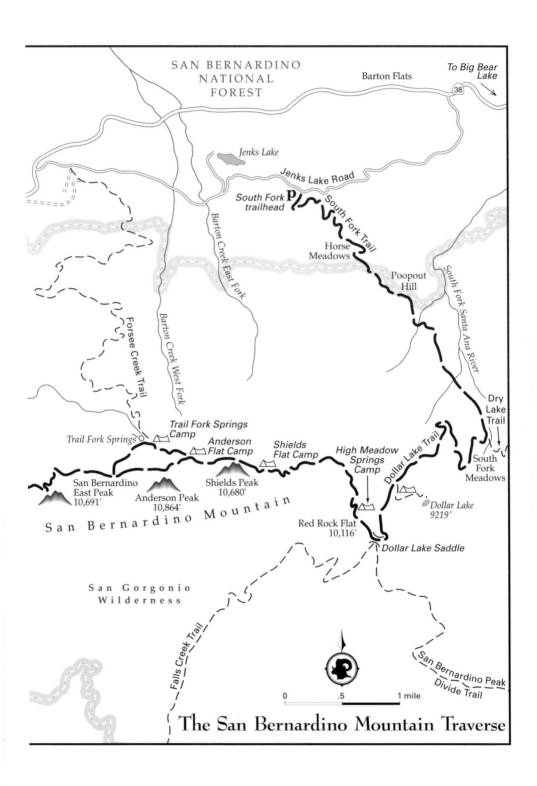

SAN BERNARDINO
NATIONAL
FOREST

Barton Flats

To Big Bear Lake

38

Jenks Lake

Jenks Lake Road

South Fork trailhead **P**

South Fork Trail

Horse Meadows

Poopout Hill

South Fork Santa Ana River

Barton Creek East Fork

Forsee Creek Trail

Barton Creek West Fork

Dry Lake Trail

Trail Fork Springs *Trail Fork Springs Camp*

Anderson Flat Camp

Shields Flat Camp

High Meadow Springs Camp

Dollar Lake Trail

South Fork Meadows

San Bernardino East Peak 10,691'

Anderson Peak 10,864'

Shields Peak 10,680'

Dollar Lake 9219'

S a n   B e r n a r d i n o   M o u n t a i n

Red Rock Flat 10,116'

Dollar Lake Saddle

San Gorgonio Wilderness

Falls Creek Trail

San Bernardino Peak Divide Trail

0   .5   1 mile

The San Bernardino Mountain Traverse

7

The San Bernardino Mountain Traverse

—Jerry Schad

Route	Days	Elev. Gain/Loss	Difficulty	Miles
↗	**2 or 3**	**5500'/4500'**	*****	**21.6**

Campsites: Limber Pine Bench Camp: 5.7 miles (for 3-day trip)
various trail camps atop the San Bernardino Peak divide:
11–14 miles
(see the Trip Description for recommendations, depending on 2- or 3-day trip)

Map: USGS 7.5-min *Moonridge, San Gorgonio Mtn., Forest Falls, Big
Bear Lake* (The US Forest Service Guide to the San Gorgonio
Wilderness topographic map is an excellent alternative to the
USGS maps.)

Best season: Late spring, summer, and fall

Take this trip!

The peaked roofline of Southern California's highest watershed divide—
San Bernardino Peak to San Gorgonio Mountain—features eight named summits, which are all over 10,000 feet in elevation. Four of the eight peaks lie no
more than a few minutes scramble from the two-day backpack route described
here. If you wish, schedule in an extra day for dayhiking to and from the other
four peaks. Either way, you'll experience a good piece of the largest subalpine
wilderness area south of the Sierra Nevada.

Trailhead

From Interstate 10 at Redlands, exit at Orange Avenue (Highway 38), and
drive 0.7 mile north to Lugonia Avenue. Turn right (east) staying on Highway

West shoulder, San Bernardino Peak

38, and continue 8 miles to the US Forest Service Mill Creek Station (stop here for information and a Wilderness Permit). Continue another 11 miles east (up into the mountains) on Highway 38 to the small community of Angelus Oaks, where a large sign on the right directs you toward the San Bernardino Peak trailhead, a short distance away via dirt road. This being a car-shuttle trip, drive your other car 5 miles farther east on Highway 38 to Jenks Lake Road on the right. Go 2.5 miles east on Jenks Lake Road to the spacious South Fork trailhead on the left.

TRIP DESCRIPTION

Heads Up! Like every other route into San Gorgonio Wilderness, this traverse over the high peaks is challenging and exhausting to anyone without recent altitude experience or training. The north-facing aspect of the ascent and descent plus the 10,000+ foot elevation of the midsection of this route shorten the season for backpacking to as little as six months. Lightning-struck pines atop of the divide speak of the violence of thunderstorms, which visit the area regularly and somewhat unpredictably in the summer. Alternately, intense July and August sunlight and heat can easily sap your energy. Pre-

Memorial Day and post-Labor Day trips are usually best. Trail campsites are abundant and several itineraries are possible. If you can reach Trail Fork Springs or Anderson Flat camps (about halfway along the route) on the first day of a weekend trip, then you can let gravity help repay your efforts the following day.

From the San Bernardino Peak trailhead, commence a relentless, switch-backing ascent south and east, up a timbered slope graced with fine, aromatic specimens of Jeffrey pine, sugar pine, plus large and small varieties of oak trees. A sign at 2 miles announces the boundary of San Gorgonio Wilderness. As you continue upward, the oaks rather suddenly disappear, and the trail climbs more moderately atop a rounded, linear ridge about 8000 feet in elevation. On that ridge you eventually emerge from parklike stands of Jeffrey pines into a sunny landscape of low-growing chaparral—mostly manzanita. Blocky San Bernardino Peak looms ahead on this plateau phase of the hike, and you clearly realize the magnitude of the remaining ascent.

Amid the manzanita you come to a trail junction at 4.3 miles. Seasonal Manzanita Springs and Columbine Spring camps lie to the west, and an obscure, unmaintained trail meanders east toward Johns Meadow. Ahead at 5.7 miles and about 1000 feet higher on a spacious and viewful bench dotted with lodgepole pines is Limber Pine Bench Camp—too short a destination for a first night's camp but fine if you intend to spend three days on the traverse. Cool water fairly dependably issues from a ravine (Limber Pine Springs) alongside the trail about 0.3 mile east.

Continue your ascent on lengthy, well-graded switchback segments to the west shoulder of San Bernardino Peak, where the trail turns abruptly left (east) and a panoramic view opens to the south. As you continue east, watch for the Washington Monument, a cairn and wooden debris marking the initial survey point of the San Bernardino meridian and baseline. To this day, township and range descriptions of surveyed property in Southern California refer to this important reference point.

Ahead, along the undulating crest, the trail passes just north of 10,649-foot San Bernardino Peak (8.0), and even more narrowly north of the talus-strewn, 10,691-foot high point of San Bernardino East Peak (9.4). From the latter summit you can look south into the yawning chasm of Mill Creek Canyon, and spot the unmaintained Momyer Peak Trail cutting precipitously across talus slopes below.

At 10.2 miles you reach a split in the trail. Both trails reconverge about 0.8 mile ahead. Trail Fork Springs Camp (10.7; and the seasonal Trail Fork Springs in a ravine nearby) lie to the left, while the right fork passes 0.2 mile north of the 10,864-foot summit of Anderson Peak. Dry Anderson Flat Camp (11.0) lies just north of where the trails reconverge.

The trail continues east across the north slope of 10,680-foot, rock-strewn Shields Peak, descends moderately to Shields Flat Camp (12.0), and rambles east and south to a trail turnoff for High Meadow Springs Camp on the right (13.7). Water can usually be found in a ravine near the camp. Red Rock Flat Camp, with a number of perfectly flat if dry campsites, lies next to the trail about a half mile beyond. If you intend to spend a half-day or more bagging any or all of the four peaks to the southeast (10,806' Charlton Peak, 10,696' Little Charlton Peak, 11,205' Jepson Peak, and 11,502' San Gorgonio Mountain), it's nice to set up your second night's camp at either High Meadow Springs or Red Rock Flat.

At the four-way trail junction atop Dollar Lake Saddle (14.5), turn left and descend north past the trail turnoff for Dollar Lake and farther down to South Fork Meadows (17.0). Even during the driest months of the driest years, the clear waters of the South Fork Santa Ana River tumble through this sylvan spot. Stay left at the trail intersection here and at every other trail junction ahead to remain on the descending course that takes you almost straightway to South Fork trailhead and your parked car. You've traveled 21.6 miles from the start, not including any side trips.

Permits

A Wilderness Permit is required for entry into San Gorgonio Wilderness. Get one at the Mill Creek Ranger Station (open 7 A.M. or earlier on the weekends) or, better yet, obtain one in advance by mail. Call (909) 794-1123 for information. All cars parked at the trailhead must display a National Forest Adventure Pass, $5 daily or $30 annually.

San Bernardino National Forest Web site: **www.r5.fs.fed.us/sanbernardino/**

To learn about Southern California author Jerry Schad's multifarious activities and accomplishments, and for a list of his titles available from Wilderness Press, see "Author Bio & Bib" on page 492.

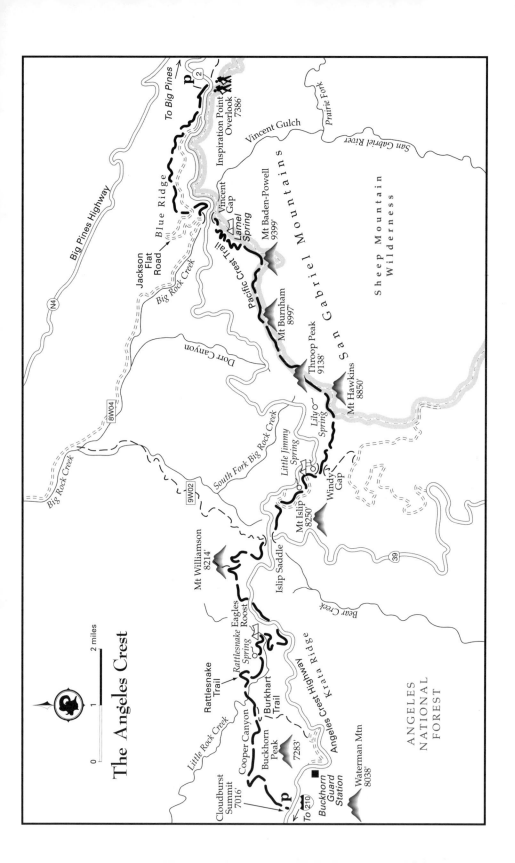

The Angeles Crest

0   1   2 miles

To Big Pines
2
P
Inspiration Point Overlook 7386'
Vincent Gulch
Prairie Fork
San Gabriel River
Big Pines Highway
Blue Ridge
Vincent Gap
Lamel Spring
Mt Baden-Powell 9399'
San Gabriel Mountains
Sheep Mountain Wilderness
N4
Jackson Flat Road
Big Rock Creek
Pacific Crest Trail
Mt Burnham 8997'
Dorr Canyon
Throop Peak 9138'
Mt Hawkins 8850'
8W04
Lily Spring
Big Rock Creek
South Fork Big Rock Creek
Little Jimmy Spring
9W02
Windy Gap
Mt Islip 8250'
Mt Williamson 8214'
39
Islip Saddle
Bear Creek
Rattlesnake Trail
Eagles Roost
Rattlesnake Spring
Little Rock Creek
Cooper Canyon
Burkhart Trail
Krata Ridge
Angeles Crest Highway
ANGELES NATIONAL FOREST
Cloudburst Summit 7016'
Buckhorn Peak 7283'
Waterman Mtn 8038'
P
To 210
Buckhorn Guard Station

8

The Angeles Crest—
Inspiration Point to Cloudburst
Summit via the PCT

—Ben Schifrin

Route	Days	Elev. Gain/Loss	Difficulty	Miles
↝	3	6600'/6440'	**	27.0

Campsites: just after Lamel Spring Trail junction: 6.4 miles
Little Jimmy Camp: 14.0 miles
Little Rock Creek: 21.5 miles
(see the Trip Description for others)

Map: USGS 7.5-min *Mount San Antonio, Mescal Creek, Valyermo, Crystal Lake, Waterman Mtn.*

Best season: Early summer through late fall

Take this trip!

This is the best big hike within sight of America's greatest metropolis. Our route traverses the Angeles crest, which forms the northern boundary of the Los Angeles basin. Non-Angelenos will be surprised that it is a real wilderness experience, mostly unchanged from the days when John Muir described it as "the most ruggedly inaccessible range I have known." High-mountain forests, steep climbs, gorgeous creekside camping, and the chance to surmount two big peaks for windswept vistas, make this the crown jewel of Angeles National Forest.

Trailhead

Our segment of the Pacific Crest Trail begins at the busy, paved Inspiration Point overlook parking area, 2 miles west of Big Pines, at the junction of Angeles Crest Highway 2 and Big Pines Highway (4 miles west of Wrightwood).

Wrightwood can be reached most easily from Interstate 15. Exit on Highway 138, about 3 miles south of Cajon Pass, and drive west to Highway 2. Turn southwest up Highway 2 to Wrightwood.

Drive about 22 miles farther west on Highway 2 to forested Cloudburst Summit, the terminus of this hike. Park in the dirt turnout.

Alternatively, both points can be reached by starting from the other end of Highway 2, in La Cañada. Exit from Interstate 210. It is a bit over 50 miles northeast to Inspiration Point.

TRIP DESCRIPTION

Heads Up! Be very careful with fire, as camper-caused wild-fires have devastated Angeles National Forest many times in the past. Please note that CAMPFIRES ARE NOT ALLOWED at any site outside of designated campgrounds, anywhere in the Angeles National Forest. Use only self-contained camp stoves (see Permits).

In addition, parking for any time along any forest roads requires that the vehicle display a National Forest Adventure Pass, which costs $5 daily or $30 for an annual permit. They are available from any USFS ranger station, or from many vendors in and around the Forest. Additionally, they can be purchased over the Internet:

www.trailworks.com/adventure_pass/

Before leaving the paved parking area, which has bathrooms but no water, take a moment to carefully cross the highway to Inspiration Point, a sweeping overlook of the East Fork San Gabriel River basin. A white-metal Pacific Crest Trail post marks your route, which starts uphill from the parking lot. It almost immediately branches left (west) from the short Lightning Ridge Nature Trail. Ascend easily, then drop west through flats of whitethorn and bitter cherry to reach forested Grassy Hollow Picnic Area (1.0), with water, toilets, and a large new visitor center.

About ½ mile northwest of the campground the PCT route goes along Jackson Flat Road 3N26 for 100 yards, before returning to trail tread on the north side of Blue Ridge. Next on the itinerary is a short spur to walk-in Jackson Flat Group Campground (2.3; available by advance reservation only), among shading pines and firs. After passing north of Jackson Flat and curving Blue Ridge, the PCT drops south across Road 3N26, then switchbacks moderately down past interior live oaks and ocean spray to Angeles Crest Highway 2 at Vincent Gap.

At a junction south of the highway, beside a parking area and a trail east to the interesting Big Horn Mine, is the trailhead for Mt. Baden-Powell Trail

8W05—a popular pilgrimage for Southern California Boy Scouts. Take this trail, which starts southwest before switchbacking gently-to-moderately up in Jeffrey-pine/white-fir groves on crunchy Pelona schist tread. After a number of switchbacks, you reach a side trail (6.3) that contours 100 yards south to Lamel Spring. This makes a good rest stop, and you could camp at either of two, very small, level spots a minute farther along the main trail.

Above, the switchbacks become tighter, the air grows crisper, and firs give way to lodgepole pines, which yield in turn, above 8800 feet, to sweeping-branched, wind-loving limber pines. These hunched, gnarled conifers, believed by some botanists to be 2000 years old, are the only obvious living things at the Mt. Baden-Powell Spur Trail, almost 4 miles and 2800 feet above Vincent Gap. Take this side hike to the 9399-foot summit. Here you get superlative views north across desert to the southern Sierra, west to Mt. Gleason, south down Iron Fork San Gabriel River (in Sheep Mountain Wilderness) to the Santa Ana Mountains, and east to Mts. San Antonio and San Gorgonio and San Jacinto Peak. On the clearest days, Mt. Whitney and Telescope Peak, overlooking Death Valley, can be seen far to the north. A concrete monument here is a tribute to Lord Baden-Powell, founder of the Boy Scout movement almost 100 years ago. This summit marks the terminus of the Silver Moccasin Trail, scouting's 53-mile challenge through the San Gabriel Mountains, which is congruent with the PCT until Three Points, about 23 miles away.

Back on the PCT, your route bears west, descending the steep ridge under Mt. Burnham, and passing a signed spur trail that heads north down the shoulder of Throop Peak to Dawson Saddle. You climb briefly in open pine/fir forest, with an understory of manzanita, whitethorn, and sagebrush, to navigate Throop Peak's east and south slopes, where you briefly enter Sheep Mountain Wilderness. More descent follows, past a signed lateral to the summit of Mt. Hawkins. Then, on the sparsely conifered ridge west of that peak, you pass a lateral (12.0) that drops ⅓ mile north to Lily Spring. Just a bit later, you pass another signed lateral trail, this one south to South Mt. Hawkins, before an aggressive descent ensues, bringing you to aptly named Windy Gap. Here, a side trail drops south to campgrounds in the Crystal Lake Recreation Area. From here, the PCT descends north off the ridge to Little Jimmy Spring, lying just below the trail. This is the last water until Little Rock Creek, in 7.7 miles. Little Jimmy Camp (14.0), the best second night's camp, is just a couple of minutes farther, with toilets, tables, and firepits.

Beyond the campground you curve west on a trail that soon passes above Windy Spring. Now your route parallels dirt Road 9WO3, keeping some distance below it. Presently, the road hairpins across the trail, and here you should find a sign identifying the PCT route. The trail heads west moderately down to Angeles Crest Highway 2, reaching it just east of its Islip Saddle intersection with now-closed Highway 39. Just west of the parking area and restrooms on

Islip Saddle, turn right on Mt. Williamson Trail 9WO2 and ascend moderately northwest past white firs and whitethorn ceanothus to the Mt. Williamson Summit Trail, which climbs 0.4 mile north to good views of fault-churned Devils Punchbowl. While you switchback west down from the ridgetop, you can look south down deep ravines in the friable granitic rock, tonalite, to the San Gabriel Wilderness, which is a Southern California refuge of mountain bighorn sheep. Ending the descent, the route merges with a jeep road for 200 yards, and then again crosses Angeles Crest Highway 2.

Your trail resumes about 50 yards west, to ascend Kratka Ridge in a heterogeneous forest of white fir, sugar and ponderosa pines, interior live oak, and mountain mahogany. Soon, you descend back to Angeles Crest Highway. Now you walk along the southern road shoulder, past a large, tan-metal, highway-maintenance shed for 180 yards to waterless Eagles Roost Picnic Area. At its entrance just west of the highway, turn west down a rocky, unsigned dirt road and descend to its end at the Rattlesnake Trail 1OW03, in a shady gully. This little-used path drops north under the stone gaze of Eagles Roost, which is now a popular rock-climbing challenge. We leave behind an older, poor path that climbs south and soon cross melodious Little Rock Creek (21.5), in cedar-lined Rattlesnake Canyon. While a cozy camp can be made beside the stream, no other sites are available here as the PCT continues down-canyon, out onto a steep hillside. The easy trail contours to Rattlesnake Spring in about one-half mile and then to another unnamed spring about a mile later. Past the second spring, a pleasant descent leads to several delightful camps beside Little Rock Creek, where the PCT merges with Burkhart Trail 1OW02. Now we turn south, easily cross the stream, and ascend southwest into Cooper Canyon. Past a pristine waterfall and the south-branching Burkhart Trail, which climbs to Buckhorn Flat Camp, the PCT route becomes an often-steep jeep road, Road 3NO2. It passes Cooper Canyon Camp (25.3), which, though often crowded, has reliable water. After a well-deserved break, continue the climb to forested Cloudburst Summit, where you meet the Angeles Crest Highway again, and find your transportation home.

Permits

No Wilderness Permit is required for this hike, since it only barely touches the borders of Sheep Mountain and San Gabriel wilderness areas. However, the use of camp stoves, even at trail camps, requires an annual California Campfire Permit, which is available from any Forest Service or California Division of Forestry office, including:

Angeles National Forest
701 North Santa Anita Avenue
Arcadia, CA 91006
(626) 574-1613, FAX (626) 574-5233

www.r5.fs.fed.us/angeles/

Build-Up/Wind-Down tips

Hey, this is L.A! Anything is available for a price, once you get back down to town. But if you want to linger for a few hours above the cars, crowds, and smog, and get an education to boot, be sure to stop at the Mount Wilson Observatory. This historic astronomical station, home of the 100-inch Hooker Telescope, has been pushing the frontiers of astrophysics for almost 100 years. It continues to be the site of cutting-edge solar research. Stories of the turn-of-the-century pioneers who first toiled to this peak are almost as interesting as the fantastic discoveries they made in the heavens above Los Angeles. It is open for inspection on weekends from 10 A.M. to 4 P.M., with guided tours at 1 P.M. To reach Mount Wilson, turn off of Highway 2 at Red Box, 14 miles above La Cañada, and follow the pavement 5 miles to the observatory parking area. There is a nice picnic area nearby.

Mount Wilson Observatory
(626) 793-3100

www.mtwilson.edu

However self-effacing he might wish to be, Sierra native Ben Schifrin has been a longtime author of, or contributor to, Wilderness Press' most important California backpacking guides (see "Author Bio & Bib" on page 492).

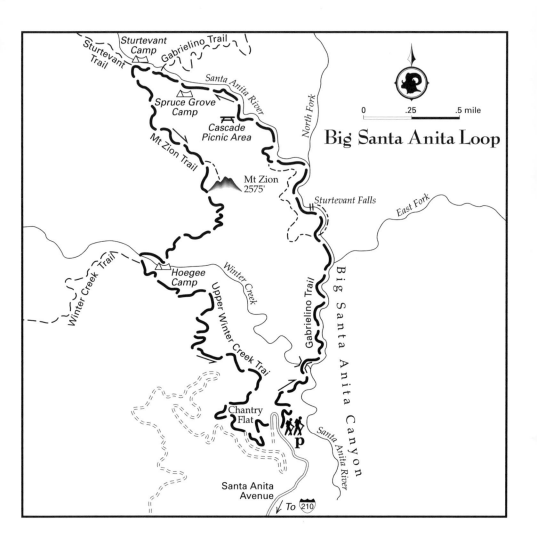

Sturtevant Camp

Gabrielino Trail

Sturtevant Trail

Santa Anita River

North Fork

Spruce Grove Camp

Cascade Picnic Area

Mt Zion Trail

Mt Zion 2575'

Sturtevant Falls

East Fork

Big Santa Anita Loop

0   .25   .5 mile

Winter Creek Trail

Hoegee Camp

Winter Creek

Upper Winter Creek Trail

Gabrielino Trail

Big Santa Anita Canyon

Chantry Flat

P

Santa Anita River

Santa Anita Avenue

To 210

Big Santa Anita Loop (Mt. Zion Loop)

—Jerry Schad

Route	Days	Elev. Gain/Loss	Difficulty	Miles
⟳	2	2100'/2100'	**	9.4

Campsites: Spruce Grove Camp: 3.5 miles
(see the Trip Description for others)

Map: USGS 7.5-min *Mount Wilson*

Best season: Fall, winter, and spring

Take this trip!

In the lush and shady recesses of the Front Range of the San Gabriel Mountains you can easily lose all sight and sense of the hundreds of square miles of dense metropolis, and the millions of Angelenos, that lie just over the ridge to the south. With easy access from the San Gabriel Valley by city street and mountain road, you can be laying bootprints down a fern-lined path less than half an hour after leaving the freeway traffic behind.

Trailhead

Exit Interstate 210 at Santa Anita Avenue in Arcadia and drive 6 miles north (first through the suburbs then up a curvy mountain road) to the large trailhead parking area at Chantry Flat.

TRIP DESCRIPTION:

Heads Up! Anticipate smog conditions: try to avoid days when a strong temperature inversion exists and stagnant air drifts into the lower canyons of the San Gabriel Mountains.

On weekends, it's wise to arrive early at Chantry Flat; otherwise parking is hard to come by. Also be aware that Spruce Grove Camp may be crowded with Boy Scouts and other campers on weekends. Weekdays are always a better bet.

In this scenic and varied loop trip from Chantry Flat, you'll climb by way of the Gabrielino National Recreation Trail to historic Sturtevant Camp, and return by way of the Mt. Zion and Upper Winter Creek trails. Two days easily suffices for the whole loop, but you have the option of stretching it to three days of very leisurely hiking if you spend a second night at Hoegee Camp.

From the lower parking lot at Chantry Flat, hike the first, paved segment of the Gabrielino Trail down to the confluence of Winter Creek and Big Santa Anita Canyon (0.6 mile). Pavement ends at a metal bridge spanning Winter Creek. Pass the restrooms and continue up alder-lined Big Santa Anita Canyon on a wide path following the left bank. The trail edges alongside a number of small cabins and various flood-control check dams built with concrete "logs," and soon assumes the proportions of a foot trail.

At 1.4 miles, amid a beautiful oak woodland, you come to a three-way split. The right branch goes up-canyon to the base of 50-foot-high Sturtevant Falls, a worthy side trip during the wet season. The middle and left branches join again about a mile upstream. The middle, more scenic trail slices across a sheer wall above the falls and continues through a veritable fairyland of miniature cascades and crystalline pools bedecked with giant chain ferns.

You pass Cascade Picnic Area (2.8) and arrive at Spruce Grove Camp, 3.5 miles from the start, named for the bigcone Douglas-fir (bigcone spruce) trees that attain truly inspiring proportions hereabouts. Stoves and tables are included at each of the seven sites.

Next morning climb a little farther, staying left on the Sturtevant Trail as the Gabrielino Trail veers right. After another 0.1 mile, Sturtevant Camp comes into view. This is both the oldest dating from 1893 and the only remaining resort in the Big Santa Anita drainage. Run by the Methodist Church as a retreat, the camp remains accessible only by foot trail.

Next, cross the creek via a check dam, continue another 0.1 mile, and look for stone steps rising on the left—the beginning of the Mt. Zion Trail, 3.9 miles from Chantry Flat. This restored version of the original trail to Sturtevant Camp winds delightfully upward along north slopes shaded by timber.

When the trail reaches a crest, take a short side path up through manzanita and ceanothus to the unremarkable summit of Mt. Zion, where a broad view can be had of the surrounding ridges and a small slice of the San Gabriel Valley.

Return to the main trail and begin a long, switchback descent (1000 feet of elevation loss in about 1.5 miles) down the dry, north canyon wall of Winter Creek—a sweaty affair if the day is sunny and warm. At the foot of this stretch you reach the cool canyon bottom and a T-intersection with the Winter Creek

Trail, 6.7 miles around the loop so far. Just below this point lies Hoegee's Camp, with 15 table-and-stove sites.

At the T-intersection, turn right, going upstream momentarily, follow the trail across the creek, and climb to the next trail junction. Bear left on the Upper Winter Creek Trail and complete the remaining 2.6 miles of easy, mostly level hiking—cool and semi-shaded nearly all the way—back to Chantry Flat.

Permits

For information on Big Santa Anita Canyon, contact Angeles National Forest, (818) 574-1613 or (818) 790-1151. All cars parked at the trailhead must display a National Forest Adventure Pass, $5 daily or $30 annually.

Angeles National Forest Web site: **www.r5.fs.fed.us/angeles/**

To learn about Southern California author Jerry Schad's multifarious activities and accomplishments, and for a list of his titles available from Wilderness Press, see "Author Bio & Bib" on page 492.

Big Leaf maple in the fall

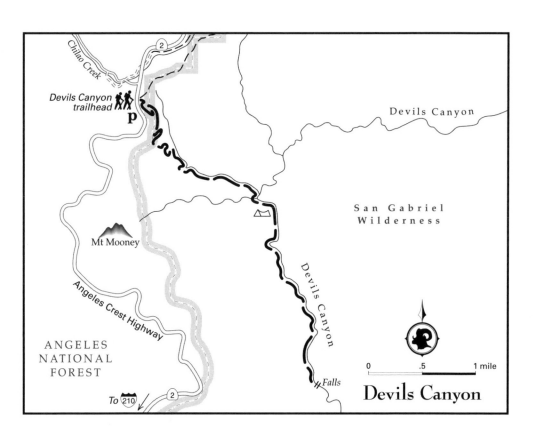

Chilao Creek

2

Devils Canyon
trailhead

P

Devils Canyon

San Gabriel
Wilderness

Mt Mooney

Devils Canyon

Angeles Crest Highway

ANGELES
NATIONAL
FOREST

To 210   2

Falls

0   .5   1 mile

Devils Canyon

10

Devils Canyon

—Jerry Schad

Route	Days	Elev. Gain/Loss	Difficulty	Miles
↰	2	2100'/2100'	**	9.8

Campsites: 2.7 miles

Map: USGS 7.5-min *Chilao Flat, Waterman Mtn.*

Best season: Fall, winter, and spring

Take this trip!

The varied, rough, and remote habitat of the San Gabriel Wilderness harbors mule deer, Nelson bighorn sheep, black bears, and mountain lions—facts that hint at the quality of the wilderness experience you can get there. Only one trail stabs deeply into the corrugated heart of this wilderness: the Devils Canyon Trail. It leads you to a clear cascading stream, fringed by a green ribbon of vegetation, hidden in the crease of a 2000-foot-deep canyon. Splash around in shallow pools, watch ducks and water ouzels at work or play, fish for trout, or trek down-canyon to visit the upper lip of a waterfall.

Trailhead

From Interstate 210 in La Cañada-Flintridge, drive up Angeles Crest Highway (State Highway 2) for 27 miles to the Devils Canyon trailhead. The well-marked trailhead is 3 miles past the Charlton Flats Picnic Area. If you reach the turnoff for the Chilao Visitor Center you have gone about 200 yards too far.

TRIP DESCRIPTION

Heads Up! Rare, torrential floods may visit Devils Canyon after heavy winter rains, rendering the canyon stream impossible to ford. The hike into and along the canyon is entirely

---

77

downhill on the way in and uphill on the way out. If the weather is warm and sunny, you may want to wait until afternoon before you start the steep climb out to ensure that you get plenty of shade.

The zigzagging descent on the trail takes you across slopes clothed alternately in chaparral and mixed-conifer forest. By 1.5 miles you reach a branch of what will soon become a trickling stream—one of the several tributaries that contribute to Devils Canyon's ample springtime flow. The deeply shaded trail leads to the main canyon, 2.6 miles (be sure to mark this spot or take note of surrounding landmarks so you can recognize this place when it's time to head back up the trail), and then downstream a bit farther to the site of a former trail camp on a flat bench west of the Devils Canyon stream. In accordance with the philosophy of returning wilderness areas to as natural a condition as possible, this former trail camp has had its stoves and tables removed.

Downstream, some real fun ensues if you're sure-footed and want to do some further exploring. You follow a fairly distinct path in places; otherwise you boulderhop and wade. Mini-cascades feed pools 3–4 feet deep harboring elusive brook trout. Water-loving alders and sycamores cluster along the stream, while patriarchal live oaks and bigcone Douglas-firs stand on higher and dryer benches and slopes, waiting in the wings, as it were, for the next big flood to sweep the upstarts away. Watch for poison oak as the canyon walls narrow; and keep an eye out for a silvery, two-tier waterfall at the mouth of a side canyon coming in from the east, nearly 2 miles down from the campsite.

Beyond the two-tier fall, 0.4 mile of rock scrambling and wading takes you to a constriction in the canyon where water slides down a sheer incline some 20 vertical feet. Avoiding the slippery lip of these falls, you might try scrambling up the rock wall to the right for an airy view of the cascade and shallow pool below. Without rapelling gear, this is basically the end of the line for downstream travel through the canyon.

Permits

As of this writing you may enter San Gabriel Wilderness without having the usual Wilderness Permit that is required for most other wilderness areas around the state. This does not absolve you from obtaining a fire permit, assuming seasonal regulations allow it. For more information, contact Angeles National Forest, (818) 574-1613 or (818) 790-1151. In addition, all cars parked at the trailhead must display a National Forest Adventure Pass, $5 daily or $30 annually.

Angeles National Forest Web site: **www.r5.fs.fed.us/angeles/**

Build-up/Wind-down tips

Before or after your trip visit the Chilao Visitor Center, open daily, just north of the Devils Canyon trailhead. This is the major interpretive facility for Angeles National Forest, with exhibits, free printed information, books for sale, and rangers on duty.

To learn about Southern California author Jerry Schad's multifarious activities and accomplishments, and for a list of his titles available from Wilderness Press, see "Author Bio & Bib" on page 492.

Pine slopes in the San Gabriel Wilderness

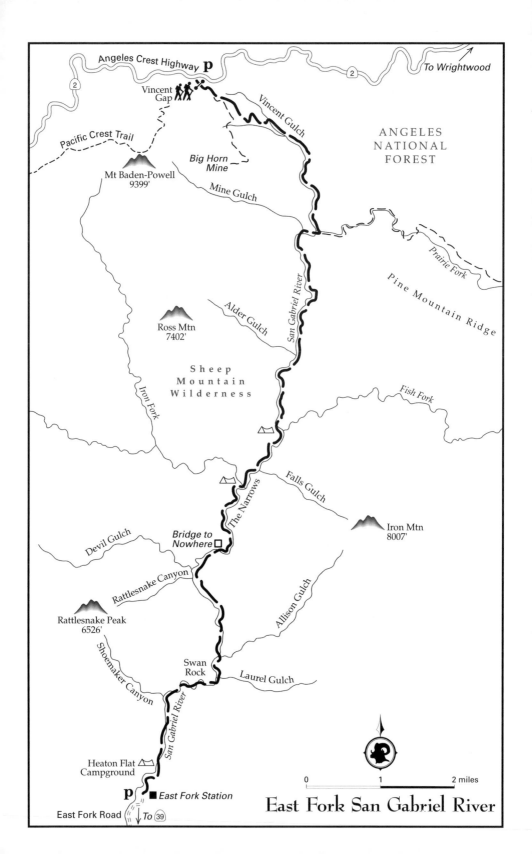

Angeles Crest Highway p

2 2 To Wrightwood

Vincent Gap

Vincent Gulch

Pacific Crest Trail

ANGELES
NATIONAL
FOREST

Big Horn
Mine

Mt Baden-Powell
9399'

Mine Gulch

Prairie Fork

San Gabriel River

Pine Mountain Ridge

Alder Gulch

Ross Mtn
7402'

Sheep
Mountain
Wilderness

Fish Fork

Iron Fork

Falls Gulch

The Narrows

Iron Mtn
8007'

Devil Gulch

Bridge to
Nowhere

Rattlesnake Canyon

Allison Gulch

Rattlesnake Peak
6526'

Shoemaker Canyon

Swan
Rock

Laurel Gulch

San Gabriel River

Heaton Flat
Campground

0   1   2 miles

p ■ East Fork Station

East Fork Road To 39

East Fork San Gabriel River

11

East Fork San Gabriel River

—Jerry Schad

Route	Days	Elev. Gain/Loss	Difficulty	Miles
↰	2	200'/4800'	***	14.5

Campsites: Fish Fork: 7.3 miles
Iron Fork: 8.4 miles
(see the Trip Description for others)

Map: USGS 7.5-min *Crystal Lake, Mount San Antonio, Glendora*

Best season: Late spring, summer, fall

Take this trip!

On this epic journey along the banks of the East Fork San Gabriel River, you'll descend nearly a mile in elevation, traveling from high-country pines and firs to sun-scorched chaparral. On the first day of hiking, you could experience a temperature increase of as much as 50° F. At one spot called The Narrows in the East Fork canyon, the stream lies 5200 feet below Iron Mountain to the east and 4000 feet below the ridge to the west—making this the deepest gorge in Southern California.

Trailhead

It's best to have someone drop you off at the start (Vincent Gap) and later pick you up at the end (East Fork Station), an 85-mile drive around by way of Interstate 15 to the east. The Vincent Gap trailhead is on Angeles Crest Highway, 9 miles west of Wrightwood. To reach East Fork Station, drive north from Azusa on Highway 39 for 10 miles to East Fork Road, then go 6 miles east to the end of the road.

TRIP DESCRIPTION

Heads Up! High water levels in the East Fork after a rainy winter or spring can make this route impassable or dangerous. Contact the Forest Service (or check out for yourself water levels in the lower canyon) before attempting this one-way, downhill trip. Long, hot June and July days are fine as long as you keep cool by getting wet at frequent intervals.

From the parking area on the south side of Vincent Gap, walk southeast down the gated road. After only about 200 yards, a footpath veers left, into Sheep Mountain Wilderness. Take it; the road itself continues toward the posted, privately owned Big Horn Mine, an inholding in the wilderness.

Intermittently shaded by bigcone Douglas-firs, white firs, Jeffrey pines, and live oaks, the path descends along the south slope of Vincent Gulch. The gulch itself follows the Punchbowl fault, a splinter of the San Andreas fault. After a few switchbacks, the trail crosses Vincent Gulch (usually dry at this point, wet a short distance below) at 1.6 miles. Thereafter it stays on or above the east bank as far as the confluence of Prairie Fork, 3.8 miles. At Prairie Fork a trail heads east to Cabin Flat. You veer right (west) down a gravelly wash, good for setting up a camp. Shortly after, at the Mine Gulch confluence, you bend left (south) into the wide bed of the upper East Fork. For several miles to come, there's no well-defined trail.

Proceed down the rock-strewn floodplain, crossing the creek (and battling alder thickets) several times over the next mile. The canyon becomes narrow for a while starting at about 5.0 miles, and you must wade or hop from one slippery rock to another. Fish Fork, on the left (east) at 7.3 miles, is the first large stream below Prairie Fork. Flat sites suitable for camping are nearby. The mouth of Iron Fork, on the right (west) at 8.4 miles, has more possible campsites.

If you have the time for an intriguing side trip, Fish Fork canyon is well worth exploring. Chock full of alder and bay, narrow with soaring walls, its clear stream tumbling over boulders, the canyon boasts one of the wildest and most beautiful settings in the San Gabriel Mountains. About 1.6 miles upstream lies a formidable impasse: there, the waters of Fish Fork drop 12 feet into an emerald-green pool set amid sheer rock walls.

Below Iron Fork you enter The Narrows. A rough trail, worn in by hikers, traverses this 1-mile-plus section of fast-moving water. You'll pass swimmable pools cupped in the granite and schist bedrock, and cross the stream when necessary. Listen and watch for water ouzels (dippers) by the edges of the pools.

At the lower portals of The Narrows (9.7), you come upon the enigmatically named Bridge to Nowhere. During the 1930s, road-builders managed to push a highway up along the East Fork stream to just this far. The arched, concrete bridge, similar in style to those built along Angeles Crest Highway, was to be a key link in a route that would carry traffic between the San Gabriel Valley and the desert near Wrightwood.

Fate intervened. A great flood in 1938 thoroughly demolished most of the road, leaving the bridge stranded.

Below the bridge, on remnants of the old road washed out in 1938, you'll run into more and more hikers, fishers, and other travelers out for the day. At 12.0 miles, Swan Rock—an outcrop of metamorphic rock branded with the light-colored imprint of a swan—comes into view on the right. At 14.0 miles you come upon Heaton Flat Campground. From there a final, easy 0.5-mile stroll takes you to the East Fork parking lot at the end of East Fork Road.

Permits

You should obtain a Wilderness Permit for the East Fork backpack route, which crosses Sheep Mountain Wilderness. Self-issuing permits are available at East Fork Station—but you end rather than start your trip there. So contact Angeles National Forest beforehand: (818) 574-1613 or (818) 790-1151. Cars parked at all trailheads must display a National Forest Adventure Pass, $5 daily or $30 annually.

Angeles National Forest Web site: **www.r5.fs.fed.us/angeles/**

To learn about Southern California author Jerry Schad's multifarious activities and accomplishments, and for a list of his titles available from Wilderness Press, see "Author Bio & Bib" on page 492.

The Coast Ranges I

The Ventana Wilderness of the Santa Lucia Range

The Ventana Wilderness (also referred to as the "Big Sur Mountains" by locals) is a 260-square-mile refuge beginning about 25 miles south of the Monterey Peninsula along the California coast. Elevations range within Ventana Wilderness as low as 300 feet to over a mile high. One of the most inaccessible wilderness areas, Ventana's four paved roads and three dirt roads get you to trailheads around the perimeter. With few trailheads, and trail routes that barely scratch its surface, cross-country travel here is virtually impossible. Though seasonal springs and tributary creeks abound throughout this wilderness, there are only four main rivers flowing out of its canyons. Only one of these rivers is dammed, the other three flow as unfettered today as they have for millions of years.

Such a setting has spawned a nearly unrivaled diversity. Animals as varied as cougars, bears, rattlesnakes, and condors inhabit its terrain. You will find plant life here as common as coastal oaks and manzanita, and as rare as giant redwoods and Santa Lucia firs. One minute you are hiking under a canopy of towering sequoias and the next you emerge onto an open, grassy hillside covered with California live oaks. A few hot springs can be found within Ventana but only one provides both the discharge and temperature optimal for a wilderness bath. And the setting in which you find Sykes Hot Spring is worthy of the time and energy required to reach it. While Ventana Wilderness is small enough that a strong and serious hiker can do a circumnavigation of its core in 3–4 days, a nearly 65-mile grand loop treats you to every facet of its varied terrain—of its plant and animal life. (JVM)

Upriver end of Los Padres Dam, Carmel River

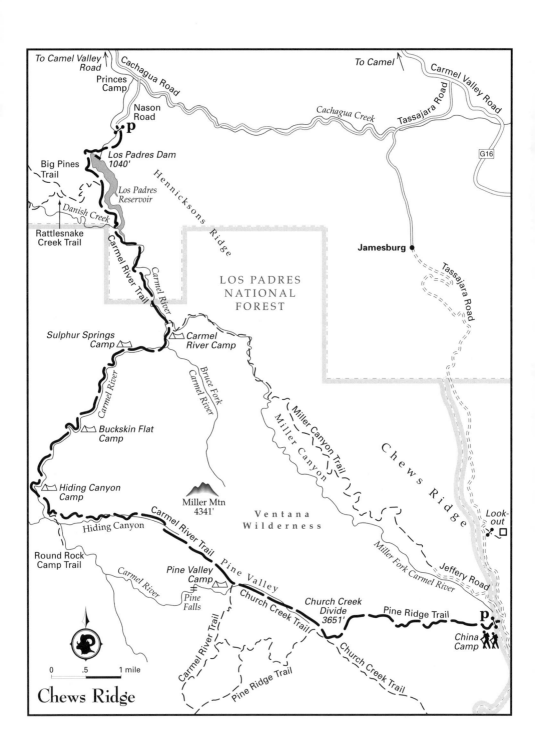

To Camel Valley Road
Cachagua Road
Princes Camp
Nason Road
p
To Camel
Carmel Valley Road
Cachagua Creek
Tassajara Road
G16

Los Padres Dam
1040'
Big Pines Trail
Los Padres Reservoir
Danish Creek
Rattlesnake Creek Trail
Hennicksons Ridge

Carmel River Trail
Carmel River

LOS PADRES
NATIONAL
FOREST

Jamesburg

Tassajara Road

Sulphur Springs Camp
Carmel River Camp

Carmel River

Bruce Fork Carmel River

Buckskin Flat Camp

Miller Canyon Trail
Miller Canyon
Chews Ridge

Hiding Canyon Camp

Miller Mtn
4341'

Ventana Wilderness

Carmel River Trail

Hiding Canyon

Look-out

Round Rock Camp Trail

Carmel River

Pine Valley Camp
Pine Falls
Carmel River Trail

Pine Valley

Church Creek Trail

Miller Fork Carmel River

Jeffery Road

Church Creek Divide
3651'

Pine Ridge Trail

p
China Camp

Church Creek Trail

Pine Ridge Trail

0   .5   1 mile

Chews Ridge

12

Chews Ridge—China Camp to Los Padres Dam via Pine Valley

—Jeffrey Van Middlebrook

Route	Days	Elev. Gain/Loss	Difficulty	Miles
↗	3	980'/4350'	***	18.8

Campsites: Pine Valley Camp: 5.3 miles
Hiding Canyon Camp: 9.6 miles
(see the Trip Description for others)

Map: USGS 7.5-min *Carmel Valley, Ventana Cones, Chews Ridge*

Best season: Late fall through spring (but accessible year-round)

Take this trip!

A globe-trotting adventurer told me 30 years ago, "The Ventana Wilderness is second only to the Amazon in ruggedness and shear inaccessibility." He was half right. While Ventana is very rugged, the trails make access to its beauty attainable by anyone willing to make the effort. This mostly downhill hike provides a taste of Ventana' s variety of plant life, views, and terrain. You traverse open, southwest-facing grassy slopes—a riot of wildflower colors in spring—gazing on tilted sandstone rock formations that beckon climbers and explorers. You trace a valley framed by sandstone cliffs among giant yellow pines. Oak and madrone abound along your route. And best of all, as the trail route zig-zags to the reservoir at trail's end, you cross a wonderful river 34 times and have your pick among dozens of clear-water swimming holes. If you can hike mid-week from late fall through early spring, you will likely have the entire route to yourself—wilderness exemplified!

Trailhead

Take Highway 1 to the Carmel Valley Road turnoff in Carmel. Turn east onto Carmel Valley Rd. and drive a pleasant 11 miles through a narrow valley strewn with large new homes, flower-farming fields, golf courses, and a budding wine-grape industry to Carmel Valley Village. This is your last source of gasoline and any variety of food and other supplies. Then continue (a total distance of 25.5 miles from Highway 1) to a junction with Tassajara Road. Turn right (south) and drive on pavement for only another 1.8 miles. Where the long washboard and rutted dirt road begins is a sort of phantom community known as Jamesburg. You climb almost steadily, on now-dirt Tassajara Rd., for the next 6 miles to the crest of Chews Ridge. Note: this route can be impassable in wet, winter months without a high-clearance 4WD vehicle, and snow cover is common then on 4000'+ Chews Ridge.

A gated fire road (left) at the high point offers a worthy side trip to the disintegrating, abandoned Chews Ridge fire lookout (there's parking opposite). But for your trailhead, descend more than 1.5 miles beyond the turnoff to a prominent dip and temporary widening of the road at China Camp. Park here and find your trailhead—signed for the Pine Ridge Trail—immediately right (west).

Since this hike requires either a car shuttle or an arranged drop-off and pickup by a friend, you need directions to the end point. Leave a vehicle here before you drive to the starting trailhead at Chews Ridge. From the short paved section of Tassajara Road turn onto Cachagua Road and head west. After several windy miles you reach a junction with Nason Road at a mobile home park. Nason Rd. leads directly to the gated Los Padres Dam trailhead and the Carmel River Trail. It's a 13-mile slog between trailheads over mostly washboard dirt roads.

TRIP DESCRIPTION

Heads Up! The Ventana Wilderness suffered a very extensive and protracted fire in the fall of 1999. Over 100,000 acres were burned. Because much of this route lies within the fire zone, before setting out contact the Forest Service office to learn if any trail closures might affect your hike (see Permits).

I prefer hiking the Ventana trails from late fall until early spring because there are fewer people, and the weather is cooler and more inviting. Yet what are enjoyable, 2-foot-deep crossings (34 between Hiding Canyon Camp and Los Padres Dam) in the spring, summer, and fall, turn into roaring torrents soon after. Choose your hiking routes and times well; know the weather forecasts.

Among other hazards note: the trails, not regularly maintained by the USFS, are subject to seasonal washout; little flies can harrass you from late spring through early fall; and some hikers have encountered mountain lions. Consequently, solo hiking is only for the most experienced wilderness traveler.

From the start of this route, and for just over a mile, you climb steadily west. For the duration of this uphill stretch you are under a dense canopy of mixed trees, until finally breaking into the open at a stand of oaks. Immediately the trail begins a long and gentle descent west across open grassy hillsides interspersed with brush and mostly oak trees. In spring these hillsides are covered in wildflowers. As you traverse downward for the next 2.5 miles you get expansive panoramas of sandstone rock formations, distant toothlike Cone Peak (5155) to the southwest, and Pine Ridge dominating the western skyline. After 3.6 miles from the trailhead you reach Church Creek Divide, an obvious broad saddle with a four-way junction. To your left the Church Creek Trail drops toward Tassajara, passing Indian caves and the sandstone rock formations you saw during your initial descent. Straight ahead the Pine Ridge Trail continues its long ascent to the crest of Pine Ridge.

If you continued along the Pine Ridge Trail, you would eventually reach the Big Sur River canyon, following a long and steep descent from Pine Ridge. It's in the Big Sur River canyon that you would find Sykes Hot Springs and a well-deserved hot soak in one of the most beautiful natural settings. The overall distance from the trailhead at Chews Ridge/China Camp to Big Sur, via the Pine Ridge Trail, is roughly a marathon's length, 26 miles. Though that route offers many wonderful, overnight campsites, the entire distance could be covered in a single day. I've hiked it this way, with and without a backpack, and I've led three, full-moon hikes of the route, arriving in Big Sur for breakfast.

This hike's route follows the Church Creek Trail (right) from the divide. The trail begins an immediate and gentle descent into Pine Valley. For the first mile or so you follow a small seasonal creek (the headwaters of the Carmel River) through a narrow canyon. Soon the canyon opens into a broad valley defined by Pine Ridge to the west and inviting sandstone cliffs to the east: this is Pine Valley. Following the trail northwest through Pine Valley you pass dozens of large yellow pines. Both the ponderosa and the Jeffrey varieties are present. You'll know the Jeffrey from its distinctive bark pattern and dominating size. In addition, a "smell check" of its bark confirms its type. Depending upon your nose, you will either detect a vanilla or pineapple aroma to the bark. It was here in 1972 that I discovered a yellow pine I dubbed the "Jeffrey Ponderwood." The tree in question had characteristics of both varieties. I sent the data to a UC Berkeley botanist and he concurred that the tree was a hybrid.

You reach Pine Valley Camp 5.3 miles from the trailhead. If the great fire of 1999 didn't destroy the private cabin in Pine Valley, it will serve as the best landmark for the campground, which is immediately to the west. The cabin itself was built in 1976 by a man from Salinas. Having learned of a 40-acre private inholding in Ventana Wilderness to be auctioned in Monterey, he went prepared to pay more than the only competition's—the USFS'—ceiling price. I first encountered him in the fall of 1976. As I approached Pine Valley Camp, I could hear the sounds of construction before I drew a bead on the site. Dumbfounded, I confronted the man and told him he couldn't build a cabin in Ventana Wilderness. He smiled, got down from his ladder, and invited me for coffee at his campfire. He then recounted how he'd acquired his own wilderness retreat—how he'd become a hero to some and an object of scorn to others. In 1998 that beautiful little cabin was still standing.

If you were to go no farther and stayed in Pine Valley for a couple of days, returning to Chews Ridge, your trip would be far from wasted. This little valley is a worthy destination all in itself. From Pine Valley Camp you can take a hike to the upper Pine Falls pool or you can climb atop the sandstone cliffs and sunbathe.

To continue toward Los Padres Dam, your destination, you pass through the gate left of the cabin and begin a northwest traverse across a meadow. First ascending gradually to a saddle, you reach another gate and the start of a long and steep descent through Hiding Canyon. The trail zigzags its way along the banks of a creek you cross nine times during your descent. Since the creek tends to be seasonal, be sure to leave Pine Valley with a full water bottle. At the end of this 4-mile descent you climb briefly up and around a brush-covered slope, meandering in and out of gullies. The trail here is often overgrown, requiring you pay close attention to the obscure path. And pushing through this tick-infested area demands you stop occasionally to check yourself for these nasty little critters.

Just beyond this relatively short section, you pass the junction with the Round Rock Camp Trail (9.2). You reach Hiding Canyon Camp and the Carmel River after 9.6 miles from the trailhead. Here begins your first of 34 Carmel River crossings to come. At the camp just across the river upstream, you'll find picnic tables (if they haven't been chopped up for firewood) and fire rings. You will also find the Puerto Suelo Trail junction.

If you took the Puerto Suelo Trail, you'd begin a long and arduous climb for over 4 miles to the Skinners Ridge Trail. At this higher junction you could take a left (heading south) toward Ventana Double Cone Peak, or right (heading northwest) toward Pat Springs, Turner Creek, and Botchers Gaps. Ventana Double Cone Peak once sported a fire lookout, and from the peak's tabletop the hiker is afforded a commanding 360° panorama of the entire wilderness. Only three peaks in Ventana offer such views: Cone Peak (5155) at the southwestern border of the wilderness; Junipero Serra Peak (5910) at the southeastern boundary; and Ventana Double Cone Peak (4853) here in the Ventana heart. Ventana Double Cone, my favorite, requiring a 17-mile, one-way hike from the closest trailhead at Botchers Gap, is also the most demanding peak to reach.

Consider carrying a pair of waterproof sandals to wear from Hiding Camp until your last river crossing just before the Los Padres Dam. Removing shoes and socks for 34 crossings in 7 miles will drive you crazy. Even in low-water conditions there are several crossings that require wading. Running shoes work great for this task but it's not comfortable hiking in saturated shoes.

If you enjoy skinny-dipping in crystal clear (and cold) swimming holes, then you'll be in paradise as you wind your way down the Carmel River. Dozens of enticing pools tempt you along this way. If you hike in the hotter months, you will not be able to resist doffing your sweaty hiking clothes and jumping in for a refreshing swim. Those who like to fish will find the best fishing in Ventana Wilderness. And there's little competition from other anglers, as few of them take the arduous hike required to access these wilderness fishing holes.

There are a couple trail junctions along the Carmel River (Big Pines Trail and Miller Canyon Trail), but the route is obvious. There are also a few camp-sites in the 9 miles between Hiding Canyon Camp and the Los Padres Dam: Buckskin Flat Camp (11.4), Sulphur Springs Camp (13.0), Carmel River Camp (13.9), and Bluff Camp (14.7). Water is abundant, of course, but I advise you to filter or treat it. Keep your eyes and ears open for rattlesnakes along this river route. In 1998 I encountered the largest rattler I've ever seen in the Ventana. It was coiled and rattling right in the middle of the trail at Sulphur Springs Camp.

For the last couple of miles the trail veers away from the Carmel River to skirt Los Padres Reservoir about 200 feet above its west shore. Soon you reach the dam itself, crossing just beneath its edifice and dropping down to a steel bridge across the spillway. Beyond the bridge you follow the obvious dirt road

Upper Carmel River near Hiding Camp

that climbs northeast out of the basin. After a brief climb the dirt road descends to the gated dirt parking lot. Unless you have a vehicle parked here, you have a half-mile walk downhill to Princes Camp (for a cold beer at the funky bar; see below) or to Cachagua Road. Cachagua Road, taken left, leads back to Carmel Valley Road, or, taken right, to Tassajara Road.

Permits

While neither Wilderness Permit nor trail quota is in effect at this writing for Ventana Wilderness, contact the Forest Service to learn current trail conditions:

USFS Administrative Office
406 S. Mildred Avenue
King City, CA 93930
(831) 385-5434

Build-up/Wind-down tips

If you were to continue your drive south on Tassajara Road for another 10 miles beyond China Camp, you would reach the gated entrance to the Zen Buddhist retreat. From May until October the monks open the retreat to the general public. While the entrance fee increases periodically, the last time I was there the cost was $15 per person for day-use only. Reservations are required for overnight accommodations. For your day-use fee you have access to both clothing-optional hot springs and swimming holes along Tassajara Creek. This is a great place for families as well as individuals seeking a safe and meditative environment for alternative wilderness enjoyment. Needless to say, showing respect for the Buddhist monks and their year-round home is essential.

Besides hiking and trail running in Ventana Wilderness, Jeffrey Van Middlebrook has many times "gone the distance" on the John Muir Trail as he states in "Author Bio & Bib" on page 492.

The Coast Ranges II

Henry W. Coe State Park in the Diablo Range

Henry W. Coe State Park at 81,000 acres is the largest state park in Northern California. Formerly settled by cattle ranchers, the lands have been acquired in sections since the first gift to Santa Clara County by Sada Coe Robinson in 1953. Excellent trails, sheltered by oaks, lead up ridges and over grasslands with distant views of the entire Bay Area and, on clear days, of the Sierra Nevada crest. In spring a glorious wildflower display is spread before the hiker; in fall the golden hillsides epitomize California's beauty.

Its close proximity to urban areas of southern San Francisco Bay and "Silicon Valley" make it ideal for ambitious dayhikes and backpacking trips. The western parcel near park headquarters, the former ranch of the Coe family, is well known for its miles of trails, deep canyons, upland meadows, and flowing streams. Here there are a visitor center with memorabilia of the Coe family, car-camping facilities, miles of trails, and 18 backpack camps.

The southwestern parcel lies on the east side of Coyote Creek and offers access to the most recently acquired ranch lands. Its two entrances, Coyote Creek and Hunting Hollow, are at lower elevations, thus offering you immediate uphill challenges. Here are grand views of the southern Diablo Range, new campsites, and opportunities to reach previously unknown regions. (JR&BC)

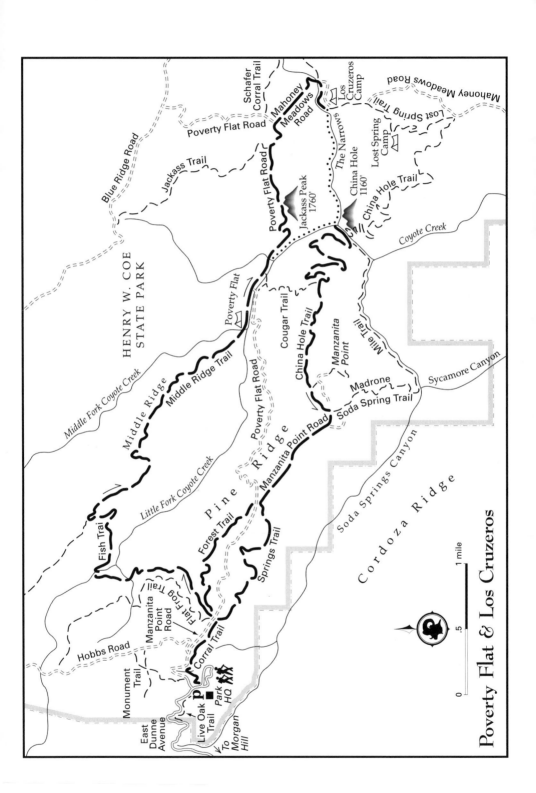

Poverty Flat & Los Cruzeros

HENRY W. COE STATE PARK

Blue Ridge Road

Schafer Corral Trail

Poverty Flat Road

Mahoney Meadows Road

Jackass Trail

Poverty Flat Road

Los Cruzeros Camp

Lost Spring Trail

Jackass Peak 1760'

The Narrows

Lost Spring Camp

China Hole 1160'

China Hole Trail

Coyote Creek

Middle Fork Coyote Creek

Poverty Flat

Middle Ridge

Middle Ridge Trail

Poverty Flat Road

Cougar Trail

China Hole Trail

Manzanita Point

Mile Trail

Little Fork Coyote Creek

Pine Ridge

Madrone

Soda Spring Trail

Sycamore Canyon

Fish Trail

Forest Trail

Manzanita Point Road

Springs Trail

Soda Springs Canyon

Cordoza Ridge

Flat Frog Trail

Hobbs Road

Manzanita Point Road

Corral Trail

Monument Trail

Park HQ

Live Oak Trail

East Dunne Avenue

To Morgan Hill

0   .5   1 mile

Poverty Flat & Los Cruzeros or Lost Spring from Coe Park Headquarters

—Jean Rusmore & Betsy Crowder

Route	Days	Elev. Gain/Loss	Difficulty	Miles
↺	2 or 3	2160'/2160'	**	13.9

(via Jackass Peak Road)
13.6
(via Middle Fork and The Narrows)
(Add 4.6 miles for a second-day loop side trip to
Lost Spring and Mahoney Meadows)

Campsites: Poverty Flat: 5.1 miles (sites farthest from creek have the most shade)

Los Cruzeros: 6.9 miles (site farthest upstream on East Fork before confluence with Kelly Cabin Creek has good shade and fine views)

Lost Spring: 7.6 miles (has fairly reliable water, and good shade, but room for only one party)

(see the Trip Description for others)

Map: USGS 7.5-min *Mt. Sizer, Mississippi Creek;*
Pine Ridge Association's *Henry W. Coe State Park* map

Best season: Spring; and fall, depending on water

Take this trip!

This trip takes you on a circle route around the western area of Henry W. Coe State Park—sampling high ridges, dense manzanita forests, oak savannas, and campsites beside two forks of Coyote Creek. You will climb two of the main ridges that run northwest-southeast, and descend to historic Native American and Spanish explorer sites. In years of plentiful rain, frocks of spring wildflowers clothe the hillsides and swimming holes tempt hot hikers. By skipping the Los Cruzeros night and the exploratory side trips, you could do this trip as an overnight.

Trailhead

From Highway 101 east of Morgan Hill take East Dunne Avenue 13 miles east, climbing via innumerable switchbacks, to park headquarters.

TRIP DESCRIPTION

Heads Up! When you make your campsite reservation, inquire about the availability of water in the creeks, and be sure to carry a water purifier. Due to the heat and exposure, it's best to get an early morning start up Middle Ridge, and carry plenty of water. While no open fires are allowed, you can use a backpacking stove.

Start your trip on the Corral Trail, beginning just across the road from park headquarters near the stop sign. This trail goes left (downhill) into a little gully below the barn, and heads toward Manzanita Point. In and out of oak-wooded ravines, the trail gently contours along the hillside where chaparral grows on the drier, south-facing slopes. In less than ½ mile you come out on a tree-studded grassland, an oak savanna. The large black oaks growing on the north-facing slopes have shiny, deeply lobed 6"-long leaves with sharp points. The new leaves, fuzzy and reddish in spring, become deep green in summer. By fall—especially in colder locations—they turn yellow tinged with red.

When the Corral Trail meets the Springs Trail (0.6), you veer left (north) to cross the wide Manzanita Point Road to a well-marked trail junction. You take the Fish Trail heading north, pass the Flat Frog Trail on the left, and note the Forest Trail taking off for Manzanita Point on your right. The latter would be a fine route on your return to headquarters. Heading north you may see uphill to the right (east) the fences of a corral that Sada Coe built when she managed Pine Ridge Ranch. Today a backpack site, Old Corral Camp, stands under the oak and pine trees just north of the corral.

The Fish Trail then bends around the hillside to enter a tight, shady little canyon. On a hot day this is a welcome, cool stretch under dark bay trees beside a watercourse that is dry by summer, as are several other small tributaries of Little Fork Coyote Creek that you cross. After a few switchbacks through the woods, you arrive at an open, grassy valley where deep-blue heads of tall brodiaea wave above the emerging oats in spring. In summer and fall, the magnificent specimens of valley oak here stand out darkly against the pale gold grass.

In the fall you might watch for holes in the ground the size of a quarter, where the hairy-bodied, long-legged tarantula lines its little underground well with a silky web that catches the insects it eats. Also in Coe Park lives the tarantula hawk, an insect that stings the tarantula, paralyzes it, and lays its eggs in the victim's body.

Contouring along the east-facing hillside you make a quick switchback down to boulder-strewn Little Fork Coyote Creek. Now you climb 0.6 mile through mixed woodland and chaparral on the south-facing slope to reach the Middle Ridge Trail junction (2.8).

Here, from your 2480' vantage point on Middle Ridge you see northeast to 3000' Blue Ridge, which cuts diagonally northwest-southeast through the park for about 7 miles. The Middle Ridge Trail, for hikers and (except after rain) for bicyclists—no horses—lies on the sloping plateau of Middle Ridge. Your route first goes through the shade of a dense growth of huge manzanitas. Their glistening, mahogany-red trunks support a broad canopy of leaves that casts a deep shadow. On a still, late-summer day you might hear the faint rustle of little papery curls of bark peeling from the trunks and falling to carpet the ground.

Then the path emerges onto grasslands, which soon widen, and you walk through a magnificent, broad, undulating savanna with immense, widely spaced valley and blue oaks. The trail slopes down on the south side of the broad ridge past a few old oaks riddled with woodpecker holes. As you descend, your view south over the canyon of the Little Fork is of Pine Ridge. You can pick out the Poverty Flat ranch road winding up through rugged woodlands of the ridge's north-facing slope, where this route will eventually take you.

About a mile from the Fish Trail junction, the trail turns northeast, crosses the ridge, dips into a few ravines and then drops down the north side. Here the forest deepens, and trees of many species crowd the steep slopes— madrones, tall ponderosa pines and gray pine, blue and black oaks interspersed with a few canyon oaks. Toyon, manzanita, and poison oak fill the understory and hardy, native bunchgrass flourishes on this hillside. You feel truly remote from civilization here—privileged humans in this wilderness. Often the only noises are the calls of many birds and the splashing of the creek in the canyon below.

On many switchbacks you continue southeast and down the steep slope for more than a mile. Arriving at the confluence of Little and Middle Forks of Coyote Creek, you are on a narrow peninsula between them. Sunlight filters through the trees, and patterns of light dance on the waters of grass-edged pools (5.0).

The first Poverty Flat backpack camp is just across the Middle Fork on a broad flat under great oaks. Hop across on the rocks—there's no bridge here. Four other campsites are downstream beyond the ford where the Poverty Flat Road crosses. These campsites now are served by a very modern outhouse, something an early, unnamed homesteader did not have. The story goes that this settler held out for years against Henry Coe, who wanted to purchase this pleasant site—thus the name Poverty Flat. Here, also, was one of the park's largest Native American settlements, with abundant fish and game, and berries and other fruit nearby.

On your second day out, heading for Los Cruzeros Camp, you have two options—one cross-country, the other on a road. The first is the shortest, entails less uphill, but depends on the season and the depth of water in the Middle Fork. It requires more than a mile of scrambling downstream over rocks and boulders in the narrow confines of the creek's passage between the two promontories of Jackass Peak and Manzanita Point to reach China Hole. (This shortcut is not shown on the park map.) If the weather is warm, you might try a dip in one of the deep pools at the confluence of the Middle and East forks there. From China Hole it is another mile of off-trail rockhopping or walking over the gravelly streambed (if the water is low) along The Narrows of East Fork Coyote Creek to reach Los Cruzeros (6.6). At high water, neither of these interesting scrambles should be attempted.

The second option requires a stiff 0.8-mile pull up Poverty Flat Road as it switchbacks up the north side of 1760' Jackass Peak. Do this climb in the early part of a hot day to take advantage of the intermittent shade of overhanging valley oaks and occasional blue oaks. Coe Park's wide patrol roads can be hot in midday, so carry plenty of water. At the road's highest point there is an informal trail heading (right) for the tree-topped summit of Jackass Peak. But this trip continues on the main road, passes the Jackass Trail coming down from Blue Ridge on the left, and then reaches the junction with the Mahoney Meadows Road. Here the Poverty Flat Road veers off left, but you bear right on the Mahoney Meadows Road (6.5).

Descending rapidly through rolling grasslands, you see northeast to Willow Ridge and the ragged Eagle Pines atop it, and south to the long Mahoney Meadows ridge lands. In spring the hillsides are gloriously strewn with an array of yellow, blue, and orange wildflowers. The meadows to the northeast, known for their brilliant spring flower displays, are called Miller Field, named for former land baron Henry Miller, who grazed great herds of cattle here.

In less than ½ mile Mahoney Meadows Road crosses the East Fork Coyote Creek and heads uphill, but you can follow a narrow trail south along the east bank of the creek to its confluence with Kelly Cabin Creek. Situated on broad flats above the East Fork and shaded by sizable valley oaks are the three Los Cruzeros campsites (6.9).

When the explorer Juan Bautista de Anza and his men came through here from the San Antonio Valley, they named this place Arroyo del Coyote. The Spanish word *cruzeros*, meaning "cross" or "creek," could be the basis for its present name—Los Cruzeros. Was it named for the creek crossing? Or did the small band of explorers set up a cross for prayer here before continuing on their journey? Today's travelers will find the site of their second night's stay a peaceful place, where several white-trunked sycamores survive and three beautiful valley oaks flourish on a gravel bar in the middle of the creekbed. The presumed Anza campsite at Los Cruzeros is now quite eroded by the floods of recent years, but the other campsites are fine.

Since the trip to Los Cruzeros from Poverty Flat is short, you may want to leave your pack and camping gear here, explore upstream along the East Fork's gravelly creekbed, and join the Schafer Corral Trail at the base of Miller Field. Or you could visit the Lost Spring campsite on the flanks of Mahoney Meadows. If you choose the latter, continue uphill (south) for 0.4 mile on Mahoney Meadows Road, past the original Los Cruzeros campsite, then veer right (southwest) on the Lost Spring Trail, zigzagging uphill through light shade. The campsite at Lost Spring, just 0.7 mile from Los Cruzeros in a shady, black-oak woodland, has a picnic table and fairly reliable year-round water.

If you feel like continuing farther, follow the well-graded trail 0.6 mile up to the junction of the main Mahoney Meadows Road and the China Hole Trail. Here on the wide, rolling grasslands are 360° views—ridge after ridge of mountains—and on either side the canyons of Coyote and Kelly Cabin creeks. In spring the grasslands are ablaze with color—blue lupines contrasting with yellow johnny jump-ups. In fall, too, there is brilliant color—poison oak turned red, pink, and orange and the gray-leaved, scarlet California fuchsia.

You could return to your Los Cruzeros campsite from the Mahoney Meadows Trail junction by way of the 2.2-mile China Hole Trail and The Narrows (if the water is low enough), descending on switchbacks through a cover of bay trees, with occasional black oaks towering overhead. At the base of the trail you come out on the east side of Coyote Creek and bear right (north), upstream to the deep pools and rocky beaches of China Hole, which invite you to stop for a swim or a snack. At the confluence of Middle and East Coyote creeks you bear right (due east) for 1 mile through The Narrows to reach Los Cruzeros—a 4.6-mile side trip. (See previous description of The Narrows.)

To return to Coe Park headquarters after your stay at Los Cruzeros, take The Narrows route to China Hole (unless high water determines your return route via Poverty Flat and the 0.7-mile Cougar Trail along the north side of Manzanita Point). Then proceed downstream over and around rocks, under willows, alders, and young sycamores for 0.1 mile on the west side of Coyote Creek (8.0). Pick up the well-graded China Hole Trail and zigzag up the south-facing, grassy hillside, shaded by great oaks. In spring blue-flowered iris bloom beside the trail; in fall the small purple-flowered aster brightens the trailside. Then you walk into a 1994 prescribed-burn area now regrown with chaparral plants—chamise, ceanothus, and mountain mahogany, surmounted by skeletons of tall, dead manzanita.

Beyond the burn you step back into a mature manzanita forest of deep mahogany trunks and gray-green leaves, where occasional madrone and black oak trees pierce the manzanita canopy. At 10.6 miles you pass the Cougar Trail coming in on your right, and continue on the China Hole Trail 0.8 mile to reach Manzanita Point Camp 7 (11.4). Take the wide, unpaved Manzanita Point Road back toward headquarters. At the junction of Poverty Flat and Manzanita Point roads (12.3) you can turn right (northeast) on the shady 1.1-mile Forest Trail—your best trail for a hot day—or take the 1.0-mile Springs Trail on the left (southwest side of ridge). Each trail contours gently back to its junction with the 0.6-mile Corral Trail, on which you continue to headquarters (13.9 or 14.0).

Permits

There is a park fee and campsite reservations are required; contact

Henry W. Coe State Park
Box 846
Morgan Hill, CA 94038

Phone: (408) 779-2728; Web site at **www.coepark.parks.ca.gov**
(Register with park staff before starting your trip.)

San Francisco Bay trail aficionados and authors Rusmore & Crowder have made lasting contributions to promoting environmental awareness through their guidebooks. To learn more see "Author Bio & Bib" on page 492.

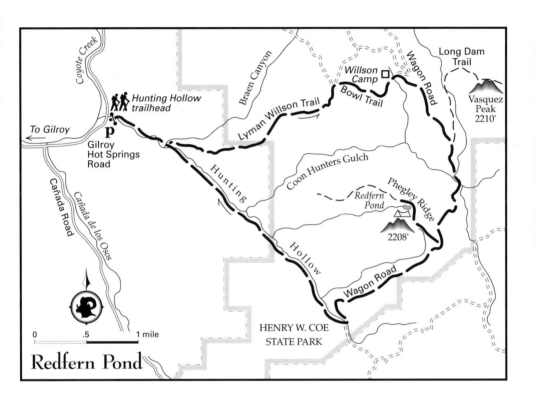

Coyote Creek

Braen Canyon

Long Dam Trail

Willson Camp

Wagon Road

Vasquez Peak 2210'

Hunting Hollow trailhead

Lyman Willson Trail

Bowl Trail

p

To Gilroy

Gilroy Hot Springs Road

Coon Hunters Gulch

Phegley Ridge

Redfern Pond

2208'

Hunting

Cañada Road

Cañada de los Osos

Hollow

Wagon Road

0   .5   1 mile

HENRY W. COE STATE PARK

Redfern Pond

14

Redfern Pond from Hunting Hollow

—Jean Rusmore & Betsy Crowder

Route	Days	Elev. Gain/Loss	Difficulty	Miles
↻	2	1352'/1352'	**	11

Campsites: Redfern Pond: 6.4 miles

Map: USGS 7.5-min *Gilroy Hot Springs;*
Pine Ridge Association's *Henry W. Coe State Park* map

Best season: Spring or fall.

Take this trip!

In the more recently opened, southwestern corner of Henry W. Coe State Park, this trip takes the backpacker up high, steep-sided ridges above tree-shaded canyons, and through remote grasslands dotted with oaks and punctuated by rocky outcrops. This area is heavily used by equestrians, as it has easy access for horse trailers, but its beauty deserves much wider acquaintance. Numerous small ponds are remnants of the cattle-grazing era, and this trip's overnight destination to Redfern Pond is one of the park's most attractive.

Trailhead

From Highway 101 on the north side of Gilroy, take Leavesley Road east about 1 mile to New Road and turn left (north). Turn right (east) onto Roop Road, which then becomes Gilroy Hot Springs Road, and continue east beside Coyote Creek, passing Coyote Creek County Park Road on the left. The pavement gives way to gravel and after 9 miles you reach the large Hunting Hollow parking lot on your right. Here you pay your State Park fee at the kiosk and register for overnight camping (previously reserved—see Permits below).

On the Madrone Spring Trail

TRIP DESCRIPTION

> **Heads Up!** Be sure to treat pond water before drinking it, and use a stove instead of a campfire for cooking.

This trip begins through the gate at the southeast end of the Hunting Hollow parking lot. The first half mile along one of the tributaries of Coyote Creek is along a dirt road, through a wide valley with magnificent sycamores growing in the creekbed and huge bay trees nearby. In the fall ground squirrels busy themselves in the meadow near the creek, gathering winter supplies. The road/trail crosses back and forth over the creek four times in the first half mile. In a wet spring you might get your shoes wet; carrying a hiking stick helps you leap across to dry ground.

After 0.5 mile you reach the junction of Lyman Willson Ridge Trail on the left—actually a wide trail that formerly was a ranch road. If you hear a squeaking noise here it will not be a worried animal but a windmill, pumping water into a nearby horse trough. Beyond the junction under a large oak, a small fenced camping spot complete with picnic table, cupboard, and barbecue, makes a good starting place for an equestrian trip.

Following the Lyman Willson Ridge Trail through a gate, past a corral shaded by walnut trees, your route heads east steeply uphill. You are now in oak woodland with typical, Henry Coe open grassland visible on Middle Steer Ridge left across the canyon. In spring iris, brodiaea, and buttercups are seen everywhere; in fall the smell of tarweed permeates the air. As you ascend the ridge you see to the south the tree-covered slope of the next canyon, part of Phegley Ridge, and at an open spot catch a glimpse of distant Pacheco Peak and Lovers Leap near the Pacheco Pass Highway. If you look down-canyon west across the Santa Clara Valley, you can see Loma Prieta, the highest peak in the Santa Cruz Mountains.

After an uphill mile some rocks in the shade of blue oaks provide a convenient rest stop. Then comes a long stretch of open grassland before the trail contours right into shade of some black oaks. As you climb, scan the trail for tracks of deer, coyote, fox, and bobcat, plus an occasional horse or human.

After 1.5 miles the trail levels out a bit and crests a knoll on the ridge, where there are wide views east, south, and west. While Vasquez Peak to the east is the highest nearby point at 2210 feet, from here it's a rounded grassy knob. The trail crosses open grasslands for another mile to the junction with the Bowl Trail (2.6). At this writing there is no sign, but it is easy to identify using your map. The Lyman Willson Trail continues straight uphill; the northward branch of the Bowl Trail, apparently little used, contours left. Your route follows the eastward-trending branch of the Bowl Trail right. Yellow tarweed smells very strong in the fall. You see two dammed cattle ponds, one below right, one immediately left. Grazing is no longer permitted in this part of the park, but wild animals also appreciate getting a drink.

Increasing numbers of rocky outcrops—a part of the Franciscan Formation composed of blue schist—add interest to the scene. Oaks grow picturesquely around these rocks. After passing a small nearby spring, and attaining the trip's highest elevation at 2208 feet, the trail—now a rough road—begins to drop down to Willson Camp, the former cattle ranch of Lyman Willson (3.5). Nestled in the shade of a huge live-oak tree, the old house looks south across grasslands and canyons toward Pacheco Peak. It takes about 2½ hours to reach this place, whose remains include an old cowshed, two derelict house trailers, various shacks, and remnants of waterlines.

Lyman Willson was the son of an early Gilroy pioneer, Horace Willson, who immigrated from New Hampshire in 1853 to what was then known as San Ysidro. Horace accumulated large landholdings by homesteading and purchase in the Diablo Range east of Gilroy. Sons Edwin and Lyman ranched property of their own near Gilroy Hot Springs. While bringing a deer down Middle Ridge to Hunting Hollow from the family hunting camp in 1915, Lyman was thrown from his horse and killed. While Edwin lived until 1937, the ranch was sold 8 years earlier. (The peak named for the Willson family and their ranch location are incorrectly spelled—only one "l"—on the USGS *Gilroy Hot Springs* quad in the 7.5-minute series.)

From Willson Camp continue a short distance southeast to a trail junction with Wagon Road, a graded dirt road that follows Steer Ridge. As you head right (south) along the ridge, note the sign at the junction that says it is 6.9 miles north to Pacheco Camp, and 1.8 miles north and then east to Vasquez Peak. Great views east, south, and west stretch before you. Looking below the trail at another stock pond you may catch a glimpse of a wild pig and piglets quenching their thirst. These descendants of escaped domestic pigs crossed with wild European boars have proliferated in the Diablo Range; you frequently see their rootings in the ground. Their tracks are similar to those of deer. Do not approach too closely because boars can be aggressive, as can a sow with piglets.

At another trail junction (4.6), the Long Dam Trail leads north then east toward Vasquez Peak. But you continue south alternately descending steeply to cross three creeks, then again struggling steeply uphill. At 5.8 miles an unsigned track cuts off right toward the Redfern Pond Trail. In some seasons this may be hard to find, so continue on Wagon Road to the main junction (6.0). Here, next to a small stock pond, the Redfern Pond Trail heads right (north), rising gently uphill across the open grasslands of Phegley Ridge.

When you crest the ridge, about 0.5 mile farther on, you reach a 2200' vantage point of your hike. Below you lies a large linear pond about 1½ acres in size, partly encircled by tall reeds. The small dam is at the far end, and the pond drains to the west. Songs of red-winged blackbirds rise from the inviting bowl, and you may hear the cry of a red-tailed hawk cruising high above. Blue- and live-oak trees dot the grassy knolls above the pond, providing many inviting campsites. The state park map suggests a campsite above the pond to the right, and another beyond the pond left of the trail. While the trail continues on a short distance, this is your welcome home for the night.

You have the option of camping here two nights and taking a 5.2-mile round-trip dayhike east to Vasquez Peak. This trip would be partly on roads, partly on a trail. To take this hike, return north on Wagon Road 1.4 miles and turn right on the Long Dam Trail. Curving around past a stock pond (Long Dam Pond), the trail climbs past Edith Pond and, 1.2 miles from Wagon Road, reaches Vasquez Road near Vasquez Peak.

When you continue your loop trip the next day, return from Redfern Pond to Wagon Road, which the route follows all the way to Hunting Hollow. First the road climbs steeply uphill, with very little shade until the ridgetop. Here you feel on top of the world (or at least Henry Coe Park), before making your final descent south to the tributary of Coyote Creek along which you began your hike.

The final 3 miles of this hike are along the valley of Hunting Hollow, with numerous creek crossings as you head northwest. Here again are the ground squirrels and brush rabbits that like meadows and bushes. In the fall tarantulas emerge from their holes looking for mates; they aren't dangerous, but give them room to escape your tread. Among other tracks in the dust are linear grooves; these are made by snakes—occasionally rattlers—so watch your step.

At 10.5 miles you have completed the loop to the junction with the Lyman Willson Trail. Retracing your steps another half mile gets you to the trailhead parking. While this entire loop trip can take 6–8 hours and be done by strong hikers in a day, it makes a relaxing weekend getaway to a little-visited part of our Bay Area wildlands.

Permits

There is a park fee and campsite reservations are required; contact

Henry W. Coe State Park
Box 846
Morgan Hill, CA 94038

Phone: (408) 779-2728; Web site at **www.coepark.parks.ca.gov**

San Francisco Bay trail aficionados and authors Rusmore & Crowder have made lasting contributions to promoting environmental awareness through their guidebooks. To learn more see "Author Bio & Bib" on page 492.

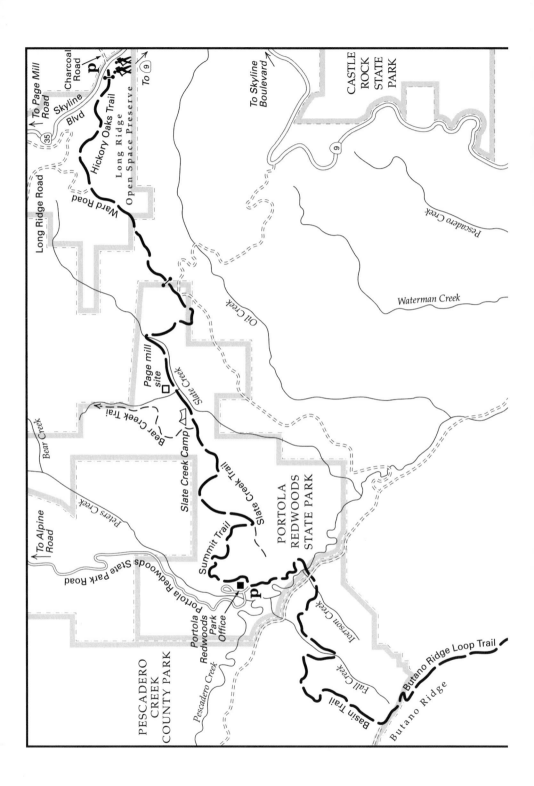

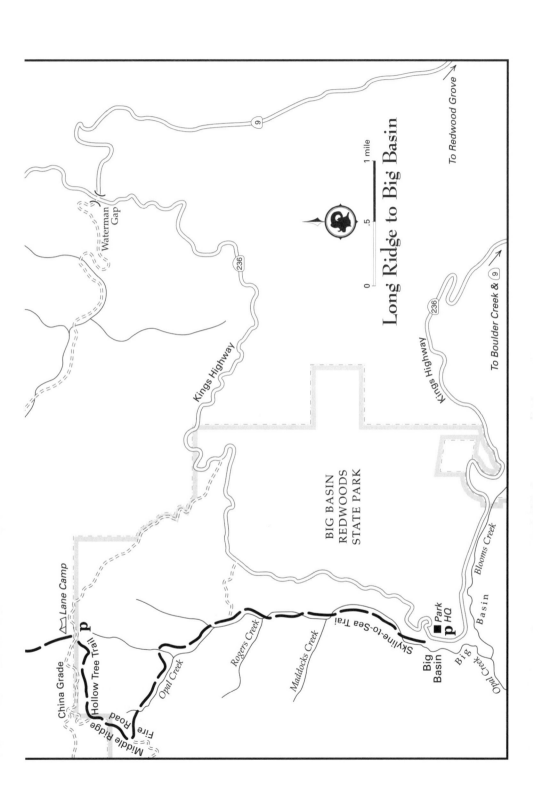

Long Ridge to Big Basin

BIG BASIN
REDWOODS
STATE PARK

Waterman
Gap

9

236

Kings Highway

To Redwood Grove

To Boulder Creek & 9

236

Kings Highway

Blooms Creek

Big
Basin

Big
Basin

Opal Creek

Park
HQ
p

Skyline-to-Sea Trail

Maddocks Creek

Rogers Creek

Opal Creek

China Grade

Lane Camp

p

Hollow Tree Trail

Middle Ridge
Fire Road

0   .5   1 mile

15

Long Ridge Open Space Preserve to Portola Redwoods & Big Basin Redwoods State Parks

—Jean Rusmore & Betsy Crowder

Route	Days	Elev. Gain/Loss	Difficulty	Miles
↱	**2 or 3**	**2017'/3630'**	**	**19.7**

Campsites & SP Offices: Slate Creek Camp: 3.75 miles
Portola Redwoods SP office: 6.6 miles (100'/2190')
Lane Camp: 13.6 miles (2017'/2350')
Big Basin Redwoods SP office: 19.7 miles (2017'/3630')

Map: USGS 7.5-min *Mindego Hill, Big Basin*; MROSD *Long Ridge and Saratoga Gap OSP*; California State Parks maps *Portola Redwoods, Big Basin Redwoods*

Best season: Late spring, summer, and early fall

Take this trip!

The first leg is an easy downhill trip from the heights of the Santa Cruz Mountains to a trail camp above Slate Creek set among madrones, oaks, and slender redwoods. First through rolling grasslands with dramatic views of forested ridges and deep canyons, you then hike under a canopy of mixed evergreen forest and pass an historic logging mill site en route to your campsite. The next day's downhill hike takes you to Portola Redwoods park office where backpackers choosing the shorter trip could be met by a shuttle.

More experienced backpackers then continue on the Basin Trail over wooded Butano Ridge for a second night at the Lane Camp (no water) on

China Grade Road in Big Basin Redwoods State Park. From this camp it is an exhilarating 5.9-mile hike through quiet redwoods, past an old logging camp, and over and along lively creeks to park headquarters in the center of Big Basin Redwoods.

Trailheads

Put-in trailhead: Long Ridge Open Space Preserve (Hickory Oaks Trail): From I-280 in Palo Alto, take Page Mill Road south 10 miles to Skyline Blvd., turn left (southeast), and continue 4.9 miles to the signed entrance to Long Ridge OSP on the right (west). There is roadside parking on east side of Skyline Blvd. at Charcoal Road. From Saratoga take Hwy. 9 west to Saratoga Gap, turn right (northwest) onto Skyline Blvd., and continue to parking at Charcoal Rd. It is illegal to leave a car parked beside Skyline Blvd. in most places (and also unwise), so try to arrange a ride to the starting point.

Take-out trailhead (for shorter trip): Portola Redwoods State Park (for shuttle car driver): From I-280 in Palo Alto, take Page Mill Road south 10 miles to Skyline Blvd., cross Skyline to Alpine Road, go south for 3.1 miles to the left turnoff onto Portola State Park Road. Continue 3.4 miles to the park office and visitor center, then proceed to nearby parking areas.

Take-out trailhead (for longer trip): Big Basin Redwoods State Park (China Grade Road for shuttle car driver) From Saratoga or Ben Lomond take Hwy. 9 to its junction with Hwy. 236 at Waterman Gap. Take Hwy. 236 west for 4.8 miles, turn right (northwest) onto China Grade Road, and then drive 4.2 miles to the Butano Ridge Loop trailhead. For Big Basin Park headquarters, continue on Hwy. 236 past China Grade Rd. to its end at the park office.

TRIP DESCRIPTION

Starting from Long Ridge Open Space Preserve's south entrance on the west side of Skyline Boulevard, go over the stile at the gated fire road to pick up an old ranch road, the Hickory Oaks Trail. In 100 yards turn right (northwest), continuing under the wide-spreading trees for which the trail is named. From their massive, clear trunks—some up to 5 feet in diameter—grow huge, horizontal, and often contorted limbs. This oak, *Quercus chrysolepis*, also called canyon, gold cup, and maul oak, has fine-grained hardwood that was prized for wagon wheels and farm implements.

Beyond the grove and uphill to the left (west; 0.2) a short spur trail leads 0.1 mile to a parklike meadow, rimmed with handsome trees and dotted with great, sandstone outcrops. Views down Oil Creek canyon from the top of the meadow are worth the short detour. The western panorama of successive forested ridges creased by wooded canyons is an uncluttered pastoral scene to nourish your spirit. From the north side of the meadow, continue for a short, pleasant stretch under more oaks before rejoining the wide Hickory Oaks Trail, to climb over rolling pasturelands that fall off to the forested canyons below.

At the junction with Long Ridge Road (0.8), turn left (west), go 0.3 mile on the Hickory Oaks Trail, and then arc southwest on Ward Road, beginning your descent along this wide old ranch road. At first you amble along through broad grasslands gloriously green in spring, golden in summer and fall. Off to the east is the ridge where Highway 9 winds its curving way down along the west boundary of Castle Rock State Park, the approximate route of the Skyline-to-the-Sea Trail and the shuttle-car driver's route to Big Basin. To the southeast are the deep, lush canyons of Oil and Waterman creeks, sometimes clothed in mist, sometimes so clear that individual trees are discernible.

Descending steadily for 0.3 mile, you reach a broad plateau where the 0.9-mile Ranch Spring Trail circles the site of the former Panighetti family ranch, now part of Long Ridge Open Space Preserve, which the Midpeninsula Regional Open Space District bought in 1990. Near this remote ranch site you could pause on the sunny, south-facing grasslands to admire the views, to explore this small flat enclosed by venerable trees, or take the loop trail that swings around the plateau and into woods of black oak and Douglas-fir, passes an old spring, and returns to the main trail.

Continuing your descent beside banks clothed with creeping manzanita bushes and lavender-flowered yerba santa, the Ward Road Trail reaches the gate of Portola Redwoods State Park (1.6), beyond which bicyclists and horses are not permitted. Hikers walk around the gate and continue downhill, winding around the southeast-facing slope. After passing a forsaken farm site on the left, you enter the shade of an evergreen forest, and go up a little rise. Look here on your right for the marked trail down to Slate Creek and Portola Redwoods State Park.

Along this circuitous trail are huge, old redwood logs cut into 3-8' lengths, evidence of an abandoned logging and shingle-making operation. Steps cut into the steep hillside take you to a crossing of Slate Creek, the place to fill your water bottles for purifying by boiling or filtering. Then turn left (southwest) and follow the creek through the cool redwood forest. This is an excellent, well-graded trail—a pleasure to walk on.

After a short uphill stretch beyond the creek crossing, you'll find a large, rustic wooden sign declaring that William Page had a mill at this site, although there are no logs, buildings, or old wagons to verify the fact. This was his second mill, the other being on Peters Creek below its confluence with Bear Creek, now on private property. A pause here will give you time to ponder how Page hauled his lumber out of this canyon.

Shortly you reach your destination, the Slate Creek Camp, on the left (south) side of the trail (3.75). Here at the junction with the Bear Creek Trail are six campsites separated by small logs and low shrubbery, mostly huckleberry, situated under a high forest canopy of madrone, fir, and young redwood.

Each has a sturdy picnic table and benches. The authors found a few mosquitoes when we stayed here in early August. You will need a campsite reservation, your backpack stove (no open fires are allowed) and, of course, your camping gear.

An option to consider in your trip plans: You could stay an extra night at the Slate Creek Camp and take the Bear Creek Trail down to the Peters Creek Loop, which is near Page's first mill. The Bear Creek Trail takes off north from the campsite for a 5.5-mile round trip with an initial elevation gain of 400 feet, a loss of almost 800 feet, and then equivalent gains and losses on the return. Although a bit strenuous, this trip takes you to some of the most magnificent, ancient redwoods in San Mateo County, still thriving near the junction of Peters and Bear creeks.

When you are ready to head for the Portola Redwoods park office, follow the Slate Creek Trail southwest. High hedges of shiny, narrow-leaved huckleberry with long, pliant branches border the trail, tall second-growth redwoods tower overhead, and the path is soft underfoot. At the Slate Creek and Summit trails junction, bear right (north) on the Slate Creek Trail for a 1.5-mile stretch to the park office. If you choose to make this an overnight trip (6.6), your shuttle driver can wait for you at the excellent visitor center.

If you are continuing 6.8 miles to Lane Camp at China Grade Road in Big Basin Redwoods State Park, the park office at Portola Redwoods is the place to replenish your water supply and fill several extra bottles for a dry camp at Lane Camp. Although this segment of the trip begins in Portola Redwoods State Park, the first half is mostly in adjoining Pescadero Creek County Park, reached from Portola Redwoods park office by following the service road to the right (east) past the park maintenance area, crossing Pescadero Creek, and then hiking on an elevated bank above a tight meander of the creek beyond the former Iverson Cabin site. Just 50 feet farther you enter Pescadero Creek County Park at the Old Haul Road (7.7). On the other side of this road/trail, pick up the Basin Trail (aka the Portola Trail) heading uphill under alder, toyon, and oak.

At first paralleling Iverson Creek, you then cross it and contour through a pretty dell under some second-growth redwoods, enlivened in late summer by orange redwood lilies and yellow mimulus. Following the east side of Fall Creek, you climb steadily and then cross it in an opening in the forest. Just before the creek crossing is a lively little waterfall; farther upstream a cascade ripples over mossy rocks. Look here for blue-flowered iris and white-blossomed, fragrant azalea in spring. Around more zigzags and out on a few knolls you continue upward through redwood and Douglas-fir forest.

When you reach a fork in the trail, go left on the Butano Ridge Loop Trail (9.0)—the other fork heads north down to the Old Haul Road. Now seriously climbing on a surfeit of switchbacks up Butano Ridge, you gain altitude at every zigzag as you round shoulders of the ridge, go between great columns of redwoods, and pass burned shells of monarch trees. Here, too, you will find small caves in great sandstone boulders worn away by wind, rain, and chemical action. Look for trees growing out of the rock, and other rocks that have broken loose and tumbled down the hillside.

Occasional madrone or tan oak trees have sprung up in gaps where old or diseased trees have fallen and left a clearing. But in general, this is a very shady redwood/fir forest, cool in summer, and exposed to ocean winds and fogs, which condense on tree branches and drip on the ground (and on hapless hikers). This environment is just right for white milkmaids, creamy-white and maroon trillium in spring, pretty little bluebells in summer, and the predominant, evergreen huckleberry shrub.

At one of the numerous switchbacks, look for a deep ditch that loggers once used to haul logs up the mountain on a cable attached to trees at top and bottom of the ridge. Near this ditch are cut ends of two large trees buried when the ditch was dug some 60 or 70 years ago.

At the Basin/Butano Ridge Loop trails junction (10.3), take the Basin Trail left (south) toward Big Basin Redwoods State Park. Following this trail, you round the nose of a ridge and contour 0.8 mile (sometimes along a very steep-sided canyon) through scattered redwoods and Douglas-firs to a small clearing, the Scenic Overlook. A log above the trail is a good place for a viewful lunch. If the day is fair, many high points in the Midpeninsula Regional Open Space Preserves along the Skyline Ridge are visible from here—Mt. Melville in Russian Ridge OSP, Lambert and Peters creek canyons, which feed into Pescadero Creek, and the high grasslands in Long Ridge OSP. Bring your binoculars to identify these and other features of the southern peninsula.

Ward Road to Portola State Park

After reaching the boundary of Pescadero Creek County Park (11.3), just 0.2 mile from the overlook, the Basin Trail's next segment goes through the private Redtree Properties L.P., formerly the Santa Cruz Lumber Company, which granted a 15-foot-wide hiking and equestrian trail easement to Sempervirens Fund, the oldest land conservancy in California. No bicycles are allowed. Logging roads intersecting the trail are blocked off, but are used to haul logs during the regular harvesting season, which follows a 16–20 year sustained-yield cycle.

Park staff and volunteers from the Santa Cruz Mountains Trail Association built this section of trail, and volunteers patrol and maintain it as well. It undulates up and down along a ridgetop under Douglas-firs and redwoods on a carpet of spent leaves. At a few points en route you can look east to other lands of the State Park system—Castle Rock and Big Basin—on Highway 9, which descend from Skyline Ridge. Soon you emerge from the woods at China Grade Road, the north boundary of Big Basin Redwoods State Park (13.4). To stay in nearby Lane Camp (with advance reservations from Big Basin Redwoods SP), just cross China Grade Road and walk 0.2 mile west to one of the six campsites laid out under live oaks, madrones, and tall tan oaks (13.6). (Alternatively, you could have a shuttle meet you here.)

From Lane Camp to Big Basin Redwoods State Park headquarters, take the beautiful Hollow Tree Trail west toward Middle Ridge Fire Road and the site of the Johansen Shingle Mill, built in 1927 and now abandoned. Remnants of dwellings, steam boilers, and scattered shingles are all that survive. You are in the headwaters of Opal Creek, where a serious fire once burned and scarred many redwoods. As you follow the Hollow Tree Trail south and then east, you cross several branches of beautiful Opal Creek. Just after one of these crossings you can see the burned-out but still-living redwood—the hollow tree.

Turn south on the Skyline-to-the-Sea Trail (17.0), following Opal Creek past the site of an early logger's home, the Maddock's Cabin, and continue 2.7 miles under huge redwoods to Big Basin headquarters. There you will find water and refreshments, a very good backpack camp—Jay Camp—and a place to meet your shuttle at the visitor center (19.7).

Permits

The Slate Creek Camp must be reserved at Portola Redwoods SP, Box F, Route 2, La Honda, CA 94020-9717, or by phone at (650) 948-9098. The Lane Camp in Big Basin Redwoods SP must be reserved at the park office, 21600 Big Basin Way, Boulder Creek, CA 95006, or by phone at (831) 338-8860. Remember that there are parking fees at the state parks.

San Francisco Bay trail aficionados and authors Rusmore & Crowder have made lasting contributions to promoting environmental awareness through their guidebooks. To learn more see "Author Bio & Bib" on page 492.

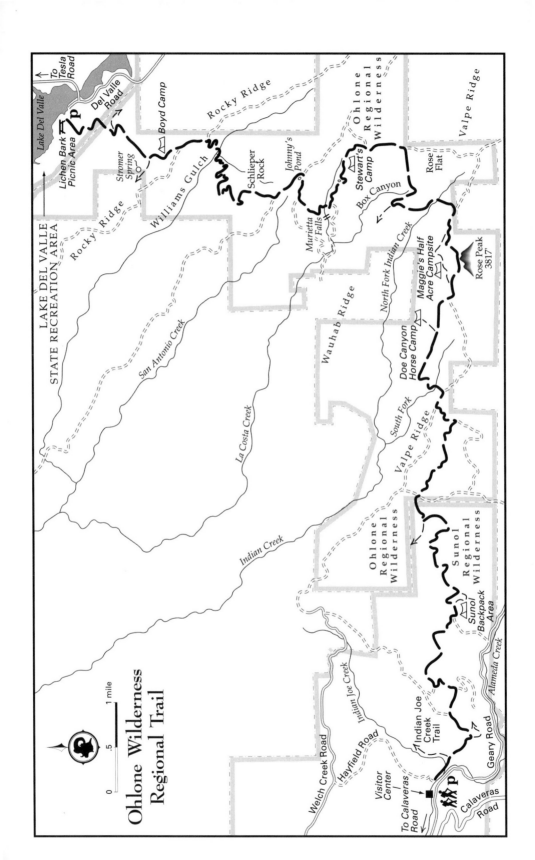

Ohlone Wilderness Regional Trail

LAKE DEL VALLE STATE RECREATION AREA

To Tesla Road

Lake Del Valle

Lichen Bark Picnic Area

Del Valle Road

Boyd Camp

Rocky Ridge

Ohlone Regional Wilderness

Valpe Ridge

Stromer Spring

Rocky Ridge

Williams Gulch

Schlieper Rock

Johnny's Pond

Stewart's Camp

Box Canyon

Rose Flat

Murietta Falls

Wauhab Ridge

North Fork Indian Creek

Maggie's Half Acre Campsite

Rose Peak 3817'

San Antonio Creek

Doe Canyon Horse Camp

La Costa Creek

South Fork

Valpe Ridge

Indian Creek

Ohlone Regional Wilderness

Sunol Regional Wilderness

Sunol Backpack Area

Welch Creek Road

Hayfield Road

Indian Joe Creek Trail

Indian Joe Creek Trail

Visitor Center

To Calaveras Road

Alameda Creek

Geary Road

Calaveras Road

1 mile

.5

0

16

Ohlone Wilderness Regional Trail—Sunol to Del Valle

—David Weintraub

Route	Days	Elev. Gain/Loss	Difficulty	Miles
⌒	3	6988'/6517'	***	19.4

Campsites: Sunol Backpack Area: 3.5 miles
Stewart's Camp: 13.6 miles
(see the Trip Description for others)

Map: *Ohlone Wilderness Regional Trail map* (this permit/map may be
all you'll need);
USGS 7.5-min *Niles, La Costa Valley, Livermore*

Best season: Spring

Take this trip!

This backpacking trip, the only one of its kind in the East Bay Regional
Park system, puts you in the heart of the Ohlone Wilderness, a rugged, remote,
and beautiful area. Along the way, you will also pass through Sunol Regional
Wilderness and Del Valle Regional Park, and spend two nights (or more if you
like) camped in oak woodland, surrounded by wildflowers and birds, perhaps
listening to the howl of a coyote or the hoot of an owl.

Trailhead

This is a car shuttle trip, starting at Sunol Wilderness and ending at Del
Valle Regional Park. Drive first to Del Valle Regional Park, leave a car there, then
proceed to Sunol Regional Wilderness.

Take-out trailhead (Del Valle Regional Park): From Interstate 580 in
Livermore, take the North Livermore Ave./Central Livermore exit, and follow N.
Livermore Ave. south through town, where it becomes S. Livermore Ave., and

then, at a sharp left-hand bend on the outskirts of town, Tesla Rd. At 3.7 miles from I-580, you reach a junction of Tesla and Mines roads. Turn right and go 3.6 miles to a junction with Del Valle Rd. Bear right and follow Del Valle Rd. 3.2 miles to the entrance kiosk, where you go straight. Continue 1.2 miles past the kiosk, cross a bridge, and turn right at a T-junction, to reach a large parking area at the end of the road, near the Lichen Bark Picnic Area.

Put-in trailhead (Sunol Regional Wilderness): To reach it from Del Valle return to central Livermore and follow 1st St. west 0.6 mile to Holmes St. Bear left and go 2.1 miles and bear right onto E. Vallecitos Rd. Follow E. Vallecitos and Vallecitos roads 6.6 miles to the Highway 84/Sunol/Dumbarton Bridge exit. Go under Interstate 680, and at a stop sign turn left onto Paloma Rd. Go back under I-680, stay in the left lane, and from the next stop sign continue straight, now on Calaveras Rd. Go 4.2 miles to Geary Rd., turn left, and go 1.8 miles to the entrance kiosk. Go 0.1 mile past the kiosk and turn left into a parking area in front of the visitor center, a green barn.

To reach Sunol from I-680 southbound in Scotts Corner, take the Calaveras Rd. exit, and at a stop sign turn left onto Paloma Rd., then follow the directions as described above. To reach Sunol from I-680 northbound in Scotts Corner, take the Calaveras Rd. exit, bear right onto Calaveras Rd., and follow the above directions.

TRIP DESCRIPTION

Heads Up! A visitor center, picnic tables, water, toilet, phone, and horse staging are available at the Sunol trailhead. There is limited water with unimproved campsites along the trail. Picnic tables, water, toilet, phone, and horse staging are provided at the Del Valle trailhead.

An East Bay Regional Parks Department (EBRPD) permit, camping reservations, and sign-in are required. Also note these rules: no bicycles; no pets in campsites overnight; no campfires—use backpack stoves only. The Ohlone Wilderness Regional Trail permit, good for one year, is a large map with route description, distances, trail elevations, and regulations (see Permits). An information panel and trail register are located on the south side of Geary Rd., about 100 yards east of the visitor center.

(Boldface numbers in the following description refer to numbers on the Ohlone Wilderness Regional Trail map. Many of these numbers can be found on trail posts along the trail, but some are missing.) After signing the register at the trailhead, you walk north about 150 feet, across Geary Rd. and through a small parking area, to a wooden bridge over Alameda Creek. The entire Ohlone

Eagles Eyrie campsite

Wilderness Regional Trail is made up of many trails that, joined together, stretch 28 miles, from Stanford Avenue at the base of Mission Peak in Fremont, to the Lichen Bark picnic area on the shore of Lake Del Valle. For the next three days you will be following the Ohlone Wilderness emblem on trail posts: a white oak leaf in a red or brown disk.

After crossing Alameda Creek and turning right, you follow the Canyon View Trail, a wide dirt path lined with white alder, big leaf maple, western sycamore, and willow, with the creek on your right. You may also notice here some of the trees and shrubs that will keep you company for most of the way to Lake Del Valle, including California bay laurel, California buckeye, coast live oak, California sagebrush, bush monkey flower, and poison oak. Approximately 100 feet past the bridge, Hayfield Road, 13, climbs left, and about 30 feet beyond, a path leads to the creek (right). Continuing straight, you soon pass another path (left), and after crossing Indian Joe Creek, you follow the Canyon View Trail over rolling terrain to a Y-junction, 14, with the Indian Joe Creek Trail.

Here you bear right on the Canyon View Trail and begin a steep climb through mixed oak woodland and grassland, seasonally colored blue and yellow by Ithuriel's spear and Mariposa tulip. At a four-way junction, 15, you leave the Canyon View Trail, which continues straight, and turn left on the McCorkle Trail. The route, now a dirt road, continues climbing steeply, then gradually lev-

119

els off to contour around a rocky ridge, and finally switchbacks upward toward a notch in the hills to the northeast.

Soon you reach the notch and a junction with a cutoff to Cerro Este Road, **16** (1.4). The large bulk of Mission Peak (2517), with its companion summits Mt. Allison (2658) and Monument Peak (2594), appears to the west, while the waters of Calaveras Reservoir shimmer to the south. Bear right, staying on the McCorkle Trail, here a narrow track, and begin descending through an area of chaparral, a striking contrast to the oak woodland and rolling grassland of a few minutes ago. California quail and wrentits may be heard and sometimes seen here, as you climb on a steep, rocky course through a wooded area to a high ridge, where California poppies dot the grassy hillsides with orange.

At a T-junction, **17**, you come to the Cerro Este Road; here your route, still part of the McCorkle Trail, turns left and continues uphill in the open to another T-junction, **18**, where you turn right, staying on the McCorkle Trail, a dirt road here. A nearby cow pond provides habitat for a robin-sized bird called the killdeer, which you may hear giving its alarm call, "kill-dee, kill-dee." This shorebird, a member of the plover family, is at home in many areas besides the shore, and can be found throughout North America. In addition to cows and birds, other wildlife here includes amphibians: watch the ground closely for baby frogs in spring. Now heading east again and descending slightly, you pass large rock outcrops and a barbed-wire fence, where a narrow dirt path heads left and your route bends right.

After ambling a while on level ground, you descend via switchbacks to a small valley, where a wet area may provide a colorful display of spring wildflowers, including lupine, Ithuriel's spear, blow wives, owl's clover, and Mariposa tulip. If the creek that drains this valley is running, you may have to cross it on rocks. At about 3.4 miles, you cross another creek and reach a trail junction, **19**, with Backpack Road. A gate ahead marks the entrance to the Sunol Backpack Area, and a sign board lists campsites—Eagles Eyrie, Hawks Nest, Sycamore Camp, Stars Rest—reached by a steep uphill trail. Water and a toilet are available in the backpack area.

If you are spending the night here, Eagles Eyrie is an excellent campsite, but like all the others it requires advance reservation. To find it, climb about 0.25 mile from the backpack-area entrance and watch for a junction with a signed spur trail veering right. This trail leads to several campsites, including Eagles Eyrie, which is perched at about 1600 feet. The main trail continues straight and is rejoined by the spur trail, in about 0.25 mile, at a gate on the border of San Francisco Water Department land. Eagles Eyrie is a grassy area with a picnic table in the shade of a large blue oak, a magnet for birds such as woodpeckers, western bluebirds, nuthatches, and hummingbirds. Water is available from a faucet beside the trail, just below the campsite in a muddy area where you may find golden monkey flower blooming in the spring. Expansive views west from a rock outcrop above the picnic table—a great spot to watch the sunset—reveal much of the terrain back to the visitor center.

To rejoin the main route from Eagles Eyrie, walk northeast on an unsigned path across a grassy hillside, past a huge valley oak, joining a trail coming up from the water faucet and a lower campsite. A steep climb brings you to the San Francisco Water Department gate, which has a sign requesting you stay on the trail while traversing their lands. Once through the gate, now back on the main route, you continue climbing through open grassland, above 2000 feet for the first time on this route, heading generally northeast. Heavily forested Alameda Creek canyon is downhill and right; beautiful oaks grace the hillsides ahead.

Your route dips to cross several small creeks lined with bay and sycamore, then passes through an area of rock outcrops colored by orange lichen. From time to time, dirt paths take off from the main route: ignore them. In open grassland here you may find blue dicks and winecup clarkia, spring bloomers. This part of the route has a supreme feeling of isolation, with no signs of civilization other than jets on approach to San Francisco International Airport. After passing a trail post and an unsigned trail joining from the left, you soon you reach a junction, **20**, with unsigned Goat Rock Road (right). Here your route turns left and climbs north toward the skyline ridge. In the distance to the south rise the Santa Cruz Mountains. At the next trail post, **21**, the route bends right, and in 100 yards reaches a fork, where you bear left. After climbing a slight rise, you descend to a four-way junction, **22**, with Billy Goat Road (5.9).

After crossing Billy Goat Road, you continue straight on Mid Road and contour southeast, reaching a gully with oak, blue elderberry, and California buckeye—the first shade in miles. Soon you reach a high point with views west, and then come to another gully with a culvert under the road. At about the 7-mile point, there is a T-junction, **23**, with Bluff Road, where your route turns left and climbs steeply. After cresting a small ridge near a cattle pond, you continue across grassy hillsides and through oak woodland to a junction, **24**, with Valpe Ridge Road (left). Here you walk through a cattle gate and turn right, passing another pond, and in about 0.25 mile, **25**, make a sharp left and descend steeply on rocky ground into a small canyon, which holds the South Fork Indian Creek.

Now in an oasis of shade and water, you may find an abundance of spring wildflowers in bloom, including fiddleneck, a coiled stem with orange flowers, and Chinese houses, pagoda-like tiers of purple flowers. A steep climb brings you out of the canyon and into a beautiful savanna—a haven for birds—where the grass, brown elsewhere by late spring, stays green in the shade of tall oaks. At a bend in the route, you get your first good look on this route of San Francisco Bay, and at the next bend, just above 3000 feet, you encounter a stunning vista that sweeps from Mt. Diablo to the Santa Clara Valley and Santa Cruz Mountains. If you like being up high, with unobstructed views, this is the place!

As the route, here called the Buckboard Trail, swings southeast, you have a pleasant walk along a ridgecrest, and soon reach a spur road, **26**, descending steeply left to Doe Canyon Horse Camp, where a water faucet and toilet await (8.9). Water and a toilet are also available at Maggie's Half Acre campsite, about 0.8 mile ahead but off the main route. Now you continue east through oak savanna, home to acorn woodpeckers, toward Rose Peak (3817), the high point on the Ohlone Wilderness Regional Trail. At a junction with Portuguese Point Road, **27**, you turn left, pass a small pond on your left, and soon reach a road, **28**, heading left to Maggie's Half Acre. If you are doing this trip in four days instead of three, Maggie's Half Acre makes a good second camp, about 6 miles from the Sunol backpack area. If you are not camping here, bear right on the main trail.

Continuing east, the route steepens and passes over rocky terrain as you near the summit of Rose Peak, the highest point in Alameda County. About 0.2 mile past the last junction, an unsigned road, steep and rocky, heads left and climbs Rose Peak, while the main route skirts the peak's south side. Having come this far, be sure not to miss the 360° views from the summit, and a chance to sign the summit register. After some effort, you arrive, seemingly, on top of the world (9.8). Using your trail map/permit—which has bearings and distances to prominent landmarks visible from Rose Peak—and a compass, you can pick out many features of the Bay Area, including Altamont Pass, Mt. Diablo, Pleasanton Ridge, Coyote Hills, Mission Peak, the Santa Cruz Mountains, and Mt. Hamilton. Beyond the Central Valley lies the Sierra Nevada, visible on clear days. You have come nearly 10 miles from the Sunol visitor center; Rose Peak marks the halfway point to Lake Del Valle.

After you have relaxed for a while, continue east and descend steeply to the main road, which you can see below and right. Once back on the main road, you may notice as you continue your descent two trees not seen so far, black oak and gray pine, both found in hotter, drier areas of the East Bay. Canyon live oak is also here, along with blue oak, loaded with mistletoe, and valley oak, making this a good place to compare these species. Just past the 10-mile point, you pass the road, **29**, coming from Maggie's Half Acre (left).

At the next junction, **30**, a road goes straight to the wilderness boundary and Rose Flat, but you turn left and continue downhill, under large black oaks and gray pines—notice the huge pine cones—to the North Fork Indian Creek, losing the most elevation so far, more than 600 feet. The steep, rocky descent brings you to the bottom of a cool, shady canyon, where maple, alder, and bay line the creek, which may be flowing over the road. Climbing back into the open, you have views west to San Francisco Bay and Mission Peak.

As you begin to get a good view southwest across the canyon to Rose Peak, a road joins from the left, **31**, and your route bends sharply right and continues climbing. As you gain a ridgetop, you can look left into Box Canyon, headwaters of La Costa Creek. Descending beside a barbed-wire fence to the head of this canyon, you pass beautiful hillsides of colorful Chinese houses, which lie in the shade of gray pines. With La Costa Creek on your left, the route climbs gently past large rock outcrops through a little valley at the head of Box Canyon. A road to the wilderness boundary and Rose Flat joins your route at a T-junction, **32**, where you turn left and begin a gradual descent (12.4). From here, the Ohlone Wilderness Regional Trail, generally eastbound since the Sunol visitor center, begins a northward march to Lake Del Valle, about 7 miles away.

If you are taking three days to complete the route, you will spend the second night at Stewart's Camp, on the road to Murietta Falls. When you reach the next junction, **33**, turn left, leaving the Ohlone Wilderness Regional Trail, and descend via a series of gentle switchbacks through an oak-and-pine forest, past stumps of old oaks riddled with woodpecker holes and fine displays of Chinese houses. Stewart's Camp (13.6) is located just above a pond where red-winged blackbirds nest in marsh vegetation, and the surrounding hillsides are decorated with lupine. The main camping area, which can accommodate up to 20 people, is south of the road. Water and a toilet are located nearby.

At just over 3000 feet, a night at Stewart's Camp can be a cold one, and don't be surprised by serenades from owls and coyotes. No need for an alarm clock here, as the chattering of birds at sunrise will get you started early. After passing the pond, you soon come to a junction with a road heading left to the wilderness boundary; your route continues straight and arrives at a small grove of trees. To visit seasonal Murietta Falls, turn left here, before crossing a tributary of La Costa Creek, and follow a narrow path that traverses and then winds behind large rock outcrops. Be careful here as you approach steep terrain. After a short distance the waterfall comes into view, tumbling perhaps 100 feet from a narrow channel in the rocks to a gully below.

The Murietta Falls area is a perfect spot to lounge in the sun, especially if the night has been cold. Once underway again on the main route, you cross the creek and immediately begin to climb north, out of a valley. Yellow Mariposa tulips and goldfinches add touches of color to the scene. At a T-junction, turn right and walk along the open crest of a ridge, toward Johnny's Pond—called simply JOHNIES on a sign beside the trail—and your reunion with the Ohlone Wilderness Trail.

You rejoin the Ohlone Wilderness Trail at a junction, **35**, and turn left (14.1). Much of the land that became the Ohlone Regional Wilderness was at one time owned by a rancher and cowboy named Harry Rowell. Rowell, a British merchant seaman who jumped ship in 1912 when he was 21 years old, settled in Alameda County and had a ranch on Dublin Canyon Road. Rowell died in 1969, but his legacy lives on in the form of the Rowell Ranch Rodeo, which he started in 1920, and Rowell's Saddlery in Castro Valley, founded in 1942. A sign beside the trail reads SCHLEPER, and the map shows Schlieper Rock, named for Fred Schlieper, a silversmith at Rowell's Saddlery in the 1940s.

Lake Del Valle

Johnny's Pond, left, was named for John Fernandes, who worked in Rowell's slaughterhouse and was his occasional sparring partner.

After descending slightly, the route climbs to a great vantage point, with views of Mt. Diablo, Morgan Territory, Livermore, Altamont Pass, and the Central Valley. Shade is at a premium here, offered by a few groves of oak, oases for birds. California quail, western tanager, and lark sparrow may be found nearby. Even in death, oaks attract birds, providing nesting habitat and food storage for species as varied as woodpeckers and swallows.

At a fork in the route, **36**, bear right past an old pear orchard and begin descending steeply on loose ground. At about the 3000-foot level, the route becomes a narrow trail and begins to drop across a steep, brushy hillside on switchbacks built by the California Conservation Corps. As you enjoy this well-graded descent, you may be treated to a fine display of spring wildflowers, such as Chinese houses, Ithuriel's spear, blue dicks, and globe tulips.

Alternately open and wooded, the trail makes a long, switchbacking traverse across a north-facing hillside, where you may find canyon live oak and black oak; here the trees may be alive with dark-eyed juncos. The sound of rushing water rises from Williams Gulch, a deep canyon ahead. When you reach its shady bottom, after putting your knees and hiking boots to the test, you will have dropped nearly 2000 feet from yesterday's high point, the summit of Rose Peak. Now is the time to relax and enjoy cool, peaceful surroundings. Two creeks—one from the southwest, the other from the southeast—join in

Williams Gulch, and the resulting stream flows northwest, eventually reaching San Antonio Creek. Your route crosses their cold, clear waters on rocks, then emerges as a dirt road on an open hillside.

Maples and sycamores growing here indicate a high water table, but as you turn left at a T-junction, **37**, and gain Rocky Ridge, the dryland species—gray pine, black oak, blue oak—again become dominant (16.7). California buckeye, with its spring profusion of white, candle-like blooms, is also here. You have just completed the most remote section, from Rose Peak to Williams Gulch, of the Ohlone Wilderness Regional Trail. (When I reached this point, I had not seen any other people for 24 hours, a level of seclusion I have encountered only once before, on the John Muir Trail.)

At a Y-junction, **38**, bear right and descend toward Boyd Camp; there is a toilet here, but water is available only at Stromer Spring, just west of the next junction, **39**, about 0.33 mile farther. (This is the last water until you reach Lake Del Valle.) After getting water, return to the main road, turn northeast and walk steeply downhill through an area of bush monkey flower, toyon, and coyote bush to the Ohlone Wilderness Regional Trail sign-in board, **40**, and a junction at 18.4 miles with the Vallecitos Trail (right). To reach the parking area at the Lichen Bark Picnic Area, continue straight and descend through an area of chaparral—mostly chamise—and wildflowers. Several switchbacks finally bring you to Lake Del Valle and the parking area.

Permits

Trail permits are available for a small fee at the entrance kiosks at Sunol Wilderness and Del Valle Regional Park, the visitor center at Coyote Hills Regional Park in Fremont, and the EBRPD reservation office, 2950 Peralta Oaks Ct., Oakland. Permits for overnight parking are available at the entrance kiosks. Reservations for backpacking camps are required; phone EBRPD reservations, (510) 636-1684, 8:30 A.M.-4 P.M., Monday through Friday.

While outdoor-photographer David Weintraub published his first guidebook for Wilderness Press in 1998, he has built a solid reputation in New England as well as the Bay Area. Check out "Author Bio & Bib" on page 492 to learn more.

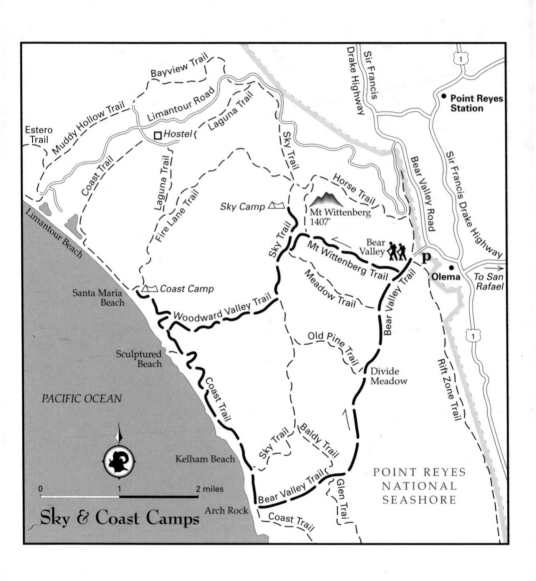

Bayview Trail

Muddy Hollow Trail

Limantour Road

Laguna Trail

Sir Francis Drake Highway

Sir Francis Drake Highway

1

Point Reyes Station

Estero Trail

☐ Hostel

Laguna Trail

Coast Trail

Sky Trail

Laguna Trail

Fire Lane Trail

Sky Camp △

Horse Trail

Bear Valley Road

Mt Wittenberg 1407'

Sir Francis Drake Highway

Limantour Beach

Sky Trail

Mt Wittenberg Trail

Bear Valley 🚶🚶

p

Meadow Trail

Bear Valley Trail

Olema

To San Rafael

Santa Maria Beach

△ Coast Camp

Woodward Valley Trail

Old Pine Trail

Sculptured Beach

Divide Meadow

PACIFIC OCEAN

Coast Trail

1

Rift Zone Trail

Sky Trail

Baldy Trail

Kelham Beach

POINT REYES NATIONAL SEASHORE

0   1   2 miles

Bear Valley Trail

Glen Trail

Sky & Coast Camps

Arch Rock

Coast Trail

17

Sky & Coast Camps Loop from Bear Valley

—Dorothy Whitnah

Route	Days	Elev. Gain/Loss	Difficulty	Miles
↻	3	1400'/1400'	*	14.5

Campsites: Sky Camp: 2.7 miles
Coast Camp: 6.4 miles

Map: *Point Reyes National Seashore* (from Wilderness Press);
or USGS 7.5-min *Inverness, Double Point*

Best Season: Year-round

Take this trip!

The San Francisco Bay Area is uniquely fortunate in having a huge semi-wilderness—Point Reyes National Seashore, containing 71,000 acres—located less than 40 miles north of the city of San Francisco. The seashore contains over 140 miles of hiking trails and features four hike-in campgrounds. On this route, you'll traverse the southernmost Douglas-fir temperate rain forest, enjoy expansive coastal views, and explore fascinating beaches rich with tidepool life. You'll awake to spectacular vistas of the white cliffs of Drakes Bay from Sky Camp, and sleep a few hundred yards from the beach at Coast Camp.

Trailhead

There are three principal routes from the San Francisco area north to the headquarters at Bear Valley. The quickest is from Highway 101 west on Sir Francis Drake Blvd. (subsequently Sir Francis Drake Hwy.) through Samuel P. Taylor State Park to Olema, where signs point the way to park headquarters ½ mile west. A slower, more scenic route from San Francisco or southern Marin is via winding Highway 1 north to Olema. Another scenic route is by Highway

101 and Lucas Valley Road through Nicasio to Point Reyes Station and south to Olema. During heavy storms, some of these routes may be closed due to flooding or downed trees. For road conditions, call Caltrans at (800) 427-7623.

Not only is this wilderness a short drive from a densely populated area, it can be reached by public transportation! Golden Gate Transit Bus 65 runs on the weekends and holidays from San Rafael to Olema, Point Reyes National Seashore Headquarters, Point Reyes Station, and Inverness. San Rafael is a major transfer point for buses from San Francisco, Sonoma County, and the rest of Marin County. For information on schedules and fees, phone Golden Gate Transit: from San Francisco and the East Bay (415) 923-2000; from Marin (415) 455-2000; from Sonoma County (707) 541-2000.

The Bear Valley Visitor Center should be your first stop in the park and is where you pick up your camping permit. You can also pick up free maps and information sheets, find out about nature programs and other activities, and browse the bookstore. The Visitor Center, (415) 464-5100, is open from 9 A.M. until 5 P.M. on weekdays, and from 8 A.M. until 5 P.M. on weekends and holidays; it has water, restrooms, and a phone. The Bear Valley trailhead is just south of the visitor center parking lot.

TRIP DESCRIPTION

Heads Up! Without potable water along the trails or at the camps, you've got to carry it in, or treat the water at Sky and Coast camps. The Point Reyes Peninsula gets a lot of summer fog; come prepared for cool weather even in midsummer. Bear in mind that weather frequently varies within the park: for example, the Coast Trail may be fogged-in while the Bear Valley trailhead enjoys brilliant sunshine. While a sign at the trailhead advises that Point Reyes is mountain lion country, sightings are rare, and poison oak and ticks are far more ubiquitous hazards.

Begin your trip on the Bear Valley Trail from the Bear Valley trailhead. Just before entering the forest, in 0.2 mile, turn right on the clearly marked Mt. Wittenberg Trail at the great multiple-trunked bay tree. Once part of the Sky Trail, in 1995 the Park Service rechristened this stretch the Mt. Wittenberg Trail. It is the most direct hiking route to Sky Camp (except for via the Sky trailhead on Limantour Road) but also the steepest. (Inverness Ridge's grade becomes more gradual closer to the ocean.) The trail ascends under hazelnut, tanbark oak, and Douglas-fir; luxuriant sword ferns form much of the understory. About halfway up the ridge, catch your breath when you reach a near-level clearing somewhat larger than a football field, which is less distinct in recent years due to thriving, young Douglas-firs. In fall you can search for huckleberries in the lush growth bordering the clearing.

The trail continues up another open slope dotted with firs, then goes steeply through forest again and finally emerges on a hillside not far from the top. A short spur trail leads 0.2 mile to the summit, where you are rewarded with 360° views of the entire Point Reyes peninsula and the esteros, Tomales Bay, Black Mountain (aka Elephant Mtn.) behind Point Reyes Station, the lush Olema Valley, and Bolinas Ridge; in clear weather you can even see Mts. St. Helena, Diablo, and Tamalpais. Descend via the same spur trail and rejoin the Mt. Wittenberg Trail for 0.4 mile. On a clear day, coastal views from Chimney Rock to the expanse of Limantour accompany you along this stretch. At the junction with the Sky Trail, turn right and follow it 0.6 mile north to Sky Camp.

On the western side of Mt. Wittenberg, Sky Camp (2.7/1025) is located in a small sheltered meadow overlooking Drakes Bay. One of the many dairy ranches on the Point Reyes Peninsula in the mid-1800s used to be located on the site. Nothing remains of the ranch today except some trees (including eucalyptus) and the spring that now provides water to the camp. You'll find 12 individual sites and one group site, a toilet, picnic tables, and lockers to protect your food from voracious raccoons. There are also charcoal grills (wood fires are not allowed), a hitchrail, and water (which must be treated).

In October 1995 an illegal campfire near the summit of Mt. Vision ran wild and ultimately destroyed 45 homes on Inverness Ridge, as well as 15% of the National Seashore. The fire raged over Sky Camp, destroying it. The fact that it was reopened the following year is a tribute to nature's regenerative powers; you would hardly guess at its previous destruction. Charred trees and blackened trunks dot the foreground of spectacular westward views of Drakes Bay and Chimney Rock, but vigorous new growth covers the chaparral slopes. Most of the park's large mammal and bird population survived the fire, and you may see deer lazing in a meadow and covies of quail scurrying across the trail.

Retrace your steps along the Sky Trail to the junction with the Mt. Wittenburg and Meadow trails, and then continue south along the Sky Trail. You reach the junction with the westward-trending Woodward Valley Trail in approximately 1.3 miles. A small meadow here, bordered by a lovely grove of old-growth Douglas-fir, can be quite dry and dusty in summer.

Cross the meadow along the narrow single-track trail, and reenter forest. Douglas-firs intersperse dense overgrown vegetation—blackberry brambles, ferns, and coyote brush. Charred trees, vestiges of the 1995 fire, line the trail, but the understory is vibrant and exploding with growth. Brilliant green moss coats blackened trunks and branches. The trail goes in and out of the woods, and you'll catch glimpses of Drakes Bay to the west. The descent is gradual at first, but becomes steeper where chaparral-covered slopes drop to the ocean. Here panoramic views extend from Chimney Rock to the San Mateo coastline. If the weather is clear enough, the Farallon Islands are visible on the horizon

20 miles out to sea. Coffeeberry, sticky monkey flower, coyote brush, and sweet-smelling grasses cover these open slopes; yellow buttercups line the trail in spring.

At 1.8 miles from the Sky Trail junction, the Woodward Valley Trail joins the Coast Trail. An old farm road, this trail runs along an ancient marine terrace now raised a couple of hundred feet above the ocean. Effects of the Vision Fire are not so dramatic here as on the higher trails because the vegetation consists mainly of coastal scrub, which regenerates more quickly than the lofty forests. Turn right on the Coast Trail, following it as it makes a V inland to cross Santa Maria Creek via a wooden bridge. The creekbed is lush with willows, alders, currants, and lupine. The trail then passes under a jutting rock formation to arrive at Coast Camp (6.4), 0.6 mile from the Woodward Valley Trail.

Coast Camp is located just 200 yard above attractive Santa Maria Beach, protected from ocean winds by a sandy ridge. Closed for a few months after the Vision Fire burned it, the camp now sports green grass and wildflowers in spring. Though the camp is on the site of another long-abandoned dairy ranch, the only remnant is the large eucalyptus tree that stands sentinel over the beach approach to the camp. Eucalyptus trees were popular among ranchers in the 19th Century, and they are often the only surviving emblems of these abandoned ranches.

Coast Camp accommodates 12 individual and two groups sites. Two faucets supply nonpotable water, and a new toilet building (with two unisex toilets, one of which is wheelchair accessible) stands adjacent to sites 8 through 14. Located up a hill 100 yards southeast, sites 1 through 7 are more private and individually sheltered by scrub and coyote brush, but offer great views of Drakes Bay.

To return to the Bear Valley trailhead, begin by retracing yesterday's route along the Coast Trail. About 0.5 mile after the junction with the Woodward Valley Trail (1.1 miles from Coast Camp), you come to the short spur trail to Sculptured Beach. If the tide is low, you can take a well-deserved side trip to this fascinating beach. Eroded, layered rocks offer marvelous opportunities for studying sea anemones and other tidepool life. The ochre cliffs form bizarrely contoured canyons. Keep an eye on the tide, as these cliffs are much too steep to climb.

South of the Sculptured Beach junction, the Coast Trail narrows from a wide road to a single-track trail. Grasses, iris, lupine, poison oak, and coyote brush line the trail. Ceanothus grows in abundance, reaching high on either side. An "opportunist," ceanothus is often one of the first chaparral plants to sprout after a fire, and thrives under post-fire conditions. After about 2 miles, you reach an access trail to Kelham Beach, under an old eucalyptus. This tree is the last remnant of yet another Point Reyes dairy ranch.

You leave the burn zone about where the Sky Trail joins your trail, 0.5 mile before the junction with the Bear Valley Trail. In a meadow about 50 feet above the sea, you reach the Bear Valley Trail, where you have a couple of spur options. A steep trail to the beach takes you to Arch Rock, a natural rock tunnel through which the creek flows. A short distance south, Millers Point (named for Clem Miller, the Congressman who was so influential in establishing the National Seashore) offers spectacular views up and down the coast.

To return to the trailhead from the Coast Trail, however, turn left and follow the Bear Valley Trail, soon leaving the coast behind and entering a lush forest. An easy, fairly level 4 miles remain in your trip, along murmuring streams, under towering trees, and through a broad meadow. On weekends this trail is generally thronged with hikers. After 0.8 mile, the trail to Glen Camp branches off to the right. (This is where bicyclists headed for the beach on the Bear Valley Trail must dismount and continue the rest of the way to the coast on foot.) Your trail follows Coast Creek upstream, away from its ocean outlet. The unusually large buckeyes along this part of the trail are magnificent in late spring, when their candles of pinkish-cream flowers are blooming.

In places large trees overarch the trail, forming leafy tunnels through which sunlight filters. Ferns abound on the mossy banks—five-finger and maidenhair, as well as the more common sword and bracken ferns. If you are hiking in spring, you will find buttercup, iris, miner's lettuce, bleeding heart, wild cucumber, blue forget-me-not, English daisy, milkmaids, and—if you look closely along the stream bank—wild ginger. The trail opens up in a gentle ascent of long Divide Meadow, which is 2.4 miles from the coast. Toilets and picnic tables invite tired hikers to rest in this peaceful expanse, where San Francisco's elite Pacific Union Club maintained its hunting lodge from the 1890s until the Great Depression.

On this last stretch, you enter an area wooded with bay, Douglas-fir, bishop pine, buckeye, hazelnut, elderberry and, along the stream, alder. Beyond Divide Meadow you follow Bear Valley Creek, running north—the opposite direction from the south-flowing Coast Creek, bordering the trail earlier. Odd drainage patterns are characteristic of this San Andreas fault zone. Just 1.6 miles after leaving the meadow, you complete your loop at the Bear Valley trailhead.

Variations

The network of trails in this area provides abundant alternatives to the loop trip described here. The Meadow Trail offers a more gradual ascent to Sky Camp than the Mt. Wittenberg Trail, and in approximately the same distance. For a one-night trip, consider a shorter loop: spend the night at Sky Camp and return the next day via the Meadow or Old Pine trails. (Sky Camp can also be accessed by a 1.2-mile hike from the Sky trailhead on Limantour Road.) To extend your trip, take the Fire Lane and Laguna trails from Coast Camp to the Point Reyes Hostel off of Limantour Road, spend another night there, and continue back to the trailhead via the Fire Lane Trail, retracing your steps from Sky Camp.

A couple of car-shuttle route variations are also possible. From Coast Camp, continue 1½ miles northwest on the Coast Trail to Limantour Beach, and plan to have a car there. Or leave a car at the hostel and follow the Fire Lane and Laguna trails 2.1 miles from Coast Camp to reach it.

Permits

Point Reyes has four walk-in campgrounds, each with pit toilets, water (which must be treated), picnic tables, charcoal grills, and food storage lockers (to protect it from raccoons). Wood fires are not permitted at the campsites. (Boat-in camping is allowed on beaches on the west side of Tomales Bay.)

Obtain a camping permit from Bear Valley Visitor Center before starting your trip. Campsites can be reserved up to three months in advance. Weekends and holidays fill up quickly, especially group sites. Summer months are the most crowded and reservations are usually filled the first day they are accepted. Since summer brings more fog than any other time of year, other seasons, such as spring and fall (and sometimes even winter), can be more enjoyable on the Point Reyes Peninsula.

The campground reservation phone line is (415) 663-8054. Phone reservations are only accepted Monday through Friday, between 9 A.M. and 2 P.M. You can make reservations in person any time the Bear Valley Visitor Center is open or by fax to (415) 663-1597.

Find maps and additional information at the park Web site: http://www.nps.gov/pore.

Build-up/Wind-down tips

You might treat yourself to a delicious oyster dinner in Point Reyes Station! Or refresh yourself with an invigorating Pacific swim at Stinson Beach, a few miles south on Highway 1!

Dorothy Whitnah was a longtime Wilderness Press author of Bay Area hiking guides; see "Author Bio & Bib" on page 492 for more information.

The Coast Ranges III

The Klamath Mountains

Occupying all of northwest California, the Klamath Mountains are a complex geologic mosaic formed from a wide variety of metamorphic rocks, which accreted to the continent over the past few hundred million years. Once connected with the northern Sierra Nevada, the mountain range was intruded by magma rising through the crust in enormous subterranean bubbles between 150 and 120 million years ago. Solidifying as granite before reaching the surface, these bubbles became exposed as erosion stripped away the overlying rock. Unlike the heavily intruded central and southern Sierra, the Klamath Mountains contain only isolated pockets of granite—the Trinity Alps is the most spectacular example.

The Klamath Mountains are sliced by deep river canyons that support a rich diversity of life. At relatively lower elevations, the Klamath escaped the thick ice sheets that have intermittently covered the Sierra Nevada over the past few million years. They occupy the geographic crossroads of three other major ranges—the Sierra Nevada, Cascade Range, and Coast Ranges. As a result of all this, the flora and fauna of the region are lush, diverse, and include many rare and unusual species found nowhere else.

The Lost Coast

The Lost Coast stretches from the Eel River delta near Ferndale south to Highway 1, a distance of more than 70 miles. Offshore is the Mendocino Triple Junction, the point where three tectonic plates meet. North of the junction, the Juan de Fuca Plate dives beneath the Pacific Northwest, triggering the volcanoes of the Cascade Range. South, the San Andreas fault reaches its offshore terminus, knitting the landscape with a host of faults. All this tectonic mayhem combines to cause dramatic uplift, creating cliffs that tower more than 1000 feet above the crashing sea. The dark cliffs weather to form unusual black-sand beaches, accessible only where small creeks have carved deep gullies between the bluffs. Sinkyone Wilderness State Park encompasses the southernmost section of the Lost Coast, an area of 7367 acres that protects more than 22 miles of shoreline.

Prior to 1850, the peaceful Sinkyone Indians inhabited the area, living in small permanent settlements along the coast and harvesting the rich diversity of land and sea. Black-tailed deer, Roosevelt elk, rabbits, grizzly bears, black bears, salmon, seals, sea lions, berries, and seaweed were all part of their varied diet. As elsewhere, with the coming of white settlers it all came to a sad end. In 1856 the Sinkyones were rounded up with fellow North Coast Indians and forced onto reservations. Many subsequently returned to their homeland only to become involved in violent disputes with the white settlers. By 1865, the Sinkyones no longer composed a recognizable tribe.

Loggers and livestock made use of the vacant land. Ranchers built small farms and communities near the open bluffs where their sheep and cattle grazed. The buildings in the Needle Rock area represent the remains of such an operation, with today's visitor center located in the former ranch house. Extensively harvested tan oak and Douglas-fir were transported by wagon and railroad, milled near the coast, and shipped from small ports. These "doghole" ports and their accompanying wharfs were precarious, typically destroyed by the turbulent seas within a few years. Logging continued intermittently until as recently as 1986, stripping most old-growth timber from the region. Sinkyone Wilderness State Park is a relatively new park, established in 1975, expanded in 1986, and lost to commercial interests forever.

Despite all the human activity, wildlife thrives in the park today. A herd of Roosevelt elk, reintroduced from Prairie Creek Redwoods State Park, wanders the coastal bluffs. Black bears and mountain lions prowl inland. Whales and seals can be spotted offshore. Raptors of all varieties soar above. And a few stands of old-growth redwood still remain. (MH)

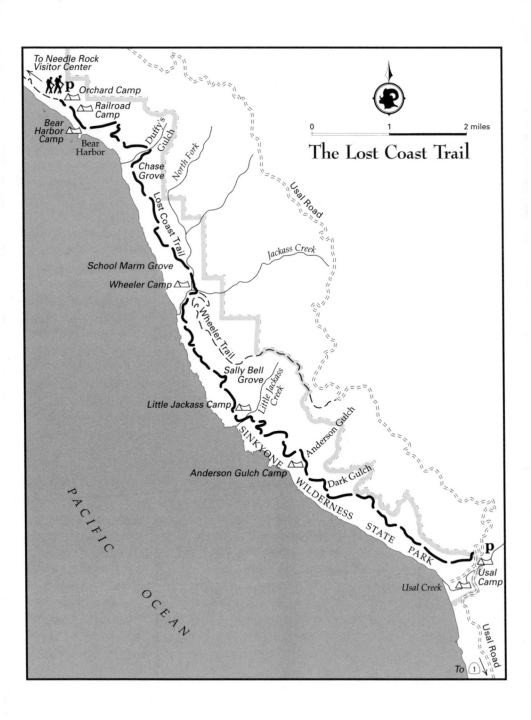

The Lost Coast Trail

To Needle Rock
Visitor Center

Orchard Camp

Railroad Camp

Bear Harbor Camp

Bear Harbor

Duffy's Gulch

Chase Grove

North Fork

Lost Coast Trail

Usal Road

Jackass Creek

School Marm Grove

Wheeler Camp

Wheeler Trail

Sally Bell Grove

Little Jackass Creek

Little Jackass Camp

Anderson Gulch

SINKYONE

Anderson Gulch Camp

Dark Gulch

WILDERNESS STATE PARK

PACIFIC

OCEAN

Usal Camp

Usal Creek

Usal Road

To 1

0   1   2 miles

18

The Lost Coast Trail, from Orchard Camp to Usal Camp

—Matt Heid

Route	Days	Hiking Time Hours/Days	Elev. Gain/Loss	Difficulty	Miles
↱	3	16–24/2–3	3800´/3800´	***	16.7

Campsites: Wheeler Camp: 4.7 miles
Little Jackass Camp: 9.2 miles
Anderson Gulch Camp: 11.7 miles

Map: USGS 7.5-min *Hales Grove, Mistake Point, Bear Harbor*
Trails of the Lost Coast, Wilderness Press

Best season: Spring and Fall (see Heads Up!)

Take this trip!

The Lost Coast can hardly be considered undiscovered. Ranching, logging, railroads, mills, and seaports have all left their mark on the land. But it is remote, too rugged for Highway 1, keeping all but the adventurous away. This backpacking trip follows the Lost Coast Trail between Orchard Camp and Usal Beach, a strenuous hike best done in three days. For being along the coast, there is virtually no level walking on this hike: the trail constantly encounters sheer creek canyons, descending quickly and ascending steeply hundreds of feet at a time.

Trailheads

The two ends of the Lost Coast Trail are far apart by road (2–3 hours' driving time) and two vehicles are required for transportation to and from the trailheads. The hike can be done in either direction; if you wish to hike south to north, simply follow the description given below in reverse order.

To reach the northern trailhead, take the Highway 101 exit for Redway and Shelter Cove. From Redway, take Briceland-Thorn Road 16.5 miles west toward Shelter Cove to Chemise Mtn. Road—turn left (south). The road's surface soon becomes dirt, and you reach a four-way junction in 6.3 miles—bear right onto the least significant road. The descent from here is steep, narrow, and not passable for trailers or RVs. While 4WD vehicles will have an easier time, low-clearance cars can make a slow descent. The Needle Rock Visitor Center is 3.2 miles from the junction. Here, day-use fees ($2/vehicle) are collected and backpackers need to pay their trail-camp fees. The trailhead at Orchard Camp is an additional 2.4 miles south at the roadend. After the first big rains of the season, the road is closed at the visitor center, making it necessary to walk this final stretch.

To reach the southern trailhead, take Mendocino County (Usal) Road 431 north from Highway 1. Along Highway 1 the unmarked and easily missed turnoff is 13.9 miles west of its junction with Highway 101, and approximately 3 miles north of Rockport at milepost 90.88. The one-lane dirt road is impassable for trailers and RVs but easily handled by all other vehicles. In 5.4 miles you reach the area's first campsites, located in a large grassy field. Trailhead parking is 0.3 mile farther on the left, immediately before a small bridge. From here, it's a short walk to the posted trailhead at the roadend.

TRIP DESCRIPTION

Heads Up! Backcountry camping is allowed only at the three designated trail camps: Wheeler, Little Jackass, and Anderson Gulch (see Permits). While no water is available at the trailhead, sources are plentiful along the trail.

Timing is key. Fog blankets the region from June through mid-September, obscuring views and chilling the air for days on end. Heavy storms usually strike by late October and can inundate the coast with torrential rainfall well into April. The wettest points in California are on the Lost Coast and winter storms are best not trifled with. Avoid holidays and weekends and crowds will be light. Those planning a winter visit should call ahead to check access as flooding and slides can close the access roads for weeks on end.

From the trailhead at Orchard Camp (0.0/40), the trail is quickly joined by a spur trail from Railroad Camp before winding down to Bear Harbor (0.4/00), a doghole port in the late 1800s. Today nothing remains but pleasant campsites tucked away from the ocean and a spectacular coastal vista. Next is a general introduction to the Lost Coast Trail experience of constant ascent and descent. Climbing a steep and narrow stream gully, the trail passes through lus-

The Lost Coast

cious greenery. Sword ferns splay everywhere, moss coats the thick trunks of overhanging alder and California bay, the large leaves of blue elderberry hug the stream, and every possible nook and cranny bursts with life. You have time to enjoy all this because the trail is remarkably vertical. Cresting the ridge, the trail traverses around Duffy's Gulch and through the first grove of old growth redwoods before gently climbing along the blufftop. Views into the sheer gulch of Jackass Creek open up as the trail makes its steep descent to Wheeler Camp (4.7/10), passing through another old-growth redwood grove immediately prior to the first campsites.

Wheeler Camp was the location of a wood-processing facility from 1951 until 1960, run by The Wolf Creek Timber Company. A small company town with store, bunkhouse, and school was constructed here as well, although this was deliberately burned for liability reasons in 1969. Remnants of the mill include knee-high periscope-like tubes protruding from the ground, which were used to test the underground flow of toxic diesel fuel that leaked from the facility. While no fuel is known to have reached Jackass Creek, to be safe obtain your water upstream from the site. If it's raining or windy, the campsites nearest the redwood grove are nicest. If it's sunny and clear, continue along the trail to the sites uphill and south of the beach.

Heading to the beach, a trail diverges left as you enter the more open meadow—continue straight, winding along the edge of the beach before climbing steeply to almost 1100 feet. Keep an eye out for the small trees that line the clifftop as you ascend. Bonsai'd by exposure to the elements, these trees can be as old as those in the surrounding forest, with remarkably stout trunks hidden beneath their twisted foliage. Shelter Cove can be spotted north from near the cliff top, before the trail plummets down through dense tan oak forest. Little Jackass Creek Camp (9.2/20) is at the bottom. Sites are fewer than at Wheeler Camp, and farther from the wonderfully secluded beach.

The trail continues inland opposite the creek, quickly entering the Sally Bell Grove, another old-growth redwood stand named for a Sinkyone woman who fled here after a brutal attack on her village at Needle Rock (May 1864) by Lieutenant William Frazier and the Battalion of Mountaineers. Passing many substantial redwoods, the trail makes another very steep ascent to 800 feet before immediately dropping to Anderson Gulch Camp (11.7/250), where campsites are small and hidden among the trees. You pass the best sites in the redwoods shortly after crossing the creek.

Another brief up-and-down brings you to Dark Gulch (12.3/350), where the final and most arduous section of the hike begins. A prolonged stretch of climbing brings you to—at over 1100 feet—the highest point on this hike, almost directly above the ocean. The thick forest of tan oak, big leaf maple, and redwood opens into fields of low-lying coyote brush and blackberry tangles. South, the trail can be seen winding along the bare ridgetop. Views of the ocean are exceptional, Usal Beach is visible, and a keen eye can identify Highway 1, 7 miles south of here, twisting along the coast before turning inland. It's a gradual descent from here to Usal Beach, ending with several steep switchbacks that deposit you near some nice campsites.

Permits

There is a fee of $3 per person per night for the trail camps, payable outside the Needle Rock Visitor Center or at the Usal Beach fee station. There is no trail quota. The Needle Rock Visitor Center (see Trailhead) is staffed year-round by volunteers, and open approximately 20 hours per week. Sinkyone Wilderness State Park headquarters, (707) 986-7711, located in Whitethorn on Briceland Road, is also open intermittently. There is no visitor center at the southern end.

Build-up/Wind-down tips

For those wishing to camp near the northern trailhead before setting off, there are 18 walk-in campsites scattered around the Needle Rock area ($7/night October-April, $11/night May-September). At the southern trailhead are 15 campsites scattered around the Usal Beach area, all accessible by vehicle.

Matt Heid, avid backpacker and recent Wilderness Press author, is leading a new generation of adventurers in the footsteps of John Muir; see "Author Bio & Bib" on page 492.

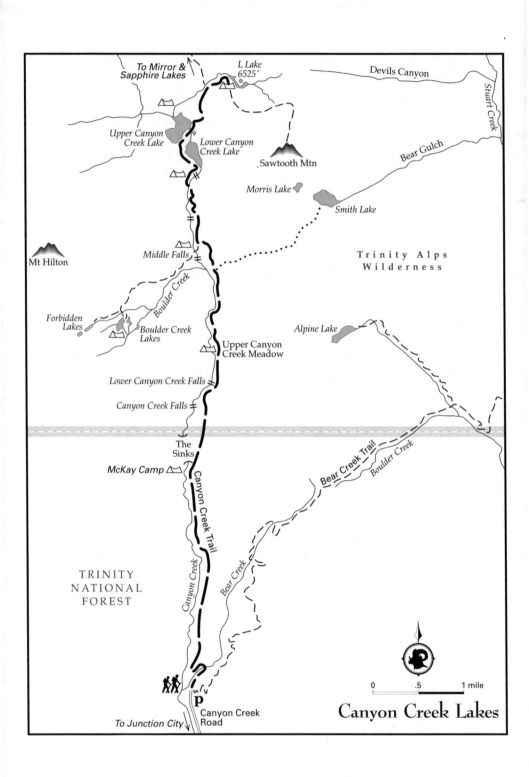

To Mirror &
Sapphire Lakes

L Lake
6525'

Devils Canyon

Stuart Creek

Upper Canyon
Creek Lake

Lower Canyon
Creek Lake

Bear Gulch

Sawtooth Mtn

Morris Lake

Smith Lake

Mt Hilton

Middle Falls

Boulder Creek

Trinity Alps
Wilderness

Forbidden
Lakes

Boulder Creek
Lakes

Alpine Lake

Upper Canyon
Creek Meadow

Lower Canyon Creek Falls

Canyon Creek Falls

The
Sinks

Bear Creek Trail

Boulder Creek

McKay Camp

Canyon Creek Trail

Bear Creek

Canyon Creek

TRINITY
NATIONAL
FOREST

P

To Junction City

Canyon Creek
Road

0   .5   1 mile

Canyon Creek Lakes

19

Canyon Creek Lakes & L Lake

—Michael White

Route	Days	Elev. Gain/Loss	Difficulty	Miles
↰	2	4260'/4260'	***	16.5
		(to L Lake and back)		
		3325'/3325'	**	13.5
		(to Lower Canyon Creek Lake)		

Campsites: L Lake: 8.25 miles
Lower Canyon Creek Lake: 6.75 miles

Map: USGS 7.5-min *Mt. Hilton*

Best season: Summer through early fall

Take this trip!

A hiking companion posed this question on a recent trip, "What if you could hike only in one mountain range for the rest of your life, which would it be?" After careful thought, I firmly responded, "The Trinity Alps!" From dense, low-elevation coastal forests to glaciated granite peaks and everything in between, few other mountain regions possess the wide range of diversity found in the Trinities.

The Canyon Creek Trail takes backpackers into the best of the Alps: sapphire-blue lakes, tumbling creeks, dramatic waterfalls, wildflowers, rugged granite peaks flanked by permanent snowfields, exquisite scenery, and splendid vistas are all here in abundance. Beyond the backpacking, peak-baggers, amateur naturalists, anglers, rock climbers, and cross-country enthusiasts will find diversions aplenty in the heart of the range. This is a popular trail by Trinity Alps standards—with good reason—but perhaps also is the best sampling of what makes this area so spectacular and so unique.

Trailhead

From Weaverville, head west on Highway 299 for 8 miles to Junction City and turn right (north) onto Canyon Creek Road. Travel 13.8 more miles to the large parking area at the road end. The trailhead is equipped with a pit toilet and a picnic table.

TRIP DESCRIPTION

> **Heads Up!** Since this trail is perhaps the most popular one in the Trinity Alps, if yours is a weekend trip, get an early start to secure the best campsites.

From the well-signed trailhead, the Canyon Creek Lakes Trail branches left from the Bear Creek Trail as you head north on a slightly rising grade. Soon leveling off, you then follow the trail on a moderate descent among big-leaf maple and dogwood down to the crossing of Bear Creek. One-third mile from the trailhead you boulderhop across Bear Creek and then climb around the shoulder of Canyon Creek into the main canyon, well above the creek. A long steady ascent ensues, where you pass through the dry vegetation of an open, mixed forest of canyon and black oak, incense-cedar, Douglas-fir, and ponderosa pine. The climb continues uninterrupted until you reach an informal junction (2.8) with a use trail heading down 200 yards to a large flat and the relocated McKay Camp just below The Sinks, a large rockslide where Canyon Creek adopts a subterranean channel. For interested backpackers, McKay Camp offers fine campsites and good fishing nearby.

From the junction, a moderate climb leads to your first source of water since the crossing of Bear Creek. A pleasant little stream glides across the trail through a narrow swath of lush vegetation, ½ mile from the junction. As refreshing as this water appears, you may wish to wait a little while as the trail quickly crosses the stream two more times above via a pair of switchbacks. Leaving the thrice-visited creek behind, you continue the ascent up the trail on the east side of the canyon. The old trail used to follow directly along the creek bottom and up past spectacular Canyon Creek Falls, but nowadays hikers must settle for the distant roar of the falls and perhaps an incomplete and unsatisfying glimpse cross-canyon through dense brush and moderate forest. Farther up the trail, ¼ mile from the creek, the newer path draws near to the creek and passes by Lower Canyon Creek Falls, a less prestigious fall but one with a wonderful swimming hole at the base, providing a fine opportunity to beat the afternoon heat (3.8).

Another ¾ mile of climbing leads you to a level stretch of trail where there are some pleasant campsites under the trees. Just beyond the campsites you stroll through waist-high ferns alongside the quiet surroundings of Upper Canyon Creek Meadows. In early season, the marshy meadows are carpeted with a wide array of wildflowers. Early evening may provide a good chance to see deer grazing on the lush foliage.

Past the meadows, the moderate climb up-canyon resumes through light to moderate forest cover, crossing some typically dry seasonal streams along the way. Near the 5-mile mark you climb over granite ledges and soon reach a large forested flat. Littered with boulders, here you will find some decent campsites not far from Canyon Creek.

For the adventurous, a rugged and steep cross-country route leaves this flat and climbs the gulch to the east toward Smith and Morris lakes, a pair of beautiful subalpine lakes situated at the southeastern base of craggy Sawtooth Mountain. The beginning of the route is the most difficult section, as you must beat some heavy brush at the base of the ridge. Once above the band of brush the way is much easier, but it still requires a good dose of stamina, route-finding skill, and some mountaineering ability. The total distance from the flat to Smith Lake is only 1½ miles, but plan on the better part of a morning or afternoon for the trailless ascent.

At the far end of the flat, just before the Canyon Creek Trail steeply ascends up a cliff, a faint use trail branches west through the trees for about 0.1 mile to the base of Middle Falls, a dramatic series of cascades tumbling over granite ledges and finally plunging into a deep bowl. From the use-trail junction, the main trail turns east and begins a series of switchbacks across the cliff, following a little creek up the slope. The grade eases above the cliff in a forested azalea dell, and proceeding up the mild trail you soon reach the junction with the Boulder Creek Trail (5.7). A steep, 0.2-mile descent down the Boulder Creek Trail leads to some excellent campsites on forested flats alongside Canyon Creek.

Remaining on the Canyon Creek Trail, you near the creek again and pass some more good campsites before reaching the end of the azalea dell (and the easy walking) at the base of another set of switchbacks. You climb around the next falls on Canyon Creek, where you will find more campsites near the stream and scattered around the cliffs above the falls. At 6.4 miles you come to a place where newer trail branches away from the old path that led directly to the outlet of Lower Canyon Creek Lake. The trail was rerouted after a fatal accident in which a hiker was killed attempting to cross the creek in 1983.

On the newer section of trail you travel upstream not far from the creek until a small sign-marked trail leads you to a crossing of Canyon Creek. You can either ford the creek, or use a fallen log to span it. From the crossing you continue up-canyon through forest to the base of another falls and the last campsites below the lakes, before a winding ascent over granite slabs leads you up and over the southwest rim of the basin to the shore of Lower Canyon Creek Lake (6.75).

The pristine waters of Lower Canyon Creek Lake fill a deep granite bowl where a smattering of weeping spruces, red firs, and Jeffrey pines cling to the

On the route to L Lake

limited pockets of soil scattered around the basin. The lack of significant forest grants visitors the delight of widespread views in every direction. To the east, steep hillsides rise up toward the sky, culminating at the top of rugged Sawtooth Mountain. Lower cliffs on the west grant vistas of snowcapped Mt. Hilton, while to the north the jagged summit of Thompson Peak—at 9002 feet the highest mountain in the Trinity Alps—fills a notch above the head of the canyon.

Although numerous campsites dot the shoreline, camping at Lower Canyon Creek Lake is not recommended as most of those sites are way too close to the lakeshore. The lack of adequate soils for waste disposal combined with the lake's popularity create a potentially serious environmental problem. The Forest Service is extremely reluctant to ban camping at Lower Canyon Creek Lake, so the proper response of earth-friendly backpackers is to camp in the forest below and dayhike up to the lake.

If Upper Canyon Creek Lake or L Lake is your goal, turn northwest from the southern tip of the lower lake and climb toward the low ridge above. Many years ago there were orange blazes sporadically painted on rocks to help guide your way, but these marks have fortunately faded away over time—ducks have more recently replaced the paint marks. With the aid of the ducks, you should be able to locate a scramble trail which eventually turns north, surmounting the cliffs high above the west side of Lower Canyon Creek Lake. Beyond the lake, the path rounds a rock rib, quickly ascends a short gully, and tops out on the dike between the two lakes.

Even grander views than the ones from the lower lake appear from the top of the dike. Joining Thompson Peak, jagged Wedding Cake springs into view along with the arcing expanse of the upper canyon, where myriad waterfalls, born from springs and snowfields high above, spill across the steep granite walls of the horseshoe-shaped basin. Above the east shore, you can catch a glimpse of the stream that drains L Lake 800 feet higher. At the far end of the upper lake the inlet creek meanders through the pastoral scene of a deep-green, grassy delta. As with the previous lakeshore, campsites along the water's edge should not be used. With a little effort more appropriate sites can be found near the far edge of the delta, or sprinkled around the upper basin beyond the lake. The verdant delta was formerly submerged when miners built a wood-timbered dam raising the level of the lake by 6–8 feet. Today the only evidence of the dam is the white bathtub ring on the granite walls around the lake. Despite the heavy traffic, fishing is still reported to be good at Upper Canyon Creek Lake for fair-sized eastern brook and rainbow trout.

A defined path continues around the southeast shore to the outlet stream's exit from the lake. To get across the quick-moving creek, you will either have to make a knee-to-waist-high ford or be very agile and quite bold as you long jump the rocky gorge. (If you choose the latter option, make sure you don't fall into the creek; it could be disastrous.) Beyond the creek a faint path continues a short distance and dead-ends at a strip of beach near a campsite, which is much too close to the water. Just above this campsite a use trail climbs steeply up the hillside, beginning the climb to L Lake.

Most backpackers are content to go no farther than Canyon Creek Lakes, satisfied with the rewards that their moderate effort has reaped. The ascent to L

Lake—at least while burdened with a backpack—is another story altogether. Although a trail of sorts leads to the lake and the distance is less than a mile from Upper Canyon Creek Lake, the route can hardly be considered an improved trail and the elevation gain is nearly 1000 feet. Campsites at L Lake are limited as well, but the few hearty souls willing to make the journey will have a good chance of solitude, when the last of the dayhikers have headed for lower regions.

To reach L Lake, follow the use trail from the illegal campsite on the strip of beach along the northeast shore of Upper Canyon Lake up a steep gully for a short distance and then bend northeast, making an upward traverse across the top of the first granite knob. Continue to climb across open terrain of the east face of the canyon, following the ducked route over sloping granite ledges and through steep gullies, until you reach the outlet stream from L Lake, about ½ mile from where you left Upper Canyon Creek Lake. Along the way you are blessed with splendid views of both Canyon Creek Lakes, the Canyon Creek drainage, and Mt. Hilton, dominating the western skyline. Once you reach the outlet stream, turn east-northeast and then climb along the ducked route next to the creek another 0.4 mile to the lake. As you approach the lake, you enter a light forest cover and then pass a narrow strip of meadow alongside the creek.

Obviously the lake was named for its irregular shape roughly resembling the letter "L," although a small circular pond near the northeast shore must have once been part of the lake, when the shoreline didn't bear this resemblance. Shallow at the western end, L Lake gains some depth at the far end and provides a home for a healthy population of eastern brook trout. Mountain hemlock, weeping spruce, and red fir grace the shoreline, adding a somewhat somber effect to the lake's atmosphere.

The 2-acre lake is jammed into the narrow cleft of a cirque, the deep chasm very nearly surrounded on all sides by steep rock walls. The southeast flank of the basin rises up sharply to culminate in the very summit of towering Sawtooth Mountain, 2350 feet above. Permanent snowfields below the peak give the area a decidedly alpine feel, even though the lake is only 6525 feet above sea level. The northern rim of the basin steeply divides the Canyon Creek drainage from that of the equally popular Stuart Fork.

Campsites near the lake are limited, but seemingly sufficient for the small percentage of backpackers willing to lug their gear all the way up here. The best-forested spots occur near the meadows below the lake, while exposed sites with a great view can be found on top of the rocky hill south of the outlet. Since mosquitoes can be a nuisance for a few weeks in midsummer, a campsite on top of the hill offers the benefit of a potential breeze.

A base camp at L Lake offers backpackers with an extra day or two many opportunities for additional adventures. For those with mountaineering abilities, a climb of Sawtooth Mountain can be quite rewarding, including an incomparable view from the summit. However, bear in mind that the final part of the ascent requires Class 3–4 climbing skills, and possibly crampons, an ice axe, and a rope, depending on conditions. Cross-country enthusiasts have the option of following a strenuous route north across a saddle in the ridge and down the other side to Mirror and Sapphire lakes. Even if you lack the desire for such rigorous pursuits, L Lake can be a great spot for simply whiling away the day in relaxation. At the conclusion of your stay in the Canyon Creek and L Lake area, retrace your steps back to the trailhead.

If you have yet to get your fill of the Trinity Alps, you can follow the Canyon Creek Lakes Trail back to the junction with the Boulder Creek Lakes Trail at the 5.7-mile mark, and take the 1½ mile path up to a set of delightfully scenic lakes. Compared to the Canyon Creek Lakes, the Boulder Creek Lakes see far fewer visitors, perhaps due to a section of trail that is one of the steepest in the Alps, gaining about 600 feet in a half mile. However, perseverance brings great rewards as the picturesque lakes and a host of smaller ponds fill glacier-scoured depressions in the nearly treeless granite basin, where vistas of rugged peaks and ridges abound. A side trip to Boulder Creek Lakes adds a round trip of 3 miles and a one-way elevation gain and loss of 825/100 feet to your overall journey.

Permits

A Wilderness Permit is required for all overnight stays in the Trinity Alps Wilderness. Campfire permits are also required if you plan to have one. You can self-register for both permits at the ranger station in Weaverville:

Weaverville Ranger District
Box 1190
Weaverville, CA 96093
(530) 623-2121

Build-up/Wind-down tips:

The Brewery, located on the main drag in the historic section of Weaverville, has been dispensing fine food and drink for quite some time. Although beer hasn't been produced here since the old mining days, modern-day patrons can choose from a fine selection of local microbrews, on tap or in the bottle—a pleasant accompaniment to the hearty but reasonably priced dinners. Plenty of unique artifacts from bygone days adorn the walls and dangle from the ceiling, augmenting the rustic atmosphere of the old brewery. For breakfast, the beer-batter pancakes are a sure-fire hit, especially when paired with the Polish sausage. The Brewery is open for breakfast, lunch, and dinner, seven days a week.

Mike White tells how he jettisoned an engineering career for backpacking and writing about it in the "Author Bio & Bib" section on page 492.

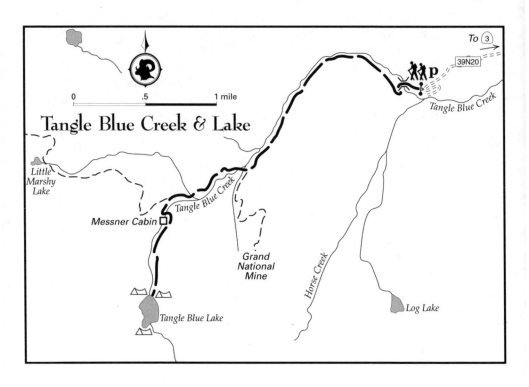

Tangle Blue Creek & Lake

0   .5   1 mile

To ③

39N20

Tangle Blue Creek

Little Marshy Lake

Tangle Blue Creek

Messner Cabin

Grand National Mine

Horse Creek

Tangle Blue Lake

Log Lake

20

Tangle Blue Creek & Lake

—Michael White

Route	Days	Elev. Gain/Loss	Difficulty	Miles
↝	2	1265'/1265'	**	6.5
		1265'/150' (one way to Tangle Blue Lake)		

Campsites: Tangle Blue Lake (north shore): 3.25 miles
(see the Trip Description for others)

Map: USGS 7.5-min *Tangle Blue Lake*

Best season: Summer through early fall

Take this trip!

A dose of mystique surrounds the naming of Tangle Blue Lake: an early resident journeying to the delightful area after a long evening of hearty celebration awoke to find his feet tangled and the air blue. Whether or not the legend rings true, the sheer beauty of Tangle Blue Lake deserves such a whimsical appellation. Nearly enclosed by a backdrop of rock walls and craggy pinnacles, serene waters of the lake mirror dramatic surroundings. Above the south shoreline, the pristine inlet creek dances over rock slabs and rambles through wildflowers of a damp meadow before entering the lake. Smaller flower-laden meadows are scattered elsewhere above the lakeshore.

If Tangle Blue Lake had the misfortune to be located near a major population center, it would doubtless be overrun by a plethora of worshipping admirers, but due to such a remote location it sees relatively few visitors. Backpackers seeking overnight accommodations are treated to a nearly ideal campsite above the north shore. More secluded campsites can be found around the south and west shores.

Trailhead

Approximately 50 miles north of Weaverville, Forest Service Road 39N20 leaves Highway 3 and heads west 3.4 miles to the trailhead. There should be a sign at the junction reading TANGLE BLUE LAKE, TRAILERS NOT ADVISED. If not, you can find the turnoff at a hairpin turn between two concrete bridges that cross Scott Mountain Creek. Initially the dirt road is quite steep, and may be impassable after a heavy rain. Bear left at a junction with Road 39N20A, 1.9 miles from Highway 3, and continue on the main road to the trailhead at a broad sweeping intersection. The trail begins on the continuation of the road beyond a locked steel gate.

TRIP DESCRIPTION

From the trailhead, you follow the dirt road 200 yards downhill to an old steel and wood bridge across Tangle Blue Creek. Once across the creek you climb steeply up the dry and dusty roadbed on a couple of switchbacks, where seeps refresh a narrow strip of lush plants and wildflowers along the edge. Through scattered forest the climb continues beside the tumbling creek, never more than a stone's throw away, until you reach the wilderness boundary (1.5).

The Trinity Alps Wilderness boundary is marked by a series of signs and a steel gate that have been vandalized. In former days, driving all the way to this point was possible, but fortunately the Forest Service decided to push the trailhead back to the current location. One wonders how much more vandalism would occur if this were still the trailhead. Away from the boundary, you continue up the road past some primitive campsites. Soon you are greeted by lushly vegetated hillsides covered with deep green grasses and colorful wildflowers. A short climb up a hillside brings you to an informal junction (1.9) with the overgrown road that used to take miners a steep mile up to the Grand National Mine.

A brief descent from the junction leads you through drier surroundings and across a tributary of Tangle Blue Creek. A short distance farther you cross the main channel of the creek and turn upstream on a single-track trail. Passing through a mixed forest of Douglas-fir, incense-cedar, and sugar pine, you quickly reach a switchback where you pick up the old road again for another ¼ mile—until a single track trail leads to the crossing of the stream coming down from Little Marshy Lake. In early season you may have to hunt around for an old log to make this crossing without getting wet.

On the far side of the creek you once again pick up the old road and make a moderately steep climb over rocky tread up to a signed junction (2.5). Turn left (southwest), leaving the road behind for good, and follow the trail into a beautiful sloping meadow filled with tall grasses and dotted with seasonal wildflowers. Up-canyon you glimpse through trees the cliffs that surround Tangle Blue Lake, now less than a mile away. Toward the far end of the meadow, the trail dives down to the crossing of Tangle Blue Creek. On the opposite bank you can see the tangled pile of old boards and rusting stove parts that constitute the remains of Messner Cabin.

Meadow near Messner Cabin

Away from the creek, the trail begins a moderately steep climb through a light, mixed forest. Continuing the climb, you enter a lush area of willow thickets, alders, ferns, grasses, and wildflowers. A number of creeklets trickle across your path and give life to tiger lilies, columbines, and other assorted flowers. After ½ mile of climbing from Messner Cabin, the trail's grade eases as you break out into the meadow below the lake. A pleasant stroll across the meadow brings you to the north shore of Tangle Blue Lake (3.25).

Nearly surrounded by steep gray cliffs, Tangle Blue Lake nestles at the bottom of a deep basin, reflecting the walls and pinnacles above in its serene waters. Above the north shore a lake view, mortared rock fireplaces, and a level spot beneath grand white firs near a creek—all add up to make a coveted campsite. Additional campsites, offering a chance for more solitude, can be found west of the outlet stream near a small meadow, or at the lake's far end. An informal path encircles the lake, but is muddy in some areas and overgrown with brush in others. Anglers will appreciate the shoreline access, but the fair-sized eastern brooks and rainbows may test your skills and patience. Swimming in the cool waters provides a refreshing break from the normally warm afternoon temperatures. Rock climbers and scramblers will find plenty of opportunities to ply their craft and obtain fine views from the top of the cliffs. At the conclusion of your stay at Tangle Blue Lake, retrace your steps to the trailhead.

Typical mountainous-coastal flora

Permits

A Wilderness Permit is required for all overnight stays in the Trinity Alps Wilderness. Campfire permits are also required if you plan to have a one. You can self-register for both permits at the Weaverville or Coffee Creek ranger stations.

Coffee Creek Ranger Station
Star Route 2, Box 3640
Trinity Center, CA 96091
(530) 266-3211

Build-up/Wind-down tips

The Forest Café in Coffee Creek is well-named, tucked into the shade of dense evergreen trees on the east side of Highway 3. Tasty country cooking is served up with a local flair, in portions that are more than suitable for even the hungriest hikers. Definitely a hangout for regulars, an entire wall of the Forest Café is graced with a mural honoring characters from the Coffee Creek Area who routinely visited a nearby bar in the 1950s. However, strangers are more than welcome to savor the tasty meals and the down-home ambiance either inside the café or outside on the attached deck. Don't show up too early for breakfast though, the café doesn't open until 9 A.M. During the summer of '99 the Forest Café was closed on Tuesdays, and only served dinner on Mondays after 5:30. Otherwise, Wednesday through Sunday, you could enjoy breakfast, lunch, and dinner between the hours of 9 A.M. and 8:30 P.M.

Mike White tells how he jettisoned an engineering career for backpacking and writing about it in the "Author Bio & Bib" section on page 492.

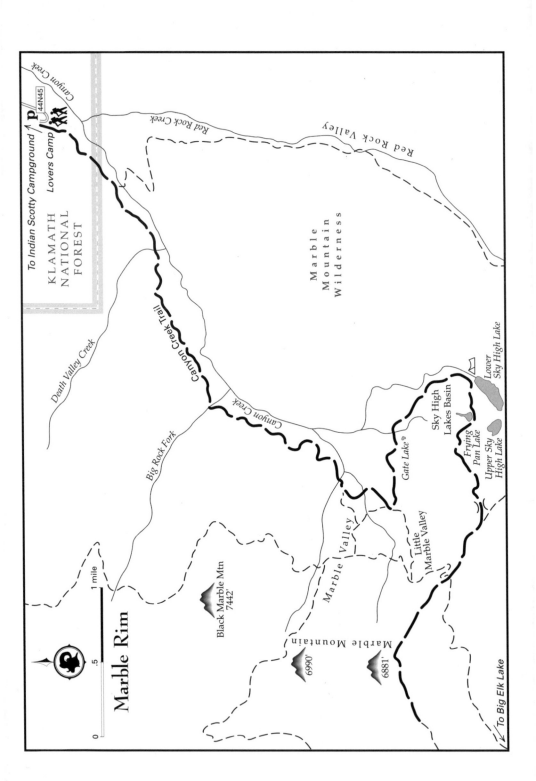

Marble Rim

To Indian Scotty Campground

Lovers Camp

44N45

Canyon Creek

KLAMATH NATIONAL FOREST

Death Valley Creek

Big Rock Fork

Canyon Creek Trail

Canyon Creek

Red Rock Creek

Red Rock Valley

Marble Mountain Wilderness

Black Marble Mtn 7442'

6990'

Marble Mountain

6881'

Marble Valley

Little Marble Valley

Gate Lake

Sky High Lakes Basin

Frying Pan Lake

Upper Sky High Lake

Lower Sky High Lake

To Big Elk Lake

1 mile

.5

0

21

Marble Rim from Lovers Camp via Sky High Lakes Basin

—Matt Heid

Route	Days	Hiking Time Hours	Elev. Gain/Loss	Difficulty	Miles
↲	2	10–14	2800′/2800′	**	17.0

Campsites: Sky High Lakes Basin: 6.0 miles

Map: USGS 7.5-min *Marble Mtn.*

Best season: Mid-June through October

Take this trip!

Designated a primitive area in 1931 and established as one of California's first wilderness areas in 1953, Marble Mountain Wilderness protects nearly a quarter million acres of pristine California. You might think that the deep lakes, striking mountains, lush forest, abundant wildlife, and isolation would attract droves of backpackers. But they don't. You will ascend impressive cliffs of the Marble Mountains via serene Sky High Lakes Basin, a moderate overnight trip that could be done as a long, strenuous dayhike. This is (deservedly) the most popular hike in the wilderness, but crowds will be light relative to other alpine regions of the state. Fishing is possible in the Sky High lakes.

Trailhead

Take Scott River Road 13.4 miles west from Highway 3 at Fort Jones to Indian Scotty Campground and turn left (south) onto Forest Service Road 44N45, posted for Lovers Camp. Bear left at the immediate fork and continue on the sinuous, one-lane paved road as it climbs 6.8 miles to a large parking lot at the roadend.

TRIP DESCRIPTION

Heads Up! Water is available at the trailhead until late September and sources are plentiful along the hike. Snow typically arrives by late October and can linger well into June—call ahead if you are planning a trip during these times (see Permits).

From the trailhead (0.0/4150), start out on Canyon Creek Trail, passing two established campsites and entering the lush forest. Douglas-fir, tan oak, and big leaf maple are common sights overhead; and trail markers, wild ginger, and ferns line the path. In 0.1 mile, the trail reaches a confusing intersection of unpaved roads—continue on the trail found diagonally across the road. After passing a wilderness-boundary sign hammered to a Douglas-fir, you soon reach a posted fork (0.7/4250) in the level trail. The trail to Red Rock Valley heads left, but you continue right on Canyon Creek Trail toward Marble Valley.

While the hike parallels rushing Canyon Creek for several miles, it remains unseen below you for the duration. Crossing flowing Death Valley Creek, the trail then climbs briefly before dropping to cross Big Rock Fork. The logs that litter the bouldery watercourse provide evidence of the ferocity that winter rains and flood bring to the region's otherwise small streams. Shortly thereafter, the trail abruptly turns upslope and begins climbing steeply uphill. Intermittent switchbacks eventually bring you to the junction for Marble Valley (4.1/5320). Marble Valley provides faster and more direct access to the Marble Mountains but entirely misses Sky High Lakes Basin. To follow this shorter route, bear right and continue uphill to the Marble Valley Cabin (closed to the public) and the Pacific Crest Trail junction. Head south on the PCT until you reach the Marble Rim Trail. This marble-strewn route also makes an excellent return trail the following day.

Bearing left toward Sky High Lakes, you climb more gradually and soon pass another junction for Marble Valley (4.4/5500) on the right. Curving east, the trail offers the first views of the Marble Mountains to the west before making a final ascent into Sky High Lakes Basin. After you crest a final rise, diminutive and willow-choked Gate Lake welcomes you to the gently rolling basin.

Carved out by recent glaciation within the past two million years, the basin holds several lakes. While use paths crisscross the area, the actual trail leads first to larger Lower Sky High Lake (6.0/5775) in the basin's southeast corner, before turning west toward tiny Frying Pan Lake, and then climbing out of the basin. The trees are diverse—white fir, red fir, mountain hemlock, western white pine, and large groves of aspen can all be found. In addition, a rare stand of subalpine fir grows here as well. A common tree throughout the Pacific Northwest, subalpine fir's range extends north to the subarctic. But in Northern California it only occurs here and in scattered locations within nearby Russian

Marble Rim

Wilderness, and both populations are more than 50 miles distant from the next closest stand in southern Oregon. Despite existing at the extreme southern limit of their range, the trees seem to be thriving. Identify them by their narrow spire shape, strongly aromatic crushed needles, and close resemblance to red fir. Within the lakes amphibians thrive: frogs, tadpoles, and the ubiquitous, orange-bellied rough-skinned newt all entertain along the shorelines. In early October, cattle graze here as well.

Continuing west toward the Marble Mountains, the trail climbs steeply up the slopes and offers superlative views of the entire basin before attaining the divide and reaching a junction with the PCT (7.1/6400). From the ridge, the entire drainage of Wooley Creek reveals itself within a horseshoe of peaks dominated west-southwest by granite Medicine Mountain (6837). From its headwaters here, Wooley Creek plummets more than 5000 feet through dense, undisturbed forest to join the Salmon River 20 miles away. Its entire pristine watershed is protected within the wilderness.

Once on the ridge, turn right and follow the PCT descending gently northwest to a four-way junction (8.6/6230), where you continue straight toward Marble Rim. Right leads down into Marble Valley, the possible return route mentioned above. Left drops down in just over a mile to Big Elk Lake, visible southwest in an open grassy area. Now climbing again toward the marble slopes, the trail remains below the divide until it reaches the low, treeless notch along Marble Rim (8.7/6480).

Part of the complex geologic mix of the Klamath Mountains, the Marble Mountains most likely originated more than 200 million years ago from coral reefs surrounding an ancient, offshore island or landmass. Over the millenia, the reefs' skeletal remains collected in thick layers that eventually solidified into the sedimentary rock, limestone. Smashed into North America, the limestone was transformed to marble and exposed by erosion to form the spectacular cliffs before you. North, Rainy Valley trails away more than a thousand feet below. Southeast are the jagged peaks of the highest mountains in the wilderness, and the Trinity Alps can often be seen on the distant southern skyline. Return as you came via Sky High Lakes Basin or take the Marble Valley short-cut.

Permits

No Wilderness Permit is necessary, but a valid campfire permit is required. Sites are abundant in the Sky High Lakes Basin. Contact Scott River Ranger Station, (530) 468-5351, located in Fort Jones by the intersection with Scott River Road. It's open Monday through Friday 8 A.M.-4:30 P.M.

Build-up/Wind-down tips

Free overnight camping is permitted in sites around the trailhead. Otherwise, try Indian Scotty Campground (28 sites, $10) at the Lovers Camp turnoff from Scott River Road.

Matt Heid, avid backpacker and recent Wilderness Press author, is leading a new generation of adventurers in the footsteps of John Muir; see "Author Bio & Bib" on page 492.

The Southern Sierra Nevada

Sequoia-Kings Canyon National Parks, John Muir, & Golden Trout Wildernesses

The wildest part of California's most beautiful mountain range, the rugged Sierra Nevada, lies within the designated wilderness of two national parks, Sequoia and Kings Canyon (administered jointly) and two wildernesses, Golden Trout and John Muir. Here, 13,000- and 14,000-foot peaks soar above a glacier-sculpted landscape of polished granite, sheer cliffs, sparkling lakes and streams, wildflower-spangled meadows, towering giant sequoias, and forested valleys. Twelve-thousand-foot peaks are so numerous that few are named.

Roads bring casual visitors to the fringes of these wonders, and from road-ends they can see some fine scenery—but that is as close as most visitors ever get to the backcountry. Pity them! Only those who venture into the Sierra's remote backcountry on foot or with stock can immerse themselves in its awe-inspiring splendor, solitude, and even danger. This section will help you get there.

The parks together—Sequoia to the south, Kings Canyon contiguous to the north—protect 863,741 acres of the Sierra's most remote backcountry. Since World War II, these parks have been administered as a single unit. They are accessible by road only from the west because the narrow belt of John Muir Wilderness curves like a protective arm around both parks' eastern boundaries, over the northern boundary of Kings Canyon, and then down the west side almost to Kings Canyon itself. Golden Trout Wilderness, a land of vast meadows and glittering streams, cups Sequoia securely on the south. Together, these wilderness areas protect about 887,916 more acres. Smaller wildernesses, worthwhile but not featured in this book, help protect more backcountry on the parks' west sides: Monarch, Dinkey Lakes, and Kaiser, as well as Jennie Lakes (see trip 25).

The parks exist because ruthless commercial exploitation of the western Sierra so alarmed people that they campaigned for federal protection. Congress established Sequoia National Park in 1890 along with General Grant National Park, a grove of giant sequoias well to the north. The parks grew nearly to their present size in 1940, but the legislation excluded Kings Canyon proper, Tehipite Valley, and Mineral King. Eventually these areas were added to the parks after fierce political battles. The Wilderness Act of 1964 established John

Muir Wilderness, legislation in 1978 created Golden Trout Wilderness, and the Wilderness Act of 1984 designated nearly all of the backcountry of both parks as federally protected wilderness, too.

Two of the nation's most famous trails, the Pacific Crest and John Muir trails, which largely follow the same tread here, rise to their greatest heights and finest landscapes as they pass north-south through these parks and wildernesses. This book uses parts of both for its trips in this area. Major trails mean you're likely to meet people. Even if it's not part of a trip in this book, get off on a use trail for perhaps no more than a half mile, or go cross-country for a quarter mile, and you'll probably have part of this thrilling landscape all to yourself.

Ansel Adams (formerly Minarets) Wilderness encompasses some 220,000 acres of spectacular country between and contiguous with John Muir Wilderness on the south and Yosemite National Park on the north. Golden Trout, John Muir, and Ansel Adams wildernesses and Sequoia, Kings Canyon, and Yosemite national parks together protect the heart of the Sierra Nevada for a north-south distance of roughly 140 air miles, from Sherman Pass on the south to Tioga Pass on the north. No roads cross the range between those points, and only one road crosses its crest: the one that leads down to little Devils Postpile National Monument and vicinity. The monument features the eponymous columnar-basalt volcanic formation as well as exquisite Rainbow Falls, and its vicinity includes three popular trailheads as well as parts of the John Muir and Pacific Crest trails.

Remote and rugged, this land is also ecologically very fragile, and use is therefore strictly regulated. Know, respect, and follow those regulations as well as the principles of no-trace camping. We recommend you avoid campfires; use only stoves. Treat all water used for cooking, drinking, clean-up, and first aid.

Grizzlies are extinct in California. However, American black bears are numerous and actively seek human food day and night throughout this region. Protect food with bear-resistant containers, the use of which is required in some areas. Hanging food from trees is almost completely useless. California's black bears are rarely aggressive toward people unless protecting cubs or food. Look upon the possibility of seeing black bears as a privilege, not a deterrence.

Federally designated wilderness is forever at the mercy of politics. Bad ideas like "wise use"—for example, "undesignating" wilderness so that it can be commercially exploited—never die, as any environmental activist knows. Animated by greed, they rise from what should be their political graves again and again. We urge you not only to visit and enjoy these very special lands but also to become active in ensuring their continued protection.* (KM)

---

* Conservationists rejoiced in April 2000 when President Clinton proclaimed Giant Sequoia National Monument to preserve those giant sequoia groves that had remained outside of federal or state protection. Though the giant sequoias themselves were not in danger of being logged— happily, their wood is virtually unusable because it's extremely fragile—they were at risk from the disturbance caused by logging and recreation around them. One part of the two-part monument

lies west and the other south of Sequoia and Kings Canyon National Parks; no trips in this book pass through it as of this writing.

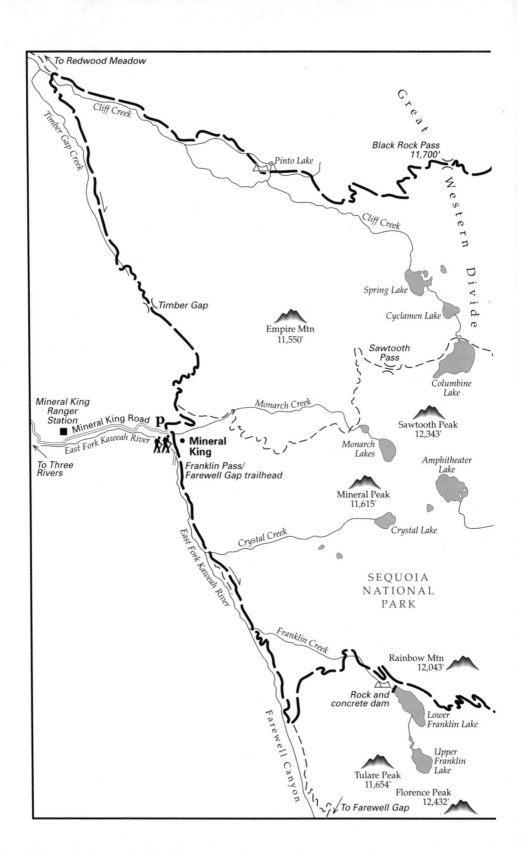

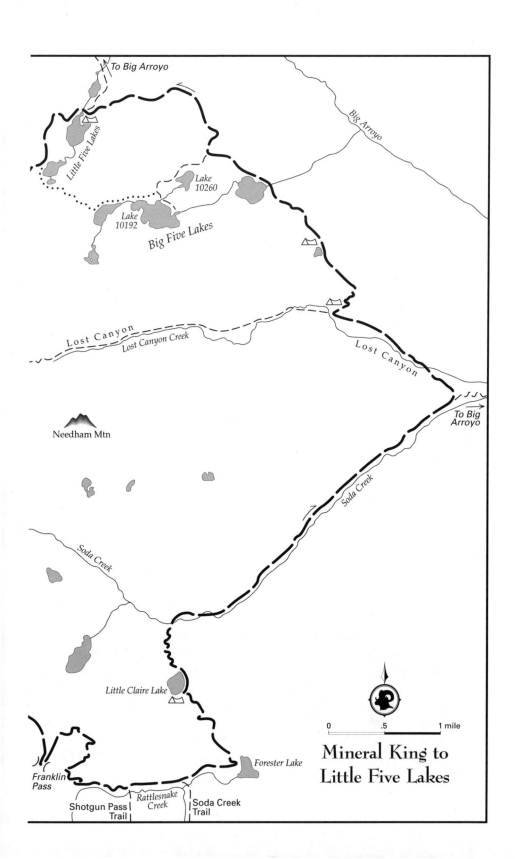

To Big Arroyo

Big Arroyo

Little Five Lakes

Lake 10260

Lake 10192

Big Five Lakes

Lost Canyon

Lost Canyon Creek

Lost Canyon

To Big Arroyo

Needham Mtn

Soda Creek

Soda Creek

Little Claire Lake

Forester Lake

Franklin Pass

Shotgun Pass Trail

Rattlesnake Creek

Soda Creek Trail

0   .5   1 mile

Mineral King to Little Five Lakes

22

Mineral King to Little Five Lakes

—Kathy Morey

Route	Days	Elev. Gain/Loss	Difficulty	Miles
↻	5–7	10,712'/10,712'	****	40.5

Campsites: Lower Franklin Lake: 6 miles
Little Claire Lake: 13 miles
Lake at 10,080': 20 miles
Little Five Lakes (main lake, at 10,550'): 25 miles
Bench by Pinto Lake: 32 miles
(check the Trip Description for others)

Map: USGS 7.5-min *Mineral King, Chagoopa Falls*

Best season: Late summer through early fall

Take this trip!

This is a trip that makes great demands—huge elevation gains and loss-es—and returns equally great rewards: some of the most spectacular scenery in the southwestern Sierra. You'll see lavish displays of wildflowers, watch morn-ing light over Franklin Lake pick out the marbled colors on Tulare Peak, gasp your way up high passes and then gasp again and again at the panorama revealed at the top, visit remote alpine basins, and see more beautiful lakes than you can count.

Make room for a layover day with a great dayhike somewhere, too. For example, you can use the saddle between the highest Little Five lake and the next-to-highest Big Five lake to make a part cross-country loop through both lakes basins. Or, from the bench by Pinto Lake, you can cross-country up Cliff Creek to visit Spring Lake, the lowest of a chain of classic cirque lakes.

Yes, by all means, take this trip—but it's not for beginners, and you'd bet-ter be in top shape! There are no easy trails out of Mineral King.

Trailhead

From State Route 99 just west of Visalia, go east on State Route 198 through Visalia, past Lake Kaweah, and beyond the little town of Three Rivers. On the outskirts of Three Rivers, turn right on Mineral King Road to begin a 90-minute drive on this tortuous one-lane road, through Sequoia National Park's Lookout Point Entrance Station (fee), past Silver City Resort and the Mineral King Ranger Station, where you'll pick up your permit. There are a couple of short, unpaved stretches. (Fans of bad "main" Sierra roads consider Mineral King Rd. one of the worst.) Across from the ranger station there's a shed, with a spring lock to keep out bears but make it accessible to you 24 hours a day, where you can leave any food and toiletries that, left in your car, would attract bears. At 24.4 miles from Three Rivers, park in the lot for Sawtooth Pass/Timber Gap trailhead, which straddles the road. There's a toilet here.

TRIP DESCRIPTION

Heads Up! Wood fires are prohibited in several backcountry areas through which this trip passes; plan on using a stove. Know the regulations for Sequoia-Kings Canyon National Park wilderness. In particular, this trip is entirely in Sequoia National Park, on whose trails pets are prohibited. Bears are a problem along this route, but several popular campsites, including three of the ones listed above under Campsites, have large steel food lockers popularly called "bear boxes." I'll note the presence of bear boxes at any campsites. By late season in a normal year, there may be long, dry stretches on this route; however, campsites mentioned below will almost certainly have water. Mineral King's marmots are known to have nibbled on car engine hoses and to have stowed away in engine compartments. Before you drive away, check under the hood for leaks and scare any marmots out of the engine area. Fill your gas tank in Three Rivers; there is no gas in Sequoia National Park.

Continue up Mineral King Road on foot a quarter mile, and turn left onto the spur road to the pack station, where the paved road curves south, and the Franklin Pass/Farewell Gap Trailhead. (Parking here is reserved for pack-station clients.) The spur road soon dwindles to a footpath. Looking up-canyon from this point , you can readily make out Farewell Gap at the top of V-shaped upper Farewell Canyon. Just west of the trail/road, the hurrying waters of the Kaweah River are hidden by a screen of willows. Here, the early morning hiker is apt to see a marmot surveying its territory. Scattered clumps of juniper and red fir contrast with the ghostly white of cottonwood trunks just before the route fords

From Black Rock Pass: center, Little Five; to right, Big Five

Crystal Creek and, veering left where the road continues straight, begins an unrelenting ascent of several miles.

Along the shaley trail savory sagebrush assails your nostrils and, between the sagebrush and the gooseberry of the lower slopes, wildflower color is provided by purple Indian paintbrush, lavender fleabane, cream cow parsnip, red ipomopsis, and the tall, five-petaled, satiny, electric-blue explorers gentian. Soon the trail fords dashing Franklin Creek (difficult in early season) just below a lovely fall and begins a steep, exposed, switchbacking ascent above a section of the Kaweah River that flows through a deep, eroded gash.

High on the steep slope, your route doubles back north, passing a junction with the trail to Farewell Gap. Turn left (east) to Franklin Pass and begin a long, stuttering traverse around the northwest slopes of Tulare Peak. This traverse provides excellent views back down the Kaweah River canyon to Mineral King, and beyond to Timber Gap. But looking up-canyon (south), the contrast between the green hillside and the red of Vandever Mountain is especially striking in the morning light. Then you enter a sparse forest cover of mature foxtail pines and cross red-hued rocky slopes dotted with spring flowers and laced with little snowmelt rills, as you turn northeast into Franklin Creek's upper canyon.

After descending briefly to ford the creek, the trail passes a campsite with a bear box and rises steeply to the rock-and-concrete-dammed outlet of lower Franklin Lake (6). The colors in this dramatically walled cirque basin are a bizarre conglomeration. To the northeast, the slopes of Rainbow Mountain are a study of gray-white marble whorls set in a sea of pink, red, and black meta-morphic rocks. To the south, the slate ridge joining Tulare Peak and Florence Peak is a chocolate red that sends color photographers scrambling for view-points, to contrast lower Franklin Lake's blue against this colorful headwall. Some small, sandy ledges with a few trees well above the northeast shore of the lower lake make pleasant campsites with good lake views; there are two more bear boxes here as well as a pit toilet by a clump of willows, above most of the campsites.

From this lake the trail rises steadily and then steeply on switchbacks. Views of the Franklin Lakes cirque improve with altitude, and it isn't long before both the upper and lower lakes are in view. This ascent leaves the forest cover behind, as it crosses and recrosses a field of coarse granite granules dot-ted with bedrock outcropping. Despite the sievelike drainage of this slope, flowers abound. High up on the slope two adjacent year-round streamlets nourish gardens of yellow monkey flower and lavender shooting stars. At the high point of 11,840 feet, a little higher than the saddle that's the official Franklin Pass (11,760), views are panoramic. Landmarks to the northwest include Castle Rocks and Paradise Peak; to the east are the immediate unglaciat-ed plateau about the headwaters of Rattlesnake Creek, and Forester Lake (on the wooded bench just north of Rattlesnake Creek). East of the Kern Trench and plateaus, you can make out Mt. Whitney on the Sierra crest. Below to the north is a large, beautiful, unnamed lake in a lonely, steep-walled cirque and, on a bench to the south east of the Shotgun Pass Trail, an intriguing lake with a large beach. While neither is visited on this trip, if you've been swearing on the way up that you'll never climb Franklin Pass again, these sights may inspire you to change your mind.

The trail on the east side of Franklin Pass zigzags down a slope mostly cov-ered with a layer of disintegrated quartz sand and oddly dotted with small, wind-sculpted granite domes. After crossing this bench, the trail drops steeply down rocky, rough, blasted switchbacks that twine back and forth over some of the headwaters of Rattlesnake Creek. The trail levels out on the north side of the creek, and enters a friendly forest of young lodgepole pines broken by pleasant meadow patches; there are a few campsites here.

Now the trail descends moderately through an increasingly dense forest cover of lodgepole pine. In a quarter mile you pass a junction with the Shotgun Pass Trail and continue ahead. In another 0.5 mile you reach a junction with the Soda Creek Trail; go left (northeast). A short distance beyond the junction, the trail fords a little stream and then ascends gently over a rocky slope. Soon the trail arrives at the charmingly meadowed west side of Forester Lake, where fine campsites look across the azure waters to a dense forest fringe, and an occa-sional surface dimpling indicates the presence of brook trout.

Curving away from Forester Lake, the trail ascends a low ridge, dips through a swale, and climbs another ridge to overlook Little Claire Lake, to whose east side the track descends (13). There are a number of good campsites here, particularly around the outlet.

The next 7-mile leg of this trip is perhaps the least scenic, and you have the dubious pleasure of losing 1800 feet in the first 5 miles and gaining most of it back—1500 feet—in the last 2. Your route crosses the outlet and shortly begins a long series of well-graded switchbacks down a steep, forested slope for over a mile. At the foot of this precipitous duff-and-rock slope, the route fords Soda Creek, descends gently over duff and sand through a moderate forest cover, and then becomes steeper. Marmots on the rocky slopes south of the creek whistle excitedly as unexpected visitors pass by, but they do not usually stir from their watching posts unless the traveler shows more than passing interest.

During the next several miles of rolling descent through lodgepole forest, somewhat away from Soda Creek, you detour out onto the canyon's hot, rocky slopes at times, at others cross occasional tributaries—one of which even rates a boardwalk—and pass campsites of uneven quality. The appearance of Jeffrey pines heralds your approach to the junction where a trail down into Big Arroyo branches right and your route turns left (north) to start a very steep, rocky, exposed ascent to the foot of Lost Canyon.

Nearing the creek in this canyon, the trail doubles back to the northwest and suddenly leaves the dry south slope for a cool, moist, verdant bower at a ford of Lost Canyon Creek (difficult in early season). Beyond the ford you veer away from the creek on a steady ascent up a duff-and-sand trail. More than a mile beyond the ford, just before a second ford of Lost Canyon Creek, you reach a junction where, in a lovely creekside meadow, the trail forks: left (west) up Lost Canyon to Sawtooth Pass, right (north) to Big Five Lakes. There are campsites and a bear box near this junction, where you go right to begin climbing the steep north wall of Lost Canyon.

This ascent makes a clear series of short, steep switchbacks which afford fine views west to the barren headwaters of Lost Canyon and the cirque holding Columbine Lake. Mostly lodgepole and foxtail pine, the timber cover thickens as the trail approaches a small, unnamed lake (20), due east of a granite spur. Fields of red heather highlight the luxuriant wildflower growth around this lake's meadow fringes and, above the treetops in the north, the barren, massive, brown hulk of Mt. Kaweah rises just barely higher than the serrated Kaweah Peaks Ridge west of it. With an excellent campsite here, this little lake allows the dusty hiker to have a leisurely swim in water much warmer than can be found most places in the Sierra.

From the north side of this unnamed lake, you rise a little on a sometimes faint trail that crosses a long ridge heavily overlain with fallen snags. Above Big Five Lakes, the trail tops the ridge and you have views of Black Rock Pass to the west, and the lowest of the Big Five Lakes immediately below. The descent to the bear box and good campsites near the outlet and along the north side of this lake is a rocky, steep downgrade. Just between us, the Big Five Lakes are prettier than the Little Five Lakes, and I hope your travel plans include an overnight at one of them.

Beyond the log-jammed outlet of the lake, the trail curves west above a reed-filled bay before embarking upon a steep, rocky, switchbacking climb of a mile. Just before the top of this climb, at a T-junction, the left fork leads to the highest and loveliest of the Big Five Lakes—but you go right to Little Five Lakes. After topping the ridge, your trail undulates for a dry mile, offering periodic great views of Mt. Kaweah, the Kaweah Peaks Ridge and, at the ridge's west end, Red Kaweah and Black Kaweah.

The dry stretch ends when the trail dips into a small, intimate valley spanned by a boardwalk, where a stream flows at least until late summer. From this brook you ascend for several hundred vertical feet in a moderate lodgepole forest, level off, and then gain sight of the main Little Five Lake (25.5) and its large bordering meadow. In a few minutes the trail reaches the base of the lake's north-end peninsula, which contains many overused campsites and a bear box. There's also a junction here with a trail leading right (north) down past another of the basin's lakes and into Big Arroyo. Beyond the campsites and the meadow southeast of them, there is a summer ranger station.

You go ahead (left, southwest) at the junction to climb up the basin, where you find the highest Little Five lake, nearly treeless and with a couple of Spartan campsites well above the lake but below and hidden from the trail. Views from these campsites are unbeatable. The ridge southeast separates Little and Big Five Lakes basins; as mentioned above, those with a layover day and comfortable with Class 2–3 travel can make a superb dayhike by using the obvious saddle on the other side of this lake to make a loop through both basins. The ridge is relatively low and rocky on the Little Five Lakes side, much higher and looser on the Big Five Lakes side. Note that the "trail" shown along the higher Big Five Lakes is a faint angler's path at best and vanishes around the north shore of the largest lake (10,192). Be prepared go cross-country almost to Lake 10260, around whose northwest shore the track becomes quite plain. From here, you can return to Little Five Lakes by trail.

Back on the main trail above the highest Little Five lake, the stony track rises more moderately than you'd expect, up to Black Rock Pass (11,700) on the Great Western Divide, where a needed rest stop affords time to take in the vast panorama. Break out the camera to record this incredible view, one of the very best on the whole loop. The companion basins of Little Five Lakes and Big Five Lakes drop off into Big Arroyo, and beyond this chasm rise the multicolored, cliffbound Kaweah Peaks. In the east is the 14,000-foot Whitney crest, backbone of the Sierra.

Leaving this breathtaking spot behind, the trail heads moderately to steeply on exposed switchbacks down rocky, mostly treeless slopes. From south-trending switchback legs, you gradually gain, and then lose, wonderful views of the chain of classic cirque lakes at the head of Cliff Creek: highest

Columbine Lake below Sawtooth Peak, middle Cyclamen Lake, and lowest Spring Lake. Continuing, Pinto Lake far below comes into view. In season, you'll find wonderful hillside meadows to enjoy as you descend nearly 3000 feet before the trail levels out in a meadow on the large bench holding Pinto Lake. Screened by willow thickets, Pinto Lake offers swimming in waters warmer than your typical Sierra pond. A use trail heads through the meadow over to Pinto Lake (and also up-valley toward cascades on Cliff Creek and Spring Lake). On the forested rise west of the meadow, there are campsites and a bear box (32). (If you are reversing this trip and heading from the campsites to Black Rock Pass, don't be fooled by the use trail up the meadow. The main trail veers into and across the meadow and promptly heads up the obvious scree slope to the east.)

The main trail curves toward the rise and one of the lake's inlets but, instead of fording the creek to the campsites as a use trail does, angles away to drop into a lush, ferny pocket, and then descends steeply on rocky switchbacks through dense willow, sagebrush, whitethorn, and bitter cherry. The descent levels out at the foot of the fine, high cascade unofficially called Cliff Creek Falls, where the trail continues down a bouldery wash before entering a verdant, forested stretch on its final descent to a ford of Cliff Creek (difficult in early season). There are campsites and a bear box here. There's also a junction with a trail leading right (northwest) down to Redwood Meadow and the Middle Fork Kaweah River; you go ahead (left, south) across the creek to Mineral King.

Cross the creek and on the west bank confront your last long climb, almost 2400 feet to Timber Gap. It begins with forested switchbacks to attain a ridge, which the trail traverses as it curves through a lush meadow. Still climbing, you work your way up an extraordinary, mile-long flower garden nurtured by numerous seeps in the fractured metamorphic rock. Reentering forest and still climbing, you reach Timber Gap at last. Trees conceal most of the view here, though it is possible to see north across the canyon of Middle Fork Kaweah River to pick out Alta Peak on the Tableland Divide far beyond.

Leaving Timber Gap, you descend to traverse a broad hillside meadow overlooking Mineral King—truly a bird's-eye view!—before switchbacking down steeply to moderately through dense forest. The trail breaks out of the forest to continue descending a chaparral-clad slope that's recovering from a fire in the early 1990s. Shortly before the trailhead, you reach a junction with the trail left (east) to Monarch Lakes and Sawtooth Pass; go right here to the trailhead.

Don't forget—scare those pesky marmots out of your engine compartment and pick up anything you left in the shed across from the ranger station!

Variations

Reverse the direction of this loop.

Permits

There is a quota for this trailhead and a permit is required for overnight stays. Permits may be available from Mineral King Ranger Station. Apply for reserved permits ($10/reservation) to Wilderness Permit Reservations, Sequoia-Kings Canyon National Park, HCR 89 Box 60, Three Rivers, CA 93271, (559) 565-3708 or FAX (559) 565-4239. You will receive *only* the reservation, and you must exchange it for a real permit at the ranger station. Check out **www.nps.gov/seki** for more info!

Build-up/Wind-down tips

The towns of Visalia, Lemon Cove, and Three Rivers offer stores, lodging, and restaurants (but have neither Chamber of Commerce nor Visitors Bureau; check your auto-club tour guide or my book *Hot Showers, Soft Beds, and Dayhikes in the Sierra*). The best dinners in Three Rivers are at the Gateway Lodge, the last lodgings and food before the Ash Mountain Entrance to Sequoia National Park. I like to "stage" myself in Visalia or Three Rivers a couple of nights before *starting* a Mineral King trip and again when coming out of Mineral King or another Sequoia National Park trailhead. Because of the long drive to Mineral King and the great elevation difference between Three Rivers, the closest town, and Mineral King, I recommend that you stay in Mineral King at least the night before you start your trip. Consider delightful Silver City Resort (summer: Box 56, Three Rivers, CA 93271, (559) 561-3223), which offers rustic cabins, deluxe chalets, a tiny store, and a little café. Or stay at one of the Mineral King campgrounds—Atwell Mill and Cold Spring (the latter is closer to the trailhead).

To find out how Kathy Morey got started hiking the Sierra and the Hawaiian islands and writing about her hikes for Wilderness Press, and for a list of her titles, see "Author Bio & Bib" on page 492.

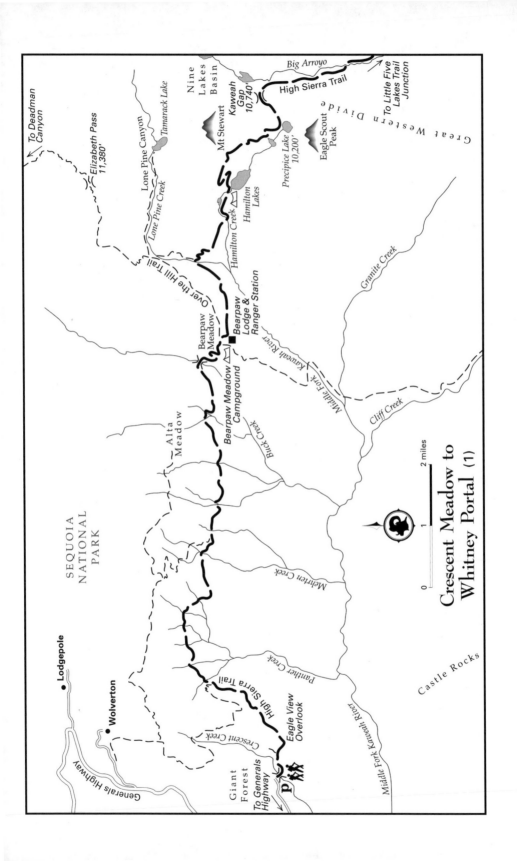

Crescent Meadow to
Whitney Portal (1)

To Deadman Canyon

Nine Lakes Basin

Big Arroyo

High Sierra Trail

To Little Five Lakes Trail Junction

Elizabeth Pass 11,380'

Lone Pine Canyon

Tamarack Lake

Mt Stewart

Kaweah Gap 10,740'

Great Western Divide

Eagle Scout Peak

Precipice Lake 10,200'

Lone Pine Creek

Lone Pine Creek

Hamilton Lakes

Hamilton Creek

Over the Hill Trail

Granite Creek

Bearpaw Meadow

Bearpaw Lodge & Ranger Station

Kaweah River

SEQUOIA NATIONAL PARK

Bearpaw Meadow Campground

Middle Fork

Cliff Creek

Alta Meadow

Buck Creek

Lodgepole

Wolverton

Mehrten Creek

2 miles

1

0

Castle Rocks

Panther Creek

Generals Highway

Crescent Creek

High Sierra Trail

Eagle View Overlook

Giant Forest

To Generals Highway

P

Middle Fork Kaweah River

23

Crescent Meadow to Whitney Portal via the High Sierra Trail

—Kathy Morey

Route	Days	Elev. Gain/Loss	Difficulty	Miles
↝	8–14	13,354'/11,854'	****	68.5

(Mileage does not include 3.8-mile out-and-back to Mt. Whitney's summit)

Campsites: Bearpaw Meadow: 11 miles
Big Arroyo junction: 22 miles
Moraine Lake: 30 miles
Kern Hot Spring: 37 miles
Junction Meadow: 45 miles
Crabtree Ranger Station: 53.5 miles
Outpost Camp: 65 miles
(see the Trip Description for others)

Map: USGS 7.5-min *Lodgepole, Triple Divide Peak, Mt. Kaweah, Chagoopa Falls, Mt. Whitney, Mt. Langley*

Best season: Late summer through early fall

Take this trip!

What would it be like to walk across the entire Sierra? many hikers wonder. *What magical places are hidden in the heart of the range, far from any trip I've attempted yet? I want to see them!* If you're such a hiker, this is the trip for you, for it crosses the range almost entirely on the famed High Sierra Trail, passing through remote and beautiful regions on its way to climbing Mt. Whitney, highest peak in the contiguous 48 states. True, many people find their way to Bearpaw Meadow and even Hamilton Lakes from the west, and up Mt. Whitney from the east. But very few ever see the splendor of Big Arroyo, from whose

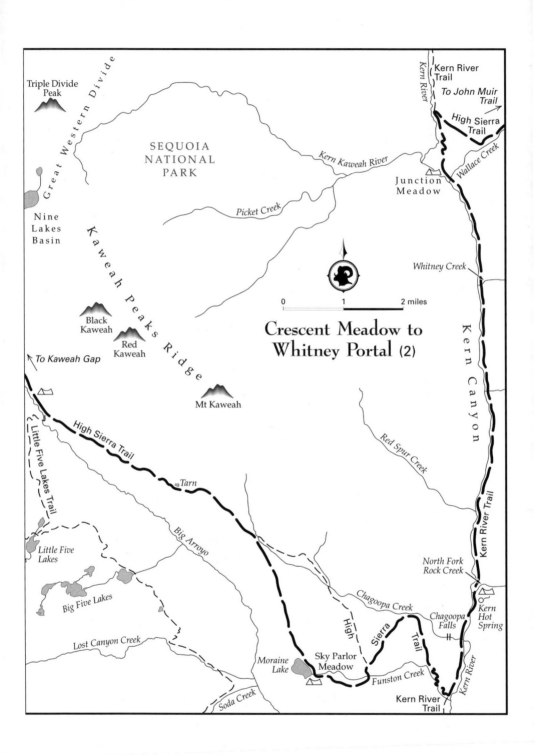

Triple Divide
Peak

Great Western Divide

SEQUOIA
NATIONAL
PARK

Kern River

Kern River
Trail

To John Muir
Trail

High Sierra
Trail

Kern Kaweah River

Wallace Creek

Junction
Meadow

Nine
Lakes
Basin

Kaweah Peaks Ridge

Picket Creek

Whitney Creek

0   1   2 miles

Crescent Meadow to
Whitney Portal (2)

Black
Kaweah

Red
Kaweah

To Kaweah Gap

Mt Kaweah

Kern Canyon

High Sierra Trail

Little Five Lakes Trail

Tarn

Red Spur Creek

Little Five
Lakes

Big Arroyo

Kern River Trail

Big Five Lakes

Chagoopa Creek

North Fork
Rock Creek

Lost Canyon Creek

High

Sierra

Trail

Chagoopa
Falls

Kern Hot
Spring

Moraine
Lake

Sky Parlor
Meadow

Funston Creek

Kern River

Soda Creek

Kern River
Trail

meadowed floor you look up to hanging valleys carved from almost-white granite. Fewer still are those who cross remote Chagoopa Plateau, enjoying the tranquil loveliness of Moraine Lake. And even though people tend to congregate at Kern Hot Spring for obvious reasons, they are just a handful who, like you on this trip, are privileged to be in the greatest of all the Sierra's "yosemites," awesome Kern Canyon. There are other places and other trails on which to cross the range, but I think none is more exciting and spectacular than this, the High Sierra Trail.

Plan a few layover days so that you can explore some of the more remote niches that the High Sierra Trail passes near but not through, like Nine Lake Basin, the basin at the headwaters of the Kern River, and Wallace Lake.

Trailheads

This is a difficult shuttle to set up because it means getting cars to opposite sides of the range; a lesser trip wouldn't justify the trouble. Consider using State Route 58, mostly a 4-lane freeway, over Tehachapi Pass between Bakersfield on the west and Mojave on the east, instead of closer but narrower, more winding, and slower roads like State Route 178 (Walker Pass) on the south or State Route 120 (Tioga Pass) on the north. Better yet, persuade non-hiking friends—cherish these people!—to drop you off and pick you up.

Put-in trailhead: Follow the driving directions for trip 24 to Lodgepole Visitor Center (you must go there to get your permit and also a ticket to leave on your dashboard indicating that your put-in car will be left at Crescent Meadow for some time). Then head south on the Generals Highway for about 6 miles to the turnoff for Moro Rock and Crescent Meadow in the Giant Forest area, turn east, and follow this spur about 2 more miles to its end at the parking lot for Crescent Meadow.

Take-out trailhead: From US Highway 395, go 13 miles west on Whitney Portal Road from Lone Pine to parking near the road's end.

TRIP DESCRIPTION

Heads Up! Wood fires are prohibited in several backcountry areas through which this trip passes; plan on using a stove. Know the regulations for Sequoia-Kings Canyon National Park wilderness. In particular, this trip is almost entirely in Sequoia National Park, on whose trails pets are prohibited. Bears are a problem along this route, but many popular campsites, including five of the ones listed above under Campsites, have large steel food lockers popularly called "bear boxes." I'll note the presence of bear boxes at any campsites. By late season in a normal year, there may be long dry stretches on this route; however, campsites mentioned below will almost certainly

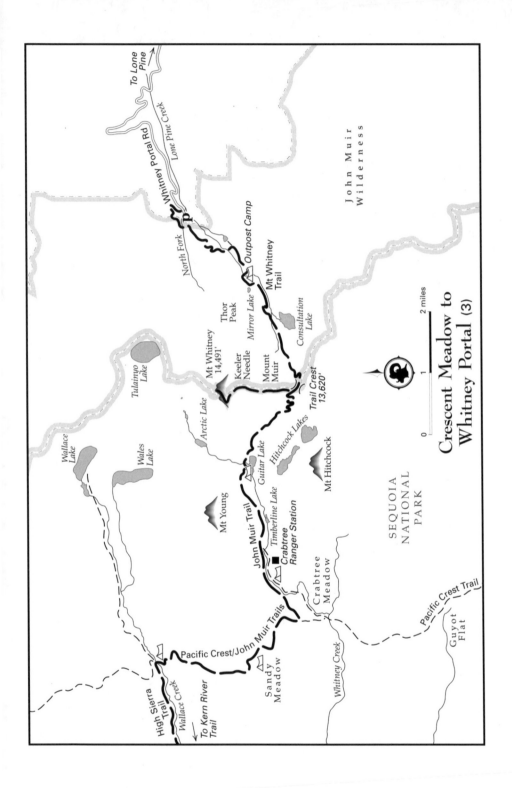

Crescent Meadow to Whitney Portal (3)

To Lone Pine

Lone Pine Creek

Whitney Portal Rd

North Fork

Outpost Camp

Mt Whitney Trail

Thor Peak

Mirror Lake

Consultation Lake

Mt Whitney 14,491'

Keeler Needle

Mount Muir

Trail Crest 13,620'

Tulainyo Lake

Arctic Lake

Guitar Lake

Hitchcock Lakes

Mt Hitchcock

Wallace Lake

Wales Lake

Mt Young

John Muir Trail

Timberline Lake

Crabtree Ranger Station

Crabtree Meadow

Pacific Crest/John Muir Trails

High Sierra Trail

Wallace Creek

To Kern River Trail

Sandy Meadow

Whitney Creek

Pacific Crest Trail

Guyot Flat

SEQUOIA NATIONAL PARK

JOHN MUIR WILDERNESS

John Muir Wilderness

0   1   2 miles

have water. A bit of bad news: this area's trail signs offer mileages that can't be taken at face value. Fill your gas tank in Three Rivers; there is no gas in the parks.

For the description of Crescent Meadow in Giant Forest to Bearpaw Meadow, the initial 11-mile leg of this hike, reverse the directions given for the Bearpaw Meadow-Crescent Meadow final leg of trip 24, "Lodgepole Campground to Deadman Canyon."

At the junction with the Over The Hill Trail, go right (generally west) to stay on the High Sierra Trail past Bearpaw Lodge and Ranger Station. The magnificent views from Bearpaw Meadow and the subsequent trail include Mt. Stewart and Eagle Scout Peak on the Great Western Divide, Black Kaweah beyond, the Yosemite-like depths of Hamilton Creek and the Middle Fork Kaweah River, and the Cliff Creek drainage below.

Continuing past Bearpaw Ranger Station, the trail descends moderately through mixed, sparse forest stands. As the trail rounds the slope and descends toward River Valley, it traverses a section blasted from an immense, exfoliating granite slab. Views of clear-cut avalanche chutes on the south wall of the canyon accompany the descent to the culvert fording wild, turbulent Lone Pine Creek. This stream cascades and plunges down a narrow granite chasm below the culvert. The force of the torrent and the narrow V of the chasm are clear evidence of the cutting power of the water. From the creek, the trail ascends an exposed slope, passing a side trail to Tamarack Lake and Elizabeth Pass (with good campsites at this junction).

Continuing the steady ascent, the traveler is overwhelmed by the gigantic scale of the rock sculpting by ice, rock, and snow to the east and southeast. The final climb to the ford of Hamilton Creek is overshadowed by mighty rock on all sides: the sheer granite wall to the north called Angel Wings, the sharply pointed granite sentinels atop the south wall, and the wall's avalanche-chuted sides—all are a constant source of wonderment and awe.

Under these heights you boulderhop across the stream a few hundred yards below the lowest lake of the Hamilton Lakes chain. From this ford the trail climbs steeply over shattered rock to the good campsites (with bear boxes) at the northwest end of Lake 8235. Views from the campsites, including the silver ribbon waterfall at the east end, are superlative, but the lake is highly overused, camping is restricted to two nights, and you should head for Kaweah Gap.

The 2500-foot steep climb to Kaweah Gap is an engineering marvel of trail construction, which has literally blasted the way across vertical cliff sections. Beginning at the northwest end of Lake 8235, the trail ascends steadily up the juniper-and-red-fir-dotted slope with constant views of the lake and its dramatic walls. Despite the rocky terrain, many wildflowers line this ascent and among the manzanita and chinquapin one will find lush lupine, yellow

View over Middle Fork Kaweah from Bearpaw Meadow Lodge

columbine, penstemon, Indian paintbrush, white cinquefoil, false Solomon's seal and Douglas phlox.

After some doubling back, the trail turns south on a steep ascent to a point just above the north shore of Precipice Lake (10,200), at the foot of the near-vertical north face of Eagle Scout Peak. The jagged summits of the peaks of the Great Western Divide dominate the skyline to the east during the final, tarn-dotted ascent to U-shaped Kaweah Gap. As you approach the gap you can see the equally spectacular summits of Kaweah Peaks Ridge beyond. This colorful ridge dominates the views east from Kaweah Gap (10,740), and you can see Nine Lake Basin to the north. Hikers with a bent for exploring barren high country can detour across granite slab-and-ledge routes north to Nine Lake Basin.

The trail continues its steady-to-moderate southward descent along the west side of the headwaters of Big Arroyo Creek, fording over to the east side midway down. This descent crosses unjointed granite broken by substantial pockets of grass and numerous runoff streams even in late season. Open stretches afford fine views of the U-shaped, glacially wrought Big Arroyo below, and the white, red, and black rocks of Black Kaweah and Red Kaweah peaks to the east. The trail then reenters timber cover and arrives at some good camp-sites along the stream (22; with bear box). These campsites and an abandoned trail-crew cabin are about a quarter mile above the Little Five Lakes/Black Rock Pass Trail junction, and a layover day here permits a visit to Little Five Lakes.

Continuing past the Little Five Lakes Trail junction, the High Sierra Trail begins a long, moderate ascent along the north canyon wall of Big Arroyo. This route parallels the course of a trunk glacier that once filled Big Arroyo, overflowed the benches on either side, and contributed to the main glacier of Kern Canyon. Your route climbs the wall of this trough, and the timber cover of this ascent is sparse, but there is no shortage of wildflowers tucked among the sage, manzanita, and chinquapin. Most colorful are yellow columbine, bright red Indian paintbrush, and purple lupine.

The trail levels off near a small, mirror-faced tarn, and, swinging away from the lip of Big Arroyo, begins a gradual descent through alternating timbered and meadowed stretches. Tree-interrupted views of the jagged Great Western Divide skyline accompany your descent to a trail junction in a meadow on the south side of a tributary of Chagoopa Creek. At this junction your route temporarily leaves the High Sierra Trail and branches right (south) through meadows with clumps of shooting stars. This descent becomes steeper over coarse granite sand, through dense stands of lodgepole and foxtail pine, with superlative views down into Big Arroyo and across the arroyo to the drainages of Soda and Lost Canyon creeks. This steadily down-winding trail brings you to the wooded shores of beautiful Moraine Lake (30), where one morning I watched a loon paddle and heard it warble its haunting call. Good campsites on the south side of the lake provide lake-fronted views back to the Kaweah Peaks and gardens of wild azalea in season.

After traversing a moraine just east of Moraine Lake, the trail descends moderately, then gently, passing an old stockman's cabin before reaching superb Sky Parlor Meadow. Views back across this flower-filled grassland to the Great Western Divide and the Kaweahs are excellent. Shortly beyond the ford of Funston Creek at the east end of the meadow, your route rejoins the High Sierra Trail, on which you turn right (northeast) to begin the moderate, then steep, descent to the bottom of Kern Canyon. The initial descent sees the lodgepole being replaced by the lower-altitude white fir and Jeffrey pine; and still lower down, the trail descends steeply through manzanita and snow bush that are overshadowed by an occasional juniper and oak. The unmistakably U-shaped Kern Trench is a classic "yosemite," typical of glacially modified valleys. The final climb down to the valley floor is accomplished via a series of steep, rocky switchbacks generally paralleling the plunging drop of Funston Creek.

On the Kern Canyon floor you join the Kern River Trail, on which you turn left (north), upstream. The Kern River Trail drops into a marshy area and then crosses two meadows on wooden walkways. Then the trail leads gently upward through a forest of Jeffrey pine and incense-cedar. High on the western rim of the canyon you catch glimpses of Chagoopa Falls, a fury of plunging white water when full. Past a manzanita-carpeted open area the trail crosses the Kern on a fine bridge and arrives at the south fork of Rock Creek, which you ford. Then, around a point, you arrive at the delightful mountain spa of Kern Hot Spring (37)—a treat for the tired, dusty hiker. To the traveler, the crude, cemented bathtub here becomes a regal, heated pool. Just a few dozen yards away, the great Kern River rushes past. If camping near the spring, you must stay in the campground just north and east of it (with bear boxes). The sites are, unfortunately, very close together and very overused, but the spring and the setting are worth it.

Continuing north, you ford the north fork of Rock Creek and traverse the gravelly canyon floor below immense granite cliffs of the canyon's east wall. Past the confluence of Red Spur Creek this route ascends gently, sometimes a bit stiffly, beside the Kern River, heading almost due north. The Kern Trench is remarkably straight for about 25 miles as it traces the Kern Canyon fault. The fault, a zone of structural weakness in the Sierra batholith, is more susceptible to erosion than the surrounding rock, and this deep canyon has been carved by both glacial and stream action. Many times glaciers advanced down the canyon, shearing off spurs created by stream erosion and leaving some tributary valleys hanging above the main valley. The glaciers also scooped and plucked at the bedrock, creating basins in the granite that became lakes when they melted and retreated.

The walls of this deep canyon, from 2000 to 5000 feet high, are spectacular, and a number of streams cascade and fall down these walls. The fords of streams draining Guyot Flat, and of Whitney and Wallace creeks, can be difficult in early season. Beyond the ford of Wallace Creek the trail enters a parklike grove of stalwart Jeffrey pines that provide a noble setting for the overused campsites at Junction Meadow (45) on the Kern River.

Leaving the Jeffrey pines of Junction Meadow, the trail ascends steeply on rocky underfooting over a slope covered by manzanita and currant. Views down the Kern Trench improve constantly, as the occasional Jeffrey, lodgepole, and aspen offer frames for the photographer who would compose a shot of the great cleft. After a mile you arrive at the junction of the Kern River Trail and the High Sierra Trail, where your route turns right (southeast), back toward Wallace Creek canyon. At 10,400 feet you reach a junction with the John Muir Trail. Turn right (south) onto it—here, it's also the Pacific Crest Trail and the High Sierra Trail. You immediately ford Wallace Creek (difficult in early season), and pass some campsites (with a bear box). A layover day here would let you explore up Wallace Creek to Wallace, Wales, and Tulainyo lakes (the latter officially the highest named lake in the Sierra). Back on the High Sierra/Pacific Crest/John Muir Trail, you continue southward on generally gentle gradients through sporadic stands of lodgepole and foxtail pine, and climb over a saddle west of Mt. Young before skirting pretty Sandy Meadow (with campsites in this area as long as the water holds out).

At a junction between Sandy Meadow and Whitney Creek, the High Sierra/John Muir Trail and the Pacific Crest Trail diverge: you take the left fork, the John Muir Trail, toward Crabtree Ranger Station and the fair campsites (53.5; with bear box) nearby, on either side of Whitney Creek around a junction with a spur trail southeast to the ranger station and then to Crabtree Meadow and the Pacific Crest Trail. Emergency services are sometimes available at the ranger station.

Contrary to what appears on the 7.5-minute topo, your route stays high on the north bank of Whitney Creek, eventually meeting the creek near a charming meadow below delightful Timberline Lake (closed to camping). The sight of Mt. Whitney's corrugated west slopes—Whitney like you've never seen it before!—mirrored in the lake's still waters will send you scrambling for your camera. Beyond Timberline Lake, the trail rises moderately steeply over sparsely timbered, rocky slopes to the slopes above barren Guitar Lake, heavily used by people planning to bag Mt. Whitney the next day. Look for campsites above the "guitar's neck," along the outlet of Arctic Lake (which you ford), and on the bench above that lake. Adventurous travelers may even want to seek out campsites at the Hitchcock Lakes.

On the main trail, you make a moderate traverse through the very wet alpine meadows above Guitar Lake before beginning a long series of well-graded switchbacks up the west side of Mt. Whitney. Beside the trail, large yellow flowers called hulsea, or Alpine gold, have anchored themselves in the most unlikely places. Expansive views westward make for pleasant rest stops. Gasping in the thin air, you arrive at last at the junction (13,560) with the trail to Mt. Whitney's summit.

Mt. Whitney Tip

Most people drop their backpacks at the junction with the trail to Mt. Whitney's summit and put on a daypack with sufficient food and water, extra clothing in case of bad weather, and any valuables (e.g., money, credit cards) they may be carrying, for the 3.8-mile round trip to the summit. I've never heard of a backpack being stolen here: who needs even one more ounce to carry at this point? When breaking camp the morning of your summit bid, prepare by packing up so that all the things you'll transfer to your daypack are easily accessible in your backpack.

With or without your full pack, you turn left (north) on this rugged trail and in about 20 yards pass a use trail that descends very steeply to high, dry campsites clinging to the rocky west side of Mt. Whitney. You wind among large blocks of talus, passing Class 3–4 Mt. Muir—"The Sierra's most insignificant 14,000-footer," huffs one writer who feels John Muir has thus been slighted. Hikers enjoy astonishing views westward, where the striking Hitchcock Lakes huddle under the steep, fluted slopes of Mt. Hitchcock, as well as eastward through the notch-like windows around Day and Keeler needles, down to barren glacial cirques containing brilliant turquoise lakes, over Consultation Lake and beyond it to the Owens Valley and the town of Lone Pine, 10,000 feet

Domes from High Sierra Trail (west end)

below. Multiple routes confuse your final climb to the broad plateau that is Whitney's summit, but the sight of the metal-roofed summit building guides you to the top (14,491). Sign the summit register just outside the building, but stay out of the building in a thunderstorm: the metal roof conducts lightning to its occupants, and some have been killed here. The true summit is a little east of the building, reached by scrambling among huge, flattish boulders. The summit on a summer's day is very crowded—there's even a pit toilet north of the building!—but nothing can detract from the incredible views from this highest point in the Sierra Nevada, which also happens to be the official southern terminus of the John Muir Trail.

But the end of your trip lies some 6000 feet below, so retrace your steps to the junction, retrieve your backpack, and turn left (east) for a few more to the highest pass on this journey, Trail Crest (13,620), where you leave Sequoia National Park and enter John Muir Wilderness. From Trail Crest the Mt. Whitney Trail, exposed and rocky, angles east around the top of a steep chute before beginning an interminable series of tight switchbacks down the mountain's east face. A short section about halfway down is notorious for being ice-covered most of the time, and there is a cable you can cling to if necessary. The powder-blue flower heads of a fragrant phlox called "sky pilot" brighten the gray trail. Building the trail required much blasting with dynamite—the natural fracture planes of the granite are evident in the blasted slabs.

Finally, the grueling 1600-foot descent ends at barren Trail Camp (12,000), the highest legal camping area along the Mt. Whitney Trail. Numerous hard tent-sites huddle among the giant boulders here, and there are a pair of solar toilets at the east end of the camp. Bears aren't a problem on this side of Mt. Whitney, but food must be protected from marmots here. Below the camp you descend some poured-concrete steps, then continue steeply down a granite trail, finding ivesia, cinquefoil, creambush, currant, and gooseberry growing in cracks in the boulders. The outlet of Consultation Lake—sometimes called "Consolation Lake" by people who have just staggered down the miserable switchbacks from Trail Crest—cascades down the ravine southeast of the trail. You ford Lone Pine Creek and pass a tiny meadow bright with shooting stars (camping prohibited). Then, switchback down to sparse timber, with your route finally leveling out near Mirror Lake, cradled in its cirque beneath the south face of Thor Peak (and closed to camping). You make a rocky ford of the lake's outlet and descend again, this time on a slope blooming with senecio, fireweed, pennyroyal, currant, Newberry's penstemon, Sierra chinquapin, Indian paintbrush, and creambush.

Where the trail levels out, you ford Lone Pine Creek and enter a large meadow and camping area, Outpost Camp (65). Like Trail Camp, Outpost Camp has a pair of solar toilets. The trail curves southeast along Outpost Camp's upper edge, passing several campsites, then turns northeast to trace the meadow's edge and cross the creek twice in quick succession. Leaving Outpost Camp, you climb slightly before descending switchbacks through large boulders to a junction with the lateral to Lone Pine Lake, visible below (campsites). Going ahead (left, north) to stay on the main trail, you shortly ford Lone Pine Creek again before beginning the final, long series of dusty, sunstruck switchbacks through sagebrush, Sierra chinquapin, mountain mahogany, and other members of the chaparral community. Two fords of North Fork Lone Pine Creek (the first may be difficult in early season) provide cool nooks on the hot descent. Breather stops on this leg provide a V-framed views down Lone Pine Creek's canyon of the Alabama Hills—a filming location for many western movies.

Having exited John Muir Wilderness, you presently reach the paved road loop at shady Whitney Portal, where your shuttle ride should be waiting for you. In season, Whitney Portal offers a campground, a picnic area, a small store, a café, potable water, and plenty of parking.

Variations

Instead of going out over busy Mt. Whitney, continue south at the junction where the High Sierra Trail turns east toward Crabtree Ranger Station, and stay on the Pacific Crest Trail longer to go out either through Cottonwood Lakes via New Army Pass or at Horseshoe Meadow via Cottonwood Pass. (See trip 27 for some of the spectacular country this alternative would take you through.)

Or turn north where you meet the John Muir Trail, to visit the magnificent basin at the headwaters of the Kern River, and then go out over very demanding Shepherd Pass.

I don't recommend reversing this trip. Carrying the heaviest load of the trip up the worst climb of the trip, the east face of Mt. Whitney, makes no sense to me, and *those* permits are extremely hard to get.

Permits

This is a quota trailhead, and a permit is required for overnight stays. Permits may be available from the Wilderness Office next to Lodgepole Visitor Center. Apply for reserved permits with a Whitney Zone Stamp ($10/reservation plus fee for stamp) to Wilderness Permit Reservations, Sequoia-Kings Canyon National Park, HCR 89 Box 60, Three Rivers, CA 93271, (559) 565-3708 or FAX (559) 565-4239. You will receive *only* the reservation, and you must exchange it for a real permit at the Wilderness Office. Check out **www.nps.gov/seki** for more info!

Build-up/Wind-down tips

See the Build-up/Wind-down section of trip 24 ("Lodgepole Campground to Deadman Canyon") for suggestions about where to stay the night before you begin this trip. Also see trip 27 ("Cottonwood Lakes to Upper Rock Creek") for suggestions about where to stay after you come out near Lone Pine.

To find out how Kathy Morey got started hiking the Sierra and the Hawaiian islands and writing about her hikes for Wilderness Press, and for a list of her titles, see "Author Bio & Bib" on page 492.

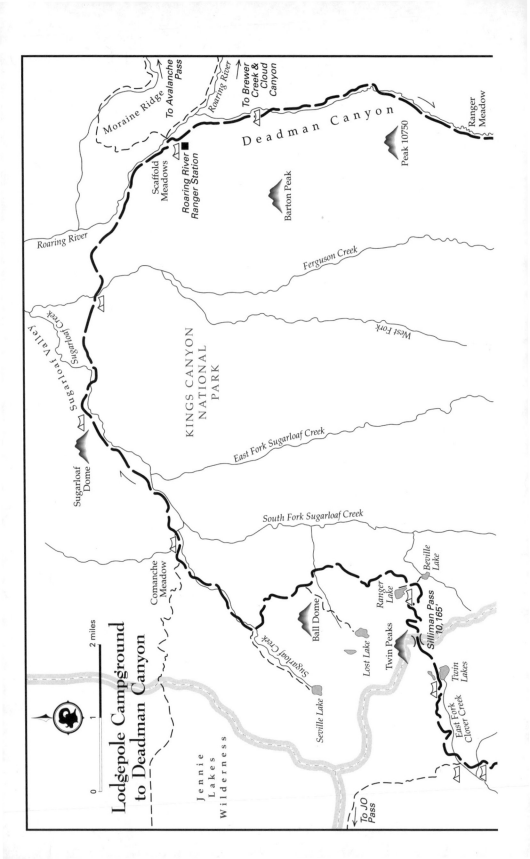

Lodgepole Campground to Deadman Canyon

2 miles

0   1

To Avalanche Pass

Moraine Ridge

Roaring River

To Brewer Creek & Cloud Canyon

Deadman Canyon

Ranger Meadow

Peak 10750

Scaffold Meadows

Roaring River Ranger Station

Barton Peak

Roaring River

Ferguson Creek

West Fork

Sugarloaf Valley

Sugarloaf Creek

KINGS CANYON NATIONAL PARK

East Fork Sugarloaf Creek

Sugarloaf Dome

South Fork Sugarloaf Creek

Comanche Meadow

Beville Lake

Ball Dome

Ranger Lake

Silliman Pass 10,165'

Sugarloaf Creek

Lost Lake

Twin Peaks

Twin Lakes

Jennie Lakes Wilderness

Seville Lake

East Fork Clover Creek

To JO Pass

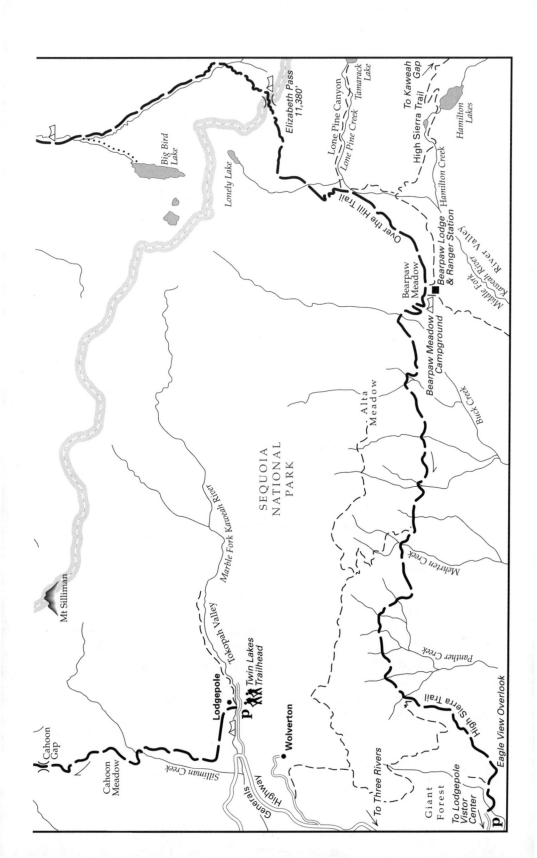

24

Lodgepole Campground to Deadman Canyon

—Kathy Morey

Route	Days	Elev. Gain/Loss	Difficulty	Miles
↝	8–14	9217'/9105'	****	52

Campsites: Twin Lakes: 6.7 miles
Ranger Lake: 10 miles
Comanche Meadow: 15.5 miles
Roaring River Ranger Station vicinity: 23 miles
Upper Ranger Meadow: 30 miles
Bearpaw Meadow Campground: 41 miles
(see the Trip Description for others)

Map: USGS 7.5-min *Lodgepole, Mt. Silliman, Sphinx Lakes, Triple Divide Peak*

Best season: Late summer through early fall

Take this trip!

Yosemite Valley is far from being the only "yosemite"* in the Sierra; there are many of them. On this trip, you'll pass through one of the most beautiful of all Sierran yosemites, Deadman Canyon, noted for its polished walls and fantastic peaks of light colored granite. A layover day at the mouth of Deadman Canyon would give you a chance to visit another yosemite, adjacent Cloud Canyon—less spectacular to hike through than Deadman because more forested, but even more remote. You'll also visit some charming lakes around Mt. Silliman and enjoy breathtaking views from the famed High Sierra Trail. If possible, plan one or two layover days to take advantage of dayhiking opportuni-

* Yosemite Valley is the prototype of what John Muir called a "yosemite" (a valley carved by glaciers out of the granite).

ties in this great backcountry. Thanks to Sequoia National Park's free shuttlebus service, inaugurated in 1999, you can complete this trip by simply taking a shuttlebus from Crescent Meadow to Lodgepole.

Trailhead

From State Route 99 just west of Visalia, go east on State Route 198 through Visalia, past Lake Kaweah, and the little town of Three Rivers. From here, the drive takes about an hour. Continue past the turnoff to Mineral King and enter Sequoia National Park at Ash Mountain. The high granite dome rising in the distance is Moro Rock above Middle Fork Kaweah River's canyon. The winding two-lane road climbs through foothills covered with native chaparral and into a grove of giant sequoias at Giant Forest. Your trip will end at a trailhead and shuttlebus stop on its eastern edge.

But for now, you continue 6 more miles on this road, the Generals Highway, to the turnoff for Lodgepole Visitor Center, Campground, and Village Store. Stop at the Visitor Center to get your permit and long-term-parking chit at the adjacent Wilderness Office and perhaps have a last "front country" snack from the store and snack bar next door. Back at your car, continue east on the Lodgepole access road past campground loops to the long-term parking area near the Lodgepole Nature Center. There are bear boxes here where you can stash any food and smelly items that might otherwise attract bears to rip your car apart. Here, you will also find toilets and water.

TRIP DESCRIPTION

Heads Up! Wood fires are prohibited in several backcountry areas through which this trip passes; plan on using a stove. Know the regulations for Sequoia-Kings Canyon National Park wilderness. In particular, this trip is entirely in these parks, on whose trails pets are prohibited. Bears are a problem along this route, but several popular campsites, including five of the ones listed above under Campsites, have large steel food lockers popularly called "bear boxes." I'll note the presence of bear boxes at any campsites. By late season in a normal year, there may be long dry stretches on this route; however, campsites mentioned below will almost certainly have water. This area's trail signs offer mileages that can't be taken at face value (e.g., the sign at Comanche Meadow says Roaring River is 11 miles away, and at Roaring River someone has altered the sign to read 8 instead of 7 miles back to Comanche Meadow; we still say it's 7.5 miles between the two). Fill your gas tank in Three Rivers; there is no gas in the parks.

The Twin Lakes trailhead in Sequoia National Park, where you start, is a short walk from the long-term parking area east down the road to a fork where the left fork crosses a bridge over Marble Fork Kaweah River. Turn left and cross the bridge to find two trailheads, one for Tokopah Valley (a delightful little yosemite itself and a fine dayhike) and your trailhead, Twin Lakes.

The dusty trail climbs away from bustling Lodgepole Campground, at first north and then west above the campground. Campground and road sounds finally fade away as you curve north again through a dense forest cover of fir, pine, and cedar, understoried by abundant stickseed, pennyroyal, lupine, gilia, and pussypaws. These woods teem with wildlife, and the traveler is very apt to see a few mule deer, many squirrels, and a host of birds. This ascent, over alternating rocky and sandy stretches, crests the moraine you have been walking on, then turns north and levels to a ford of Silliman Creek.

After passing shooting-star-fringed Cahoon Meadow, the trail continues the moderate ascent over duff-and-sand underfooting through patchy, dense stands of red and white fir and some meadow sections, crossing several streamlets, to Cahoon Gap. The trail then descends moderately to ford the unnamed tributary just south of East Fork Clover Creek (with campsite and bear box). One-fourth mile beyond this ford your trail veers right (east) at a junction (with campsite and bear box) where the trail to JO Pass goes ahead (right, north); you then ford East Fork Clover Creek.

The sometimes gentle, sometimes moderate ascent up East Fork Clover Creek introduces lodgepole and mountain white pine into the forest cover, and as the trail approaches Twin Lakes, open stretches between the trees are a tide of colors. In season, you'll find rank, knee-high corn lily, blue and white lupine, white mariposa lily, orange wallflower, purple larkspur, lavender shooting star, white cinquefoil, violet aster, and golden senecio. The last half mile to the heavily timbered flats and knolls around Twin Lakes (6.7) is a steep ascent, and the flats offer many overused campsites, a bear box, and a pit toilet on the higher knoll north of these sites. There is a quieter campsite on the lower knoll, west of the smaller of the Twin Lakes. By late summer you're unlikely to find campsites with water between Twin Lakes and Ranger and Beville lakes.

Continuing toward Silliman Pass, the view of two large boulder stands of exfoliating granite (Twin Peaks) dominates your horizon during the steep progress to the pass. This ascent sees the end of the fir and almost exclusive domination of the lodgepole pine. At the pass (10,165) views are surprisingly good for this relatively low, timbered saddle: flat-topped Mt. Silliman to the south, the heavily wooded Sugarloaf Creek drainage to the northeast, the Great Western Divide to the east, and the barren flats of the Tableland Divide to the southeast. The pass is on the boundary between Sequoia and Kings Canyon national parks.

From the pass the trail enters Kings Canyon National Park on a switchback, turns north to the nose of a viewful granite ridge, and then switchbacks

Camp high in Deadman Canyon

down. From the switchbacks there are good views of Ball Dome and much of the Kings River watershed, including the Monarch Divide. At the foot of the switchbacks a level duff trail leads north, passing signed junctions with spur trails to Beville Lake and then to Ranger Lake, which has excellent campsites and a bear box on its southwest side (10). A layover day spent in this pleasant environment allows you to visit the nearby scenic settings of Beville and Lost lakes.

Lush in early and even mid-season, by late summer the low-elevation route from Ranger Lake to Roaring River through Sugarloaf Valley may be a hot, dry, dusty slog. One factor is that the area is still recovering from a devastating forest fire. Keeping in mind the beauty of Deadman Canyon to come, on the main trail you go east, then north, from the Ranger Lake junction toward Comanche Meadow, traversing granite slabs at first. After climbing a little ridge, the trail passes the turnoff to Lost Lake and Rowell Meadow and circles Ball Dome. Passing through moderate-to-heavy forest cover, the trail emerges at a meadowed crossing of the outlet stream from Seville Lake (campsite). Beyond this crossing is the signed junction of the Seville Lake/Rowell Meadow Trail. Going east on the northwest side of Sugarloaf Creek, the route descends sometimes steadily and sometimes moderately over duff-and-sand underfooting. This descent crosses an unnamed tributary, and a short distance beyond passes a trail to Rowell Meadow and Marvin Pass. About 100 yards farther on, the trail passes the Kanawyer Gap Trail (which leads north and then west to Marvin Pass), and then fords the rocky creek emptying Comanche Meadow (15.5). There are fair if overused campsites and a bear box on the west side of this ford (the east side has been taken over by the young trees of the recovering forest).

Beginning a half mile after the ford, the trail drops moderately on sandy underfooting over a heavily forested slope that still shows the effects of fire. You pass through a drift fence and presently level out on the floor of Sugarloaf Valley, where the trail follows the course of an old glacier. Through the trees, you can see round, smooth, 1000-foot-high Sugarloaf Dome, like a giant ice-cream cone of rock. More resistant than the surrounding rock, this granite island withstood the ice onslaught. The trail passes Sugarloaf Meadow (campsites, with a bear box west of the dome) and parallels and then fords Sugarloaf Creek.

On the south side of this wide, shallow ford, the trail passes more campsites before crossing a series of sharp wrinkles in the terrain to reach Ferguson Creek and still more campsites. After fording this creek, the trail rounds a long, dry, timbered ridge nose before dropping down a steady slope to a drift fence with a stout, swinging gate and signs announcing the area is closed to grazing from here to Roaring River. Living up to its name, Roaring River can be heard a few yards to the left. With this pleasant accompaniment the trail ascends the last, gentle mile and a half under fire-scarred pines. It passes Scaffold Meadows (reserved for NPS grazing) on its way to the good campsites—with bear box and pit toilet—near Roaring River Ranger Station, fording Barton Peak stream on the way (23). Emergency services are perhaps available from the resident summer ranger, whose cabin is nearby—then again, the ranger may be out on patrol. Check the signboard outside the cabin fence and sign the register here to let the ranger know who's passing through. A layover day or two here would let you explore Cloud Canyon, the source of Roaring River, and Brewer Creek before heading up Deadman Canyon.

There's also a junction here, which we'll call the Roaring River junction. One fork goes left (north) to cross Roaring River on a footbridge. It meets yet another junction, which we'll call Cloud-Avalanche junction. Here, one fork goes southeast up Cloud Canyon and over Colby Pass to the Kern-Kaweah River and then Kern Canyon; the other fork goes north over Avalanche Pass and drops to Bubbs Creek. Back at your Roaring River junction, the second fork goes ahead (east); this is a use trail to campsites for parties with stock. The third fork—your fork—turns right (south), curves around the ranger station, and climbs into Deadman Canyon, eventually going over Elizabeth Pass to connect with the High Sierra Trail.

Your trail veers away from Roaring River on a gentle-to-moderate ascent past well-charred Jeffrey pines. Over-the-shoulder views include a fine example of a lateral moraine in the form of Moraine Ridge, the northeast wall of the canyon. The route passes through several drift fences in Deadman Canyon; be sure to close the gates. At the right time of summer, flowers seen during the initial climb include buckwheat, sagebrush, Indian paintbrush, mariposa lily, pennyroyal, penstemon, and shooting star. Campsites are few until a little before the trail fords Deadman Canyon Creek for the first time—there are four fords of this creek between Roaring River and Elizabeth Pass. From here, you have a good view of the sculpted canyon walls, a view dominated for now by Peak 10750. There's another campsite in 1.5 miles and still more campsites ahead as you ascend this well-watered canyon. About 50 yards southeast of the campsite, at the north end of a large wet meadow, lies the gravesite from which Deadman Canyon takes its name. The battered wooden sign says, HERE REPOSES ALFRED MONIERE, SHEEPHERDER, MOUNTAIN MAN, 18– TO 1887. Legend has it he took ill and died here before his partner could make the two-week round trip to Fresno and back with a doctor. As others have observed, not even the pharaohs of Egypt have tombs as magnificent as this poor sheepherder has.

From the grave your ascent continues, offering good views up-canyon of the spectacularly smoothed, unjointed, barren walls. Soon the trail refords the creek and then climbs alongside a dramatic, green-water, granite-slab chute. The trail levels out in a dense stand of lodgepole and fir and, passing a campsite, emerges at the north end of the open grasslands of Ranger Meadow. Precipitous canyon walls dominate the views from the meadow, the cirque holding Big Bird Lake is clear on the west wall, and dramatically shaped Big Bird Peak soars on fantastic pinnacles into the clear Sierra sky. By midsummer this meadow is a colorful carpet of purple and red wildflowers, including shooting star, penstemon, and red heather.

From Ranger Meadow the trail resumes its steady ascent over duff and sand through stands of lodgepole and clumps of aspen. Below a forested bench, the creek streams picturesquely down granite slabs. Just before the Upper Ranger Meadow flat, the route fords the creek to the east side. Here you have awesome glimpses of the headwall of the Deadman Canyon cirque, and this view continues to rule the skyline from the good campsites at the north end of Upper Ranger Meadow (30). A layover day here would let you follow the unofficial route to Big Bird Lake: a use trail takes off west across the creek here, becoming a well-worn tread as it ascends the slope south of the lake's outlet, and leads to a bench overlooking the main lake and several small ones.

As you leave Upper Ranger Meadow, the trail ascends gently through boulders on the meadow's east side. Low-growing willows line the stream, and clumps of wildflowers dot the green expanse. The ascent increases to moderate and then very steep as you switchback up the cirque's steep east wall. As if to spite the increasing steepness, plentiful moisture nourishes tall meadow grasses and flowers here in such profusion that they obscure the trail, which may at times be reduced to a line of trampled vegetation. The main stream drops by foaming cascades on the west.

The very steep section isn't long, and you level out on a granite bench to cross the stream for the last time, above a long, dashing granite chute. Note ahead southwest a strikingly narrow, sharp, gray peak reminiscent of a ship's prow; it's a good landmark on your way to Elizabeth Pass. Parallel rows of boulders indicate the route you should take across the granite, curving slightly right to pick up a relatively new, well-engineered trail of riprap (fist-sized pieces of broken rock) laid between boulders to form an obvious trail winding up the cirque's southwest wall, mostly through a talus field. Don't curve left over the worn rut ascending the steep alpine meadows that dominate the head of this cirque; this is the old, abandoned, hard-to-follow route. Instead, the Elizabeth Pass Trail is now this gradual to moderate riprap highway, with occasional patches of meadow. When in doubt as to where to go next, look for the next section of riprap. Soon you see another gray peak left of the ship's-prow peak; as you rise higher, you see a trio of red-and-gray peaks to the left of this second gray peak. The broader saddle between these red-and-gray peaks is Elizabeth Pass.

The riprap ends near the base of the pass, where year-round snowfields provide water and there are one or two very Spartan campsites. By late season, this may be the last water before the ford of Lonely Lake's outlet on the other side of the pass. (For now, hikers coming the other way, from Bearpaw Meadow, have been climbing a well-ducked route through alpine meadows. On the Deadman Canyon side of the pass, hikers should look for the riprap path in the talus rather than ducks as they descend.)

By this time, you can see the last few, steep switchbacks heading to the pass. Light-colored granite slabs forming cliffs at the cirque's head contrast with the darker metamorphic rocks (around an old copper mine site) seen to the east, and this contrast is even more marked from Elizabeth Pass (11,380). Views at the pass are astonishing: upper Deadman Canyon falls away to the north; southwest, they include parts of the Middle Fork Kaweah River watershed and Moose Lake; and northwest, the jumbled peaks of the southernmost prominences of the Tableland Divide. Below to the south, a row of striking, shark-tooth-shaped peaklets lines one side of the cirque you next descend. Like Silliman Pass, Elizabeth Pass borders the two parks.

From the pass, the trail initially descends into Sequoia National Park on steep switchbacks, then follows a well-ducked, moderate traverse through a huge alpine meadow, curving west and southwest to ford Lonely Lake's outlet (with a possible nearby campsite) on the cirque's steep west wall. Beyond the ford, you drop through dense chaparral on a series of rocky switchbacks. At the foot of these zigzags, the route passes a spur trail left (east) to Tamarack Lake. Travelers ready to stop for the night can take the spur trail a short way up Lone Pine Canyon to campsites in the first wooded area near refreshing Lone Pine Creek.

In another quarter mile you reach a second junction: left (south) to descend along Lone Pine Creek to the High Sierra Trail; right (southwest) on the Over The Hill Trail to make a steep and mostly shadeless ascent across the sparsely timbered nose of the ridge above Bearpaw Meadow. Turn right onto the Over The Hill Trail to begin cursing—sorry, climbing—to an open high point on this ridge that offers breathtaking views up Lone Pine Canyon to Triple Divide Peak and across the unseen Middle Fork Kaweah River to the Great Western Divide.

The steep, rocky, and mostly dry descent from this ridge passes through stands of lodgepole and red fir to join the High Sierra Trail 150 yards west of a ranger station and backcountry lodge which share a magnificent view—alone worth a visit!—over the Middle Fork Kaweah country. Emergency services are probably available at the ranger station. Meals and lodging at Bearpaw Lodge are by reservation only, but there is a tiny "store" where you can buy film, freeze-dried food, and trail snacks (supplies are very limited). Those wishing to camp in the vicinity should turn right (west) for 0.3 mile on the High Sierra Trail to a junction with a trail left (south) 200 yards down to overused Bearpaw Meadow Campground (41) under heavy forest cover (with piped, treated water, bear boxes, and toilet). Open fires are not allowed around here.

Staying on the High Sierra Trail and continuing generally west, you ramble through moderate to dense forest before descending a very loose slope to the bridge across Buck Creek (with campsite and bear box). Climbing away from Buck Creek, the undulating trail re-enters forest, crosses a couple of Buck

Creek's tributaries and, near the westernmost tributary, passes a bear box surrounded by a clutch of very poor campsites under dense forest.

As you continue west, the forest thins to reveal what it has heretofore mercifully been hiding: this trail traverses a very steep slope with thousands of feet of exposure. Far from being level, it rises and falls, sometimes by almost 400 feet. At times the trail seems little more than a ribbon blasted out of a steep, granite sheet. Watch your step here, although it's tempting to keep your eyes on views across the chasm—granite domes and those jagged formations known as Castle Rocks. Water and safe resting places are scarce along this stretch, and the heat can be enervating on a warm afternoon. Shortly after passing a junction with a trail branching right (uphill, north) to Alta Meadow and Wolverton, you find the next camping area between the branches of Mehrten Creek. Reportedly, campsites and a bear box are accessed by a steep and very slippery climb up the creek's west branch.

Leaving the cool recess of Mehrten Creek, the trail heads west to Crescent Meadow. Soon you notice the warm, herbal scent of kit-kit-dizze ("mountain misery"), a shrub very characteristic of the southern Sierra at these altitudes, which lines the trail here and there. A moderate to patchy forest of ponderosa and sugar pine, black oak, and incense-cedar offers some shade, and the trail presently begins crossing the tributaries of Panther Creek. West of a very steep, loose pair of gullies holding tributary streams, you pass above a gentle, dry, forested gully offering campsites below the trail and access to water from the next tributary, about 100 yards farther west in another loose gully. You cross Panther Creek's westernmost tributary a little before the junction with the old Wolverton Cutoff Trail (right, uphill). This tributary marks the last legal camping area for those headed to Crescent Meadow, and reportedly there is a tiny campsite somewhere around here.

Beyond Panther Creek, the trail traverses slopes scorched by a forest fire ignited by a carelessly dropped cigarette. You leave the forest for the open slopes around Eagle View Overlook, with awesome views west to Moro Rock, far below to the river, and east to the glaciated peaks of the Great Western Divide. Curving northwest toward a knoll now, in a few hundred yards the trail reaches a junction on a saddle in the shade of giant sequoias: left (west) on the High Sierra Trail for 0.6 mile to the trailhead; right (north) to dayhiking destinations in Giant Forest. You bear left here, on the shady north side of the knoll, and end your hike by curving around lush Crescent Meadow on a gentle descent. Cross a footbridge to the trailhead, where there are toilets, water, and a shuttlebus stop at the meadow's west edge—ignore a signed spur trail just before the footbridge and branching left to the parking lot. Take the shuttlebus back to Lodgepole Visitor Center and walk from there to your car.

Variations

Reverse the direction of this semi-loop. For a relatively easy trip—a weekender or a trip suitable for novices—take this trip only as far as Twin Lakes or, better yet, Ranger Lake.

Permits

This is a quota trailhead, and a permit is required for overnight stays. Permits may be available from the Wilderness Office next to Lodgepole Visitor Center. Apply for reserved permits ($10/reservation) to Wilderness Permit Reservations, Sequoia-Kings Canyon National Park, HCR 89 Box 60, Three Rivers, CA 93271, (559) 565-3708 or FAX (559) 565-4239. You will receive *only* the reservation, and you must exchange it for a real permit at the Wilderness Office. Check out **www.nps.gov/seki** for more info!

Build-up/Wind-down tips

The towns of Visalia, Lemon Cove, and Three Rivers (in order of their proximity to Lodgepole) offer stores, lodging, and restaurants (no Chamber of Commerce or Visitors Bureau; check your auto-club tour guide or my book *Hot Showers, Soft Beds, and Dayhikes in the Sierra*). Even from low-altitude Three Rivers, it's an hour's drive to your 6740-foot trailhead.

So, better yet, stay at altitude at one of the lodgings or campgrounds along the Generals Highway the night before starting your trip. From south to north, lodgings are Wuksachi Village (the replacement for Giant Forest Village), for reservations call (888) 252-5757, Stony Creek Lodge, (559) 335-5500, Montecito-Sequoia Lodge, (800) 227-9900, and Grant Grove Village, (559) 335-5500. Campgrounds at altitude, from south to north along or near the highway, are Lodgepole*, Dorst*, Stony Creek**, Upper Stony**, Horse Camp, Buck Rock, Big Meadows, Azalea, Crystal Springs, and Sunset. (* indicates a NPS campground; sites may be reserved, 1-800-365-2267 or **http://reservations.nps.gov**, up to 5 months in advance; ** indicates a USFS campground; sites may be reserved, 1-800-280-2267; otherwise, first come, first served.) These facilities are in very high demand in summer. Make your plans and reservations early!

To find out how Kathy Morey got started hiking the Sierra and the Hawaiian islands and writing about her hikes for Wilderness Press, and for a list of her titles, see "Author Bio & Bib" on page 492.

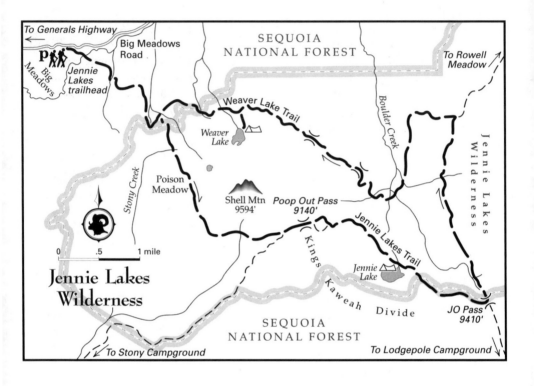

25

Jennie Lakes Wilderness

—Ruby Johnson Jenkins

Route	Days	Elev. Gain/Loss	Difficulty	Miles
♀	3	3430'/3430'	**	8.9

Campsites: Jennie Lake: 6.9 miles
Weaver Lake: 15.9 miles

Map: USGS 7.5-min *Muir Grove, Mt. Silliman*

Best season: Late summer, early fall.

Take this trip!

This 10,500-acre wilderness, snuggled between Kings Canyon and Sequoia National Parks, features numerous grassy meadows, refreshing creeks, and pine-shaded trails. Its two secluded lakes, backdropped by craggy peaks, are its most winsome enchantments. Although attractive and accessible, this wilderness still provides a measure of solitude even though it's located between two famous national parks. Allow extra days to explore the parks' wonders.

Trailhead

On Highway 180 east of Fresno, drive 1.7 miles from the Big Stump entrance of Kings Canyon National Park (entrance fee) to the triangle junction with the Generals Highway. Turn right and drive 6.7 miles to the T-junction of paved Big Meadows Road. Turn left and drive 3.8 miles to the Jennie Lakes trailhead. It has a phone and restrooms; a non-fee campground is 0.3 mile farther.

TRIP DESCRIPTION

Heads Up! In a hurry to get to one of the stellar lakes? Continue straight ahead at the Jennie Lake Trail junction on Weaver Lake Trail 30E09. Turn right on the Weaver Lake access trail to Weaver Lake (8707). It's an easy 3.6-mile one-way hike.

Jennie Lake Trail 29E05 (0.0/7600) leaves the trailhead parking lot, soon bridges Big Meadows' soggy outlet stream, and gently rises at the foot of one of the many exfoliating domes on this rolling tableland. It then turns to follow a frolicking branch of Big Meadows Creek 0.1 mile before crossing it. The path climbs another dome and while on top curves to the right. (Note this curve for your return trip lest you veer off course.)

Tiny blue-eyed Mary and yellow dwarf monkey flower announce the end of winter along the path, which is sparsely shaded by Jeffrey pines. The trail rounds a ridge offering open views of the lofty mountains of Kings Canyon National Park and then descends to pass an unmapped path traveling north to Big Meadows Campground. Shortly, at a forked junction (2.1/8160) with Weaver Lake Trail 30E09, on which you will return, your trail turns right.

From here to Poop Out Pass you climb around the flanks of Shell Mountain, ascending almost continuously on a moderate grade. In a dark forest of red firs, lodgepole and western white pines, you pass into Jennie Lakes Wilderness, hop across the spring-fed outlet stream of Poison Meadow, and then saunter past the meadow, which lies laterally on the east side of the trail. Beyond a pocket glade, you leave the trees to enjoy views southwest of Big Baldy Ridge, Chimney Rock, and the quilted plains of the San Joaquin Valley.

Turning east around a Shell Mountain ridge, the rocky path descends among pinemat manzanita to cross a seasonal headwaters branch of Stony Creek. It then climbs past a T-junction (4.8/9040) with a 5.0-mile, ridge-straddling trail to Stony Campground (another trailhead access to this wilderness). Your trail next arrives at well-named Poop Out Pass (5.1/9140). This broad pass offers camping room or places to stash packs for those with compass and map who wish to enjoy the supreme views from atop Shell Mountain.

Several trail choices lead down-canyon beyond Poop Out—all steep. The best choice, probably the newest trail, descends along the ridge and switchbacks. Beyond the switchback it crosses a snowmelt creek where the fragmented paths meet. Now the path traverses east, largely on exfoliating granodiorite slopes. Views of the ragged Sierra begin to appear. Then curving southeast, the trail rises easily through forest to an unmarked junction (6.8/9020) with a short 0.1-mile path to Jennie Lake (9012), prior to the lake's outlet.

In 1897 the head ranger for the Kings River District, S.L.N. Ellis named this lake for his wife. Cradled next to the fractured façade of a Kings Kaweah Divide peak, Jennie Ellis Lake rests in all its splendor: campsites cluster on the red fir-shaded north shore; mountain chickadees and solitary vireos serenade early risers; brook and rainbow trout swim in its placid waters.

Upon leaving, a climb of five switchbacks takes you east from Jennie Lake's north shore; then the trail curves right reaching a saddle. The ensuing path touches the park border and stays near or on the crest, offering en route a few views southeast of deeply gouged Mount Silliman. A 1.6-mile hike from the Jennie Lake spur junction takes you to JO Pass (8.4/9410). Ellis named this pass for the letters jo cut on a tree, probably by a sheepherder. (The trail south from the pass would take you to Lodgepole Campground in about 8 miles.)

You turn sharply left on JO Pass Trail 30E11, and head north past a brook and campsites, over peeling rock and boulder steps. You descend easily in a stately forest to boulderhop a Boulder Creek tributary. Generous campsites are located nearby. In the upstream meadow—close to the receding snowline if you are hiking in early season—you will see a garden of marsh marigolds in bloom. A 4- to 12-inch leafless stem supports this bowl-shaped flower of six to nine pure white, petal-like sepals around a sometimes large, yellow, center cushion of many stamens. When in bud, this lovely flower looks pale blue.

A gain of elevation on switchbacks and an easy walk take you to a junction (10.9/8980) with Weaver Lake Trail 30E09, onto which you turn left. (If you took a right turn, you would travel several miles via Rowell Meadow to Big Meadows Road, a point 7.0 miles east of your trailhead.)

Heading west, you drop sometimes steeply, then turn south to slant down west-facing slopes in Boulder Creek's scenic headwater bowl. At the south curve of the bowl, where Jennie Lake's mountain hovers distantly up-canyon, you ford four branches of Boulder Creek. Originating at Jennie Lake, this creek often requires a wade across but, in late summer, a boulderhop will suffice. Boulder Creek gathers numerous streams to eventually become a major tributary to the South Fork Kings River.

After the creek crossings you regain your lost elevation by the time you reach an obvious saddle. Beyond that, you descend to a broader saddle and 0.6 mile later arrive at the signed Weaver Lake access trail (15.6/8620). After a 0.3-mile ascent on the access trail, you gain the north shore of Weaver Lake (8707) with its several campsites.

Weaver is smaller than Jennie Lake but similarly striking. Both lakes cuddle against towering glacial-scooped rocks: here the face of Shell Mountain. At both, rock shadows dance on the rippling water and white-flowered Labrador tea edge their forested shores; both lakes invite an extended stay. To reach Shell Mountain's summit, angle up along either vegetated side of the rocky face, and then curve in toward the highest point.

Upon returning on the 0.3-mile path to Weaver Lake Trail 30E09, you turn left and head west. Cross Weaver Lake's outlet stream, pass out of the wilderness, ford a tarn- and spring-fed brook, and meet you incoming route at a T-junction (16.8/8160) next to the brook. Follow your footsteps on Jennie Lake Trail 29E05 to your starting point (18.9/7600).

Permits

None required

Ruby Johnson Jenkins first hiked the John Muir Trail to celebrate her 50th birthday, and thereby inaugurated a career as a Wilderness Press guidebook author; see "Author Bio & Bib" on page 492 for the surprising story.

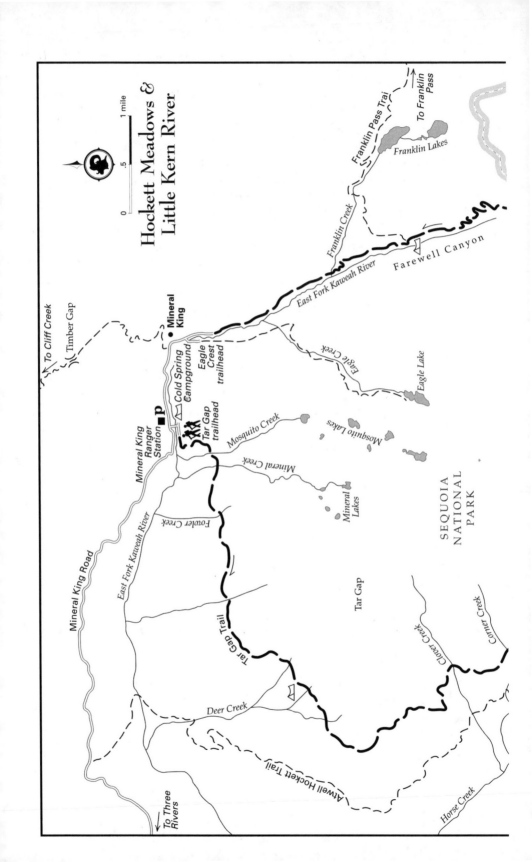

Hockett Meadows & Little Kern River

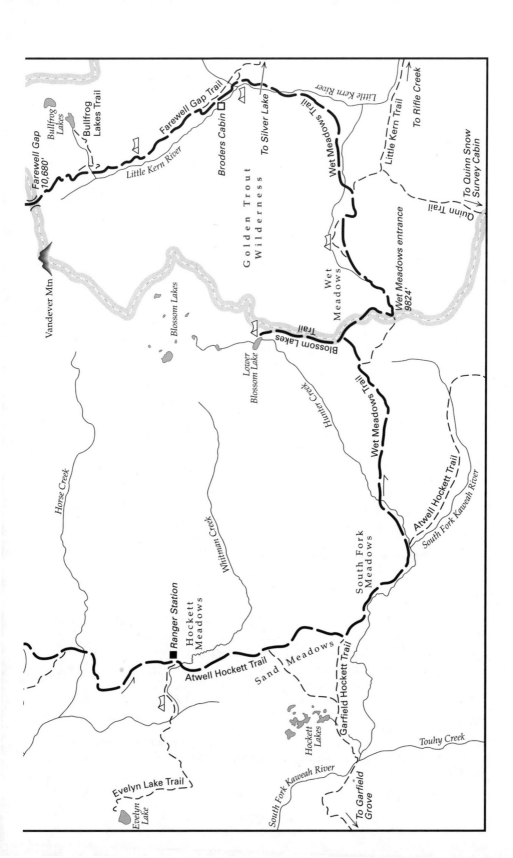

26

Hockett Meadows
& Little Kern River

—Ruby Johnson Jenkins

Route	Days	Elev. Gain/Loss	Difficulty	Miles
↻	5–7	4950'/4950'	**	31.8

Campsites: Hockett Meadows (0.1 mile west of ranger station): 9.8 miles
Lower Blossom Lake (1.0 mile north of trail): 16.6 miles
Little Kern River headwaters: 22.4 miles
Farewell Canyon shelf: 26.6 miles
(see the Trip Description for others)

Map: USGS 7.5-min *Mineral King, Silver City, Moses Mtn., Quinn Peak*

Best season: Late summer through early fall

Take this trip!

This adventure takes you to the land of the Hockett plateau, where wildflowers thrive in nature's gardens, deer herds congregate in tall grass meadows, and lakes repose in glaciated bowls. The route then loops around to the rushing Little Kern River, whose headwater freshets plunge down flaming rock walls. The numerous side trips offered expand and extend your adventures.

Trailhead

From Highway 99 drive 39 miles east on Highway 198 through Visalia and Three Rivers. At a T-junction drive Mineral King Road 23.6 miles east to Tar Gap parking lot just beyond the ranger station. Allow 90 minutes to negotiate the 700 curves on the mostly paved Mineral King Rd., which is not recommended for RVs or trailers. The signed trailhead is above Cold Spring Campground near the ranger station.

TRIP DESCRIPTION

Heads Up! Plan to overnight in Mineral King Valley at 7800' elevation to acclimate yourself. You must stay in one of two campgrounds that fill up fast; they're first-come, first-served only. You may neither car camp at trailheads nor camp off-trail within 4 miles of the valley. Silver City village, (559) 561-3223, in the valley has cabins, showers, a restaurant with a few groceries, and a gas pump.

To locate the trail, enter Cold Spring Campground and hike west up the road found next to the bulletin board and pay station. You will see the trail to the left past the campsites. (The parking lot to the right affords parking for the walk-in campsites, not for the trailhead.)

The Tar Gap Trail (0.0/7490) rises quickly under white fir shade on an ascent that is moderate to steep despite several switchbacks designed to ease the grade. Where the trail crosses slopes moistened by seeps, it passes among ferns and thimbleberry bushes; on drier soils it passes among infrequently seen dainty, white-petaled sargent's campion. This flower's clefted petals open from a sac at their base, and its thin leaves grow opposite on an equally thin stem.

You soon pass an abandoned Mosquito Lakes Trail (0.5/8044), which ascends left. Although no longer maintained, this trail is preferred over its replacement by many who seek the Mosquito Lakes. You immediately hop across Mosquito Creek and, after climbing over a minor ridge, ford Mineral Creek, another dashing stream.

Beyond the creek's recess, you begin a long scalloped pattern, traversing around ridges and retreating into creases; the latter often shelter impetuous creeks crowded with seasonal efflorescence—one such is Fowler Creek, the next stream you ford. Namesake State Senator Thomas Fowler, a flamboyant Irish-emigrant entrepreneur, took control of Mineral King mining in 1878 after the original investors had pulled out, declaring its silver too costly to extract. Under Fowler's direction, mines on Empire Mountain near Timber Gap were enlarged and connected via tramway with a mill near the valley floor. He learned the hard way that the first investors were right, and retired from mining bankrupt, discouraged, and ill.

Ahead the undulating but overall ascending path passes through a boulder chute. On the ridge above, the rock displacement caused by weathering and by the scraping effect that glaciers had on the Sierra is clearly visible. The next open boulder field presents the best views in this trip of the East Fork Kaweah

River canyon, the serpentine road to Mineral King, and the ever-encroaching brown smog of the San Joaquin Valley.

You next ford the several branches of Deer Creek. About 0.2 mile after the initial branch, you find a large campsite (4.2/8240) laid out in the forest below the trail, the first site beyond the trailhead's 4-mile zone of no camping. There is another large campsite below the trail near a meadow and its stream within the next mile. Soon you outflank a ridge, the end of the rim above that contains Tar Gap—far removed from this Tar Gap Trail. You pass a cabin-sized boulder standing trailside as you enter into the Horse Creek watershed.

The varied trail along this watershed presents in intervals: sloping granite dynamited to create the path, sun-baked terrain covered with manzanita and snow brush, moist slopes filigreed by seasonal flowers, and cool forests of red fir replacing lodgepole pine. In time the route crosses the braided effervescence of Clover Creek, then of Corner Creek; it then descends to the forked junction (8.0/8580) with the Atwell Hockett Trail, which paralleled below your path for many miles.

Now on the Atwell Hockett Trail you pass the obscure, unsigned Horse Creek Trail, which angles into the woods a few dozen feet from the junction, and soon reach capacious campsites under red firs next to the crossing of Horse Creek. At this excellent place to camp, the handy cable relieves your locating a branch to safely hang your food from marauding bears.

Several logs aid in a dry crossing of Horse Creek (8.2/8545) during high water and, later on the trail, log bridges span bogs alight with shooting star wildflowers. After Horse Creek, your ascending course deflects west to round a ridge, separating the Horse Creek and Whitman Creek watersheds, and drops to a T-junction with the Evelyn Lake Trail (9.7/8505).

Expansive and verdant Hockett Meadows spreads impressively before you. At its north end just ahead, you see a log cabin where a park ranger resides from June to September. When not on patrol, a raised flag indicates his presence. Feel free to seek advice. While a small part of the meadow by the cabin is fenced off for administrative use, the vast spread of grass beyond the fence attracts large gatherings of deer, most often seen at dusk.

Most of the campsites along the Evelyn Lake Trail are closed for restoration. The best site is just west of the ranger station off the Atwell Hockett Trail. With a great view of the meadow, it is large and, thankfully, has a bear-proof food box. Two three-sided outhouses are located off the Evelyn Lake Trail. Plan, if you can, to stay two nights at Hockett Meadows to allow a full day at Evelyn Lake, 8.0 miles round trip on the Evelyn Lake Trail. This cirque lake, hugged by boulders, offers a few campsites and has excellent swimming and fishing.

Continuing on the Atwell Hockett Trail beyond the Evelyn Lake junction, you pass west of the ranger station and Hockett Meadows, bridge Whitman Creek, and ascend easily into a fringe of lodgepole pines that obstructs meadow views. During snowmelt this vast meadow is transformed into a glossy lake.

You stay left while, in quick succession, your path reaches three junctions: at the first (10.8/8580) a trail cuts across Sand Meadows to Hockett Lakes; from the next the Garfield Hockett Trail (11.7/8530) leads to Garfield Grove; the last (12.0/8525) is a cutoff to the Tuohy Trail. After cutting across a lobe of peaceful South Fork Meadows, bisected by the South Fork Kaweah River, and passing a lateral to a packers' campsite with a food storage box, you fork left onto the Wet Meadows Trail (12.9/8603), leaving the Atwell Hockett Trail just before it fords Hunter Creek.

Here you climb gently east among wildflowers that bloom well into summer. In early season the whole plateau resembles a park, with plush meadows of tall grass; slopes of ferns, lupines, and soft thimbleberry plants; numerous trees whose spreading crowns offer shade; and flowers that bloom everywhere like tossed confetti. Most of the better known flowers nod in the soft breezes here, but look for the delicate, little elephant heads. Their tiny pink blooms alternate on the stems and each has a "head, trunk, and two elephant ears." The plant prefers moist soil.

To conclude your romp on the Hockett plateau, you first boulderhop Hunter Creek, the outlet of lower Blossom Lake, then embark on a steady ascent. Your trail curves about, gaining elevation among lodgepole pine and red fir, then at length levels out and meets a cutoff trail (15.2/9562) to the Wet Meadows Entrance. Since lower Blossom Lake is an ideal place to camp, espe-

Middle Blossom Lake

cially following above average wet seasons when the lake is brimming, continue straight ahead, again ascending, until you meet the Blossom Lakes Trail (15.6/9860), which follows the watershed divide between the Kaweah and Kern rivers and the boundary between Sequoia Park and Sequoia Forest. (The cutoff trail, bypassing Blossom Lakes, saves you 0.3 mile.)

In its hidden setting, days away from all trailheads (but only 1.0 mile north of this junction), scenic lower Blossom Lake, with its chain of lovely upper lakes, invites you to sample splendor and solitude, and encourages you to spend an extra day swimming, fishing, and exploring the upper lakes. A large camping area extends along the lower lake's east side. Reach the upper lakes by climbing near their outlets.

From the Blossom Lakes junction, the trail heads south along the divide, where it leaves Sequoia National Park at the Wet Meadows Entrance (16.3/9824) and enters the Forest Service's Golden Trout Wilderness. Here the Wet Meadows Trail acquires a number, 31E11, and begins a long descent east to the Little Kern River. After three switchbacks it reaches a roofless log cabin built by the Pitt Brothers and large campsites near a splashing stream.

As the descent continues, you cross the inlet stream to Wet Meadows, observe paths branching left to campsites, and see bits of the meadow to the north framed by red firs and backdropped by the rugged, nameless peaks of the Great Western Divide. After another set of switchbacks you arrive at Deadman Camp, spread next to a glade housing a rain gauge and "snow pillow." The pillow constantly measures the snowpack's water content and radios measurements to the water resource agencies.

A little further travel leads you to a broad, forested flat with several campsites and a trail junction (18.3/8965). (Quinn Trail 31E13 heads south to the Quinn Snow Survey Cabin. Unmaintained Little Kern Trail 31E12 branches east to travel through the superb country along the Little Kern River to Rifle Creek.)

You continue on Wet Meadows Trail 31E11, descending past more campsites. Boulderhop Wet Meadow's outlet creek below a cascade moistening creek dogwoods and willows. As you curve north into drier climes, the canyon of the Little Kern River opens to your view, and you can identify the distant, distinctive Needles south of the canyon. After miles of descent you now begin a 2500-foot ascent along the Little Kern River that culminates at Farewell Gap, 4.3 miles ahead. The river is heard but unseen until it explodes before you in a thundering falls over russet metamorphic rocks. Shortly after, you bridge the Little Kern (19.9/8440) on a broad red fir log.

Several campsites appear at the junction. Advancing upriver on open slopes, you pass a cutoff (20.4/8800) to the Farewell Gap Trail above. Just beyond, you step over a small creek. Then in several minutes lower-tiered logs, remnants of Broders Cabin, appear between the trees on a bluff across the river. A sign nailed on one of two large red firs marks the steep path that crosses the river to the cabin site and ideal campsites.

Your trail switchbacks once and ends at an acute-angle junction (20.9/9085) with Farewell Gap Trail 31E10. Your route turns left (north) and heads up-canyon on this trail. (Heading south here would take you to Silver Lake.) Quickly the path crosses a creek redolent of swamp onions, then continues to ascend on a bias across southwest-facing slopes luxuriant with plants watered by snowmelt creeklets. The path presently gains elevation through switchbacks.

You may forget to watch your footing as your gaze lifts to the steep canyon walls composed of Pre-Cretaceous metamorphic rock. These muted gold, red, rust, magenta, and brown slopes, dotted with green of foxtail pine and red fir, soar around 2000 feet. Lofty cirque-tucked snowpacks lasting well into summer give birth to silvery streams that plummet down these precipitous slopes. The bowl resounds with the symphony of falling water.

Soon you pass several fine campsites perched among foxtail pines flanking the river. This is the best place to camp if you are planning a side trip to Bullfrog Lakes or a climb of Vandever Mountain. Shortly beyond, you pass a large, exposed camping area near the junction of the unsigned, 0.8-mile, steep Bullfrog Lakes Trail (22.6/9920), a side trip that makes an enjoyable dayhike. If you take it, hang your backpacks off the ground, as unattended they will surely be chewed by marmots. The lakes lie in a fractured-rock crescent, glistening intense blue against the austere, treeless beauty that surrounds them.

On a traverse, still heading north, after the Bullfrog Lakes junction, you cross one creek that drains overflow from the lakes and a second that tumbles from a tiny tarn near the crest. You hike along sodden slopes spattered with the ephemeral colors of numerous wildflowers. Across the canyon a peak points to Vandever Mountain. You pass the unmarked northern end of the cutoff trail (22.8/10,080) to Bullfrog Lakes, then, shortly after, climb a set of 10 switchbacks to reach Farewell Gap (24.0/10,680). Here you leave Golden Trout Wilderness and the headwaters of the Little Kern River to reenter Sequoia National Park. Here, also, you have a chance to climb Vandever Mountain. By turns inviting or foreboding, Vandever is one of the most widely visible and identifiable peaks of the Mineral King basin. From Farewell Gap it's not a hard cross-country climb, just straight up the rocky slope for 0.6 mile.

Dry camping here at the gap is possible but undesirable due to the usual fierce winds. Now the long, long descent to the trip's end—via innumerable switchbacks, zigzags, and U-turns into highly scenic Farewell Canyon—looms ahead. On the ninth switchback from the gap, photographers will find the ideal setting to capture Mineral King framed in the foreground by a sturdy foxtail pine. On the slopes along the way, some backpackers will notice powder blue forget-me-nots. The tiny five-petaled flower, with a yellow ring at its throat, blooms in loose clusters atop a stem with alternate, oblong leaves. At length a welcome spring sends water across the trail to join the juvenile East Fork

Upper Little Kern River headwaters

Kaweah River. Stop here for a breather and—if you plan to spend another, recommended night on the trail—fill your water bottles here.

Eventually, you pass the only camping area on this stretch: a broad, tree-covered shelf way below the trail to the left, with steep access to the river. (Campgrounds are usually full in the valley, and driving Mineral King Road requires a rested person behind the wheel.) A few minutes after the campsite, you pass the Franklin Pass junction (26.7/9358), and many curves later you wade across Franklin Creek. In time your trail straightens for the last leg. Eventually you pass corrals and reach the bridge where you turn left—to approach the Eagle Crest trailhead (30.4/7830). From here, find the road through old Mineral King village. It takes you to the path—becoming a nature trail with wayside plaques—that leads to your starting site, Cold Spring Campground (31.8/7460).

Permits

A Wilderness Permit is required. Apply at Mineral King Ranger Station or make advance reservations ($10.00 fee) by contacting:

Wilderness Permit Reservations
Sequoia-Kings Canyon National Parks
HCR 89, Box 60
Three Rivers, CA 93271
(559) 565-3708; FAX (559) 565-4239

Ruby Johnson Jenkins first hiked the John Muir Trail to celebrate her 50th birthday, and thereby inaugurated a career as a Wilderness Press guidebook author; see "Author Bio & Bib" on page 492 for the surprising story.

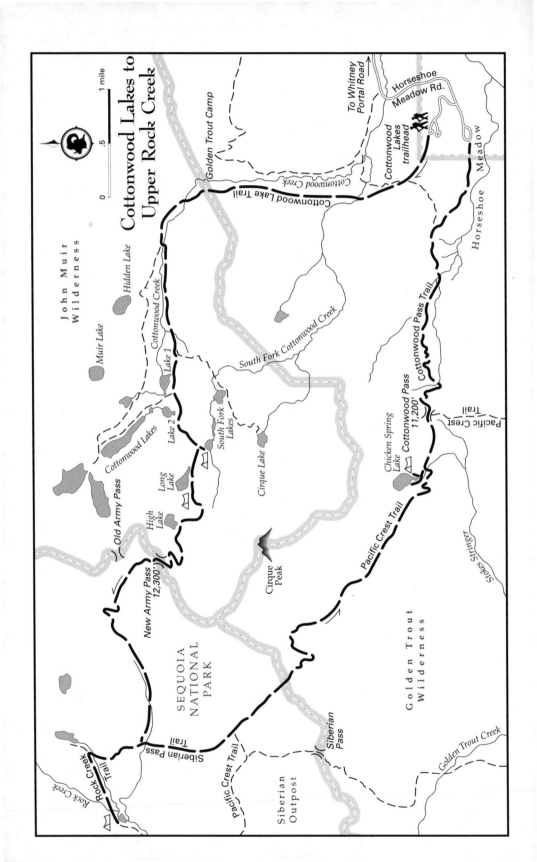

Cottonwood Lakes to Upper Rock Creek

John Muir Wilderness

Muir Lake

Hidden Lake

Cottonwood Lakes

Lake 1

Lake 2

Cottonwood Creek

Old Army Pass

High Lake

Long Lake

South Fork Lakes

South Fork Cottonwood Creek

Cirque Lake

New Army Pass 12,300'

SEQUOIA NATIONAL PARK

Cirque Peak

Pacific Crest Trail

Rock Creek Trail

Rock Creek

Siberian Pass Trail

Pacific Crest Trail

Siberian Pass

Siberian Outpost

Golden Trout Wilderness

Chicken Spring Lake

Cottonwood Pass 11,200'

Cottonwood Pass Trail

Pacific Crest Trail

Stokes Stringer

Golden Trout Creek

Cottonwood Lake Trail

Cottonwood Creek

Golden Trout Camp

To Whitney Portal Road

Horseshoe Meadow Rd.

Cottonwood Lakes trailhead

Horseshoe Meadow

0   .5   1 mile

27

Cottonwood Lakes to Upper Rock Creek

—Kathy Morey

Route	Days	Elev. Gain/Loss	Difficulty	Miles
↻	5–7	3080'/3080'	**	23.8
		(includes 1.5-mile walk between trailheads)		

Campsites: South Fork Lakes (westernmost): 5.3 miles
Lake on Rock Creek at 10,440': 11.8 miles
Chicken Spring Lake: 17.8 miles
(see the Trip Description for others)

Map: USGS 7.5-min *Cirque Peak, Mt. Whitney, Johnson Peak*

Best season: Late summer through early fall (wait till late summer
after a heavy winter, to get over 12,300-foot New Army
Pass)

Take this trip!

I'm always looking for trips with huge dividends per hiking mile. This one
nears the top of my list. Magnificent alpine basins defined by sculpted peaks
cradle shining blue lakes and are linked by high passes with awe-inspiring
views, all on a relatively short trip that's about half in Sequoia National Park.

But don't cut it short! One layover day in the Cottonwood Lakes or the
South Fork Lakes would let you climb Mt. Langley—the Sierra's southernmost
14,000-footer—or easier Cirque Peak, or explore Cottonwood Basin. Another
layover day, this one near the lake on Upper Rock Creek, would permit a dayhike into breathtaking Miter Basin or a visit to dramatic Siberian Outpost.

Trailheads

The two trailheads on this route are so close together that you just walk between them. Both are off Horseshoe Meadow Road south of Lone Pine.

Put-in trailhead (Cottonwood Lakes): From the center of Lone Pine on US 395, go 3.5 miles west on Whitney Portal Road, turn left onto Horseshoe Meadow Road, and following it 20 airy, winding miles to a turnoff (right) at the sign for the Cottonwood Lakes trailhead. Go about 1 mile more to the parking lot. Adjacent is a backpackers' campground (one overnight only) with restrooms and potable water.

Take-out trailhead (Horseshoe Meadow, labeled "Kern Plateau" on some maps): Follow the directions for the Cottonwood Lakes trailhead except don't turn right for that trailhead. Instead, continue 0.5 mile more to the road's end at a parking lot with restrooms, potable water, and an adjacent (one-overnight) backpackers' campground.

To close the loop, walk the roads between these trailheads. (Drop packs and relax at Horseshoe Meadow while the peppiest member of the party walks the 1.5 miles to retrieve the car.)

TRIP DESCRIPTION

> **Heads Up!** Bears are active along this route and counterbalance bear-bagging may be ineffective; I recommend a bearproof food canister. There's a bear box at the lake on Rock Creek. Know Sequoia National Park plus Golden Trout and John Muir wilderness regulations! No wood fires are permitted in Cottonwood Lakes Basin, at South Fork Lakes, or within 0.25 mile of Chicken Spring Lake. Pets are *not* permitted on national park trails.

The first mile and a half of trail for this trip doesn't appear on the *Cirque Peak* topo, though the Cottonwood Lakes trailhead does—go figure. The trail leads west, then north on a gentle and brief ascent through an open stand of lodgepole and foxtail pine, passes a spur to the equestrian area, and soon enters Golden Trout Wilderness. The sandy trail soon begins to descend gently, then levels out. In about 1 mile you cross South Fork Cottonwood Creek.

In another half mile you pick up the trail as it's shown on the topo; the junction is imperceptible, the old trail south of it overgrown, and you ignore it, anyway. Skirt the west side of the meadows along Cottonwood Creek and ascend steadily, passing privately operated Golden Trout Camp. Soon you enter John Muir Wilderness and cross Cottonwood Creek. Beyond this crossing the trail swings west, with the creek and its meadows to the southwest. The ascent levels during these stretches.

At the next trail junction, turn left and cross Cottonwood Creek. Now the trail climbs moderately above the creek. Beside a large meadow, we reach another junction. Here you take the right fork for New Army Pass, instead of the left fork to South Fork Lakes, because you're heading for the westernmost, highest South Fork lake, which is slightly closer via the right fork. Ascend a forested moraine to a junction at the meadowed west end of the lowest Cottonwood lake, Cottonwood Lake 1, and to a fine view of Cottonwood Basin and Mt. Langley. Check current fishing regulations to see which lakes are open to angling; lakes 1–4 have been closed for many years.

Taking the left fork here, you pass Cottonwood lake 2 and then veer southwest through a jumbled area of near-white granite blocks. From the point where the trail turns west-northwest, a short spur trail descends a few yards to good campsites at the west end of the westernmost South Fork lake (5.3). These campsites are located in a sparse grove of foxtail pines with fine views of Cirque Peak to the southwest. You'll find other campsites at the easternmost South Fork lake, Cirque Lake, and Long Lake.

From the westernmost South Fork lake, the trail ascends westward through thinning timber to Long Lake. After skirting the south shore, the route begins a long, steadily rising traverse that takes you above campsites at the west end of the lake. Views of the lake are photographers' favorites, but save some film for the panoramic shots farther up. This traverse brings you above treeline as the trail skirts a wet area covered with grass, willows, and wildflowers. Where the trail touches the south edge of High Lake, a pause will brace you for the upcoming rocky switchbacks.

The trail soon begins a series of long, gently graded zigzags that climb the cirque wall up to New Army Pass (12,300). The higher you climb up, the better are views east of the lakes immediately below and of the Cottonwood Creek drainage. It's a pleasant if bouldery half-day ramble to and from Cirque Peak from here (views from it are outstanding). Allow a full day to bag the peak if you start from the lakes below the pass.

Descending from New Army Pass into Sequoia National Park, the trail crosses a long, barren slope of coarse granite sand sprinkled with exfoliating granite boulders. A half mile north of the pass our route passes an unmaintained trail (not shown on the topo map) that branches right to Old Army Pass, the original pass built by the Army in the 1890s. Beyond this junction our route swings west and descends steeply over rocky tread to level off on a more gentle descent in a barren cirque. The trail crosses to the north side of the unnamed stream in the cirque and reenters moderate forest cover. About 2 miles from New Army Pass the trail meets a trail to Siberian Outpost—wonderfully barren and wild, with varicolored soils—and Siberian Pass, and there are good campsites on the south side of the stream just south of this junction.

Your route turns right (north), continuing to descend through denser lodgepole pine. When the forest gives way to the open spaces of a lovely meadow, the route fords a little tributary of Rock Creek and turns left on the Rock Creek Trail. This trail descends steeply alongside a willow-lined tributary of

From the vicinity of Cottonwood Pass, looking down Stokes Stringer to Big Whitney Meadow

Rock Creek until the rocky slope gives way to a meadow just above the lake on Rock Creek at 10,440 feet (11.8). Around these meadows you may sight the relatively rare white-tailed jackrabbit. There are fair campsites at the head of this meadow, others are located at the lake's outlet, and more primitive ones are to be found on the south side of the lake. There's also a bear box, usually on the dry "peninsula" on the lake's northwest side.

This marshy-meadowed lake makes a fine base camp for side trips to the rugged Miter Basin and adjoining unnamed Soldier Lakes. A use trail to Miter Basin makes a hard-to-spot exit along the north side of the large, overused campsite just east of our lake's meadow. This trail is easy to follow to the place where Rock Creek cascades out of the basin; from there, it's cross-country, and you can return via the Soldier Lakes. Other fine side trips include a looping cross-country exploration of the Boreal Plateau via Siberian Outpost.

To continue your trip, retrace your steps 1 mile to the meadowed Siberian Pass Trail junction passed earlier. Fill your water bottles here; this is the last reliable water source before Chicken Spring Lake. From the junction this trail ascends southward gently over a moderate-to-densely forested slope of foxtail and lodgepole pine. Our route crosses a barren area, climbs over an easy ridge and, 1 mile south of the last junction and on the upper edge of Siberian Outpost, turns left onto the famous Pacific Crest Trail.

As you ascend through moderate-to-dense lodgepole forest, you enjoy good views west of large, bleak Siberian Outpost and of Mt. Kaweah and the

Great Western Divide. The sandy trail provides soft, sometimes trying under-footing as it exits Sequoia National Park for Golden Trout Wilderness on a ridge west of Cirque Peak, contours above a meadow, and traverses viewful slopes at the headwaters of Golden Trout Creek. You presently switchback east down the wall of Chicken Spring Lake's cirque. When you cross the lake's outlet (often dry by late season), turn upstream to the lake (17.8), where there are good campsites on the east side in foxtail pines, and fair campsites on the west side.

Return down the outlet to the Pacific Crest Trail and turn left (east) to meet the Cottonwood Pass Trail in an easy two-thirds mile. Turn left (east) to Cottonwood Pass (11,200) just a few steps away, offering great views west toward the Great Western Divide, and east toward the Inyo and Panamint ranges. Reluctantly leaving this viewpoint, you zigzag down switchbacks to a lit-tle meadow, then descend more gradually over a couple of quick stream cross-ings. From here, the trail descends gradually eastward in the forested north mar-gin of sizable Horseshoe Meadow, leaving Golden Trout Wilderness a mere 150 yards before the parking lot. From here, close the loop on the road as described under Trailheads.

Variations

Reverse this great trip. Or extend it by camping in or just below Miter Basin.

Permits

This is a quota trailhead, and a permit is required for overnight stays. You'll start and finish in Inyo National Forest wilderness, so contact them in Lone Pine, at the Mt. Whitney Ranger Station, (760) 876-6200, or at their main office in Bishop—873 N. Main St., Bishop, CA 93514, (760) 873-2500—for your permit, or see **www.r5.fs.fed.us/inyo/**. For Sequoia National Park back-country information, call (209) 565-3708 or see **www.nps.gov/seki**.

Build-up/Wind-down tips

Nearest your trailheads, the pleasant town of Lone Pine offers lodgings, restaurants, and stores for the nights before you go in and after you come out (Chamber of Commerce: Box 749, Lone Pine, CA 93545, (760) 876-4444). Get up early to watch dawn's alpenglow on Mt. Whitney's east face—preferably over a hot breakfast at P.J.'s. There are also a number of campgrounds near Lone Pine in addition to one-overnight backpackers' campgrounds at each trailhead.

To find out how Kathy Morey got started hiking the Sierra and the Hawaiian islands and writing about her hikes for Wilderness Press, and for a list of her titles, see "Author Bio & Bib" on page 492.

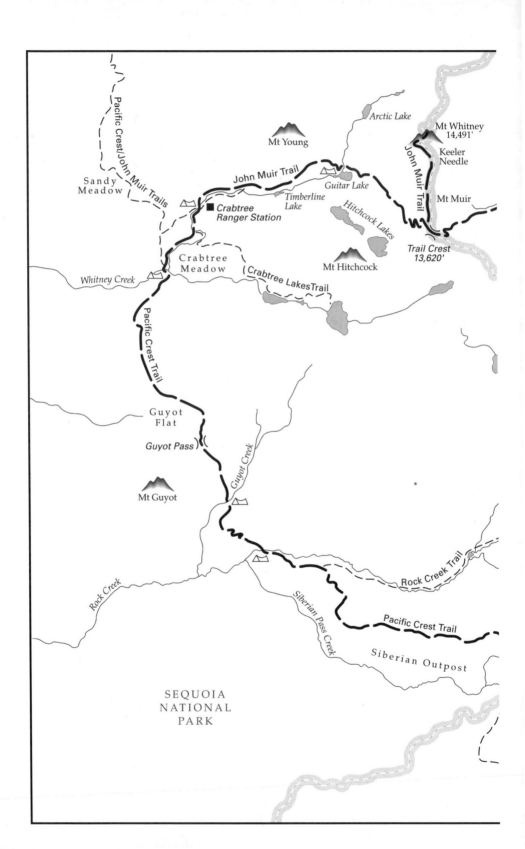

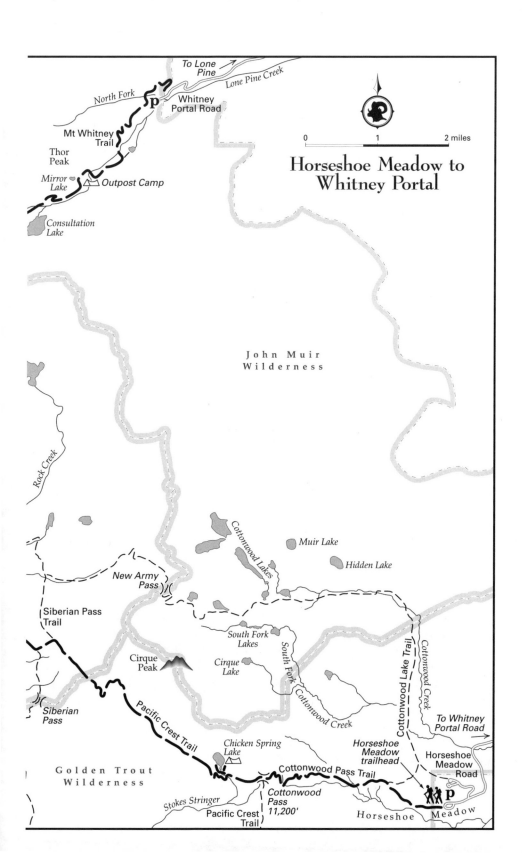

To Lone Pine

Lone Pine Creek

North Fork

P

Whitney Portal Road

Mt Whitney Trail

Thor Peak

Mirror Lake

Outpost Camp

Consultation Lake

Horseshoe Meadow to Whitney Portal

0   1   2 miles

John Muir Wilderness

Rock Creek

Cottonwood Lakes

Muir Lake

Hidden Lake

New Army Pass

Siberian Pass Trail

South Fork Lakes

South Fork Cottonwood Creek

Cottonwood Lake Trail

Cottonwood Creek

Cirque Peak

Cirque Lake

Siberian Pass

Pacific Crest Trail

To Whitney Portal Road

Chicken Spring Lake

Horseshoe Meadow trailhead

Horseshoe Meadow Road

Golden Trout Wilderness

Cottonwood Pass Trail

Stokes Stringer

Cottonwood Pass 11,200'

Pacific Crest Trail

P

Horseshoe   Meadow

28

Horseshoe Meadow to Whitney Portal

—Kathy Morey

Route	Days	Elev. Gain/Loss	Difficulty	Miles
↱	5–7	7407'/8887'	***	36

Campsites: Chicken Spring Lake: 4.5 miles
Lower Rock Creek ford: 14 miles
Crabtree Ranger Station: 21 miles
Outpost Camp: 32.5 miles
(see the Trip Description for others)

Map: USGS 7.5-min *Cirque Peak, Johnson Peak, Mt. Whitney, Mt. Langley*

Best season: Late summer through early fall

Take this trip!

No time for the High Sierra Trail (trip 23)? No problem! This trip combines the splendid scenery of trip 27, "Cottonwood Lakes to Upper Rock Creek," and the last leg—over Mt. Whitney—of the High Sierra Trail to reveal one superb alpine beauty spot or view after another: clear lakes, a splendidly barren basin, forested ridges, rushing streams, and high peaks. Combine that with the opportunity to bag Mt. Whitney from the west, and you've got a real winner.

Trailheads

This point-to-point backpack is an easy shuttle to set up compared to that for the High Sierra Trail, because both trailheads are accessed from Lone Pine. Allow 3–4 hours for the setup.

Put-in trailhead (Horseshoe Meadow): Follow directions for trip 27's Take-out trailhead.

Take-out trailhead (Whitney Portal): Follow directions for trip 23's Take-out trailhead.

TRIP DESCRIPTION

Heads Up! Wood fires are prohibited in several backcountry areas through which this trip passes; plan on using a stove. Know the regulations for Sequoia-Kings Canyon National Park wilderness. In particular, this trip is largely in Sequoia National Park, on whose trails pets are prohibited. Bears are a problem along this route, but many popular campsites, including five of the ones listed above under Campsites, have large steel food lockers popularly called "bear boxes." I'll note the presence of bear boxes at any campsites.

From Horseshoe Meadow trailhead, reverse the description for the last leg of trip 27 as you skirt Horseshoe Meadow, zigzag up to viewful Cottonwood Pass, turn right on the Pacific Crest Trail, and then traverse to Chicken Spring Lake's outlet (and up to the campsites at the lake (4.5), if you're ready to stop for the night). Continue beyond the outlet, into Sequoia National Park, and from there to the junction at the upper edge of Siberian Outpost, where you go left (west), staying on the Pacific Crest Trail.

Your route shortly meets the Siberian Pass Trail. Go right (northwest) to stay on the Pacific Crest Trail, which begins a long, rolling descent along the forested ridge atop the south wall of Rock Creek canyon. Where the trail is close to the right side of the ridge, it is well worth stepping off a few hundred feet right to get excellent views of the peaks surrounding Miter Basin. After 2.5 miles from the junction the trail makes a steep descent toward Siberian Pass Creek but turns north before reaching it. Then it drops via rocky switchbacks through a dense forest down the south wall of Rock Creek canyon. When the underfooting turns to duff, you meet, and turn left (west) onto, the Rock Creek Trail and descend 1 mile down-creek to the overused campsites at the ford of lower Rock Creek (14; with a bear box).

After fording the creek, the trail climbs steeply up the north wall of the canyon, then levels somewhat to the ford of Guyot Creek (with a campsite and the last water for more than 4 miles). The jumbled, symmetrical crest of Mt. Guyot takes up the western skyline, and highly fractured Joe Devel Peak looms east, as the trail begins another steep ascent through a moderate forest cover of lodgepole and foxtail pine. This bouldery climb culminates at a saddle—sometimes called Guyot Pass—from which there are good views north across Kern Canyon to the Kern-Kaweah drainage, and of Red Spur, Kern Ridge, and the

Timberline Lake

Great Western Divide. From the saddle, the trail descends moderately to the large, sandy basin of Guyot Flat, then traverses the forest east of the flat. Like the Chagoopa Plateau west across Kern Canyon, this flat and the subsequent "shelf" traversed later in this hiking day were part of an immense valley floor in preglacial times. However, much of the granular sand deposits are a result of later weathering and erosion of the granite peaks to the east.

Beyond Guyot Flat the trail undulates through a moderate forest cover, bobbing over a pair of sandy ridges, before dropping steeply on very rocky switchbacks into the Whitney Creek drainage. The descent into this drainage affords views eastward to Mt. Whitney—the long, flat-topped, avalanche-chuted mountain that towers over the nearer, granite-spired shoulder of Mt. Hitchcock. This descent concludes over a barren, rocky stretch to lower Crabtree Meadow, where, just beyond a good campsite with a bear box, your route fords Whitney Creek and turns right (east) along its north bank, leaving the Pacific Crest Trail. A half mile of gentle ascent ends at Upper Crabtree Meadow, where the route passes the unmarked Crabtree Lakes Trail. Continuing northeast beside Whitney Creek, the trail ascends gently, fords the creek, passes an unmapped spur trail north to Crabtree Ranger Station, fords the creek again, and climbs a little to meet the John Muir Trail. At the junction with the spur to the ranger station—where emergency services may be available—you'll find an oversized bear box and fair campsites. There are more campsites near the junction with the John Muir Trail.

From the campsites near Crabtree Ranger Station, follow the final leg of trip 23 up Whitney Creek's north bank, past Timberline Lake (closed to camping) and Guitar Lake, and up the west face of Mt. Whitney. Take the side trip to Mt. Whitney's summit, then descend the peak's east face through Trail Camp, past Mirror Lake, and through Outpost Camp to Whitney Portal.

Variations

Start at trip 27's Cottonwood Lakes trailhead and follow that trip's directions through South Fork Lakes and over New Army Pass as far as the lake on upper Rock Creek at 10,440 feet. From there, continue down Rock Creek to lower Rock Creek ford and pick up the rest of this trip's directions from there.

Permits

This is a quota trailhead, and a permit is required for overnight stays. Request a Mt. Whitney Zone stamp with your permit and include the extra fee for that stamp, too. Apply for permits to Inyo National Forest, 873 N. Main Street, Bishop, CA 93514, (760) 873-2500, or see **www.r5.fs.fed.us/inyo/**.

Build-up/Wind-down tips

Refer to this section of trip 27, "Cottonwood Lakes to Upper Rock Creek."

Mt. Whitney Tip

See page 183 [where this is placed in trip 23].

To find out how Kathy Morey got started hiking the Sierra and the Hawaiian islands and writing about her hikes for Wilderness Press, and for a list of her titles, see "Author Bio & Bib" on page 492.

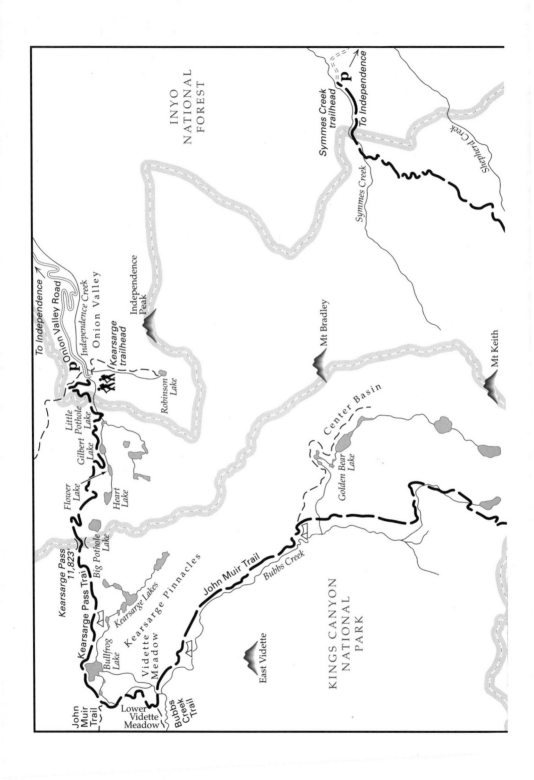

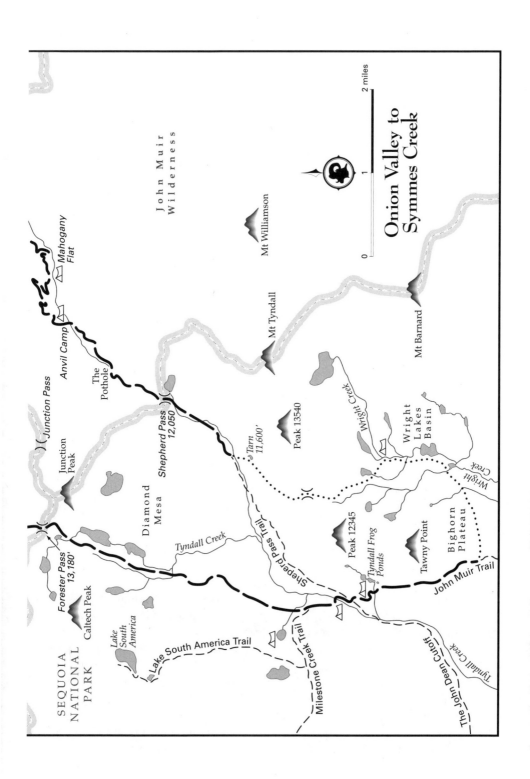

Onion Valley to
Symmes Creek

29

Onion Valley to Symmes Creek

—Kathy Morey

Route	Days	Elev. Gain/Loss	Difficulty	Miles
⌐	8–14	7921'/10,870'	***	40.5

Campsites: Kearsarge Lakes (northernmost): 6.7 miles
above upper Vidette Meadow: 8.5 miles
upper Bubbs Creek: 13.3 miles
lake at 11,400': 21.5 miles
Wright Lakes: 27.5 miles
Anvil Camp: 33 miles
(see the Trip Description for others)

Map: USGS 7.5-min *Kearsarge Peak, Mt. Clarence King, Mt. Brewer, Mt. Williamson*

Best season: Late summer through early fall

Take this trip!

If you love treeline country, this is the trip for you! With most of its length near or above treeline, on this backpack you cover a vast alpine landscape of lofty passes; high basins full of beautiful, icy lakes; remote and rugged peaks on the Sierra crest (so near you may be tempted to bag a few); Spartan but viewful campsites; and mountain panoramas that seem to stretch a hundred miles.

And talk about opportunities for dayhiking on layover days! You'll definitely want some in order to explore farther afield. If you have but one layover day, plan at least one at the 11,400-foot lake on the edge of the remote plateau beneath the Kings-Kern Divide, which holds dozens of lakes and ponds composing the headwaters of the Kern River. Other layover days would let you see Center Basin (lightly visited since it was bypassed by the John Muir Trail), and lovely Wallace and Wales lakes in the drainage just south of Wright Lakes. Part of this route as described is easy to moderate cross-country, but see Variations below if you prefer to stay on trail.

Trailheads

Put-in trailhead (Onion Valley): From US Highway 395 in Independence, turn west on Market Street (Onion Valley Road) and drive 13.3 miles to a circular parking lot serving three trailheads. Yours is the Kearsarge Pass trailhead, the middle one. Onion Valley has toilets, water, and an adjacent campground.

Take-out trailhead (Symmes Creek): Follow the Put-in trailhead directions to go west on Market Street (Onion Valley Road) for 4.5 miles. Turn left on Foothill Road and go 1.3 miles to a fork. Take the right-hand fork and go past an old corral on the left, then immediately cross Symmes Creek. In 0.5 mile take the right fork, and take the right fork again at the next two forks. Then go 0.5 mile more to the trailhead near Symmes Creek. Some of these forks may have small signs, but don't count on it.

TRIP DESCRIPTION

Heads Up! Wood fires are prohibited in several backcountry areas through which this trip passes; plan on using a stove. Know the regulations for John Muir and Sequoia-Kings Canyon National Park wildernesses. In particular, this trip is almost entirely in these parks, on whose trails pets are prohibited. Bears are a problem along this route. If you will spend a night east of the Sierra crest along the Kearsarge Pass Trail in John Muir Wilderness, Inyo National Forest requires you to carry your food in bear-resistant canisters; bear problems have become very severe here, and there are no bear boxes. A canister will give you maximum freedom of choice in camping spots, anyway. In Sequoia and Kings Canyon national parks, several popular campsites, including most of the ones listed above under Campsites, have large steel food lockers popularly called "bear boxes." I'll note the presence of bear boxes at any campsites.

The trail leaves the road a few yards north of the Onion Valley campground and switchbacks up a dry, manzanita-covered slope. Switchbacks always seem to come in bunches, and this ascent is no exception. The first set of switchbacks is relatively open and exposed, offering fine views back onto Onion Valley and south to the heavily diked summit of Independence Peak. After about 0.3 mile there is a short level stretch where one may study the distinctive shapes of the large foxtail pines nearby. Found only at high altitudes in the mountains of California, foxtail pines have distinctive dark, purple cones that take two years to mature. The densely needled (in clusters of five) branches do look like tails and do look inviting to touch—but you'll probably get

229

Little Pothole Lake

sticky fingers if you do. Then the trail enters John Muir Wilderness and switchbacks steadily again, until after a mile it comes close enough to tumbling Independence Creek.

On a more gradual slope, your path crosses many runoff rills in early and mid-season, where a neophyte botanist can identify specimens of Queen Anne's lace, paintbrush, wallflower, tiger lily, columbine, shooting star, and whorled penstemon. At the top of this gentle grade is Little Pothole Lake, not much for camping, but boasting two beautiful, willow-lined cascades pouring into its south and west bays.

After another set of rocky switchbacks, the trail levels off in a slightly ascending groove across glacial moraine and then reaches small, round Gilbert Lake (10,417). Poor-from-overuse campsites dot the shores of this fine swimming lake, and fishing for rainbow and brook trout is good in early season. This small lake absorbs much of the dayhiking impact from people camping at Onion Valley, as does Flower Lake, at the top of the next set of switchbacks. There are many highly used campsites along the north and east sides of this shallow lake (10,531). Bears are very serious problems in this basin.

From Flower Lake the Kearsarge Pass Trail turns north and ascends steeply to a viewpoint overlooking Heart Lake. Now the trail switchbacks up to another overlook—this time the lake is the nearly perfect blue oval of Big Pothole Lake. From the trail high above the water, the lake, with its backgrounding granite finger, is particularly photogenic. Continuing, the trail rises above the trees—except for a few hardy whitebark specimens—and then makes two long-legged traverses across an exposed shaley slope to the low saddle of Kearsarge Pass (11,823). To the west, the impressive view encompasses the Kearsarge Lakes, Bullfrog Lake, and the serrated spires of the Kearsarge Pinnacles.

Entering Kings Canyon National Park on the west side of the pass, your route descends steeply on a loose, rocky traverse high above the basin holding the Kearsarge and Bullfrog lakes. You soon reach a junction with a trail—incorrectly shown on the USGS *Mt. Clarence King* topo—that drops steeply left (south) to the several Kearsarge Lakes. Turn left to the lakes here, where there are many overused campsites with great views of the jagged Kearsarge Pinnacles as well as multiple bear boxes; near the next junction, with the trail that goes west through the Kearsarge-Bullfrog lakes basin, there's usually a map showing bear-box locations at the various lakes where camping is legal. Continue ahead (south) about 0.3 more mile to the northernmost lake (6.7), which is the first reached by this trail, but make your camp at whichever lake pleases you most.

Regain the trail that runs through the Kearsarge-Bullfrog lakes basin and head west on it, presently curving around beautiful Bullfrog Lake (closed to camping) and then dipping southwest past a couple of pretty ponds on its outlet. Beyond these ponds you intersect the John Muir Trail; turn left (south) onto it, and wind steeply down through dense forest, fording Bullfrog Lake's outlet twice, to a junction with the Bubbs Creek Trail at Lower Vidette Meadow (with a bear box). Turn left (east) here below the north face of East Vidette, ford the outlet of Bullfrog Lake for the last time, and begin a gradual to moderate climb along a stretch of Bubbs Creek to hardened campsites (9.5) located at about 9600 feet, above upper Vidette Meadow. Excellent and less crowded camping continues over the next mile up-canyon, and there's a bear box serving campsites around 9900 feet.

The trail ascends steadily yet moderately through a lodgepole-pine forest alongside Bubbs Creek. Take advantage of this short day's hike to explore the creek's smooth granite ledges and irresistible pools. Trees soon get so sparse that you may as well be above treeline, and the views around this pretty basin just get better as you go. In 2.8 miles you pass the Center Basin/Junction Pass Trail going east. Just beyond this junction and below the trail, there's a flat with a bear box and overused campsites. The Center Basin/Junction Pass Trail was part of the old John Muir Trail, which went over Junction Pass before the Forester Pass section was built in 1932. Golden Bear Lake, 1.3 miles and 700 vertical feet up the Center Basin Trail, is one of the gems of the Sierra. However, to be nearer Forester Pass, your hike continues south and uphill another 2 miles to treeline (14.3). A number of campsites have been carved out of the rock among the whitebark pines on the west side of the trail. Just past this point, at the top of the rise where the trail turns due east, there may be exposed, Spartan campsites, and there is a site between the two ponds to the north, at about 11,250 feet.

From your treeline campsite, you climb along a wall with the outflow from Lake 12248 splashing down beside you, and then cross the stream several times. The trail then ascends the west wall of the canyon, reaches the south wall, and switchbacks steeply up to the visible notch of Forester Pass (13,180). As you approach the pass, Junction Peak is a near-perfect pyramid due east of you just 0.3 mile away. Snow may linger on the north side of the pass well into the summer. Views from the pass to the northeast include Mt. Pinchot, University Peak, Mt. Bradley, and Mt. Keith. To the south are Mt. Kaweah, Kaweah Peaks Ridge, Red Spur, Kern Point, and Black Kaweah. Close by, Caltech Peak stands out to the west. Delicate blue-purple sky pilot, denizen of the sky-high country, grows in crevices in the rocks around the pass.

From here, the trail descends into Sequoia National Park on steep switchbacks, some blasted out of the rock. The first 20 feet of descent make you wish the trail builders had made it a little wider. Below you to the south, you can see the two lakes immediately west of Diamond Mesa, a distinctive flat-topped table with sheer sidewalls. These two lakes are set in open granite slabs and sand, and provide a few very Spartan campsites. After you pass them and Diamond Mesa, spectacular views open up of the Tyndall Creek headwaters and Mt. Tyndall in the east. Near treeline, shortly past the outflow of a small lake, you reach the signed junction with Lake South America/Milestone Creek Trail to the west. Turn right (west) at this junction and follow the outflow a lit-

tle north of the trail up to this lake (21.5/11,400), where you will find beautiful camping in the nearby foxtail pines on the north shore. This is the spot for
a layover day to explore the Kern River's headwaters.

Return to the John Muir Trail and turn right to continue southward.
Within a short half mile you cross Tyndall Creek (with campsites and a bear
box on the west bank), pass the junction with the Shepherd Pass Trail going
northeast along the west side of Tawny Point, and pass the junction with the
old trail going south down Tyndall Creek. There's a summer ranger station
about a mile down this old trail, now informally referred to as the John Dean
Cutoff. (Yes, the order in which these junctions occur is incorrectly shown on
the *Mt. Brewer* topo.) Stay on the John Muir Trail at both of these junctions,
soon passing a spur to the little ponds called Tyndall Frog Ponds (with campsites and a bear box).

After passing the steeper slopes of Tawny Point, look for an unmarked trail
eastward that crosses the Bighorn Plateau's margin into the Wright Lakes basin.
(Can't spot the trail? No problem: just stay on the John Muir Trail to its next
low point, where it crosses Wright Creek, and turn northeast into the basin's
huge meadow to follow the creek upstream.) Here you cross a vast meadow,
sloping upward, to reach Wright Lakes, which are tucked under Peak 13540
west of Mt. Versteeg. You will find fair campsites at about 11,200 feet (27.5),
where the outlet stream of Lake 11952 meets the other two outflows draining
the upper basin. Occasional foxtail pines and granite erratics provide wind
shelter for camping. You may hear a coyote pack howl, and you will probably
share the basin with mule deer, for they summer here. A layover day lets you
explore these lakes which—unusual in the Sierra—are set in a vast expanse
rather than hemmed in by mountain walls. Another unforgettable layover day
lets you visit Wallace and Wales lakes in the next drainage south. Peak-baggers
should note that this basin is a good place from which to climb some worthy
peaks, including 14,018-foot Mt. Tyndall, 13,470-foot Mt. Versteeg, and
13,990-foot Mt. Barnard, all reportedly having at least a Class 2 route (meaning a trailless but rather easy walk-up route, possibly with some straightforward
boulderhopping) in addition to more difficult ones.

When you're ready to leave Wright Lakes, walk northwest cross-country
toward the northwesternmost lakelet shown on the topo map. An obvious
angler's trail works up the northeast wall of the western shoulder of Peak
13540. The saddle between Peak 13540 and Peak 12345 is visible for your
entire ascent. The panoramic view from this saddle includes the noble series of
summits of the Great Western Divide—Junction Peak; Mts. Keith, Brewer,
Kaweah, Guyot, and Young—and the top of Mt. Whitney, as well as the Kern
River Trench. From the saddle, head straight down; it does not help to try to
contour northeastward. Only when you have left very steep terrain should you
begin to contour northeastward, planning to meet the Shepherd Pass Trail near
the tarn shown at 11,600 feet on the topo map. Beyond the tarn this trail

ascends gently yet steadily toward Shepherd Pass. The lake just a few feet before the pass has several chilly, windy campsites: this lake is often half frozen even in midsummer. At Shepherd Pass (12,050) views of the Great Western Divide spread out behind you; and before you—8000 feet below—you can see Owens Valley.

The trail down the first 500 feet of Class 3 talus though periodically rebuilt deteriorates rapidly. Often this north-facing slope is covered by a snowfield well into summer, so that you descend a ladder of snow pockets rather than unstable talus. When the steepest part of the descent ends, the trail continues through a jumble of huge boulders. Just below treeline you reach The Pothole and pass a trail going northwest to Junction Pass (see above). In another mile, descending over rough, rocky trail, you cross Shepherd Creek for the first time, and in the welcome foxtail-forest cover you reach good campsites at Anvil Camp (34), on either side of the creek. No wood fires are permitted.

Leaving Anvil Camp, you descend on good trail through talus. Abruptly, the foxtails end and you begin a long series of gentle switchbacks down through eastside terrain—mountain mahogany, sage, and other plants of dry slopes—to Mahogany Flat. There are several campsites here, and water if you leave the trail and descend to the creek. Continuing your switchbacking descent, you cross the only year-round creek between Mahogany Flat and Symmes Creek. You then pass the burned remaining stubs that were once a mountain mahogany "forest" of very large shrubs. A final stream crossing at 8700 feet (often dry by midsummer) marks the beginning of a discouraging 500-foot ascent. The first steep section of climbing gets you to a small ridge; there is a dry campsite with views that make up for the absence of water. Shepherd Creek has carved a steep canyon to the south, capped by towering Mt. Williamson, the only 14,000-foot Sierra peak not on the crestline.

The trail then traverses from Shepherd Creek Canyon to the Symmes Creek watershed by crossing two small ridges, continuing to ascend over slopes so steep they seem to exceed the angle of repose. Frequent rockslides take out sections of this trail. You reach a final welcome but waterless saddle with ample campsites among the trees. From this saddle the trail descends, moderately steeply, through western white pine and red fir on innumerable switchbacks 2240 feet to Symmes Creek, the first water since Shepherd Creek. You ford Symmes Creek four times as the steep canyon narrows—easy in a dry year or in late summer, but sure to wet your feet and threaten your footing the rest of the time. Between crossings, the trail is overgrown by alders, willows, creamberry bushes, and cottonwoods. A scant quarter mile after the last crossing, the stock trail leaves to your left, and you continue another half mile to the Symmes Creek trailhead.

Variations

You can reverse this trip if you are in top shape, but the Shepherd Pass Trail is notorious as one of the toughest trails over the Sierra crest. Also, if you don't want to tackle the cross-country leg through Wright Lakes and would prefer to stay on trail, cut the trip a little short by taking the Shepherd Pass Trail at the junction near Tyndall Creek.

Permits

This is a quota trailhead, and a permit is required for overnight stays. Apply for permits to Inyo National Forest, 873 N. Main Street, Bishop, CA 93514, (760) 873-2500, **www.r5.fs.fed.us/inyo/**.

Build-up/Wind-down tips

Independence is the town nearest these trailheads. Contact the Lone Pine Chamber of Commerce, which handles Independence, too, for more information, at Box 749, Lone Pine, CA 93545, (760) 876-4444. When staying in Independence, I'm partial to the Winnedumah Hotel, a bed-and-breakfast in what was built in the 1920s as the Owens Valley's first high-class lodging. If Independence is booked solid, Lone Pine, with more rooms and restaurants, is only about 15 miles south.

To find out how Kathy Morey got started hiking the Sierra and the Hawaiian islands and writing about her hikes for Wilderness Press, and for a list of her titles, see "Author Bio & Bib" on page 492.

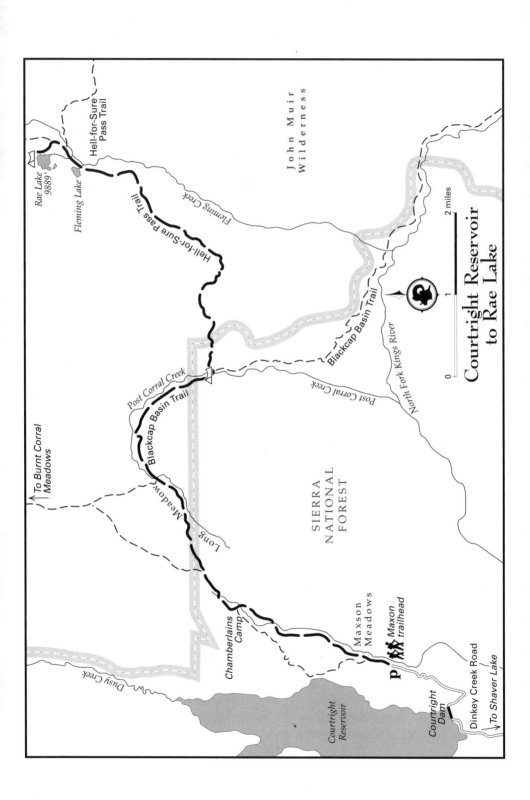

Courtright Reservoir to Rae Lake

Rae Lake 9889'

Fleming Lake

Hell-for-Sure Pass Trail

Hell-for-Sure Pass Trail

Fleming Creek

J o h n   M u i r
W i l d e r n e s s

Post Corral Creek

Blackcap Basin Trail

Blackcap Basin Trail

To Burnt Corral
Meadows

Long Meadow

Post Corral Creek

North Fork Kings River

Dusy Creek

Chamberlains Camp

SIERRA
NATIONAL
FOREST

Maxson Meadows

Maxson trailhead

P

Courtright Reservoir

Courtright Dam

Dinkey Creek Road

To Shaver Lake

0   1   2 miles

30

Courtright Reservoir to Rae Lake

—Jason Winnett

Route	Days	Elev. Gain/Loss	Difficulty	Miles
⌇	3	3455'/3455'	**	26

Campsites: Post Corral Creek ford: 7.0 miles
Rae Lake (north side): 13 miles

Map: USGS 7.5-min *Courtright Reservoir, Ward Mtn.,*
Blackcap Mtn., Mt. Henry

Best season: Summer to early fall

Take this trip!

There is a lot of wilderness to the west of Kings Canyon National Park. The North Fork Kings River was not granted National Park status because this drainage was coveted by the logging and grazing industries. And for good reason: the lower elevations contain cathedral forests of towering conifers while the higher elevations support a vast wonderland of subalpine meadows. Most of this area is now within the John Muir Wilderness where logging is prohibited and grazing has been reduced. This beautiful trip passes through some of these meadowy flower gardens, and Rae Lake provides easy access to many out-of-the-way lake basins west of the LeConte Divide.

Trailhead

Courtright Reservoir (8200). Go northeast 42 miles from Clovis (near Fresno) on State Highway 168 and in Shaver Lake turn right onto Dinkey Creek Road. Follow this 26 miles to the Courtright/Wishon Y. Courtright Reservoir is 7½ miles north. From the junction above the reservoir, cross the dam, and in ⅔ mile the road ends at a paved parking lot signed MAXSON TRAILHEAD.

TRIP DESCRIPTION

Heads Up! The drive is fairly long from either San Francisco or Los Angeles, about 6–7 hours, including a stop for Wilderness Permits. Early season travelers should weigh both the prevalence of mosquitos and a possible wet ford of Post Corral Creek. Because this area is popular with deer hunters, you may want to check when the season is (it varies from year to year); midweek is better than weekends for avoiding hunting activity.

From the west side of the Maxson trailhead parking lot our trail descends northeast along with the Duty Ershim OHV Route. Soon the 4WD road levels off and begins a gentle ascent under a moderate cover of lodgepole pine. After 1 mile the road forks left at a sign declaring that motor vehicles are not allowed. Our trail goes right and soon we pass another welcome sign announcing our arrival into designated wilderness.

Our shaded trail now ascends moderately along the west side of a flower-lined creek before fording it at the foot of Maxson Meadows. Staying east of the meadows we pass Chamberlains Camp before climbing 500 feet to a signed Y-junction with the trail to Burnt Corral Meadows. Here, we turn right, cross a small seasonal creek, and descend to the head of aptly named Long Meadow. For most of a mile the sandy trail winds east along the margins of the nearly level meadow before passing another trail going left toward Burnt Corral Meadows. Just beyond it, we boulderhop the small creek and enter denser forest cover. Soon our route begins the gentle descent to the meadowy environs of Post Corral Creek. Nearing the meadows we pass a faint trail leading across the creek to a small cabin owned by the party that leases grazing rights from the Forest Service. Coming at a much lower cost than those on private land, these cattle-grazing allotments effectively provide a welfare system for those privileged enough to get a lease.

It's another mile to the ford of Post Corral Creek but you may prefer to avoid the sometimes busy campsites there by finding secluded campsites this side of the ford, between the trail and the creek on your left. The nearby meadowy areas boast a variety of wildflowers in season, such as Indian paintbrush, meadow rue, streamside columbine, marsh marigolds, and bright-orange tiger lilies. Birdlife is also to be found including grouse, robins, and small, black and white, dark-eyed juncos, which flit about looking for insects. Higher up the food chain, goshawks, Cooper's hawks, and sharp-shinned hawks prey upon these smaller birds. A sudden blur and a burst of feathers floating to the ground may be all you see of these fast and powerful raptors. In the creek the most common predator is the eastern brook trout, which is known to mistake hook-concealing imitations for the living insects. Larger, native land animals include a gentle vegetarian, the deer. Aside from humans, the other large omnivore in these parts is the black bear, so store your food accordingly.

Just east of the ford of Post Corral Creek (may be wet in early season) our route leaves the Blackcap Basin Trail and turns left onto the Hell-for-Sure Pass Trail. At first the ascent is shaded and moderate, but in less than a mile the grade steepens as it ascends the ridge separating Post Corral Creek from Fleming Creek. The trail crosses several sections of granite slabs that have been dynamited to provide traction for the steel-shoed feet of horses.

As we near the ridgetop, the trail crosses a small, forested flat and then switchbacks the last few hundred feet before leveling off and turning northeast. After 1½ miles of rolling ascent we turn north and climb steep, rocky switchbacks that lead to the meadows surrounding small Fleming Lake. Now the landscape takes on a more subalpine character with the meadow species of plants tending to grow a little lower to the ground. Soon after crossing the outlet of Fleming Lake we turn left off of the Hell-for-Sure Pass Trail and climb to a shaded hillside junction with the spur trail going left to Rae Lake. In another ¼ mile we arrive at meadow-fringed Rae Lake (9889). There are excellent campsites among the trees on the north side of the lake.

Fishing is good for brook trout (to 12″) at Rae Lake. Unlike true members of the trout family, eastern brook trout need no running water to spawn, so they thrive at Rae Lake with its minimal inlet and outlet streams. This medium-sized lake used to be called Wolverine Lake, presumably because someone once saw one of these rare and solitary creatures here. Built more like a beaver-sized bear, the largest and least seen of the weasel family has exceptional strength and endurance and is known to be extraordinarily ferocious. Whether taking down animals a big as deer or just appropriating old carrion, these creatures have reputably defended their claim against lions and bears 5–10 times their size. When your allotted time at Rae Lake is over, retrace your route to the trailhead.

Permits

Wilderness Permits can be reserved between March 1 and August 15 by writing to:

Sierra National Forest
Pine Ridge Ranger District
Box 559
Prather, CA 93651
(559) 855-5360

Include your name, address, day phone, number of people, entry and exit trailhead (Maxon), approximate itinerary (with alternate dates), and $3 per person (nonrefundable) payable to USFS. Note, also, that 33% of the permits are issued on a first-come, first-served basis on the day of, or day before, your departure. From 8 A.M. to 5 P.M., seven days a week, you can get permits at Pine Ridge Ranger Station (29688 Auberry Rd., at the junction of Highway 168 in the little town of Prather, on your way). During the summer, permits may also be available at Dinkey Creek Ranger Station, located a short distance upstream from where Dinkey Creek Road turns right to cross Dinkey Creek. You can contact Sierra National Forest on the Internet at **www.r5.fs.fed.us/sierra/**.

Build-up/Wind-down tips

Between Dinkey Creek and the Courtright/Wishon Y is the McKinley Grove of giant sequoias. Right alongside the road, it makes a nice place to stretch and relax after a hot trip through the valley. And, it's not every day that you get to sit by the largest living things on the planet.

Long a coauthor with his father of our earliest hiking guidebooks for the Sierra, Jason Winnett continues to glean spiritual gifts there, as our "Author Bio & Bib" on page 492 makes clear.

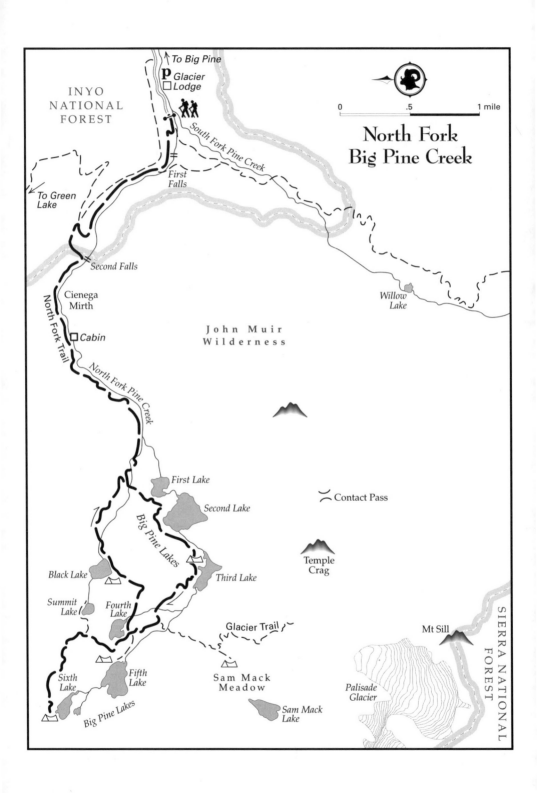

North Fork
Big Pine Creek

INYO
NATIONAL
FOREST

To Big Pine

P Glacier
Lodge

South Fork Pine Creek

First
Falls

To Green
Lake

Second Falls

Cienega
Mirth

North Fork Trail

☐ Cabin

North Fork Pine Creek

John Muir
Wilderness

Willow
Lake

First Lake

Second Lake

Contact Pass

Big Pine Lakes

Temple
Crag

Black Lake

Third Lake

Summit
Lake

Fourth
Lake

Glacier Trail

Mt Sill

Sixth
Lake

Fifth
Lake

Sam Mack
Meadow

SIERRA NATIONAL FOREST

Palisade
Glacier

Big Pine Lakes

Sam Mack
Lake

0   .5   1 mile

31

North Fork Big Pine Creek

—Andy Selters

Route	Days	Elev. Gain/Loss	Difficulty	Miles
♀	3	3600'/3600'	***	16.0

Campsites: Third Lake: 5.5 miles
Fifth Lake: 6.9 miles
Sixth Lake: 8.2 miles
(see the Trip Description for others)

Map: USGS 7.5-min *Coyote Flat, Split Mtn., North Palisade*

Best season: Late summer through early fall

Take this trip!

At the head of Big Pine Creek soars the longest spine of 13–14,000-foot peaks in the lower 48 states, the legendary Palisades. At every turn the North Fork Trail reveals new perspectives on these splintery crests, all while touring past nine inviting lakes. The largest glaciers in the Sierra gather in benches below the peaks, completing the setting for an alpine tableau unmatched in California.

Trailhead

From the center of Big Pine on US 395, the road west up Big Pine Creek begins as Crocker Street, and is signed for Glacier Lodge. Just out of town the road climbs steeply into Big Pine Creek's canyon. Once in the forest zone it passes a couple of Forest Service campgrounds, and ends at the trailhead 11.6 miles from 395. Dayhikers can park here at the roadend if there is space, but overnight hikers must leave their cars 0.6 mile below the trailhead in the large lot provided.

TRIP DESCRIPTION

> **Heads Up!** Because this trail's quota often fills up early in summer, for weekends especially apply for an advance reservation (see Permits below). Campfires are prohibited above 10,000 feet in this area, which includes all campsites on this trail; use a stove.

Our hike starts behind the locked gate at the roadend, beside rushing Big Pine Creek and below some private summer cabins. Walk past the cabins and follow trail signs pointing uphill past a couple of access paths, then climb a pair of short switchbacks. The second takes you across a bridge over the North Fork, right below crashing First Falls. Beyond the streamside birches you come to where the trail up Big Pine Creek's south fork continues traversing, and where you resume switchbacking uphill. Already the first great mountain vista appears above the South Fork canyon, with Middle Palisade poking over a ridge, and the "Twilight Pillar," the north buttress, which prominently shadows the canyon at twilight, of Norman Clyde Peak dominating the skyline.

In the shade of Jeffrey pines and aspens, we climb to a bench, an old roadbed. Hikers once drove this road to a high trailhead below Second Falls. But in September 1982 a tropical storm drenched this canyon with an estimated 6 inches of rainfall in one night, flooding out the road below First Falls. Just up-canyon along this path another bridge takes us back across the creek, and on the other side we see a picnic site, a former campground. Here we turn up-canyon on sandy footing and leave the shade of cottonwoods and Jeffreys. In midsummer, an early start makes the ensuing stretch of sunny climbing more pleasant.

With a couple of gentle switchbacks we turn uphill among manzanita and tobacco brush, and then our trail angles up to a triple intersection. Here the route to Green Lake continues east-southeast up this moraine; the stock trail from below Glacier Lodge arrives here from the southeast; our trail cuts back and continues climbing west toward Second Falls. With a last uphill chug we round the steep corner near the falls, and then regain forest cover next to the churning creek.

Our trail now passes through an aspen grove and the sylvan flats known as Cienega Mirth. On our left we reach a cabin built as a summer retreat by actor Lon Chaney in the 1920s. The Forest Service has since taken over the cabin, and now uses it to house their wilderness ranger. Beyond here you have easy walking through some moist glades rich in shooting star, tiger lily, and columbine. With a couple of slight rises we reach a dry meadow and our first view of some towering ramparts ahead—the flying buttresses of Temple Crag. Although this citadel stands below the Sierra crest and doesn't quite reach 13,000 feet, its Gothic battlements are the most impressive in the area. As we climb a bit more the tip of the region's highest peak also comes into view, the North Palisade.

Next we hop across a tributary, swerve around a rise, then re-ford the tributary, and regain forest cover. Here we encounter another trail, the path descending from Black Lake, which will be the return leg of our loop. Keep left and again cross the stream we've been following to resume a steady but gentle, winding climb, under lodgepole pines and past outcrops, to a slope above First Lake. A bit farther southwest we pass a couple of woodsy campsites and ascend through a granite portal to an overlook of Second Lake, the largest in the group. Here and at Third Lake, Temple Crag really dominates the terrain.

The trail continues rising gradually past shady cliffs to Third Lake. Small campsites on the north, east, and south rim of this lake's basin probably get more use than any others in the area. Whether you camp or rest here, the grand view includes a couple of interesting features. In summer Third Lake has a milky-aqua hue, the result of water rich in superfine silt, rock ground to a fine powder by the Palisade Glacier out of sight above. Another curiosity here is the contrast between Temple Crag's dark granodiorite, studded with inclusions, and the blond granite of the massive hill just east of it. The notch between them— where the two distinct rock types meet—is known as Contact Pass. The darker rock of the Palisades is part of an older pluton, and millions of years ago the lighter-toned granite intruded around it.

From Third Lake we curve north and weave up a few short switchbacks, then head to a small meadow and a crossing of a freshet issuing from Fourth Lake. Just beyond this ford the Glacier Trail forks southwest. For those ready to hike high and hard, this trail takes you up to the foot of the Palisades (see description below). Our North Fork Trail curves north and gently climbs to a three-way junction. The left pathway rounds a ridge to Fifth Lake, where fine campsites, decent fishing, and more great panoramas await, just 0.2 mile away. The right fork is the trail to Black Lake, the return leg to the trailhead. For now hike straight ahead and wind past campsites near the west shore of Fourth Lake. This is the lake with the most woodsy view, good for anyone ready for a break from the stimulation of awesome peaks. Just beyond Fourth Lake, the trail comes to another fork.

The left branch here is the direct, unmaintained and unsigned path to Sixth Lake. It heads up along a swale and makes a couple small switchbacks to reach a spur overlooking Fifth Lake. A sign there indicates this route is just a footworn, rocky path, heading northwest up and around a knob and then a short distance to Sixth Lake.

Back at the fork, we take the right branch northeast and quickly meet the canyon's final junction, with the 0.2-mile spur to tiny Summit Lake. Keep left on the signed horse path for Sixth Lake, climbing gently toward treeline on the west side of a small meadow. Near the base of the long rock slope ahead we veer west over a spur, then gain a final 250 feet to the ridge above Sixth Lake. This highest section of rough trail through spindly whitebark pines gives us some of the best panoramas of the Palisades, in a sense more spectacular than the closer view from the top of the Glacier Trail. From the ridgetop a brief rocky descent completes the North Fork Trail near the north shore of Sixth Lake. Seventh Lake lies at treeline, a short walk west. The best camping near these highest lakes is on the low rise between them.

Sixth and Seventh lakes are sites where the California Department of Fish & Game is attempting to reestablish the mountain yellow-legged frog. In recent years biologists have found that this frog, once common in most of the higher Sierra lakes, has become fairly rare. The primary reason for their decline has been the widespread introduction of trout, which eat the tadpoles. Starting in 1999, Fish & Game has netted out the alien trout, with the expectation that the frogs will recolonize the lakes from tiny adjacent ponds where a few have hung on. Failure to fully involve the public in this decision has upset some, but most people—including many anglers—are happy to see native fauna returned to some high lakes where fishing was never particularly good.

For the return loop, hike back down to the wooded intersection near the southwest shore of Fourth Lake, at the Fifth Lake turnoff. Take the eastbound trail here to cross Fourth Lake's outlet. Next you'll climb slightly around a ridge, and then descend northeast to Black Lake. Although less popular, this lake makes an excellent base, as fine campsites await above the trail here, deep water may offer the best fishing in the area, and a short scramble up the slope north of the lake presents a view as grand as any in this basin.

East from Black Lake the trail continues descending, crossing the outlet stream and then breaking out of the lodgepole forest to another Palisade panorama. Next, stair-step down some long switchbacks across open slopes of sagebrush, mountain mahogany, and whitebark and lodgepole pine (which would be hot slopes to climb on a midsummer afternoon). The descent takes you to the former junction with the North Fork Trail, 4.4 miles from the trailhead.

Variations (Glacier Trail Spur)

This difficult path climbs nearly 2000 feet within a steep couple of miles, but for anyone who thrills at the highest peaks of the High Sierra this is a necessary pilgrimage. From the North Fork Trail 1.0 mile northwest of Third Lake, the Glacier Trail descends southwest to cross the main creek and then begins a steep, rocky climb. After quickly gaining about 600 feet the grade eases at Sam Mack Meadow, a treeline hollow with several campsites. From here the rough path climbs steeply east in tight switchbacks up the adjacent ridge. Once atop this ridgeline, you should be able to trace a route southwest through the krummholz and barren rocks along its crest. To get the awe-inspiring view you're seeking, continue another half mile along this low spine up to nearly 12,500 feet, where you're ensconced in the Sierra's most alpine amphitheater

—the cirque of the Palisade Glacier. Reigning centrally over you is the third highest peak in California, North Palisade with its icy couloirs, proud buttresses, and distinctive, high snowfield. To the left juts the big thumb of Mt. Sill, and to the right splintery crests extend through Starlight and Thunderbolt peaks. The Palisade Glacier fans out below you. After taking it in, retrace your steps to the North Fork Trail.

Permits

All overnight travelers on this trail must have a permit. Sixty percent of the 24 daily permits are issued by reservation, and forty percent on a first come, first served basis. Because this trail is quite popular, summer weekend backpackers (with a quota in effect from the last Friday in June through September 15) should apply for permit reservations well in advance. Inyo National Forest accepts reservations beginning March 1 or three weeks before the trip date, and each reservation costs $5 per person. Your reservation will be confirmed with a letter, which you must redeem for the permit at the ranger station some time before 10 A.M. on the day of your trip. Obtain reservation forms from: Wilderness Reservations, White Mountain Ranger Station, 798 N. Main St, Bishop, CA 93514, or call (760) 873-2500. You can fax a reservation form to (760) 873-2484, or go online at **www.r5.fs.fed.us/inyo/**. The (free) first come, first served permits will be available at the White Mountain Station starting at noon the day before entry.

Build-up/Wind-down tips

Wilson's Eastside Sports in Bishop (12 miles north of Big Pine) is well stocked with gear for the backpacker and climber, and their staff has experience and knowledge not usually found in urban-based stores. Anyone interested in climbing the Palisades might want to hire a guide through the Sierra Mountain Center, also in Bishop.

For those coming from sea level, a night before the trip spent at 7500 feet in one of the campgrounds in Big Pine Creek canyon can provide some acclimatization to the relatively high altitudes, and make for easier, more enjoyable hiking. Glacier Lodge, a fine old inn and restaurant, stood for many years right across the canyon from the trailhead, where the famous mountaineer Norman Clyde once worked as its winter caretaker. But in the spring of 1999 the lodge burned down. At this writing some small cabins there are available for rent, and the owners hope to rebuild the lodge before the 2001 season.

From an L.A. childhood Andy Selters's route to custodian of the Sierra Club's Mt. Shasta hut, to a career leading treks and climbs from Alaska to Nepal, and writing about some of them for Wilderness Press, is briefly described in "Author Bio & Bib" on page 492.

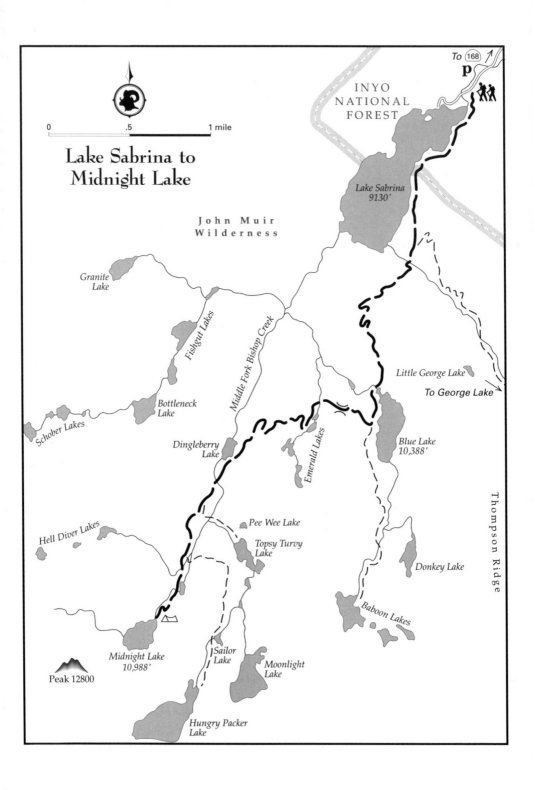

Lake Sabrina to
Midnight Lake

INYO
NATIONAL
FOREST

To (168)
P

Lake Sabrina
9130'

John Muir
Wilderness

Granite
Lake

Fishgut Lakes

Middle Fork Bishop Creek

Little George Lake

To George Lake

Schober Lakes

Bottleneck
Lake

Dingleberry
Lake

Emerald Lakes

Blue Lake
10,388'

Hell Diver Lakes

Pee Wee Lake

Topsy Turvy
Lake

Donkey Lake

Thompson Ridge

Baboon Lakes

Midnight Lake
10,988'

Sailor
Lake

Moonlight
Lake

Peak 12800

Hungry Packer
Lake

0   .5   1 mile

32

Lake Sabrina to Midnight Lake

—Jason Winnett

Route	Days	Elev. Gain/Loss	Difficulty	Miles
↰	3	2620'/2620'	**	11.5

Campsites: Midnight Lake: 5.75 miles
(see the Trip Description for others)

Map: USGS 7.5-min *Mt. Thompson, Mt. Darwin*

Best season: Late summer through early fall

Take this trip!

This trip offers unusually quick and easy access to some of the most spectacular alpine wilderness in California. A cluster of striking granite peaks surround the headwaters of Middle Fork Bishop Creek, with glacier-clad Mt. Darwin topping the bunch at 13,830 feet. With many beautiful, trout-filled lakes in this superlative landscape, it is easy to find sweet, out-of-the-way spots.

Trailhead

Lake Sabrina (9130). Go 18 miles southwest from Bishop on State Highway 168 to the backpackers' parking area below the lake, at the North Lake turnoff.

TRIP DESCRIPTION

From the designated backpackers' parking area below Lake Sabrina, your route follows the road ½ mile up to the trailhead, which is about 100 yards below the Sabrina Dam on the left. The well-used trail, signed SABRINA BASIN TRAIL and BLUE LAKE TRAIL, climbs around the dam and begins a long traverse of the slope above deep blue Lake Sabrina. You cross lush greenery and small streams initially, but soon the hillside becomes dry with a sparse forest of aspen, juniper, Jeffrey, lodgepole, and western white pine, and mountain mahogany. In this landscape fewer trees permit awesome views, and the tall peaks to the west beckon us onward. About halfway around the lake the trail begins climbing steadily, and at 1.5 miles passes the trail branching left to George Lake. Just beyond this junction, our route crosses the splashing outlet from George Lake, where we find our first reliable water and shade since the north end of Lake Sabrina.

From here the trail switchbacks up through lodgepole pine, crosses a small stream, and swings south over a ridge. Continuing up a ravine, our route soon overlooks picturesque Blue Lake (10,388). A short descent past overused campsites leads to the outlet where the views are classic, with rugged Thompson Ridge reclining above clear Blue Lake.

After you rockhop the outlet, the trail winds through granite outcrops along the lake's west side. About halfway along the lake there is a trail junction where going straight would lead to Baboon Lakes (a fabulous hike of its own). Our route turns right toward Dingleberry Lake. Heading northwest, the trail tops a low saddle and crosses a steep, rocky slope on granite ledges. On this northern exposure snow can linger into summer, so use extreme caution crossing any steep snowbanks: they can appear deceptively easy, masking obstacles below, especially rocks. Turning southwest our route soon crosses the outlet from Emerald Lakes. Although small, these lakes are indeed gems. From here, a short climb brings us to the ridge east of Dingleberry Lake. An easy descent then takes us to the swampy south side of the lake, a haven for mosquitoes.

Staying with the main trail to Midnight Lake we cross the Middle Fork Bishop Creek and continue southwest, passing an unsigned spur trail that goes left to Topsy Turvy Lake. A few switchbacks then lead us to the signed junction with the trail to Hungry Packer Lake on the left. Soon thereafter we ford the outlet from Hell Diver and Blue Heaven lakes. As the canyon walls rise on either side we pass a tarn and climb granite terraces to arrive at Midnight Lake (10,988). Rising above the west shore of the lake is Peak 12800+, and behind it the massive east face of Mt. Darwin towers 13,830 feet into the sky. In this pristine environment you'll enjoy the kind of priceless slumber that comes only from climbing high into the mountains. Excellent campsites can be found from the tarn to the lake's outlet. After a recommended day exploring the environs at Midnight Lake, retrace your route to the trailhead.

Permits

Wilderness Permits can be reserved from March 1 to August 15 by writing to:

Inyo National Forest
798 N. Main St.
Bishop, CA 93514
(760) 873-2500

Include your name, address, day phone, number of people, entry and exit trailhead (Lake Sabrina), itinerary (with alternate dates), and $3 per person (nonrefundable) payable to USFS. Note, also, that 40% of the permits are issued on a first-come, first-served basis on the day of, or day before, your departure at the White Mountain Ranger Station (see above address), 8 A.M. to 5 P.M. seven days a week. If you are coming down Highway 395 from the north, you can get permits at the Mono Basin National Forest Scenic Area Visitors Center (0.5 mile north of Lee Vining), or at the Mammoth Ranger Station (just before the town of Mammoth Lakes, 3 miles west of Hwy. 395). You can contact Inyo National Forest on the Internet at **www.r5.fs.fed.us/Inyo/**.

Build-up/Wind-down tips

Because this trip takes you to 11,000 feet on your first day out, if you are coming from a low-elevation locale I recommend you acclimatize by spending at least the night before at 9200 feet, camping 2 miles farther up Highway 168 at North Lake. If you are heading north after the trip, consider stopping at Hot Creek State Park in Long Valley, southeast of Mammoth. Here you will find a geologic wonder where hot springs well up into a wide pool in the river, providing an unusual setting for a gratifying soak.

Long a coauthor with his father of our earliest hiking guidebooks for the Sierra, Jason Winnett continues to glean spiritual gifts there, as our "Author Bio & Bib" on page 492 makes clear.

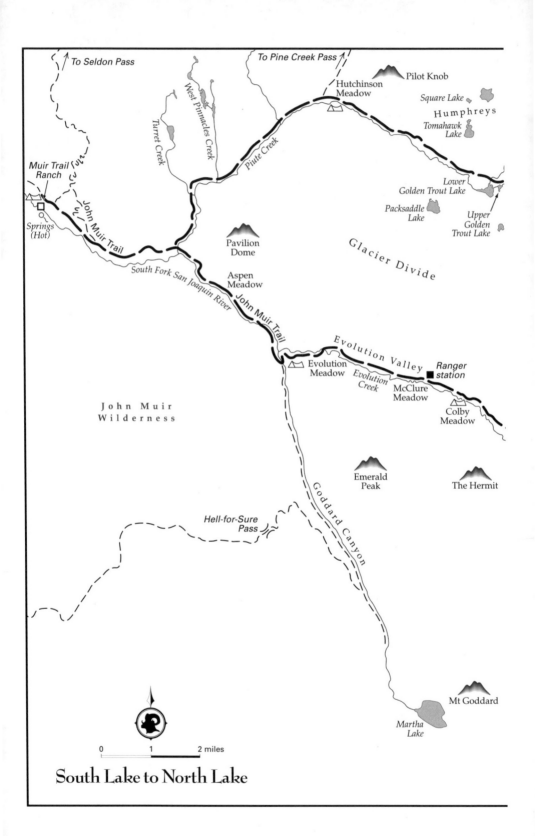

To Seldon Pass

To Pine Creek Pass

Pilot Knob

Hutchinson
Meadow

Square Lake

Humphreys

West Pinnacles Creek

Turret Creek

Piute Creek

*Tomahawk
Lake*

Muir Trail
Ranch

Springs
(Hot)

John Muir Trail

*Lower
Golden Trout Lake*

*Packsaddle
Lake*

*Upper
Golden
Trout Lake*

Pavilion
Dome

Glacier Divide

South Fork San Joaquin River

Aspen
Meadow

John Muir Trail

Evolution Valley

Ranger
station

Evolution
Meadow

*Evolution
Creek*

McClure
Meadow

Colby
Meadow

**John Muir
Wilderness**

Emerald
Peak

The Hermit

Goddard Canyon

Hell-for-Sure
Pass

Mt Goddard

*Martha
Lake*

0   1   2 miles

South Lake to North Lake

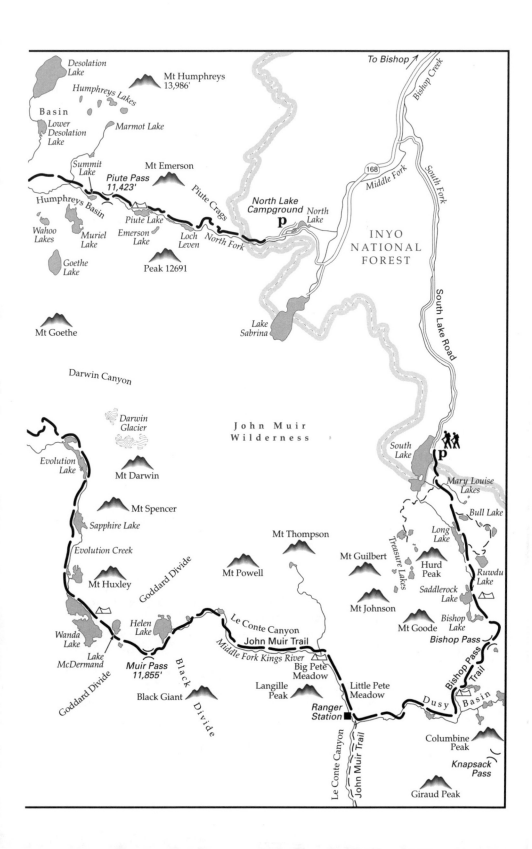

33

South Lake to North Lake

—Kathy Morey

Route	Days	Elev. Gain/Loss	Difficulty	Miles
↱	5–7	8923'/9401'	****	60.5

Campsites: northernmost large lake in Dusy Basin: 7 miles
Big Pete Meadow: 13 miles
Wanda Lake: 21.5 miles
Colby Meadow: 28 miles
Blayney Hot Springs: 40.5 miles
Hutchinson Meadow: 49 miles
Piute Lake: 57 miles
(see the Trip Description for others)

Map: USGS 7.5-min *Mt. Thompson, North Palisade, Mt. Goddard, Mt. Henry, Mt. Hilgard, Mt. Darwin.* (Also have the *Mt. Tom* topo if you plan to camp afield and dayhike in Humphreys Basin.)

Best season: Late summer through early fall

Take this trip!

This is one of the great classic trips of the Sierra, visiting some of the range's most beautiful features: three superb alpine lakes basins, Dusy, Evolution, and Humphreys; three magnificent Sierra canyons, Le Conte Canyon, Evolution Valley, and lower Goddard Canyon; one of the Sierra's few backcountry hot springs, Blayney Hot Spring; and two magnificent creek-and-lake drainages, South Fork Bishop Creek and North Fork Bishop Creek. Even though the route is heavily traveled—much of it is on the John Muir Trail—the country through which it passes is vast, and you'll find alpine solitude if you want it, look for it, and perhaps walk a little off-trail for it. Did I mention the fabulous dayhiking available at many places along this trip? More on that in the Trip Description!

Trailheads

Put-in trailhead (South Lake): From US Highway 395 in Bishop, head southwest on State Route 168 (West Line St.) for 15.5 miles to a junction with South Lake Road. Turn left and drive 7 more miles to the backpackers' parking at South Lake (where there's a toilet). If you're taking this trip as described, leave a second car, or arrange a pickup, at the Take-out trailhead.

Take-out trailhead (North Lake): Follow the directions above as far as the junction with South Lake Road. Don't turn here; instead, continue ahead for another 2.5 miles, almost to Lake Sabrina, to the turnoff right to North Lake. Follow this airy, one-lane dirt road steeply up to North Lake, pass the lake, look for the next turnoff and, after the pack station, turn right on the spur road to the hikers' parking lot (with a toilet)—about one-half mile short of your trailhead in North Lake Campground. (Willows flourishing along North Lake Rd. may conceal the sign for the spur road.)

If you're reversing the route of this trip: from the lot, walk back to North Lake Rd., turn right, and walk through the campground to the trailhead, which is next to the restrooms (with water here, too). Although you can't leave your car at the trailhead, you can drive up here long enough to drop off packs and all of your party but the driver, who gets to hoof it back to the trailhead from the lot.

TRIP DESCRIPTION

Heads Up! Wood fires are prohibited at some sites along this route; use a stove. Know the regulations for Kings Canyon National Park and John Muir wildernesses! Bears are a problem all along this route, as are marmots in the alpine basins; use appropriate food-storage techniques.

Starting from the roadend (9760)—about a quarter mile above the South Lake dam—the somewhat rocky Bishop Pass Trail ascends through a moderate-to-dense forest cover of lodgepole, fir, and aspen. This ascent traverses the morainal slope on the east side of South Lake, bearing toward Hurd Peak, and then passes a trail to the Treasure Lakes. After turning southeast, your trail soon crosses the Mary Louise Lakes outlet on a log bridge, and then passes the unsigned trail to these lakes. Frequent patches of lupine, forget-me-nots, wallflowers, and swamp onions delight travelers as they ford streamlets and cross swampy sections.

The trail then switchbacks up to a junction with the Bull/Chocolate Lakes Trail and levels off to reach the islet-dotted north end of Long Lake. You're near treeline now; trees are stunted and few, while views are sweeping—you'll be scrambling to get your camera out. After crossing this popular lake's outlet, the trail undulates along the east side of the lake. Near the lake's south end anoth-

View from Muir Pass

er trail goes east to Ruwau Lake, and then we cross the sparkling outlet stream from that lake to arrive at the overused campsites on knolls above the south end of Long Lake. A layover day in this area permits a wonderful dayhike up the steep, rough trail to Ruwau Lake and the saddle high above it, then down through the Chocolate Lakes and Bull Lake, and back on the main Bishop Pass Trail.

The memorable vistas of the wooded and meadowed shores of Long Lake stay with visitors as they ascend through sporadic, subalpine, tarn-dotted meadows. Sometimes steep, this trail climbs steadily past spectacular Saddlerock Lake (with campsites on the rise to the east) and the unmarked fisherman's spur trail to Bishop Lake (with poor, exposed campsites).

Beyond Saddlerock Lake, the trail begins a series of steep switchbacks at the head of a spectacular cirque basin. Excellent views of Mt. Goode appear on the right, and the incredible comb-tine spires of the Inconsolable Range on the left accompany the panting climber, making breather stops unforgettable. Glacially smoothed ledge granite and quarried blocks on every hand line this well-maintained trail. Because occasional pockets of snow sometimes blanket the approach to Bishop Pass (11,972) late into the season, exercise care in the final, steep ascent. Views from the pass are excellent of the Inconsolable Range to the north; Mt. Agassiz to the southeast; Dusy Basin immediately to the south, flanked by Columbine and Giraud peaks; and the Black Divide on the distant western skyline.

From the pass your route, the main trail, descends on a sometimes switch-backing traverse southwest. There are a couple of use trails diverging here, but the westbound main trail is the most heavily used and generally features hoof-prints and dung of pack animals, too. This sandy descent contours over rock-bench systems some distance north of the basin's northernmost large lake near 11,350 feet—not the small lake just west of Mt. Agassiz. Where the trail comes near the lake's inlet, our route branches left, leaving the trail and crossing smooth granite and tundra to the fair campsites at the west end of this lake (7). Other fair campsites can be found a few yards to the southwest, along the outlet stream.

Alpine scenery from the above campsites is breathtaking in its vastness. You can see the Inconsolable Range as it rises behind Bishop Pass, and the climber's mecca, the Palisades, fills the eastern skyline. Also to the east towers symmetrical Isosceles Peak. A very sparse forest cover of gnarled whitebark pines dots the granite landscape on all sides, and the fractures in the granite are filled with grassy, heather-lined pockets.

You'll find more campsites by going cross-country to the cluster of lakes east and south of this one, below Isosceles and Columbine peaks. By late season, campsites nearer the trail and below this lake may be limited by a scarcity of water between here and the lowest Dusy Basin lakes (the long string of lakes just below 10,800). Adventurous hikers can use a layover day here to make an exciting visit to Palisade Basin (the next drainage to the southeast) via trailless Knapsack Pass. Or ramble through the basin, enjoying its many lakes.

Dusy Basin Sighting

Down the trail through Dusy Basin, I once saw a line of kayakers carrying on heads and shoulders their bright but now battered kayaks. Some were still smiling; others were losing enthusiasm with each heavily laden step. On the kayakers' backs the kayaks were going bump, bump, bump, down the trail like Pooh Bear down stairs behind Christopher Robin. In their wake, the rough granite rocks wore small, curled strips of colored material. Had they authorization for what still strikes me as a dumb stunt? In case they were all stark, raving mad, I tried to smile and say hello to each. Seeing one with a very unhappy face, I dared to ask, "Are you people crazy?" He sighed, shifted the kayak on his obviously aching back, and said, "Yeah, now I think we are!" They planned to continue down through Le Conte Canyon to kayak the Middle Fork Kings River. Does anybody know if they made it?

From the northernmost large lake of Dusy Basin, the trail descends over smooth granite ledges and tundra sections. Occasional clumps of the flaky-barked, five-needled whitebark pine dot the glacially scoured basin, and impressive Mts. Agassiz and Winchell and Thunderbolt Peak continue to make up the eastern skyline. To the south the heavily fractured and less-well-defined summits of Columbine and Giraud peaks occupy the skyline. This moderate descent swings west above the lowest lakes of the Dusy Basin, and begins a series of steady switchbacks down into Le Conte Canyon along the north side of Dusy Branch creek. Colorful wildflowers along this descent include Indian paintbrush, pennyroyal, lupine, white cinquefoil, penstemon, shooting star, and some yellow columbine. Just below a waterfall, a wooden bridge crosses to the creek's east side. Views of the U-shaped Middle Fork Kings River canyon are seen constantly during the zigzagging downgrade, and on the far side of the valley you can see the major peaks of the Black Divide, foregrounded by The Citadel and Langille Peak.

As the trail descends, the very sparse forest cover of stunted whitebark seen in most of Dusy Basin gives way to the trees of lower altitudes, including western white pine, juniper, lodgepole, aspen, and some red fir near the foot of the switchbacks. The creek descends by beautiful, steep cascades down the granite east wall of this beautiful canyon. The trail recrosses Dusy Branch creek at the head of a stepladdering bench (with campsites), and then makes the final 1.5-mile switchbacking descent, passing through a drift fence, to a junction with the John Muir Trail in Le Conte Canyon. Emergency services are perhaps available from the ranger station just a few yards northwest of the junction.

Your route turns right (north) onto the famous John Muir Trail, and ascends moderately over duff through moderate-to-dense stands of lodgepole. Langille Peak dominates the views to the left, and its striking white, fractured granite face is a constant reminder of the massive forces exerted by the river of ice that once filled this canyon. Abundant fields of wildflowers color the trailside, including corn lily, tiger lily, fireweed, larkspur, red heather, shooting star, monkey flower, pennyroyal, penstemon, goldenrod, and wallflower. As the trail approaches the south end of Little Pete Meadow, occasional hemlock is found mixed with the lodgepole; the view north at the edge of the meadow includes Mts. Powell and Thompson. There are good but heavily used campsites at Little Pete Meadow.

The trail from Little Pete to Big Pete Meadow makes a moderate ascent on rock and sand through a sparse-to-moderate forest cover of lodgepole and occasional hemlock. Looking back over your shoulder rewards you with fine views of Le Conte Canyon, while ahead the granite walls where the canyon veers west reveal glacially smoothed, unfractured faces. Some quaking aspen can be seen as the trail passes through a drift fence, ascends through Big Pete Meadow (more forest than meadow) and reaches a large area of campsites (13).

As the trail turns west, you have excellent views of the darker rock of Black Giant, and a few yards beyond the turn the trail fords the stream draining the slopes of Mts. Johnson and Gilbert. Passing more campsites, the trail continues west on an easy-to-moderate ascent through grassy extensions of Big Pete Meadow. Most of the rock underfooting encountered to this point has been of

Highest large lake in Dusy Basin with Columbine Peak

the rounded morainal variety, but as soon as the trail leaves the westernmost fringes of Big Pete Meadow, the rock exhibits sharp, fractured edges. Over this talus, the trail ascends more steeply through a partial forest cover of western white, lodgepole and whitebark pine, and some hemlock. Loose rock and sand make poor footing, while the dashing cascades of the Middle Fork offer visual relief on this steep, rugged ascent. The meadowed flat where the trail jogs north toward the tiny, unnamed lake east of Helen Lake supports a sparse forest fringe.

The ascent to Muir Pass starts with a steady climb over sand and rock through a sparse timber cover of whitebark pine. That timber cover soon disappears, giving way to low-lying heather. Snow may linger in big patches across the trail on this side of the pass until late season. At the talus-bound, round, unnamed lake east of Helen Lake, the trail veers west, crossing and recrossing the trickling headwaters of the Middle Fork Kings River. Excellent views southeast of the Palisades and Langille, Giraud, and Columbine peaks make the breather stops doubly welcome. The trail becomes rocky and the slope more moderate as it passes the next unnamed lake and winds up the terminal shoulder of the Black Divide to Helen Lake. Rocks in the colorful reds, yellows, blacks, and whites that characterize this metamorphic divide are on every hand. The trail rounds the loose-rocked south end of this barren lake, and ascends steadily over a rocky slope that is often covered with snow throughout the summer. Looking back, you can see the striking meeting of the black meta-morphic rock of the Black Divide and the white granite just east of Helen Lake.

Muir Pass (11,955) is marked by a sign and a unique stone shelter. This hut, erected by the Sierra Club in memoriam to John Muir, the Sierra's best-known and most-loved mountaineer, stands as a shelter for stormbound trav-elers. In a sense, it is a wilderness monument, and should be treated as such—leave nothing but your boot tracks. (Even human waste has become a problem in the vicinity; camping is prohibited in and around the shelter except in an emergency.) From this pass the views are magnificent. In the morning light, the somber crags north and south relieve the intense whites of the lighter granite to the east. Situated in a gigantic rock bowl to the west, Wanda Lake's emerald-blue waters contrast sharply with its lower white edges, which, on the south side, merge into the darker rock of the Goddard Divide.

The descent from the pass is moderate and then gentle over fragmented rock, and then it levels out, passing the southeast end of campsite-less Lake McDermand. Skirting the east side of Wanda Lake, the trail affords excellent views of snow-and-ice-necklaced Mt. Goddard, and then arrives at the margin-ally legal—too close to water—Spartan campsites near the lake's outlet (21.5). Look for a campsite well back from the water's edge. The expansive views from these campsites include Mt. Goddard and the Goddard Divide to the south, and Mts. Huxley, Spencer, Darwin, and Mendel to the north.

Soon occasional wildflowers, including heather, wallflower, and penste-mon, can be seen as the trail descends over rock and sand. Below Wanda Lake the trail crosses Evolution Creek and stays on the west bank on a moderate descent that becomes switchbacks above Sapphire Lake. Fine views east of the Sierra crest make watching your footing a difficult task. Sapphire Lake is indeed a high-country gem, fringed with green, marshy grass, and situated on a large glacial step—unfortunately with virtually no campsites. Your route traverses its steeper west side and, after a steady descent, refords Evolution Creek just above Evolution Lake on a row of very large boulders. Rerouted out of the lake's meadowed shoreline, the trail crosses a rocky slope, staying high above the lake's east shore. Glacial smoothing and some polish can be seen in the gran-ite surrounding the lake, and on the abrupt walls on each side. There are a few small campsites huddled below the trail near the lake's northwest end.

After passing several campsites just below the lake, the trail makes a brief northward swing before switchbacking down to Evolution Valley. This north-ward swing passes the trail ascending to Darwin Canyon and the route to the Darwin Glacier. The zigzagging downgrade over morainal debris reenters forest cover and passes clumps of seasonal wildflowers that include penstemon, paintbrush, swamp onion, lupine, forget-me-not, cinquefoil, buckwheat, and tiger lily. At the foot of the grade, where the trail fords the stream emptying Darwin Canyon, you pass more campsites and then continue down a series of small benches through moderate stands of lodgepole to the good campsites at

Colby Meadow (28). There are more campsites farther on, along the dry margins of McClure and Evolution meadows.

It's almost all downhill from here to Blayney Hot Springs. From Colby Meadow the route continues west, passing lovely McClure Meadow. Although the region is heavily used, its beauty is still breathtaking, especially now that these meadows are recovering from decades of stock grazing. Pause to look east, back up the valley, to enjoy the sight of The Hermit towering over McClure Meadow—a classic subject for Sierra photographers. The trail between McClure and Evolution meadows is a pathway that winds through moderate and dense stands of lodgepole and, midway down McClure Meadow, passes a ranger station (with emergency services perhaps available here).

The duff trail passes the drift fence below McClure Meadow on a moderate-to-steady descent that fords several tributaries draining the Glacier Divide. Now get ready to ford Evolution Creek; the old, official ford below the meadow has washed out and become very dangerous. Instead, where the stream broadens and slows over a sandy bottom near the head of Evolution Meadow, veer out into the meadow and ford carefully, picking up a use trail through campsites on the creek's south bank. You soon rejoin the official trail, just above the old ford, and begin a steady, switchbacking descent out of Evolution Valley alongside the dashing creek and into Goddard Canyon.

Midway down the switchbacks, there are impressive views of Goddard Canyon. The forest cover along the zigzags is sparse-to-moderate lodgepole, juniper, and some aspen, and mountain flowers seen along the trail include pennyroyal, larkspur, penstemon, cinquefoil, currant, monkey flower, buckwheat, and paintbrush. The switchbacking trail crosses glacial polish exhibiting some striations, and, at the bottom, passes several good campsites as it leads through a heavy stand of lodgepoles. Just beyond these campsites, the trail crosses a footbridge and meets the Goddard Canyon/Hell-for-Sure Pass Trail branching left (south); you turn right (north), staying on the JMT. You make a gentle descent on dusty underfooting through stands of quaking aspen, lodgepole, and some juniper. Gardens of wildflowers line the trail, including sneezeweed, penstemon, yellow cinquefoil, pennyroyal, Mariposa lily, and lupine. As the trail approaches a wood-and-steel bridge crossing of the South Fork San Joaquin River, the canyon walls narrow and rise V-shaped from the canyon floor. On the north wall one can make out unmistakable striations carved by ice-driven rocks in the latest glacial stage.

Our route passes several more campsites on the right, and then, just before we cross the bridge, a short spur trail leads west to some campsites on the south side of the river. Beyond the bridge, we descend a short, rocky stretch over morainal debris. This steady descent levels out through the densely forested flat of Aspen Meadow, which is made up of postglacial alluvial deposits. An occasional Jeffrey and juniper add variety to the forest cover as the route leaves the flat and descends steeply on a rocky, dusty trail. Looking back, you have a last look at Emerald Peak, V'd by the steep canyon walls.

Your route passes some campsites in the chaparral under big Jeffrey pines, and then a sign indicating the boundary of Kings Canyon National Park and your entry into John Muir Wilderness. Next, you cross Piute Creek on a wood-and-steel bridge, where the trail to Piute and Pine Creek passes branches right (with a possible campsite). Turn left (west) to stay on the JMT, which soon branches right (north) to climb the steep canyon wall toward Selden Pass. You continue ahead (left, northwest) toward Florence Lake.

From this junction your route undulates via rocky trail down the South Fork San Joaquin River canyon. The mostly sparse forest cover has changed from a predominance of lodgepole to Jeffrey, juniper, some red and white fir, and the seepage-loving quaking aspen. Now in heavy forest cover, you continue along a series of moderate ups and downs to a junction with a spur trail climbing north (right) to meet the JMT on the canyonside. You continue west (left, ahead) toward Florence Lake, shortly reaching a lateral that branches left, down toward rushing South Fork San Joaquin River, to overused campsites (40.5). This lateral is just before an inholding, private Muir Trail Ranch, a resort that hosts guests by the week and caters to equestrians. There are no facilities available to non-guests except that they will hold resupply packages for people traveling the John Muir and Pacific Crest trails.

Across the river (dangerous in early season) are more campsites and a use trail leading to a wonderful public hot-spring pool in a little meadow. The pool's sides are soft and vulnerable to erosion, so take care entering and exiting the water. An early morning soak here, watching dragonflies flitting over the dew-spangled meadow—well, it doesn't get much better. The use trail leads from here to a little swimming lake, "Warm Lake." The entire area is fragile and heavily used; please minimize your own impact.

Retrace your steps to the JMT and turn right (southeast) on it, away from Muir Trail Ranch. Continue retracing your steps to the junction with the trail to Piute and Pine Creek passes, by the wood-and-steel bridge over Piute Creek. Don't cross the bridge; instead, go ahead (left, north) on the Piute Creek Trail next to rushing, icy Piute Creek. The rocky trail climbs and then descends briefly to the creek (late in a dry year, your last easy access to water until West Pinnacles Creek). From here, the trail keeps to the west side well above the creek and fords multibranched Turret Creek (may be dry in a dry year). You climb and descend hot chaparral slopes on switchbacks affording poor footing, but you're rewarded by the excellent views of highly fractured Pavilion Dome and the surrounding, unnamed domes composing the west end of Glacier Divide.

The trail then swings east through a narrowing canyon, crosses a couple of gullies on log bridges, fords tiny West Pinnacles Creek, and pursues a steep, rocky course until it enters a moderate lodgepole forest cover before reaching

Long Lake and Mt Goode

the East Pinnacles Creek ford. Views of the cascading tributary streams are frequent along this trail section. From the ford, the trail ascends gently to beautiful Hutchinson Meadow (49), where travelers will find excellent campsites near the Pine Creek Pass Trail junction. The lovely meadow setting provides excellent campsite views of several granite peaks, including Pilot Knob east-north-east.

Turn right (east) at the Pine Creek Pass Trail junction, toward Piute Pass, ascending moderately through seasonal gardens displaying paintbrush, shooting star, fleabane, swamp onion, red mountain heather, buttercup, cinquefoil, penstemon, buckwheat, yarrow, senecio, Douglas phlox, Labrador tea, lemon willow, and alpine willow. As you climb, the forest cover thins to sparse lodgepole as it enters vast Humphreys Basin and crosses the outlet of the Desolation lakes. Humphreys Basin (see trip 34) offers numerous scattered campsites, but those nearest Piute Creek and especially Upper Golden Trout Lake are badly trampled and dusty from overuse; look for campsites farther afield. You will find a few Spartan ones off the use trail north to the Desolation lakes as well as by going cross-country to more remote lakes like Tomahawk and Square. Lower Golden Trout Lake is closed to camping. Wood is scarce in this high basin; use stoves. Mt. Humphreys is particularly striking, with its alternating, vibrantly colored layers. Dayhiking in Humphreys Basin is excellent, with so many remote lakes to explore.

From here, reverse the steps of trip 34 to climb out of Humphreys Basin, over Piute Pass, and down North Fork Bishop Creek past numerous lakes and ponds (with campsites at Piute Lake (57) and Loch Leven), past Piute Crags, and finally through North Lake Campground, down North Lake Road, and left at the spur road to the pack station, just beyond which you'll find the hikers' parking lot. It's a fittingly splendid finale to one of the great classic Sierra trips.

Variations

Reverse the direction (and Trip Description) of this trip.

Permits

This is a quota trailhead, and a permit is required for overnight stays. Apply for permits to Inyo National Forest, 873 N. Main Street, Bishop, CA 93514, (760) 873-2500, or see **www.r5.fs.fed.us/inyo/**.

Build-up/Wind-down tips

Because these are high trailheads, start acclimatizing by spending at least the night before you set off in the vicinity. There are numerous Forest Service campgrounds along State Route 168 and South Lake Road. If you're reversing the trip, North Lake Campground is right at your starting trailhead.

There are also three resorts near the trailheads, each offering lodgings, a store, and a café. Along South Lake Road and under the same management are Bishop Creek Lodge (Rt. 1, South Lake Road, Bishop, CA 93514, (760) 873-4484) and Parcher's Resort (Rt. 1, South Lake Road, Bishop, CA 93514, (760) 873-4177). Parcher's is closer to the South Lake trailhead. On 168 a little beyond the South Lake Road turnoff is Cardinal Village Resort (Route 1, Box A-3, Bishop, CA 93514, (760) 873-4789). The nearest town with lodgings, stores, and restaurants—and lots of them—is Bishop at 4000 feet (Bishop Chamber of Commerce, 690 N. Main Street, Bishop, CA 93514, (760) 873-8405).

To find out how Kathy Morey got started hiking the Sierra and the Hawaiian islands and writing about her hikes for Wilderness Press, and for a list of her titles, see "Author Bio & Bib" on page 492.

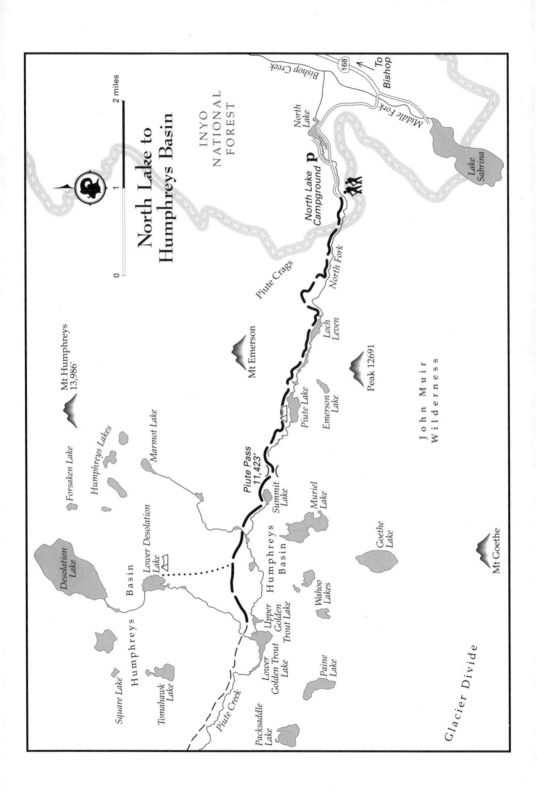

North Lake to
Humphreys Basin

34

North Lake to Humphreys Basin
—Kathy Morey

Route	Days	Elev. Gain/Loss	Difficulty	Miles
↲	3	2544'/2544'	**	14.6

Campsites: Piute Lake: 3.5 miles
(vicinity of) Lower Desolation Lake: 7.3 miles
(see the Trip Description for others)

Map: USGS 7.5-min *Mt. Darwin, Mt. Tom*

Best season: Late summer through early fall

Take this trip!

Your wonderfully scenic hike up North Fork Bishop Creek features flowery meadows, a fine waterfall on the creek, plenty of lovely lakes, and a wonderland of alpine ponds and streams just before you cross viewful Piute Pass to one of the Sierra's finest alpine basins, huge, lightly timbered, lake-filled Humphreys Basin. I've been to Humphreys Basin many times and *still* haven't explored every lake and pond—there are just too many! There's great cross-country day-hiking in every direction throughout the basin. Nature seems to have outdone herself creating splendid waterways here, and you can spend the entire day happily following a stream up and down its length. Few trips yield as much alpine beauty and sheer enjoyment for as little effort as this one.

Trailhead

See directions for North Lake, the Take-out trailhead for trip 33, "South Lake to North Lake."

TRIP DESCRIPTION

Heads Up! Although campfires are technically legal, because wood is very scarce here they are inappropriate; please use a stove. Know John Muir Wilderness regulations! Bears may be a problem; store food appropriately. Humphreys Basin is badly overused by stock parties, especially east of and around Upper Golden Trout Lake. To help reduce the overall impact, watch where the stock parties go—or where the poop leads— and then head elsewhere in the basin. See the suggestions below.

Just beyond the trailhead the route enters John Muir Wilderness, and then ascends gently along slopes dotted with meadowy patches, aspen groves, and stands of lodgepole pine. In season the traveler will find wildflowers galore in little meadows and in sandy patches among the granite slabs, including paintbrush, columbine, tiger lily, spiraea, and penstemon. After the trail fords and quickly refords North Fork Bishop Creek, the ascent becomes moderate. Aspen is left behind, the lodgepole becomes sparse, and some limber pine is seen. This glaciated canyon is flanked by slab-topped Peak 12691 on the south and 13,118-foot Mt. Emerson on the north. The High Sierra newcomer will marvel at how the great granite slabs maintain precarious perches atop Peak 12691, seeming almost vertically above you. But they all topple eventually, due to the action of frost wedging, and add to talus piles at the foot of the peak.

The trail grows steeper as it switchbacks up the open slopes of orange-tinted Piute Crags over shattered rock shed from the crags. If the going gets hot, cool your senses by gazing over at the beautiful waterfall the creek makes cascading out of Loch Leven.

Approaching Loch Leven—the prettiest lake this side of Piute Pass—the trail levels off. There's a campsite north of the trail, near the lake's west end. The trail then ascends moderately through a cover of sparse lodgepole and whitebark, winds among large, rounded boulders, passes through a drift fence, and skirts a pair of small lakes before arriving at the next bench up-canyon, which contains this day's destination, Piute Lake (3.5). Consider the wind in selecting a campsite, as it often blows stiffly in Piute Pass country. There are overused campsites on the north side close to the trail. To find out-of-the-way seclusion ford the creek and scramble southeast up a fairly steep slope to granite-bound Emerson Lake.

From Piute Lake, the trail ascends an open, rocky slope to treeline, overlooking alpine meadows threaded by streamlets and dotted with bright pools. Sooner than you might expect, it switchbacks up to the last traverse before Piute Pass. Here, even in midsummer, you'll probably pass through a "road cut" in a snowbank, created by packers using sand and shovels. At the pass (11,423) there are grand views west to Pilot Knob and the canyon of the South Fork San Joaquin river, south to Glacier Divide (the north boundary of Kings Canyon National Park), and north over barren blue lakes to the unnamed ridge separating Humphreys Basin from French Canyon, and to Mt. Humphreys, highest

Piute Crags

peak this far north in the Sierra. If it could acquire 14 feet from somewhere, Bishop residents would have their own 14,000-footer. (I can see Bishop Chamber of Commerce members streaming up Mt. Humphreys, each bearing a huge boulder—wait a minute, the easiest route up that peak is Class 4.)

The rocky-dusty main trail descends briefly toward pale blue Summit Lake and then curves northwest high above it, along the treeless edge of the great cirque that is Humphreys Basin. Below you to the south, the headwaters of Piute Creek spill ribbonlike down the basin, forming a lake here, a pond there.

Unseen above you north lie the Marmot and Humphreys lakes, whose outlets you splash across where they nourish trailside patches of willows, shooting stars, and sneezeweed. A few small, high campsites with panoramic views cling to open slopes between the trail and these remote lakes. You will also find a windy, exposed campsite or two around Muriel Lake's north shore.

At a point where the main trail is above and north of a small lake with a green island, you reach a well-beaten spur trail north to the Desolation lakes. Except late in a dry year, a number of small ponds lie here and there off this trail, along with the occasional Spartan campsite. Those fond of treeless, open camps will find a site or two east of the use trail above Lower Desolation Lake (1.3 miles more), and some wind-raked flats among the great white boulders surrounding aptly named Desolation Lake, 1.5 miles farther along this spur. I recommend you seek your campsite in the vicinity Lower Desolation Lake (about 7.3). Or consider campsites even farther afield and cross-country, such as on the high, open benches holding Tomahawk Lake or Square Lake, or around meadowed Packsaddle Lake and its ponds.

The main trail continues to descend to the cascading outlet of the Desolation lakes—the last reliable water before Hutchinson Meadow in a dry year. If you missed the use trail to the Desolation lakes, you can follow their outlet north from here. Below, the Golden Trout lakes gleam lustrously down in the cirque bottom. Dusty use trails lead off to poor, terribly overused campsites around Upper Golden Trout Lake, about half a mile south depending on your route. Lower Golden Trout Lake is closed to camping within 500 feet of its shoreline.

Any site you choose provides your base from which to explore the basin's many wonders. A few suggestions for great cross-country rambles: 1) climb steeply to the lower of the shallow, rocky Wahoo Lakes and then traverse over to big Muriel Lake and up to the boulder-bounded lakes in Goethe Cirque; 2) climb to one of the saddles overlooking French Canyon and take a peek at the many lakes below; 3) make a challenging loop through the Humphreys Lakes, over the Class 2–3 saddle northeast of Peak 12030 down to Forsaken Lake and its huge, flower-strewn meadow, and return via the Desolation lakes. Accomplished peak-baggers can try Mt. Humphreys; more casual ones can attempt easier Pilot Knob. Of course, to enjoy one of the basin's best shows you don't have to hike at all: with most sites offering views of Mt. Humphreys, just wait till alpenglow enhances its multicolored layers! When your allotted time has dwindled, retrace your steps over Piute Pass to the trailhead.

Permits

This is a quota trailhead, and a permit is required for overnight stays. Apply for permits to Inyo National Forest, 873 N. Main Street, Bishop, CA 93514, (760) 873-2500, or see **www.r5.fs.fed.us/inyo/**.

Build-up/Wind-down tips

See the the ones for trip 33, "South Lake to North Lake."

To find out how Kathy Morey got started hiking the Sierra and the Hawaiian islands and writing about her hikes for Wilderness Press, and for a list of her titles, see "Author Bio & Bib" on page 492.

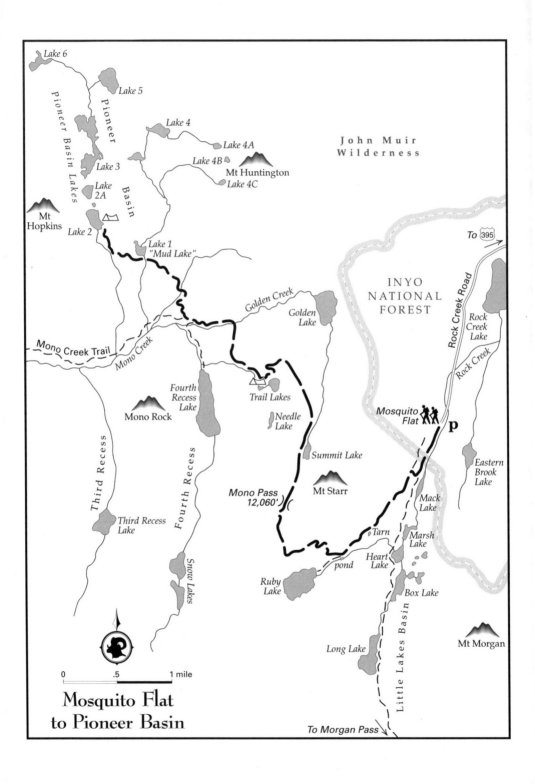

Lake 6

Lake 5

Lake 4

Lake 4A

Lake 4B

Mt Huntington
Lake 4C

Pioneer Basin Lakes

Pioneer

Basin

Lake 3

Lake 2A

Lake 2

Mt
Hopkins

Lake 1
"Mud Lake"

Golden Creek

Golden
Lake

John Muir
Wilderness

To 395

INYO
NATIONAL
FOREST

Rock Creek Road

Rock
Creek
Lake

Rock Creek

Mono Creek Trail

Mono Creek

Fourth
Recess
Lake

Trail Lakes

Mono Rock

Needle
Lake

Summit Lake

Mosquito
Flat

p

Eastern
Brook
Lake

Third Recess

Fourth Recess

Mt Starr

Mono Pass
12,060'

Third Recess
Lake

Snow Lakes

Tarn

pond

Ruby
Lake

Heart
Lake

Mack
Lake

Marsh
Lake

Box Lake

Little Lakes Basin

Long Lake

Mt Morgan

0   .5   1 mile

Mosquito Flat
to Pioneer Basin

To Morgan Pass

35

Mosquito Flat to Pioneer Basin

—Kathy Morey

Route	Days	Elev. Gain/Loss	Difficulty	Miles
⌇	3	4590'/4590'	***	18.8

Campsites: Trail Lakes: 5.5 miles
Pioneer Basin Lake 2: 9.4 miles
(see the Trip Description for others)

Map: USGS 7.5-min *Mt. Morgan, Mt. Abbott*

Best season: Late summer through early fall

Take this trip!

It's a tough hike into high, lightly forested Pioneer Basin, but the spectacular views along the way and the opportunities for superb dayhiking from your scenic base camp deliver ample rewards. Pioneer Basin is on the north side of the canyon of Mono Creek; the south side is pierced by the famous Mono Recesses. Fourth Recess is a moderate dayhike from Pioneer Basin. The basin is ringed by peaks named for a quartet of California's 19th Century robber barons (the "pioneers"), and peak-baggers can set their sights on Mts. Huntington, Stanford, Crocker, and Hopkins. Ramblers will enjoy simply following anglers' trails, or going cross-country from lake to pond to lake.... Amateur botanists will delight in the variety of wildflowers encountered in season.

Trailhead

From US Highway 395 at Toms Place, turn west on Rock Creek Road. Follow it 10.7 miles southwest, past Rock Creek Lake to the roadend at Mosquito Flat. Get here early; on a summer weekend or holiday, this parking lot can be jammed by mid-morning, and cars can be parked up to a mile down the road.

TRIP DESCRIPTION

Heads Up! Know John Muir Wilderness regulations! Bears may be a problem here; store food properly. This is a fragile ecosystem where wood quickly consumed in fires can take years to grow. While campfires may technically be legal at your Trail Lakes and Pioneer Basin campsites, please use a stove.

Roughly paralleling Rock Creek along its west side, the broad, sandy trail is nearly level at first, soon enters John Muir Wilderness, and begins climbing moderately through a dazzling flower garden, which is perhaps the best in the Eastern Sierra in season. In a little short of half a mile you reach a Y-junction: left (south) to Little Lakes Valley and Morgan Pass; right (southwest) to Mono Pass (the southernmost of two with this name in the Eastern Sierra). Be sure to top the little rise you've been climbing to find a spectacular viewpoint: of Mack Lake below, left (east), and beyond it of Mt. Morgan; of hulking, bare Mt. Starr to the west; and of the glorious semicircle of peaks at the head of Little Lakes Valley south, including Mts. Mills, Abbot, and Dade, and Bear Creek Spire.

Bear right (south-southwest) at the Y for Mono Pass, to begin a long climb on a sandy but viewful trail up the east slope of Mt. Starr. You soon pass a spur trail coming in on your right from the pack station. Continuing ahead, the trail intersects seasonal runoff nourishing surprising, though also seasonal, wildflower displays. Excellent views open up over Little Lakes Valley. You pass a pretty tarn near 1.5 miles, and at almost 2 miles you turn into a swale and reach a junction with a signed lateral to Ruby Lake, a quarter mile away if you were to head left. Near this junction, Ruby Lake's outlet, with a charming pond on it, provides your last reliable water until Summit Lake, a little beyond Mono Pass.

Bypassing Ruby Lake, you take the right fork and continue relentlessly up, with a view of Ruby Lake below and of the peaks around Little Lakes Valley soon commanding whatever attention you can spare from the steep, dry trail—superb views and photo opportunities provide good excuses for rest stops. Finally, leaving views behind, the trail turns into a sandy draw that may hold snow till very late in the season. For this reason, you may find multiple tracks between here and the far end of Summit Lake, made by hikers trying to avoid the retreating snow—or you may have to make your way across the snow itself.

At 4.5 miles you arrive at viewless Mono Pass (12,060', though an old sign here says 11,970) and step across the Sierra crest, from Inyo to Sierra National Forest, in a stark landscape of shattered granite. A close ground inspection soon dispels any impression of lifelessness by revealing numerous ground-hugging plants. While many are familiar from lower elevations, here they are dwarfed by severe conditions. Panoramic views are available by ascending Mt. Starr to the east.

The trail descends a little toward the shore of Summit Lake, a turquoise oval set in cream-colored rock and gray-brown sand. The trail—or multiple tracks—roughly parallel Summit Lake's outlet before converging on a flat below the lake to veer northwest. Don't drop into the meadow around the outlet stream unless you are desperate to find a campsite now. Golden Lake is invisible at the bottom of the "pit" into which the stream descends.

You climb a little ridge (possibly through more snow) and begin a switchbacking descent of a dry slope from which you have breathtaking views over the great glacial canyon of Mono Creek. Especially prominent in these views are Needle Lake (misspelled as "Neelle Lake" on the 7.5' topo) to the west, with the Trail Lakes emerging just below it, and the lowest lake in Pioneer Basin to the northwest, set in a wide, inviting meadow.

As you near the Trail Lakes, you'll notice a tiny stone hut that's a California snow-survey shelter—no trespassing! The main trail actually swings away from the Trail Lakes (11,200) just before touching their shores, but you'll see the smaller lake on your left as you come abreast of them. A rocky plateau a few feet above the larger lake provides several overused campsites (5.5) among stunted whitebark pines, and there is also a small flat about 0.1 mile below the lakes, across the trail from the meadow lining the lakes' outlet. While campfires may technically be legal here, dirty fire-rings deface the area. In an ecosystem where down-and-dead wood is nonexistent and tree growth is extremely slow due to harsh conditions, a campfire is unthinkable. Avoid campfires here and use your stove.

From your campsite, return to the main trail to begin a dusty, stony descent of nearly 800 feet to a welcome ford of Golden Creek, where a use trail turns upstream (east) toward Golden Lake on the north bank, and your route turns west and downstream, paralleling Golden Creek and generally staying well above it. The descent eases, though the trail remains deep in dust and full of loose rocks, and you are soon in moderate forest cover.

You presently reach the signed lateral left (south) to Fourth Recess; Fourth Recess Lake is an enjoyable dayhike from Pioneer Basin. For now, though, you go right (ahead, west) on the Mono Creek Trail and shortly find the signed lateral that goes right (ahead, west) to Pioneer Basin. This junction can be confusing: the main trail curves left here, while you take the lateral, which goes ahead.

At first the lateral avoids climbing into the basin, instead undulating over a couple of little ridges. But soon the trail descends to a year-round stream at a junction where a use trail leads left (southwest, downstream) to a few campsites.

Staying on the lateral, you curve right (generally north and upstream) through a moderate forest of lodgepole pines with a meadowy understory and hordes of mosquitoes, to begin a sometimes-steep climb into Pioneer Basin. You ford the stream to ascend rocky switchbacks through patchy forest. The grade eases as you approach the ridgetop east of Lake 1, and the trail soon dips into the meadow around the lake, fording its outlet. This lake, called "Mud Lake" by packers, offers the most popular campsites in the basin because they're the easiest to reach and have moderate forest cover. Being the lowest lake, it has the most comfortable temperature for swimming. But it's the least interesting and most crowded of the many available lakes.

Campsites are scattered throughout the basin; you may have to hunt for them. Consider Lake 2, above and northwest of Mud Lake. To get there, follow the trail across Mud Lake's outlet. Where the meadow gives way to forest again, the trail begins a brutally steep and stony climb of almost two-thirds mile to Lake 2 (9.4), much of the climb through a lovely hillside meadow. The grade eases a little below Lake 2, and the trail peters out around the lake. The sparsely-forested bench south of the lake is bisected by a meadow and offers several campsites with fine views either of the lake or across Mono Creek's canyon and into the Mono Recesses. There are also a couple of campsites on the rise east of the lake. Anglers' tracks doodle along Lakes 2, 2A, and the pond between them, and along Lake 3.

To reach the medium-sized lake on the east side of the basin and long, multilobed Lake 10862 on the west side ("Lake 4" and "Lake 3," respectively), pick up a wide, rocky-dusty use trail that strikes north about 100 yards before you top the ridge east of Mud Lake. (If you see Mud Lake as you climb into the basin, you have overshot this junction.) The use trail climbs moderately through dry lodgepole forest before coming alongside a rushing creek across which there's a forested ridge. You ford the creek to a prominent fork: the left fork leads shortly to ridgetop packer campsites with fine views; the right fork follows the stream's west bank, up three, splendidly meadowed benches. On the third bench, a faint use trail forks right at an obscure junction to cross the stream and lead to Lake 4. The "main" use trail you have been on passes a large pond and almost peters out in a marshy area, but then leads to another pond and a peninsula on Lake 3 with several overused campsites huddled among waist-high whitebark pines. Better sites along Lake 3 are worth searching out. The additional trek up the use trails to one of these lakes adds about 1.5 miles one way.

Getting to the highest lakes requires easy and beautiful cross-country rambling. Lake 6 is nearly rockbound and lacks campsites, and Lake 5 has very few. From wherever you camp, you must eventually retrace your steps to Mosquito Flat.

Variations

Consider extending your trip to head for one or more of the Mono Recesses for a night or two, or pick a convenient campsite in Mono Creek's canyon from which you can dayhike into some of the recesses. There are also Hopkins and Grinnell basins on the north wall.

Permits

This is a quota trailhead, and a permit required for overnight stays may be available from summer ranger kiosk near the trailhead (sometimes right at trailhead, sometimes just inside campground). Otherwise, apply for permits to Inyo National Forest, 873 N. Main Street, Bishop, CA 93514, (760) 873-2500, or see **www.r5.fs.fed.us/inyo/**.

Build-up/Wind-down tips

At 10,230 feet, Mosquito Flat is the highest, readily accessible trailhead in the Sierra, so acclimatize yourself by spending at least the night before your trip somewhere in its vicinity. There are two lodgings along Rock Creek Road, Rock Creek Lodge (Route 1, Box 12, Mammoth Lakes, CA 93546, (760) 935-4170), FAX (760) 935-4172) and Rock Creek Lakes Resort (Box 727, Bishop, CA 93515, (760) 935-4311). There are also several campgrounds along Rock Creek Road, including one right next to the trailhead: a small, one-overnight backpacker campground (with a valid Wilderness Permit required to prove eligibility). Back on 395, Tom's Place Resort offers lodgings, a store, and a café (Rural Station, Bishop, CA 93514, (760) 935-4239). North of Toms Place on 395 and west on Convict Lake Road is Convict Lake Resort (Route 1, Box 204, Mammoth Lakes, CA 93546, (800) 992-2260, (760) 934-3800, FAX (760) 934-0396).

The nearest towns are Bishop to the south (Bishop Chamber of Commerce, 690 N. Main Street, Bishop, CA 93514, (760) 873-8405), and Mammoth Lakes on the north (Mammoth Lakes Visitors Bureau, Box 48, Dept. P, Mammoth Lakes, CA 93546, (760) 934-2712, FAX (760) 934-7066). Both offer plenty of lodgings, stores, and restaurants, but Mammoth is higher (Mammoth, 7600–8000'; Bishop, 4000').

To find out how Kathy Morey got started hiking the Sierra and the Hawaiian islands and writing about her hikes for Wilderness Press, and for a list of her titles, see "Author Bio & Bib" on page 492.

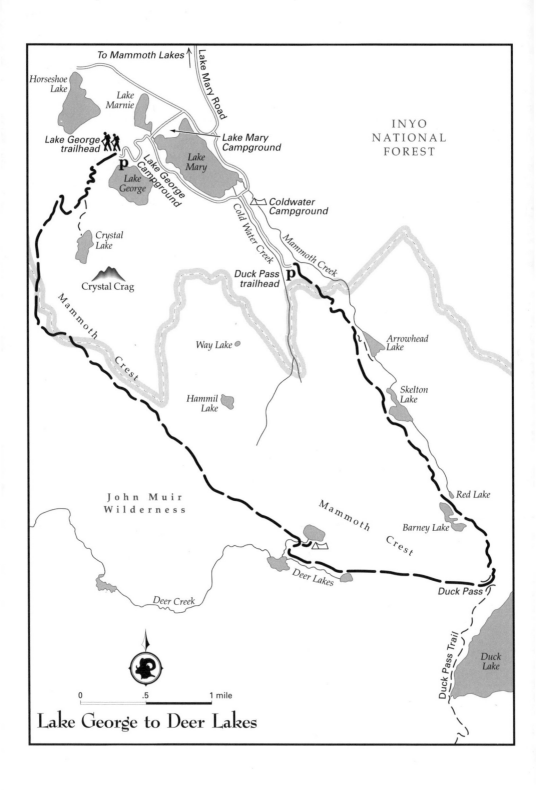

Lake George to Deer Lakes

To Mammoth Lakes

Lake Mary Road

INYO
NATIONAL
FOREST

Horseshoe
Lake

Lake
Marnie

Lake George
trailhead

p

Lake George
Campground

Lake Mary
Campground

Lake
Mary

Lake
George

Coldwater
Campground

Crystal
Lake

Cold Water Creek

Mammoth Creek

Duck Pass
trailhead

p

Crystal Crag

Mammoth   Crest

Way Lake

Arrowhead
Lake

Skelton
Lake

Hammil
Lake

Red Lake

John Muir
Wilderness

Mammoth   Crest

Barney Lake

Deer Lakes

Duck Pass

Deer Creek

Duck Pass Trail

Duck
Lake

0   .5   1 mile

36

Lake George to Deer Lakes

—Kathy Morey

Route	Days	Elev. Gain/Loss	Difficulty	Miles
↗	2	2755'/2689'	***	13

Campsites: Deer Lakes basin: 7 miles
(see the Trip Description for others)

Map: USGS 7.5-min *Bloody Mtn., Crystal Crag*

Best season: Late summer through early fall

Take this trip!

Dramatic, far-reaching views unfold as you climb toward Deer Lakes—across startling terrain. You begin on light-colored, coarse granite sand that abruptly ends at dark red cinders near the ridgetop, where a well-formed cone rises from a bowl of red cinders into the mountain sky. While this is the Sierra, it's a landscape distinctly reminiscent of Maui's famed Haleakala Crater. There has been considerable volcanism from here north in the Sierra, and the contrast between the typical Sierran gray granite and these colorful volcanic features is a source of joy and wonder along this stark, airy, alpine route. The tiny lakes basin is an alpine gem in the barren terrain setting, and it's so little used that you may have it all to yourself. Finish your journey with an interesting cross-country leg and then a descent through a fine lodgepole forest—quite a contrast with the treeless route to Deer Lakes!—past several attractive lakes and ponds. The trailheads for this shuttle trip are fairly close to each other in the same lakes basin, and energetic hikers can make a loop of this trip by walking the roads back to their starting point. That's a lot packed into a mere weekend's trip!

Trailheads

Put-in trailhead (Lake George): From US Highway 395 at the Mammoth Lakes junction with State Route 203, turn west and drive through the town of Mammoth Lakes on 203, now called Main Street. At the second traffic light, where 203 turns right toward Mammoth Mountain Ski Area/Mountain Bike Park, zero your odometer and continue straight ahead on what's now called Lake Mary Road. As the road approaches the lowest of the lakes southwest of town, it curves left to keep climbing while a spur road to Tamarack Lodge Resort, Twin Lakes, and Twin Lakes Campground turns right. Stay on the Lake Mary Road past an art gallery and then a pack station to a Y-junction. Take the right fork here—briefly tracing big Lake Mary's east shore—to a junction with a spur road to Lake George. Turn left along Lake Mary's north shore and go west past Lake Mary Campground to the next junction (a T-junction), where you turn right and climb to a parking lot on the edge of Lake George, between Lake George Campground and Woods Lodge. Park here (4.7). There are two trailheads; you want the one for Crystal Lake, which is nearer Woods Lodge, on the north end of the parking lot. You'll find toilets and water in the campground.

Take-out trailhead (Duck Pass): If you're driving from town straight to this trailhead, follow the directions above as far as the Y-junction beyond the pack station. Take the left fork around Lake Mary's east shore and past Pine City Campground. As the narrow road begins to curve around Lake Mary's head, there's a turnoff left into Coldwater Campground. Turn left and follow this road up through the campground to a large parking lot serving three trailheads. Park here, 5.0–5.2 miles from the second traffic light in Mammoth Lakes depending on where you park. You want the middle trailhead for the Duck Pass Trail, next to the easternmost of two restrooms (with water here, also).

To walk to the trailhead at Lake George from the one at Duck Pass, follow the road down through the campground (northwest) to a T-junction with Lake Mary Road. Turn left on the slim shoulder of Lake Mary Road and follow it past the Lake Mary Store (Barrett's Landing), along Lake Mary's west shore, to a Y-junction (appearing like a T when you're going west). Take the left fork up to the parking lot at Lake George. Someone once told me there is a use trail between Lakes Mary and George, but I happen to know that he later got hopelessly lost when he tried to follow it. (Reverse the directions above to walk to the Duck Pass trailhead.)

TRIP DESCRIPTION

Heads Up! Wood is scarce to non-existent at Deer Lakes; use a stove. Know John Muir Wilderness regulations! Because Inyo National Forest National Forest prohibits backcountry camping outside of designated wilderness, you can't camp at tempting places on or near this route, like Crystal Lake, before entering John Muir Wilderness near the top of the initial climb. Don't expect to catch your dinner in Deer Lakes. Because these lakes are extremely poor in nutrients, rainbow trout survive here by not growing: one not much bigger than a fingerling can be an adult 20 years old. Leave the few and tiny starvelings in peace. There may be no water (and therefore no acceptable campsites) between the Lake George trailhead and Deer Lakes: fill those water bottles before you hit the trail!

Climbing above the cabins of Woods Lodge, your trail switchbacks fairly steeply up through tall mountain hemlocks and lodgepole pines, affording views down to Lake George and east to "Red and Gold Mountain." At a signed junction with the trail to Crystal Lake (left, south), your route continues ahead (southwest) toward Mammoth Crest. If you've the energy, take this spur down a little over a half mile and 131 feet to this gem of a little lake (no camping).

Back on the main trail, a long switchback leg ends at a view of Horseshoe Lake almost directly below you, and each succeeding switchback leg north offers more open views. From granite, the rock underfoot abruptly changes to volcanic red cinders; stunted whitebark pines record the prevailing wind direction.

Just past the John Muir Wilderness boundary (signed, but mislocated) the trail descends briefly, and you pass a pair of unsigned trails to the right. Consider dropping your packs here and taking one of these use trails—for fantastic views and a closer look at the volcanic rubble—to the summit of the obvious, handsome cinder cone, which is an amazing mix of colors: cream, orange, brick red, dark brown, golden brown, ochre, gray, black, even a dusty lavender. Barren Mammoth Mountain north is the remaining, west side of an extinct volcano—ironic, considering in winter it's a major ski resort.

As you continue south—bearing left—crunch along over cinders dipping through the remnant of a crater, pass another unsigned trail to the right, and reach the crest. Now you can see the Ritter Range west, and southwest, the Silver Divide and the Middle Fork San Joaquin River canyon, converging with Fish Creek's canyon. Your rocky and sandy route continues south, where the crest broadens to a moonscape of red and white pumice, dotted with rounded clumps of wind-pruned whitebarks. By making brief excursions east, you'll get spectacular views of Crystal Crag, Crystal Lake, and the Owens Valley.

The often sandy trail climbs moderately, then steeply, just west of the crestline, with expanding views into Crater Meadow. The trail briefly touches the crest on an east-facing knife edge that offers a dizzying view down a sheer, snow-filled chute to Hammil and Way lakes far below—a view reminiscent of those from the Mt. Whitney Trail east from Day and Keeler needles. It's easy to confuse the geography from here—Deer Lakes are *not* in the bowl to the right, but Deer *Creek* is. The trail follows the crest curving eastward, and then descends fairly steeply into Deer Lakes basin. The trail terminates near the middle (northernmost) Deer Lake (7). Find a Spartan campsite near this lake or along the stream connecting it with the lowest Deer Lake.

Crystal Crag

The terrain is gentle and rocky, and several indistinct trails head toward the pass that overlooks Duck Lake, directly east of the highest (easternmost) Deer Lake. One use trail leaves from the east end of the middle Deer Lake. Your route, over often indistinct trail, leaves just east of this lake's outlet. If you lose your trail, continue straight toward the very obvious low point just east of the highest Deer Lake. When you reach the edge of the talus, walk along its base, almost reaching a small tarn not shown on the topo map. From this point an obvious steep use trail snakes 200 feet up on loose scree and dirt footing to a lovely, wide meadow.

The trail crosses this meadow eastward past a lone, very large boulder in a low saddle. Ignore the ducks and the use trail that lead upward to the left (north) face from this boulder, and continue directly ahead (east) toward Duck Lake. Soon the trail descends among whitebark pines. It is occasionally hard to see. If you lose the trail, head straight downhill (avoid contouring left), and you will soon intersect the well-maintained Duck Pass Trail. Turn left (north) onto the trail, which leads levelly to Duck Pass, 350 yards ahead. Take a moment to enjoy the beautiful view over Duck and Pika lakes below (with campsites, but there's no camping within 300 feet of Duck's outlet, and no fires permitted) and to the picturesque, jagged little crest beyond them.

On the north side of Duck Pass, the trail descends steeply by numerous rocky switchbacks down the granite headwall of the cirque. Especially after a heavy winter, snow may linger late into the season on this north-facing, sheltered headwall. The descent eases in beautiful alpine meadows as the trail approaches barren Barney Lake (with campsites, but no fires within 300 feet of the lake). You wind between Barney Lake and smaller Red Lake (with more campsites), crossing the stream between them. The trail then tops a little knoll past avalanche-downed trees before descending gradually to moderately through handsome forest and patches of blossom-dotted meadows to lovely Skelton Lake (with overused campsites). Continuing beyond Skelton Lake, you descend to a junction with the side trail right (southeast and downhill) to Arrowhead Lake, barely visible below (with campsites).

Now the dusty trail makes a series of lazy switchbacks through moderate-to-dense lodgepole forest before straightening out for a final moderate, rocky descent. You leave John Muir Wilderness and veer left across a little stream channel (usually dry by mid-season) before curving past information signs and cinderblock restrooms to the trailhead parking lot.

Variations

Do this trip as a dayhike. Or reverse the direction, although I'm told it is harder to find Deer Lakes from the Duck Pass area than it is to take the trail along the crest to them.

Permits

This is a quota trailhead, and permits are required for overnight stays. Apply for a permit to Inyo National Forest, 873 N. Main Street, Bishop, CA 93514, (760) 873-2500, or see **www.r5.fs.fed.us/inyo/**.

Build-up/Wind-down tips

The adjacent town of Mammoth Lakes (Visitors Bureau, (800) 367-6572) has ample lodgings, restaurants, and stores as well as several campgrounds in the general area. Even better, there are four lodges and four campgrounds in the lakes basin where your trip starts and ends—with a campground immediately adjacent to each trailhead (Lake George Campground at that trailhead and Coldwater Campground at Duck Pass). The lodges are Woods Lodge (Box 108, Mammoth Lakes, CA 93546, (760) 934-2261), beside your starting trailhead at Lake George; Wildyrie Resort (Box 109, Mammoth Lakes, CA 93546, (760) 934-2444) at Lake Mamie (and under the same management as Woods Lodge); Crystal Crag Lodge (Box 88, Mammoth Lakes, CA 93546, (760) 934-2436) on Lake Mary and nearest your ending trailhead; and Tamarack Lodge Resort (Box 69, Mammoth Lakes, CA 93546, (760) 934-2442, FAX (760) 934-2281), with an outstanding restaurant (Lakefront Restaurant, serving breakfast and dinner) on the lowest Twin Lakes (actually a series of three; go figure).

To find out how Kathy Morey got started hiking the Sierra and the Hawaiian islands and writing about her hikes for Wilderness Press, and for a list of her titles, see "Author Bio & Bib" on page 492.

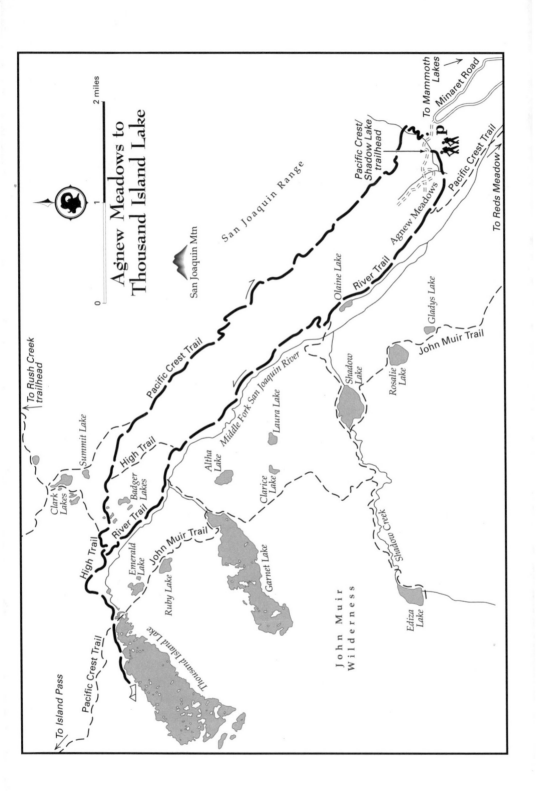

Agnew Meadows to
Thousand Island Lake

2 miles

1

0

San Joaquin Range

San Joaquin Mtn

To Mammoth Lakes

Minaret Road

Pacific Crest/
Shadow Lake
trailhead

Agnew Meadows

Pacific Crest Trail

To Reds Meadow

River Trail

Olaine Lake

Pacific Crest Trail

To Rush Creek
trailhead

Summit Lake

High Trail

Badger
Lakes

Middle Fork San Joaquin River

Laura Lake

Altha
Lake

Clarice
Lake

Shadow
Lake

Rosalie
Lake

Gladys Lake

John Muir Trail

Clark
Lakes

River Trail

High Trail

Emerald
Lake

John Muir Trail

Ruby Lake

Garnet Lake

Shadow Creek

Ediza
Lake

John Muir
Wilderness

Thousand Island Lake

Pacific Crest Trail

To Island Pass

37

Agnew Meadows
to Thousand Island Lake

—Kathy Morey

Route	Days	Elev. Gain/Loss	Difficulty	Miles
↻	3	1707'/1707'	**	17.6

Campsites: northwest side of Thousand Island Lake: 7.1 miles
(plus distance to your campsite—a minimum of another
0.25 mile)
(see the Trip Description for others)

Map: USGS 7.5-min *Mammoth Mtn., Mt. Ritter*

Best season: Late summer through early fall

Take this trip!

Your destination, Thousand Island Lake, is one of the Sierra's great beauty spots, a huge—by Sierra standards—sheet of sky-blue water dotted picturesquely with granite islands and situated at the foot of the wild, jagged Ritter Range. The area around Thousand Island Lake is chock-full of more lakes and ponds than you can count, including Thousand Island's big neighbor, Garnet Lake. There's spectacular dayhiking, especially for those willing to tackle some easy cross-country travel. Finally, there are three major trail routes you can take to Thousand Island Lake, all of them marvelously scenic, so that getting to and from the lake are joys in themselves. I combine two of the routes into a loop trip here and mention the third under Variations (below).

I describe a favorite dayhike, looping through Thousand Island and Garnet lakes via the saddle between their southwest ends and the John Muir Trail, in the Take this trip! section of trip 46, "Tuolumne Meadow to Agnew Meadows." Another I highly recommend is ascending to 10,203-foot Island Pass, a little to the north on the John Muir Trail, and enjoying a cross-country ramble around the many little ridges, meadows, and ponds on the interesting plateau east of the pass.

Trailhead

Agnew Meadows, your trailhead for this trip, is the same trailhead described as the Take-out trailhead for trip 46.

TRIP DESCRIPTION

> **Heads Up!** Camping at Thousand Island Lake is prohibited within a quarter mile of the outlet; read and know the posted regulations here, as well as those for Ansel Adams Wilderness! Bears are a very serious problem at Thousand Island Lake; use canisters or kiss your chow goodbye.

Look for a Pacific Crest Trail marker at the trailhead on the south side of the first of the two parking lots. The trail departs southbound, crossing two branches of a little creek, bobs over a low ridge, and skirts a lobe of Agnew Meadows; colorful San Joaquin Ridge rises steeply to the north. Cross the creek again, leaving the meadow behind, and follow the nearly level trail as it winds under lodgepoles between rocky knobs. You pass an unsigned track coming in on the right and presently reach a junction: left (southeast) on the PCT to Reds Meadow; right (ahead, northwest) on the River Trail to Olaine and Shadow lakes.

Go right to descend into the canyon of the Middle Fork San Joaquin River on the open, scrub-dotted trail. Reaching the flats bracketing the river, you reenter forest cover and not long after skirt the east side of shallow Olaine Lake. Just beyond is a Y-junction: left (west) to Shadow Lake; right (northwest) to continue on the River Trail. Turn right to stay on the River Trail, which begins a gradual-to-moderate ascent along the Middle Fork San Joaquin River. The trail switchbacks up through fragrant scrub, then climbs gradually under patchy forest cover, crossing streams draining San Joaquin Ridge and passing potential campsites. Below the trail on your left, the river splashes along, occasionally forming inviting pools.

You skirt a meadow before reaching another Y-junction: right (northeast) on a spur to the PCT—here also called the High Trail; left (northwest) on the River Trail to Garnet and Thousand Island lakes. Go left across a stream, ascend switchbacks, and curve west to yet another junction: right (west) to Thousand Island Lake, left (southwest) to Garnet Lake. There is a campsite west of this junction. Take the right fork uphill through dense lodgepole and fir, sometimes along cascades dashing over stone ledges right next to the trail, to meet the PCT at a T-junction: left to Canada via Thousand Island Lake, right to Mexico via Agnew Meadows.

Thousand Island Lake

Go left (generally west) on the Pacific Crest Trail to curve northwest and then southwest, passing several snowmelt tarns with beautiful views of Banner Peak, to the meadowy outlet of Thousand Island Lake and a junction with the John Muir Trail: right (northwest) to Island Pass, left (southeast) to cross the lake's outlet on a footbridge. Turn left for a few steps on the Muir Trail to another junction, this one a use trail branching right around Thousand Island Lake's northwest shore. Camping is prohibited within a quarter mile of the lake's outlet, as shown by a map on a signboard where you enter the Thousand Island Lake area (7.1). Take the use trail along the lakeshore; the campsites get better the farther you go toward the head of the lake. There are almost no acceptable campsites along the lake's southeast shore. Bears are a very serious problem here. Please observe the posted regulations to help preserve this magnificent but overused area, perhaps even helping it to recover.

Views across the island-dotted lake to the rugged Ritter Range, dominated by Banner Peak, are awesome. You'll immediately notice the difference between the predominantly darker rock of the Ritter Range and the lighter granite of the Sierra crest's alpine peaks. Geologically, the Ritter Range is made up of somewhat older rocks originally volcanic in nature, and the spectacularly jagged skyline from Banner Peak southward attests to the strength of this rock, which resisted the massive glaciers that eroded the range.

When it's time to leave, return to the Muir Trail-Pacific Crest (High) Trail junction just north of the lake's outlet. Pick up the High Trail and retrace your steps of the to the junction where the High Trail meets the River Trail. Go left (ahead, east) on the High Trail and shortly reach the next junction: right (east, then southeast) on the High Trail to the Badger Lakes and Agnew Meadows; left (east-northeast) to the Clark Lakes and Rush Creek trailhead. You go right on the High Trail, through lodgepoles and past the mosquito-heaven Badger Lakes (with campsites).

On this first slope the trail emerges from the dense forest cover, and then it winds up and down through a ground cover that, except for a few scattered stands of pine, is sagebrush, bitterbrush, willow, and some mountain alder. Passing three junctions in the mile beyond Badger Lakes, the trail then contours along the side of San Joaquin Mountain. The dry sage slopes are slashed by streams lined with wildflowers as far up as you can see: larkspur, lupine, shooting star, columbine, penstemon, monkey flower, scarlet gilia, and tiger lily. You may even spot the occasional, Spartan campsite.

For several miles the views are excellent of the Ritter Range to the west; particularly impressive are those of Garnet Lake's outlet and the V'd view of Shadow Lake directly across the San Joaquin River canyon (about 2.8 miles from the trailhead). The trail then descends through a forest of pine and fir. Five hundred feet of well-graded switchbacks bring you to the parking lot north of the pack station.

If you drove a car to this trailhead, turn right (northwest) on the road that runs by the pack station and follow it to the parking lot at your starting trailhead. If you need to catch a shuttlebus back to parking beyond Minaret Summit, turn left (southeast) on the road and walk about a quarter mile to the shuttlebus stop on Devils Postpile Road.

Variations

Very sturdy hikers can do this loop as a dayhike. Another variation would be to return on the John Muir Trail instead of on the High Trail. Learn the details of this variation by following trip 46 from Thousand Island Lake past Emerald, Ruby, Garnet, and Shadow lakes—with more ups and downs than the High Trail and fewer far-ranging views, it's very beautiful in its own right thanks to all those lakes.

Permits

This is a quota trailhead, and permits are required for overnight stays. Apply for permits to Inyo National Forest, 873 N. Main Street, Bishop, CA 93514, (760) 873-2500, **www.r5.fs.fed.us/inyo/**.

Build-up/Wind-down tips

Agnew Meadows, your trailhead, is down in the canyon of Middle Fork San Joaquin River along with Devils Postpile National Monument, and is also just west of the town of Mammoth Lakes (Visitors Bureau, (800) 367-6572). The town has ample lodgings, restaurants, and stores. Its campgrounds include those off Devils Postpile Road; there's a resort at the end of that road (Red's Meadow Resort, (760) 873-3928; lodgings, café, store). Many of these facilities are in very high demand during the summer; make your plans and reservations early!

To find out how Kathy Morey got started hiking the Sierra and the Hawaiian islands and writing about her hikes for Wilderness Press, and for a list of her titles, see "Author Bio & Bib" on page 492.

Banner Peak behind Thousand Island Lake

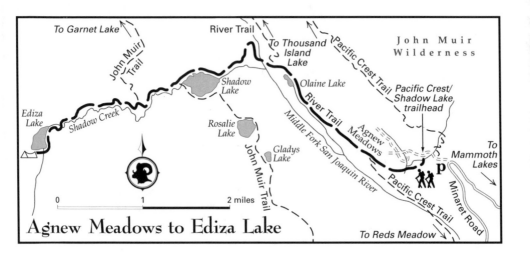

To Garnet Lake

River Trail

To Thousand
Island
Lake

Pacific Crest Trail

John Muir
Wilderness

John Muir Trail

Shadow
Lake

Olaine Lake

Pacific Crest/
Shadow Lake
trailhead

Ediza
Lake

Shadow Creek

River Trail

Rosalie
Lake

Middle Fork San Joaquin River

Agnew
Meadows

To
Mammoth
Lakes

Gladys
Lake

John Muir Trail

Pacific Crest Trail

P

Minaret Road

0   1   2 miles

Agnew Meadows to Ediza Lake

To Reds Meadow

38

Agnew Meadows to Ediza Lake

—Ron Felzer

Route	Days	Elev. Gain/Loss	Difficulty	Miles
⌇	3	1495'/1495'	**	14

Campsites: The first legal campsites are 3½ miles from the trailhead along Shadow Creek, but only across the creek from the trail above Shadow Lake. (Because the creek crossing can be hazardous until late in the season, use the bridged JMT crossing above Shadow Lake.) Camps may be made above the trail (100' or more), but are not recommended. Camping is allowed at Ediza Lake on the far side of the lake opposite the outlet: 7 miles. No campfires are allowed in this area; use a stove.

Map: USGS 7.5-min *Mammoth Mtn., Mt. Ritter*

Best season: Summer to early fall (you'll encounter snow in early summer after heavy winters; in July wildflowers are best, but so, too, are mosquitos)

Take this trip!

With only moderate effort this trail places you among peaks of the spectacular Ritter Range—capped by Mt. Ritter, Banner Peak, and the Minarets—in the Ansel Adams Wilderness. Some say that the alpine beauty of all Sierra lakes culminates at Ediza Lake where, amid towering evidence of mountain building and glacial action, the visitor can readily appreciate the colossal forces that shaped these awe-inspiring landforms. For more than a century, climbers have used the shores of Ediza Lake as their base camps for scaling these classic peaks. However, hikers without climbing experience should not attempt them without the guidance of capable climbers.

Trailhead

To reach the trailhead at Agnew Meadows, drive 3.8 miles west on State Highway 203 from US Highway 395 through the town of Mammoth Lakes. At Minaret Junction (the 2nd traffic light), turn right onto Minaret Road and go 4.2 more miles to the main lodge of Mammoth Mountain Ski Area. Here you will have to park your car and take a Mammoth Shuttle System bus, unless you arrive before or after operating hours or qualify for certain exceptions. (Most campers will not qualify; check at the Mammoth Ranger Station for current regulations.) Minaret Summit is 1.4 miles farther along, and the road beyond it is closed to private vehicles during normal shuttle-bus operating hours. Past Minaret Summit 2.7 miles is the turnoff to Agnew Meadows; down this turnoff are two trailhead parking lots at 0.3 and 0.4 mile, respectively. The second lot is closer to the trailhead, but if parking is not available there, you may be able to park at the first lot and walk by trail to the second lot.

TRIP DESCRIPTION

Heads Up! This trail tends to be in heavy demand during July and August by both dayhikers and backpackers. Those seeking solitude may not be able to find it at this time. An advance Wilderness Permit reservation is highly recommended during these months (see Permits). Also, there are fairly severe camping restrictions along this route (see above). To save the bears (and your food), I strongly recommend bear-proof food canisters for all overnight travel in this area.

Our signed route (a segment of the Pacific Crest Trail south, aka the River Trail) leaves the trailhead parking area just beyond Agnew Meadows Pack Station. As we head west, our route passes a fenced pasture, and we cross several streamlets under a cover of lodgepole pines before passing the first of several signs welcoming us to the Ansel Adams Wilderness. After about a half mile we arrive at a fork. Here we continue straight ahead (northwest), where the PCT turns left toward Devils Postpile and Reds Meadow, descend a dry slope covered with montane chaparral, and pass a connector trail to the PCT on the left. Then our dusty route levels off and skirts the northeast shore of Olaine Lake. Just beyond the lake it turns west, leaving the River Trail about 2 miles from the trailhead. Passing through aspen and sagebrush, we arrive at a bridged crossing of the Middle Fork San Joaquin River. Shortly beyond the crossing we leave the river, jog south a bit, and then begin our climb.

The trail up the west wall of the canyon is rocky underfoot but well maintained. This path rises steeply for 600 feet up juniper-dotted sagebrush slopes on switchbacks, and the hiker is rewarded with excellent views of cascading Shadow Creek, as it falls from the lip of Shadow Lake's outlet. You will be awed by the vertical orientation, glacial polish, and striations of the metavolcanic rocks along this section of trail. These rocks originally formed during violent volcanic events about 200 million years ago. Our arrival at lovely Shadow Lake is via a notch in these heavily glaciated metavolcanic rocks, where we have a water-level view of the lake, with the grand Ritter Range as a backdrop. To encourage resource recovery from camping overuse damage, the Forest Service has wisely closed the shores of Shadow Lake to all overnight camping.

Southwest from Shadow Lake's bridged inlet at about 3½ miles from the trailhead, our route ascends near rushing Shadow Creek on a 1-mile segment of the John Muir Trail. Numerous cascades along the stream invite you to stop and take a break, and there are deep holes for fishing or swimming (in late season only, as these waters are rapid and very cold, usually into August). No camping is between Shadow Creek and the trail, to encourage resource renewal as at Shadow Lake. After the JMT branches north toward Thousand Island Lake, our route continues upstream near Shadow Creek about 1½ more miles, passing through a series of colorful wet meadows, carpeted with paintbrush, monkshood, penstemon, lilies, and numerous other wildflowers well into late summer. Approaching Ediza Lake's outlet, you begin to encounter the subalpine mountain hemlock with its characteristic floppy leader. And from the lake's far shore, the impressive Ritter Range practically rises from the water's edge.

Camping is now allowed only on the opposite side of the lake north of the main inlet stream and its meadows, again to encourage the renewal of vegetation and soils after a century of heavy use here. Even though it looks shorter to cross the lake's outlet and approach the campsites over the talus slopes of the north shore, this stream crossing can be tricky. So the recommended route is to follow the well-used path along the south shore and ford the shallower (though swift and cold till late summer) inlet stream to the legal campsites there. Check the signs along the trail and at the lake's outlet for exact regulations and allowed camping areas in effect at the time of your visit. Campfires are not allowed at Ediza Lake.

While you can retrace your steps to Agnew Meadows via Shadow Lake whenever you've had your fill, I recommend at least one layover day at Ediza Lake to explore surrounding slopes, fish, swim, or just relax and soak up the ambiance of the setting. Experienced climbers will want to spend one or more days ascending peaks in the Ritter Range from their base camp here. Experienced backpackers can make an interesting loop back to the trailhead or via the shuttlebus from Devils Postpile by following a cross-country route to Minaret Lake.

Variations (Minaret Lake Cross-country Return Route)

Experienced backpackers can make an interesting and very scenic return loop via Minaret Lake, exiting at Devils Postpile (shuttle required) by following

Lake Ediza

an unmaintained route from the southeast corner of Ediza Lake up to Iceberg Lake. From the outlet of Iceberg Lake, follow the trail around the east side of the lake, and climb talus to Cecile Lake's outlet. This stretch can be icy until midseason and an ice ax may be required to negotiate it safely. Our obscure, partly ducked route skirts the lake on its east side and leads to the southeast end of the lake, from which we have awesome views of Clyde Minaret, Minaret Lake, and Minaret Creek canyon. From here drop down about 500 feet to Minaret Lake on the vague trail to the east. The maintained trail to Devils Postpile is easily found at the east end of Minaret Lake.

Permits

Wilderness Permits are required for all overnight travel into the Ansel Adams Wilderness, which includes Ediza Lake. Trailhead quota limits are in effect from late June until about mid September. Reservations can be made from six months to 48 hours in advance of your departure date. Unused reservations are available on a walk-in basis at the Mammoth Ranger Station (or the Mono Basin Visitor Center) 24 hours in advance of departure date on a first come, first served basis. Small groups departing from Sunday through Thursday will have the best chance of obtaining permits. For reservations write:

Inyo National Forest
Wilderness Reservations Office
873 N. Main Street
Bishop, CA 93514

You can download a reservation request form at **www.r5.fs.fed.us/inyo/**, or call (760) 873-2408 for information.

Build-up/Wind-down tips

The village of Mammoth Lakes has developed into a year-round full-service resort community with literally hundreds of restaurants and places to stay (see "Aunt Kathy's" restaurant recommendations on page 21). The convenient Old Shady Rest Campground just before the first main intersection in town always seems to have a few campsites available for those needing a place to camp the night before heading off to the trailhead. Your best starting source of information for all the above is the visitor center just east of town.

As "Author Bio & Bib" on page 492 tells you, author Ron Felzer has been teaching natural history of the Sierra for almost as long as he's been backpacking its trails, and his interests have sometimes taken him even farther afield.

The Central Sierra Nevada

Yosemite National Park

By the start of the Third Millennium, visitation to Yosemite National Park had been averaging 4 million visitors per year and, if history is an accurate indicator, visitation will only increase. The draw is Yosemite Valley, perhaps the world's most interpreted natural feature. Thought by John Muir to have been entirely excavated by glaciers, and by others later to have been just greatly excavated by them, glacial erosion only minimally incised into the valley's walls. The valley is a very old feature, having evolved—after the last Sierra Nevada uplift—for at least 65 million years before any glacier ever reached it. Glaciers altered the valley's dimensions in two ways. First, each major glacier, which typically was about 1500–1000 feet thick, exerted pressure on the lower walls for thousands of years, and when each rapidly retreated, the pressure was suddenly released and a round of rapid exfoliation ensued. This led to the accumulation of tremendous amounts of talus, such as you see today, some 13,000 years after the last glacier retreated. The valley, which already was wide due to mass wasting of its walls over tens of millions of years, became perhaps 10 percent wider due to the dozens of glaciations. Second, glaciers filled the valley with hundreds of feet of sediments.

Nevertheless, each year millions of Yosemite tourists will learn how glaciers deepened the valley and steepened its walls, transforming cascades into waterfalls. And each year these tourists will occupy the campsites you hope will be free when you drive up to the park. Don't count on it. You can still drive to Sequoia and Kings Canyon National Parks and easily find a campsite, but if you try to reserve a campsite in Yosemite, say two or three months in advance, you're likely to discover that all sites are taken. As visitation increased in the park, the Park Service reduced the total amount of campsites, compounding the shortfall. For Yosemite backpackers, I've mentioned specifics on obtaining a park campsite in the "High Sierra Camps Loop" trip. Outside the park, Yosemite overfill ensures that Tioga Road campgrounds east of Tioga Pass will be full. This also is true for the Devils Postpile-Agnew Meadows area and, at least on weekends, for the Pinecrest Lake area.

Emigrant, Hoover, & Ansel Adams Wildernesses

Some of the most impressive scenery and nicest lakes lie outside Yosemite National Park in the adjoining wildernesses of Emigrant on the northwest border, Hoover on the northeast border, and Ansel Adams on the southeast border. Emigrant Wilderness overwhelmingly is a granitic landscape with relatively shallow canyons and dozens of glacial lakes. Because its canyons are shallow, hiking across this wilderness is easy by Sierran standards. Hoover Wilderness is a narrow one, in effect a buffer zone between Yosemite's Sierra crest and lower lands to the east. This zone almost coincides with a belt of metamorphic rocks, so this wilderness has a very different feel: deep, near-crest canyons in various earth hues of metamorphic rocks alternating with grays of granitic rocks. This belt continues south along the Sierra crest through Yosemite's Tioga Pass, then beyond through eastern Ansel Adams Wilderness. There you'll find arguably the finest mountain scenery in the Sierra Nevada: the sawtooth Ritter Range and sparkling, reflecting lakes along its east base. In the west of this wilderness the landscape is more granitic and the relief is less, somewhat akin to Emigrant Wilderness, and therefore relatively easy hiking. Of course, if you want to challenge yourself with major ups and downs every day, Yosemite proper is for you. And since most of its lakes are above 8000 feet elevation, your effort to reach them will be compounded by the thinner air found up here. But then, the High Sierra is dramatic due in part to high elevation, which allows higher relief—towering peaks above deep valleys—to exist. (JPS)

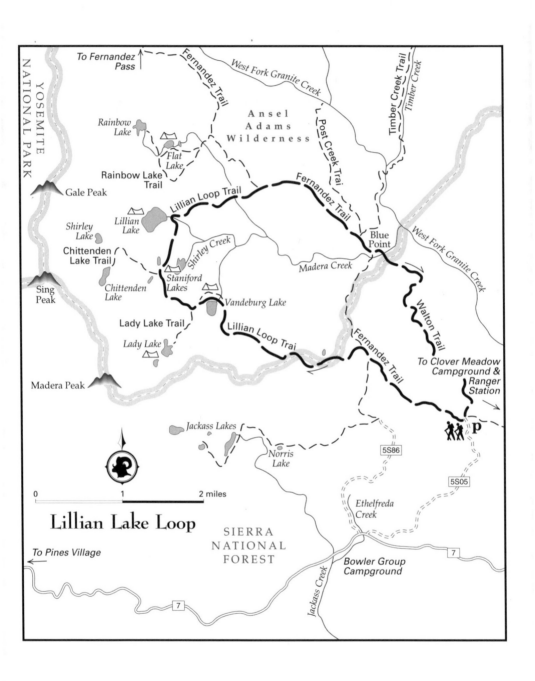

Lillian Lake Loop

To Fernandez Pass

Fernandez Trail

West Fork Granite Creek

Timber Creek Trail

Timber Creek

Ansel Adams Wilderness

Post Creek Trail

YOSEMITE NATIONAL PARK

Rainbow Lake

Flat Lake

Rainbow Lake Trail

Fernandez Trail

Gale Peak

Lillian Loop Trail

Blue Point

West Fork Granite Creek

Shirley Lake

Lillian Lake

Shirley Creek

Madera Creek

Chittenden Lake Trail

Sing Peak

Staniford Lakes

Chittenden Lake

Vandeburg Lake

Walton Trail

Lady Lake Trail

Lillian Loop Trai

To Clover Meadow Campground & Ranger Station

Fernandez Trail

Madera Peak

Lady Lake

Jackass Lakes

Norris Lake

5S86

5S05

P

0   1   2 miles

Ethelfreda Creek

SIERRA NATIONAL FOREST

7

To Pines Village

Bowler Group Campground

Jackass Creek

7

39

Lillian Lake Loop

—Jeffrey P. Schaffer

Route	Days	Elev. Gain/Loss	Elev. Low/High	Difficulty	Miles
↻	2 or 3	2440'/2440'	7470'/9050'	**	13.1

(mileage pertains to basic loop, including only spur to Lady Lake)

Campsites: Lady Lake: 5.2 miles
(see the Trip Description for others)

Map: USGS 7.5-min *Timber Knob*

Best season: Mid July through mid September

Take this trip!

If you make the basic loop, you encounter three lakes, which isn't bad for a relatively easy 12-mile hike. However, if you visit Lady Lake, you'll have a fourth lake with an easy mile of extra effort. Since many folks can hike 13 miles in a day, why backpack at all? The answer is that the country's just too scenic— and several of its lakes too beautiful—to make a whirlwind trip through it. In addition to visiting Lady, I suggest you also visit Chittenden, Flat, and Rainbow. These four add about 7.2 miles to the trip and 50% more total elevation gain and loss. With a total of 19.3 miles it is a suitable 2-day hike: set up camp at the largest Staniford Lake, make an afternoon visit to Chittenden Lake, then return to camp. Still, I recommend a more leisurely 3 days, spending your first night at Lady Lake then your second at Flat Lake. Situated on a large flat bench, this lake has one of the largest camping areas bordering any Sierran lake, and makes an ideal base camp to reach one of my favorites, Rainbow, situated on a bench above it.

Trailhead

From the Highway 49 junction in Oakhurst, drive north on Highway 41 for 3.5 miles to a junction with Road 222, signed for Bass Lake. Follow this east 3.5 miles to a fork, veer left and continue east 2.4 miles on Malum Ridge Road

274 to a junction with north-climbing Forest Route 7, or Beasore Road. (Immediately before this junction, south-dropping Beasore Road goes briefly to Pines Village, just above the north shore of Bass Lake, and it is your last opportunity for food and fuel.) Forest Route 7 climbs 11.4 miles to an intersection at Cold Springs Summit, then winds 8.6 miles before coming to a junction with Road 5S04, opposite Globe Rock, losing its good pavement along the way (this may change in the future). Continue along your road, an obvious route, 7.5 miles to a junction with Road 5S86 (27.5 miles along Forest Route 7). This junction is 0.4 mile past the Bowler Group Camp entrance and 100 yards *before* Forest Route 7 crosses Ethelfreda Creek. Road 5S86 climbs 1.9 miles to a trailhead at its end. From it, a steep trail provides the shortest route to Vandeburg Lake via Staniford Lakes. On the down side, however, it is a still initial, 600-foot climb to a ridge, and when you've almost completed this loop, you'll have a 500-foot climb back up to it, only to soon start your 600-foot descent. Therefore, I suggest the following route. Fork left onto Road 5S05 just 100 yards *after* Forest Route 7 crosses Ethelfreda Creek, and ascend it 2.3 miles to its end, complete with a large turnaround/parking lot.

TRIP DESCRIPTION

Heads Up! Most of this route is above 8000 feet, which means that you can expect lots of early-season snow. Even in a year of normal precipitation you're likely to find a few small patches of snow on the trail well into July. This is not a problem, but in early July there are enough patches that you could lose the trail. Madera Creek basin is large and forested, and without a compass and map you could get lost. The same applies if you get caught in, say, a September snow storm.

From your trailhead, you can make the Lillian Lake Loop in either direction. The clockwise direction begins north on a continuation of your road, which is blocked off to prevent motor vehicle traffic. The advantage of this is that you have more views and not much elevation gain over the first 3 miles. It, however, is lakeless. I prefer the counterclockwise direction, since you get the route's only significant ascent out of the way in 2 miles and then have a generally easy ramble to Vandeburg Lake over the next 2¼ miles.

In this direction we start west on the Fernandez Trail. (In the opposite direction the trail descends about a mile to the Clover Meadow Campground, then ends near its entrance, just west of the Clover Meadow Ranger Station.) Westward, you begin an easy ascent through a typical mid-elevation Sierran forest, but after ⅓ mile your trail steepens. For almost a mile you climb moderately, then briefly up short, steeper switchbacks below a small, exfoliating "dome." Just past it you reach a near-crest junction with a steep, mile-long trail ascending north from the alternate trailhead (at the end of Road 5S86), and 0.2 mile later reach a crest junction with the Lillian Loop Trail (1.8). With major climbing done, you fork left (west) for an easy stroll, soon entering Ansel Adams Wilderness. Just within it, on the north side of a broad ridge, you spy a waist-deep pond on your right; then hike later past two often wet, moraine-dammed meadows—both mosquito havens before August. After about 2 miles of easy hiking on your trail, you then climb moderately to steeply to reach a notch in a granitic crest. In about 300 yards you pass two ponds on a short descent to a junction near Madera Creek. From the junction the right branch—for horses—descends north to Madera Creek, then circles counterclockwise ⅓ mile to rejoin the left branch above the lake's west shore. On foot, you take the left branch, climbing to nearby good-to-excellent campsites just above the north shore of Vandeburg Lake (4.3). From them, steep, granitic Peak 9852 along with dark, saddle-shaped Madera Peak to its right are reflected in the lake's placid early morning waters.

From where the horse and foot branches of the Lillian Loop Trail reunite, you start a 250-yard, moderate climb up bedrock to a junction on a lodgepole flat with the Lady Lake Trail (4.7). Here you can take a spur trail south, which climbs, mostly gently, just over ½ mile to a large campsite on the north shore of granite-rimmed Lady Lake. I find this lake more attractive than Vandeburg because it has an irregular shoreline not a roundish one, because it is speckled with several boulder islands, and because it is closer to the two aforementioned peaks. You can circle this lake, although you'll have to scramble across talus that lies below Peak 9852. On such a navigation, you'll find ample campsites above the lake's north, west, and northeast shores. At the lake's south and southwest shores are expansive, glacier-smoothed slabs that are good for basking, particularly after a dip, which at 8900 feet elevation is always brisk. In this vicinity you have views of Mts. Ritter, Banner, and the Minarets—another incentive for camping here (as well as catching the warming rays of the early morning sun). Just beyond the south slab is Lady Lake's 1½-acre satellite, in a stark, alpine setting, from which you can begin an ascent to looming, metamorphic Madera Peak. Like all the lakes you might visit along this hike, except for the shallow Staniford Lakes, Lady Lake has trout (as does its satellite).

Beyond the Lady Lake Trail junction your Lillian Loop Trail crosses the lodgepole flat, then climbs a couple of hundred feet up fairly open granitic slabs. On them you can stop and appreciate the skyline panorama from the Minarets south to the Mt. Goddard area in Kings Canyon National Park. During past glaciations virtually all of this panorama except for high crests and mountain peaks was under ice. At ½ mile from the junction you top a ridge, then on a moderate-to-steep descent northwest, you reach, in ¼ mile, a junction with the Chittenden Lake Trail (5.4). Here, close to a Staniford Lakes creek, one can start a mile-long climb up to cliffbound Chittenden Lake. The trail, which is largely across bedrock, is ducked, but even so it is obscure in places. Essentially

Staniford Lake

it winds about ⅔ mile northwest up to a small, often boggy meadow, from where you could continue ¼ mile northwest up to extremely shallow Shirley Lake, which is not worth most hikers' efforts. From the meadow the trail is more pronounced, and it climbs steeply southwest ⅓ mile to Chittenden Lake. The last slabby trail section to it is so steep that equestrians rarely visit it. Chittenden may be the most beautiful of all the lakes in this part of Ansel Adams Wilderness, though Lady and Rainbow lakes offer stiff competition. Although Chittenden's water usually does not rise above the low 60s, the lake's three bedrock islands will certainly tempt some swimmers. Anglers also will find the lake attractive, and from a low ridge above its northeast shore you have a fine view of your Madera Creek basin plus much of the upper San Joaquin River basin. At your lake only one good campsite exists, a large one about 40 yards above the north corner. Because camp space is at a premium, I suggest you camp among the slabs bordering the largest Staniford Lake, and only day-hike to Chittenden.

About 100 yards past the junction your Lillian Loop Trail offers a view of a waist-deep, grass-lined lakelet, just off your left. Then, in another 200 yards, you reach a small trailside pond, also on your left, and from here you can branch right (east), and stroll cross-country for 200–250 yards across low-angle slabs to the largest Staniford Lake (5.8). This is certainly the best lake to swim in, and if any sizable lake along this route will warm up to the low 70s in early August, it will be this one. The great bulk of the lake is less than 5 feet deep, its only deep spot being at a diving area along the west shore. Gentle terrain surrounds the lake, providing many sites for camping.

Along the northbound Lillian Loop Trail you pass two more ponds, before briefly traversing open slabs. You then diagonal up slopes to a minor ridge with many glacier-polished slabs. From the ridge, you descend 90 yards to Lillian Lake's outlet creek, which drains southeast into Shirley Creek. Cross the outlet creek for a 50-yard walk upstream to a low dam on Lillian Lake (6.5). Here is an adjacent, lodgepole-shaded area that once comprised the largest campsite in this part of the wilderness. Since camping is prohibited within 400 feet of the northeast shore, be inventive and try elsewhere. For example, there is a large camp about 40 yards above the lake's north corner. Being the largest and deepest lake you'll see along this hike, Lillian Lake is also the coldest—not good for swimming. However, its large population of trout does attract anglers.

With your basic hike now half over, leave the lake's outlet and descend the Lillian Loop Trail a mile east through forest down to a two-branched creek with easy fords. Your trail ends in ¼ mile, after a short, stiff climb over a gravelly knoll. Here, at a junction on a fairly open slope, we rejoin the Fernandez Trail (7.7).

On it we climb a mile northwest up granite slabs through an open forest to a meadowside trail junction immediately below a minor gap. From here a trail climbs 1.5 miles up to rewarding Rainbow Lake. Should you want to visit it—and I recommend you do—go but ¼ mile to a junction. From it the Rainbow Lake Trail climbs ½ mile southwest up a broad crest before turning northwest to soon drop over 100 feet to the lake's outlet creek. The more direct approach to this lake is to branch right and traverse westward about ⅓ mile to the south shore of Flat Lake, which is deep enough to swim in and to support trout. However, the shoreline water is shallow, which is not conducive to good fishing. The land adjacent to the south shore is flat, lodgepole-shaded, and extensive, capable of holding dozens of campers. Because camping is banned within ¼ mile of Rainbow Lake, perched on a bench above Flat Lake, you should camp here, then dayhike to Rainbow. With that goal in mind, head briefly southwest to Rainbow's outlet creek, which feeds into Flat Lake, then, with the creek on your right, ascend moderately steep slopes to the brink of the creek's cascading course, about 150 feet higher. Here you'll meet the Rainbow Lake Trail. Cross the creek and traverse a bench for 0.1 mile to reach a lakelet. You could camp along this bench and experience a hopefully wondrous sunset and sunrise. However, once you pass the lakelet, you're within the banned-camping zone. On the trail you climb shortly north to a ridge, then from it drop momentarily to Rainbow Lake's outlet. Just beyond it is a small ridge that pro-trudes into the prized lake, offering you a fine spot to photograph, fish, or dive from. One can cross this multi-lobed lake by swimming from islet to islet.

After your visit to Flat and Rainbow lakes, backtrack to the junction of the Lillian Loop Trail with the Fernandez Trail. On the latter, you descend ⅓ mile east to a linear gully, cross its seasonal creek and then in ¼ mile first parallel it a bit before drifting over to the crest of a moraine. On it you traverse a similar distance, have views east, then plunge straight ahead, the steep descent aided by a few short switchbacks. Below them your Fernandez Trail descends ½ mile to a trail junction. If you were to follow the trail north 70 yards to a crest saddle, you would see that it forks into the Post Creek Trail (left) and the Timber Creek Trail (right), both lightly used.

From this junction the Fernandez Trail descends 0.2 mile to a gravelly flat along the north bank of Madera Creek. This spacious flat is well suited for camping, and from it you can inspect the dark-gray plug of olivine basalt of Blue Point above you, which was once part of the throat of a cinder cone. Glaciers removed the cinders but were too feeble to erode the lava. Here on the flat is the Walton Trail (9.0), your route forking east from the southbound Fernandez Trail. Take the Walton Trail 150 yards east over to Madera Creek, which through mid-July, when runoff is still high, is a 10-yard-wide ford. If so, look for boulders 100–200 yards downstream to keep your feet dry.

Now you make a short, steep climb, reaching a minor gap in 200 yards. Having completed the only significant climb on this trail, you can rest and absorb the vistas. Here you leave Ansel Adams Wilderness to commence a 2¾-mile ramble, dipping and winding in and out of gullies and through groves of conifers, but emerging at vistas, particularly northwest of the serrated crest of the Ritter Range. Your easy trail ends as you descend ¼-mile southeast from a minor gap to a closed road, on which you walk a level ¼ mile back to your trail-head.

Permits

A Wilderness Permit is required year-round for all those spending the night in Ansel Adams Wilderness. Additionally, a quota system is in effect from late June through September 15, and up to two thirds of the daily quota can be reserved in advance. Reservations may be made by mail from March 1 through August 15, and should be made at least three weeks before your trip. These cost you $3 *per person*. Permits are not mailed; rather, pick yours up in person up to 48 hours before your hike's starting date. You get these only at the Mariposa-Minarets Ranger District Office (Box 10, North Fork, CA 93643; phone: (559) 877-2218). As stated just above, the drive from North Fork to the trailhead is a long one. You can take your chances and drive up FR 7 to the Clover Meadow Ranger Station (see Trailhead) and get one in person. The quota limit should be no problem if you are starting Sunday through Thursday, but weekends are risky.

Build-up/Wind-down tips

Unless you're a group, you can't stay in Bowler Group Camp. The closest campground along Forest Route 7 is Upper Chiquito, about 1 mile east of the Globe Rock junction. However, I find it unappealing and prefer Clover Meadow Campground. To reach it, from the Road 5S05 junction continue 2.1 miles east on FR 7 to a junction with entirely paved FR 81 (aka Minarets Road). From the small community of North Fork, this is a long, winding road north, albeit a very scenic one. (If you're not in a hurry before or after your hike, it is worth taking.) The route has three roadside campgrounds (plus others on lateral roads), and Soda Springs is the one farthest north, about 35 miles above North Fork and 17 miles before the junction with FR 7. From this junction, take Road 5S30 northeast 1.8 miles to Clover Meadow Ranger Station, and get your permit there if you haven't gotten one earlier. To reach the primitive Clover Meadow Campground, which has only several sites, take the narrow road branching left from the ranger station. This road can be rutted and sometimes boggy. If the campground hasn't opened for the summer season, that's a good sign you'll find lots of snow along your hike.

Jeffrey P. Schaffer provides background on his path to guidebook writing, detailed mapmaking, and challenging received views of Sierra geological formation, besides a list of his titles from Wilderness Press, in "Author Bio & Bib" on page 492.

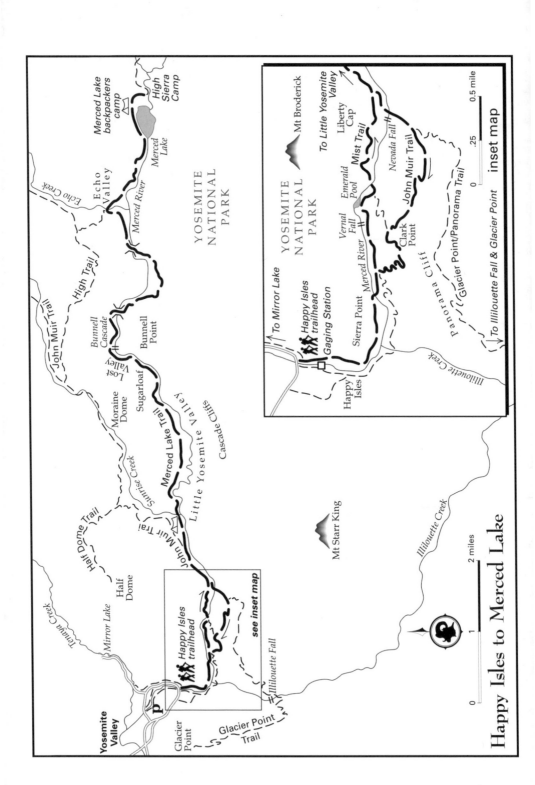

Happy Isles to Merced Lake

40

Happy Isles to Merced Lake

—Jeffrey P. Schaffer

Route	Days	Elev. Gain/Loss	Elev. Low/High	Difficulty	Miles
↻	3	4670'/4670'	4030'/7230'	**	26.6

Campsites: Little Yosemite Valley: 4.2 miles
Merced Lake backpackers' camp: 13.1 miles
(see the Trip Description for others)

Map: USGS 7.5-min *Half Dome, Merced Peak*

Best season: Early July through mid September

Take this trip!

This is the very first backpack trip I ever made in the Sierra Nevada, back in 1964. I've repeated it, and in the '90s enjoyed it even more, in part because backpacker paraphernalia have considerably improved, but additionally because of its grand, canyon scenery. You have to work for it, but the ascents past Vernal and Nevada falls are well worth the effort. Mile for mile, this very popular ascent may be the most scenic one in the park. The first part goes up the famous (or infamous) Mist Trail—a steep, strenuous route where you encounter Vernal Fall's mist, which cools you on hot afternoons. Take raingear or, if it is a warm day, strip down to swimwear, since you can dry out on slabs above the fall. For best photos start after 10 A.M. Above Nevada Fall climbing is quite minimal, and beyond Little Yosemite Valley and its crowds, the multi-stepped stretch to Merced Lake is lined with dramatic, towering, glacier-smoothed canyon walls. Over much of this distance you are accompanied by the musical sounds—if not the sight—of the Merced River, which alternates between quiet pools and dashing cascades.

Trailhead

Arbitrarily, this is at the Happy Isles shuttle-bus stop (stop 16) in south-eastern Yosemite Valley. If you have a vehicle, you'll have to leave it at the backpackers' parking lot, which is about midway between Curry Village and Happy Isles. When you get your Wilderness Permit, you'll be told how to reach it. If you don't take a shuttle bus, you'll have a ½-mile walk via trail or road southeast to Happy Isles.

TRIP DESCRIPTION

Heads Up! The steep Mist Trail up to the top of Vernal Fall is wet, especially before August, and a careless slip in the wrong place could be fatal. (Still, most tourists make it up and down without injury.) Higher up, when you ascend past Nevada Fall, your trail's short switchbacks are steep and often have loose gravel. Again, you could slip, especially if you decide to descend this route, although unlike the lower part, none of this upper part is seriously exposed.

Above the two falls is Little Yosemite Valley, which has one of the largest backpackers' camps you'll find anywhere in the state, and hence, it attracts bears. Fortunately, at its camp and at the large one at Merced Lake, bearproof food-storage boxes exist. The problem is that if you or your tent smells of food, you'll likely have a nighttime food inspection. This can be unnerving, especially when the bear slashes your tent to provide entry. Avoid this by leaving the fly unzipped so that bears can poke their heads inside your tent without damaging it (still unnerving!).

Finally, pools in the Merced River are tempting and I've swum in some. However, the water is cold and can be swifter than you might imagine, so enter it with caution, and certainly *not* in the pools just above Nevada Fall. Emerald Pool, just above Vernal Fall, can be safe when the river flow is slow, although occasionally a careless swimmer is swept over the fall. Again, use caution and good sense.

Strong hikers can dayhike this route, while others attempt it as an overnight backpack. But because there is considerable elevation gain and loss, I recommend you take two days to reach Merced Lake, then one long day—mostly downhill—to return.

From the Happy Isles shuttle-bus stop you begin by walking briefly east across an adjacent bridge and head south, soon reaching a stream-gaging station. From this station the famous John Muir Trail heads about 212 miles southward to the summit of Mt. Whitney. Bay trees, Douglas-firs, and canyon live oaks dominate the forest canopy as you start up it, and after a few minutes you meet a trail on the right that descends to the nearby Merced River. In a few more yards is a small spring-fed cistern with questionably pure water.

Beyond it the climb south steepens, and before bending east you get a glance back at Upper Yosemite Fall, partly blocked by the Glacier Point Apron. This smooth, curving apron contrasts with the generally angular nature of Yosemite's topography. Note the canyon wall south of the apron, which has a series of oblique-angle cliffs—all of them remarkably similar in orientation since they've fractured along the same series of joint planes. At the canyon's end Illilouette Fall plunges 370 feet over a vertical, joint-controlled cliff. Just east of the fall is a large, light-colored scar that marks the site of a major rockfall that broke loose during the winter of 1968-69. If you look west from your vantage point, you'll see the talus of a more-recent major rockfall, one that broke loose from high on the Glacier Point environs in 1996. Another one broke loose from midway up its north slope in 1998, and its debris came close to obliterating your trailhead parking lot. Now climbing east, you head up a canyon whose floor in times past was buried by as much as 2000 feet of glacier ice. Hiking beneath the unstable, highly fractured south wall of Sierra Point, you cross a talus slope—an accumulation of rockfall boulders. The May 1980 Mammoth Lakes earthquakes perhaps set up three rockfalls here, which finally occurred in conjunction with heavy rains in late spring 1986. With each rockfall the valley widens slightly, as it has for millions of years.

Entering forest shade once more, you ascend a steep stretch of trail before making a quick drop to your destination, the Vernal Fall bridge (0.9). From it you see Vernal Fall, a broad curtain of water plunging 320 feet over a vertical cliff before cascading toward us. Looming above the fall are two glacier-resistant masses, Mt. Broderick (left) and Liberty Cap (right). Just beyond the bridge are restrooms and an emergency telephone (heart attacks, slips on dangerous rocks).

About 200 yards beyond the bridge you come to a junction, the start of a loop. Here the Mist Trail, which we'll ascend, continues upriver while the John Muir Trail (1.1), which we'll descend, makes a switchbacking route to this junction. In swimsuit or raingear, start up the Mist Trail and soon, rounding a bend, receive your first spray. If you're climbing this trail on a sunny day, you're almost certain to see one, if not two, rainbows come alive in the fall's spray. The spray increases as you advance toward the fall, but you get a brief respite behind a large boulder. Beyond it, complete your 300-plus steps, most of them wet, which guide you up through a verdant, spray-drenched garden. The last few dozen steps are under the shelter of trees; then, reaching an alcove beneath an ominous overhang, you scurry left up a last set of stairs. These, protected by a railing, guide you to the top of a vertical cliff. Pausing here you can study your route, the nearby fall, and the river gorge. The railing ends near the brink of Vernal Fall but, unfortunately, people venture beyond it, and every year it seems that one or more are swept over the fall. Sunbathers, trying to reach the far side

View of Liberty Cap and Vernal Fall from the Mist Trail

of Emerald Pool, which lies just above the brink, may underestimate the danger of the river's slippery rocks and the danger of its treacherous current. Don't be taken in.

Plunging into the upper end of chilly Emerald Pool is churning Silver Apron. Late in the summer when the Merced's flow is noticeably down, one is tempted to glide down this watery chute into Emerald Pool. This is hazardous, for one can easily crash on some boulders just beyond the end of this silvery chute. Rivers are not to be taken lightly. You'll see a bridge spanning the narrow gorge that confines the Silver Apron, and this structure is your immediate goal. The trail can be vague in this area, due to use paths, but the correct route leaves the river near the pool's far (east) end, and you'll find outhouses here. After a brief climb south, the trail angles east to a nearby junction. From it a view-packed connecting trail (2.0) climbs almost ½ mile to Clark Point, where it meets the John Muir Trail. We, however, stay low and curve left over to the Silver Apron bridge. Beyond it you have a short, moderate climb up to a broad bench which was once the site of La Casa Nevada. Opened in 1870 it was managed by Albert Snow until 1891, when a fire burned the main structure to the ground.

Spurred onward by the sight and sound of plummeting Nevada Fall, you climb eastward, soon commencing a series of more than two dozen compact switchbacks. As you ascend them, Nevada Fall slips out of view, but you can see towering Liberty Cap. Your climb ends at the top of a joint-controlled gully where, on brushy slopes, you once again—at the Nevada Fall junction (3.2)—meet the John Muir Trail (with outhouses just up it).

From this junction you climb up a gully that is generally overgrown with huckleberry oak, a shrubby though still true oak. From the top you quickly descend into forest cover and reach a fairly large swimming hole on the Merced River. Though chilly, it is far enough above the river's rapids to provide a short, refreshing dip. A longer stay would make you numb. Beneath conifers you continue northeast along the river's azalea-lined bank, then quickly encounter a trail fork. The left fork climbs and then descends the low east ridge of Liberty Cap—a shortcut to the Half Dome Trail. On the JMT we go a short half mile to another junction, from where this trail branches north while our Merced Lake Trail continues east. Here, in Little Yosemite Valley (4.2), on the short stretch of JMT north, you first reach a large backpackers' camp, with bearproof storage boxes, then outhouses, and beyond them a spur trail northeast over to a rangers' station. The camp is the recommended place to spend your first night.

Next day, you embark on a shady 2-mile stroll, following the Merced Lake Trail through broad, flat-floored Little Yosemite Valley. The valley's floor has been largely buried by glacial sediments, which like beach sand make one work even though the trail is level. Progressing east through it, you stay closer to the base of glacier-polished Moraine Dome than to the Merced River, and along this stretch you can branch off to riverside campsites that are far more peaceful than those near the JMT junction, which tends to be a "Grand Central Station." The valley's east end is graced by the presence of a beautiful pool—the receptacle of a Merced River cascade. However, these sites lack bearproof food-storage boxes.

Onward, you climb past the cascade and can glance back to see the east face of exfoliating Moraine Dome. Your brief cascade climb heads toward the 1900-foot-high Bunnell Point cliff, which is exfoliating at a prodigious rate. Rounding the base of a glacier-smoothed dome, unofficially called the Sugar Loaf, you enter shady Lost Valley, in which no fires are allowed. At the valley's east end, you switchback up past Bunnell Cascade, which with the magnificent canyon scenery can easily distract one from the real danger of this exposed section of trail. Although the scenery may overpower you, past glaciers, which completely buried Bunnell Point, were powerless to effectively erode this part of the canyon. They overtopped the point by several hundred feet, yet their massive thicknesses, exerting over 100 tons per square foot on the lower slopes, failed to transform this canyon from a V to a U shape.

Just beyond the V gorge, the canyon floor widens a bit, and in this area we meet our first bridge (8.5) over the Merced River. Your up-canyon walk soon reaches a series of more than a dozen switchbacks that rise 400 feet above the river—a bypass route necessitated by another V gorge. Our climb reaches its zenith amid a spring-fed profuse garden bordered by aspens, which in mid-summer supports a colorful array of various wildflowers. Beyond this glade we soon emerge onto a highly polished bedrock surface. Here you can glance west and see Clouds Rest—a long ridge on the horizon. Now descend back into tree cover and, among the white boles of aspens, brush through a forest carpet of bracken ferns and cross several creeklets before emerging on a bedrock bench above the river's inner gorge. From the bench you can study the features of a broad, hulking granitic mass opposite you whose south face is bounded by an immense arch. A hairline crack along its east side indicates that a major rockfall is imminent. Traversing the bench, you soon come to a bend in the river and our second bridge (10.4) of the Merced just above the brink of its cascades. Strolling east, you soon reach the west end of spacious Echo Valley. Proceed to its north edge, which has a junction with the Echo Valley/High Trail (11.2).

Now you immediately bridge Echo Creek, strike southeast through formerly burned, boggy Echo Valley, and climb about ¾ mile east past some of the Merced River's pools and cascades to the outlet of Merced Lake (12.6). Don't camp here, but rather head about 250 yards past the north shore to the spacious Merced Lake backpackers' camp (13.1). Complete with bearproof food-storage boxes, this is situated about ¼ mile before the High Sierra camp. Nearby 80-foot-deep Merced Lake, being a large one at a moderate elevation, supports three species of trout: brook, brown, and rainbow.

After your stay at the lake, backtrack about 9 miles to the junction with the John Muir Trail in Little Yosemite Valley. Here you follow the trail description of the Tuolumne Meadows to Happy Isles trip, first 1.0 mile to the junction with the upper end of the Mist Trail, then 3.6 scenic miles beyond it on the JMT down to the Happy Isles shuttle-bus stop.

Permits

See the similar section under the "High Sierra Camps Loop" trip. If you get a permit in person, stop at the valley's Visitor Center, where you'll find its Wilderness Center. Don't expect to walk in and get a permit for a weekend trip; the day's quota may be full.

Build-up/Wind-down tips

See the similar section under the "High Sierra Camps Loop" trip, especially the second half, for wind-down tips. As in Tuolumne Meadows, getting a Yosemite Valley campsite is virtually impossible, especially during the summer season, so plan to drive to the valley on the day you'll start your hike.

Jeffrey P. Schaffer provides background on his path to guidebook writing, detailed mapmaking, and challenging received views of Sierra geological formation, besides a list of his titles from Wilderness Press, in "Author Bio & Bib" on page 492.

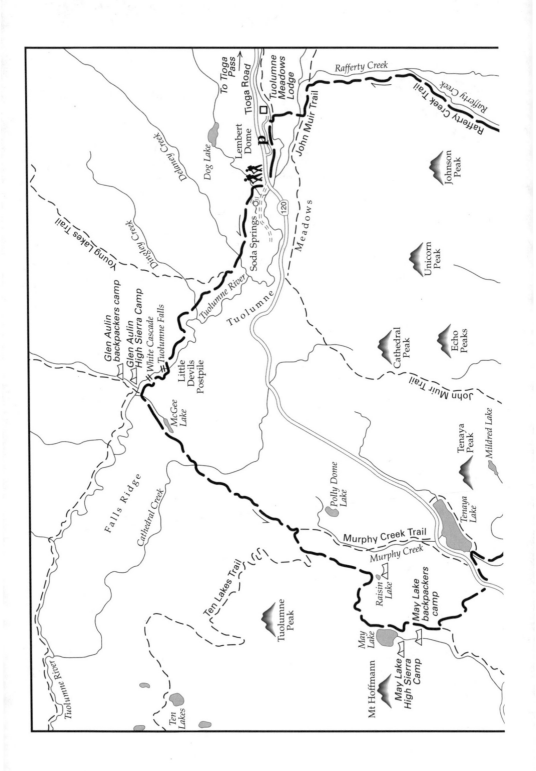

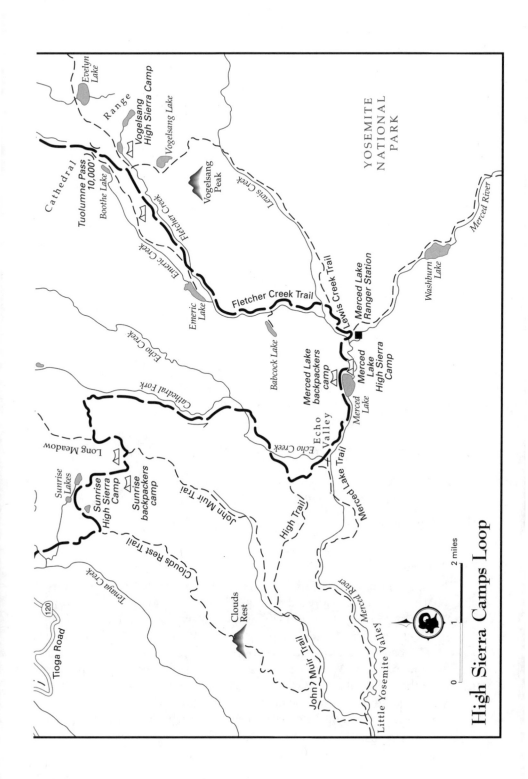

High Sierra Camps Loop

41

High Sierra Camps Loop

—Jeffrey P. Schaffer

Route	Days	Elev. Gain/Loss	Elev. Low/High	Difficulty	Miles
↻	5–7	8830'/8830'	7100'/10,170'	***	51.0
					(miles without side hikes)

Campsites: Glen Aulin backpackers' camp: 6.5 miles
McGee Lake: 7.5 miles
Raisin Lake: 13.2 miles
May Lake backpackers' camp: 15.0 miles
Sunrise backpackers' camp: 23.8 miles
Merced Lake backpackers' camp: 34.0 miles
Vogelsang High Sierra Camp: 42.5 miles
(see the Trip Description for others)

Map: USGS 7.5-min *Falls Ridge, Merced Peak, Tenaya Lake, Tioga Pass, Vogelsang Peak*

Best season: Late July through early September

Take this trip!

This lengthy trip is unique in that you can backpack for 6 days without carrying a backpack. You can carry a day pack and spend each night at one of the High Sierra camps, complete with bedding and meals. But it's easier said than done, for demand far outstrips supply. Therefore, a lottery is held each December to determine the lucky relative few for the following summer. To enter the lottery, contact Yosemite Concession Services between September 1st and November 15th. Phone them at (209) 252-4848, or write to Central Reservations, Yosemite Concession Services, 5410 East Home Ave., Fresno, CA 93727, or reach them on the Internet at **www.yosemitepark.com/lodging/**.

The unlucky majority still should take this trip. There is a reason why the camps are located where they are: they are along a High Sierra loop trail that offers a sampling of some of the best scenery in Yosemite National Park. To avoid crowds, simply camp at sites situated between the High Sierra camps.

Trailhead

The Tioga Road makes an east-west traverse across Yosemite National Park, and on that road are two appropriate trailheads, both obvious. The western one is at a small parking lot near the southwest corner of Tenaya Lake, while the eastern one is in Tuolumne Meadows at a spur-road junction by the base of Lembert Dome, which is immediately northeast of a bridge across the Tuolumne River. You could park along the start of the spur road or westward along it. I prefer to continue briefly east on the Tioga Road to the Tuolumne Meadows Lodge spur road, go right on it a short distance, then branch right into a large backpackers' parking lot (the Trip Description begins from here). Adjacent, a small office dispenses Wilderness Permits. Finally, you could continue on this road to another large parking lot, reached about ⅓ mile before road's end at the lodge's parking lot, which is reserved for guests only.

TRIP DESCRIPTION

> **Heads Up!** Yosemite has lots of bears that leave you alone, but not your food—see a discussion of this problem in this book's introductory section. Campsites by the High Sierra camps have bear boxes or other bearproof devices to safely store your food. Should you try to avoid crowds by hiking in early July, before the High Sierra camps open, you'll encounter some snow patches. By hiking in mid or late September, after they close, you'll run the risk of being caught in a snowstorm. And, before early August, mosquitoes can be quite abundant.

You could begin this loop trail either clockwise or counterclockwise from either the Tuolumne Meadows or the Tenaya Lake environs. I prefer counterclockwise from the former, since this way on your first day, when your pack is heaviest and you are perhaps not in the best of shape, your route is mostly level and downhill.

From the parking lot with the wilderness-permit office, take a trail which heads briefly west to the Tioga Road and its westside Lembert Dome parking lot. Here you walk ⅓ mile west on a dirt road to a gate, then continue west along the lodgepole-dotted flank of Tuolumne Meadows, with fine views south across them toward Unicorn Peak, Cathedral Peak, and some of the knobby Echo Peaks. You soon reach the vicinity of Soda Springs. A nature trail goes to them and then on to the conspicuous Parsons Memorial Lodge. From this general area, your trail undulates northwest through a forest of sparse lodgepole pines and, in just under one mile, descends to a boulder ford or log crossing of

Polly Dome and Tenaya Lake

Delaney Creek. Just before it, a stock trail from the stables back in the meadows comes in on the right. Immediately beyond the creek you hop a branch of Delaney Creek, hop another in ⅙ mile, and in ⅙ mile more pass the Young Lakes Trail (2.5).

At this junction your route goes left, and after more winding through scattered lodgepoles, it descends some bare granite slabs and enters a flat-floored forest. A mile's pleasant walking since the last junction brings one to the bank of the Tuolumne River, just before three branches of Dingley Creek, near the west end of the huge meadows. From here, the nearly level trail often runs along the river, and in these stretches by the stream, there are numerous glacier-smoothed granite slabs on which to take a break—or take a dip in the river if the current is slow.

After a mile-long winding traverse, the trail leaves the last slabs to climb briefly up a granite outcrop to get around the river's gorge. You can leave the trail and walk toward a brink, from where you'll see—on the south side of the gorge below you—Little Devils Postpile. This 9.4-million-year-old remnant of a basalt lava flow, despite repeated attacks by glaciers, remains, a mute testimony to the impotence of glaciers' ability to erode.

Back on the trail you wind down eventually toward a sturdy bridge over the river, and parallel it down-canyon. As the river soon approaches nearby Tuolumne Falls, it flows down a series of sparkling rapids separated by large pools and wide sheets of water spread out across slightly inclined granite slopes. Beyond this beautiful stretch of river the trail descends, steeply at times, past Tuolumne Falls and White Cascade to a junction with the trail to May Lake—tomorrow's route. We, however, descend to a nearby bridge below roaring White Cascade. During high runoff, you may have to wade just to reach this bridge! Just past the bridge is a spur trail right to Glen Aulin High Sierra Camp, and behind it is your first night's destination, the Glen Aulin backpackers' camp (6.5).

On the second day, recross the Tuolumne River bridge and climb to the nearby junction.

From here you briefly curve northwest through a notch and then ascend gently southwest, soon crossing and recrossing McGee Lake's *northeast*-flowing outlet, which dries up by late summer. Where the trail levels off, McGee Lake, long and narrow and bordered on the southwest by a granite cliff, comes into view through the lodgepole trees. The dead snags along the shallow margin, and the fallen limbs and downed trees make fishing difficult, and in late summer the lake may dwindle to a stale pond. Adept campers can find isolated, level spots, some with views, on slopes north of McGee Lake (7.5), beneath the east end of Falls Ridge.

Beyond the lake your trail descends along its *southwest*-flowing outlet for ¾ mile, crossing this stream, and in ¼ mile it reaches a Cathedral Creek tributary. A few hundred yards beyond it is a boulderhop of wide Cathedral Creek. Then, after 3 miles of walking through forest, you have a welcome panorama. In the distant northeast stand Sheep Peak, North Peak, and Mt. Conness, encircling the basin of Roosevelt Lake. In the near north, Falls Ridge is a mountain of pinkish granite, which contrasts with the white and gray granite of the other peaks. When you look back toward McGee Lake, the route appears to be entirely carpeted with lodgepole pines. The trail continues up a moderate slope on gravel and granite shelves, through a forest cover of hemlock, red fir, and lodgepole. After arriving at a branch of Cathedral Creek, you cross it, then more or less parallel it for almost a mile to a junction with the Murphy Creek Trail (11.0), which descends 3.0 miles to Tenaya Lake. A short ½ mile before the lake, a lateral trail departs southwest from it, parallels the Tioga Road, and after one mile ends at a bend in the highway by a trailhead parking area. We'll reach this spot by a longer route.

Just ½ mile from the junction, you reach another one with the Ten Lakes Trail (11.5), which first climbs slopes beneath the very steep east face of Tuolumne Peak. Here you branch left and ascend briefly to a long, narrow, shallow, forested saddle beyond which large Tenaya Lake is visible in the south. After traversing somewhat brushy slopes, you reach a spring, then momentarily come to a series of switchbacks. Progress up the long, gentle gradient of these zigzags is distinguished by the striking views of Mt. Conness, Mt. Dana, and the other giants on the Sierra crest/Yosemite border. The trail then passes through a little saddle just north of a glacier-smoothed peak, and suddenly ahead is another Yosemite landmark, Clouds Rest, the largest expanse of bare granite in the park.

Now the trail descends gradually over fairly open granite to a forested flat and bends west above the north shore of Raisin Lake (13.2), which is one of the park's warmer "swimming holes." It also has campsites, including waterless, isolated ones with views, located about ¼ mile south of the lake. From the lake's vicinity, the trail continues beside a flower-lined runoff streambed under a sparse forest cover of conifers, and then swings west to cross several seasonal creeks. Finally the trail makes a ½-mile-long ascent steeply up to May Lake. Views improve constantly, and presently you have a panorama of the peaks on the Sierra crest from North Peak south to Mt. Gibbs. The Tioga Pass notch is clearly visible. At the top of this climb is a gentle upland where several small meadows are strung along the trail. In the west, Mt. Hoffman dominates. Now you head south along the east shore of the lake to the conspicuous High Sierra camp, immediately beyond which is the May Lake backpackers' camp (15.0), complete with outhouse and piped water, and stretched out along the south shore.

This day's hike is only 8½ miles, with minimal elevation change, so if you arrive at the camp still full of energy, there's always a "run" up to the summit of Mt. Hoffmann, at 10,850 feet about 1500 feet above May Lake and only 1¾ miles distant via trail. Should you take the challenge, leave your backpack behind, wear dark glasses, and apply lots of sunscreen, for there's ⅓ less air on the summit than at sea level, so the ultraviolet rays come on strong. Avoid altitude sickness by taking it easy, for the route is short. From the southwest corner of May Lake an obvious trail climbs southwest, then northwest to the summit plateau, which has several small summits. Choose the highest one, on your left. Situated near the geographic center of the park, this summit provides you with a commanding view. If you've brought along a topo map of the park, you should be able to identify dozens of features. Few peaks provide so much scenery for so little effort.

On your third day, you have an easy start—about 2½ miles downhill to the Tioga Road. You quickly encounter views and switchbacks, but these rapidly give way to about a mile traverse south to the May Lake trailhead (16.2). From here you follow the road northeast momentarily to where it is blocked off, then descend the closed stretch of road southeast to the Tioga Road. Cross the road and parallel it on an obvious trail 0.6 mile northeast to the Tenaya Lake trailhead (18.2), near the southwest corner of the lake. During the summer season, shuttle buses ply the road between here and Tuolumne Meadows, offering you a free ride back to your trailhead, should you want or need to cut your trip short.

Your downhill stretch is now over, and you'll do some serious climbing before reaching the next High Sierra camp. From the trailhead parking area, take a broad path east 200 yards to the usually flowing outlet of Tenaya Lake,

which often requires wading across. Onward, you continue 150 yards generally south to a trail junction. The trail left makes a loop around the lake, and
along it you may see stumps protruding from the lake. A myth is that the lake
was dry for centuries and a forest grew on the lake bed. In actuality, occasional, large rockfalls carried trees and talus into the lake, and while most trees sank
to the bottom, a few lodged heavy-end first into the sediments, the light end
protruding above water.

From the junction you veer right along a trail that heads south for ¼ mile
beside Tenaya Creek. Then over the next ½ mile it reaches a ford of Mildred
Lake's outlet creek, which, like the other streams between Tenaya Lake and the
Sunrise trail junction, can dry up in late season. Beyond the creek the trail
undulates and winds generally south, passing several pocket meadows. You
then begin to climb in earnest, toiling up short, steep switchbacks. As your trail
rises above Tenaya Canyon, you pass several vantage points from which you can
look back upon its polished granite walls, though you never see Tenaya Lake.
To the east the canyon is bounded by Tenaya Peak; in the northwest are the
cliffs of Mt. Hoffman and Tuolumne Peak. Your switchbacks are mercifully
shaded, and where they become steepest, requiring a great output of energy,
they seasonally give back the beauty of the finest flower displays on this trail.
Finally, after about 1000 feet of ascent—the amount you lost in your descent
from May Lake—the switchbacks end and the trail levels as it reaches a shallow
saddle and a junction with the Clouds Rest Trail (21.0).

Here you turn left, contour east, cross a low gap, and then descend north
to lower Sunrise Lake. Above its east shore are excellent examples of exfoliating
granite slabs, and the large talus slope beneath them testifies to the slabs' insta-
bility. However, after your recent, arduous climb, you're more likely to jump
into the lake for a refreshing swim.

Climbing from this lake and its small campsites, you reach a crest in several minutes, and from it could descend an equally short distance north to
more isolated, island-dotted middle Sunrise Lake. The trail, however, veers east
and gains a very noticeable 150 feet in elevation as it climbs to upper Sunrise
Lake, the largest lake of the trio. Due to former heavy use, the shoreline was
degraded and now camping is banned.

Leaving this lake, the trail climbs south up a gully, crosses it, then soon
climbs up a second gully to the east side of a broad gap, from which you see
the Clark Range head-on, piercing the southern sky. From the gap, 600 feet
above the shallow saddle you reached earlier, you descend south, veer east, and
then veer north to make a steep descent to the Sunrise backpackers' camp
(23.8), encountered immediately before the High Sierra camp, perched on a
granite bench just above the southern half of Long Meadow. Your overnight stay
here gives you an inspiring sunrise over Matthes Crest and the Cathedral Range.

On your fourth day you drop momentarily to the meadow, immediately
below you, then tread the John Muir Trail ¾ mile through it, first east and then

north to the Echo Creek Trail (24.7), on which you immediately cross the meadow's creek on boulders. The trail quickly switchbacks up to the top of a forested ridge and then descends through dense forest to a tributary of Echo Creek. Cross this, descend along it for ⅓ mile, recross, then momentarily reach the west bank of Echo Creek's Cathedral Fork. Here you have fine views of the creek's water gliding down a series of granite slabs, and then the trail veers away from the creek and descends gently above it for more than a mile. Even in late season these shaded slopes are watered by numerous rills that are bordered by still-blooming flowers. On this downgrade the trail crosses the Long Meadow creek, which has found an escape from that meadow through a gap between two domes high above our trail. The route then levels out in a mile-long flat section of this valley where the wet ground yields a plus of wildflowers all summer but a minus of many mosquitoes in early season. Beyond this flat "park" the trail descends more-open slopes, and eventually you can see across the valley the steep course of Echo Creek plunging down to its rendezvous with its western Cathedral Fork.

In this area your trail levels off and passes campsites immediately before you take a bridge over Echo Creek. Beyond it, your trail leads down the forested valley and easily fords a tributary stream, staying well above the main creek. This pleasant, shaded descent soon becomes more open and steep, and it encounters fibrous-barked juniper trees and butterscotch-scented Jeffrey pines as it drops to another bridge 1⅓ miles from the first one. Beyond it, the trail rises slightly and the creek drops precipitously, so that you are soon far above it. Then the sandy tread swings west away from Echo Creek and diagonals down a brushy slope. There the views are excellent of Echo Valley, which is a wide place in the great Merced River canyon below. On this slope you arrive at a junction with the High Trail (31.2), which goes 3 miles west to a junction with the John Muir Trail. Leaving the dense growth of brush behind, start southeast and make a drop 450 feet into Echo Valley. In it you quickly arrive at another junction, this one with the Merced Lake Trail (31.9). On it you go east, immediately bridging Echo Creek, passing through a burned-but-boggy area, then climb east past the Merced River's pools and rapids to the west shore of Merced Lake (33.4). Don't camp here, but rather continue 0.6 mile, going about 250 yards past the north shore to the Merced Lake backpacker's camp (34.0). Complete with bearproof food-storage boxes, this is situated about ¼ mile before the High Sierra camp. If you haven't gotten water from the lake, then get it from the camp.

Begin day five by hiking a level mile east to the Merced Lake Ranger Station and an adjacent junction with the Lewis Creek Trail (35.1). On it you struggle 1½ mile in a 1000-foot climb northeast up to a junction with the Fletcher Creek Trail (36.4). The ascent to here provides views, and Merced Lake, to the west, serves as a gauge as one climbs increasingly above it. Take a number of rests up to the junction so that you can enjoy the changing views. On the

Medlicott Dome Summit

Fletcher Creek Trail you descend briefly to a bridge over Lewis Creek. Just 50 yards upstream is a good campsite, and then the trail enters more open slopes as it climbs moderately on a cobbled path. Just past a tributary ½ mile from Lewis Creek, you have fine views of cascading Fletcher Creek backdropped by an imposing dome. Ahead, you climb over two dozen mostly short switchbacks, and can see much of the Clark Range to the south. You then have an easier, if moderate, ascent northward, the grade easing as you approach a minor ridge, a fine rest spot.

From this spot your trail descends briefly to a junction with the Babcock Lake Trail (38.0). Consider: the native vegetation around the Vogelsang High Sierra Camp has suffered a severe impact due to overuse, and although it is still legal to camp near it, I strongly recommend you do not. You have at least four choices, of which I feel the Babcock Lake locale is the least susceptible to environmental damage. The others are at Emeric lake, or between that lake and Boothe Lake, or beyond Tuolumne Pass, say, midway down the Rafferty Creek Trail.

To Reach Babcock Lake, take the ½-mile trail, which first arcs west to nearby Fletcher Creek, often a ford before late summer, then northwest up to a low ridge. From it the trail goes southwest, crosses a second low ridge, then reaches the lake's northeast end. Among fair lodgepole-shaded campsites by the southeast shore, the trail dies out short of the lake's tiny island. Better campsites are on the opposite shore. Suitable diving slabs are along both shores of this fairly warm lake. For stealth camping, explore the relatively flat lands both north and south of this lake.

From the Babcock Lake junction, the Fletcher Creek Trail ascends steadily through a moderate forest cover, staying just east of Fletcher Creek. After ¾ mile this route breaks out into the open and begins to rise more steeply via rocky switchbacks. From these one can see nearby in the north the outlet stream of Emeric Lake—though not the lake itself, which is behind a dome just to the right of the outlet's notch. Soon you enter an expansive meadow with superb views of glaciated, barren slopes and cliffs. After about ¾ mile of meadow walking, you reach a scissors junction, about 90 yards beyond a ford of Fletcher Creek. To visit Emeric Lake, turn left here and on the Emeric Lake Trail (40.2) and traverse about ⅓ mile southeast to the lake. To camp at it, head across its meadowy northeast shore—generally boggy through July—and then traverse over to isolated sites above the lake's northwest shore. Alternatively, you can traverse along its southeast shore (good for swimming and sunbathing), but first you will have to cross blocky talus near the lake's dome before heading to the northwest shore.

Both Babcock Lake and Emeric Lake require at least a mile of extra hiking, round trip, so if you'd rather not make the effort to visit either, or don't want to have a 10+ mile hike out on your last day (although most of it is level or downhill), then consider forking left at the scissors junction. Northeast, a trail first goes through the forest fringe of the long meadow that straddles Fletcher Creek. It then climbs farther from the meadow and passes northwest of a bald prominence that sits in the center of the upper valley of Fletcher and Emeric creeks, separating the two. Here you can look for isolated camping sites in this vicinity, particularly above the far bank of Emeric Creek. Camping is not allowed at Boothe Lake. After topping a minor summit, your trail descends slightly and then winds almost level past several lovely ponds that are interconnected in early season. Next is a lakelet, 100 yards in diameter, which would offer good swimming in some years. Just beyond it, the trail traverses northeast to a little swale with another possible swimming pond before reaching an overlook above Boothe Lake. Your trail then contours along meadowy slopes just east of and above the lake, passing a junction with a use trail down to the lake. About ¼ mile farther you pass another trail descending to this lake. Just ahead is your high point, 10,000-foot Tuolumne Pass.

If you're a purist and want to follow the precise route of the High Sierra Camps Loop, then from the scissors junction branch right (east), and climb 2.3 miles to Vogelsang High Sierra Camp (42.5). Most of this ascent is constrained between chorusing Fletcher Creek on the right, and cliffs or steep slopes on the left, so campsites are essentially nonexistent unless you make a determined off-trail search. The camp marks the route's high point elevation-wise at 10,170 feet, so if the dramatic views you get from it don't leave you breathless, the ascent to it will. Fletcher Peak towers above the camp, and is flanked on the south by Vogelsang Lake, and on the north by a chain of lakes, starting with nearby, trailside Upper Fletcher Lake (interestingly, there is no Lower Fletcher Lake). Signs will direct you to where you can camp, which can vary over the years. Scattered clusters of lodgepole or whitebark pines offer little protection from the wind, which can be quite strong in the afternoon.

On your final day, make a short-mile trek over to broad, open Tuolumne Pass (43.4), a major gap in the Cathedral Range, which is a crest extending from the park's highest summit, Mt. Lyell, northwest to Cathedral Peak. You now have more than 1½ miles of easy descent through a long meadow, which provides you with continuous views of the Sierra crest from about Mt. Conness east to Tioga Pass. Your next 3½+ miles of descent is mostly viewless or tree-filtered views, and except near the end, where the descent is fairly steep, you stay quite close to Rafferty Creek. After the first ½ mile along this descent, you reach another meadow, about ½ mile long, and then over the next mile—to a point where Evelyn Lake's creek joins Rafferty Creek—you can head east across Rafferty Creek and find abundant gentle slopes and flats suitable for tree-shaded, protected camping. About a mile below the two creeks' union, you can find a similar, expansive camping environment, although by then you're only about 3 miles from your trailhead, instead of about 5.

You know you're getting near the John Muir Trail when you start a noticeably steep descent. Over ½ mile, short switchbacks help to ease the grade, then the trail starts to ease off just before reaching the High Sierra backpackers' highway, the John Muir Trail (48.6). On it you traverse a nearly level ⅔ mile west to a junction, branch right, the route ahead contouring over to Tuolumne Meadows Campground, a mile away. Northbound on the JMT you quickly reach two bridges across the Tuolumne River, and from this lovely spot have inspiring views up-canyon toward Mt. Dana and Mt. Gibbs. A short, winding climb north, followed by an equal descent, brings you to the Dana Fork of the Tuolumne River, only 150 yards past a junction with an east-climbing trail to the Gaylor Lakes. Immediately beyond the river's bridge is a short spur trail to the Tuolumne Meadows Lodge, which can be your High Sierra Camps Loop's first or last night's stay, if you've gotten reservations.

Most likely, you'll start west, downstream, toward your original trailhead. Starting on a trail, you soon hear the Dana Fork as it makes a small drop into a pool, almost cut in two by a protruding granite finger. At the base of this finger, about 8–10 feet down, is an underwater arch—an extremely rare feature in any kind of rock. If the water is slack and you feel like braving the cold water, usually 50°F at best, you can dive down to the arch, swim through it, and add this crazy act to your life's accomplishments. Just beyond the pool you approach the lodge's road, where a short path climbs a few yards up to it and takes one to the entrance of a large backpackers' parking lot. Now you parallel the paved road westward, passing the Tuolumne Meadows Ranger Station and quickly reaching a junction, the spur road west curving into a second large backpackers' lot—the one with the wilderness-permit office, from where this hike's description began.

Permits

Permits are required, trailheads have quotas and, in the Tuolumne Meadows area, quotas often fill quickly, especially for Fridays and Saturdays. Half of the permits can be reserved, while half are available on a first-come, first-served basis on the day of, or one day prior to, the beginning of your trip (see Trailhead for the location of the wilderness-permit office). By starting on Sunday through Thursday, you'll have a better chance of getting a free permit in person. However, the High Sierra Camps Loop is so popular that you ought to reserve a permit well in advance, and you can get one up to 24 weeks in advance of your starting date. Either phone the Wilderness Center at (209) 372-0740 or write to: Wilderness Permits, Box 545, Yosemite, CA 95389. A $3 *per person* non-refundable processing fee is charged for all reservation requests.

Build-up/Wind-down tips

If getting a Wilderness Permit can be stressful, so too can getting a campsite. The Tuolumne Meadows Campground simply cannot handle all who'd like to camp in it. I suggest three alternatives. First, skip camping; drive directly to the trailhead and start hiking. Your first night's stay in the wilderness, at Glen Aulin, can be reached by most hikers in 3 hours, so even if you arrive in Tuolumne Meadows by mid-afternoon, you'll have time to reach it. Second, camp outside the park, such as in eastside campgrounds in lower Lee Vining Canyon (forget upper), in the Bridgeport area, or in the Mammoth Lakes area. Third, camp in one of the park's campgrounds that is not on the reservation system. The appropriate ones, all on or near the Tioga Road from west to east between Crane Flat and Tenaya Lake, are: Tamarack Flat, White Wolf, Yosemite Creek, and Porcupine Flat. These typically open mid-July and close by mid-September. Checkout time is 10 A.M., so try to be at one of these camps around then, from Sunday through Thursday (forget Friday and Saturday).

Jeffrey P. Schaffer provides background on his path to guidebook writing, detailed mapmaking, and challenging received views of Sierra geological formation, besides a list of his titles from Wilderness Press, in "Author Bio & Bib" on page 492.

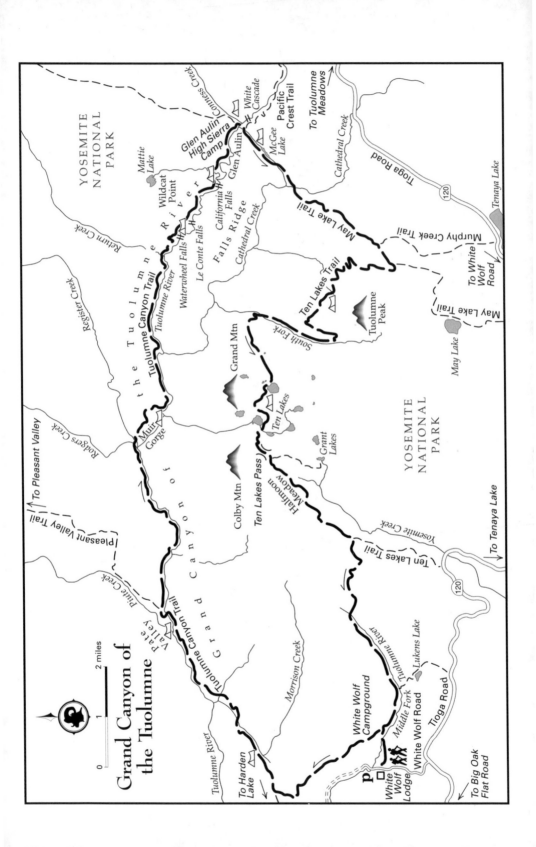

Grand Canyon of the Tuolumne

42

Grand Canyon of the Tuolumne

—Jason Winnett

Route	Days	Elev. Gain/Loss	Difficulty	Miles
↺	5–7	8800'/8800'	***	48.75

Campsites: near Morrison Creek: 5.5 miles
Pate Valley: 10.5 miles
above Muir Gorge: 16.5 miles
flat above Waterwheel Falls: 20.75 miles
near river in Glen Aulin: 22.75 miles
McGee Lake: 24.75 miles
pond near Tuolumne Peak: 32.0 miles
largest of Ten Lakes: 38.5 miles

Map: USGS 7.5-min *Hetch Hetchy Reservoir, Ten Lakes, Falls Ridge*

Best season: Summer through early fall

Take this trip!

Over a 100 years ago, John Muir declared the Sierra Nevada "the most Divinely beautiful of all the mountain chains I've ever seen." Millions of people have since made pilgrimage here to experience the famous "Range of Light." And of all the mighty canyons and valleys in the incomparable Sierra—including the valley of Yosemite—there is only one that has earned the appellation "Grand Canyon": the Grand Canyon of the Tuolumne River.

With mile-high canyon walls, vast expanses of granite, spectacular waterfalls, and abundant wildlife, this Grand Canyon also features a much rarer quality: it's in backcountry wilderness. Protected within Yosemite National Park, the closest section is at least a day's hike from the nearest road. This classic loop trip takes you to the canyon bottom at 4200 feet in Pate Valley, and then all the way up through it to 9800-foot Tuolumne Peak. En route you'll experience the heart of this diverse wilderness, the result of millions of years work by the mighty Tuolumne River and its once-massive glaciers.

Trailhead

White Wolf (7910). On State Highway 120 in Yosemite National Park, go 14.5 miles northeast from Crane Flat, or 32.3 miles west from Tioga Pass, to the White Wolf turnoff, and follow the access road 1 mile down to the trailhead opposite the lodge (toilets, water). The access road is closed usually by the end of September.

TRIP DESCRIPTION

> **Heads Up!** Camping out in Yosemite National Park the night(s) before or after your trip can be problematic as area campgrounds are often full during the summer months. Some can be reserved up to five months ahead of time by calling the National Park Reservations System at 1-800-436-7275. Other campgrounds, such as the one at White Wolf, are on a first-come, first-served basis.

We begin our trek just across the access road from White Wolf Lodge. Here, the trail skirts the south side of White Wolf Campground and heads east for a level mile through a lodgepole pine forest. After crossing seasonal Middle Fork Tuolumne River, we meet a signed junction with a trail to Lukens Lake. Turning left, we continue through almost level forest for another mile and cross a nearly imperceptible ridge. Now descending, our route follows a flower-lined creek to a beautiful, forest-fringed meadow. We skirt this meadow to the east and climb a gentle mile to a more open, distinctive ridge. We are standing on the crest of a moraine deposited by a glacier that once flowed down the Grand Canyon of the Tuolumne.

From this point, we begin descending a slope that eventually leads to the bottom of the canyon. At first, we cannot see the canyon as our trail crosses several more lateral moraine crests. As we lose altitude, the forest cover changes quickly; lodgepole pine and red fir soon give way to western white pine, Sierra juniper, and Jeffrey pine.

As the grade steepens and the forest cover thins, you get your first glimpses across the canyon to the surrounding uplands to the north, though the canyon itself is still hidden out of sight below. Where the trail crosses some glacially polished bedrock, consider that glacial ice once filled the canyon to this height, during ice ages of the Pleistocene Epoch. Descending into denser forest again, you encounter incense cedar, white fir, and quaking aspen, which indicate a high water table here. After many switchbacks you reach a signed junction with a trail to Harden Lake; turn right. The grade eases as you descend east across a forested slope, where you see even lower-elevation trees including black oak, sugar pine and, near an unmarked creek, some alder.

Soon you can hear Morrison Creek on your right; the trail crosses a flat bench where a rough boardwalk keeps our feet dry. Just beyond it, the forest cover opens and there are good campsites near the creek. (If you start heading down steep switchbacks, then you've gone too far.) A few minutes climb north of the campsites is a granite ridge. To the east (right) of its high point there is a great view down into the canyon. By carrying water up here, you could camp near several majestic ponderosa pines, and behold dawn fill Piute Creek's broad chasm to the north and illuminate the Grand Canyon of the Tuolumne River below.

Leaving the Morrison Creek campsites, you begin the final plunge to the bottom of the Grand Canyon, still over 2500 feet below. First the trail steepens into a series of switchbacks beside splashing Morrison Creek in a forest of white fir, incense-cedar, sugar pine, and dogwood. After dropping about 500 feet the trail veers north, and views open up dramatically. At 5700 feet the trail crosses a bench where you can stop for some in-depth viewing of this phenomenal canyon, including the incongruous reservoir of Hetch Hetchy to the west. You could camp here on this bench, as Morrison Creek is nearby and usually flows down to this elevation through midsummer. With the appearance of canyon live oak the environment reflects the lower elevation.

After crossing now-seasonal Morrison Creek, you begin the last 1500 feet to the bottom. Although extremely steep in places, the trail has been expertly constructed with many sections of riprap, where wedge-shaped rocks were painstakingly fitted together to form a sort of staircase with no two steps the same. You can see and hear the Tuolumne River far below and, on a hot summer's day, anticipate a refreshing dip. At 5000 feet the trail crosses a gully where water runs seasonally, sometimes in the form of winter avalanches. At 4500 feet you cross another seasonal creek (this one marked as perennial on the topo map). Both of these water courses can become dangerous torrents late in spring during a heavy snow year. At 4400 feet the grade levels off briefly as you pass a moraine-dammed pond. Re-entering tall forest cover again, your route makes a short descent through an area that was mildly burned by natural fire in 1994.

Upon reaching the canyon floor, the trail heads upriver. The now-gentle grade soon leads you through a magnificent cathedral forest of white fir and ponderosa pine, where there are several excellent campsites. Because there are only a few low-elevation wilderness valleys left in the Sierra, the idyllic sanctuary of Pate Valley is a rare gem. Here, we can appreciate why they say John Muir died of a broken heart after Hetch Hetchy Valley was dammed. In what would be his final and most passionate campaign, he worked feverishly to save "this most precious and divine feature of the Yosemite National Park." Tragically, however, big bucks prevailed and the City of San Francisco completed O'Shaughnessy Dam in 1923.

Continuing briefly upriver, our level trail crosses several channels of the river via bridges; the short section between them can flood in a very wet year.

Once on the north side of the river—where the trail remains until Glen Aulin—we enter another burned area and reach a junction with the Pleasant Valley Trail. Turning right, our route passes through a narrowing of the valley floor where bedrock, acting like an underground dam, has forced groundwater near the surface, thereby producing a lush, muddy area. Though too wet for tree growth, many species of water-loving shrubs thrive here including cow parsnip and rushes. The trail returns to riverside for awhile and crosses a short section of riprap, set in cement to withstand flooding. Wading may be required here during high runoff. In the unlikely event that the river is so high that you are unsure of your safety here (or anywhere else), please turn back or find a safe alternative rather than risk a watery grave.

Still gently ascending, the trail crosses another, older burn, where the fire was hot enough to torch large trees as well as the ground cover. Just beyond this area our route passes some fantastically large and deep pools in bedrock—a fine swimming and fishing spot. From here the canyon narrows and the trail stays close to the river for a mile, where again some wading may be required during high runoff. This shady stretch of canyon gives way to a wider valley where the nearly vertical cliffs soar skyward in classic Yosemite style. Partway through this wilderness Yosemite, the trail climbs to overlook the river. Near the beginning of this short climb is an excellent campsite near a large pool, lying at the base of granite slabs down which the river slides and tumbles. In these sunny, lower-elevation sections of the canyon, you are likely to encounter many reptiles, especially blue-bellied lizards. There are many species of snakes in the Grand Canyon, including the reclusive rattlesnake.

As you approach Muir Gorge the canyon becomes narrow and steep, and the trail passes two live-oak-shaded campsites as it climbs away from the river. Named after a man who eagerly sought out inaccessible places, Muir Gorge is the only part of the canyon too steep to build a trail, so we're obliged to climb around it. Just before the footbridge over seasonal Rodgers Creek, you can look straight up into the dark chasm of Muir Gorge. Soon thereafter, you bridge seasonal Register Creek, and climb its side canyon briefly before swinging south over a low, shady ridge. After a short descent the trail climbs steeply for 400 feet to an open, granite ridgetop. It is well worth the short hike down to an overlook of mysterious Muir Gorge—a real eagle's perch—but be careful because, unlike an eagle, if you take off you will fly only one way, down.

The descent back to the river is mostly shady, and the canyon again widens above Muir Gorge. Where granite slabs come down to the river, the trail can be wet in early season, though climbing above high water is easy. Beyond these slabs ¼ mile is a small, seasonal creek channel in white gravel. Between the river and the trail is an excellent campsite, and you are unlikely to meet many people here as it is almost equidistant many steep miles to the nearest road.

The ascent continues to be gentle for about 1 mile until looming canyon walls again close in, challenging even the most flexible neck to take in the high skyline. Before the canyon steepens, the trail passes some seasonally flooded campsites. The last Douglas-fir and bay laurel fall behind as you climb alongside the tumbling river for about a mile. As your trail swings away from the river, the grade levels off in a dense forest. With the river once again in sight, you pass two small waterfalls that hint at upcoming attractions. Bridging Return Creek, the trail begins climbing steeply. Waterwheel Falls loom above, and in early season are at their thunderous and uniquely spectacular best: protrusions in the granite bedrock deflect the falling water into wheeling sprays that shoot far into the air. Don't be in a hurry here as the falls are best viewed from below, and on a hot day their cooling mist provides a soothing respite. The well-routed trail returns to the river just above the falls, where there's a small lake. The trail climbs away from the river again behind a low bedrock ridge for ¼ mile to an open, juniper-dotted slope, where an unsigned trail leads down to a wide, forested flat by the river. This flat offers some excellent campsites situated beneath a cathedral-like forest of towering Jeffrey pine, white fir, and incense-cedar.

Above this flat the trail again steepens and climbs past a short lateral trail to a view of LeConte Falls, which are well worth seeing at a close but safe distance. Leaving behind the last incense-cedar and sugar pine, the trail becomes quite steep and sunny as you come under the towering buttress of Wildcat Point. Again, the trail tread is riprap—a construction choice consistent with building materials in this land of granite. The grade eases before reaching California Falls, the third and lowest of the three major ones below Glen Aulin. A short climb past these falls brings you to Glen Aulin, where the slow and lazy river here winds through a wide, level valley for over a mile. Much of Glen Aulin was burned near the end of the millennium, and many former campsites are now undesirable due to exposure and potential deadfall. Where the trail swings near the river, there is a campsite under old, unburned forest. Fire is normal in the forest, and nature continues her cycles with the timely succession of tree species. Aspen is quick to grow back after fires because, unlike conifers, it can resprout from the crown of its roots. Aspen is an early successional species while red fir, which grows better in the shade of already established forest, is a late successional species.

A short climb out of Glen Aulin proper brings you to the Pacific Crest Trail. Glen Aulin High Sierra Camp is across the trail, beyond Conness Creek. Behind its buildings is a backpacker's camp with bear-proof poles for hanging food. Some food supplies can be purchased at the office during summer. White Cascade plummets into a large pool above the nearby bridge, and while the trail can be flooded for a short distance beyond it, the trail is easily negotiated.

Here, at long last, you part ways with the river, and climb to a junction where you leave the Tuolumne Canyon Trail and turn right onto the May Lake Trail. Now hiking in forest, the grade is easy and soon you arrive at the north shore of quiet McGee Lake. The secluded campsites at this lake are found on the south side of the outlet at either end of the lake; curiously, McGee Lake drains both east into the Tuolumne River and west to Cathedral Creek. From the west end of the lake the trail descends southwest, crossing the seasonal west outlet before arriving at Cathedral Creek. Although Cathedral Creek flows to a trickle by late summer, it can be a wet crossing in early summer. From the creek the trail climbs steeply at first, and then more gently as you cross a low ridge and continue for about 2 miles to a signed junction with the Murphy Creek Trail. Turning right you proceed for a level ½ mile to another signed junction. Here you leave the May Lake Trail and the High Sierra Camps loop and turn right onto the Ten Lakes Trail.

Off the beaten path again you continue southwest a little longer before turning northeast and beginning the 1200-foot climb toward Tuolumne Peak. Both the grade and the views increase until the trail reaches several high points on the northeast ridge of Tuolumne Peak. You have now reached the highest point of the trip, at nearly 10,000 feet above sea level. The views here are a worthy reward: to the east beyond Tuolumne Meadows rises the Sierra crest; south of the meadows stands the ice-sculpted Cathedral Range; northeast is the massive, white-granite, southwest face of Mt. Conness; to the north the Grand Canyon of the Tuolumne lies hidden beyond dome-topped Falls Ridge. A Class 2 scramble up Tuolumne Peak to the west gives even better views. Centrally located in Yosemite National Park and higher than any thing else around (except nearby Mt. Hoffman), Tuolumne Peak offers perhaps the most comprehensive terrestrial view of the park.

The trail drops briefly to a pond where you will find little-used campsites. Snowmelt can linger late into summer here on the north side of Tuolumne Peak, along with attendant mosquitos and cool nights. Heading west and then northwest, the winding trail climbs up and down for over a mile to an overlook of the South Fork Cathedral Creek canyon. The trail then switchbacks down to the west, contours south, and switchbacks west again to reach the South Fork. Turning north, you descend moderately, then gently along the creek's east side for 2 miles to a seasonally wet ford. From here the trail soon leaves the creek and once again climbs west out of the canyon. As you switchback up this open slope you can look back down into this deep, glacially scoured canyon and beyond to the much deeper Grand Canyon, which is mostly hidden below. As the slope eases you once again find yourself in forest. After a nearly level mile the trail begins heading down and soon reaches the north shore of the eastern-most and largest of the Ten Lakes. Good campsites are plentiful on the north and west sides of the lake.

Heading northwest from the lake your route is nearly level for ½ mile before turning southwest to descend to the south side of the next largest of the Ten Lakes. The Ten Lakes basin is a popular destination for both people and wily bears who desire your food. Just west of this lake you meet a spur trail going left to the higher, southwestern Ten Lakes. Just beyond it you cross their outlet and begin climbing 600 feet to the broad ridge on the west side of Ten Lakes basin. As you cross the top of this gently sloping upland, for the only time on this trip you walk over a non-glaciated surface—a remnant of the pre-ice age Sierra. From here you get a final, superlative overview of the Tuolumne River drainage.

Descending southwest the grade is at first gentle as you pass the trail to Grant Lakes on your left. But the grade soon steepens, until you reach the north side of Halfmoon Meadow. Skirting the meadow, the trail again descends more or less southwest for a long 2 miles to a signed junction where you leave the popular Ten Lakes Trail and turn right towards White Wolf. Ascending gently, the usually shaded trail climbs 1½ miles to a broad, forested ridge. Here, you begin the final grade of the trip, which is downhill, smooth, and shady. Following the headwaters of the Middle Fork Tuolumne River, you saunter gently down a quiet path for about 2 miles to a junction with a trail to Lukens Lake on the left. Continuing west for a level mile you meet the trail to Pate Valley, thereby completing the loop. From here you simply retrace your steps back to White Wolf Campground. Savor this final wilderness mile and reflect on how the Grand Canyon of the Tuolumne has enriched your life, as it did John Muir's over 100 years ago.

Variations

A brief variation of this trip (and one that is relatively easy to get a permit for) is to do an out and back, 2–4 day backpack from Tenaya Lake up the Murphy Creek Trail. You then partially follow this Trip Description in reverse, to camp at the forested flat above Waterwheel Falls, especially in early summer when the falls are most spectacular.

Permits

You may reserve a Wilderness Permit for Yosemite up to 24 weeks ahead of time by calling the Wilderness Center at (209) 372-0740, or by writing to:

Wilderness Permits
Box 545
Yosemite, CA 95389

Include your name, address, day phone, number of people, itinerary (with alternate dates), entry and exit trailheads (White Wolf), and $5 per person (nonrefundable) payable to Yosemite Association. Permits are issued on demand at Big Oak Flat Information Station (at the west entrance on Hwy. 120), and at Tuolumne Meadows Lodge, at the east end of Tuolumne Meadows (sometime after Labor Day this may shift to the Information Center). Arrive early (as early as 6–7:30 A.M. at the Meadows, 8 A.M. at Big Oak Flat or Yosemite Valley), as permits go fast during the summer.

Build-up/Wind-down tips

For a wonderful dip in a huge, deep pool, visit Rainbow Pool on your westward return home. It is 10.5 miles west of the Big Oak Flat Park entrance at Highway 120's third crossing of South Fork Tuolumne River. Just across the bridge, turn south on a short spur road to parking above the pool. This deep pool has very high diving rocks and nice surrounding trees.

Long a coauthor with his father of our earliest hiking guidebooks for the Sierra, Jason Winnett continues to glean spiritual gifts there, as our "Author Bio & Bib" on page 492 makes clear.

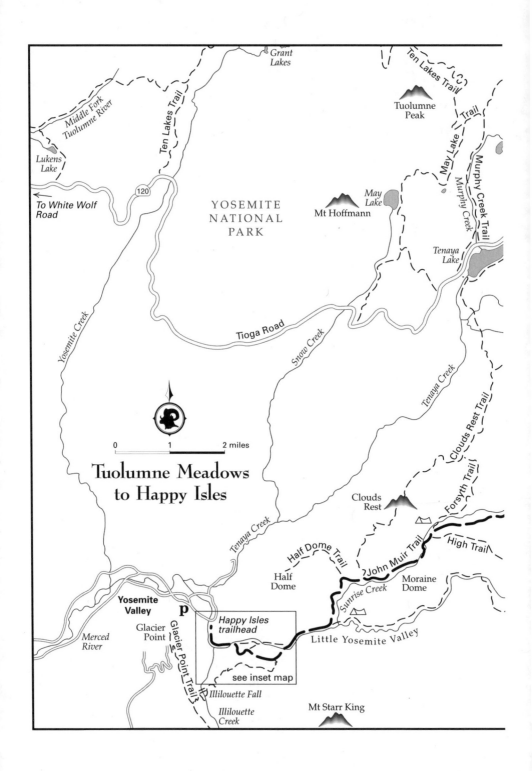

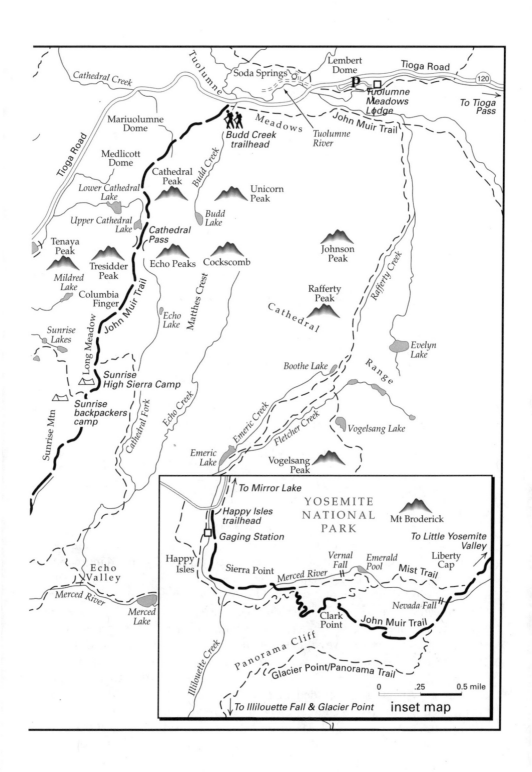

Cathedral Creek

Tuolumne

Soda Springs

Lembert Dome

Tioga Road

120

Mariuolumne Dome

P

Tuolumne Meadows Lodge

To Tioga Pass

Meadows

Budd Creek trailhead

John Muir Trail

Tuolumne River

Medlicott Dome

Tioga Road

Lower Cathedral Lake

Cathedral Peak

Budd Creek

Unicorn Peak

Upper Cathedral Lake

Budd Lake

Cathedral Pass

Johnson Peak

Tenaya Peak

Tresidder Peak

Echo Peaks

Cockscomb

Rafferty Creek

Mildred Lake

Columbia Finger

Matthes Crest

Rafferty Peak

Cathedral

Sunrise Lakes

John Muir Trail

Echo Lake

Long Meadow

Evelyn Lake

Range

Boothe Lake

Sunrise High Sierra Camp

Sunrise backpackers camp

Sunrise Mtn

Cathedral Fork

Echo Creek

Emeric Creek

Fletcher Creek

Vogelsang Lake

Emeric Lake

Vogelsang Peak

To Mirror Lake

YOSEMITE NATIONAL PARK

Mt Broderick

Happy Isles trailhead

Gaging Station

To Little Yosemite Valley

Happy Isles

Sierra Point

Merced River

Vernal Fall

Emerald Pool

Liberty Cap

Mist Trail

Echo Valley

Merced River

Merced Lake

Clark Point

Nevada Fall

John Muir Trail

Illilouette Creek

Panorama Cliff

Glacier Point/Panorama Trail

0   .25   0.5 mile

To Illilouette Fall & Glacier Point

inset map

43

Tuolumne Meadows to Happy Isles via John Muir Trail

—Jeffrey P. Schaffer

Route	Days	Elev. Gain/Loss	Elev. Low/High	Difficulty	Miles
↗	3	2790´/7320´	4030´/9950´	**	21.6

Campsites: Sunrise High Sierra Camp (2nd trail): 7.9 miles
Forsyth Trail (near Sunrise Creek): 12.7 miles
Little Yosemite Valley backpackers' camp: 16.9 miles
(see the Trip Description for others)

Map: USGS 7.5-min *Half Dome, Merced Lake, Tenaya Lake*

Best season: Late July through Labor Day

Take this trip!

This northernmost section of the 212-mile-long John Muir Trail is perhaps the most popular trail route from Tuolumne Meadows to Yosemite Valley, and justifiably so. Along it you pass relatively close by sheer, glaciated landmarks, which include Cathedral Peak, Matthes Crest, and Columbia Finger, and descend past the famous Yosemite Valley landmarks of Liberty Cap, Nevada Fall, and Vernal Fall. Most of this trip is downhill, which adds to its enjoyment. Nevertheless, there is considerable climbing, which says something of the more than considerable descent. Therefore, I recommend it be done in three days instead of two, just to save your knees. If you insist on two, then camp by Sunrise Creek in order to break your descent in half. If you take three days, then camp by Sunrise High Sierra Camp and in Little Yosemite Valley. To jazz up this already great hike, I've included three very rewarding side trips of variable effort. In the order you encounter them, these are Mariuolumne and Medlicott domes and Lower Cathedral Lake (extra 2½ miles distance/extra 400 feet of ascent), Moraine Dome (1/200), and Half Dome (4/1900). For the last side trip you'll want to use a small day pack; you certainly won't want to carry a backpack to the top of Half Dome! (Anyway, overnight camping there is no longer allowed.) Not a side trip but rather an alternate route is a descent to the Yosemite Valley floor via the Mist Trail (see Heads Up!).

Trailhead

The Tioga Road makes an east-west traverse across Yosemite National Park, and on that road, in Tuolumne Meadows, is your trailhead, located on the south side of the road about 1½ miles west of the entrance to the Tuolumne Meadows Campground. Note: since this is a point-to-point hike, a shuttle is required. Rather than do it with two vehicles, take a hikers' bus, which plies between Yosemite Valley and Tuolumne Meadows from about late June through Labor Day. For information on fee, schedule, and reservations, you can call (209) 372-1240 or else stop at the valley's Visitor Center, where you can also get a Wilderness Permit. Leave your vehicle in the valley and enjoy a stress-free bus ride up to Tuolumne Meadows.

TRIP DESCRIPTION

> **Heads Up!** See the "High Sierra Camps Loop" Heads Up! Additionally, if you do any of the three side trips, some scrambling with hands and feet (Class 3 climbing) is required, and caution is a must. Furthermore, the summit of Half Dome can be struck with lightning in thunderstorms. These, however, usually occur in mid or late afternoon, so if you start your ascent from Sunrise Creek or beyond, you should be able to reach the summit well before noon. Finally, if you take the alternate descent route, the Mist Trail, be aware that the trail is very steep and wet. If you are not careful, you stand a good chance of slipping and falling. Even up above, where the alternate route is dry as it descends beside Nevada Fall, the switchbacks are steep and the loose gravel on them can cause you to slip and fall. In short, any deviation from the actual John Muir Trail has its risks and therefore upgrades the difficulty of this hike to moderately strenuous.

Starting at the Budd Creek trailhead, walk 200 yards southwest to a junction with the John Muir Trail, which you'll follow all the way down to Yosemite Valley. Continuing southwest, you now ascend moderately to steeply, and after 0.3 mile should see the obvious, if unofficial, Budd Lake Trail branching left. Lodgepoles dominate your ¾-mile ascent to the crest of a lateral moraine, from which the trail briefly descends west. This gives you a breather, as does a ½-mile traverse to a creeklet. Ahead, you then ascend short, moderate-to-steep switch-

Hiker on viewpoint (upper left) at the top of Nevada Fall

backs, and, after 300 feet of climbing, your trail's gradient eases and you traverse along the base of largely unseen Cathedral Peak, a mass of granodiorite towering 1400 feet above you.

Where your traverse soon leaves the Tuolumne River drainage for that of the Merced River, you can start the first of three side trips. To the west rises

Medlicott Dome and just north of it, rises slightly higher Mariuolumne Dome (this is near the Mariposa and Tuolumne county line, whence the name). Make an easy traverse through open forest then up to the conspicuous saddle between the two domes. Leave your pack there and head right, up easy slopes to Mariuolumne's small summit block, just under 10,000 feet elevation. You'll have to do a bit of climbing to get started up, but mostly it is not a problem. If you decide against it, your near-summit view is almost identical to the summit view, which is only from slightly higher. For a minimal amount of effort, you have an incredibly spectacular view. The views from slightly lower Medlicott Dome are similar, though not as good, so if you don't want to carry your backpack up to it, then just traverse southwest along the dome's lower flank. This quickly gives way to a broad ridge, which you follow easily down to the outlet of lower Cathedral Lake, a great lunch stop with impressive scenery. Then head along the lake's southern perimeter, start an ascent northeast, and quickly find the lake's trail.

Those not taking this excursion continue about 0.5 mile on the JMT to a junction with this Lower Cathedral Lake Trail (3.2). Visiting this scenic lake adds about 1½ miles to your mileage. Bear-frequented, roomy campsites lie near the north shore, but campfires are not allowed. (Even where they are, don't make them; save the downed wood for the local decomposers.) Unless you're going at a very leisurely pace, you won't want to set up your first night's camp so early in your trek.

From the junction with the trail to lower Cathedral Lake, you climb an easy ¾ mile to upper Cathedral Lake (4.0). If you head west over toward the lake's outlet, you'll encounter slabs, great for basking from after a quick (chilly!) dip. Even better slabs lie across the outlet, as do campsites. The JMT traverses a meadow to the lake's south-shore peninsula, which offers a fine view of two-towered Cathedral Peak. The trail then climbs ¼ mile to broad Cathedral Pass (4.3), where the excellent views include Tresidder Peak, Cathedral Peak, Echo Peaks, and Matterhorn Peak far to the north.

Beyond the pass is a long, beautiful swale—the flowery headwaters of Echo Creek. Your path traverses up the east flank of Tresidder Peak on a gentle climb to the actual high point of this trail, at a marvelous viewpoint overlooking most of the southern park. The inspiring panorama here includes the peaks around Vogelsang High Sierra Camp in the southeast, the whole Clark Range in the south, and, farther away, the peaks on the park's border. Your high trail soon traverses under steep-walled Columbia Finger, where, by heading yards left up to the top of a minor ridge, you have another great view. The JMT then switchbacks quickly down to the head of the upper lobe of Long Meadow. Here it levels off and leads down to a gradually sloping valley dotted with lodgepole pines to the head of the second, lower lobe of *long* Long Meadow, which has a junction with the Echo Creek Trail (7.0).

Cathedral Peak from Cathedral Pass

Now the route heads south ½ mile before bending west ¼ mile to pass below Sunrise High Sierra Camp, perched on a granite bench just above the trail. You should see two trails to it: one climbing up to the north end of the camp; the other (7.9), just beyond it, to its south end. South of the camp are some backpacker campsites from where you can take in the next morning's glorious sunrise. From the camp the JMT continues through the south arm of Long Meadow, then soon starts to climb up the east slopes of Sunrise Mountain. About 1.6 miles past the camp and 400 feet higher, you top a broad ridge, and now can celebrate, because the route ahead is almost entirely level or downhill.

You begin by paralleling the headwaters of Sunrise Creek, descending steeply on switchbacks down a rocky canyon. At the foot of this descent you cross a trickling creek, then climb a low moraine to another creek, and in a short ½ mile top the linear crest of what has been interpreted as a giant lateral moraine. More correctly, it is a bedrock ridge with a veneer of gravel and with gigantic granite boulders left by the last Ice Age glacier as it was retreating up Little Yosemite Valley. Lower down, additional morainal crests appear on both sides of the trail, and you see Half Dome through the trees before your route reaches a junction with the Forsyth Trail (12.7). Fair campsites lie along Sunrise Creek, about 150 yards north of this junction.

Here you turn south and in a moment reach the High Trail (12.8) coming in on the left. Turn right and descend southwest, your path being bounded first on the north by the south buttress of the Clouds Rest eminence and then, about ½ mile past the trail junction, on the south by the northeast end of a ridge, Moraine Dome. For admirable views and interesting geology, I strongly recommend you take my second side trip and ascend south some 200 feet in elevation to attain the broad ridgecrest, then walk southwest along it to the obvious summit of Moraine Dome. This is named for a lateral moraine that descends southwest from just below the dome's summit. This moraine, hanging on the south side of Moraine Dome about 1750 feet above the floor of Little Yosemite Valley, does not represent the approximate thickness of the last glacier, geological experts to the contrary. It and earlier glaciers topped it by hundreds of feet. Atop Moraine Dome you'll see—besides a fabulous 360° panorama—two geologically interesting features. One is an 8-foot-high dike of resistant aplite, which stands above the rest of the dome's surface because it weathers more slowly. Nearby just downslope is a large erratic boulder which, unlike the rock of Moraine Dome, is composed of Cathedral Peak granodiorite, easily identified by its large feldspar crystals. Ongoing exfoliation of adjacent bedrock, aided by a lengthy root from a nearby Jeffrey pine, has left the erratic perched precariously atop a 3-foot-high pedestal. From the dome you can descend initially southwest, following the descending lateral moraine as you descend bedrock slopes of about 20° steepness. Where the moraine bottoms out only to rise again—a dead giveaway that it is a recessional lateral moraine—you branch north for an easy ¼-mile jaunt down to Sunrise Creek, reaching it and the adjacent JMT where both curve from southwest to west.

Meanwhile, along the JMT a mile from the last junction, you ford Sunrise Creek in a red-fir forest, then in ¾ mile see a good campsite on a large, shady creekside flat. You then curve northeast to quickly cross the creek's tributary, which has two west-bank campsites. Immediately past these is a junction with the Clouds Rest Trail (14.9), and after an easy ½-mile descent from it there is a junction with the Half Dome Trail (15.4). This is an incredible side trip that shouldn't be missed, especially since any year the Park Service may decide to remove the cables to the dome's summit; if you're not a climber, you'll have missed a golden opportunity.

From this junction your shady path switchbacks down through a changing forest cover that includes some stately incense-cedars, with their burnt-orange, fibrous bark. At the foot of this descent you reach the floor of Little Yosemite Valley. Here you encounter a cutoff trail (16.8), which is the more direct route to Nevada Fall, albeit one with a bit of ascent and descent. The JMT heads south, and you're likely to see a spur trail east to a Park Service camp, a home for summer rangers. Nearby is a group of very conspicuous outhouses—necessitated due to the incredible day traffic up to Half Dome and back—and just south is Little Yosemite Valley's backpackers' camp, complete with bearproof food-storage boxes. And just south of it is a junction with the Merced Lake Trail (17.0).

"Happy Isles to Merced Lake" describes this trail in considerable detail, so it won't be repeated here. Basically, you reverse the description, although you have options. First you follow the John Muir Trail a level, short ½ mile west to a reunion of the cutoff trail, this beside the Merced River. Next, you continue a long ½ mile, briefly ascending before descending to a junction with the Mist Trail's upper end (18.0), complete with a nearby outhouse. This trail is arguably the more scenic one, descending past Nevada and Vernal falls, although by taking it you miss the JMT's dramatic views of Liberty Cap, Mt. Broderick, and Half Dome. Also, because it is about ½ mile shorter, it is quite steep and is potentially treacherous (see Heads Up!).

On the JMT you meander briefly over to a bridge just above the brink of Nevada Fall. Just a few yards before the bridge you can strike northwest on a short spur trail down to a viewpoint beside the fall's brink. This viewpoint's railing is seen from the fall's bridge, thereby giving you an idea where the trail ends. Don't stray along the river bank or the cliff's edge, as people have fallen to their deaths. Standing near the tumultuous brink of the Merced River, you can look across its canyon—minimally eroded by glaciers—to *unglaciated* Glacier Point. Vernal Fall, which lies just beyond Emerald Pool, plunges over a vertical wall that is perpendicular to the steep one Nevada Fall plunges over. This part of the canyon contains major fracture planes, or joint planes, which account for the canyon's angular landscape.

From the Nevada Fall bridge we strike southwest, immediately pass glacier polish and erratic boulders like those seen just before it, and shortly end a gentle ascent at a nearby junction just beyond a seeping spring, where we meet the Glacier Point-Panorama Trail (18.4). Our trail starts with a high traverse that provides an ever-changing panorama of domelike Liberty Cap and broad-topped Mt. Broderick—both testaments to the ineffectiveness of glacial erosion. As you progress west, Half Dome becomes prominent, its hulking mass vying for your attention. Eventually you descend to Clark Point, where you meet a scenic connecting trail (19.4) that switchbacks down to Emerald Pool. Backpackers wishing to keep dry and avoid a possible slip continue down the JMT, which curves south into a gully, switchbacks down to the base of spreading Panorama Cliff, then switchbacks down a talus slope. Largely shaded by canyon live oaks and Douglas-firs, it reaches a junction with a horse trail (no hikers allowed) that descends to the Valley's stables. Continue a brief minute more to a junction with the Mist Trail's lower end (20.5), turn left, and quickly reach the Vernal Fall bridge. Soak in the view of the fall, crowned with the more-distant Liberty Cap, then join hordes of tourists for a brief ascent, then a generally steep, if reasonably short descent to Happy Isles. There, take a bridge west across the Merced River, near where you can purchase snacks and souvenirs, and walk shortly north to the Happy Isles shuttle-bus stop (21.6).

Permits

See the "High Sierra Camps Loop" information on Wilderness Permits and related advice.

Build-up/Wind-down tips

This is a popular trail, so get a Wilderness Permit in advance—see the "High Sierra Camps Loop" information on Wilderness Permits and related advice, as mentioned below. Further, as mentioned in Build-up/Wind-down tips in that hike, it's very difficult to get a campsite within the park, so plan to drive in to Yosemite Valley, park your vehicle, then take the hikers' bus up to Tuolumne Meadows.

By the time you finish your hike, you'll be hot and sweaty, having descended to lower climes. Therefore, you might stop at Yosemite Lodge for refreshments—food or beverages, particularly the latter—before heading out. If you're leaving the valley via Highway 140, note that the Merced River warms about ½-1°F for every mile it traverses. In the valley, the water's about mid-60s, but a few miles below El Portal, the river's swimming holes typically are in the 70s by afternoon. Quite refreshing. If you're leaving by Highways 120 and 41, take heart. On Highway 120, cross the South Fork Tuolumne River bridge, midway between the park boundary and Groveland, and immediately turn left for a short descent to Rainbow Pool Picnic Area, with warm swimming and high diving. Those on Highway 41 park in Wawona near the covered bridge and walk about 200 yards up the South Fork Merced River to some excellent swimming holes.

Jeffrey P. Schaffer provides background on his path to guidebook writing, detailed mapmaking, and challenging received views of Sierra geological formation, besides a list of his titles from Wilderness Press, in "Author Bio & Bib" on page 492.

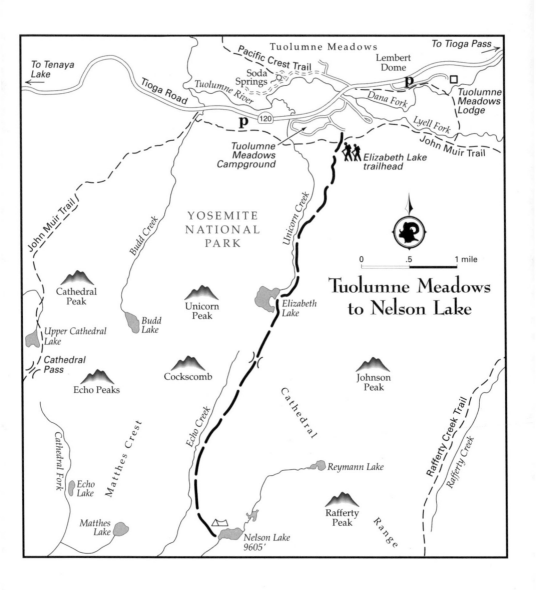

Tuolumne Meadows

To Tioga Pass

To Tenaya Lake

Pacific Crest Trail

Soda Springs

Lembert Dome

Tioga Road

Tuolumne River

Dana Fork

Tuolumne Meadows Lodge

Lyell Fork

p

120

Tuolumne Meadows Campground

John Muir Trail

Elizabeth Lake trailhead

Unicorn Creek

YOSEMITE NATIONAL PARK

John Muir Trail

Budd Creek

Tuolumne Meadows to Nelson Lake

0   .5   1 mile

Cathedral Peak

Unicorn Peak

Elizabeth Lake

Budd Lake

Upper Cathedral Lake

Cathedral Pass

Echo Peaks

Cockscomb

Johnson Peak

Cathedral

Echo Creek

Matthes Crest

Rafferty Creek Trail

Rafferty Creek

Cathedral Fork

Echo Lake

Reymann Lake

Matthes Lake

Rafferty Peak

Range

Nelson Lake 9605'

44

Tuolumne Meadows to Nelson Lake

—Thomas Winnett

Route	Days	Elev. Gain/Loss	Difficulty	Miles
↲	2	2924' /2924'	**	11.8

Campsites: Nelson Lake: 5.9 miles

Map: USGS 7.5-min *Vogelsang Peak, Tenaya Lake*

Best season: Mid- or late summer

Take this trip!

Never to have hiked out of Tuolumne Meadows in Yosemite National Park would be a significant oversight for the serious backpacker. The meadows are the hub of some of the best backpacks in the whole world. As such, they are well populated during the season, but since the trail to Nelson Lake is not on the topo map and not diligently maintained, you have a chance for solitude there. You will also have world-class views north and south from the high points of the trip, and no trail route offers finer close-up views of those geologic wonders called Unicorn Peak and the Cockscomb.

Trailhead

Your trailhead, signed for ELIZABETH LAKE, is located across a road from a masonry building just before the turnaround in the Group Camping section of the Tuolumne Meadows Campground on Highway 120 in Yosemite.

TRIP DESCRIPTION

Heads Up! Bears are a hazard (see the chapter "Bears & Other Hazards"). No open fires are allowed in Yosemite above 9600 feet; use a stove when camping at Nelson Lake. Also, there is no camping within 4 trail miles of Tuolumne Meadows.

In a few hundred feet you cross the John Muir Trail and then continue a steady southward ascent. The shade-giving forest cover is almost entirely lodgepole pine as the trail crosses several runoff streams that dry up by late summer. More than a mile from the start your route veers close to Unicorn Creek, and the music of this dashing, gurgling, cold-water stream makes the climb easier. When the ascent finally ends, the hiker emerges at the foot of a long meadow containing lovely Elizabeth Lake (2.4) at the foot of striking Unicorn Peak.

Past Elizabeth Lake, the meadow gives way to a moderately dense forest cover of lodgepole interspersed with mountain hemlock, and the trail climbs steeply, then moderately, and steeply again. A few hundred feet before you reach the ridgecrest, you come to a late-lingering snowbank where the trail splits. If you go left, you will pass through a narrow gully between granite walls. If you go right, you will walk up a bare granite-sand slope. I recommend that if you have a full pack, you take the right trail going to Nelson Lake and the left one returning, because of some steep places on the left trail just beyond the crest.

Because of the closeness of the Cockscomb (about 1 mile due west), the hiker has excellent views of that knifelike spire from just beyond the left pass.

Mt Conness and White Mountain from Elizabeth Lake

Well-named by François Matthes, this slender crest bears clear marks of the highest level reached by ice of the last glacial episode. Its lower shoulders reveal the rounded, well-polished surfaces that betray glacial action, while its jagged, sharply etched crest shows no such markings. Further evidence of glacial action may be clearly seen on the steep descent into the head of long, typically U-shaped Echo Creek valley. The shearing and polishing action of the ice mass that shaped this rounded valley is evident on the cliffs on the west side.

About 0.3 mile from where the trail split, and several hundred yards beyond the crest, the forks come together again on a steep, tree-dotted hillside. As your route descends along winding, clear, meadowed Echo Creek for about 2 miles, the valley floor is lush with wildflower growth. During midsummer the passerby can expect to see Davidson's penstemon, Douglas phlox, senecio, red heather, lupine, and swamp whiteheads. At the end of the second large meadow in this canyon, your trail leaves Echo Creek and veers east up a low, rocky ridge, undulating through sparse forest. You are almost at Nelson Lake (9605) before you can see your destination, meadow-fringed at the foot of imposing granite Peak 11357. Good campsites may be found on the northeast and southwest sides (5.9). Anglers will find the lake's waters good fishing for brook trout.

Permits

To get information about permits, contact:

Wilderness Center
Box 545
Yosemite National Park, CA 95389
(209) 372-0740

Obtain your actual Wilderness Permit at the booth a short way down the Tuolumne Lodge spur road or, after Labor Day, at the Information Center in the meadows.

Build-up/Wind-down tips

If you forgot something, you may find it before your trip at the store in Tuolumne Meadows. Good food at reasonable prices is sold at the Tioga Pass Resort, 2 miles outside the park beyond Tioga Pass. For a first-class dinner, go to Mono Inn, north of Lee Vining on Highway 395.

Since Tom Winnett is always modest and succinct, consult "Author Bio & Bib" on page 492 to learn little more than our Publisher Emeritus' titles currently in print.

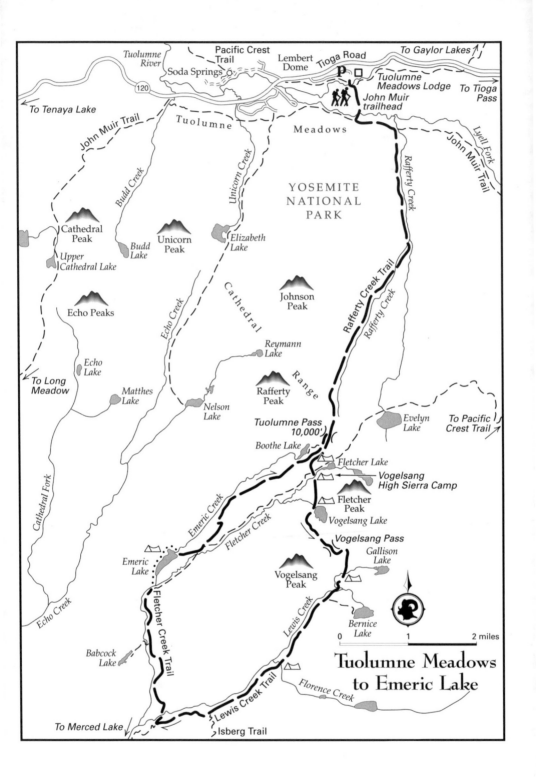

Tuolumne Meadows to Emeric Lake

45

Tuolumne Meadows to Emeric Lake

—Thomas Winnett

Route	Days	Elev. Gain/Loss	Difficulty	Miles
	5–7	**4100'/4100'**	***	**28.9**

Campsites: Upper Fletcher Lake (northeast): 6.2 miles
Vogelsang Lake: 6.8 miles
meadow below Gallison Lake: 8.8 miles
Florence Creek: 10.5 miles
Emeric Lake (northwest): 14.7 miles

Map: USGS 7.5-min *Vogelsang Peak, Merced Lake, Mt. Lyell, Tenaya Lake*

Best season: Late summer

Take this trip!

With Tuolumne Pass as the neck of the "noose," this trip "lassos" Vogelsang Peak by dashing down the valley of Lewis Creek and then cruising back up the valley of Fletcher Creek. In addition to the spectrum of views of this fine peak, the hiker will constantly have good vistas of many parts of the Cathedral Range, and anglers will find good fishing in both creeks and at Emeric Lake.

Trailhead

Your trailhead, signed for the JOHN MUIR TRAIL, is located at the large parking lot 0.3 mile west of Tuolumne Meadows Lodge. If you are approaching from Tuolumne Meadows Campground, drive 0.6 mile northeast up the Tioga Road, turn right on the lodge spur road, and follow it 0.4 mile to the lot, on your left.

TRIP DESCRIPTION

> **Heads Up!** Bears are a hazard (see the chapter "Bears & Other Hazards").

Begin by hiking up the road to the trail sign beside the lodge's parking lot. Hike through the employee tents and reach a bridge over the Dana Fork Tuolumne River. Turning left, you meet a trail that leads upriver toward the Gaylor Lakes, and you veer right (south). Now you ascend a slight rise and descend to the beautiful Lyell Fork, over which there is a substantial double bridge. Just past it, at a T-junction, you turn left (east). Soon, in dense lodge-pole-pine forest, you encounter the signed trail (1.5) to Tuolumne Pass and Vogelsang High Sierra Camp. Turn right onto this trail and immediately begin one of the toughest climbs of the entire trip. Even so, the gradient is moderate as often as it is steep, the trail is well-shaded by lodgepole pines, and the length of the climb is less than a mile.

Then, as the ascent decreases to a gentle grade, we pass through high, boulder-strewn meadows that offer good views eastward of reddish-brown Mts. Dana and Gibbs, and gray-white Mammoth Peak. Soon the trail dips close to all-year Rafferty Creek.

Then your nearly level trail passes above an orange snowcourse marker in a large meadow below and continues its long, gentle ascent through a sparse forest of lodgepole pines unmixed with a single tree of any other species. About a half mile beyond a stream that dries up in late summer, you ford another that also does in some years.

As you begin the gentle ascent to Tuolumne Pass, nearby Rafferty Creek invites you to pause and examine dense, varied wildflower displays. Finally the exclusive lodgepole pines allow a few whitebark pines to join their company, and these trees diminish the force of winds that often sweep through Tuolumne Pass (10,000). In the pass a signed trail junction indicates your route to Vogelsang High Sierra Camp as the left fork. Through breaks in this forest you have intermittent views south of cliff-bound Fletcher Peak and Peak 11799. Then your path leaves the green-floored forest and leads out into an area of bouldery granite outcroppings dotted with a few trees. Now in the west side of saucer-shaped Tuolumne Pass, a major gap in the Cathedral Range, you follow a rocky-dusty path up a moderately steep hillside below which Boothe Lake and its surrounding meadows lie serene. Finally your trail reaches the top of this climb, and suddenly you can see the tents of Vogelsang High Sierra Camp (6.2), at 10,157 feet the highest of six such camps. A few snacks may be bought here, or dinner if you have made a reservation by phone before your trip, (559) 253-5674. You must camp in the designated area just northeast at Upper Fletcher Lake.

Mt Clark and Emeric Lake

Taking the Vogelsang Pass Trail from the camp, you descend slightly to ford Fletcher Creek on boulders and then begin a 550-foot moderate ascent with occasional steep sections to the pass. Dramatic sections of the trail here cross exposed granite slopes. The panting hiker is rewarded, as always in the Sierra, with increasingly good views. Fletcher Peak rises grandly on the left, far north stands Mt. Conness, and Clouds Rest and then Half Dome come into view in the west-southwest. At 0.6 mile from Vogelsang Camp the trail skirts above the west shore of Vogelsang Lake (6.8), where windswept camping occurs among the whitebarks bordering this treeline lake. Nearer the pass, views to the north are occluded somewhat, but expansive views appear in the south. From the windswept pass (10,960) you look down on Gallison and Bernice lakes. The trail rises briefly northeast before it follows steep switchbacks down into sparse lodgepole forest where many small streams provide moisture for thousands of giant lupine plants, with flowers both dark violet and light blue in color. The singing of the unnamed outlet stream from Gallison Lake (8.8; 2.0 miles from Vogelsang Lake) becomes clear as the trail begins to level off, and then you reach a flat meadow through which the stream slowly meanders. There is a fine campsite beside this meadow, though wood fires are illegal here.

Proceeding down a rutted, grassy trail for several hundred yards, you come to a brief, steep descent on a rocky path that swoops down to the meadowed valley of multi-braided Lewis Creek. In this little valley in quick succession you boulderhop the Gallison Lake outlet and then cross Lewis Creek on a log. In a few minutes you pass the steep half-mile lateral to Bernice Lake. Then the shady trail winds gently down east of the creek under a moderate canopy of lodgepole pine mixed with some hemlock, crossing a little stream about one-half mile from the last ford. Then, after almost touching the creek opposite a steep, rusty west canyon wall, the trail winds through dense hemlock forest to Florence Creek (9200). This year-round creek cascades dramatically down over steep granite sheets to the camping area (10.5; 3.7 miles from Vogelsang Lake), and the water sounds are a fine sleeping potion at bedtime.

Leaving the densely shaded hemlock forest floor, your trail descends a series of lodgepole-dotted granite slabs, and Lewis Creek makes pleasant noises in a string of chutes not far away. Then, where the creek's channel narrows, you find on your left a lesson in exfoliation: granite layers peeling like an onion. Typically seen on Yosemite's domes, this kind of peeling provides a fine example on a canyon slope. As the bed of Lewis Creek steepens to deliver the stream's water to the Merced River far below, the trail steepens, too, and your descent reaches the zone of red firs and western white pines. After dipping beside the creek, the trail climbs away from it. At about 8700 feet you pass the Isberg Trail (12.0; 1.5 miles from Florence Creek), which leads south along the rim of the Merced River canyon.

From this junction the Lewis Creek Trail, now out of earshot of the creek, switchbacks down moderately, sometimes steeply, under a sparse cover of red fir, juniper, and pines for 1.2 miles to a signed junction with the Fletcher Creek Trail. Turn right onto this trail and descend on several switchbacks to a bridge over Lewis Creek. From here the trail begins an initial 400-foot ascent, at times moderate, often steep, over unevenly cobbled, exposed trail—a grunt on a hot day. Your path is bordered by proliferating bushes of mountain whitethorn and huckleberry oak. Just past a tributary one-half mile from Lewis Creek, we have fine views of cataracts and waterfalls on Fletcher Creek where it rushes down open slopes dotted with lodgepole pines. The trail then passes very close to the creek before veering south and climbing, steeply at times, on the now-familiar cobbling placed by trail crews. Here one has more good views of Fletcher Creek chuting and cascading down from the notch at the base of a granite dome before it leaps off a ledge in free fall. The few solitary pine trees on this otherwise blank dome testify to nature's extraordinary persistence.

At the notch, your trail levels off near some nice but illegal campsites, and then soon passes a side trail (12.7; 1.5 miles from the Lewis Creek Trail) to small Babcock Lake. From this junction the sandy trail ascends steadily through a moderate forest cover just east of Fletcher Creek. After a mile the trail rises steeply via rocky switchbacks from which one can see nearby in the north the outlet stream of Emeric Lake, though not the lake itself, which is behind a dome just to the right of the outlet's notch. For an adventurous shortcut to Emeric Lake, follow this outlet up to the lake. First, leave the trail and wade across granite-bottomed Fletcher Creek as best you can. There is no natural place to do so, and in a wet year you may get very wet yourself. Then follow up this outlet and stroll along the northwest shore of Emeric Lake (9338) to some excellent campsites (14.7; 2.0 miles from the Babcock Creek Trail). Sometimes windy, the lake was nevertheless so still one night that I saw the Milky Way clearly reflected in it.

Circle the head of Emeric Lake, staying near the lake to protect the meadow north and northeast of the lake, which is carpeted with delicate wildflowers. Cross the inlet stream and find a trail at the northeast corner of the lake, at the base of a granite knoll. This trail leads east-northeast to an X-junction (15.3; 0.6 mile from the Emeric Lake campsites) in the valley of Fletcher Creek. Taking the left branch up the valley, you follow a rocky-dusty trail through the forest fringe of the long meadow that straddles Fletcher Creek. This trail climbs farther from the meadow and passes northwest of a bald prominence that sits in the center of the upper valley of Fletcher and Emeric creeks, separating the two. Topping a minor summit, the trail descends slightly and then winds levelly past a long series of lovely ponds that are interconnected in early season. You soon pass a use trail to the south end of Boothe Lake (9845). At the top of a little swale, the trail reaches an overlook above Boothe Lake, then contours along this meadowy hillside about 50 vertical feet above the lake, passing another use trail down to it. About one-fourth mile farther you reach west Tuolumne Pass and a junction (18.8; 3.5 miles from the Emeric Lake campsites) with the trail to Vogelsang Camp. From here you retrace your earlier steps to Tuolumne Meadows.

Permits

See "Permits" in trip 44.

Build-up/Wind-down tips

See this section in trip 44.

Since Tom Winnett is always modest and succinct, consult "Author Bio & Bib" on page 492 to learn little more than our Publisher Emeritus' titles currently in print.

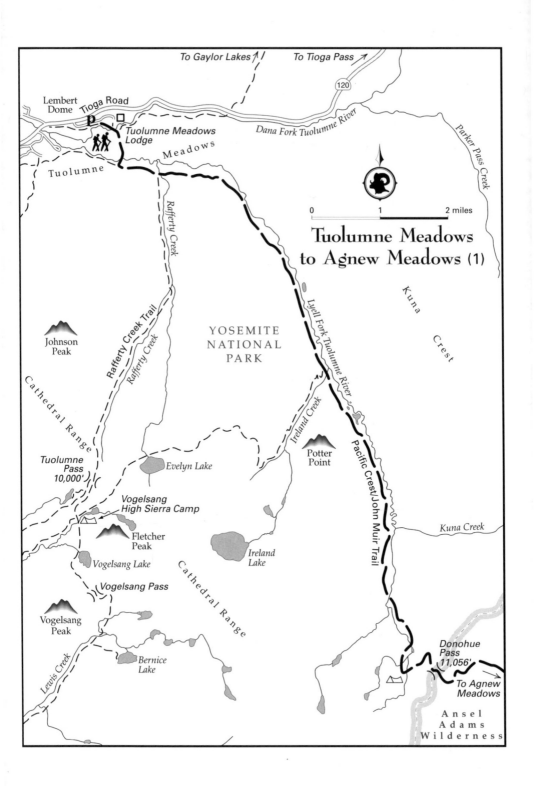

To Gaylor Lakes   To Tioga Pass

120

Lembert
Dome   Tioga Road
Tuolumne Meadows
Lodge
Dana Fork Tuolumne River
Meadows

Tuolumne

Rafferty Creek

0   1   2 miles

Tuolumne Meadows
to Agnew Meadows (1)

Kuna

Crest

Johnson
Peak

Rafferty Creek Trail

Cathedral Range

Rafferty Creek

YOSEMITE
NATIONAL
PARK

Lyell Fork Tuolumne River

Parker Pass Creek

Ireland Creek

Potter
Point

Tuolumne
Pass
10,000'

Evelyn Lake

Vogelsang
High Sierra Camp

Pacific Crest/John Muir Trail

Kuna Creek

Fletcher
Peak

Ireland
Lake

Vogelsang Lake

Cathedral Range

Vogelsang Pass

Vogelsang
Peak

Bernice
Lake

Lewis Creek

Donohue
Pass
11,056'

To Agnew
Meadows

Ansel
Adams
Wilderness

46

Tuolumne Meadows to Agnew Meadows

—Kathy Morey

Route	Days	Elev. Gain/Loss	Difficulty	Miles
↗	5–7	4000'/4350'	***	29.9
		(another 0.25 mile to shuttle stop)		

Campsites: Lyell Fork base camp: 8.8 miles (good sites starting around 7.8 miles)
just north of Rush Creek Trail junction: 17.3 miles
Island Pass: 19.1 miles
Thousand Island Lake: 20.9 miles
Garnet Lake: 22.9 miles
Shadow Creek: 25.3 miles (desperation camping: highly restricted, severe bear problems)
(see the Trip Description for others)

Map: USGS 7.5-min *Tioga Pass, Vogelsang Peak, Koip Peak, Mt. Ritter, Mammoth Mtn.*

Best season: Late summer through early fall

Take this trip!

Get swept away by the wonderfully varied scenery on this trip, a leg of the John Muir Trail—lush meadows lining sensuous river curves, breathtaking views near high passes, and the dark, jagged Ritter Range reflected in numerous lakes. In season, there are superb wildflowers. You'll enjoy great dayhiking opportunities on your layover days.

My favorite dayhike on this trip is a mostly cross-country loop or semi-loop in the Island Pass-Thousand Island Lake vicinity. Curve around the north side of Thousand Island Lake before climbing the obvious, treeless saddle

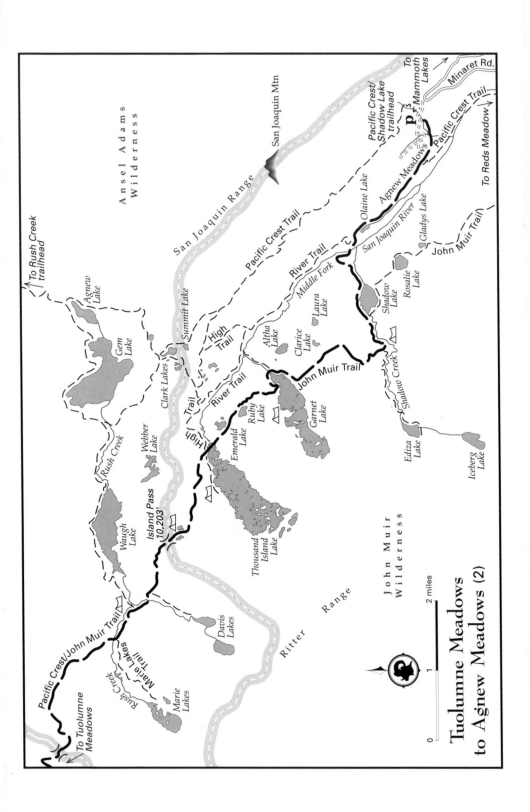

Tuolumne Meadows
to Agnew Meadows (2)

Ansel Adams Wilderness

San Joaquin Range

San Joaquin Mtn

To Rush Creek trailhead

Agnew Lake

Gem Lake

Summit Lake

Clark Lakes

Pacific Crest Trail

High Trail

River Trail

Middle Fork

San Joaquin River

Olaine Lake

Pacific Crest/ Shadow Lake trailhead

To Mammoth Lakes

Minaret Rd.

P

Agnew Meadows

Pacific Crest Trail

To Reds Meadow

Gladys Lake

Rosalie Lake

Shadow Lake

John Muir Trail

Laura Lake

Altha Lake

Clarice Lake

John Muir Trail

Shadow Creek

Ediza Lake

Iceberg Lake

Rush Creek

Webber Lake

High Trail

River Trail

Island Pass 10,203'

Waugh Lake

Emerald Lake

Ruby Lake

Garnet Lake

Thousand Island Lake

Davis Lakes

Ritter Range

John Muir Wilderness

Pacific Crest/John Muir Trail

Rush Creek

Marie Lakes Trail

Marie Lakes

To Tuolumne Meadows

0   1   2 miles

between Thousand Island and Garnet lakes' southwest ends. Descend to the beautiful ponds west of Garnet and then more gradually along Garnet's flowery north shore, where you'll pick up a use trail than connects with the JMT at an unsigned T-junction. Close the loop on the JMT.

Trailheads

I think it's better to get any hassles over with *before* you start your hike, so if you have just one car, consider leaving it at Agnew Meadows or at the ski area/mountain bike park lot near the Take-out trailhead. Then arrange for one of the Eastern Sierra's shuttle services to drive you—for a very hefty fee—to the Put-in trailhead. See the Eastern Sierra telephone directory for taxi services or call the ranger station in Bishop—see Permits below—for shuttle-service information.

Put-in trailhead: Parking lot near Tuolumne Lodge, just off State Route 120 in Yosemite National Park. Just under 7 miles west of Tioga Pass on 120, take the signed Tuolumne Meadows Lodge turnoff; it's east of the bridge over the Tuolumne River and west of the Mono Pass trailhead. Go a short way down this spur road to turn sharply right into the signed backpacker's parking lot, where there is a summer information/permit-issuing kiosk. Park and pick up your permit here. There's more backpacker parking a little farther down the spur road, this time on the left.

Take-out trailhead: Agnew Meadows, off the Devils Postpile Road out of Mammoth Lakes. From US Highway 395 between Lee Vining and Bishop, take State Route 203 west through the town of Mammoth Lakes. Zero your odometer where 203 turns right onto Minaret Road. Follow 203 for 8.2 miles as it snakes northwest to the ski area/mountain-bike park. You may have to park and take a for-fee shuttlebus from here (see Heads Up! below). Otherwise, continue over Minaret Summit down the one-lane, twisting, airy Devils Postpile Road to a hairpin curve where you turn right on the signed Agnew Meadows dirt spur road for the last quarter mile. Pass a pack station and park in one of two large trailhead lots on the left, near the road's end. Your trailhead is on the south side of the first of the two lots, signed for the Pacific Crest Trail and Shadow Lake.

TRIP DESCRIPTION

Heads Up! There's a fee to enter Yosemite National Park. At Minaret Summit, roughly between Memorial Day and Labor Day (from 7:30 A.M. to 5:30 P.M.), you must park your car at the ski area/mountain bike park and take a for-fee shuttlebus; get off at the Agnew Meadows stop and walk the rest of the way (see Take-out trailhead). Bears are active all along this route and counterbalance bear-bagging is ineffective: take a bearproof food canister and sleep soundly while your fellow campers who hung their food are up all night chasing bears away. Know Yosemite National Park and Ansel Adams wildernesses regulations! No pets; they are not permitted on national park trails.

From either backpacker parking lot (0.0), pick up a wide trail south of the spur road and bear east through lodgepole forest toward Tuolumne Meadows Lodge, to which a number of use trails take off. Staying on the main trail, you soon cross the Dana Fork Tuolumne River on a bridge and go right (ahead, east) at a junction, leaving the Dana Fork behind. The trail shortly crosses a pair of bridges over the Lyell Fork Tuolumne River. Get out the camera: the views up-canyon from these bridges are spectacular!

Beyond the bridges you meet the official route of the John Muir and Pacific Crest trails (0.9) and begin roughly paralleling the lazy, picturesque Lyell Fork eastward, leaving Tuolumne Meadows behind and entering Lyell Canyon. Camping is prohibited within 4 miles of State Route 120, but that's no hardship on such a beautiful, gradual trail. At a junction with the Rafferty Creek Trail (1.6), you go left (ahead, east) on the JMT/PCT and soon cross bubbling Rafferty Creek on a footbridge.

In another ¾ mile, the trail and the river curve south-southeast, and the forest thins till the trail is skirting, and sometimes even in, the meadows lining the river. Seasonal wildflowers, best in early and mid seasons, dot these lush meadows. The stroll upriver is wonderfully scenic, and you presently begin to spot potential campsites here and there. Just north of imposing Potter Point you reach a major camping area at a junction with the trail to Ireland and Evelyn lakes and Vogelsang High Sierra Camp (6.0). Go left (ahead, southsoutheast) on the JMT/PCT and shortly ford Ireland Creek. Continuing upstream, you notice small, dry rises west of the trail, some of which offer excellent campsites overlooking the lovely river, backed by the Kuna Crest.

The trail reaches a forested bench called Lyell Fork base camp (8.8) just before beginning a stiff climb to Donohue Pass. The site is popular with weekenders, and sites back downstream may be more peaceful and private.

From Lyell Fork base camp, begin a series of steep, exposed switchbacks up the head of Lyell Canyon, ending abruptly at a forested bench with many overused campsites. Cross Lyell Fork on a footbridge (10.2) before resuming the ascent, this time to a handsome cirque cupping a subalpine meadow and a tiny lake, with one or two campsites nestled in the whitebark pines on the sandy rise east of the lake's outlet, which you ford just below the lake (12.0). Now the rocky trail climbs steeply up the cirque's west side before leveling out in a marshy area, popping over a low rise, and dipping to a pretty pond whose outlet you ford. When still, the pond picturesquely reflects Mt. Lyell, at 13,144 feet Yosemite's highest peak, and its glacier, the largest seen on this trip.

Lyell Canyon of the Lyell Fork Tuolumne River

Next, you tackle the last steep climb east to the pass, and may spy one or two Spartan campsites along the way, usable when snowmelt provides water nearby. Views along this climb more than gratify your needed rest stops. There aren't many views from tarn-blessed, 11,056-foot Donohue Pass (13.8) on the Sierra crest. But as you begin descending on the east side, leaving Yosemite National Park for Ansel Adams Wilderness, views over the large, granite basin at the headwaters of Rush Creek are breathtaking.

The stony trail descends moderately into the nearly treeless upper basin, which is too wet and fragile for camping except for a few Spartan sites where it's dotted by dry hummocks—sites well worth seeking out. Numerous peaks, including Donohue Peak and the Koip Crest, provide a rugged backdrop for most of the basin, which drains into famous Mono Lake. Rush Creek's headwaters, often paralleled and a couple of times forded by the JMT/PCT, pour down the basin over a series of enchanting, increasingly forested benches where campsites on the higher, drier rises are worth looking for.

A more serious ford of Rush Creek, difficult in early season, precedes the junction with the Marie Lakes Trail. For those who can safely make the leap with a full pack, there is a jump-across spot just downstream of the ford. At the junction (16.8), near which there are a couple of fair campsites, go left (ahead, southeast) to begin switchbacking down to a junction with the Rush Creek Trail at an area known as Rush Creek Forks. Good campsites, not obvious from the trail, are located on its west side along a bench about 0.3 mile north of the forks

"Ham and Eggs Lakes" from Island Pass

(17.3). Campsites at the forks are badly overused and now illegal because they're too close to water. A summer ranger may be stationed 5 miles away, below Waugh Lake to the east.

At the junction with the Rush Creek Trail (17.6), stay on the JMT/PCT by going right (ahead, southeast). You make at least three fords in the next quarter mile, some of which may be difficult in early season. Climbing through dry forest, you pass a spur trail on your right, southwest to Davis Lake, and stay on the JMT/PCT. It's not long before you reach the meadows and ponds of broad, marshy, 10,203-foot Island Pass (19.1), where it's very hard to determine the high point. But just southwest of it, the trail winds between a pair of small, shallow lakes, known as "The Ham and Eggs Lakes," that offer a few campsites, pleasant swimming, and outstanding views of Banner Peak in the Ritter Range. Island Pass lies on the Sierra crest, and waters on its west side eventually drain into the Pacific Ocean.

The route south from Island Pass descends moderately to a junction at the northeast end of magnificent but overused Thousand Island Lake, where a spur trail leads to campsites on the lake's north shore—the south shore has virtually none. Views of the Ritter Range over this lake and its sister to the south, Garnet Lake, are unforgettable, especially in the morning when the peaks are mirrored in their still waters. A few more steps bring you to a signed junction (20.9) where the JMT and the PCT part company temporarily. Regulations posted near here explain that camping is prohibited within ¼ mile of the lake's outlet. You stay on the JMT, taking the right fork southeast over a crude footbridge spanning the outlet.

Climbing away from Thousand Island Lake on a moderate grade, you pass pretty Emerald Lake, whose west shore is closed to camping. The trail continues ascending past Ruby Lake, where there are fair campsites, and then climbs the ridge separating Ruby and Garnet lakes. Big, blue, windy Garnet Lake fills the view as you descend rocky switchbacks to a junction with a use trail leading to campsites on Garnet's north shore—the campsites get better the farther you go.

Staying on the JMT, you curve briefly around Garnet's north shore before crossing its outlet on a rickety-looking footbridge (22.9). Posted regulations announce that camping is prohibited within ¼ mile of Garnet's outlet. Just beyond the footbridge there's an obscure junction with a rough trail on your left that descends northeast into the canyon of Middle Fork San Joaquin River.

Again staying on the JMT, you briefly skim Garnet's southeast shore before tackling a steep but scenic climb up the ridge south of the lake. At a saddle atop the ridge, there's a swimming-pool-sized pond that warms up enough by midsummer for pleasant bathing. The 1,100-foot descent of the ridge, into the Shadow Creek drainage, offers few campsites until you're near its end, where the trail begins to level out and a shady flat near a tributary of Shadow Creek has fair campsites.

The JMT soon meets and joins the Shadow Creek Trail (25.3). As posted rules announce here, camping in the Shadow Creek drainage is very limited and strictly regulated. Please study, understand, and follow these regulations in order to help this terribly overused area recover! Turn left (east) to descend the steep, rocky-dusty trail, which parallels Shadow Creek as it tumbles in foaming cascades down its narrow canyon. You reach another junction near a footbridge (26.4), where you bid farewell to the JMT. Go ahead (left, east) here, staying on the Shadow Creek Trail, and make an easy traverse along the north shore of idyllic Shadow Lake, which is entirely closed to camping but is a choice spot for a rest stop.

Leaving Shadow Lake, the trail winds down exposed switchbacks along the outlet's notable waterfall. At the bottom of the descent, in the aspen-shaded canyon of Middle Fork San Joaquin River, the trail veers south to cross the river on a footbridge. You soon reach a junction with the River Trail back to Thousand Island Lake; go right (ahead, east) here toward Agnew Meadows. Soon curving south-southeast, the track passes lily-pad-dotted Olaine Lake and presently forks. Take the left fork southeast to Agnew Meadows and begin a moderate, open, rocky-dusty ascent to a bench above the river. Near the top of the ascent, you find yet another fork, where you again go left (southeast) to Agnew Meadows, ignoring an unsigned track that soon comes in on your left.

The nearly level, lodgepole-shaded trail threads its way between rocky knobs and crosses a little creek before skirting part of Agnew Meadows, where colorful San Joaquin Ridge rises to the north. You bob over a low ridge, cross a couple more arms of the creek, and arrive at the take-out trailhead (29.9) parking lot to find your car or meet your ride. If you're using the shuttlebus, walk through this parking lot to pick up a dirt spur road and head generally east (right as you leave the parking lot) a quarter mile, past Agnew Meadows Pack Station, to the shuttlebus stop at paved Devils Postpile Road.

Variations

You won't want to miss lovely Emerald, Ruby, and Garnet lakes. However, you can pick up a shortcut at Garnet. While it's 9 scenic miles from Garnet Lake to Agnew Meadows on the JMT and Shadow Lake Trail, you can cut off 3 miles and a steep 425' climb/1,100' descent by taking the "rough trail"—be ready for brief rock-scrambling!—at the outlet of Garnet Lake. Head northeast down to meet the River Trail in the canyon of the Middle Fork San Joaquin River, and turn right (south) to follow the River Trail to Agnew Meadows.

Permits

This is a quota trailhead, and permits are required for overnight stays. If starting in Yosemite, contact Wilderness Permits, Box 545, Yosemite, CA 95389, (559) 372-0740, or see **www.nps.gov/yose**. If starting from Agnew Meadows, contact Inyo National Forest, 873 N. Main Street, Bishop, CA 93514, (760) 873-2500, or see **www.r5.fs.fed.us/inyo/**.

Build-up/Wind-down tips

Near the put-in, the town of Lee Vining on US Highway 395 at the edge of Mono Lake (Chamber of Commerce, (760) 647-6595) offers lodgings, restaurants, and stores. Along State Route 120 (Tioga Road) between 395 and Tuolumne Meadows, you'll find several popular campgrounds and two lodgings, Tioga Pass Resort ((209) 372-4471) and Tuolumne Meadows Lodge (Yosemite Reservations, (209) 252-4848), where you can find soft beds, hot showers, and good meals before your trip.

Near the take-out, the town of Mammoth Lakes (Visitors Bureau, (800) 367-6572) has ample lodgings, restaurants, and stores as well as campgrounds to meet your needs for the night you finish this trip, including campgrounds off Devils Postpile Road and a resort at the end of that road (Red's Meadow Resort, (760) 873-3928; with lodgings, café, and store).

All these facilities are in very high demand during the summer; make your plans and reservations early!

To find out how Kathy Morey got started hiking the Sierra and the Hawaiian islands and writing about her hikes for Wilderness Press, and for a list of her titles, see "Author Bio & Bib" on page 492.

To Lundy
Canyon

Lake
Helen

Hoover
Wilderness

Hess
Mine

Mill Creek

Steelhead
Lake

Shamrock
Lake

Twin
Lakes

Odell
Lake

Cascade
Lake

20 Lakes
Basin

Lundy Pass
10,320'

Z Lake

Hummingbird
Lake

Wasco
Lake

Tioga

Crest

North
Peak

Conness
Lakes

Greenstone
Lake

Saddlebag
Lake

INYO
NATIONAL
FOREST

0   .5   1 mile

Dam
Saddlebag Lake
Resort

P

Lee Vining
Creek

To Tioga Road

20 Lakes Basin Loop

47

20 Lakes Basin Loop

—Kathy Morey

Route	Days	Elev. Gain/Loss	Difficulty	Miles
↻	2	240'/240'	*	8.5

Campsites: sub-basin west of Steelhead Lake: 3 miles (see the Trip Description for others)

Map: USGS 7.5-min *Tioga Pass, Dunderberg Peak*

Best season: Late summer through early fall

Take this trip!

This easy trip can even be done as a dayhike, and you won't believe how much alpine beauty is packed into such a short jaunt. 20 Lakes Basin is set among majestic peaks and is full of pretty lakes. Yet, in spite of its rugged setting, the trail through it is mostly gentle to moderate. Most of the basin lacks acceptable campsites, but a short cross-country jaunt brings hikers to scenic if Spartan campsites in a granite sub-basin.

There's delightful dayhiking in addition to simply looping through the basin. Just rambling through the sub-basin is great fun. If a more adventurous cross-country trip appeals to you, consider a scramble toward the crest west of the sub-basin (on the other side of which is the northern backcountry of Yosemite National Park) or up to the Conness Lakes south of the sub-basin.

Trailhead

From 2.2 miles north of the Tioga Pass entrance to Yosemite National Park on State Highway 120, go 2.6 miles north up a part-paved, part-dirt road to big, dammed Saddlebag Lake, where there is a parking lot just above the day-use-only Saddlebag Lake Resort. There are toilets and water at the trailhead (with an adjacent campground); the resort offers a café, a store, and for-fee ferry service across the lake.

TRIP DESCRIPTION

Heads Up! Wood fires are prohibited in 20 Lakes Basin; use stoves only! Know Hoover Wilderness regulations! It's the policy of Inyo National Forest (which manages this little slice of Hoover Wilderness) to prohibit backcountry camping outside of designated wilderness.

Assuming most of you will walk rather than take the ferry, you'll find your trailhead just a few steps south of Saddlebag's dam, where the trail begins as an old road that dips below the face of the dam. (Crossing on the dam isn't recommended.) Climbing up on the other side, the road becomes a footpath north-northwest along Saddlebag Lake's west side, over shattered rocks in rust, brown, gray, and cream colors, and through a surprising array of flowers in season. The splendid peaks around the head of 20 Lakes Basin come into view, with light-granite North Peak and red-brown Mt. Scowden particularly striking. To the east are the colorful, gently rounded, metamorphic summits of the Tioga Crest. This region is full of ruins left by mostly unsuccessful mining ventures. To support one such venture, the Tioga (or Great Sierra) Mine's plans in the winter of 1882 called for men and mules to haul 16,000 pounds of mining machinery—using huge sleds—up Mill Creek from the east, through Lake Canyon, over the Tioga Crest, down to Saddlebag Lake, and presumably from there to the mine, a few miles southwest of Saddlebag!

The trail fades as you approach the stream that's the outlet of Greenstone Lake (10,120) at 1.3 miles. Greenstone is one of the prettiest lakes in the basin, so toddle over to its shoreline, where you'll spot some of the greenish-gray rocks that give this lake its name. Reaching Greenstone's outlet, you cross the stream to pick up the trail coming up from the ferry landing at Saddlebag's head, and then bear west above Greenstone Lake to enter Hoover Wilderness at just over 1.3 miles. There's a sign-in station here.

Beginning a gradual-to-moderate climb on this wide, dusty trail, which was once a road to a now-defunct mine deep in the basin, you traverse above lovely ponds north of Greenstone Lake before reaching skinny, rock-rimmed Wasco Lake and crossing a divide: behind you, streams drain southeast through Saddlebag Lake and Lee Vining Creek; ahead, streams drain north into Mill Creek and through Lundy Canyon. The trail descends a bit, passing Wasco's head and the ponds on its outlet, to reach lovely Steelhead Lake at a little over 2.3 miles. The stream from higher, unseen Cascade Lake spills noisily into Steelhead's southwest side, and a use trail branches west (left) at Steelhead's south end.

Pick up that use trail to cross Steelhead's inlet and head west for about half a mile—the exact distance will depend on the route you take when the use trail fades out. You wander up ledges along the headwaters of Mill Creek, passing unnamed lakes west of Steelhead, into a handsome granite sub-basin around

Greenstone Lake and North Peak

beautiful Cascade Lake (3/10,315). Viewful though exposed campsites are scattered here and there in this sub-basin, whose south and west edges are defined by the east- and west-trending ridges of North Peak on the Sierra crest. A layover day here offers fine opportunities for cross-country exploring.

Return to the main trail near Steelhead Lake and turn north on it, along the lake's east shore. As the trail approaches Steelhead's north end, it swings east, descends a little past some lakelets, and crosses Steelhead's outlet to reach a junction: right (northeast) to Lake Helen and Lundy Canyon, left (north) to the defunct Hess Mine. Go right, climbing steeply but briefly on a trail that's well-beaten but only approximated on the 7.5-minute topo. You reach islet-filled Shamrock Lake at just over 4 miles, climb up and over a talus slope on Shamrock's north side, and then ascend a knob. Atop the knob, the trail may be indistinct—rows of rocks and ducks help—as it leads to an overlook of beautiful Lake Helen, Lundy Canyon, and some Great Basin peaks far to the east.

From this overlook, the trail curves right (northeast) and descends the knob's north face. You pass some lovely cascades and ponds southwest of Lake Helen and skirt the lake's northwest bay, touching down at last at Lake Helen's rocky outlet, where the final few feet drop to the outlet that may call for the Famous Fanny Belay (i.e., sit and ease yourself down on your rump). Ford the outlet to find a signed junction: left (northeast) to Lundy Canyon, right (south) to Odell Lake and back to Saddlebag Lake. There are lovely views over Lundy Canyon and its waterfalls a short way down the left-hand fork; however, the trail down into Lundy Canyon is extremely steep as well as easily and often washed out, and Lundy Canyon itself offers almost no acceptable campsites.

In any case, your route lies on the right-hand fork. Unless the lake's level is low, you begin with a short, steep climb to circumvent a low cliff. You trace the east shore of Lake Helen on a rocky path before climbing moderately to steeply southeast up a very rocky draw through which Odell Lake's outlet flows into Lake Helen. The trail tops out briefly above Odell, then climbs gradually to a high point, unsigned Lundy Pass (10,320). Views of the wonderfully colorful peaks around Lundy Canyon are particularly good from here. Now you begin a gradual descent to Saddlebag Lake, crossing the outlet of little Hummingbird Lake, and soon leave Hoover Wilderness. Not long after, you reach a junction: right (west) on a spur that meets the main trail near Greenstone Lake; ahead (south) on a use trail to the ferry landing; and left (east) to begin traversing Saddlebag Lake's east side.

For this trip, turn left into forest cover and pass a backcountry ranger's cabin. On an old road above the lakeshore, you stroll through an open lodgepole forest, climbing a little on a gradual grade. The forest vanishes as you cross above the peninsula that juts south into the lake. Runoff on the steep slopes above the lake supports long, narrow, flowery meadows, and there are fine over-the-shoulder views back into 20 Lakes Basin. Trees reappear as you near the south end of Saddlebag Lake, and signs may warn you out of the meadow below the trail. The old road curves around the meadow, rising slightly to a gate that separates the trail from the parking lot, where you close the loop and find your car.

Variations

Do this trip as a dayhike.

Permits

This is a quota trailhead, and permits required for overnight stays may be available from summer ranger kiosk near the trailhead—sometimes right at the trailhead, sometimes just inside the campground. Apply for permits to Inyo National Forest, 873 N. Main Street, Bishop, CA 93514, (760) 873-2500, or see **www.r5.fs.fed.us/inyo/**.

Build-up/Wind-down tips

The nearby town of Lee Vining on US Highway 395 at the edge of Mono Lake (Chamber of Commerce, (760) 647-6595) offers lodgings, restaurants, and stores. Along State Route 120 (Tioga Road) between 395 and Tuolumne Meadows, you'll find several popular campgrounds and two lodgings, Tioga Pass Resort ((209) 372-4471) and Tuolumne Meadows Lodge (Yosemite Reservations, (209) 252-4848), where you can find soft beds, hot showers, and good meals before your trip. There's also the campground right at Saddlebag

Steelhead Lake and North Peak

Lake. All of these are very popular during the summer, so make your reservations early.

To find out how Kathy Morey got started hiking the Sierra and the Hawaiian islands and writing about her hikes for Wilderness Press, and for a list of her titles, see "Author Bio & Bib" on page 492.

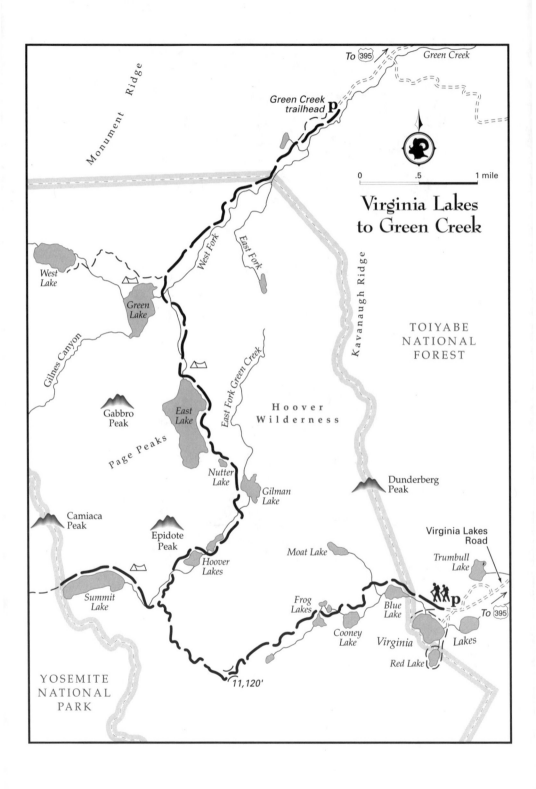

To ⑳395   Green Creek

Green Creek
trailhead **p**

Monument   Ridge

West Fork

East Fork

Virginia Lakes
to Green Creek

0   .5   1 mile

West
Lake

Green
Lake

Kavanaugh Ridge

TOIYABE
NATIONAL
FOREST

Gilnes Canyon

East Fork Green Creek

Gabbro
Peak

East
Lake

H o o v e r
W i l d e r n e s s

Page Peaks

Nutter
Lake

Gilman
Lake

Dunderberg
Peak

Camiaca
Peak

Epidote
Peak

Moat Lake

Virginia Lakes
Road

Trumbull
Lake

Hoover
Lakes

Summit
Lake

Frog
Lakes

Blue
Lake

p

To ⑳395

Cooney
Lake

Virginia   *Lakes*

11,120'

Red Lake

YOSEMITE
NATIONAL
PARK

48

Virginia Lakes to Green Creek

—Kathy Morey

Route	Days	Elev. Gain/Loss	Difficulty	Miles
↱	2	1420'/3240'	**	12
		(includes the 2-mile out-and-back to campsites at Summit Lake's head)		

Campsites: Summit Lake: 5–5.5 miles (depending on where you camp)
East Lake: 8 miles
Green Lake: 9 miles
(see the Trip Description for others)

Map: USGS 7.5-min *Dunderberg Peak*

Best season: Midsummer through early fall. Wait till late summer after a heavy winter for two reasons: the likelihood of steep snowbanks in the north-facing cirque you must descend above Summit Lake, and the fords of Green Creek, most of which are dangerous at high water.

Take this trip!

Skirting northern Yosemite National Park's eastern boundary, this scenic gem of a trip delivers plenty of alpine delights to repay its one stiff climb. Lakes, streams, high peaks, high meadows, and seasonally abundant wildflowers are all at hand throughout this beautiful trip.

There are fine dayhiking opportunities if you elect a layover day, too. From Summit Lake you can explore Yosemite's Virginia Canyon. From Green Lake you can visit pretty West Lake, or head up Glines Canyon part cross-country to Virginia Pass—a use trail takes you most of the way, fading out just below the pass. Look for artifacts of long-ago mining operations.

On this route I met the only stark naked hiker I've ever encountered in the Sierra. He had on a baseball cap, dark glasses, and tennis shoes, period. Good grief, the sunburn! Not a scenic attraction.

Trailheads

Put-in trailhead: From Conway Summit on US Highway 395 between Lee Vining and Bridgeport, drive 6.2 miles west on paved Virginia Lakes Road to the trailhead at Virginia Lakes; the pavement vanishes just before the parking lot (with toilets and water).

Take-out trailhead: From US Highway 395 south of Bridgeport and north of the junction with State Route 270 to Bodie, turn west onto minimally signed, dirt Green Creek Road. Follow it 1 mile to a junction with Summit Meadow Road; go left here. Continue another 2.5 miles to a junction with a spur road, Forest Road 20, southbound to Virginia Lakes; go right here. Continue another 5.2 miles, veering right into the signed parking lot trailhead (going left here would take you into Green Creek Campground, the location of which is incorrectly shown on the topo; trailhead facilities include toilet and water).

If you are setting up the shuttle, after you leave one car at the Green Creek trailhead, you can take scenic Forest Road 20 toward the put-in trailhead instead of going all the way back to 395. Shortly after you pass the Virginia Lakes Pack Station, FR 20 meets paved Virginia Lakes Road at a T-junction; turn right.

TRIP DESCRIPTION

> **Heads Up!** Bears can be a problem on this route; store food properly. Know Hoover Wilderness regulations! If you dayhike into Yosemite, know that pets are prohibited on all park trails. Leave Spot at the boundary or, better yet, at home.

From an information sign at the trailhead, which is next to the restroom, head west over an open slope, ignoring use trails left to the shore of upper Virginia Lake. You'll marvel at the colorful slopes around you; these peaks, part of a sub-range sometimes called the Dunderbergs, are "carved" from a roof pendant—an ancient remnant of the sedimentary rock "roof" that formerly overlay the buried plutons now pushed up as the more familiar Sierran gray granite. Throughout the range, most of the roof has eroded away as it was shoved aside, crushed, and twisted by the rising granite. Surviving roof fragments were left "hanging" (pendant) in the upthrust granite. Where roof pendant and granite meet is a "contact zone," and valuable minerals tend to precipitate out here. Miners sought gold and silver along these zones, leaving traces for history buffs to enjoy; for hikers, roof pendants offer colorful rock and mining remains.

You curve north around a patch of forest, meeting a stock trail that comes in on the right (east). Continue ahead here, curving west, passing a couple of ponds, and entering Hoover Wilderness. The trail begins to trace the shoreline of pretty Blue Lake—closed to camping. Ahead, the inlet cascades dramatically down the steep slope between this lake and higher Cooney Lake. Paralleling Blue Lake but leaving its shoreline behind, you begin climbing moderately to steeply on a rocky-dusty trail, ascending the slope northwest of the lake. In spite of its apparent barrenness, the slope supports quite a flower display, especially near the top of the climb.

Now the track crosses unseen, higher Moat Lake's outlet stream, then curves south through a flowery hillside meadow before entering forest cover and passing a tiny old cabin that's remarkably well preserved—please help it stay that way. You skirt another hillside meadow as the trail curves northwest, then south over a rocky, open slope to beautifully peak-rimmed Cooney Lake at almost 1.3 miles; there may be a campsite or two around this lake.

A steep switchback carries you above Cooney Lake to a pretty bench where you cross Cooney's inlet stream and reach the lowest of the Frog Lakes at a little over 1.3 miles. The three delightful little Frog Lakes nestle together on this bench, all at almost the same elevation, in a mostly marshy setting, with some knolls offering possible campsites.

Continuing, you splash across the stream linking two of the Frog Lakes but soon leave them behind. Follow the trail up a series of rocky, increasingly barren little benches, passing high above an unnamed pond. You make a final, steep, rocky attack on the crest ahead to stand atop an unnamed saddle, at just over 3 miles and at 11,120 feet. The view east, back over the Virginia Lakes, is simply astounding. But the view west is obscured by the terrain, so, if you wish, trek some 400 yards northwest over barren, shattered, metamorphic rock to an outcrop with awe-inspiring views: northwest to Summit Lake, far below on the eastern edge of northern Yosemite; to the Sierra crest just west of Summit Lake; and, northeast around the corner, the Hoover Lakes. The rock colors here are amazing—gray, gray-green, brown, rust, cream, and very-nearly-blue—and the rocks are splashed with lichens in brilliant rusts and chartreuses. And, somehow, tiny alpine flowers find roothold and shelter among these broken stones.

Back at the saddle, the trail drops a mile and a half moderately to steeply down the rocky slope, toward Camiaca and Epidote peaks bracketing Summit Lake, and a junction. Snow often lingers late in this north-facing cirque, and hiking sticks offer welcome stability when crossing snowbanks. The descent eases as you reach knolls near the cirque's bottom but above snow-born West Fork Green Creek. There's a campsite or two on these knolls. At the junction, it's left (west, then northwest) to Summit Lake and Yosemite; right (northeast) to Hoover Lakes. Surrounded by shattered rock, Hoover Lakes offer few campsites, so, turning left, you descend to cross the flowery marsh at the bottom of the cirque and climb up Summit Lake's outlet to this marvelous sheet of sky-blue water. In early season the outlet area can be very wet; otherwise there's a good campsite (5.0) in the sparse trees above it. There are a couple more campsites high in a pair of forested strips about midway around the lake's north shore, and more almost on the Yosemite border just beyond the lake's head (5.5), on low knolls north and south of the trail. The setting is breathtaking—especially the views of roof-pendant Dunderberg Peak from the head of the lake.

Returning from Summit Lake to the trail junction on the knolls at the bottom of the cirque, turn left (northeast) for Hoover Lakes and begin a moderate, very scenic descent. It soon brings you alongside rollicking Green Creek, which you ford above the highest Hoover Lake and then again between the two. Vistas of blue water combined with green, flower-spangled meadows set among reddish rock are stunning—and the scenery just gets better as you go.

If you don't have a hiking stick or two, look for some to help you at the next ford, between lower Hoover Lake and still-lower Gilman Lake (with campsites). Because the trail and stream drop steeply here, this ford can be difficult in early to mid season. Hang onto those sticks; there are more fords to come. Once across, the trail climbs a little as it threads past some attractive ponds and then traces pretty Nutter Lake's northeast shore.

Topping a little rise, you begin a gradual descent along the east shore of one of the loveliest lakes in this drainage, East Lake. Backgrounded by Epidote Peak, Page Peaks, and Gabbro Peak, East Lake is a scenic delight; look for snowmelt waterfalls cascading from peak drainages into the lake. Campsites are few here, but seek them out above the trail and near the outlet (8).

As the trail rounds the lake's north end, it makes an awkward crossing of East Lake's outlet streams; although the topo shows only one outlet, there are usually two streams. Now you begin a gradual descent in moderate to dense lodgepole forest to another ford. Beyond the ford, a splendid meadow spreads down the hillside, rich with flowers in season. The trail switchbacks moderately down through meadow and forest to a ford, composed of huge boulders placed across the stream above a cascade.

It's not long before you wind down to the final ford of Green Creek, this time just below beautiful Green Lake (9; with campsites along the west shore). If this ford is too daunting, try going upstream to the lake itself, where you can ford the outlet stream where it's wider and shallower, and then finish the crossing on what's left of the lake's dam. Either way you cross, the main trail promptly climbs away from the stream to a junction with the trails around the lake's north shore and to higher, unseen West Lake.

Now the trail descends moderately on a dry ridge high above the creek, at first through sunstruck chaparral. But partway down, you begin to cross seeps and streams from Monument Ridge, high above to the northwest. The water nourishes an eye-popping array of seasonal flowers, including some of the tallest rein orchids I've ever seen in the Sierra. Deep in the canyon created by

Monument and Kavanaugh ridges, you continue downward, sometimes steeply, to meet Green Creek near the wilderness boundary, where there are some handsome cascades.

Switchbacks carry you down the slope above the foaming creek. After the grade moderates, you climb a little to a ridge before resuming your descent and crossing the outlet of the unseen lake at about 8180 feet, next to which there's a gated and very bad road leading off to some kind of inholding. The trail now seems more like an old road, because it is, and you briefly touch Green Creek for the last time.

Soon you branch away from both creek and road on a dusty footpath that bears left and up into a patchy forest of Jeffrey pine, then bobs along over a marshy streamlet before curving down to the trailhead parking lot. Or you can stay on the old road, walk through the campground, and continue till you spot the trailhead parking lot off to the left. The distances are roughly the same.

Variations

Reverse the direction of this trip or do it as a dayhike.

Permits

This is a quota trailhead, and permits are required for overnight stays. Apply for reserved permits to Toiyabe National Forest, Bridgeport Ranger District, HCR 1 Box 1000, Bridgeport, CA 93517, (760) 932-7070, or see **www.fs.fed.us/outernet/htnf/toiyabe.htm**; include a $3/person fee with your application.

Build-up/Wind-down tips

The nearby towns of Lee Vining (Chamber of Commerce, (760) 647-6595) to the south and Bridgeport (no Chamber of Commerce; consult your auto-club tour guide, get the Eastern Sierra phone book, or check my book *Hot Showers, Soft Beds, and Dayhikes in the Sierra*) to the north on Highway 395 offer lodgings, restaurants, and stores.

Trumbull Lake Campground is very near the put-in trailhead. Nearby Virginia Lakes Resort rents its cabins only by the week, unfortunately; but it does have a café and store. Green Creek Campground is adjacent to the take-out trailhead, but not where the USGS 7.5-minute topo shows it. It's along the spur road branching left from (south of) the new trailhead; the spur road is off-limits to the public's vehicles, except for the part through the campground. All of these are very popular during the summer, so make your reservations early.

To find out how Kathy Morey got started hiking the Sierra and the Hawaiian islands and writing about her hikes for Wilderness Press, and for a list of her titles, see "Author Bio & Bib" on page 492.

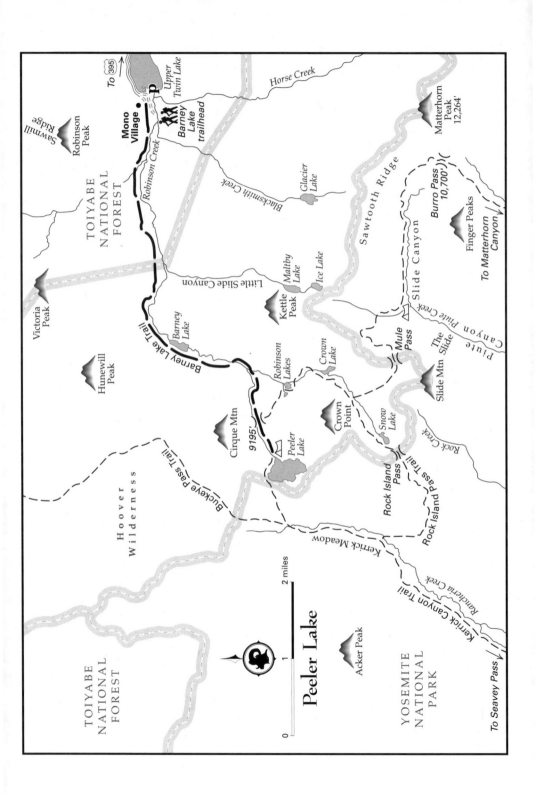

Peeler Lake

TOIYABE NATIONAL FOREST

YOSEMITE NATIONAL PARK

To Seavey Pass

Kerrick Canyon Trail

Rancheria Creek

Kerrick Meadow

Acker Peak

Hoover Wilderness

Buckeye Pass Trail

Cirque Mtn
9195'

Peeler Lake

Crown Point

Snow Lake

Rock Island Pass

Rock Island Pass Trail

Rock Creek

Robinson Lakes

Crown Lake

Mule Pass

Slide Mtn Slide

The Slide

Piute Creek

Piute Canyon

Slide Canyon

Burro Pass 10,700'

Finger Peaks

To Matterhorn Canyon

Sawtooth Ridge

Matterhorn Peak 12,264'

Kettle Peak

Maltby Lake

Ice Lake

Little Slide Canyon

Barney Lake

Barney Lake Trail

Hunewill Peak

Victoria Peak

TOIYABE NATIONAL FOREST

Robinson Creek

Blacksmith Creek

Glacier Lake

Horse Creek

Robinson Peak

Sawmill Ridge

Mono Village

Barney Lake trailhead

Upper Twin Lake

To 395

0   1   2 miles

49

Peeler Lake

—Thomas Winnett

Route	Days	Elev. Gain/Loss	Difficulty	Miles
⌇	2	2400'/2400'	**	16

Campsites: Peeler Lake: 8.0 miles

Map: USGS 7.5-min *Buckeye Ridge*

Best season: Late summer

Take this trip!

Peeler Lake is a delightfully unique Sierra experience in that one camps literally on top of the mountain chain, for this lake pours its waters down both sides of the Sierra.

Trailhead

Take Twin Lakes Road west from US 395 in Bridgeport. Go past the Twin Lakes to Annett's Mono Village. There is limited public parking near the launching ramp, though you may have to ask where you should park.

TRIP DESCRIPTION

> **Heads Up!** Bears are a hazard (see the chapter "Bears & Other Hazards").

Follow signs saying BARNEY LAKE through the campground to find the wide, level, shaded trail. Travelers setting out in the fall season should take a few minutes at the outset for a side trip to view the colorful Kokanee salmon spawning in the shallows of Robinson Creek south of the campground. Beyond the campground your sandy trail winds through a moderate-to-dense forest of Jeffrey pine, juniper, lodgepole pine, aspen, and cottonwood along Robinson Creek. In late summer, cottony catkins from the cottonwood trees here litter the initial

Peeler Lake beyond tarns south of it

section of your trail, leaving the ground surface the gray-white of spring snow. After crossing several small tributaries, the trail ascends gently, and within three-fourths mile encounters the first fir trees, but the forest cover soon gives way to a sagebrush-covered, gently sloping bench, from where you can see the headwall of the valley in the west.

As you make your way up this open bench through thigh-high sagebrush, rabbitbrush, chamise, and mule ears, you have unobstructed views of Victoria, Hunewill, and Robinson peaks on the right, and some ragged teeth of the Sawtooth Ridge on the left. About halfway up this bench the trail passes a ghost forest of drowned trees caused by beaver dams downstream. Beavers still share this fine Sierra stream with you. On the right, somnolent marmots are likely to be seen dozing among piles of scree that flow from the feet of the avalanche chute scarring Victoria Peak; on the left, the dramatic, unbroken granite wall of Blacksmith Peak at the top of Little Slide Canyon dominates the view. A sign proclaims this area as part of the federally protected Hoover Wilderness. On the left, Robinson Creek becomes a willow-lined cascade that is frequently heard but seldom seen.

About one-half mile into the wilderness area, the ascent resolves into switchbacks that ford several tributaries. In their moist banks one finds monkey flower, monkshood, red columbine, swamp onion, and shooting star scattered among clumps of bracken fern. Along the drier stretches of trail the severity of the rock is alleviated by colorful patches of Indian paintbrush, Mariposa lily, scarlet gilia, yarrow milfoil, whorled penstemon, pussy paws, strepthanthus, and goldenrod.

After the ascent levels out, your trail veers south, fords another tributary, and arrives at the outlet point of arrowhead-shaped Barney Lake (3.8/8290). Here you might elect to take a cool, quick dip under the soaring heights of Crown Point, or merely lie on the sandy beach and watch the play of the local water ouzels (also called dippers).

The trail skirts the lake's west side in a steady, long, hot ascent that takes you onto the canyon wall well above the ghost-forested delta inlet of Barney Lake. Once above the wetter sections of the delta, the trail descends to a wildflower-decorated ford of Robinson Creek. Here among the willows you can find lavender swamp onion, red columbine, orange tiger lily, and yellow monkey flower. The moderate forest cover now shows a transition to higher climes with the introduction of nodding-tipped hemlock and some robust western white pine.

About one-fourth mile upstream the trail refords Robinson Creek, then fords the outlet creek from Peeler Lake just above its confluence with Robinson Creek, and rises abruptly by steep switchbacks. After leveling off somewhat, you come to a bench junction with the Crown Lake Trail. Here your route turns right, ascends moderately near the south outlet from Peeler Lake, and then steeply up the draw just northeast of the lake, to reach this outlet. Beautiful Peeler Lake (8.0/9489) sits astride the Sierra crest, contributing water to Robinson Creek and thence to the Great Basin on the east, and to Rancheria Creek and thence to the Pacific Ocean on the west. This medium-large lake has mostly abrupt rocky shores, and the deep-blue color characteristic of deeper Sierra lakes. There are good-to-excellent campsites around most of the lake (though not all of them are legal). The best lie on the east shore, reached by leaving the trail where it starts to descend to cross the south outlet.

Permits

You'll need a Wilderness Permit from the administering agency, Bridgeport Ranger District of Toiyabe National Forest, whose office is just south of Bridgeport on US 395.

Bridgeport Ranger Station
HCR1 Box 1000
Bridgeport, CA 93517
(760) 932 7070

Since Tom Winnett is always modest and succinct, consult "Author Bio & Bib" on page 492 to learn little more than our Publisher Emeritus' titles currently in print.

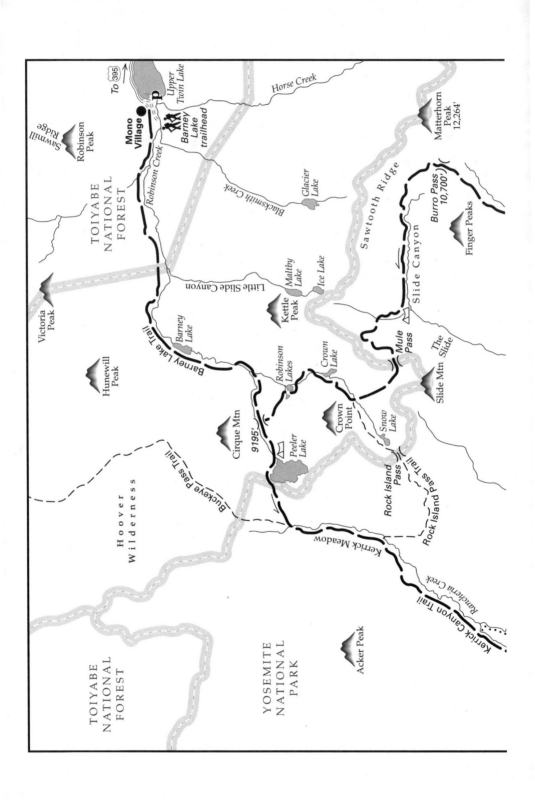

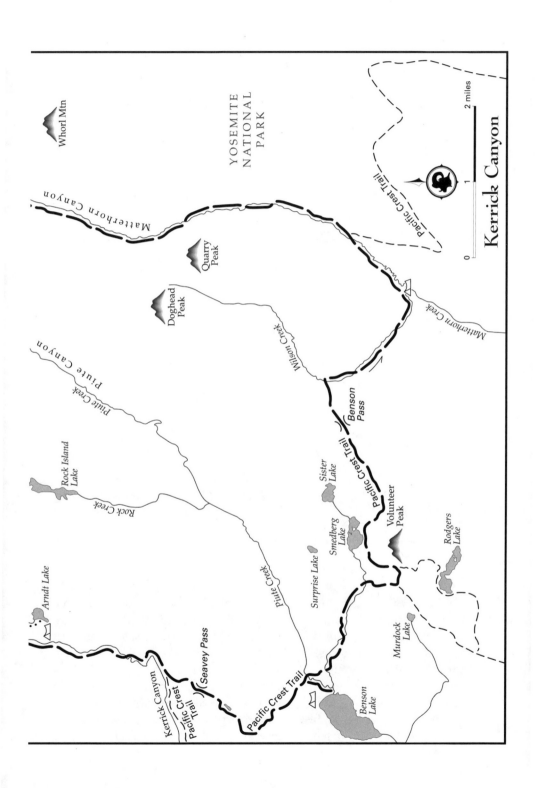

Kerrick Canyon

50

Kerrick Canyon & Matterhorn Canyon Semi-loop via Barney & Peeler Lakes

—Ben Schifrin

Route	Days	Elev. Gain/Loss	Difficulty	Miles
♀	5–7	9300'/9300'	***	53.6

Campsites: Peeler Lake: 8.2 miles
Benson Lake: 20.4 miles
Matterhorn Canyon at PCT: 31.2 miles
Slide Canyon: 40.1 miles
(see the Trip Description for others)

Map: USGS 7.5-min *Twin Lakes, Buckeye Ridge, Matterhorn Peak, Piute Mtn.*

Best season: Late summer through early fall

Take this trip!

This is Yosemite at its finest: sweeping subalpine vistas, soaring granite peaks, and intimate campsites beside delightful, trout-filled lakes and streams. And, since this semi-loop trip is far from the big-name attractions of southern Yosemite, there aren't crowds! Matterhorn Canyon, the jewel of northern Yosemite, lies halfway through our trip. This spectacular canyon is named for 12,264-foot Matterhorn Peak, which dominates its head. Here, ice-age glaciers modified the 13-mile-long trough, giving it a dazzling array of smooth cliffs and aprons, capped with lofty, frost-riven peaks that now support lasting snowfields. Cozy conifer groves make the canyon bottomlands eminently hospitable to campers.

We start via the Robinson Creek Trail, justifiably the most popular route into the Yosemite north country. It leads quickly up into breathtaking sub-alpine terrain around glittering Peeler Lake. After traversing Kerrick Canyon, which has less relief than Matterhorn but a marvelous assortment of flanking domes, this hike follows the Pacific Crest Trail to Benson and Smedberg lakes, both with good fishing. It then ascends Matterhorn Canyon, before passing right under the spiry Sawtooth Ridge at the head of little-visited Slide Canyon.

Trailhead

From Highway 395 near the west side of Bridgeport, take paved Twin Lakes Road south 13.6 miles to the entrance to Mono Village at the western head of upper Twin Lake. Park within the village for a nominal fee.

TRIP DESCRIPTION

> **Heads Up!** Note that camping is not allowed within 100 feet of Barney Lake. Due to its popularity, there is a one-day camping limit at sites just below the outlet of Barney Lake.

Begin your backpack in Mono Village, a private resort sprawling across the alluvial fan of Robinson Creek at the head of upper Twin Lake. Although this resort contains a maze of roads and facilities, there is a well-signed way to the Barney Lake trailhead at the resort's far western end.

Before starting up the Barney Lake Trail, enjoy the head of Twin Lakes, especially in the fall when the Kokanee salmon run and hillside aspens turn first amber, then red. Twin Lakes lie behind curving recessional moraines, which were left near the end of the last (Tioga) glaciation. Tioga lateral moraines form obvious bouldery, sagebrush-dotted benches high above both the north and south shores of Twin Lakes, indicating that the last glacier filled the canyon here to a depth of about 1500 feet! Summits to the north of Twin Lakes, from Eagle Peak to Robinson Peak and Sawmill Ridge, as well as Crater Crest and Monument Ridge to the south, are composed of former volcanic rocks and limestone that originated more than 200 million years ago. Volcanic eruptions ranged in composition from explosive rhyolitic lava to fluid basaltic lava, like those found east of Yosemite National Park today. During the Nevadan orogeny all these rocks were metamorphosed. They were metamorphosed again, by the much later intrusion of magma from below, about 85 million years ago. This magma solidified to form our canyon's white walls of Cathedral Peak granodiorite.

Follow signs to the start of the Barney Lake Trail, branching right, away from the pretty meadow and its tantalizing glimpses of granitic parapets south up Blacksmith and Horse creeks. The trail, if initially vague when you set out, quickly becomes well defined, in a bare-floored Jeffrey-pine forest. Your level path then strikes west, staying north of Robinson Creek under a canopy of white fir, Jeffrey pine, Fremont cottonwood, and aspen. Presently you walk under the scarp of a small roche moutonnée (a glacial knoll), where Basque shepherds carved their names on aspen trees early in the 20th Century. Then, after a few minutes of walking you reach a persistent stream chortling down, through wild-rose shrubbery, from the basin between Victoria and Eagle peaks.

The trail next winds gently up through more-open terrain, where bouldery ground moraine and alluvium support sparse conifers, sagebrush, manzanita, and barley. Soon the cobbly, dusty path comes close to Robinson Creek, where its waters veer north around a jutting granitic promontory, and here the canyon—and our vista—opens up. Our path continues westward, well above lodgepole pines in locally beaver-dammed Robinson Creek. Note the sweeping aprons of avalanche-scoured slope-wash that descend south from ruddy Victoria Peak, contrasting sharply with the spidery cliffs of light-hued granodiorite that form the sharper crests of Hunewill and Kettle peaks, guardians of the upper Robinson Creek basin. Here, the dry surroundings support mule ears, relieved by patches of gooseberry, mullein, rabbitbrush, and some curl-leaf mountain mahogany. At 7600 feet we pass through a grove of aspens, then amble through more sagebrush and boulders to the Hoover Wilderness boundary, about 2½ miles from Mono Village. From here a use trail cuts south to the mouth of Little Slide Canyon, up which can be seen the smooth granitic buttress called the Incredible Hulk, as well as other incredible, but unnamed, rock-climbing goals. Minutes later we reenter white-fir cover, and can stop for a drink beside tumbling Robinson Creek. This is a good rest spot for the climb ahead.

When you are ready to assault the canyon headwall, gear down to accommodate more than a dozen well-graded switchbacks that lead north through head-high jungles of aspen, bitter cherry, serviceberry, snowberry, and tobacco brush, staying always within earshot of unseen Robinson Creek. Above 8000 feet we step across a rivulet merrily draining the slopes of Hunewill Peak, a welcome respite that furnishes flowers of American dogwood, giant red paintbrush, Labrador tea, fireweed, aster, Parish's yampah, and Gray's lovage to delight the eye. Still climbing, we return momentarily to the creekside, where industrious beavers at times create a small pond. Then, we climb rockily, bending south, in a gully under aspen shade. Half our ascent is behind us when we level out to step across a branch of Robinson Creek that drains the 10,700-foot saddle to our west. About a yard or so beyond this creek, the easily missed use trail to South Fork Buckeye Creek branches west through a tangle of aspens and creek dogwoods. Just a few yards later, where Robinson Creek can be repeatedly plugged by small beaver dams, a level use trail branches south along the outlet stream of Barney Lake, with adjacent campsites. This short spur trail joins the paralleling main trail at the northwest corner of Barney Lake, where a sandy beach, good after a swim, makes a fine spot for a lunch break.

About 4½ miles from Mono Village, 14-acre Barney Lake (8290) is nestled in a narrow, glaciated trough, rimmed on the east by the broken, lichen-mottled north spur of Kettle Peak. The western shoreline, which our trail follows, is a dry talus slope mixed with glacial debris. Here, a pair of switchbacks elevate the trail to an easy grade, some 100 feet above Barney Lake's inlet. Below, beavers have dammed meandering Robinson Creek, drowning the meadow and a grove of lodgepole pines. Farther southwest, cirque-girdled Crown Point dominates the horizon, with Slide Mountain behind its east shoulder, while Kettle Peak flanks to the east, topped by a gendarmed cockscomb.

After a few minutes we descend several short switchbacks. Wind through broken rock and past avalanche-twisted aspens, over two freshets draining Cirque Mountain, then come to a ford of Robinson Creek. Here, we are about ¾ mile beyond Barney Lake and about 2½ miles before Peeler Lake. This crossing can be a wet ford in early season, if industrious beavers have dammed the creek just downstream. Rainbow and brook trout of handy pan size occur here, as in Barney Lake. From the far bank, we climb easily south in a pleasant forest of lodgepole pine, red fir, western white pine, and a new addition: mountain hemlock, which reflects our higher altitude. The trail soon leads back to the west bank of Robinson Creek, which we cross using a log, if one is handy. Next the trail crosses the cascading stream from Peeler Lake, beside which one might rest before ascending a long series of switchbacks, just ahead. The first set of gentle, well-engineered switchbacks traverses a till-covered slope to about 8800 feet, where we level off momentarily for a breather, before darting north for a steeper ascent. The vistas east, to stunted whitebark pines growing on rough, ice-fractured outcrops of Kettle Peak, offer good excuses to stop frequently on this energetic climb. Eventually we come to a small saddle at 9195 feet, which has a trail bound for Rock Island Pass and Slide Canyon—this is the return route which we will walk, four days hence.

Bound for Peeler Lake, we now turn northwest, walking moderately up in mixed open forest, to a small, shaded glade beside Peeler Lake creek. We step across this stream twice before switchbacking south, moderately up into a narrow gully. The wind can pick up as we ascend it, a sure sign that we're nearing the ridgetop. Sure enough, about 8 miles from Mono Village, Peeler Lake's often-windswept waters soon come into view, behind car-size granodiorite blocks that dam its outlet. A short descent leads us below this talus to dynamited trail tread on the lake's north shore. Here, the lake's startling blue waters foreground rounded Acker and Wells peaks, in the west. Most of the good campsites, under conifers, are found as we undulate rockily into forest pockets along the north shore, though the east shore has some fine ones as well, if a bit out of the way. Spend your first night here. The lake margin, mostly rock, does have a few stretches of meadowy beach, where one can fly-cast for rainbows and brookies to 14 inches.

Sawtooth Ridge

Leaving Peeler Lake near its northwest end, the path climbs slightly to a granitic bench dotted with bonsai'd lodgepoles, plus sedges and ocean spray. Here, views back across the outlet show serrated Peak 11581 rising east of Kettle Peak. Now a short descent leads to the Yosemite National Park boundary. Beyond the festoon of regulatory and mileage signs, pocket meadows covered with dwarf bilberry and sedge gradually coalesce into the northeastern arm of Kerrick Meadow. Soon we reach a junction, from which the Buckeye Pass Trail goes north and the Kerrick Canyon Trail, our route, goes south. Now about 9¼ miles into our trek, we start south through Kerrick Meadow. Covering a vast ground moraine at the head of Rancheria Creek, the meadow is a frost-hummocked expanse of sedge, rice-grass, reed-grass, and dwarf bilberry—quite typical of Sierran subalpine meadows. Numerous young lodgepole pines encroach upon the grassland, but can die if the soil gets too boggy, as happens in years of abundant snowfall.

Head down-canyon along the path, which can be rutted up to 2 feet deep in the delicate turf, and soon cross the seasonal headwaters of Rancheria Creek. Now we descend easily, ambling along the west margin of Kerrick Meadow, over slabs and dry terraces, typical habitat of sedges. At times a profusion of birds flit among the open lodgepoles near our route: yellow-rumped warblers, American robins, mountain bluebirds, white-crowned sparrows, northern flickers, dark-eyed juncos, and Brewer's blackbirds. Purple Lemmon's paintbrush and deep-blue alpine gentian blossom in early summer.

After about 1½ miles from the previous junction, we come to another one, with the Rock Island Pass Trail, which is an alternate route for our return trip. Still gently descending, we pass through a lodgepole grove, then emerge at the northern end of an even larger meadowed expanse, rimmed on the west by 400-foot bluffs. Long views south down upper Kerrick Canyon are topped by Piute Mountain and other dark, rounded summits near Seavey Pass. After another 1½ miles of rolling, sandy trail, our route crosses a trio of low moraines, then cuts close to an oxbow in 20-foot-wide Rancheria Creek where the broad canyon pinches off above a low hillock. In this area you'll find the north-flowing outlet creek of Arndt Lake. This lake, ¼ mile south, has good campsites. About 13½ miles from Mono Village, it is a good destination in itself, away from sometimes overly popular Barney and Peeler lakes.

Presently, Rancheria Creek's banks become a broken gorge, and we drop rockily down, only to strike another sandy meadow, this one with a flanking cluster of steep domes. Our path soon leads out of this lupine-flecked flat, down through a bouldery salient of lodgepoles to yet another meadow. Down this we amble south, soon to walk right along the seasonally muddy bank of meandering Rancheria Creek. At the next curve, about 2 miles below Arndt Lake's creek, we cross our creek to a clump of lodgepoles on the east bank, and continue down-canyon. Presently, a master joint in the Cathedral Peak granodiorite bedrock directs Rancheria Creek briefly east. We follow its splashing course down over broken, porphyritic (large-crystal) bedrock slabs, then turn back west on another master joint for ½ mile on shaded slopes to a junction with the Pacific Crest Trail.

Bound south (left) for Seavey Pass, 0.7 mile away, our route climbs sometimes steeply up the sandy-cobbly PCT into a dome-girded ravine, at the top of which we glimpse a small pond rimmed with corn lilies and other flowers. The PCT now bends southeast and ascends to the Rancheria Creek/Piute Creek divide, then briefly drops southwest to another gap, the real Seavey Pass (17.3).

From this point, our path winds its way down over open benches. We soon come upon a large tarn with vistas over the confusing array of rust-stained cliffs surrounding Piute Creek, to Peak 10060 and Volunteer Peak, which form the horizon. From this pond our route switchbacks west down a shaded draw, then turns steeply southeast, negotiating sometimes-brushy slopes first north, then south of a cascading stream. Glimpsing our second day's goal, Benson Lake, we finally reach the valley bottom, a sometimes-swamped tangle of willows and bracken ferns, under lodgepoles and firs. At the floodplain's south end, some 2¾ miles from Seavey Pass, is the Benson Lake spur trail. The 0.4-mile-long spur to Benson Lake ends at a broad, sandy beach—once the lake has dropped a foot or so—and campsites lie just back from shore. Along the shore you have vistas over the mile-long take to brushy domes at the outlet. Angling here is for large rainbow and brown trout.

Our third morning finds us retracing our steps to the PCT, where we turn southeast (right) across wide Piute Creek, via fallen logs. Then, climb up into the morning sunlight atop a brushy saddle. A short distance later, our route strikes the creek that drains Smedberg Lake, which poses a difficult ford in early summer. This is usually best solved in the thicket of aspens just upstream. South of that stream, the path climbs rockily up, often at a steep gradient, before crossing the creek twice more, in easier spots, along a more moderate ascent in a tight canyon walled by tremendous bluffs. Once again south of the creek, our route tackles a steep hillside, via moderate switchbacks under increasing numbers of mountain hemlocks. Red heather forms a discontinuous, showy understory here. Almost 700 feet higher, but still under the stony gazes of precipitous Peak 10060 and Volunteer Peak, we find a trail branching southwest to shallow Murdock Lake, about ½ mile away. It is a recommended destination for those desiring some isolation, which is usually lacking at Smedberg Lake. Even more isolation lies at more appealing Rodgers Lake, and by climbing east ⅓ mile on the PCT, we reach a meadowy junction with a trail that departs south to that lake, vaulting a ridge along its mile-long course.

To reach Smedberg, the PCT over the next mile switchbacks down, then up to a slabby, polished bench overlooking the lake's south shore (24.8). Named for an Army cartographer who, with Lieutenants Benson and McClure, mapped the Yosemite backcountry in the early 1900s, 30-acre Smedberg Lake is dotted with low, grassy islets, and rimmed with light-granite strips of sedge-and-bilberry meadow and pockets of conifers. Pan-size rainbow trout are common in its shallow waters, which reflect a sweeping face of streaked granite over the east shore, and the brooding vertical profile of Volunteer Peak on the south. Most camps are found on the west and north shores. Remote camps exist above its northwest and northeast shores in the vicinity of, respectively, Surprise and Sister lakes.

We leave Smedberg Lake by curving south into a hummocky, boulder-and-meadow vale, then soon step across one of its three inlet creeklets to climb northeast toward Benson Pass, an even 2 miles past the lake. The first rise is moderate, under open mixed conifers. We briefly level out in a small meadow before the last, earnest climb to the pass. Near the top, some of the sandy trail is very steep, but it is soon behind us. At the pass (26.7), sparingly inhabited by whitebark pines, we stand in coarse granitic sand, catching our breath to views west of Volunteer Peak, and northeast over Doghead and Quarry peaks to Whorl Mountain and Twin and Virginia peaks.

A steep stretch rapidly leads us from Benson Pass down to a gravelly flat; then it becomes a switchbacking descent, under pleasant shade, to the hop-across ford of Wilson Creek in a steep-walled trough. This is a classic glaciated, hanging tributary canyon, widely believed to be hanging because its glacier could not erode downward as fast as the larger glacier in the main canyon. Such is not the case. In resistant bedrock, such as that found in this part of the Sierra range, glaciers of all sizes eroded very little; all tributary canyons were hanging before glaciation.

Turning down-canyon, the PCT alternately traverses dry openings and lodgepole forests as we cross Wilson Creek twice more. Soon the gentle-to-moderate descent resolves into some two dozen tight, rocky switch-backs, as hanging-valley Wilson Creek canyon debauches into deeper Matterhorn Canyon. Bottoming out a few minutes later, we turn up Matterhorn Canyon through dry, sandy, lodgepole-filled flats and pass a large camping complex (31.2). It lies just before the wide, cobbly ford of Matterhorn Creek. On the east bank, 4½ miles from Benson Pass, is our trail, which starts up the canyon, while the PCT continues south.

Leaving the PCT, we start north for a 6-mile ascent to Burro Pass, and if you aren't camping near the ford of Matterhorn Canyon creek, you ought to consider doing so higher up in the beautiful canyon. At first, our trail climbs imperceptibly, passing some nearby good camps, and keeps near the large creek past sandy meadowlands. Views within this steep-walled trench are initially dominated by soaring Peak 10400+, above the canyon's west slopes. In about 1½ miles we enter an open, bouldery stretch, then cross Matterhorn Creek via boulders to a small, lush meadow. We later recross the creek at a horseshoe bend. About 200 yards beyond, there's evidence of past winter avalanches that, descending from high on Quarry Peak, decapitated trees even as they flowed cross-canyon and partway up the opposite wall! The massive east face of Quarry Peak, composing part of the canyon's west wall, offers rarely attempted rock climbs up to 10 pitches long in the summer months.

About ¾ mile farther upstream, we ford again to the west side, then wind into a boulder-strewn, talus-footed meadow. Willows line the streamside, inter-mittently making way for rapidly thinning forest patches. Our gently ascending sandy path passes a few very nice, remote camps—these are your last desirable camping opportunities before the pass. Ahead, it's pretty much open going, with Burro Pass clearly in sight: the low point on a light ridge, with Finger Peaks on the west and massive Matterhorn Peak on the east. Standing behind Burro Pass, the jagged Sawtooth Ridge slices into blue skies and billowing afternoon cumulonimbus clouds. Above 9800 feet, under an arc of jagged peaks that stretches from Matterhorn Peak to Whorl Mountain and its unnamed over-hanging outlier, the tread becomes steeper, crossing a delicate alpine fell-field that is sometimes replete with Lemmon's paintbrush, Sierra penstemon, and pussy paws. Soon the cobbly, riprapped trail becomes steeper still, and resolves into a chaos of eroded, miniature switchbacks. These lead through the broken granite that forms the final slope of Burro Pass (32.2), which at nearly 10,700 feet is just over 2 miles high.

Up here, where the air pressure is only 80% that at sea level, have a well-deserved rest after the short but arduous ascent. From our vantage-point, a 360° panorama unfolds. Aptly named Sawtooth Ridge, to the north, throws up a picket line of fractured granite gendarmes, culminating in 12,264-foot Matterhorn Peak. East of us, massive Twin Peaks loom beyond an unnamed peak, dwarfing Whorl Mountain and its 11,920-foot partner, which together spawn a textbook rock glacier. Vistas back down the trough of Matterhorn Canyon stop at the exfoliating slopes of Quarry Peak, save for a real treat on a clear day, when over its east flank peek Clouds Rest, Quarter Domes, and Half Dome, all near Yosemite Valley. Before our view southwest is blocked by the shoulder of Finger Peaks, we see Doghead Peak, the tip of Volunteer Peak, and distant Central Valley smog. West of Burro Pass, Slide Canyon curves down into pine-clad lower slopes from a pair of beautiful, little-visited alpine lakelets occupying a bench under the gaze of Finger Peaks.

Leaving Burro Pass, our trail drops steeply via rocky switchbacks, often obscured by long-lasting snowfields, to hop across infant Piute Creek in spongy alpine-meadow turf. It then follows that raucous, bubbling stream west on a sometimes-steep descent into clustered whitebark pines, which soon become an open forest. Soon we hop to the south bank of Piute Creek, then wind through a delicate, boggy meadow before recrossing just above an excellent campsite, complete with small waterfall, in mixed conifers. Leaving this camp, the trail stays farther from the creekside and descends, sometimes via moderate switchbacks, into denser forest. Fair camps are found all the way down to the campsites in willow-understoried forest on the floor of Slide Canyon (40.1), our trail's low point along Piute Creek. Truly remote, essentially pristine, trail-less camping lies along the creek down this canyon—a worthy layover day.

Now the trail begins to go gently up in sun-dappled forest, and soon switchbacks moderately near a small branch of Piute Creek. From here we can look down-canyon to the feature that named this canyon and the mountain south of us: the Slide. It was first noted by Lieutenant Nathaniel F. McClure, while mapping the Yosemite north country:

> After traveling three and one half miles down the canyon, I came to the most wonderful natural object that I ever beheld. A vast granite cliff, two thousand feet in height, had literally tumbled from the bluff on the right-hand side of the stream with such force that it not only made a mighty dam across the canyon, but many large stones had rolled far up the opposite side.

McClure somewhat overestimated Slide Mountain's 1600-foot wall but he understated the magnitude of the rockfall. About 2½ million cubic yards fell—some boulders the size of small houses—and the debris cut a swath across Piute Creek about ¼ mile wide and rolled almost 200 vertical feet up the far bank!

After a few switchbacks we find ourselves atop the rim of Slide Canyon, on a sloping subalpine bench. Here we step across the small stream we've been paralleling, then ascend more steeply west into a rocky gulch. This climb presents ever-improving panoramas east to Burro Pass and the headwaters of Slide

Canyon. Our trail climbs north up the gully, then descends gently south into a spongy, boulder-rimmed stepladder meadow. The final rise from this vale to the 10,460-foot saddle dividing the Piute and Robinson creek drainages proceeds on frequently steep, always cobbly tread. Possibly the most interesting view from this windy col, about 4 miles beyond Burro Pass, is to the northeast. We look over the head of Little Slide Canyon, guarded by the Incredible Hulk and then north, beyond, to the ruddy metamorphic caps of Buckeye and Flatiron ridges.

Leaving Yosemite National Park behind, our trail first descends the col by a half-dozen moderate switchbacks to a stream-braided, marshy terrace fed by an unmapped snowfield in the hollow north of Slide Mountain. At the lower end of this flat lies a small tarn, which we skirt to the south. Then, we descend rockily in a maze of head-high whitebark pines and talus blocks along its outlet stream. Soon the way becomes even steeper, plunging north, losing 500 feet elevation via excruciatingly rocky switchbacks, to another pocket meadow, where we cross to the stream's west bank. Below, we trace the sharp western lateral-moraine crest, left perhaps by a Little Ice Age glacier from Slide Mountain. It descends to upper Robinson Creek, as do we, where in a sandy, willowed flat we meet a junction, about 1½ miles from the col, with the Rock Island Pass Trail.

Anglers and hikers who desire a more secluded alpine campsite can turn southwest (left) toward Rock Island Pass. Their route up along the steep southern slopes of Crown Point later succumbs to gentle switchbacks. One is eventually rewarded with a grassy knoll at 10,260 feet, affording a breather and views over the Sierra crest to the Sawtooth Ridge. Then the trail angles briefly down past snug, sandy camps to sedge-rimmed Snow Lake, containing both rainbow and golden trout. Almost everyone who reaches here, especially photographers, will want to ascend the short, meadowed distance to broad Rock Island Pass, 1½ miles from the previous junction, for lake-reflected vistas of frost-fractured Kettle Peak. Some hikers may decide to descend the moderate trail 2 miles west from the pass, down through a quiet subalpine forest to meet the Kerrick Canyon Trail at the lower end of Kerrick Meadow, then exit Yosemite NP via Peeler Lake. This strategy would add an extra half day to their journey.

Back at the Rock Island Pass Trail junction in the sandy flat, our route turns downstream, among talus boulders and willows. Across the stream, 100 yards east, sits a large, pretty tarn, well worth the side trip for the ecological lessons, views, and secluded alternative camping to sometimes-crowded Crown Lake. This lakelet sits on a meadowed bench between granite hillocks. Its outlet stream used to flow northeast, directly down to the head of Crown Lake, but it now starts northwest down into the willow-choked meadow traversed by our trail, then goes around a rocky knob before heading down-canyon. Possibly, rapid growth of the thick bilberry, sedge, and rush turf surrounding the tarn blocked the original outlet and elevated the lake level until the water found the northwest outlet. Also, frost-heaving of the dense sod during spring months may have closed off the old outlet and further elevated the lake rim. Note that it is markedly higher than the surrounding meadow.

Leaving this interesting lakelet, return to the Robinson Creek Trail and descend east via gentle switchbacks to the sodden meadow on the west shore of Crown Lake. The path circumvents the meadow to reach Crown Lake's north outlet (44.7), from where use trails lead to the only legal campsites. These lie in grouped whitebarks and hemlocks above the lake's rocky east shore. Anglers will be pleased to find a self-sustaining fishery of rainbow trout.

The next leg of our descent leads to the two small Robinson Lakes, on a 9200-foot bench under towering Crown Point. First we hop Robinson Creek just a minute north of Crown Lake, then descend more and more steeply under open conifer shade. One-half mile below our first ford, we jump back to the west bank, just above the larger Robinson Lake. Here we get nice views north over its shallow, rainbow-breeding waters to Hunewill and Victoria peaks. Meager camps lie on the isthmus between the two Robinson Lakes, although if you do camp here, you should look for more ecologically sound ones farther from their shores.

Leaving the isthmus, our trail swings west along the north shore of the swampy, grassy western lakelet, then climbs through a chaos of mammoth talus blocks—the terminal moraine of the Crown Point cirque glacier. One-third mile of dynamited trail through this jumble ends under the quiet shade of a pure mountain-hemlock grove that lines a gully containing a seasonal creek. We hop the creek here, turn northeast, and soon climb to a sunny col to meet the Peeler Lake Trail (46.3). From here we retrace our first day's steps downhill all the way to Mono Village at upper Twin Lake.

Permits

Humboldt-Toiyabe National Forest administers the Hoover Wilderness, at the start of our trip. It is easier to get permits from them, than from very busy Yosemite National Park.

Contact:
Bridgeport Ranger Station
HCR 1
Box 1000
Bridgeport, CA 95317
(760) 932-7070

The Ranger Station is on Hwy. 395, just ½ mile south of Bridgeport. There are trailhead quotas in effect for the Robinson Creek Trail, beginning on the last Friday in June and running through September 15. So, apply for a permit as early as possible. Half of all permits are given in person on the day of the trip at Bridgeport Ranger Station. The other half can be reserved by mail, but not by phone. You can download a Wilderness Permit application form from the Hoover Wilderness Web site: **www.fs.fed.us/htnf/hoover.htm**

You can make reservations beginning January 1, up to 3 weeks in advance of your trip. A $3 per person non-refundable processing fee is charged. Make checks payable to "USDA-USFS."

Build-Up/Wind-Down tips

For gratuitous carbo-loading, either before or after your trip, there is no better place than the Bridgeport Bakery. It is right on Highway 395 in the heart of town. Although they make wholesome breads and pour a good cup of coffee, the early-morning lineup is for heavenly gooseberry streudel, pecan danish slathered with stick-to-your teeth caramel glaze, and their pièce de résistance: the most simply elegant, melt-in-your-mouth cake donut ever to grace this earth.

If you get there too late (they've often sold every crumb on their made-fresh-daily shelves by noon), or if it just doesn't feel right to be noshing on pastry when the sun is high, saunter 100 feet in either direction to one of two, classic, mom-and-pop burger joints. Each serves a delightful drip-to-your-elbows burger and fries. Let the grease settle a bit by hoofing a block west on 395 to view the lunker trout that are stored in the cooler in front of the sporting goods store; they've all been caught in the surrounding lakes and streams.

The definitive cure for trail-pounded feet and pack-sore backs is a soak in Buckeye Hot Springs. If you're already in Bridgeport, get back in the car and drive 7.3 miles back toward Mono Village on Twin Lakes Road. Turn right (north) onto dirt Buckeye Creek Road. (If you reach Honeymoon Flat Campground, you've gone 0.8 mile too far.) From the trailhead at Mono Village, Buckeye Creek Road is 6.3 miles out.

Drive the well-graded dirt road 2.75 miles along the foot of the hillside to cross Buckeye Creek via a bridge. On the other side, bear right at a junction with a road that continues up-canyon to quiet Buckeye Campground. Head down-canyon, up onto an open sagebrush-covered plateau about 100 feet above the stream. In about 0.2 mile, an unsigned, ersatz parking area on the right is where to stop for the hot springs. There are numerous intimate and shallow 1–2 person pools at the rim of the scarp, but be sure to sample the biggest and hottest spring down below, just beside a gravelly bend of Buckeye Creek. A network of use trails lead down. Clothing is optional, and the scenery is always superb. Please haul out all your glass and cans.

However self-effacing he might wish to be, Sierra native Ben Schifrin has been a longtime author of, or contributor to, Wilderness Press' most important California backpacking guides (see "Author Bio & Bib" on page 492).

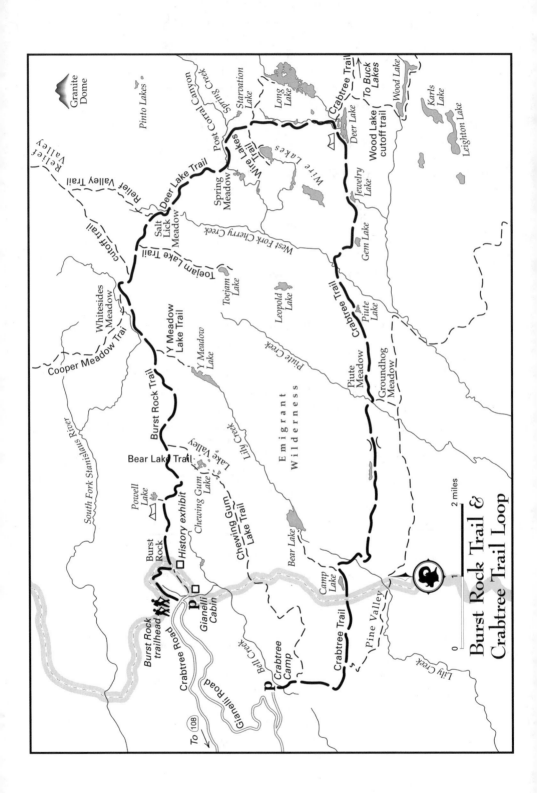

Burst Rock Trail &
Crabtree Trail Loop

51

Burst Rock Trail &
Crabtree Trail Loop
—Ben Schifrin

Route	Days	Elev. Gain/Loss	Difficulty	Miles
⌐	3	2920'/4240'	**	22.4

Campsites: Powell Lake: 1.8 miles
Chewing Gum Lake: 3.9 miles
Deer Lake (recommended camp): 11.1 miles
(see the Trip Description for others)

Map: USGS 7.5-min *Pinecrest, Cooper Peak, Emigrant Lake*

Best season: Late summer through early fall

Take this trip!

If you're an angler, this long near-loop trail is for you. Cutting directly into the granitic, lake-speckled heart of the western Emigrant Basin, hardly a mile along this easy route fails to present a lake or a stream stocked with fighting, delectable trout. The trail's destination, Deer Lake, possibly has more good fishing within a two-hour walk than any other spot in the entire Sierra. Our outbound leg is the historic western portion of the difficult Emigrant Pass wagon trail, which brought intrepid gold seekers to the Sonora mines over 140 years ago. Today, it is by far the most pleasant and scenic westside avenue into the Emigrant Basin's heart. The return path, via the easy Crabtree Trail, passes still more lakes, views, and meadows.

Trailhead

Crabtree Road 4N26.1 branches right from State Highway 108 just 0.8 mile east of Cold Springs (2.0 miles west of the Pinecrest Y). Follow Crabtree Road 9.1 miles to well-signed Crabtree Camp spur road 4N26. Crabtree Camp is the end of our semi-loop hike—head down the spur road 0.6 mile to the paved road-end loop. Leave a car here for your return shuttle. From Crabtree Camp, return to the junction with larger Gianelli Road 4N47, and turn right (east). Climb 4.0 miles farther and park at the signed Burst Rock Trail parking area, near Gianelli Cabin. Please park under the firs west of the road, to prevent further destruction of the delicate meadow around the cabin.

TRIP DESCRIPTION

The Burst Rock trailhead stands just away from the northern edge of an 8560-foot-high meadow, amid lodgepole pines and a smattering of mountain hemlocks and red firs. The first mile of the Burst Rock Trail has been shifted north, away from its previous position as an historic wagon road on the steep west flanks of Burst Rock. Be sure to walk into the meadow, along the old trail, to fill your canteens in the trickling headwaters of Bell Creek, before embarking on the new, waterless route. A minute south, just on the east bank of the creek-let, we can see what now remains of A. E. Gianelli's turn-of-the-century hunting cabin: four tiers of lodgepole logs in a 15-foot square.

The new, signed trailhead is directly north of the parking area. The path ascends gently northeast along a duff-floored moraine. We quickly reach a broad, bouldery saddle in an open stand of mixed conifers. Our way is almost level for a few minutes as we round the very head of Bell Creek, then an easy ascent resumes, via two long switchbacks. These lead us to an imperceptible fusion with the old trail, on the southwestern rim of the sandy shoulder of Burst Rock's summit massif. Now we angle easily up, northeast, to find a sign commemorating the Duckwall party's wagon train that pioneered this historic Sierran crossing. A few yards later we make a signed entry of the Emigrant Wilderness. The summit of the sandy, pine-dotted plateau called Burst Rock is just a few yards off-trail to the north.

Our level trail heads east under the high point of Burst Rock to a second, signed Emigrant Wilderness boundary. Photographers will first amble up to that summit to capture vistas north across the deep gorge of South Fork Stanislaus River to the Waterhouse Lake environs, and farther north to the Dardanelles and Mokelumne Peak. Volcanic mountains from Cooper Peak east to Leavitt Peak can be seen to advantage, while cerulean skies and lofty cumulonimbus clouds may backdrop Tower Peak, the Saurian Crest, and Mount Lyell and the Clark Range far to the southeast. Burst Rock's name is a corruption of "Birth Rock," so called because a Mrs. Wilson, a member of an overland wagon train using the punishing Emigrant Pass trans-Sierra route, gave birth to a girl here, using a natural cave in the cliffs below, for protection from the elements.

The headwaters of Bell Creek are our next objective, and the trail leads east, skirting below the slabby summit ridge. The brief descent ends at a saddle

Powell Lake and Castle Peak

and a junction with a short spur trail north to Powell Lake (1.8). This delight-ful granite-bound lakelet has two rock reefs extending into its shallow, humus-bottomed waters, which interrupt reflections of Cooper Peak and Castle Rock in the north. Mountain hemlocks fringe the lake. Nice but heavily used camps are nestled on the west and northeast shores. Keep in mind the one-night camping limit at Powell Lake, and that keeping stock there, overnight, is not allowed. Fishing for small brookies (to 8″) is very good any time but midwin-ter, and a few foot-long fish have been caught on deep lures and bait.

Beyond the Powell Lake junction, a dividing ridge causes the trail to ascend 300 feet. Then, side-hilling down northeast, the path reaches a granitic outcrop from where excellent views encompass the entirety of northern Yosemite. The meandering path of Lily Creek lies below, in Lake Valley, which is a boulder-pocked grassland. Chewing Gum Lake occupies its southern end. Thereafter, our way descends easy switchbacks down volcanic slopes cloaked in sagebrush and senecio. We soon enough level out at the Chewing Gum Lake Trail (3.1). It is only 0.8 mile down the meadowy path to the small lake, which would make a good campsite for those who get a late start on their first day.

As we continue on, consider the plight of an even tardier group of campers: a party of California-bound gold-seekers was once trapped here, at the head of Lake Valley, in an autumn snowstorm (it would seem that most Sierra crossings were ill-timed). They cut firewood from lodgepole pines near this point—but 10 feet above the ground, indicating the snowpack's depth! Some of the truncated trees still stand.

Once again, a volcanic-topped ridge stands in the way of our eastward progress on this historic pathway. A moderate, well-constructed ascent leaves some energy for gazing at the Emigrant Basin north country, or pondering the difficulties one would have had 140 years ago, nursing a family and heirloom-laden wagons over this route. Atop the ridge, slopes of pussy paws and locoweed give way to mixed, open-conifer groves. Descending, we switchback occasionally before striking the Y Meadow Lake Trail. It drops easily south 0.6 mile to the sandy shores of that dam-created lake, which, like Chewing Gum Lake, would make a pleasant intermediate night's stopover.

The next leg of the route leads over nearly level lodgepole-covered terrain on generally sandy, sometimes muddy trail to Whitesides Meadow. We swing near South Fork Stanislaus River and pass, in quick succession, the Cooper Meadow Trail (5.7) and the Relief Valley Cutoff Trail. Just yards later we top the Lily Creek-Cherry Creek divide. Dropping steeply, then more moderately, we find the Toejam Lake Trail, leaving due south. The easy 1.4-mile detour to lovely Toejam Lake is well worth the effort; pristine and little-visited Leopold Lake, another trailless 1.1 miles beyond, is an even better destination. Both bodies of water support brook trout.

From the Toejam Lake junction, uneventful walking on the Deer Lake Trail in viewless lodgepole groves leads down to level ground near our second linkage with the Relief Valley Trail. Here we turn south and arc down through bouldery forest to the banks of West Fork Cherry Creek in Salt Lick Meadow. Climbing away from Salt Lick Meadow, a southward-bearing, rocky-dusty trail leads up to a level lodgepole forest speckled with grassy tarns. Later, you pass a good camp just before stepping onto the edge of Spring Meadow, in wide Post Corral Canyon. True to its name, Spring Meadow is lush and wet, to the point of having a cluster of boggy ponds south of the trail. Ford Spring Creek; across it, our path veers southeast. One can avoid this wet stretch, and try for trout at the same time, by leaving the trail here and walking levelly east to small, meadowed Starvation Lake, tucked in a bowl under an attractive dome. Just 5 minutes from the trail, it is nonetheless little fished—a boon to those who do stop, since it supports a good fishery of brook trout.

The short remainder of the easy ascent leads to the signed Wire Lakes Trail (9.4). Most hikers will want to make the short side trip to the fantastic trio of Wire Lakes: it is only 0.6 mile to the west shore of the more-forested, upper lake, and another 1.0 mile beyond, via fading use trail, to the wilder open bowl of the rocky lower lake. All three lakes offer excellent brook trout fishing.

Returning to our Deer Lake Trail, we resume an easy southerly course. Beyond a pocket meadow, we pass a trail that leads east barely a mile to Long Lake's open, rocky north end. It is another little-visited spot with fine camps and fishing for large rainbow trout. Soon after, we climb over a pine-timbered saddle, then undertake a final, delightful descent through meadows and past tarns. The lowest tarn of the group, rimmed by red heather, dwarf bilberry, and bog kalmia, is actually a nicer camping spot than any of the larger, named lakes in this vicinity. From it, the path leads down-canyon, soon leveling out in sandy lodgepole flats north of Deer Lake. Here our route strikes the Crabtree Trail (11.1), our return route, beside Deer Lake's damp meadow rim.

Deer Lake is one of the most popular "hub" destinations in the Emigrant Basin. As such, it has been subjected to severe camping pressure. Please abide by the posted camping regulations, and camp only in designated sites. Deer Lake is off-limits to overnight camping with stock. Please spend no more than one night at this overused lake. Better still: take 15 minutes to climb the half-mile spur northeast to the check-dammed outlet of Long Lake, and use it as your base, instead.

From Deer Lake, short walks on almost any point of the compass will lead to a myriad of delightful lakes, streams and viewpoints. The author recommends three day trips:

1) Rabid anglers should traverse the west shore of Long Lake, casting lures for lunker rainbows. Cross west over our original route, fish the shores of Wire Lakes, and then drop cross-country back to the Crabtree Trail, just west of Deer Lake. After lunch, trace the Wood Lake Cutoff Trail south from the eastern end of Deer Lake. Angle a bit for large brookies in the three distinct segments of Wood Lake, then head south on anglers' trails to Karls, Leighton, Kole, Coyote, or Red Can lakes—all teeming with succulent trout.

2) Those who want to see the very heart of the Emigrant Wilderness should follow the continuation of the Crabtree Trail, east from Deer Lake, descending to the lovely Buck Lakes in their deep canyon. Then, climb up to the stupendous western end of enormous Emigrant Lake. Hike a ways along its north shore for outstanding views to Grizzly Peak, near historic Emigrant Pass. You can return the way you came (stop to fish—both lakes have trout to 20"!). Or, you can make a more-strenuous return, by descending the path along North Fork Cherry Creek, Emigrant Lake's outlet stream, to Cow Meadow Lake. From there, ascend trails west to Wood Lake and beyond to Deer Lake.

3) Cap your trek with an ascent of Granite Dome, the western summit of the Emigrant Basin. Traverse past the shores of Long Lake, up through heavenly meadows to shallow Coolidge Meadow Lake. Ascend to the head of the broad basin above it, and break out onto a bench holding similar Wilson Meadow Lake. Make your way directly to the summit over sandy hillsides and slabby outcrops. Return the way you came, or descend southwest past tiny Pinto Lakes. Ducked cross-country routes or an old horse trail will lead down to the Salt Lick Meadow environs. Retrace your steps back to your Deer Lake base camp.

After sampling the pleasures of the countryside around Deer Lake, pack up and head back towards civilization by way of the Crabtree Trail. Proceed west on sandy loam around the north shore of Deer Lake. From its wooded outlet, our path descends a slabby ravine. Below, we descend more gently to the swampy eastern end of humus-bottomed Jewelry Lake. The gravels and lagoons at the lake's head provide good spawning for rainbow trout. The dominant feature of the Jewelry Lake area, visible for miles around, is the 600-foot-high overhanging dome north of the lake. Note that keeping more than four head of any stock within ¼ mile of overused Jewelry Lake, or Gem or Piute lakes to the west, is prohibited.

Rounding muddily above the northern shores of Jewelry Lake, we find another west-trending gully, which we follow down onto sunny, glaciated slabs, speckled with sunflowers, pussy paws, buckwheat, and stonecrop. At the bottom of our brief descent, which is punctuated by small switchbacks, we find pretty Gem Lake (12.9), which sits on the edge of an open, glaciated granite bench. The best camping at this shallow, warmish lake is on the north shore, which our path parallels.

Walk west, rounding the small lake, then climb briefly to a wooded saddle. From here, we descend along a steep, forested slope on cobbly switchbacks. Almost 400 feet below, we reach a sandy ford of West Fork Cherry Creek. Now, ascend gently southwest, still following a joint-controlled depression in the granitic bedrock. Easy walking through lushly vegetated meadow reveals a trailside jungle of orange-and-maroon tiger lily, fragrant purple onion, palmate-leaved yellow cinquefoil, and stalked, white rein orchid. A few minutes' walk leads to the next small lake on our agenda: Piute Lake. The lake itself is small and grass-fringed, except where forested with lodgepoles, and its shallow, greenish waters also support rainbow trout.

We skirt the north shore. A moderate climb leads away from the overused lake to a broad saddle. From it, our path descends rockily west on switchbacks, down the east slope of Piute Creek canyon. Dry slabs and lodgepole pines demarcating the lower margin of Piute Meadow are reached at the bottom of the long descent, where we encounter, in order, the Groundhog Meadow spur trail (16.0), a broad crossing of Piute Creek, and a large campsite. Beyond, we keep to the trees south of the willowed west arm of Piute Meadow, heading uphill. First, ascend easily on a side-hill traverse, and then more aggressively up via dynamited switchbacks. Atop yet another low, brush-fringed saddle, we look back to survey the eastern horizon, with dark Bigelow Peak and the jutting prominence of Tower Peak.

Descending easily west from the gap, we soon reach a pretty lakelet, speckled with Indian pond lilies and backdropped by dancing aspens and lichen-dappled granite. Next, we make a lengthy traverse to the west, first gently up, then down. Our path soon reaches the top of a granite headwall, which it circumvents in a short, steep, rocky descent. We drop to the level of a hanging side valley and walk northwest through a meadow to an easy ford of Lily Creek.

The ascent of the west canyon wall is steeper, sandier, and hotter than was our descent. Dense manzanita and ceanothus flank the climb, which ends soon enough at the signed Bear Lake Trail (19.6). This is a recommended detour, especially for those planning to spend one more night in the wilderness: a well-beaten path ascends less than a mile past pockets of meadow to the stream-flow-maintenance dam impounding Bear Lake. This pretty but often overpopulated lake has its best camps on the west shore. Fishing is usually fair, for medium-sized rainbow trout. Because it is so close to the roadend, Bear Lake has a one-night camping limit, and is closed to camping with stock.

After retracing our steps down to the Crabtree Trail, we again strike a westerly course and walk through a small saddle, momentarily reaching a large campsite complex on the eastern end of shallow, green Camp Lake. This sparsely forested, sorely trampled small lake supports a harried population of brook trout. More campsites are found as we climb rockily above the south shore, and at the western end, as well. One hundred yards later, we exit the Emigrant Wilderness at its signed boundary. Stands of Jeffrey pine, red fir, and Sierra juniper next shade an easy traverse, which ends atop the last joint-controlled saddle of our trek, where we pass a short trail south to Pine Valley.

Now make one final steep, dusty descent via heavily eroded switchbacks in loose volcanic duff. Below, the wide trail turns north. On a sandy bench, we pass the lower end of the Chewing Gum Lake Trail, (on which ambitious hikers could toil up, 4.2 miles to the lake, then return to the Burst Rock Trail). A minute beyond that path, we strike Bell Creek at a large graceful wooden bridge. Just across it, we end our journey at the picnic tables surrounding Crabtree Camp (22.4) and its paved road-end-parking loop.

Permits

Emigrant Wilderness is managed by the Stanislaus National Forest. Get Wilderness Permits from them by writing to:

Stanislaus National Forest
Summit District Ranger
#1 Pinecrest Lake Road
Pinecrest, CA 95364
Or call (209) 965-3434.

Build-Up/Wind-Down tips

The best shop for last-minute gear and tips is Sierra Nevada Adventure Company, at the T-junction of Highways 49 and 108 in downtown Sonora. They have a complete selection of maps, equipment, freeze-dried food, plus a very knowledgeable staff. Call (209) 532-5621 or drop by 173 South Washington Street.

The last few dusty miles out to your car at Crabtree Camp will cause a terrible thirst. Slake it at Snowshoe Brewing Company, Sonora's finest brew pub. It is just a minute south of Highway 108 in East Sonora: 19040 Standard Road. Call (209) 536-1445.

You walked on the trail of the California Forty-Niners. Now, check out what all the excitement was about: visit Columbia State Historic Park, just five minutes north of Sonora on Highway 49. The entire old gold-rush town is now a walk-through museum, complete with exhibits, gold-panning demos, stagecoach rides (with holdups!), and opulent saloons. It has a number of fine restaurants (City Hotel serves the most elegant meal in Tuolumne County), and authentic Victorian bed-and-breakfast inns.

Either visit the California State Parks Web site: **www.parks.ca.gov/**, call (209) 532-0150, or e-mail: **calavera@goldrush.com**

However self-effacing he might wish to be, Sierra native Ben Schifrin has been a longtime author of, or contributor to, Wilderness Press' most important California backpacking guides (see "Author Bio & Bib" on page 492).

The Northern Sierra Nevada

Lake Tahoe

The northern Sierra, like California's portion of the Cascade Range, spans 130 miles, from about Sonora Pass northwest to the North Fork Feather River Canyon. Superficially, it bears affinities to that range, since most of its crest lands are composed of volcanic flows and deposits. What it lacks is active volcanoes, although a future eruption, specifically, in or near the Lake Tahoe basin, cannot be ruled out. Given the volcanic nature of most of its crest lands, why shouldn't it be considered a southern extension of the Cascade Range? After all, the southernmost part of that range, south of the Lassen area, also lacks active volcanoes, and the vegetation in both ranges is virtually identical. The difference between the two ranges is that beneath the northern Sierra's volcanic flows and deposits are granitic and metamorphic rocks, which are absent in the Cascade Range until you reach central Washington.

In California's Cascade Range, all its mountain lakes are nestled in volcanic basins; in the northern Sierra, they are in granitic and metamorphic ones. There are two general differences. First, lakes in granitic and metamorphic basins have clearer water, because they lack the microscopic volcanic clays that can stay suspended in volcanic-basin lakes. Second, except where dammed by moraines (a rare occasion, exhortations to the contrary) lakes in granitic and metamorphic basins are watertight. In contrast, lakes in volcanic basins can often leak through cracked lava, and hence their water level decreases once inflow becomes minimal. The only lake you'll visit in this section that drops more than a foot or two is Little Jamison's Rock Lake; it is fed only by snowmelt, and when that is gone, about three feet of evaporation can occur before October precipitation begins to replenish it.

In the northern Sierra there are a number of wildernesses and recreational areas. From north to south these are: Plumas-Eureka State Park, Lakes Basin and Grouse Ridge recreation areas, Donner Pass crest lands, and Granite Chief, Desolation, Mokelumne, and Carson-Iceberg wildernesses. All of these, except for Grouse Ridge Recreation Area, have the Pacific Crest Trail either traversing through them or passing close above them. There are some scenic stretches of this trail, including one "classic" crest-hugging stretch from Tinker Knob north to Donner Pass but, alas, adequate campsites along it are virtually nonexistent. We came up with only one great PCT hike, the stretch from Ebbetts Pass to Carson Pass. It has some wondrous scenery, ample lakes and camps, and, unlike a scenic stretch north from Sonora Pass into Carson-Iceberg Wilderness, is quite safe.

Carson-Iceberg, Mokelumne, Desolation (Lake Tahoe), & Granite Chief Wildernesses

Carson-Iceberg Wilderness has a deficiency of lakes by High Sierra standards, and those that exist generally are easily reached and overpopulated. If I were to recommend one lengthy backpack trip in this wilderness, it would be one starting just north of the eastside's Wolf Creek Meadows: the East Carson Trail. Before the 1990s this was not terribly desirable for two reasons. First, of the two routes heading over to the East Carson River Canyon, one climbed and dropped excessively, while the other was partly along roads. Between these have been added a newer trail, a direct one with minimal elevation change. Second, the myriad cattle are gone. While there are no lakes within the East Carson River Canyon, there is the river—miles of anglers' paradise—and even on weekends you have most of this canyon to yourself.

North of this wilderness is the Mokelumne Wilderness, through which our PCT hike traverses. Most of its lakes aren't; they're ponds and lakelets. The several lake-size bodies of water that do exist lie in the subalpine realm above 8000 feet, and have fragile soils or rocky nearby lands not suited for environmentally sound camping.

Next comes the most popular High Sierra wilderness north of Yosemite National Park: Desolation Wilderness, only minutes away from the urban south shore of Lake Tahoe. As its popularity has increased, so too has regulation. Where else, at the start of the Third Millennium, can you spend up to $100 for the privilege of camping overnight? Besides the hikes offered here, I could easily add more, including a westside route from Wrights Lake north to Lake Schmidell and beyond.

Beyond Desolation Wilderness is Granite Chief Wilderness, largely lakeless except for the Five Lakes bench, which is closed to camping. It does have one trail worth considering, the Powderhorn Trail down to Diamond Crossing. Except for its start, it is entirely through old-growth forest—a rarity for the heavily logged northern Sierra. But while most of us want to save old trees, few actually like to backpack among them—they block the scenery! Unless they are redwoods, we tend to avoid them. By Diamond Crossing, Five Lakes Creek executes a series of cascades, each with an adjacent swimming hole, and this feature is a worthy goal for those willing to make the effort.

I've already mentioned the PCT from Tinker Knob north to Donner Pass. North from Interstate 80, the PCT could have been a grand route past Castle and Basin peaks to Paradise and White Rock Lake, but a substandard route was built. North of White Rock Lake, you're in logging country, as you are west of these crest lands. One exception is compact Grouse Ridge Recreation Area, about 10 to 15 miles west of the crest. It is packed with lakes, but most are small and/or shallow, mostly inferior to Desolation Wilderness lakes. On the other hand, it has no permits, no quotas, and no overnight backcountry camping fee—check it out. (JPS)

Kathy Morey

Glen Alpine Falls

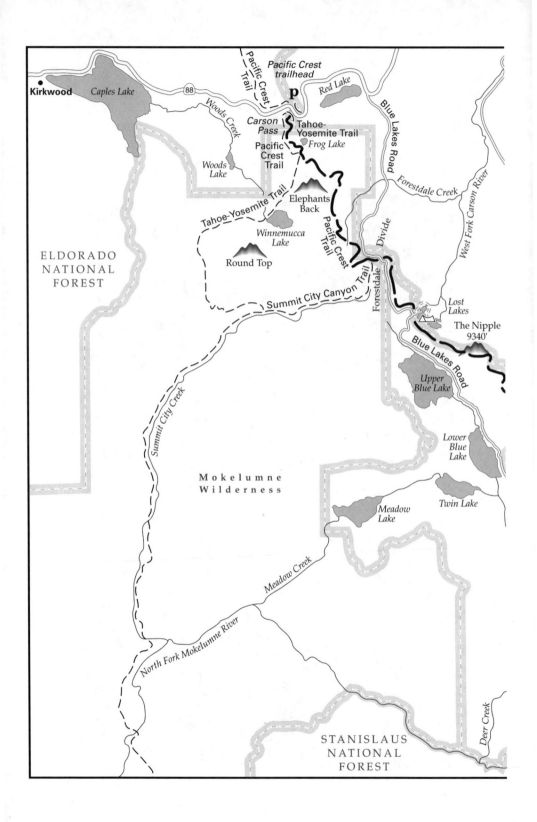

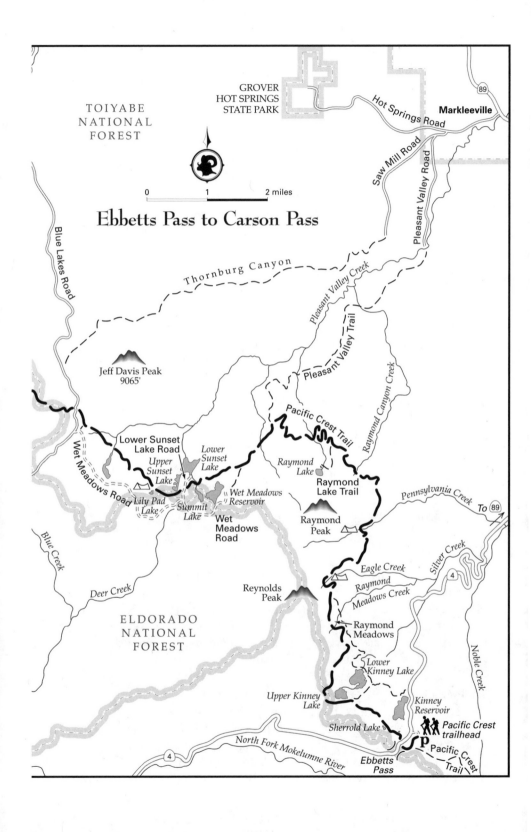

Ebbetts Pass to Carson Pass

TOIYABE
NATIONAL
FOREST

GROVER
HOT SPRINGS
STATE PARK

Hot Springs Road

Markleeville

89

Saw Mill Road

Pleasant Valley Road

Blue Lakes Road

0   1   2 miles

Thornburg Canyon

Pleasant Valley Creek

Pleasant Valley Trail

Raymond Canyon Creek

Jeff Davis Peak
9065'

Pacific Crest Trail

Wet Meadows Road

Lower Sunset
Lake Road

Upper
Sunset
Lake

Lower
Sunset
Lake

Raymond
Lake

Raymond
Lake Trail

Pennsylvania Creek

To 89

Lily Pad
Lake

Summit
Lake

Wet Meadows
Reservoir

Wet
Meadows
Road

Raymond
Peak

Silver Creek

4

Blue Creek

Eagle Creek

Raymond
Meadows Creek

Deer Creek

Reynolds
Peak

Raymond
Meadows

ELDORADO
NATIONAL
FOREST

Noble Creek

Lower
Kinney Lake

Upper Kinney
Lake

Kinney
Reservoir

Sherrold Lake

Pacific Crest
trailhead

P

Pacific Crest
Trail

North Fork Mokelumne River

4

Ebbetts
Pass

52

Ebbetts Pass to Carson Pass via PCT

—Jeffrey P. Schaffer

Route	Days	Elev. Gain/Loss	Elev. Low/High	Difficulty	Miles
↗	3	6490´/6560´	7740´/9200´	**	29.5

(mileage without side hikes)

Campsites: Eagle Creek: 5.6 miles
Pennsylvania Creek: 7.5 miles
Lily Pad Lake: 15.7 miles
Blue Lakes Road: 18.4 miles
(see the Trip Description for others)

Map: USGS 7.5-min *Carson Pass, Ebbetts Pass, Pacific Valley*

Best season: Late July through mid-September

Take this trip!

There are many sections of the Pacific Crest Trail in California that are worth hiking. This High Sierra section was chosen because it is readily accessible, because it is not overcrowded relatively speaking (no quotas), and especially because it takes you past one of the most fantastically eroded volcanic landscapes in the state. As you might expect, there are far-ranging views, particularly from The Nipple, a summit close to the trail.

Trailheads

You begin your hike from a PCT trailhead parking area at the end of a short spur road that is 0.3 mile east from Highway 4's Ebbetts Pass, and you end at a PCT trailhead parking area at Highway 88's Carson Pass. The distance between the two is considerable, about 40 miles. From Ebbetts Pass, Highway 4 descends 13 miles northeast to a junction with Highway 89, coming west from Highway 395 via Monitor Pass. Now on Highway 89, you go 5 miles northwest to Markleeville, then about 7 miles more to Highway 88. Turn left and ascend Highways 88/89 west for 6 miles to where they split, 89 heading north to Lake Tahoe via Luther Pass, 88—your highway—climbing 9 miles southwest to Carson Pass. Here, during the summer season, there is a parking fee of $3 per day.

TRIP DESCRIPTION

Heads Up! If you begin in mid-July, you're likely to encounter some snow patches; before then, considerable snow patches. Two potentially dangerous ones are on the steep northeast slopes of Elephants Back. However, with care you should be fine, even without ice ax or crampons. Also, especially in the middle section, where there are a lot of ponds and bogs, mosquitoes can be prevalent into early August.

The net change in elevation from trailhead to trailhead is a mere 70 feet, but if you walk in either direction, you'll do about 6500 feet of ascending (and a similar amount of descending). This is quite a lot, but fortunately there is only one major protracted climb, almost 1000 feet, from Forestdale Canyon up the north ridge of Elephants Back. Still, there are lots of ups and downs on the order of 200–500 feet. This hike can be done as a strenuous overnight hike, camping at Lily Pad Lake, my favorite choice. However, I suggest a more leisurely pace, one with three nights, camping by either Eagle Creek or Pennsylvania Creek, at Lily Pad Lake, and finally at the Lost Lakes.

You begin by heading ¼ mile south up to the Pacific Crest Trail, then traversing on it ⅓ mile over to a crossing of Highway 4, just east of Ebbetts Pass. For a lesson in history, walk a minute or two up to the plaque at the pass. Ahead, you climb ⅓ mile north to your first good view, then strike northwest to a notch just west of a crest pond, and descend steeply west to a pond and adjacent Sherrold Lake (1.1), with a campsite. Beyond this lakelet the PCT snakes northwest, ducking in and around obstacles of a mostly granitic landscape, then traverses west between a shallow pond and a low knoll just north of it. Following the path of least resistance, the trail traverses granitic benches and then curves northwest to a forested ridge above Upper Kinney Lake (2.2), set in a granite basin and backdropped with rugged, pyramidal, volcanic Peak 9540. From here a spur trail starts a descent north to the obvious nearby lake, although the trail almost immediately splits into several routes. This lake is much larger than Sherrold, and it has better campsites. However, usually not long after Labor Day this reservoir is drastically drained, reducing it to an oversized pond with an ugly bathtub ring.

Onward, the PCT traverses ¼ mile west to a small pond on a broad crest, from which it turns north and over the next 1½ miles skirts generally open slopes along the boundary of Mokelumne Wilderness before entering it after crossing one low ridge and reaching the crest of another. Just ahead you descend briefly west to Raymond Meadows (4.5) and its creek, below the rugged, serrated Sierra crest. Before mid-August the creek usually is flowing, and then you can set up camp in this vicinity. Onward, you traverse about ¾ mile below the east base of Reynolds Peak before reaching a low ridge, from which you're confronted with a huge dome, straight ahead. We're now in the heart of a fantastic volcanic landscape, and here is a good place to camp, so descend briefly west to the headwaters of Eagle Creek (5.6). Here you'll find a campsite just beyond its step-across ford. Late-season hikers will find water flowing just downstream, where a tributary joins this creek.

You cross this tributary and, engulfed by forest, cross many more as you traverse northeast along the lower slope of the largely unseen dome. This dome sits atop the west end of a ridge and, as you hike eastward, you'll note that it changes its profile to become very un-domelike. Also eastward you'll pass quite an array of minor ridges and pinnacles. After about a mile you will seek a gash in the ridge to make a forested, switchbacking descent about ½ mile down to Pennsylvania Creek (7.5). Because it's perennial, it's a good one to camp by, except that there is no level ground where you cross it. To find isolated camping, head about 200+ yards up-canyon. The farther you go—and you can easily go ½ mile up the broad floor of this dramatic canyon—the more you'll feel you have this fantastic volcanic landscape to yourself. Camping in the right spot, you'll catch the first rays of the morning's rising sun.

From the creek your odyssey continues with a diagonal climb north 1 mile up to a wind-cropped sagebrush saddle, followed by an easy descent to snowmelt tributaries of highly gullied Raymond Canyon. Your rollercoaster route winds in and out of these before climbing to panoramic views from a broad east-west crest. Here the PCT strikes west into a thriving forest on the long, north-descending ridge from Raymond Peak. Now you descend about 300 yards northwest to the Raymond Lake Trail (10.0), climbing south. If you're interested in visiting this lake, it's best to contour from the ridge over to the trail rather than dropping about 100 feet to the junction. In 0.7 mile this trail first climbs sagebrush slopes to a minor gap on the ridge—one with great views—then quickly starts a steep ascent to Raymond Lake, about 160 feet higher. At about 9000 feet, the lake lies in the subalpine realm, making it too cold for decent swimming. Camping is poor except in one spot, 0.1 mile west from the outlet, among protective trees at a minor saddle just above the lake's northwest corner.

Beyond the Raymond Lake Trail the PCT switchbacks down open, sagebrush slopes, which offer you far-ranging vistas. After a mile you reach the lake's multibranched creek, then traverse about ½ mile across open slopes to a ridge with a viewpoint, one with an excellent view north down-canyon to Pleasant Valley and beyond to Nevada's Carson Valley and its bordering desert lands. Ahead you traverse briefly west to an often dry gully, then climb north to a nearby saddle near the north end of Raymond Peak's long, descending north-west ridge. After an initial jog south, you switchback north ¼ mile down to another jog. Here, just off the trail, is another viewpoint, which rivals or exceeds the one you passed about 0.7 mile back. From it you have essentially the same view, but one that now includes all of Pleasant Valley plus lands around Markleeville.

From the switchback you descend 0.3 mile southwest to a junction with the Pleasant Valley Trail (12.6), ascending from its namesake valley, from which a road descends to Markleeville. Now in forest cover you traverse 0.4 mile over to a Pleasant Valley Creek tributary, which has a large, adjacent camp-site. From its west bank, over the next ½ mile you start northwest, then angle southwest in and out of gullies as you climb to a saddle. Ahead, you descend about 200 yards to a junction with a spur trail (13.6), which traverses 200 yards to the Wet Meadows trailhead. From there, a road winds about 5 miles north to end at the Blue Lakes Road, which you'll cross in a similar distance by trail.

This next PCT stretch, over to that road, is a lake-blessed one that takes you past several lakes, most raised by dams. You first descend a bit, in about ¼ mile, to cross the seasonal creek you've been paralleling, then go 0.4 mile across minor undulations to a second seasonal creek. If you followed it about 200 yards upstream, you'd reach the north corner of Wet Meadows Reservoir. Immediately past this creek you pass a trailside pond, then about 200 yards west of it cross a minor gap and start a descent southwest. Along it you see nearby Summit Lake, just to the south, and can head cross-country over to this reservoir. As at the first, you can swim and, if you search a bit, can find a spot to camp. The PCT quickly bottoms out in a gully containing a creek that drains from Summit Lake north down to nearby Lower Sunset Lake. You soon see that lake and can head directly down to it, or continue onward to Lower Sunset Lake Road (15.1) and take it down to the lake. In the opposite direction the road heads 200 yards over to the Wet Meadows Road. Bearing generally west, your trail first skirts just south of Upper Sunset Lake, flirts with an ill-defined Sierra crest, then descends briefly to Lily Pad Lake (15.7). Unlike the others, this one is completely natural and it has good campsites on granite benches. Its water is clear, thanks to lying in a granitic basin. The previous ones were at least part in volcanic land, which often yields cloudy water. Lily Pad Lake is deeper than one might first expect, and it is a fine one for swimming, given the basking slabs nearby.

Onward, the PCT winds northwest through viewless forest for 0.5 mile, then winds a shorter distance west to a creeklet, crosses it, and heads north to west slopes of a nearby, linear lake. This one is attractive and deep enough to support trout and offer swimming, but lacks good campsites and has—for most

Lost Lakes from the Nipple

of the summer—too many mosquitoes. Ahead, you soon cross the outlet creek of unseen Tamarack Lake, just to the south. Then the forest briefly opens and due north stands steep-sided Jeff Davis Peak, your best beacon to measure progress through the Wet Meadows-Blue Lakes country. Over the next 0.5 mile you head generally northwest and twice cross the headwaters of Pleasant Valley Creek, the second time just before a junction with a spur trail (18.1) that goes 200 yards southwest to the Blue Lakes Road trailhead. This large trailhead facility actually lies not on the Blue Lakes Road, but rather 0.1 mile south on the road to the Wet Meadows trailhead. You could camp at the trailhead's parking lot, which at least is flat, and it has an outhouse. Just ⅓ mile past the spur trail, your PCT crosses the Blue Lakes Road (18.4). This road gets a lot of use during the summer, so if you have to hitch out for help, here's a good spot to do it.

Your easy hiking now is over. On the last third of this hike you'll first climb to The Nipple, later drop into a deep canyon north of Forestdale Divide, then make a major climb to the Sierra crest immediately north of Elephants Back, each climb surpassing 9000 feet in elevation. It's about time to don those hats and dark glasses! Elevation does have its rewards, namely, views, which improve while making a winding, moderate ascent west. You'll see a number of peaks, including the closest prominent one, Jeff Davis Peak. Listed at 8990 feet on an earlier topo, this volcanic neck is listed at 9065 feet, 75 feet higher, on a newer one. Either the Sierra crest rose at 3 feet per year, or there was a topographer's error. Having done extensive mapping while using inaccurate topo maps, I am convinced of the latter.

About ½ mile beyond Blue Lakes Road and 300 feet above it, your trail momentarily tops out among lodgepoles and junipers, and here you have your first great view of lands west of the Sierra crest. From your vantage point you see much of the Mokelumne Wilderness landscape. Along the crest are Round Top, to the northwest, and Raymond and Reynolds peaks, to the southeast. In the canyon below you are Upper and Lower Blue Lakes, and west of the latter is *solitary* Twin Lake and beyond it, Meadow Lake. The PCT next meanders westward close to the crest for about ½ mile before trending northwest. On this general course the route meanders 1¼ miles. Halfway along it your trail comes close to a shallow crest saddle, and a minute's walk to it rewards you with far-ranging views to the north and east. These include your well-known Jeff Davis Peak, then 2 miles north to Markleeville Peak, then 6 miles farther north to Hawkins Peak—all remnants of volcanoes—and finally, 8 more miles north to granitic Freel Peak. At 10,881 feet, Freel Peak is the highest summit on the rim of the Lake Tahoe basin. The crest lands in your vicinity, being broad and gentle, look unglaciated and uneroded, but scattered erratic boulders suggest that glacier ice spilled east across the crest. Some 20,000 years ago Mokelumne Wilderness harbored an extensive ice cap, one extending from Round Top to Raymond and Reynolds peaks—and beyond.

Continuing northwest, you climb 250 feet higher to a saddle at the southeast base of The Nipple (20.8). At 9340 feet, The Nipple stands a head above the broad shoulder of the Sierra crest and offers you an exceptional 360° panorama. You can tackle its summit head-on by climbing ¼ mile northwest directly up to it, or can continue almost ½ mile up your trail, to just below a crest saddle, climb up to it, then parallel the crest east to the 15-foot-high summit block. Old registers in a can at the summit will testify to the popularity of the viewpoint. You'll see familiar views as well as new ones, which include your next destination, the Lost Lakes. With that goal in mind, from just below the saddle west of The Nipple, take the PCT, which quickly levels off at 9200 feet— your route's highest elevation—then starts a crest-hugging, very scenic descent about 1¼ miles to the Lost Lakes spur road (22.6), at about 8650 feet. This road winds around the north and east shores of the northwestern Lost Lake, then ends at the north shore of the southeastern one. This road is readily accessible for pickups and SUVs, and most folks in them camp in the spacious area along the forested west shore of the northwestern lake. To escape car campers, try the forested belt separating the two lakes.

You lost elevation descending to the Lost Lakes, now you'll have to make some of it up—about 250 feet—to vault the Forestdale Divide. You do about 200 feet of it in the first ½ mile, then have a leisurely traverse north, leaving most of the trees behind by the time you turn north, ¾ mile later. On this stretch you're treated to superb views west down deep Summit City Canyon and south across the Blue Lakes. At the bend you can supplement these views by heading over to the adjacent Sierra crest, just above you, for views of lands to the north and east.

Westbound, you descend slightly to cross the Blue Lakes Road in 0.2 mile, pass a muddy pond in about 200 yards, then in 0.2 mile reach the Summit City Canyon Trail. Just under 200 yards later, you top cross the Forestdale Divide (24.4). Up here at about 8940 feet elevation, snow patches can linger well into summer and obscure the trail. However, the Blue Lakes Road, which also crosses the divide, is quite obvious, and if you can't find the trail's crossing, then from the road hike southwest along the Forestdale Divide crest about 250 yards.

At the divide you reenter the Mokelumne Wilderness and switchback down an often snow-patched trail, passing above one conspicuous lakelet, unfortunately nestled in a boggy meadow. Your PCT then approaches a smaller, second one, only knee-deep, then circles a third, a tiny pond—none of these suitable for camping. Just past the third, you cross the outlet creek of an unseen fourth, then wind on down for ⅔ mile, dropping 300 feet, to a stream crossing beside granitic outcrops. If you need or want to camp in this vicinity, look for small sites among the bedrock.

Ahead, your trail first crosses several low outcrops, then climbs northward across mostly brushy talus slopes whose openness allows glances back at the impressive scenery of the upper Forestdale Canyon as well as views east and north, that is, down and across the deep canyon. After 1¼ miles of northward ascent and 400 feet of elevation gain, your trail reaches a granitic east-west ridge and first switchbacks briefly up it before equally briefly traversing west to the east base of dark, volcanic Elephants Back. Before mid-July you may see a continuous snowfield on its northeast slopes; in September, you may see your entire trail diagonalling up these slopes. Between then, there may be two snowfields—first a larger, lower one, then a smaller, upper one. Both can be quite iced over and potentially dangerous, so many hikers walk along the lower, gentle slopes of the first, climb up talus, then traverse along the upper, gentle slopes of the second, away from its drop-off right edge. These accomplished, you cross the often windy Sierra crest among scattered whitebark pines just north of Elephants Back, then descend ⅓ mile to a junction with the Tahoe-Yosemite Trail (28.3). Southbound, this first goes an even mile to Winnemucca Lake, near treeline. With few trees, lots of boulders, and sometimes lots of wind, it's not a desirable lake to camp at.

Anyway, you're just 1¼ miles from your hike's end, so camping does not weigh heavily on your mind (a beer might). In under 200 yards north the TYT reaches a junction immediately south of the shallow, relatively unappealing Frog Lake (especially in late season when it is little more than an oversized muddy pond). The TYT descends shortly left (west), offering views of the Caples Lake environs. It then concludes by descending briefly north before traversing over to a small visitors' center at the south end of a long parking lot at Highway 88's Carson Pass (29.5). Cheers.

Permits

Backpackers get their free Wilderness Permits at either trailhead. No quotas.

Build-up/Wind-down tips

There are several campgrounds along Highway 4 both west and east of Ebbetts Pass. West of it, the Lake Alpine campgrounds often are full on weekends, so continue east to Mosquito Lakes Campground, Pacific Valley Campground (along a spur road south), or to Hermit Valley Campground. The last one is about 3⅓ miles before Highland Lakes Road, and 1 mile down it is Bloomfield Campground, my favorite. Beyond Highland Lakes Road, Highway 4 climbs 1⅓ miles east to Ebbetts Pass. From the pass the highway winds about 5½ miles down to Silver Creek Campground, easily the closest eastside campground to the trailhead.

This hike requires a shuttle, and about midway along it you'll pass through Markleeville (don't blink or you'll miss it). Being tired, hot, and sweaty after your hike, you may want to take a bath, so drive 4 miles up to Grover Hot Springs State Park, shower, soak in water from its hot springs, then head back into town for food and spirits.

Jeffrey P. Schaffer provides background on his path to guidebook writing, detailed mapmaking, and challenging received views of Sierra geological formation, besides a list of his titles from Wilderness Press, in "Author Bio & Bib" on page 492.

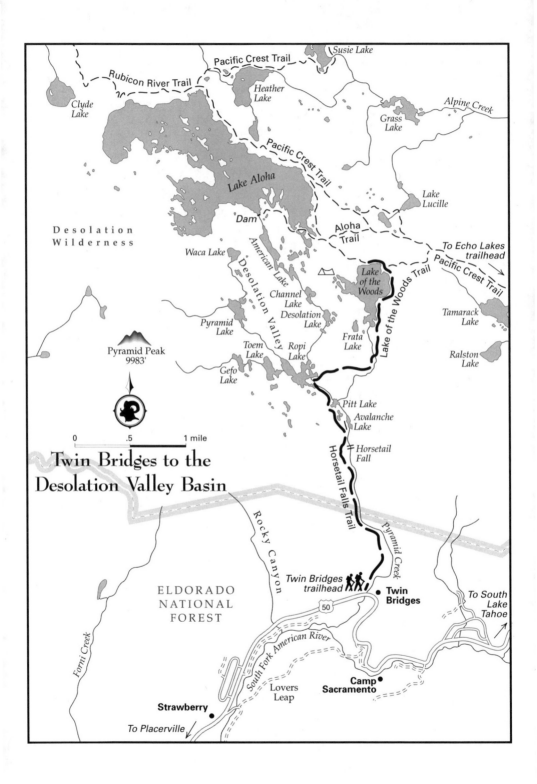

Susie Lake

Pacific Crest Trail

Rubicon River Trail

Heather
Lake

Clyde
Lake

Grass
Lake

Alpine Creek

Pacific Crest Trail

Lake Aloha

Lake
Lucille

Dam

Aloha
Trail

Desolation
Wilderness

To Echo Lakes
trailhead

Waca Lake

Pacific Crest Trail

American Lake

Desolation Valley

Channel
Lake

Lake
of the
Woods

Tamarack
Lake

Desolation
Lake

Lake of the Woods Trail

Pyramid
Lake

Frata
Lake

Ralston
Lake

Toem
Lake

Ropi
Lake

Pyramid Peak
9983'

Gefo
Lake

Pitt Lake

Avalanche
Lake

Horsetail
Fall

0   .5   1 mile

Twin Bridges to the
Desolation Valley Basin

Horsetail Falls Trail

Rocky Canyon

Pyramid Creek

Forni Creek

ELDORADO
NATIONAL
FOREST

Twin Bridges
trailhead

Twin
Bridges

To South
Lake
Tahoe

50

South Fork American River

Lovers
Leap

Camp
Sacramento

Strawberry

To Placerville

53

Twin Bridges to the Desolation Valley Basin

—Jeffrey P. Schaffer

Route	Days	Elev. Gain/Loss	Elev. Low/High	Difficulty	Miles
↲	2	2040'/2040'	6120'/8060'	***	7.0
					(mileage without side hikes)

Campsites: Lake of the Woods: 3.5 miles
(see the Trip Description for others)

Map: USGS 7.5-min *Echo Lake, Pyramid Peak*

Best season: Late July through early September

Take this trip!

This hike is an understandably popular one, for it provides the quickest route to the Desolation Valley lakes. Whereas only four lakes are mentioned in the above mileages, more exist in this vicinity; eight of them are named, the largest being Lake Aloha, with a greater acreage than all others combined. Those willing to go briefly cross-country with map in hand can find isolation even on a busy summer weekend. Should you go all the way to Lake Aloha by a cross-country route, you'll add at least 4 miles of hiking, round trip. However, it is quite easy, and searching for hidden lakes, lakelets, and campsites is very rewarding.

Trailhead

From the Highway 49 junction in Placerville, drive 5 miles east up Highway 50 to the Eldorado National Forest Information Center, get your Wilderness Permit there, then continue 35 miles up the highway to the settlement of Strawberry. Finally, drive an additional 1⅔ miles to Twin Bridges, an easily missed site. However, your highway conspicuously bridges Pyramid Creek immediately before a sharp curve right.

TRIP DESCRIPTION

Heads Up! Part of this route, up bedrock slabs past Horsetail Falls, is cross-country, quite steep, and potentially dangerous, especially when descending. Supposedly a number of hikers have fallen to their deaths by getting off route, although in the 1990s the route was very well marked (perhaps too well marked). Should you go before late July, then the crossing of swollen Pyramid Creek can be potentially dangerous.

Your trail starts along the west side of Pyramid Creek, although you may find one or more use trails. You quickly leave the creek near its bend east, then rejoin it ½ mile later and follow it 250 yards northwest through open forest to another bend, then 160 yards north to the wilderness boundary, in a shady fir grove. About ½ mile past the boundary you may have route-finding problems, although the route usually is well marked. After about 200 yards of climbing up an increasingly steep tread, you reach a vantage point from which you can look down-canyon and identify the canyon's huge east-wall lateral moraine—deposits left by a former glacier. You can also study nearby lower Horsetail Fall (1.3), often roaring as it plunges 100 feet into a splashing pool. This vantage point is on ice- and water-polished, gravel-covered, sloping bedrock. In other words, it's potentially treacherous, so exercise caution here and above.

The trail, essentially a marked cross-country route, veers away from the lower fall and starts west steeply up open slabs. In several places you'll probably have to use your hands as well as your feet, although if you are on route, you won't be climbing any cliffs or overly steep slopes. (In the past, one or more possible routes have been marked with ducks and/or with paint.) High above the lower fall the route bends north and diagonals up a talus slope before cutting 80 yards east to a small flat just above the brink of upper Horsetail Fall. The view from the flat alone *almost* justifies this arduous, 800-foot elevation gain up steep slopes, and from it you can now identify the canyon's west-wall moraine. It's hard to believe that a glacier descending Pyramid Creek filled the canyon at least to the crest of its 900-foot-high lateral moraines.

With danger behind you, drop briefly on a trail segment from the small flat, then parallel Pyramid Creek 200 yards up to small but scenic Avalanche Lake (1.8). Your route to Ropi Lake is now essentially cross-country. About ¼ mile beyond Avalanche Lake you approach relatively unappealing Pitt Lake (2.0), and near its northern end you must make a decision. To get to Lake of the Woods, you'll have to cross Pyramid creek, and this is best done before you reach Ropi Lake—if you want to keep your feet dry. Therefore, start looking for

Middle Horsetail Fall, above Twin Bridges

suitable boulders and/or logs on which you can cross the creek. The principal cross-country route stays along the creek's west bank as it climbs ⅓ mile to the outlet of Ropi Lake (2.4).

Ropi is the start of several cross-country excursions that offer isolated camping. From it, you can head west to nearby Toem Lake or, above it, to Gefo Lake. Additionally, check out isolated lakelets and ponds lying on naked granite to the south of these. You can ascend to Lake Aloha by at least two different routes, each about 2+ miles long, depending on how much you meander. Still, this is shorter than reaching it on trail first passing Lake of the Woods. The western route goes to Gefo Lake, then north to Pyramid Lake and up its northeast inlet creek to Waca Lake. From here you can zip northwest over a low ridge to adjacent Lake Aloha or east over a low ridge to nearby American Lake. The eastern route ascends Pyramid Creek, which empties into the northeast corner of Ropi Lake. If you find this ascent intimidating, then veer right of the obvious knoll just west of the creek. The gradient is less, and you'll cross behind the knoll, but will miss Desolation Lake. Ahead, paralleling Pyramid Creek you immediately pass an unnamed lakelet, just north of the knoll, and quickly reach Channel Lake. Then just beyond it, from the east bank of linear American Lake, either meander east to explore over a half-dozen lakelets in this area or else continue upstream to Lake Aloha's 20-foot-high dam, less than 200 yards beyond the north tip of American Lake. Lake Aloha, with a spread of 610 acres—almost one square mile—is far and away the largest lake in the wilderness, thanks to its dam impounding water on the nearly flat floor of spreading Desolation Valley. Soon after the Labor Day weekend, much of the lake is drained, and because most of the lake is less than 10 feet deep, this spreading lake contracts enormously. Therefore, visit the lake no later than that weekend, when the water level is still high, and you can swim to hundreds of low, bedrock islands and islets.

Another possible side trip is 9983-foot Pyramid Peak, the highest summit in Desolation Wilderness. Make a climb west from Ropi Lake past Toem Lake to Gefo Lake. From it several routes are possible, for the slopes are not too steep. You can diagonal due south up to the peak's southeast ridge, reaching it at about 8600 feet; or you can climb west up either side of the Gefo lake inlet creek and then briefly up to the ridge. Atop it you diagonal west up to the peak's south flank, then climb straight to the bouldery summit. Its views, however, are somewhat disappointing to some, since Lake Tahoe is largely hidden from view, but all else lies spread out below you.

Most hikers, upon reaching Ropi Lake, start up an official trail that begins from the lake's snag-infested east arm. This trail ascends east-northeast ⅓ mile up a straight, joint-controlled gully, crosses a tiny, seasonally boggy flat, then continues on an easier grade ¼ mile east to Lake of the Woods' outlet creek. This it follows 200 yards upstream to a crossing. Ahead, you go momentarily east just past the south edge of a small, stagnant pond, immediately turn north, then climb ¼ mile to a low ridge damming *extremely popular* Lake of the Woods (3.5), which is best visited on a weekday, not the weekend. Campsites lie around the lake, the better, more-private ones located along its west shore. If you camp here, be sure you do so at least 100 feet from the shore, and 200 feet is better. For example, camp on small, flat bedrock benches located on gentle terrain just west of the lake and just north of Frata Lake. That lake, located about 200 yards west of Lake of the Woods' outlet, is shallow but still deep enough for pleasant swimming in its slightly cloudy water.

This hike ends at Lake of the Woods, but you can continue on to Lake Aloha. At Lake of the Woods' northwest corner, which is nearly a mile by trail from its outlet, a trail climbs northwest, reaching a popular trail to Lake Aloha in less than ½ mile. Just 60 yards down it you reach a junction above a southeast arm of Lake Aloha. By your route this junction is about 5 miles from your trailhead. (From the Echo Lakes trailhead it is almost 6, however, that route starts 1300 feet higher, and because it has a lot less climbing it is the preferred route.) From the junction a de facto trail branches left and embarks on a ¾-mile course over to the lake's dam and its justifiably popular swimming area. On barren granitic benches to the south of the lake you can make a camp.

Permits

Dayhikers can fill out Wilderness Permits at the trailhead, but backpackers need to get them at Highway 50's Eldorado Visitor Center, Eldorado NF, 3070 Camino Heights Drive, Camino, CA 95709; (530) 644-6048, Fax: 295-5624. It is open year-round, seven days a week, from 8 A.M. to 5 P.M. Quotas exist from the Memorial Day weekend through September 30, so if you plan to hike on a weekend, make a reservation early, up to 90 days in advance. You have to pick up your permit in person, which you can do after hours, since your permit will be held for you in an outside box. Not everyone will be driving east up Highway 50, so during the summer season you can also pick up your permit at the William Kent Visitor Center, 2.2 miles south of Tahoe City on Highway 89, or at the Lake Tahoe Visitor Center, 3.2 miles north of the Highway 50/89 split in South Lake Tahoe.

From Sunday through Thursday, wilderness use is quite light, so you ought to be able to obtain a permit at any of the three visitor centers in person. This saves paying the reservation fee of $5 per party. There is a charge to camp overnight in the wilderness, $5 per night per person for the first two nights (free beyond that). The maximum party size is 12, which would have to pay $120 for two nights, but fortunately there is a $100 cap. There is no charge for backpackers ages 12 and under.

Build-up/Wind-down tips

If you need to camp near the trailhead, the closest campground is Lovers Leap Campground. Just east of Highway 50's Strawberry, take Strawberry Lane, which begins immediately northeast of Strawberry Lodge. The lane quickly bridges the South Fork American River, and you branch left. Be aware that this campground is heavily used by rock climbers. A short hike up from the campground gets you to the base of imposing Lovers Leap, and here you can be entertained by climbers impressively practicing their trade.

Jeffrey P. Schaffer provides background on his path to guidebook writing, detailed mapmaking, and challenging received views of Sierra geological formation, besides a list of his titles from Wilderness Press, in "Author Bio & Bib" on page 492.

Glen Alpine to Half Moon Lake

54

Glen Alpine to Half Moon Lake

—Kathy Morey

Route	Days	Elev. Gain/Loss	Difficulty	Miles
↲	2	1480'/1480'	*	10

Campsites: Half Moon Lake: 5 miles
(see the Trip Description for others)

Map: USGS 7.5-min *Emerald Bay, Echo Lake, Rockbound Valley*

Best season: Summer through early fall

Take this trip!

This trip goes into southern Desolation Wilderness, everyone's favorite wilderness in the Northern Sierra. Enormously popular and accessible as Desolation Wilderness is—right on Lake Tahoe's western edge—it's nevertheless possible to find quieter nooks like Half Moon Lake. And from there you have access to some wonderful dayhikes, including bagging Mt. Tallac, a spectacular 9735-foot viewpoint over the incomparable Tahoe region. Take at least one layover day here to enjoy this beautiful area.

Trailhead

On Lake Tahoe's western shore, take State Route 89 to Fallen Leaf Road; take it south past the turnoff right to private Stanford High Sierra Camp. Fallen Leaf Road's condition gets worse by the yard as it climbs past attractive Glen Alpine Falls to the Glen Alpine trailhead beside Lily Lake (1.9 miles from the junction with 89). There are toilets here.

TRIP DESCRIPTION

Heads Up! Know Desolation Wilderness regulations!

The trailhead, which may be unsigned, is just beyond the restrooms at a locked gate across a very rocky old road. You head generally west on that road, where the first leg is a public right-of-way through private land; please stay on the road. With side roads dodging in and out, you stay on the main road by taking the right fork if the junction is unsigned and by following signs when present. At a little over one-third mile you reach a viewpoint for a very handsome cascade on Glen Alpine Creek. You'll find that the road alternately rises or is level, is sunstruck or shady, as it continues generally west past cabins, ponds, meadows, forest stands, and patches of wildflowers. Nearing 1 mile you reach the road's end and pick up the trail to Susie, Gilmore, and Grass lakes, on which you wind gradually up rocky knolls. You dip into forest, pass the boundary of Desolation Wilderness, and reach a junction at a little over 1.3 miles: left (southwest) to Grass Lake, right (north) to Dicks Pass and Gilmore, Half Moon, and Susie lakes. Government maps incorrectly show the true wilderness boundary a little beyond, not before this junction.

You go right, winding now through forest, now over granite slabs, now up and around rocky outcrops, beneath a row of rust, gray, and brown peaks to the south and with an unmapped creek often nearby for company. At a little over 2.5 miles, you ford the creek in forest, then ford two seasonal trickles in the next half mile, as you work your way up a lightly forested gully. Continuing, the trail is at first exposed, traversing over rusty rock above the cheery creek; then it enters a lodgepole-red fir forest, fords another creek, and shortly reaches a junction at 3.3 miles: left (west) for Susie Lake and Lake Aloha, right (west-north-west) for Gilmore and Half Moon lakes and Dicks Pass.

Go right on a rocky-dusty trail through open forest, ascending as you pass a talus slope on your right. Reddish Dicks Peak looms ahead. Soon, the gully to your left sprouts a lily-pad-dotted pond, while the Sierra crest appears in the distance on your left. Near 3.7 miles you meet the Pacific Crest Trail: left (southwest) to Susie Lake, right (northeast) to Half Moon and Gilmore lakes. Go right, almost immediately reaching another signed junction. Here, it's left (north) to Half Moon Lake, right (north-northeast) to Gilmore Lake. The Pacific Crest Trail skirts Gilmore and Susie lakes but bypasses Half Moon Lake, which is one reason why Half Moon Lake is the most peaceful of these three.

Turn left for Half Moon Lake, soon veering west-northwest toward Jacks and Dicks peaks on chaparral slopes. The trail to Half Moon Lake may be faint at times. You climb gradually, and from a rubbly shoulder have a good view of dramatic Cracked Crag. Now you descend into a damp forest of mountain hemlock, red fir, and lodgepole, meeting a tiny, unmapped creek that feeds pocket meadows and little tarns. You continue this ridge-and-forest pattern, gradually gaining elevation. At almost 4.5 miles you pass a large tarn on your left; it's one of Half Moon's outlying ponds, and, if you're so inclined, you can start looking for a campsite now. The trail, sometimes very faint, threads among pretty ponds to emerge on a grassy slope above long, narrow, almost crescent-shaped Half Moon Lake, which extends deep into a wonderfully rugged cirque bounded by Dicks and Jacks peaks. In season, inlets bounding down this cirque form showy cascades. Half Moon Lake has a companion on its southwest, Alta Morris Lake, which completes the "crescent." You'll think, *Just rambling around this cirque to visit all its ponds and lakes will be fun!*

As for other dayhikes, you can retrace your steps to previous junctions and visit Susie Lake or Gilmore Lake. In particular, if you want to bag Mt. Tallac, you'll need to backtrack to the junction with the Pacific Crest Trail and turn left toward Gilmore Lake. You switchback up a hot, open slope with occasional shade from big old junipers; your effort is rewarded with expansive views that include Susie Lake. Topping the ridge you've been climbing, you trade the views for a lodgepole forest, some pocket meadows and, soon, the cascading outlet of Gilmore Lake. At the next junction, where it's left (west) on the Pacific Crest Trail to Dicks Pass, right (north) to Gilmore Lake and Mt. Tallac, you go right to an apparent fork that signals the edge of Gilmore Lake, where there are picnic sites and campsites. Mt. Tallac's gentlest slopes rise across Gilmore's outlet, above its southeast shore, so follow the trail across the outlet and head up steeply up to the summit. When it's time to pack up and go home, retrace your steps to the trailhead.

Variations

Do this trip as a dayhike.

Permits

This is a quota trailhead, and permits are required for overnight stays. Contact El Dorado National Forest Information Center: 3070 Camino Heights Drive, Camino, CA 95709, (530) 644-6048.

Build-up/Wind-down tips

The South Lake Tahoe area offers a myriad of lodging and camping choices, more than I can list here. Contact the Lake Tahoe Visitors Authority (Box 16299, 1156 Ski Run Blvd., South Lake Tahoe, CA 96151, (800) AT-TAHOE, FAX (916) 544-2386) and the South Lake Tahoe Chamber of Commerce (13066 Lake Tahoe Blvd., South Lake Tahoe, CA 96150, (916) 541-5255). Not to mention the stores, restaurants, and casinos just over the Nevada border, where you can throw your money away!

To find out how Kathy Morey got started hiking the Sierra and the Hawaiian islands and writing about her hikes for Wilderness Press, and for a list of her titles, see "Author Bio & Bib" on page 492.

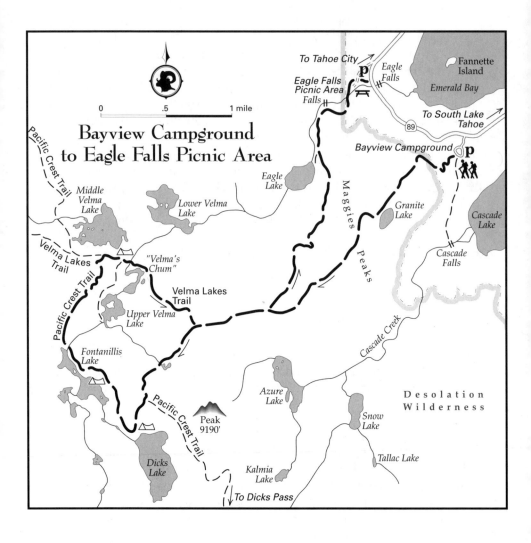

Bayview Campground
to Eagle Falls Picnic Area

To Tahoe City

Eagle Falls Picnic Area
Falls

Eagle Falls

Fannette Island

Emerald Bay

To South Lake Tahoe

89

Bayview Campground

Cascade Lake

Cascade Falls

Cascade Creek

Eagle Lake

Middle Velma Lake

Lower Velma Lake

Granite Lake

Maggies Peaks

Pacific Crest Trail

Velma Lakes Trail

"Velma's Chum"

Velma Lakes Trail

Upper Velma Lake

Pacific Crest Trail

Fontanillis Lake

Azure Lake

Snow Lake

Desolation Wilderness

Tallac Lake

Peak 9190'

Pacific Crest Trail

Dicks Lake

Kalmia Lake

To Dicks Pass

0   .5   1 mile

55

Bayview Campground to Eagle Falls Picnic Area

—Kathy Morey

Route	Days	Elev. Gain/Loss	Difficulty	Miles
↱	2	2140'/2440'	**	11.4

Campsites: Dicks Lake: 5 miles
Fontanillis Lake (southeast end): 5.3 miles
Middle Velma Lake: 6.8 miles
"Velma's Chum" (outlet): 7 miles
(see the Trip Description for others)

Map: USGS 7.5-min *Emerald Bay, Rockbound Valley*

Best season: Summer through early fall

Take this trip!

Much of the Northern Sierra lacks the polished-granite glory of the Southern Sierra. Here in the north the peaks are lower, the vegetation generally denser, the views consequently fewer and shorter, and much of the terrain has been altered by volcanism. However, *this* little trip recaptures the Southern Sierra's splendor in a granite basin of Desolation Wilderness. And it is a basin chock-full of lakes and ponds, offering far-ranging views over lovely Lake Tahoe and its beautiful satellites, Emerald Bay, Cascade Lake, and Fallen Leaf Lake. A layover day at one of the lakes mentioned for campsites would let you explore along the Pacific Crest or Velma Lakes trails, or just ramble through this basin as the fancy strikes you.

Because the Southern Sierra is my idea of what paradise should look like, I remember my first visit to this area well. I'd been working on *Hot Showers, Soft Beds, and Dayhikes in the Sierra* in the Northern Sierra for some time and, lovely though it is, was starting to long for the great, lake-filled spaces and sharp granite peaks far to the south. As I suddenly came upon this lightly wooded, lake-rich, granitic countryside, my heart leapt at the sight, and I felt as if I were truly in the High Sierra once more!

Trailheads

These two trailheads are just a mile apart off State Route 89 along Lake Tahoe's southwest shore, on the scenic stretch above the head of Emerald Bay. Bayview Campground, the put-in, is southeast of Eagle Falls Picnic Area, the take-out; so, if you're driving from South Lake Tahoe, you'll reach Bayview Campground's turnoff before Eagle Falls Picnic Area's. I strongly recommend you *not* close the loop along the road. It is far too narrow and heavily traveled by people too distracted by the great scenery, who are driving too fast—except when the traffic is bumper-to-bumper.

Put-in trailhead (Bayview Campground): From SR 89, turn south into the campground and drive through it to trailhead parking, about 0.2 mile depending on where you park (with toilets).

Take-out trailhead (Eagle Falls Picnic Area): From SR 89, turn west into the picnic area/parking lot and park here (with toilets).

TRIP DESCRIPTION

Heads Up! Know Desolation Wilderness regulations!

From the trailhead at the south end of Bayview Campground, walk about 45 feet south to a junction: left (south) to Cascade Falls (see below). You go right for Granite Lake, zigzagging steeply up a dusty duff trail through a monotonous, claustrophobic forest of spindly white firs. At half a mile you enter Desolation Wilderness near an intermittent stream and soon reach a rocky viewpoint. From here use trails lead to slightly different views, or you can scramble up on the surrounding boulders. Whatever you do, the views are simply magnificent, especially in early mornings before the midday haze settles in. You can look east across Emerald Bay to Lake Tahoe and the Carson Range; no highway view of Emerald Bay is nearly as spectacular as this one. And the next switchback up reveals another panorama, this one including the head of Emerald Bay and a bit of highway.

Cascade Falls Excursion

Some publications call Cascade Falls "White Cloud Falls" for the clouds of white mist it wreathes in season. At the junction some 45 feet from trailhead parking at Bayview, the left fork leads south through open forest and then across chaparral slopes to excellent viewpoints of Cascade Falls above mostly-private Cascade Lake. Then it slithers over granite slabs just above the falls on Cascade Creek at about 0.7 mile (depending on how far out on the slabs you go; watch your footing!). Return the way you came.

The grade eases as you follow the (unmapped) alder-lined channel that is Granite Lake's seasonally flowing outlet, through a mixed conifer forest with a flowery understory. Nearing the lake, you veer away from the outlet among bouldery chaparral. The trail soon levels out above pretty, lodgepole-shaded Granite Lake (1.5), nestled in the cleavage of Maggies Peaks, which, once upon an unenlightened time, were named more crudely not for Maggie herself but for her bosom—Maggie being a pretty young woman who worked at some long-gone Tahoe resort. This is a charming area, well worth a rest stop but too overused for camping.

To continue, resume climbing steeply as you leave Granite Lake. Don't be misled onto use trails, particularly a large one leading south from the first big switchback above Granite Lake. Your trail winds up the lightly wooded slope west of Granite Lake—the ridge between Maggies Peaks—on a series of rocky and sandy switchbacks. Views make the climb worth the trouble—increasingly excellent ones over the South Lake Tahoe area, eventually including Lake Tahoe, Emerald Bay, Granite Lake, Cascade Lake, and Fallen Leaf Lake. The forest becomes thicker and the grade eases near the top of the climb, with the most expansive views just before you round the ridgetop. You soon top out, and the other side offers fine views west over Desolation Wilderness toward the Velma Lakes. Stroll through moderate-to-open forest, descending gradually to moderately, rounding some prominent knobs, and ignoring a use trail that descends left to Azure Lake. Sometimes it seems as if you're headed toward Mt. Tallac, other times Peak 9190.

You reenter moderate forest and, at just over 3 miles, on a small, viewless saddle, meet the trail coming up from Eagle Lake at what we'll call the Bayview-Velma-Eagle junction: left (west-southwest) to the Velma Lakes and to Dicks Lake, right (northeast) to Eagle Lake. Go left and work your way up and down over a broad, sparsely-wooded saddle, from which you have rare glimpses of Azure Lake far below and even some over-the-shoulder views of Lake Tahoe.

At 3.7 miles you reach the Velma-Dicks junction: left (southwest) to Dicks Lake, right (west-northwest) to the Velma Lakes. Turn left to Dicks Lake and follow the sometimes-faint trail through a wonderful, sparsely forested granite basin. Keep a sharp eye out for the track on this hard-rock terrain, bearing in mind that you're heading generally south-southwest for prominent Dicks Peak. You pass several pretty tarns and then an unnamed lakelet whose multistranded outlet you presently ford at a low point on this leg; look for Spartan campsites in this area. You cross a seasonal stream and begin ascending, presently switchbacking moderately up the rocky slopes below Dicks Lake and enjoying over-the-shoulder views of the Velma Lakes sparkling far below. Don't worry:

Dicks Pass

you'll visit the Velma Lakes on your way to the take-out trailhead. Note that the trail section shown on the *Rockbound Valley* topo as connecting Upper Velma Lake with the trail below Dicks Lake no longer exists.

Near the top of this climb, you find a junction: left (southeast) for Dicks Pass, right (southwest) for Dicks and Fontanillis lakes. Go right for Dicks and Fontanillis lakes, pausing on the ridgetop at 8500 feet to take in a marvelous view over Desolation Wilderness, and then descend to another junction at just under 5 miles, this time with the Pacific Crest Trail: left (south) on a spur for Dicks Lake, right (northwest) for Fontanillis Lake. If lovely Dicks Lake is your choice for the night, toddle downhill a little to it (5). It's a great setting for a lake: cradled closely under Dicks Pass in half-wooded, half-talus slopes. Find a campsite here with a fine view of Dicks Peak and Dicks Pass.

And if you're game to camp at Fontanillis Lake, which I think is the most alpine of all the lakes you'll see on this trip, continue past Dicks Lake and over a little ridge before descending gradually past a pond to the southeast end of long, slender Fontanillis Lake (5.3), set in a nook carved out of the ridge that extends north from Dicks Peak. Look for the few campsites above the trail on the rocky slopes of the lake's east shore, or near the ponds at its southeast end. The Pacific Crest Trail traces Fontanillis's east shore for 0.6 mile, fording its outlet, from which there is a fine view east toward Lake Tahoe.

Leaving Fontanillis, the trail descends gradually northward, then curves northeast through dry forest down the ridge west of Upper Velma Lake to a junction—shown incorrectly or not at all on most maps—with the Velma Lakes Trail near the southeast corner of Middle Velma Lake (6.8). This popular lake, ringed by granite slabs, sits about 50 feet below the trail here, so if you'd like to visit it, carefully pick your way down to the lake's edge, where the camping, sunbathing, and swimming are good. Because this appealing lake is situated so close to the junction of two major trails, it's very heavily used on weekends; you may want to seek a quieter campsite elsewhere.

Leave the Pacific Crest Trail for the Velma Lakes Trail by turning right (east); in barely 0.1 mile there's a junction with a spur trail to Upper Velma Lake. If you want to camp at this lovely lake, turn right (southwest) and follow the trail about 0.3 mile through a damp, flowery forest and over granite slabs to its shore; the spur trail continues around the lake's west side. Fontanillis Lake's outlet spills into Upper Velma Lake, cascading beautifully down the slopes to the south-southwest.

Back on the Velma Lakes Trail, you continue east to ford the broad stream draining as an outlet from an unnamed Velma Lake down to Lower Velma Lake, which is off-trail below (northeast). In *The Tahoe Sierra*, Jeff Schaffer suggests cross-countrying northwest along the stream to less-used camping along Lower Velma Lake. The unnamed Velma Lake, which I call "Velma's Chum" (7), is the prettiest of the Velma Lakes to me. If you haven't already chosen a campsite for the night, look for one back from the shoreline here.

But this trip keeps going southeast on the Velma Lakes Trail, leaving the Velma Lakes behind as it climbs past some little ponds and soon arrives at the Velma-Dicks junction where, earlier, you turned toward Dicks Lake and away from the Velma Lakes. Turn left (east-northeast) here, leaving the Velma Lakes Trail, to retrace the trail section between this junction and the Bayview-Velma-Eagle junction. At the Bayview-Velma-Eagle junction you turn left (northeast) toward Eagle Lake.

You pass a bouldery knoll and cross a long, granite slab on which the trail seems to vanish—but just go northeast down to the slab's far edge where you pick up the trail again. You descend alongside a small, unmapped stream, presently crossing it, before climbing a little as you make a rolling, sandy traverse on the west side of the Maggies Peaks ridge between Eagle and Granite lakes. There are views from here of a lily-pad-dotted lakelet deep down in a boggy pocket to the north, but you'd need wings to reach it.

Finally you swing around the nose of the ridge and leave the splendid granite basin that holds the high lakes you've been visiting. The trail begins switchbacking down, now sandy and rocky over slabs, now duff through patches of forest. More switchbacks take you moderately to steeply down a shady slope, along which you cross another unmapped stream. Where the forest gives way to chaparral, you begin to have good views over Eagle Lake. Continue a descent that's moderate at first, then very steep at the end where it approaches a junction with the spur trail to Eagle Lake: sharply left (south) to cliff-bound

Eagle Lake's east shore, which makes a fine rest stop but whose campsites are unattractive and way overused; ahead (right, north) along the rushing creek that is Eagle's outlet to the take-out trailhead. Very soon you cross an area of juniper-dotted granite slabs with excellent views over Lake Tahoe and Emerald Bay—a shutterbug's delight.

The rocky and sandy trail gets steep again, easing briefly as you cross a footbridge overlooking a charming waterfall. The officially named Eagle Falls is below the highway, but to many visitors, *this* gem of a cascade is "Eagle Falls." After snapping a photo or two, you descend moderately to steeply on stone steps past junipers till the trail nearly levels out as a broad, sandy pathway through chaparral and under mixed conifer cover, curving east to end at a picnic area just off State Route 89. Your shuttle car or ride should be waiting for you here. Now, wasn't that a great little trip!

Variations
Reverse the direction of this trip. Or do it as a long dayhike.

Fontanillis Lake

Permits

This is a quota trailhead, and permits are required for overnight stays. Contact El Dorado National Forest Information Center: 3070 Camino Heights Drive, Camino, CA 95709, (530) 644-6048.

Build-up/Wind-down tips

See trip 54, "Glen Alpine to Half Moon Lake."

To find out how Kathy Morey got started hiking the Sierra and the Hawaiian islands and writing about her hikes for Wilderness Press, and for a list of her titles, see "Author Bio & Bib" on page 492.

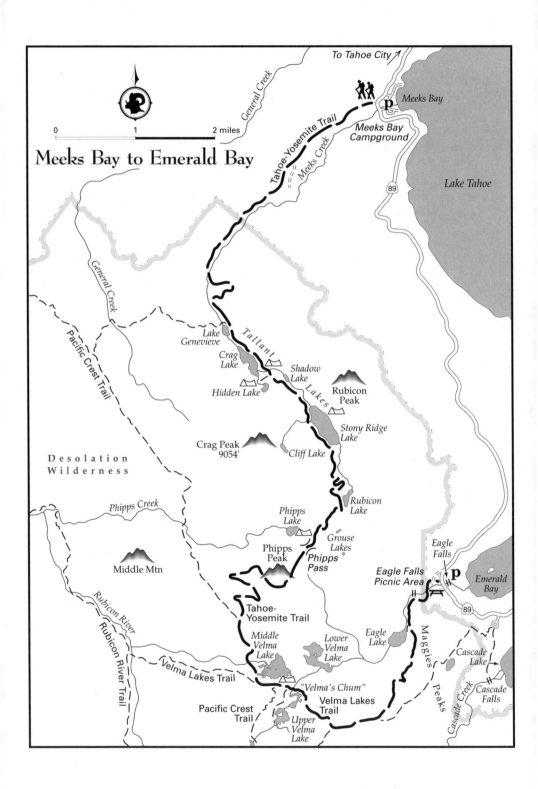

Meeks Bay to Emerald Bay

To Tahoe City ↗

Meeks Bay

Meeks Bay
Campground

Lake Tahoe

General Creek

Tahoe-Yosemite Trail

Meeks Creek

89

0   1   2 miles

General Creek

Pacific Crest Trail

Desolation
Wilderness

Lake
Genevieve

Crag
Lake

Shadow
Lake

Hidden Lake

Rubicon
Peak

Tallant Lakes

Stony Ridge
Lake

Crag Peak
9054'

Cliff Lake

Rubicon
Lake

Phipps Creek

Phipps
Lake

Grouse
Lakes

Eagle
Falls

Middle Mtn

Phipps
Peak

Phipps
Pass

Eagle Falls
Picnic Area

Emerald
Bay

89

Rubicon River

Rubicon River Trail

Tahoe-
Yosemite Trail

Middle
Velma
Lake

Lower
Velma
Lake

Eagle
Lake

Cascade
Lake

Maggies Peaks

Velma Lakes Trail

"Velma's Chum"

Velma Lakes
Trail

Cascade Creek

Cascade
Falls

Pacific Crest
Trail

Upper
Velma
Lake

56

Meeks Bay to Emerald Bay

—Jeffrey P. Schaffer

Route	Days	Elev. Gain/Loss	Elev. Low/High	Difficulty	Miles
↲	2	3690'/3350'	6240'/8880'	**	17.8
					(mileage without side hikes)

Campsites: Crag Lake: 4.9 miles
Hidden Lake: 5.7 miles
Middle Velma Lake: 13.4 miles
(see the Trip Description for others)

Map: USGS 7.5-min *Emerald Bay, Homewood, Rockbound Valley*

Best season: Late July through mid-September

Take this trip!

This relatively easy backpack route is along the subdued, northernmost part of the 186-mile Tahoe-Yosemite Trail (from Meeks Bay south to Tuolumne Meadows), and it rewards you, starting 4½ miles in, with one lake right after another. You exit down to Highway 89 at Emerald Bay, 7¾ miles south of your trailhead, but unlike virtually any other Sierran point-to-point hike, you don't need to make a car shuttle. During the summer season, take the Highway 89 bus! Summertime bus schedules seem to change yearly, so phone in advance, (530) 542-6077.

Trailheads

From where Highway 50 leaves Highway 89 in South Lake Tahoe, drive 3¼ miles northwest on Highway 89 to the Lake Tahoe Visitor Center. Get your Wilderness Permit here, if you haven't gotten it already, and also ask about the bus schedule between your starting and ending points, respectively, Meeks Bay and Emerald Bay. Continue 5½ miles on Highway 89 to the moderately large but often overflowing parking lot of Eagle Falls Picnic Area, at the head of Emerald Bay. This is where you'll end your hike. Parking here is $3 per day, an incentive to park by the starting trailhead. To reach it, continue 7¾ miles to a closed road just 230 yards past the Meeks Bay Campground entrance. If you're driving from Tahoe City, follow Highway 89 south 2¼ miles to the William Kent Visitor Center, get your Wilderness Permit, if you haven't gotten it already, and then continue 8¾ miles to the trailhead, just 250 yards past Meeks Bay Resort. Park where you can find space anywhere along the highway.

TRIP DESCRIPTION

Heads Up! Like many Sierran routes, this one has its annoyances with permits, quotas, early season snow, mosquitoes, and perhaps even bears. The only serious problem, as I see it, is a small, but long-lasting snowfield just north of Phipps Pass. It is icy enough and steep enough to be hazardous. Should you slip, you could be seriously hurt when you hit the rocks at its base. Therefore, I suggest you hike no sooner than late July; early August would be better. And while weather usually holds well into October, I cut the recommended time to mid-September. Why? Because around then the Highway 89 bus service between your starting and ending trailheads stops.

The Tahoe-Yosemite Trail starts west along a gated road and takes one on a nearly level arc southwest through a forest of white fir, incense-cedar, and lodgepole, ponderosa, and sugar pines. After 1⅓ miles the flat road nears a grassy swamp, on the left, and here a trail branches right. On the trail you climb moderately for 0.4 mile, then continue up a mostly gentler gradient to Meeks Creek, lush with creekside flowers and shrubs. Ahead, your ascent is almost negligible, which helps to make this such a fine backpack trip. As you progress southwest, you enter Desolation Wilderness, and parallel the usually unseen creek along a large, mostly forested flat. You pass three meadows—one quite swampy—and beyond the last one parallel Meeks Creek up a moderate ascent to reach a second forested flat. Up here, red fir, Jeffrey pine, and western white pine have replaced their lower-elevation look-alikes: white fir, ponderosa pine, and sugar pine. Incense-cedar was the first to drop out, but a somewhat similar tree, the juniper, will be seen on exposed rocky benches above. Lodgepole pine, which adapts to several vegetational, climatic, and soil zones, remains with us.

Next you climb briefly but steeply south to a bridge across Meeks Creek, this locality having possible camping. Ahead, you climb moderately up a path that arcs east into a shady, moist, forested cove, then, winding southwest up the cove's south slope, soon arrive at a much drier, more open ridge. This is a good resting spot from which you can just barely see Lake Tahoe. Now you climb southeast for a short, pleasant stretch beside cascading Meeks Creek as you hike up to the northeast corner of shallow, relatively warm Lake Genevieve (4.6), at

7420 feet the lowest of the Tallant Lakes. Along the lake's north shore an old, lightly used trail strikes northwest, rambling 2 miles over to General Creek. There are campsites around Lake Genevieve, some even with a good view of dominating 9054-foot Crag Peak, but since most of them are within 100 feet of the lake, you should continue up-canyon and quickly reach larger Crag Lake (4.9). I find this the most appealing of the Tallant Lakes, in part because Crag Peak is a dramatic backdrop, in part because the lake has several good campsites, but mostly because from near where your southbound trail leaves the lake by a good campsite, you can swim out to a small island, rest and warm up, then continue to a protruding bedrock mass on the east shore. That mass provides ample sites for diving into the lake and lots of space for sunbathing.

Climbing up-canyon, you soon boulderhop Meeks Creek, and then encounter a spur trail on a ridge just beyond it. This descends about 200 yards to Hidden Lake (5.7), nestled near the foot of now towering Crag Peak. Should you want to camp here, look for sites among granitic slabs along its southeast shore or on rumpled lands between this lake and Crag Lake.

From the Hidden Lake trail junction, you climb up the ridge and then curve east to another ridge, both with glacial deposits. Behind the second lies shallow Shadow Lake (5.9) and an adjacent boggy meadow with a former forest of lodgepoles, now ashen snags. Leaving this swampy, mosquito-prone environment behind, ascend a moderately graded stretch that momentarily becomes steeper as it climbs alongside rapids and cascades of Meeks Creek. Above this stretch you reach Stony Ridge Lake (6.3), largest of the Tallant Lakes. Here, at 7840 feet, cross its low dam and look for campsites above its north and northeast shores. For many overnighters, this will be as far as they want to go, since to reach the next relatively warm lakes you'll have to climb just over 1000 feet, only to descend a similar amount to the Velma Lakes.

At the lake's southwest corner you cross and immediately recross upper Meeks Creek, proceed south along the west edge of a boggy meadow, and then, near an impressive, low-angle granitic cliff, start up a series of well-graded switchbacks, bounded by two tributaries. After almost reaching a steep, churning cascade, you turn onto the last switchback, climb southwest, and get hemlock-framed views below of Stony Ridge Lake and its meadow. You soon curve south into a willowy cove, bordered by steep cliffs, then make a short climb southeast to Rubicon Lake (8.1). Dammed by a ridge of resistant bedrock, this lovely lake is the highest of the Tallant Lakes. Because they form a line of beads along the creek that connects them, they are called "paternoster" lakes, after their resemblance to beads on a rosary. At 8340 feet, the lake has nippy water, reaching at best into the low 60s, but a tempting rock just off the shore beckons one to jump or dive in. After you quickly climb out, you can then watch trout swimming lazily below as you bask atop this rock.

The lake is about the halfway point in your climb from Stony Ridge Lake to Phipps Pass. Just above the lake's south end you reach a forested ridge from where you could drop south, perhaps on a faint trail, to the northern Grouse Lake. Brushy shored and snag-bound, it is not an attractive destination. Your TYT switchbacks up westside slopes to climb up to and immediately west of a granitic outlier. Just beyond it you can see how joints really control its angular shape. Next you quickly encounter a small gully, snowbound as late as early August. This is the only snow problem you're likely to encounter after early July. When it's iced over, you have to cautiously kick-step your way up across it.

Just beyond the gully is another switchback. This spot is the first opportunity, of many ahead, from where you can get a good view to the southeast, to the north end of Fallen Leaf Lake, above which stands 10,881-foot Freel Peak, the highest peak along the rim of the Lake Tahoe basin.

Feathered Dino Digression

It was about here, while taking a break, that I was observing a junco on a cool July day in the abnormally cool summer of 1999. Why wasn't it freezing to death? The answer, of course, is that birds have amazing body-heat retention thanks to their down feathers. I started thinking about dinosaurs. Paleontologists had known for a few years that dinos thrived in Alaska. Whereas the climate back then was warmer and milder than today's, they still had to survive a long, dark winter. How could cold-blooded animals do this? The answer was that they migrated south, like birds (but on foot), thousands of miles to sunnier climes. Conceivably adults could do this, but young juveniles could not. Because the general view is that birds arose from dinosaurs, I thought maybe the Alaskan dinos were feathered and so could survive the winters. Interestingly, two months later, an article appeared in Science, *proclaiming that five fossil specimens of Chinese dinosaurs had feathers. Right or wrong, I feel that wilderness gives me inspiration.*

Ascents also give me perspiration, and your ascent takes you a switchback leg higher up the joint-controlled rocks. Then the TYT climbs moderately southward for ¼ mile and crosses a gully just before skirting above Phipps Pass (9.1), the shallow saddle on your left. Just beyond the pass the trail almost tops a crest on your right, and from it you could drop 320 feet in elevation down a steep slope to isolated camping near cold, circular Phipps Lake.

The route ahead, except for a few trivial gains to your route's high point, is all downhill. The TYT traverses granitic slabs and boulders along the southeast slope of Phipps Peak, then swings around to the peak's open south slope, from which you'll see the Velma Lakes in the gray, granitic basin below, and the rusty, metamorphic summit of Dicks Peak towering above. Onward, you curve northwest, reenter an open forest of mountain hemlocks, and lodgepole, western white, and whitebark pines, and then come to within 50 yards of a shallow saddle on a ridge. Walk out on it for views of Rubicon River lands. On the north-northwest skyline is pointed, volcanic Tinker Knob, situated about 5½ miles south-southeast of Highway 40's infamous Donner Pass.

The Pacific Crest Trail traverses crest lands on the west rim of the Lake Tahoe basin, and it skirts past Tinker Knob before finally dropping to the pass. This tri-state trail is our next goal, and from the shallow saddle we start a descent. Long switchbacks across south-facing slopes make the 660-foot drop a well-graded one, and after 1⅔ miles we arrive at a junction with the Pacific Crest Trail (12.0). At the junction you're only about a mile from and 200 feet above Middle Velma Lake, so head down to this swimmer's paradise. Your TYT/PCT makes a moderate, generally viewless, descent to the lake's outlet creek, which all too often gets hikers' feet wet. The acres of soggy soil found in this forested flat prove to be a fantastic breeding ground for mosquitoes, so before August you won't want to loiter.

The PCT then climbs ⅓ mile southeast to a junction with the Velma Lakes Trail (13.1). West, this trail descends west 2.25 miles to Camper Flat, on the spacious floor of Rockbound Valley. East, this trail, which also serves as the PCT and TYT, traverses 0.3 mile to a junction above the south shore of Middle Velma Lake (13.4). Just 70 yards before this junction, you have a good view of the lake and may want to descend to popular campsites near its shore, which is located about 50 feet lower than your trail.

From the junction, you join those on the last part of the "Bayview Campground to Eagle Falls Picnic Area" hike and head out to Highway 89. In brief, this quickly crosses a stream, then in 1 mile first skirts past an unnamed Velma Lake before climbing about 250 feet to a junction with a trail bound for Dicks Lake. Next you make a traverse 0.6 mile east to a second junction, branch left, and descend 2.5 miles to the Eagle Falls trailhead.

Permits

See the relevant information in trip 53, "Twin Bridges to the Desolation Valley Basin."

Build-up/Wind-down tips

On summer weekends, certain Tahoe Basin campgrounds, especially Fallen Leaf, are likely to be full. You'll have better luck at Meeks Bay Campground, close to the trailhead, or William Kent Campground, behind the visitor center, or at General Creek Campground, in Sugar Pine Point State Park, 7 miles south of the visitor center and 1.75 miles before the Meeks Bay trailhead. It's amazing how empty even Fallen Leaf Campground becomes by Sunday at noon, a good reason to visit the Lake Tahoe area during the week.

Jeffrey P. Schaffer provides background on his path to guidebook writing, detailed mapmaking, and challenging received views of Sierra geological formation, besides a list of his titles from Wilderness Press, in "Author Bio & Bib" on page 492.

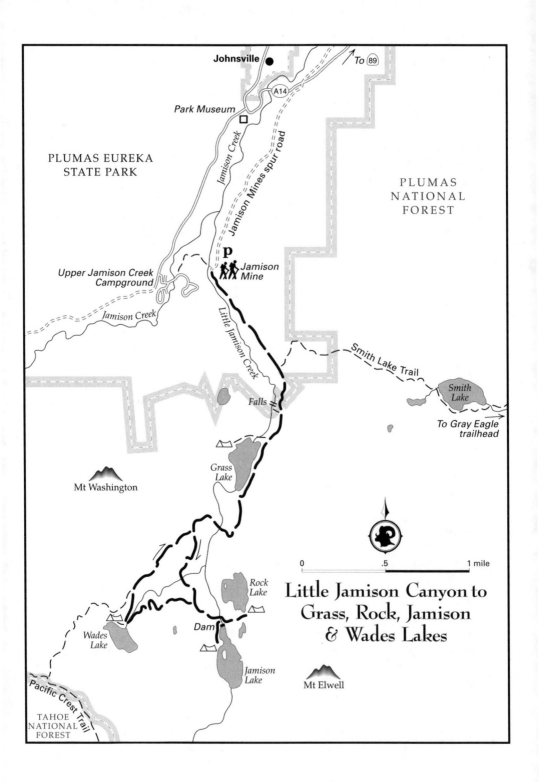

Little Jamison Canyon to Grass, Rock, Jamison & Wades Lakes

57

Little Jamison Canyon to Grass, Rock, Jamison & Wades Lakes

—Jeffrey P. Schaffer

Route	Days	Elev. Gain/Loss	Elev. Low/High	Difficulty	Miles
♀	2	**2090´/2090**	**5260´/6550´**	*	**7.5**

Campsites: Grass Lake (northeast corner): 1.3 miles
Wades Lake via older trail: 3.0 miles
Jamison Lake: 3.1 miles
Rock Lake: 3.2 miles
Wades Lake via newer trail: 3.5 miles
(see the Trip Description for others)

Map: USGS 7.5-min: *Gold Lake*

Best season: Mid-July through mid-September

Take this trip!

This hike is one of the few nice ones in the Sierra Nevada that does not require a Wilderness Permit—a taste of what Sierran hiking was like in the "good old days." At 7½ miles in length, it's short enough to dayhike and, indeed, many people do. However, each of four lakes visited is a worthy overnight goal.

Trailhead

From the north part of Graeagle, a small eastside Sierran settlement on Highway 89 just south of the Highways 70/89 junction in Blairsden, branch onto County Road A14, heading west. Drive 4⅔ miles up it to the Jamison Mines spur road, in Plumas-Eureka State Park, and veer left on it only ¼ mile before A14 bridges Jamison Creek. On the spur road, drive 1⅓ miles up to a large trailhead parking lot among the Jamison ruins. From the lot a connecting trail heads first west then south, going ⅓ mile over to the Upper Jamison Creek Campground, which is a fine place to stay before or after your hike. To reach it from where A14 bridges Jamison Creek, drive ¼ mile up to a fork and turn left. You immediately pass the park's museum, and just over a mile south past it reach the campground's entrance.

TRIP DESCRIPTION

> **Heads Up!** Avoid weekends. On a typical summer Sunday morning, Wades Lake, which has the most spacious camping area, may have two dozen campers (sometimes twice this). By noon, the lake's sites are generally empty. The lesson is clear: for relatively isolated backpacking, avoid Friday and Saturday nights.

This hike is rated "easy," because of the short distances to its lakes, but this rating is marginally so, since the hike has a noticeable elevation gain. Your route begins among the ruins of buildings that were the site of a bustle of activity in the late 1800s. From quartz veins in the nearby Jamison mine complex, over $1½ million worth of gold was extracted. You head south up-canyon on an old mining road, which becomes a trail just beyond the last building. Scattered Douglas-firs and other conifers offer some shade, while brushy spots offer views. Your southbound trail generally is moderate, but locally steep, and it has a lot of loose cobbles and boulders—left by the last glacier—so you have to watch your step when you descend. After paralleling Little Jamison Creek, about 100 feet below, the trail eases up and curves left to a small flat that has a junction with the eastbound Smith Lake Trail (0.8). Lying only about 2 miles from our trailhead, this lake is a popular destination, but it is also reached in half that distance and with about one third the climbing effort from the Gray Eagle trailhead, near Gray Eagle Lodge, which is just off the Gold Lake Road.

Continuing southward and upward, you go but ¼ mile to a short spur trail, which you can take a few paces right to a view of 60-foot-high Jamison Falls. From the spur trail you have a short, easy climb, mostly through lush vegetation, to a small canal, which served operations down at the Jamison Mine. In this vicinity you leave State Park lands behind for the Forest Service's Lakes Basin Recreation Area, and soon you arrive at the northeast corner of Grass Lake (1.3), and have a sweeping view of the upper part of the drainage basin, one often mirrored in morning, when the lake's surface is placid. There is no suitable camping along the lake's east shore, which our trail traverses, but two fine, ample ones lie along its west shore. You reach these by taking an obvious trail that first heads along the north shore to the lake's outlet and soon turns southwest. By its name, Grass Lake sounds grass-choked and shallow, but most of the shoreline is not grassy, and the lake certainly is deep enough for fishing and

Wades Lake in Little Jamison Canyon

swimming. Being the lowest lake of the four on this trip, it is also the warmest one for swimming.

Our trail south up Little Jamison Canyon passes by the shallow southern end of Grass Lake, which has aquatic vegetation that attracts ducks, especially those migrating south on the Pacific flyway. Beyond the lake's south end you climb momentarily to a bench, then continue south toward an obvious headwall, which supports hidden Rock Lake above it. Rather than tackle the headwall, your trail veers west, crosses two (or sometimes more) branches of Little Jamison Creek (a possible ford before mid-July), then climbs briefly west to a junction with the Rock & Jamison Lakes Trail.

Here, a mere 2.2 miles into our hike, most backpackers continue 0.8 mile farther, up an old trail, initially steep for 0.3 mile, to Wades Lake, which has a very spacious camping area. I prefer to avoid the crowds (if hiking on a weekend) and branch left on the Rock & Jamison Lakes Trail. On it you soon encounter several short switchbacks, and hereabouts have a good view downcanyon. You then reenter forest to cross the refreshing outlet creek from Wades Lake, about 0.4 mile up your trail. A small campsite with a view lies just past its crossing, but better sites are at the lakes. Onward, you traverse about 200 yards southeast to a low outcrop of granitelike metarhyolite, which is an attractive bouldering area for climbers. However, better climbing exists just west of Jamison Lake. About another 200 yards south past the outcrop you encounter a junction with the newer trail to Wades Lake, branching right. This we'll take later, but since Jamison Lake is a mere ¼ mile away and Rock Lake not much farther, we'll visit them first.

Through open forest you arc southeast briefly up to a low, open, bedrock ridge, from which you drop momentarily to a junction. From here a trail, beside Jamison Lake's outlet creek, goes a few paces south to the lake's dam. This is not the trail you want. Rather, look for a sometimes-cryptic one immediately branching right, back up to the bedrock ridge. Once on this ridge, adjacent Jamison Lake is apparent, and you take a use trail to its end, where a resistant mass of bedrock juts eastward into the lake (3.1). Just a hop, skip, and a jump (and a few strokes) offshore from it is a vegetated bedrock island, protruding high above the water, not leveled by glacial erosion. Also protruding from the water is the lake's only detraction, a few standing stumps of dead trees flooded when the check dam was constructed many years ago. In the north half of the lake are a couple islets, worth swimming to, basking on, then swimming back from on a hot summer's afternoon. At Jamison Lake, camping is limited. There are several sites, all small. The advantage is that if you have one, you'll not have neighbors.

You may find similar sites above the lake's northeast shore. To reach it, backtrack to the main trail, immediately cross the lake's outlet creek, then wind briefly eastward, topping a low ridge. Among bedrock and brush you can head south in pursuit of a campsite. Most stay on the trail and descend momentarily to encounter a short trail down to the south shore of nearby Rock Lake (3.2). An equally well-used trail continues briefly east to a shallow saddle, from which you can head a stone's throw south to a shallow lakelet (not worth it for most folks), or head briefly north to the southeast corner of Rock Lake. Both the south and southeast sites have ample space for a camp, especially the latter, and both get heavy use. Between them is a protruding ridge, accessible from both sites, which is great to fish or dive from. Those who like high-diving might be tempted by the much higher ridge rising high above the lake's southwest shore. The easiest and safest way to reach its summit is to go back to the first low ridge you topped and take a use trail north. From there you'll have a great view, not only of the lake but also of surrounding lands. Furthermore, you'll see that the use trail rollercoasters onward, offering opportunities for isolated camping, fishing, and swimming. You can walk all the way to the north shore, passing a glacier-defying, protruding island, barely offshore, which rises at least 20 feet above the surface of this deep, seemingly bottomless lake. Around it, bedrock reigns, and trees are scarce. While some might miss forest cover, I welcome this openness, since, as at Jamison, you can have sites with views. Furthermore, the lake is about as mosquito-free as a Sierran lake can be—thanks to lack of necessary mosquito ponds and vegetation—so if you are hiking in July, especially early July when mosquitoes are prevalent, this lake is your best bet.

Our hike continues by backtracking down to the aforementioned junction with the newer trail to Wades Lake. This 0.7-mile route was thoughtfully laid out, providing you with many views west, north, and east. In the first ¼ mile, which can be vague in a spot or two, you climb to an improbable gap on a broad ridge. (The route is easier than one first imagines.) Here you have arguably the best views on the entire circuit—a good excuse to take a rest after 200 feet of vertical ascent. Ahead, the route is easier, traversing west in and out of several gullies, winding briefly south and up, then heading momentarily west to attain a crest that you ascend, paralleling Wades Lake's outlet creek, some 200 yards. You then drop to the outlet creek, reach a large campsite above its opposite bank, and walk a few paces south to very popular Wades Lake (3.5). The prime camping area lies west of the lake's outlet, and it can hold dozens of backpackers, equestrians, and horses (packers use the lake). Therefore, I suggest you first spend a night in the Jamison-Rock environs, have a leisurely morning there, then reach Wades at noon (the later the better) and have lunch there, perhaps after a swim. From the lake's outlet you'll see some tempting diving and basking bedrock slabs at the foot of steep, dramatic slopes, on the opposite side of the lake. These slabs appear to be very difficult to reach, due to incredibly dense growth of shrubs. However, you can get fairly close to them by crossing the outlet creek and taking a use trail over to the lake's southeast corner. From there, bite the bullet and make a direct swim of about 150 yards over to them. From mid-July through mid-August, when the water's adequately warm, this exercise is a real treat.

After your visit, take the old route back toward the trailhead for new views, for variety, and for a shorter walking distance (by about ½ mile). You begin with a 0.2-mile traverse over to a main trail, which ascends your canyon to the Pacific Crest Trail, a three-state route that traverses the rim above Wades Lake. Descend the main trail—the older Wades Lake Trail—first generally moderately and with some shade, then the steep, rubbly lower part. This is shadeless, so you have views, but only while stationary, since you have to watch your footing. After 0.3 mile of cautious descent you reach a junction with the trail to Jamison and Rock lakes, and backtrack 2.2 miles to your trailhead.

Permits

None.

Build-up/Wind-down tips

Graeagle, a speck on the map through the 1960s, became by the 1990s a tourists' mecca, thanks to the construction of a golf course and a considerable number of second homes for summer recreation and winter skiing. It has a number of stores and eating establishments, so if after your hike you don't mind mingling with tourists, you can get quite a fine meal. This also applies to Truckee, another tourist town, if you're heading south on Highway 89. For those taking the very winding Highway 49 route westward back to civilization, try either Sierra City or Downieville, which have retained their mining-town charm. Finally, if you have taken this route, you might look for warm swimming holes below Downieville, along the North Yuba River. Some of the best—and your last opportunity—are found where Highway 49 bridges the South Yuba River. However, on hot summer-weekend afternoons, this vicinity will be packed; just finding a parking spot can be a problem.

Jeffrey P. Schaffer provides background on his path to guidebook writing, detailed mapmaking, and challenging received views of Sierra geological formation, besides a list of his titles from Wilderness Press, in "Author Bio & Bib" on page 492.

The Cascade Range

From about the North Fork Feather River Canyon, California's section of the volcanic Cascade Range extends about 130 miles through northern California to the Oregon border. Unlike Oregon's Cascade Range, which makes a conspicuous drainage divide along most of the length of that state and is capped by one prominent stratovolcano after another, California's section is ill-defined and much of it is relatively low. The Cascade lands extending 30 miles north from Mt. Shasta to the Oregon border have only a few minor summits, only one exceeding 8000 feet in elevation, and timber worth cutting is so sparse that Congress placed only about half of this land within the Klamath National Forest. In contrast, the southern 30 miles have a well-defined drainage divide and are in prime lumber country. In this section there only is one trail long enough for a lengthy, week-plus backpack, and that is the Pacific Crest Trail. Assuming you won't like to view past and ongoing logging operations, we've omitted them from this book.

Mt. Shasta & the Medicine Lakes Highlands

For hikers there really are only two desirable areas, the lands around Mt. Shasta and those around Lassen Peak. Mt. Shasta, at 14,162′, easily is California's tallest and most impressive volcano, and its steaming summit attracts an inordinate number of hikers and mountaineers of varying competence. Being historically active, it has fairly steep slopes and precious little land for camping. Where you do find high flats, they are undesirable, exposed sites above treeline. Therefore, the only suitable backpack is, as at some major volcanoes in Oregon and Washington, a circumnavigation around its lower slopes, a route through the Mt. Shasta Wilderness that stays near treeline. Some 40 miles east-northeast of Mt. Shasta lies isolated Medicine Lake, the center of the very large, but not towering, volcanically active Medicine Lake Highlands. Most of it is prime lumber country, and hence it has a plethora of logging roads and a deficit of trails. (JPS)

Some Shasta History

Mt. Shasta stands in solitary dominance as the most striking mountain in northern California. Its volume—estimated by various geologists at between 80 and 120 cubic miles—makes it, arguably, the largest volcanic peak in the continental United States, and its base-to-summit rise of over 11,000 feet is among the world's largest. Indeed, if Shastina, Mt. Shasta's secondary cone, stood alone, it would be the third highest mountain in the Cascade Range after Mts. Rainier and Shasta. And yet, ironically, Mt. Shasta was the last major mountain of the Pacific Northwest to be discovered by Euro-American explorers. Mts. Rainier, Hood, St. Helens, Baker, and St. Elias were all named and mapped before 1800. Shasta, midway between the British settlements at Fort Vancouver at the mouth of the Columbia River and the Spanish enclaves in San Francisco and Monterey, was not seen by explorers until they had journeyed overland nearly 300 miles from these settlements into unknown territory.

In 1846 General John C. Fremont estimated Mt. Shasta to be nearly the height of Mont Blanc and unclimbable. In 1870 Clarence King, along with pioneer Yosemite photographer Carleton Watkins, explored and photographed the first active glaciers to be identified within the United States. Explorer and ethnologist Major John Wesley Powell named four of Shasta's glaciers in the local Native American dialect. Dr. C. Hart Merriam, and other members of the US Biological Survey, completed the first Shasta treeline circumnavigation during the summer of 1898. Merriam, a central figure in American natural history, named Diller Canyon for geologist Joseph Diller, and finalized his "life-zone" theory of plant and animal distribution during this trip. Twenty-five years later, Mac Olberman, custodian of the Sierra Club cabin at Horse Camp, made the second complete circumnavigation. (MZ)

Lassen Volcanic National Park, Thousand Lakes & Caribou Wildernesses

A distant 75 miles southeast of Mt. Shasta stands 10,457' Lassen Peak, the central attraction for three national lands with wilderness: Lassen Volcanic National Park, Thousand Lakes Wilderness to its north, and Caribou Wilderness to its east. The national park was set aside in 1916, a year after major eruptions blasted from Lassen's summit, which fumed on and off from 1914 through 1921. The peak and its adjacent lands occupy the western third of the park, but most of its 150 miles of hiking trails form a mesh in the lake-blessed eastern two thirds of the park. Several backpack loops are possible, and we've selected what we feel is the optimal one.

Thousand Lakes Wilderness leaves something to be desired: lakes. It is about 990 lakes short of its touted number, and of the 10 or so lakes present, only three are worth a visit: Eiler, Everett, and Magee. Should you wish to visit them, or climb to the present rim of a formerly two-mile-high volcano, then obtain a Lassen National Forest map, which shows the pertinent roads to the wilderness' three trailheads. While Thousand Lakes Wilderness at least has a few lakes, Caribou Wilderness has no caribou, reindeer, nor even elk, which is a very similar species. What it does have are over 100 ponds and lakelets plus about a dozen lakes worth visiting. The loop we've put together visits most of these.

Currently there are no quotas for any of the wildernesses, although Shasta and Lassen do require permits. As Sacramento Valley cities and Cascade Range towns continue to increase in population, wilderness use is bound to increase. Visit these areas in the early 21st Century, before they become crowded like the High Sierra. (JPS)

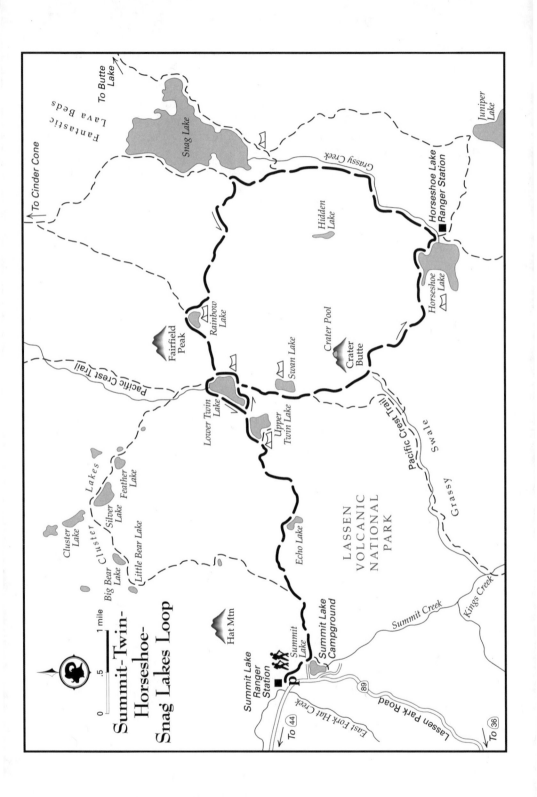

Summit-Twin-Horseshoe-Snag Lakes Loop

To Cinder Cone

Fantastic Lava Beds

To Butte Lake

Snag Lake

Grassy Creek

Hidden Lake

Horseshoe Lake Ranger Station

Juniper Lake

Horseshoe Lake

Crater Pool

Crater Butte

Rainbow Lake

Fairfield Peak

Swan Lake

Pacific Crest Trail

Lower Twin Lake

Upper Twin Lake

Pacific Crest Trail

Grassy Swale

Cluster Lakes

Silver Lake

Feather Lake

Cluster Lake

Big Bear Lake

Little Bear Lake

Echo Lake

LASSEN VOLCANIC NATIONAL PARK

Hat Mtn

Summit Lake Ranger Station

Summit Lake

Summit Lake Campground

Summit Creek

Kings Creek

East Fork Hat Creek

Lassen Park Road

To 44

To 89

To 36

1 mile

.5

0

58

Summit-Twin-Horseshoe-Snag-Lakes Loop
—Jeffrey P. Schaffer

Route	Days	Elev. Gain/Loss	Elev. Low/High	Difficulty	Miles
♀	3	2680´/2680´	6090´/7160´	**	17.7
					(mileage without side hikes)

Campsites: Upper Twin Lake: 3.2 miles
Lower Twin Lake (southwest corner): 3.7 miles
Swan Lake: 4.6 miles
Horseshoe Lake: 7.2 miles
Snag Lake (southwest shore): 10.7 miles
junction at Rainbow Lake: 12.6 miles
(see the Trip Description for others)

Map: USGS 7.5-min *Mt. Harkness, Prospect Peak, Reading Peak, West Prospect Peak*

Best season: Late July through mid-September

Take this trip!

The eastern half of Lassen Volcanic National Park is a backpacker's delight, for you traverse relatively easy terrain and encounter a lake about every two miles. Being located in northeastern California quite far from the state's major urban areas, the park's backcountry is lightly used compared to the Sierra Nevada, hence no need for trailhead quotas. This semi-loop trip—one of several possible loops—is short enough to be done in a day by strong hikers. However, I suggest you take three days to do it—since it is wonderful country to laze about in. Try hiking on weekdays, when you may get the feeling that you have the whole wilderness all to yourself.

Trailhead

The trailhead is located at a parking lot beside the Summit Lake Ranger Station. You reach this via Highway 89, the Lassen Park Road. From the Highways 44/89 junction just beyond Lassen Volcanic National Park's north boundary, drive 12.7 miles on Highway 89 to the ranger station's spur road. Or, from the Highways 36/89 junction 5½ miles south of the park's south boundary, drive 21.4 miles on Highway 89 to it. Via Highway 44, the Highways 44/89 junction is about 45 miles east of Redding and about 65 miles west of Susanville. Via Highway 36, the Highways 36/89 junction is about 46 miles east of Red Bluff and about 61 miles west of Susanville.

TRIP DESCRIPTION

Heads Up! The park's road typically opens in mid-June, providing access to your trailhead. However, your trail will lie under snow then, and not until about the Fourth of July weekend does it become passable. Even then, you'll encounter many patches of snow, so it's best not to hike before late July. Lassen's lands are volcanic, and volcanic soils can retain considerable groundwater for quite some time. Consequently, expect boggy areas through most of the summer and mosquitoes. Unless you're hiking in September, carry mosquito repellent and consider sleeping in a tent rather than under the stars.

Your trail begins with a ½-mile traverse southeast to Summit Lake, along which you pass spur trails to campsites in north Summit Lake Campground. Once along the lake's shore, you go but 90 yards to a junction with a trail circling the lake to the south campground. Because Summit Lake really isn't on a summit, a better name would be Divide Lake: perched atop a broad divide, the lake contributes water, usually as groundwater, to both East Fork Hat Creek and Summit Creek.

From the junction you start a 500-foot ascent east, one of three "major" climbs on your route. This begins up a gully, then up slopes to a ridge, from which you climb briefly northeast to a plateau. Along this ascent you'll see Lassen Peak due west, Crescent Crater on its north flank, and Chaos Crags behind it. You barely walk along the plateau before reaching a junction. This is a start of an 8½-mile loop frequented by dayhikers. It descends north to the Cluster Lakes, climbs southeast to Lower Twin Lake, then climbs west back to our junction. However, the Cluster Lakes aren't as appealing as the lake's we'll encounter and, while camping potential is less among them, mosquito potential is greater. Therefore, head for the Twin Lakes.

You begin an almost 700-foot descent to them by first dropping east to Echo Lake (2.2). This is a pleasant, photogenic lake, one suitable for a rest stop,

View north of Summit Lake

and it is the only one along your hike where camping is banned, due to proximity to the trailhead. Onward, you momentarily climb out of the depression holding the lake, then drop east, passing a meadow and a stagnant pond before heading north through a small, flat-floored valley. The lava flows exposed on the valley's steep sides yield to a shallow, linear laklet, just beyond which you drop rather steeply down more lava flows to the west corner of Upper Twin Lake (3.2). For isolated camping, take a use trail south along its shore then east to gentle lands just above its southwest shore. The official trail hugs the lake's north shore, and steep slopes prevent any camping. However, just past the lake's northeast corner you encounter a broad, spacious ridge that separates this lake from nearby Lower Twin Lake, and atop it you can find spots to camp, these about 100–200 yards from the shore of either lake. Most will continue onward, quickly arriving at the southwest corner of Lower Twin Lake (3.7), which like its twin 40 feet higher is L-shaped.

Here begins a 10¼-mile loop, which you can take in either direction. If you keep left, you pass Rainbow Lake before making a 700-foot, relatively short, and therefore quite steep, descent to Snag Lake. While many may prefer to descend rather than ascend this, I prefer the opposite. This is because the loop follows Grassy Creek for about 2 miles, and grassy (meadowy) it is, harboring myriad mosquitoes. Going right here lets you descend along it at a good, virtually effortless clip rather than sweat up it, trying to outpace pursuing mosquitoes. Though mosquito-prone, Grassy Creek is one of the loveliest creeks I've ever had the pleasure to hike.

Branching right, take the trail that skirts Lower Twin Lake's south shore, with camping possibilities just above it, to reach a junction near its southeast corner. If you were to go ¼ mile north along the lake's east shore, you'd reach our return route. Instead, climb ¼ mile south, on a very short stretch of the Pacific Crest Trail, moderately up to a broad ridge, then descend shortly and gently to the outlet creek of nearby Swan Lake (4.6). From its northeast corner, about 70 yards away, you see Crater Butte above its far shore. Most cinder cones like this one have a crater, or depression, but this circular, extinct volcano has a lakelet, Crater Pool, which is reached by equal effort from either here or later on (along my preferred route). Swan Lake is hemmed in on its north, west, and south shores, so to camp here, head for the very spacious flat along its east shore.

The Pacific Crest Trail climbs above the lake's west shore, then in ¼ mile reaches a junction. The right fork, the PCT, descends to Grassy Swale; the left fork, our route, also descends to it, but first goes ¼ mile to a minor divide before dropping ½ mile to it. Here you find a trail descending 0.6 mile to the PCT. You head east up the swale, going another ¼ mile to a meadow where the trail starts to curve right.

Should you wish to view Crater Pool (about a 1-mile hike), leave the trail here, cross the meadow and start northeast up steep slopes just ahead. These quickly ease off and, if you walk over to the southeast base of Crater Butte, you ought to see a use trail. Take this up a gully and in ¼ mile arrive at a long stretch of large boulders, on your right. These stay with you for about 300 yards, then about 100 yards past them, start a diagonal left up to the crest of an obvious ridge. The use trail continues straight ahead, up to a very broad plateau. This is the surface of a large lava flow, similar to the Fantastic Lava Beds of the park's Cinder Cone. This flow extends from Rainbow Lake in the north, to Juniper Lake in the south, and to Hidden Lake in the east, and of course its source is Crater Butte. Give the Cinder Cone and its Fantastic Lava Beds about 10,000+ years to develop soil and a forest, and then it will look like your locality. Once you top the ridge, take the path of least resistance, which varies, depending where you are. Basically, you want to get into the shallow valley just northwest and head briefly southwest up to Crater Pool, a lakelet about 100 yards across. While nothing to write home about, it is quite unique and, on a hot August afternoon, suitable for a swim. Before then, it's too cold; after August, it is mostly less than chest-deep. There is no adequate campsite.

Only the curious will visit Crater Pool; most curve right to gently climb 200 yards to a minor divide, then make a brief descent, first quickly passing a seasonal pond, then soon passing a larger lily-pad pond. Ahead, you barely descend as you go ¾ mile to the northwest arm of well-named Horseshoe Lake (7.2). As at the Twin Lakes, camping is prohibited along its northwest shore.

However, about 50 yards before the arm you can head south 75 yards to a spacious campsite on a lodgepole-pine flat. For isolated camping, continue along the lake's curving west shore. Horseshoe Lake has an interesting floor, with three quite distinct if hidden (flooded) basins. The northwest basin, along which your trail traverses, averages about 10 feet or less, having only one moderately deep spot—about 20 feet—near the west end of the lake. This deeper spot is unexpected since yellow pond lilies, which grow only in shallow water, are found nearby. The lake's southwest arm occupies a second basin up to 40 feet deep, while east of it is the deepest basin, with a maximum depth of 75 feet.

Keeping your feet dry, if perhaps only briefly, strike east about ½ mile to where your trail curves southeast to cross just above a small peninsula on the lake's northeast shore. Here the water is so shallow that you can almost wade halfway across this large lake. The depth, being less than 5 feet in places, effectively keeps out cold water from the lake's deep, southern half, making the northwest arm of the lake a very attractive swimming hole. Furthermore, the lake's pebbly bottom drops off quickly before leveling at about 10–15 feet. There are no rocks, snags, or other submerged obstacles to worry about, and no wade through 100 yards of lake-bottom ooze—all often characteristics of lakes in volcanic lands.

After perhaps a refreshing swim, continue ¼ mile southeast to the lake's outlet. Just 100 yards down it you'll meet a trail that crosses the creek to reach the Horseshoe Lake Ranger Station, above the opposite bank, complete with a locked outhouse. (You get to use the woods.) The lake has an official campsite, which you reach by first heading about 70 yards east past the station's cabin, then branching right for a 300-yard walk to an obvious site, on your right, one with a tree-filtered lake view. Since it's large enough for one party, if you get it you have this neck of the woods all to yourself.

Your loop route does not cross the lake's outlet, Grassy Creek, but rather takes the trail paralleling it downstream. Grassy Creek is a delightful, meandering, chorusing creek, one flowing through a stringer meadow rather than being encroached by trees. It invites you to dally, but mosquitoes will urge you on. After an easy ¾-mile descent north, your trail bends east and goes just 200 yards to a junction. For a rewarding side trip, start from the bend and head about 200 yards north to a seasonal creek and cross it. About here you should find a use trail, which stays just above the creek's west bank as it goes 0.6 mile to the south tip of Hidden Lake, nestled in a linear basin about 200 feet higher than your trail. On ample, gentle slopes above the south shore you can set up camp. The lake's floor generally is quite shallow near the shore, which means you'll have a bit of a wade out to deeper water. The lake certainly is deep enough for swimming and to support fish, but you'd really have to make a very far cast to reach any trout.

Past the trail's bend east to a nearby junction, Grassy Creek significantly increases its gradient, producing an increasingly livelier, louder chorus. After a mile of gentle-to-moderate descent, your trail, now northbound, veers away from Grassy Creek and its serenade, and maintains its gradient ½ mile down to a junction just shy of Snag Lake. This is the start of a 13½-mile loop, which, right (counterclockwise), skirts along the southeast shore of Snag Lake, heads 3 miles over to Butte Lake, traverses its east and north shores over to Butte Lake Campground, then strikes southwest over to the Cinder Cone before veering southeast to parallel the west shore of Snag Lake back to your junction.

Our loop goes left, and soon almost touches the very shallow south tip of Snag Lake (when the lake is full). By late July—the soonest you'll want to start this hike—the lake has dropped a foot or two, exposing a route you can take ½ mile north to the lake's prominent southwest peninsula. Along this traverse you'll encounter plenty of level ground, just within the bordering forest, suitable for camping. Should you choose to keep to the trail, then from where you almost touch the south tip, traverse ⅓ mile to a trail junction just west of the southwest shore of Snag Lake (10.7). From this junction you can descend directly east to spacious campsites or else traverse northeast across the hummocky southwest peninsula and search for additional sites. Out there, where cottonwoods grow, you have a view north of a recent, essentially unvegetated lava flow and the top of Cinder Cone, protruding behind it. Back around A.D. 1567, a rather fluid lava flow spilled across the broad valley Grassy Creek flowed through. The flow was followed, perhaps only days or weeks later, by the construction of a cinder cone. At least three more flows and two more cinder-cone eruptions followed, the last flow and eruption happening during the winter of 1850–51. Today these fresh landmarks are called Cinder Cone and its Fantastic Lava Beds. Some of the lava flows reached Butte Lake and reduced its size. One of the flows, perhaps one of about A.D. 1720, blocked Grassy Creek, and consequently, a lake pooled up behind the flow. As the lake grew, it drowned the forest, leaving only myriad snags, which the first emigrants saw and thus gave our lake its name. Grassy Creek still flows into Butte Lake, but it does so by flowing under the Fantastic Lava Beds.

At only 7 miles from your trailhead, Snag Lake, with its abundant camping potential, is a fine place to overnight. Then the next morning, while temperatures are still cool, you can begin a steep climb west from the trail junction. About half of your 700-foot climb is done in the first ½ mile, as your trail arcs from southwest to northwest. It then climbs west ⅓ mile to a hanging valley, where you have a short respite before veering northwest for a ¼-mile climb up a gully to the top of a lava plateau. After you make a ½-mile, gently undulating traverse west, you make a short but brief drop northwest to the east shore of Rainbow Lake (12.6). Just ahead is a junction, but should you want to camp at this desirable lake, look for campsites on the spacious flat beside its southeast shore.

From the junction a trail departs northeast, making a beeline for Cinder Cone, 2½ miles distant. Our route makes a rainbow curve around Rainbow's north and west shores, then in ½ mile reaches the northeast shore of slightly lower Lower Twin Lake (13.4). Here you meet the Pacific Crest Trail and go a mere 300 yards northwest on it to a junction. The PCT, bound for Canada, continues north, reaching a spur to the Twin Lakes Ranger Station in another 300 yards. You, however, veer west from the junction, to tread past the lake's north tip. Through most of July you'll see a long reflection pond extending several hundred yards north from this tip, and then you may have to wade. You could walk north to the pond's end, then south along its opposite side, but in the time required to do this, you could have taken off your shoes, waded west, and put them back on. Most hikers will have a dry traverse across the tip, then all will make the ½-mile traverse along Lower Twin's northwest shore to reach its southwest corner, where you started your loop. From this point, retrace your steps 3.7 miles to your trailhead.

Permits

Wilderness Permits are required for backpackers, but there are no trailhead quotas. You can get a permit in advance by phoning Lassen Volcanic National Park's headquarters at (530) 595-4444 and requesting a wilderness-permit packet. Allow at least two weeks for processing. You can also get a permit in person. If you're arriving via Highway 44, get one at the Loomis Museum or, when it's closed, at the Manzanita Lake Entrance Station. If you're arriving via Highway 36, get one at the Park Headquarters, at the Southwest Information Station, or at the Southwest Entrance Station. The maximum number of people you can have in your party is 10.

Build-up/Wind-down tips

Summit Lake Campground, almost next to the trailhead, can be full on a summer weekend, so if you are driving up on a Friday or Saturday, it may be safer to camp sooner rather than be turned away. If you're arriving via Highway 44, then try the very large Manzanita Lake Campground, although it is also popular and too may be full. However, Crags Campground, 4 miles farther east, should have space. If you're arriving via Highway 36, then stay at Southwest Campground, with walk-in sites, located immediately beyond the park's Southwest Entrance Station.

Jeffrey P. Schaffer provides background on his path to guidebook writing, detailed mapmaking, and challenging received views of Sierra geological formation, besides a list of his titles from Wilderness Press, in "Author Bio & Bib" on page 492.

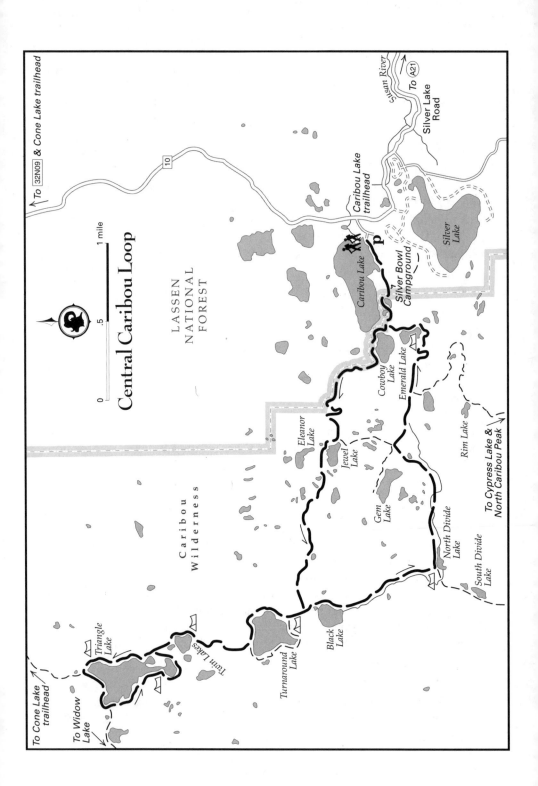

Central Caribou Loop

To 32N09 & Cone Lake trailhead

To 32N09

To 10

Susan River

To A21

Silver Lake Road

Caribou Lake trailhead

LASSEN NATIONAL FOREST

1 mile

.5

0

Caribou Lake

Silver Bowl Campground

Silver Lake

Cowboy Lake

Emerald Lake

Eleanor Lake

Jewel Lake

Gem Lake

Rim Lake

To Cypress Lake & North Caribou Peak

North Divide Lake

South Divide Lake

Caribou Wilderness

Triangle Lake

Twin Lakes

Turnaround Lake

Black Lake

To Cone Lake trailhead

To Widow Lake

59

Central Caribou Loop

—Jeffrey P. Schaffer

Route	Days	Elev. Gain/Loss	Elev. Low/High	Difficulty	Miles
↻	2	1190′/1190′	6580′/7100′	*	12.3
			(mileage with side hike to Jewel Lake)		

Campsites: Turnaround Lake: 3.6 miles
northeastern Twin Lake: 4.5 miles
Triangle Lake (northeast tip): 5.4 miles
North Divide Lake: 9.0 miles
Emerald Lake: 10.5 miles
(see the Trip Description for others)

Map: USGS 7.5-min *Bogard Buttes, Red Cinder*

Best season: Mid-July through late September

Take this trip!

John Muir called the Sierra Nevada a gentle wilderness, but take almost any Sierra hike in this book, and you'll find you may climb 2000–3000 feet in any given day. That's not gentle. To experience a really gentle wilderness, take this trip. Along it, you have only one "major" escarpment to tackle, a whopping 250-foot elevation gain. Other than that, your route is almost level, with minimal ups and downs (except the descent of the escarpment.) So far as I know, there is no other place in California where you experience a lake-blessed mountain wilderness with such a minimal effort than here in the Caribou Wilderness.

Trailhead

First you have to reach County Road A21. From Redding, drive 45 miles east on Highway 44 to the Highways 44/89 junction just north of Lassen Volcanic National Park. Drive 13 miles north on Highways 44/89 to where they split about ½ mile north of Old Station, then drive 28 miles east on Highway 44 to the north end of CR A21. This junction is 24 miles west of Susanville. Or, from Red Bluff, drive 46 miles east on Highway 36 to the Highways 36/89 junction south of Lassen Volcanic NP, then 12 miles southeast on 36/89 to a junction with Highway 32 (52 miles northeast from Chico). Still on 36/89, go 10 miles east to where they split, then continue first 3 miles to Chester, then 13 miles to the south end of CR A21. This junction is 22 miles west of Susanville. You want the Silver Lake Road (Forest Route 110), which is 4.5 miles south of the north junction, 13.8 miles north of the south junction. Leaving CR A21, drive 5.0 miles west on the Silver Lake Road to Forest Route 10, coming north from Highway 36. Rocky Knoll Campground is just to the left. Keep right, now on FR 10, and go 0.4 mile to another junction. Road 31N14, straight ahead, goes over to Silver Bowl Picnic Ground and Silver Bowl Campground just 0.1 mile beyond it. To reach the trailhead, continue on FR 10, which angles right, and go but 0.3 mile north to a short spur road. This quickly forks, the right branch climbing momentarily to just above Caribou Lake and a boat ramp and parking area for the reservoir's users. You keep left and quickly reach the Caribou Lake trailhead parking area.

TRIP DESCRIPTION

Heads Up! There is very little to worry about, other than mosquitoes, which in virtually every lake-studded mountain wilderness of California are a nuisance into early August. However, there is a possibility that if you hike before mid-July, when snow patches abound, or if you get caught is an unexpected late-summer or early-fall snowstorm, you may not be able to follow your trail. Then, given the area's flatness and general lack of prominent peaks, you could lose the trail and get seriously lost. However, if it looks like a real storm may be heading your way, you should be able to make it back to your trailhead in under three hours, reaching the safety of your vehicle before the storm hits.

At only 12.3 miles of total hiking over mostly level land, almost anyone in adequate shape can do make this circuit as a dayhike. So why backpack? The reason is that there are some fine camping opportunities, especially at Triangle Lake. This lake is better reached from the Cone Lake trailhead, just north of Caribou Wilderness and only 1.8 miles from the lake's north tip. But taking this fast way in, you'd miss Jewel Lake, Turnaround Lake, and the northeastern Twin Lake, all with good camping and attractive settings. If, after making the Triangle Lake loop, you backtrack, you'll hike 11.4 miles, not much less than my proposed route. However, by completing the route back (with a possible side trip to South Divide Lake, which will add about 0.6+ mile to your route), you will experience new scenery. While South Divide Lake is not too attractive once its water level goes down, it's near the center of the wilderness and only lightly visited. I've included the brief diversion to Emerald Lake, which for me rivals Jewel Lake and Triangle Lakes as among the best in the wilderness.

From your parking area a brief trail climbs to an outhouse and the main trail, both immediately above the southeast shore of heavily fished Caribou Lake. Being a reservoir, its water can fluctuate wildly, and even before Labor Day can be 10+ feet lower than its maximum level, thereby leaving a conspicuous bathtub ring. After a 0.4-mile westward traverse, you'll meet a feeder trail, which ascends 0.4 mile from Silver Lake. Here you sign in, for the wilderness boundary is just a few heartbeats ahead. Continuing briefly west, you round a lily-pad pond, glimpse two ponds below the trail and also Caribou Lake's west end, then, 0.3 mile into the wilderness, reach a junction. Branching left is a trail that provides access to Emerald Lake, North Divide Lake, and others; we'll take this trail on the way back.

Keeping straight ahead, we reach, in only 200 yards, photogenic Cowboy Lake (0.8), backdropped by a lava cliff. Swimming and fishing are out, since most of the lake is barely 2 feet deep (frogs, take note: this is your paradise). Our trail then wanders through a shady forest for ½ mile before switchbacking 250 feet higher, ascending a long escarpment to reach a gully. Congratulations, you've just done the only real climb on this entire trip, and Jewel Lake (2.0), at the head of the gully, is your reward. And what a jewel it is! Like most of the trailside lakes in the volcanic lands of Lassen and Caribou, this one is deep enough to swim in and to support fish. But unlike most of them, this one has several bedrock ledges just above shore to bask on or fish from. Your trail traverses west above the lake's north shore and between trail and shore lie several fine campsites on glacier-polished-and-grooved lava bedrock. On your traverse west, you can leave the trail and descend north to nearby Eleanor Lake. While not as attractive and definitely more likely to have more mosquitoes, it is less frequented, and so has somewhat secluded camping.

Past these lakes your trail winds through an open forest on a nearly level bench, then climbs easily west along the base of a brushy escarpment. You top out near a lily-pad pond, then in 200 yards see an early-season pond/late-season meadow, and from it continue easily ¼ mile down to a junction between Black and Turnaround lakes (3.4). Should you want a very short hiking trip—a mere 7.7 miles, including Emerald Lake—turn left here, head south past Black Lake to North Divide Lake, then east toward your trailhead. My recommended route is 4.6 miles longer: a hike north to Triangle Lake, a circle around it, and then a return to this junction.

With this plan in mind, you turn right and start a nearly level walk north, quickly reaching the southeast shore of Turnaround Lake (3.6). If you're hiking in early summer, when the lake is largest, you'll first encounter its very shallow, linear finger, extending south from this shore. If you're a large group, you might consider camping on the spacious, nearly level lands by its south shore, west of

View of Black Butte from the west shore of Triangle Lake

the finger. You can continue onward to the lake's southwest lobe, cross a boggy meadow south of it, then follow a trail along its west shore. This side provides the lake's most isolated camping, with two good camps located midway along it. On the main trail, you hike first along the east shore, then the north shore. On the latter, you can find a camp or two, particularly north of the trail. On this shore are some conspicuous rocks that are good for a lunch break, for drying off after a swim, or just to sit and admire the lake and its lava-butte backdrop. Where the trail turns north to leave the lake, you'll see the north end of the west-shore use trail.

Northbound, your trail makes a momentary climb to start a 0.4-mile traverse to the northeastern Twin Lake (4.5). A twin it is not, but it does have two smaller siblings, both shallow and definitely not worth visiting, unless you're a duck. This lake is a worthy goal in itself, since, as at Turnaround Lake, there is a spacious area for camping on flat, lodgepole-shaded lands just above its south shore. From one or more sites you have pleasant views across the lake toward the small, forested butte just northeast of the lake. This lake can be a good one for swimming once you wade out, say 30 yards, to where the water is deep enough. Fishing is another matter, since fish are unlikely to swim in the shallows near shore.

Onward, you traverse Twin Lake's east shore, then just beyond its shallow north lobe arrive at a junction with Triangle Lake's loop trail (4.7). Starting southwest, this takes about 1¼ miles to reach the lake's northeast tip, and we'll return along it. Directly ahead, your route to Triangle Lake's northeast tip is ½ mile shorter, and, like the loop trail, offers fine views, which is why I suggest you circle the entire lake. From Twin Lake you may have noticed *reddish* Black Butte rising above the forest. As you traverse north along the east shore of *untriangular* Triangle Lake, this stratovolcano wanna-be is conspicuous as it rises more than 800 feet above the lake. Its lava was pastier, more andesitic than basaltic, hence it produced a short, thick lava flow, which you see extending southwest from it.

You'll quickly see a narrow peninsula extending north from the southern part of Triangle Lake. In early season when the lake is highest, this peninsula is an island. In late season, after the lake drops a few feet, the shallow necks connecting the lake proper with the south lobe and the southeast lobe (near your trail) almost become exposed. Regardless how much the lake drops, the south lobe, though relatively shallow, still is plenty deep for swimming, and between it and the southeast lobe is a fine campsite. You'll find another one just north of the southeast lobe, and can find additional suitable sites just east of your trail, among lodgepole-shaded flats and gentle slopes.

After a ½-mile traverse along the southeast lobe and the east-shore proper, you arrive at Triangle Lake's northeast tip (5.4), from where a trail departs north to descend 1.8 miles to the Cone Lake trailhead. The route from the trailhead up to the lake is so short and easy that anglers sometimes carry in rafts to fish this large, deep lake. At the junction you turn southwest to start a pleasant walk along the lake's arcing north shore. Within 60 yards you'll pass a good, obvious campsite, the only legal one. You'll also likely see illegal shoreline sites; legal ones can be found on gentle slopes or on the broad, low ridge, all just north of the lake. From the lake's northeast corner a relatively new trail strikes west about 2½ miles, winding from pond to pond along a nearly level route. This back-door entrance to northeastern Lassen Volcanic National Park reaches a north-south trail about ¾ mile south of (and above) Widow Lake.

Now you start south, then soon ascend briefly southeast up to a lava bench. This has two small projections into the lake, and on each is a great campsite, each being—in my opinion—among the best in Caribou Wilderness. Each spot offers inspiring views across the lake, easy access for great swimming and fishing, and early-morning warmth from the rising sun. Immediately past the second, you turn south to parallel the narrow neck connecting Triangle Lake proper with its south lobe. Beyond this good swimming hole your trail quickly turns northeast for a short traverse, passing possible campsites both left and right, to reach the end of Triangle Lake's loop trail (6.7).

Now you backtrack 1.3 miles past Twin Lake and Turnaround Lake to the junction between Black and Turnaround lakes (8.0). *Greenish* Black Lake (8.1)—another misnomer—lies just 200 yards south of this junction. It is pleasant enough, but has only a rather mundane backdrop. The lake is good for a rest, food break, swim, or possibly even angling, but it lacks nearby campsites.

Actually, there is plenty of room for camping, although you may be 100+ yards away from the shore. Check out the spacious level and gentle-sloping lands above its north, east, and south shores.

Past the lake you parallel its seasonal outlet creek, which after ¼ mile has such a flat gradient that after the creek dries up, it's hard to tell if it was flowing north or south. South, in another ½ mile you reach a junction just above the northwest corner of linear North Divide Lake (9.0). By this junction is a spacious lodgepole-shaded flat with abundant space for camping. This lake, being only about waist deep, is not suitable for swimmers, be they humans or fish. A nearby lake that is suitable is its twin, linear South Divide Lake, about ¼ mile away by a trail that starts west, then curves south through a seasonally wet meadow. Before about mid-August, you may get your shoes wet. In it you'll see, 2 miles due west, the small summit of Red Cinder, which at 8374 feet is easily the highest summit in the wilderness. After the meadow dries out, South Divide Lake's water level drops enough to expose land between its north and south lobes. Both lobes are deep enough for swimming and to support fish, even when the lake level is low. You can camp near it, away from most of the wilderness' traffic, but when it is ringed with its seasonal shoreline, it's not too attractive.

From the junction by North Divide Lake, your loop route over the next mile first makes a very easy traverse past changing, interesting scenery, then, after passing a lily-pad lakelet, it makes a short drop to a junction with the Gem Lake Trail (10.0). This steep trail climbs 0.2 mile up a gully to reach hemmed-in Gem Lake, whose adjoining steep slopes preclude camping. If you like to fish, this lake certainly is worth trying.

Onward, your trail east first traverses past a long, linear meadow, which is a knee-deep lake in early summer, then it makes a ¼-mile descent to a junction with the Emerald Lake Trail (10.4). Take it. About 200 yards south up this moderately climbing trail you reach a flat bench of lava perched about 15 feet above the northeast shore of Emerald Lake (10.5). This has a fine campsite, and on weekends probably will be occupied. For me, it's a great swimmers' lake, since from rocks at the base of the lava bench, you can dive right in, then later sun yourself atop the bench. Beyond Emerald Lake, a very windy, contorted trail climbs about 1.0 mile to Rim Lake, then 0.7 mile past it to Cypress Lake, located just beyond a waist-deep, unnamed lake. Both Rim and Cypress lakes are worth visiting, but the stretch of trail before Rim Lake is up sparsely forested bedrock slabs and, for some people, it is hard to follow. If you are going to get lost on any of the wilderness' trails, it will be along this stretch. Those who do make it to Cypress Lake can make a straightforward cross-country hike to the popular summit of North Caribou peak, about 600 feet above the lake. From it you see not only all of Caribou Wilderness, but many miles beyond it in most directions, including a view west to Lassen Peak 17 miles away, and northwest to Mt. Shasta, a very distant 84 miles away.

After a visit to Emerald Lake (and perhaps beyond), return to the main trail and start a descent east. Within ¼ mile you begin a switchbacking descent of the same long escarpment you ascended early on your hike, except that your route is located about ¾ mile to the southeast. In the downward direction, you complete your descent in several minutes, then quickly reach the south shore of an unnamed, bilobed lake, along whose east shore you walk north. Its narrow constriction is shallow enough to wade across, but both lobes are plenty deep for swimming or fishing (your last opportunity in the wilderness). Onward, you barely leave the lake before you arrive at a junction near Cowboy Lake (11.6). Now you're at your original trail and you make an easy 0.7-mile backtrack to your trailhead.

Permits

No permits are required, but sign in anyway at the Caribou Wilderness boundary.

Build-up/Wind-down tips

There are two campgrounds close to your trailhead, Rocky Knoll and Silver Bowl. I prefer the latter, since it is more level and has fewer mosquitoes.

After your hike, if you're driving through Chester, check out the Creekside Grill, at 278 Main Street, just 0.3 mile southwest of Feather River Drive (a route to southeastern Lassen Volcanic National Park). This restaurant serves dinners only, and is closed Mondays and Tuesdays. On weekends, reservations are desirable, (530) 258-1966. It has both indoor and outdoor creekside seating, and has an excellent menu and wine list. While it may be pricey by Chester standards, it's not by urban restaurant standards.

Jeffrey P. Schaffer provides background on his path to guidebook writing, detailed mapmaking, and challenging received views of Sierra geological formation, besides a list of his titles from Wilderness Press, in "Author Bio & Bib" on page 492.

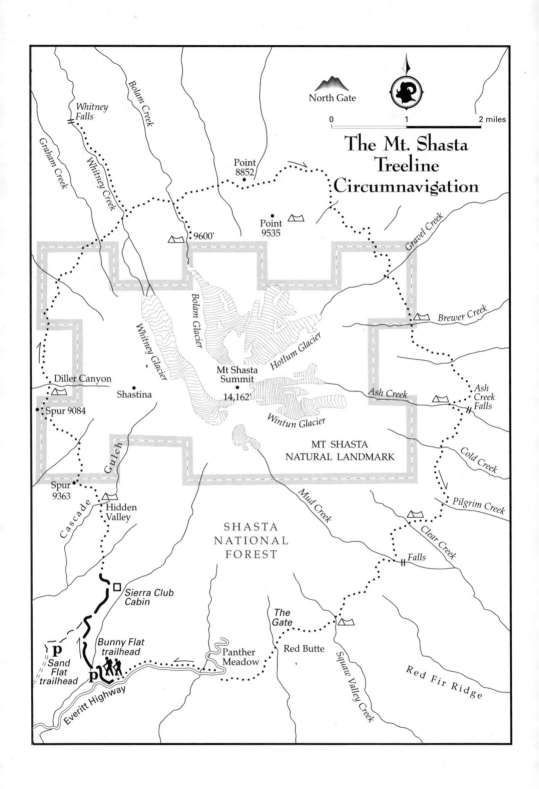

North Gate

0   1   2 miles

The Mt. Shasta Treeline Circumnavigation

Whitney Falls

Bolam Creek

Graham Creek

Whitney Creek

Point 8852

Gravel Creek

Point 9535

9600'

Bolam Glacier

Whitney Glacier

Hotlum Glacier

Brewer Creek

Diller Canyon

Shastina

Ash Creek

Ash Creek Falls

Spur 9084

Mt Shasta Summit 14,162'

Wintun Glacier

Cold Creek

Pilgrim Creek

MT SHASTA NATURAL LANDMARK

Spur 9363

Gulch

Cascade

Hidden Valley

Mud Creek

Clear Creek

SHASTA NATIONAL FOREST

Falls

Sierra Club Cabin

The Gate

P

Bunny Flat trailhead

Panther Meadow

Red Butte

Squaw Valley Creek

Red Fir Ridge

Sand Flat trailhead

P

Everitt Highway

60

The Mt. Shasta Treeline Circumnavigation

—Michael Zanger

Route	Days	Elev. Gain/Loss	Elev. Low/High	Difficulty	Miles
⟳	5–7	2500'/2500'	7000'/9500'	***	25–30

Campsites: While there are no developed campsites along the circumnavigation route, water sources are frequent and comfortable sites nearby can always be found. Clockwise from the Bunny Flat trailhead, some of the best are:
Hidden Valley (Day 1)
basin at 9600', below Bolam Glacier (Day 2)
Brewer Creek (Day 3)
Ash Creek or Clear Creek meadows (Day 4)
Squaw Valley Creek meadows (Day 5)
(see Trip Description for others)

Map: *Mt. Shasta Map* from Wilderness Press includes the recommended circumnavigation route
USGS 7.5-min *Mt. Shasta, Hotlum*

Best season: July through September

Take this trip!

When John Muir, America's most eloquent and far-traveled naturalist, first caught sight of Shasta from the Sacramento River canyon in 1875, he exclaimed, "...I was fifty miles away and afoot, alone and weary. Yet all my blood turned to wine, and I have not been weary since." Muir, the quintessential mountaineer, who circled the mountain in segments over more than a decade, found Shasta's circumnavigation to be perhaps more appealing than the ascent:

Arctic beauty and desolation, with their blessings and dangers, all may be found here, to test the endurance and skill of adventurous climbers; but far better than climbing the mountain is going around its warm, fertile base, enjoying its bounties like a bee circling a bank of flowers.... As you sweep around so grand a center the mountain itself seems to turn.... One glacier after another comes into view, and the outlines of the mountain are ever changing.

Relatively few people take this ultimate Shasta backpack, partly because it's a fairly committing endeavor, with no trail to follow. But in these days of abundant trails on most mountains and in nearly every wilderness area, this kind of trip poses a welcome, off-trail adverture. Indeed, you can easily imagine that you're following John Muir's footsteps. Crossing the toes of several Shasta glaciers offers superb views, and the short side trips to view waterfalls—in particular Whitney and Ash Creek falls—are well worth the extra time. Experienced backpackers who are comfortable with occasional scrambling should not be deterred from taking this trip, one of California's finest and least-traveled backcountry hikes.

Trailhead

Horse Camp (1.7 miles from Bunny Flat): There are two trails to Horse Camp off Everitt Highway, from Bunny Flat and from Sand Flat. More people take the trail from Bunny Flat because it climbs more gradually, starting 100 feet higher. From the town of Mt. Shasta, Bunny Flat is 10.9 miles up Everitt Highway, and the trailhead is right beside the road. A large parking area, an outhouse, and a bulletin board with information and self-issuing wilderness permits are located here (see also Permits).

TRIP DESCRIPTION

Heads Up! In route finding, strenuousness, and terrain, this trip should be considered a moderate but long mountaineering endeavor. Very fit hikers can complete the route in four days, and five would be comfortable for most backpackers. Plan your route carefully to camp at water sources, and find passages across some of the canyons. Shasta's relatively open slopes help make route finding fairly easy, but soft, ashy underfooting occasionally gets tedious. Knowing how to self-arrest and carrying an ice ax can be necessary in early season on high snowfields.

While backpackers can choose to circle Mt. Shasta at different elevations, a clockwise direction, usually beginning and ending at the Sierra Club's cabin

Ash Creek Falls

at Horse Camp, is preferred: water sources, campsites, and scenery continually improve in this direction, and most of the tiresome scree is dealt with initially. Though many route variations are possible—especially on the mountain's west flanks—most hikers will stay near the 8000-foot level (approximately treeline). What follows is a *very general* description of the route, with mention of key canyon crossings, important landmarks, and campsites.

Starting from Horse Camp, you can stay low, perhaps planning a first camp at Cascade Gulch or Diller Canyon. In dry years these canyons might not offer water, although you can always count on finding snow to melt in Diller Canyon. An alternative route is to go high and spend the first night in Hidden Valley, where water is always available. This enables a slightly higher traverse around Shastina, over spurs 9363 and 9084. Staying high gives you a wonderfully scenic and somewhat shorter route, but it takes you across some trying scree slopes, and you have to negotiate some short cliff bands, 0.25 mile south of Diller Canyon and about 0.75 mile north of it.

To traverse the Graham Creek-Bolam Creek area, it's best to avoid the morainal hills below the Whitney and Bolam glaciers by going somewhat high across the terminus of the Whitney glacier. There are small grassy areas and springs for camping west of the Whitney Glacier toe, but they can be difficult to find. (A worthy side trip is to scenic Whitney Falls: follow Whitney Creek downhill for almost a mile, staying on the east side of the canyon for easier going and excellent views.) For those who go high, good campsites await in the basin below the Bolam Glacier, at about 9600 feet. To continue clockwise from this area, it's best to descend along the east side of Bolam Creek to treeline.

In the North Gate vicinity, most hikers contour south of Point 8852, and gradually lose elevation as they continue east. Another option is to climb over the morainal benches near Point 9535, where there's excellent camping on flat, sandy ground, and almost always snowmelt for water. To continue east off these benches, descend sandy gullies through some cliff bands east-southeast of Point 9535 and contour toward Gravel Creek. Those who are relatively high will find some difficulty in crossing Gravel Creek's canyon. The canyon walls consist of steep, unstable ash with large, precariously perched boulders. Members of a party must take special care to avoid knocking rocks onto one another, and not climb directly below or above one another. Below 7500 feet the canyon walls are safer and not as high. Excellent campsites in a beautiful hemlock forest are found at Brewer Creek (reliable and clear).

The next key point is Ash Creek right about the falls. To get there, hike through whitebark parklands near the 8000-foot level across Brewer Creek. Contour left around the ridge just north of the falls at 7800 feet and then cut back west to descend into the canyon above the falls. An 8-foot cliff on this descent requires some scrambling. Solid snow—avalanche debris—usually offers a convenient bridge across Ash Creek until late in summer. A short walk east offers spectacular views of the almost 300-foot Ash Creek Falls, one of John Muir's favorite sights on Mt. Shasta. On the south side of the canyon, climb directly upslope through a band of whitebarks.

Cold Creek, Pilgrim Creek, and Clear Creek are all reliable and silt-free. Contour around Clear Creek's canyon at about 7800 feet to set up for the crucial crossing of intimidating Mud Creek canyon. From around 7700 feet on the canyon rim, drop straight into the canyon on a loose, sandy rib, at the uppermost grove of full-size Shasta red firs, just up-canyon from a bare, obvious landslide area. Near the canyon bottom, again take special care to avoid sending rocks onto partners. Cross Mud Creek a couple hundred yards above the falls, and climb directly up a steep, faint drainage to get back out of the canyon. This exit is important; large rocks offer reliable stepping stones to the rim. From the southwest rim of the canyon, a course that contours near 7800 feet will take you around Red Fir Ridge to Squaw Valley Creek. The lush meadows here offer one of the nicest campsites on the mountain. From here you can traverse north of Red Butte on an excellent trail of use through The Gate to Panther Meadow (or the old ski bowl) and return to Everitt Highway. Two miles down this road (or 3 miles from the old ski bowl) is the Bunny Flat trailhead.

Permits

While there is currently no quota limiting backpacking, the Forest Service requires a permit for overnight stays in the Mt. Shasta Wilderness. You can get one at the Ranger District office (otherwise, self-issue a permit at the bulletin board outside, or at the trailhead):

204 W. Alma Street
Mt. Shasta, CA 96067
Phone (530) 926-4511

Build-up/Wind-down tips

Two establishments in the town of Mount Shasta should not be missed in preparing for the Mt. Shasta circumnavigation. The Fifth Season outdoor store (300 N. Mt. Shasta Blvd., (530) 926-3606) has a complete range of outdoor equipment, including rental gear. Guidebooks, maps, and the latest information on mountain conditions are also available. Berryvale Market (305 S. Mt. Shasta Blvd., (530) 926-1576) has an excellent selection of organic, natural, and hard-to-find foods, including lots of "goodies" for a backpack trip. Castle Lake and the many excellent swimming holes on the South Fork Sacramento River above Lake Siskiyou are fine places to wash off the trail dust, and to soak aching muscles after a long backpack.

Shasta Mountain Guide Michael Zanger has coauthored the book on Mt. Shasta; see "Author Bio & Bib" on page 492.

The Warner Mountains

Roughly half of California's population lies in southwest California, concentrated in a coastal megalopolis stretching from Santa Barbara to San Diego. At its antipode in northeast California's Modoc County is a vast volcanic landscape, in which cattle far outnumber people. Besides a dozen hamlets too small for traffic lights, there's the county seat of several thousand people, Alturas. Here you'll find no malls, no auto row, no fast-food establishments, no subdivisions, and no air pollution—just pure, untrammeled Americana. If you want to get away from it all, this place is for you. Alturas is a distant 140 miles from the city of Redding via eastbound Highway 299, and 185 miles from the city of Reno via northbound Highway 395. Where the two highways meet—at the north end of Alturas—is the locus for trailhead directions in the Warner Mountains.

The Warner Mountains are California's northeasternmost range, separating the Modoc Plateau to the west from the Great Basin to the east. Bearing affinities to both geologic provinces, it's composed of multiple, thick lava flows like the Modoc Plateau, and is a dipping fault-block range like those of the Great Basin. The Surprise Valley fault system trailing the Warner's eastern escarpment is the principal site of still-active faulting here. The system is stretching the land, causing Surprise Valley to sink over time. Today it is filled with deep sediments capped by three, large, muddy, and extremely shallow Upper, Middle, and Lower Alkali lakes. Thinning of the crust has allowed magma to work toward the surface here, heating groundwater and giving rise to a string of hot springs, which parallel eastside County Road 1. About 12 miles north of Cedarville, County Road 13 branches east from it toward nearby mud volcanoes, which have erupted and steamed away in historic time. Indeed, after the hamlet of Cedarville civilization ends. Highway 299 heads 9 miles east of it to the Nevada border, where a dirt road, with a dire warning on lack of services, carries onward. We, Californians, tout our Sierra wildernesses that are, really, neither that wild nor remote. For wilderness, northwestern Nevada, and this less traveled corner of California, are some of the most remote areas in the Lower 48.

Highway 299 bisects the Warner Mountains, the lower northern half of which is traversed by roads and the higher southern half is traversed by trails. This roadless area is home to the 70,385-acre South Warner Wilderness. The west-dipping range is a miniature Sierra Nevada, and just as the southern part of that range is highest and mostly roadless with the north-trending John Muir Trail along its crest, so the South Warner Wilderness has the Summit Trail. And just as the John Muir Trail doesn't take you to Mt. Whitney, the Summit Trail doesn't take you to the Warner's highest mountain, 9,892' Eagle Peak. I'd have you climb *lowly* 8,646' Squaw Peak, just off the Summit Trail's northern section, and the first of two recommended hikes in this range. Should you have to bag Eagle Peak, you can reach it by either taking the Slide Creek Trail from Soup Spring Campground or the Poison Flat Trail from Mill Creek Campground. Both lead east to the Summit Trail, but where the first reaches it you'll ascend the peak's northwest ridge, and where the second reaches it you'll ascend its southwest ridge.

Like the Sierra Nevada the Warner Mountains have lakes. But rather than occupying glacier-excavated basins, about half the lakes lie uniquely behind or atop massive rockfall deposits. Along the Pine Creek Trail on the second recommended hike, you can visit three such lakes found in this drainage. The two largest rockfall-dammed lakes are Clear Lake, just east of Mill Creek Campground, and, south of the wilderness, 0.75-mile-long Blue Lake.

Also quite unique, the range is one of the few areas to harbor all three of California's yellow pines: ponderosa, Jeffrey, and the relatively rare Washoe. These grow at lower elevations—Mill Creek Campground is a classic site—but as you ascend you'll encounter white fir, western white pine, lodgepole pine, and finally whitebark pine. Conspicuously absent is red fir, a conifer common to the Klamath Mountains, Cascade Range, and Sierra Nevada. On drier slopes grow lots of sagebrush plus lesser amounts of mountain mahogany, mule ears, and western juniper. In localized areas with sufficient groundwater, aspens grow in tight clusters and, in late summer, add yellow dabs of color to the landscape. (JPS)

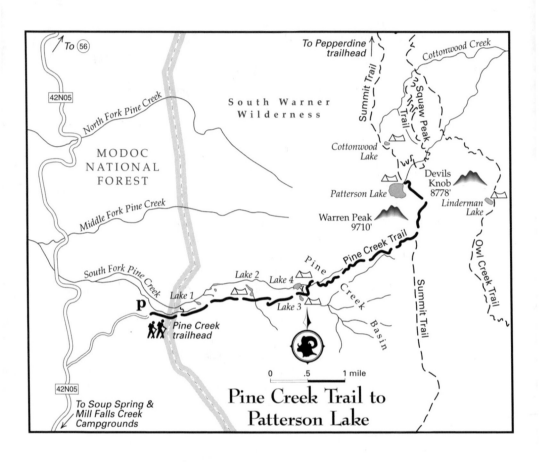

To (56)

42N05

North Fork Pine Creek

South Warner Wilderness

To Pepperdine trailhead

Cottonwood Creek

Summit Trail

Squaw Peak Trail

MODOC NATIONAL FOREST

Middle Fork Pine Creek

Cottonwood Lake

Devils Knob 8778'

Patterson Lake

Linderman Lake

Warren Peak 9710'

Pine Creek Trail

South Fork Pine Creek

Lake 2

Lake 4

Pine

Owl Creek Trail

Lake 1

p

Lake 3

Creek Basin

Summit Trail

Pine Creek trailhead

0   .5   1 mile

42N05

To Soup Spring & Mill Falls Creek Campgrounds

Pine Creek Trail to Patterson Lake

61

Pine Creek Trail to Patterson Lake

—Jeffrey P. Schaffer

Route	Days	Elev. Gain/Loss	Elev. Low/High	Difficulty	Miles
↗	2	3000´/3000´	6780´/9380´	***	11.6
					(mileage without side hikes)

Campsites: second lake: 1.5 miles
third lake: 2.5 miles
fourth lake and the Pine Creek crossing: 2.6 miles
Patterson Lake: 5.8 miles
(see the Trip Description for others)

Map: USGS 7.5-min *Eagle Peak, Soup Creek, Warren Peak*

Best season: Late July through mid-September

Take this trip!

This hike has a split personality. First, you have 2.6 miles of easy strolling up a "glaciated," flat-floored, steep-walled canyon to the crossing of Pine Creek, just past your third trailside lake (and a fourth just off the trail). This stretch is an easy hike, one that stands alone for those with children or those who want to put forth a minimum effort. Then from the creek, you shift gears for a 3.2-mile-long, serious ascent. The second stretch first climbs 1600 feet to the Summit Trail, then 400 feet higher to a ridge above Patterson Lake, to which you descend steeply. Overall, this hike is a tad shorter than hike 62, but it involves about 25% more climbing. So why take it? First, the lakes; second, the crest's southern views, obscured along the next hike; and third, access to the summit of Warren Peak, second highest in the Warner Mountains.

Trailhead

From the Highways 299/395 junction in Alturas, drive 1.0 mile south to east-heading County Road 56. This marks the north end of a major loop along the western flank of South Warner Wilderness, terminating at Likely, 18 miles south of CR 56 on Highway 395, but about 43 miles away via this loop. Those heading east on Highway 299 take CR 56, but those heading north on Highway 395 branch east on the loop from Likely. For hike 62, also take CR 56.

Those arriving to the area via Highway 299 drive 12.6 miles east on County Road 56 to the Modoc National Forest boundary, where the road becomes Forest Route 5. Take this 1.1 miles to a junction, where Forest Road 31 splits left (east), then continue on FR 5, winding 10.2 miles south to an east-climbing road signed for the Pine Creek trailhead. Take this road 1½ miles up to its end.

This trailhead lacks an adjacent campground, the nearest one being Soup Spring. To reach it, continue 0.9 mile south on FR 5, then branch left (east) onto a loop road. Over 3.1 miles, this essentially curves south to a spur road, then continues 5.2 winding miles back to FR 5. On the spur road, drive ⅓ mile southeast to Soup Spring Campground and the adjacent Slide Creek trailhead. Because it's not particularly attractive, I recommend Mill Creek Falls Campground. From the south end of the loop road, about 4.2 miles south of its north end via FR 5, drive 1.6 miles south to an east-branching road at the northern end of spacious Jess Valley, and ascend it 2.0 miles to the campground.

Those arriving via Highway 395 reach this campground by driving to Likely, turning right (east), and driving a scenic 8.3 miles east up a Pit River gorge to a split at the east edge of Jess Valley. Right (south), County Route 258 climbs 8 miles to highly desirable Blue Lake and its namesake campground. You turn left (north) and drive 2.8 miles to the start of the Mill Creek Falls road.

For hike 62, drive 12.6 miles east on County Road 56 to the Modoc National Forest boundary, where the road becomes Forest Route 5. Take this a mere 1.1 miles to a split, where FR 5 curves southwest. You branch left (east) onto Forest Route 31 and drive 6.6 miles to a junction, and turn right (south) to ascend 0.6 mile to the Pepperdine trailhead. Immediately beyond it is diminutive Pepperdine Campground.

TRIP DESCRIPTION

Heads Up! If, about 2.6 miles into your hike to the Pine Creek crossing, you see lots of snow ahead on the crest lands of the range, don't attempt to ascend the trail any farther than the junction with the Summit Trail. That spot will provide splendid views of the southern part of the range. Ahead is a traverse across steep slopes to a ridge above Patterson Lake, and those slopes can be treacherous when snowbound. A fall could be fatal. By late July, this stretch is usually snow-free, and then the trail is safe.

Starting in a shady forest of white firs, you parallel Pine Creek eastward, reaching, in 250 yards, an old road descending to a spacious creekside flat just below the trail. Were it not so close to the trailhead, I'd be tempted to set up camp there. For the next ¼ mile you'll see evidence of former logging, but then you enter South Warner Wilderness and its undefiled forest. Immediately ahead is additional creekside camping, but still too close to the trailhead for me. And that applies to the first lake (0.8) you'll see, about ¼ mile farther. This shallow, picturesque lakelet is not like others in this drainage, for it is human-made, ponded behind a low dam.

Eastward, you do a bit of climbing before reaching a corn-lily meadow, located a mere ¼ mile before a second lake (1.5), the first of about a half-dozen lakes and lakelets all with a common origin. You are hiking up a classic "glaciated" canyon—one with a broad, nearly level floor and steep walls. But this canyon was never glaciated! It was broadened through massive backwasting of its steep walls, probably occurring mostly during earthquakes along the Surprise Valley fault system. In times past the wasting was massive—tremendous rockfalls, whose deposits now on the canyon floor form dams across Pine Creek, creating lakes, or rumpled topography with lakes occupying some hollows. What may call your attention to the second lake—at least before all the snow melts—is a creek noisily cascading into it. This linear lake just north of the trail has two distinct parts: a broad, deep south half and a narrow, shallow north half. You can hunt and peck for campsites, but for isolated camping, look on level ground above the north half of the west shore.

Past the second lake you make a brief traverse, then make a short climb before commencing another one. After almost ½ mile on it, you leave dense forest cover behind as you come to the edge of a meadow, in which lies the nearby third lake (2.5). Its backdrop is the Pine Creek Basin, a classic headwaters glacial landscape—sans glaciers. This lake has a dam, so its origin is partly human-made. It, like the second lake and nearby fourth lake, is deep enough to support fish. From the dam you can take a spur trail above its northeast shore 50 yards to a fine campsite. This lake drains into adjacent Pine Creek, and from near the dam you can take a use trail paralleling the west bank of the creek downstream 0.1 mile to the fourth lake (2.6), the largest in the drainage. This deep lake is perhaps the most interesting, for it is so conspicuously rockfall-dammed. Giant boulders are strewn along its shores, especially chaotically above the southwest shore, from where you can view the source of the rockfall: Pine Creek canyon's overly steep north wall. Level camp space is hard to find around this lake, which is one of the best for swimming and fishing in the wilderness.

Chaotic rhyolite blocks in Pine Creek Basin

From the third lake's dam the trail descends about 100 yards to Pine Creek and here levels off by the upper end of the creek's minigorge. While a misleading trail continues east, you ignore it, descend a few steps to the creek, ford it (if a log is unavailable), and then on a sometimes vague trail head about 100 yards north-northeast through the western part of expansive Pine Creek Basin meadow. From the meadow's northwest corner, the trail up forested slopes ahead is quite obvious. Your generally moderate climb, although with short, steep stretches, is not nearly as steep as you'd think by viewing it from the meadow. It first climbs northward, soon crosses and recrosses a minor tributary feeding into the fourth lake, then ascends momentarily to a stand of aspens. Among them—a beautiful sight when in September color—you view Pine Creek Basin in its entirety, from meadow bottom to crest summits. As you climb the forest thins, and in one stretch among sagebrush, about a third the way up to the Summit Trail, you can rest and have a view west toward distant Mt. Shasta. Higher up, sagebrush starts to yield to forest, and over the last 0.5 mile or so of ascent, the trees are whitebark pines, the harbingers of treeline.

Unless your pack is too heavy, you reach the Summit Trail (4.8) in fine shape. Here, at about 9000 feet, you have far-ranging views: ranges east beyond Middle and Lower Alkali lakes; south, the backbone of the southern Warner range, capped by its highest summit, 9892′ Eagle Peak; distant Tahoe National Forest lands far beyond its west flank; and Lassen Peak to the southwest. Now in thin air you labor up a steep, though mercifully short, trail segment ⅓ mile north along the crest. Should you choose to climb to the summit of nearby Warren Peak, the range's second highest at 9710 feet, leave your trail before it starts an ascending traverse across steep slopes. You should be able to pick a fairly obvious route to its summit, making an ascending traverse that parallels the ridge west up to it. You'll definitely want to leave your backpack behind, but certainly not your camera.

Where the Summit Trail leaves the crest, it veers right on a ⅓-mile-long ascending traverse across steep slopes to a conspicuous ridge, on which you trade southeastern views for northeastern ones. The route ahead is direct, a steep, ⅓-mile-long descent, which drops 400 feet in elevation through a subalpine forest, to the outlet of Patterson Lake (5.8). Here you'll find campsites on both sides of the lake's outlet creek, as well as a bit to the northeast, farther from the lake. Patterson Lake, just below treeline, easily is the largest of the range's glacier-formed lakes (others being Cottonwood, Linderman, and the North and South Emerson lakes). Patterson Lake lies in a conspicuous cirque, a deep, steep-sided bowl with foreboding, dark cliffs rising to the summit of Warren Peak. Especially with snow patches that can persist well into July, the environment is a chilly one, but hopefully you'll be warmed by a hearty dinner, great hiking companions, and the next morning, a memorable sunrise.

Permits

None.

Build-up/Wind-down tips

In Alturas, which is in the middle of nowhere, is Nipa's restaurant, which offers Thai cuisine (as well as American). It has exotic birds and fish, which, if not environmentally appropriate here, definitely fit that culture. Mill Creek Falls Campground (mentioned above) is nestled in a magnificent grove of yellow pines, a peaceful site in itself. The trail from it leads to nearby Mill Creek Falls and just beyond it to not so *clear* Clear Lake, both worthy hikes. Finally, Blue Lake (mentioned above) is the range's largest lake, and it has a spacious campground. The Blue Lake National Recreation Trail circles the lake, and along it you're apt to see beaver lodges.

Jeffrey P. Schaffer provides background on his path to guidebook writing, detailed mapmaking, and challenging received views of Sierra geological formation, besides a list of his titles from Wilderness Press, in "Author Bio & Bib" on page 492.

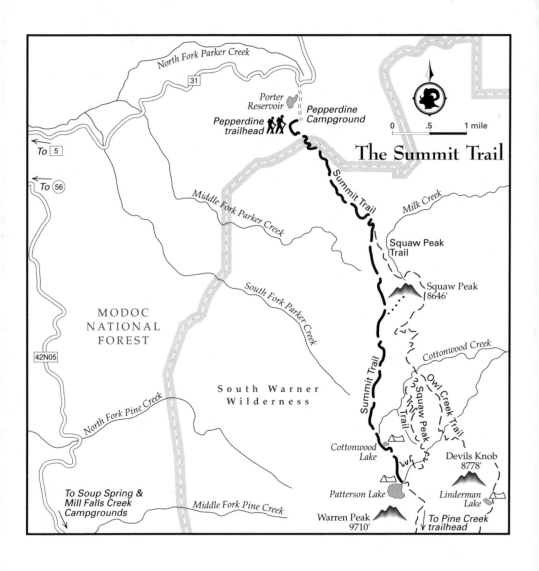

The Summit Trail

North Fork Parker Creek

31

Porter Reservoir

Pepperdine Campground

Pepperdine trailhead

To 5

To 56

Middle Fork Parker Creek

Summit Trail

Milk Creek

Squaw Peak Trail

Squaw Peak 8646'

South Fork Parker Creek

Cottonwood Creek

MODOC NATIONAL FOREST

Owl Creek Trail

42N05

Summit Trail

Squaw Peak Trail

South Warner Wilderness

North Fork Pine Creek

Cottonwood Lake

Devils Knob 8778'

Patterson Lake

Linderman Lake

To Soup Spring & Mill Falls Creek Campgrounds

Middle Fork Pine Creek

Warren Peak 9710'

To Pine Creek trailhead

0   .5   1 mile

62

The Summit Trail, from Pepperdine Trailhead south to Patterson Lake

—Jeffrey P. Schaffer

Route	Days	Elev. Gain/Loss	Elev. Low/High	Difficulty	Miles
↰	2	2400´/2400´	6820´/9020´	**	12.0

Campsites: Cottonwood Lake: 5.4 miles
Patterson Lake: 6.0 miles
(see the Trip Description for others)

Map: USGS 7.5-min *Warren Peak*

Best season: Mid-July through late September

Take this trip!

Imagine your own mountain range! Along this hike, you'll have its scenery almost all to yourself. Because the Summit Trail offers views up and down this compact range, you rapidly become well acquainted with and embrace it. With high-trail views rivalling those of the Sierra Nevada's highest peaks, you can see over 100 miles in most directions on clear days—well into desert lands of northwestern Nevada and southern Oregon, and west through south into northeastern California. Prominently northwest stands the Crater Lake rim 140 miles away; west, Mt. Shasta 100 miles away; southwest, Lassen Peak 90 miles away; and south, Tahoe-area summits as much as 150 miles away.

Trailhead

See Trailhead in hike 61.

TRIP DESCRIPTION

Heads Up! In years of heavy snowfall, the stretch of trail from Cottonwood Lake south can be mostly snowbound well into mid-July. Fortunately, the route to Patterson Lake is safe and quite easy to follow.

The first ¼ mile of your trail—a moderate, forested climb—offers no clue to what's to come. However, you quickly reach a crest saddle, enter the South Warner Wilderness in this vicinity, and just minutes south up the lava crest are treated to a developing panorama. Expansive vistas come into view—westward ones including Alturas and its upper Pit River valley, and Mt. Shasta, and eastern ones down into Surprise Valley and its Alkali lakes. Save your film, for the views only get better—ones that include Lassen Peak and other summits and ranges not seen at this elevation. The trail is well graded, making the climb southwest a joy. About 2.1 miles from the trailhead you reach a crest junction, one that provides breathtaking views, both north along the spine of the Warner Mountains and east and west to distant lands.

We stick to the Summit Trail, which branches right to climb toward nearby Squaw Peak. However, you ought to know what lies along the Squaw Peak Trail (2.1), which branches left to start a descending traverse around Squaw Peak. Its north section rambles about 3¼ miles south, losing about 500 feet in elevation as it descends, to a junction just south of and above Cottonwood Creek. From there the Owl Creek Trail climbs about 2 miles up to the east ridge of Devils Knob and, now 1000 feet higher, provides views southeast across and beyond Lower Alkali Lake. From the ridge the sometimes cryptic trail descends about 0.4 mile to Linderman Lake's east-shore campsites, at about 8100 feet elevation some 200 feet below you. Why visit this subalpine lake? Well, there's no quick route to it—I've just described the easiest route, which has spectacular scenery in the range's eastern escarpment—so the lake is one of the most isolated, seldom-visited mountain lakes in the state. You can't swim or fish in this waist-deep lake, but you certainly can enjoy the solitude and perhaps even admire a pair of bald eagles performing aerial acrobatics in the pristine sky.

From the junction near Cottonwood Creek, the southern part of the Squaw Peak Trail climbs a hefty 1700 feet in elevation over a switchbacking, 2¾-mile ascent to a junction with the Summit Trail 0.3 mile north of Patterson Lake. Believe me, you won't want to ascend this trail, although this scenic stretch is a possible alternate return route for those with good knees. Be aware that it's about 3½ miles longer than the Summit Trail, and involves about 500 more feet of ascent.

From the north end of the Squaw Peak Trail, the Summit Trail climbs moderately southward, first offering views east, then, after a crest crossing, views west. You ascend moderately for ½ mile, cross Squaw Peak's northwest

Trailside lake

ridge, then traverse another ½ mile to a saddle (3.4) at the base of Squaw Peak's southwest ridge. The peak's 8646´ summit is a popular dayhike, a mere ½ mile away and 400 feet above you. You could climb either ridge to the summit, but the southwest ridge is more open and viewful. From the summit you have a 310° panorama, with the southern part of the range hidden behind 9710´ Warren and its eastern subordinate, 8778´ Devils Knob. At or near the afore-mentioned saddle is sufficiently flat space to dry-camp (nearby snow patches last usually into mid-July). There, you can either take in a sunrise over Nevada or a sunset over northern California.

Although the Summit Trail overall is well graded, it surpasses 8000 feet elevation as it crosses Squaw Peak's flanks, and because you will top out just over 9000 feet around Patterson Lake, the thin air can leave you breathless. Southbound from the saddle, the views can leave you breathless as you revel along 1¼ miles of classic, crest-hugging trail. This ends with a brief veering onto western slopes before you climb shortly back to the crest. From it you drop momentarily to a reliable creeklet, lined with corn lilies, and by walking just up or down from this point, can find small sites for stealth camping. Most hikers continue onward, climbing briefly to a similar creeklet, then an equally short climb past it to Cottonwood Lake (5.4). Though small and shallow, it is never-theless deep enough for swimming. At about 8700 feet elevation, swimming is brisk at best, but better here than in deep, perpetually chilly Patterson Lake. Camping around Cottonwood Lake is limited to hidden sites above the northwest shore, opposite from the trail; better, obvious ones lie ahead, so continue onward. First you climb steeply southeast 0.3 mile to a junction with the south end of the Squaw Peak Trail (5.7), mentioned earlier, then climb south a similar distance over an easier grade to Patterson Lake (6.0). See the end of hike 61 for ambiance, features, and camping opportunities.

Permits

None.

Build-up/Wind-down tips

See Build-up/Wind-down tips in hike 61.

Jeffrey P. Schaffer provides background on his path to guidebook writing, detailed mapmaking, and challenging received views of Sierra geological formation, besides a list of his titles from Wilderness Press, in "Author Bio & Bib" on page 492.

Appendix 1

The Backpacks—at a Glance

See page 5 for an explanation of the icons used below.

Easy (*) Backpacks—

NO.	NAME	MILEAGE	DAYS	ROUTE	GAIN/LOSS (in feet)	FEATURES
1.	Horsethief Canyon	3.0	2		500/500	riparian creek, waterfalls
3.	San Mateo Canyon	7.4	2		1300/1300	riparian creek, canyons
57.	Grass & Wades Lakes	7.5	2		2090/2090	lakes basin—no permits!
47.	20 Lakes Basin Loop	8.5	2		240/240	lakes, peaks, granite basin
2.	Noble Canyon Trail	10.0	2		650/2400	creek, flora, mining ruins
54.	Half Moon Lake	10.0	2		1480/1480	lake, Mt. Tallac-access
59.	Central Caribou Loop	12.3	2		1190/1190	volcanic lakes basin
17.	Sky & Coast Camps	14.5	3		1400/1400	coastal views and access

Moderate (**) Backpacks—

NO.	NAME	MILEAGE	DAYS	ROUTE	GAIN/LOSS (in feet)	FEATURES
20.	Tangle Blue Lake	6.5	2		1265/1265	lake, peaks, meadow, flora
9.	Big Santa Anita Loop	9.4	2		2100/2100	riparian creek, waterfalls
10.	Devils Canyon	9.8	2		2100/2100	creek, flora, waterfalls
14.	Redfern Pond	11.0	2		1352/1352	outcrops, oak savannas
55.	Bayview to Eagle Falls	11.4	2		2140/2440	granitic lakes basin, falls
32.	Midnight Lake	11.5	3		2620/2620	lake, peaks, glacier
44.	TM to Nelson Lake	11.8	2		2924/2924	landmark peaks, lake
48.	Virginia Lakes	12.0	2		1420/3240	lakes, peaks, meadow, flora
62.	Pepperdine-Patterson	12.0	2		2400/2400	range-divide views, lakes

NO.	NAME	MILEAGE	DAYS	ROUTE	GAIN/LOSS (in feet)	FEATURES
4.	San Jacinto Peak	12.0	2		2600/2600	peak experience—views
39.	Lillian Lake Loop	13.1	2		2400/2400	3 (or more) Sierran lakes
13.	Poverty Flat	13.9	3		2160/2160	ravines, creek, savannas
38.	Ediza Lake	14.0	3		1495/1495	lake, peaks, waterfalls
34.	Humphreys Basin	14.6	3		2544/2544	lakes basin, meadows, falls
49.	Peeler Lake	16.0	2		2400/2400	lake, peak divide, views
21.	Marble Rim	17.0	2		2800/2800	lakes, peaks, flora, wildlife
37.	Thousand Island Lake	17.6	3		1707/1707	huge lake, peaks, flora
58.	Summit-Snag Lakes	17.7	3		2680/2680	volcanic lakes basin
56.	Meeks Bay-Emerald Bay	17.8	2		3690/3350	granitic lakes basin, views
25.	Jennie Lakes Wilderness	18.9	3		3430/3430	lakes, meadows, peaks
15.	Long Ridge to Big Basin	19.7	3		2017/3630	coast redwoods, canyons
43.	TM to Happy Isles	21.6	3		2790/7320	classic Yosemite descent
51.	Burst Rock/Crabtree	22.4	3		2920/4240	granitic lakes basin—fish
27.	Upper Rock Creek	23.8	5–7		3080/3080	peaks, lakes, alpine basins
30.	Rae Lake	26.0	3		3455/3455	lake, meadows, flora
40.	Merced Lake	26.6	3		4670/4670	river canyon, falls, lake
8.	The Angeles Crest	27.0	3		6600/6440	peak-bagging, views
52.	Ebbetts-Carson Pass	29.5	3		6490/6560	volcanic peaks, lakes, views
26.	Little Kern River	31.8	5–7		4950/4950	lakes, meadows, peaks

Moderately Strenuous (***) Backpacks—

NO.	NAME	MILEAGE	DAYS	ROUTE	GAIN/LOSS (in feet)	FEATURES
53.	Desolation Valley Basin	7.0	2		2040/2040	granitic lakes basin, falls
61.	Pine Creek-Patterson Lk.	11.6	2		3000/3000	lakes, views, peak-bagging
36.	Lake George to Deer Lks.	13.0	2		2755/2689	lakes basin, geology
11.	East Fork San Gabriel	14.5	2		200/4800	gorgeous trip—downhill
6.	San Gorgonio Mountain	15.6	2		5700/5700	peak experience—views
31.	North Fork Big Pine Crk.	16.0	3		3600/3600	lakes, peaks, glaciers

NO.	NAME	MILEAGE	DAYS	ROUTE	GAIN/LOSS (in feet)	FEATURES
19.	L Lake	16.5	2	↲	4260/4260	lakes, peaks, flora, falls
18.	Lost Coast Trail	16.7	3	↗	3800/3800	rugged & remote coast
12.	Chews Ridge	18.8	3	↗	980/4350	outcrops, flora, river route
35.	Pioneer Basin	18.8	3	↲	4590/4590	lakes basin, peaks, flora
16.	Ohlone Wilderness	19.4	3	↗	6988/6517	oak savannas, high ridges
7.	San Bernardino Traverse	21.6	2	↗	5500/4500	peak-bagging, views
45.	TM to Emeric Lake	28.9	5–7	℗	4100/4100	landmark peaks, lakes
46.	TM to Agnew Meadows	29.9	5–7	↗	4000/4350	river, peaks, meadow, lake
60.	Mt. Shasta Treeline	25-30	5–7	○	2500/2500	glaciers, views—trailless
28.	Horseshoe to Whitney	36.0	5–7	↗	7407/8887	peaks, lakes, alpine basins
29.	Symmes Creek	40.5	8-14	↗	7921/10870	peaks, lakes, alpine basins
42.	Grand Canyon/Tuolumne	48.75	5–7	○	8800/8800	river canyon, falls, lakes
41.	High Sierra Camps Loop	51.0	5–7	○	8830/8830	lakes, peaks, falls, camps
50.	Kerrick/Matterhorn	53.6	5–7	℗	9300/9300	canyons, peaks, lakes

Strenuous (****) Backpacks—

NO.	NAME	MILEAGE	DAYS	ROUTE	GAIN/LOSS (in feet)	FEATURES
22.	Little Five Lakes	40.5	5–7	○	10712/10712	lakes, peaks, flora, wildlife
24.	Deadman Canyon	52.0	8–14	↗	9217/9105	lakes, peaks, canyons, flora
5.	San Jacinto Traverse	55.9	5–7	↗	8240/12240	desert-to-peak flora, views
33.	South Lake to North Lk.	60.5	5–7	↗	8923/9401	canyons, lakes, hot spring
23.	The High Sierra Trail	68.5	8–14	↗	13354/11854	lakes, peaks, flora, wildlife

Appendix 2
Author Bio & Bib

Ron Felzer has backpacked in the Sierra—both as a student and a teacher of its natural history—since the late 1960s. His Wilderness Press High Sierra Hiking Guide to *Devils Postpile* has been in print since 1971 and is currently in its 6th edition. With degrees in forest management and forest science, Ron has taught biology, forestry, and natural history at Merritt College in Oakland since 1975. Hiking and nature pursuits have led him and his students to the Sierra, the Southern Alps of New Zealand, and the Peruvian Amazon.

Other Wilderness Press books authored by Ron Felzer are:
- High Sierra Hiking Guide for *Mineral King*
- High Sierra Hiking Guide for *Hetch Hetchy* (out of print)

Matt Heid—I backpack because wilderness offers escape and opportunities to commune with Nature in its timeless flow, while reflecting on the trappings of society. Please see *101 Hikes in Northern California* for other wilderness backpacks and dayhikes throughout the northern two thirds of the state.

Ruby Johnson Jenkins was a latecomer to backpacking. Her first trip—to celebrate her 50th birthday—was to hike the entire John Muir Trail. Because of that experience she later felt confident to continue the work of her son, J.C. (Jim) Jenkins, who was killed in an automobile accident. Ruby updated Jim's books, *Self-Propelled in the Southern Sierra: Vols. I & II*, and later wrote new editions with new titles. While doing her field work, she hiked over 5000 miles (covering every trail in the Southern Sierra at least twice), climbed over 100 mountains of 5000-feet elevation or more, and drove every twisting ribbon of unpaved road mentioned in her books.

Wilderness Press books coauthored by Ruby Johnson Jenkins are:
- *Exploring the Southern Sierra: East Side*
- *Exploring the Southern Sierra: West Side*
- *The Pacific Crest Trail, Vol. 1: California*

Kathy Morey—The backpacking bug bit her hard in the 1970s and hasn't let go yet. In 1990 she abandoned an aerospace career to write for Wilderness Press, authoring four guidebooks on Hawaii and *Hot Showers, Soft Beds, and Dayhikes in the Sierra*, and becoming a coauthor for *Sierra South, Sierra North*, and *Guide to the John Muir Trail*.

Hawaii Wilderness Press books authored by Kathy Morey are:
- *Hawaii Trails*
- *Maui Trails*
- *Oahu Trails*
- *Kauai Trails*

Jean Rusmore & Betsy Crowder—In 1995 Betsy Crowder replaced Frances Spangle as Jean's principal hiking companion as well as coauthor of her popular Bay Area hiking guides. Since then they "have hiked through every park and preserve, Bayland marsh, and creekside park chain, on loops and round trips, exploring and marveling at the rich variety of landscape and the magnificent heritage of natural beauty showcased [here]." In a freak automobile accident, Betsy was killed instantly on September 29, 2000 not more than a mile from her home in Portola Valley. Her death is a great loss to the Bay Area environmental community as well as to family and friends. Jean writes, "I miss her good humor, her determination, her dedication to our books, and her company on the trail."

Wilderness Press books coauthored by Jean Rusmore & Betsy Crowder are:
- *Peninsula Trails*
- *South Bay Trails*
- *The Bay Area Ridge Trail* (by Jean Rusmore)

Jerry Schad is the author of nine books on outdoor recreation in Southern California, and is a recognized expert on its trails. A fifth-generation Californian born in the Bay Area, Schad arrived in San Diego County in 1972, and has remained there ever since. He is professor of physical science and astronomy at San Diego Mesa College, writes newspaper columns on topics of local interest for the *San Diego Reader*, and hosts the *Afoot and Afield in San Diego* series on KPBS-TV. Schad is an accomplished stock photographer with over 1000 photo credits in publications throughout the world. He may be contacted through his Web site: **www.skyphoto.com**.

Wilderness Press books authored by Jerry Schad are:
- *Afoot and Afield in San Diego County*
- *Afoot and Afield in Orange County*
- *Afoot and Afield in Los Angeles County*
- *101 Hikes in Southern California*

Ron Felzer

Matt Heid

Michael White

Thomas Winnett

Jean Rusmore

Kathy Morey

David Weintraub

Betsy Crowder

Jerry Schad

Jeffrey P. Schaffer

Michael Zanger & son

Ben Schifrin

Jeffrey Van Middlebrook

Ruby Johnson Jenkins

Andy Selters

Jeffrey P. Schaffer made his first backpack trip in a 1962 traverse of the Grand Canyon, at age 19. The following year the climbing frenzy seized him, which lasted until about 1972, some 200 roped ascents later. In that year he began work on his first book for Wilderness Press, *The Pacific Crest Trail*. Between then and the late 1980s he was sole or principal author of 12 guidebooks, and had mapped about 4000 miles of trail for us and for a few 15' topographic maps. Innumerable observations while hiking led him to seriously question conventional geological wisdom on the origin of mountain ranges, which led to a lengthy book on the origin of the Sierra Nevada landscapes, particularly Yosemite Valley. At the start of the millennium he was teaching geology and geography at Napa Valley College, introducing students to the Sierra Nevada and other lands.

Wilderness Press books authored by Jeffrey P. Schaffer are:
• High Sierra Hiking Guides for *Tuolumne Meadows, Yosemite, Merced Peak* (out of print), and *Sonora Pass* (out of print)
  • *The Pacific Crest Trail, Vol. 1: California* (coauthor)
  • *The Pacific Crest Trail, Vol. 2: Oregon-Washington* (coauthor)
  • *Crater Lake National Park and Vicinity*
  • *Lassen Volcanic National Park & Vicinity*
  • *Yosemite National Park*
  • *Carson-Iceberg Wilderness*
  • *Desolation Wilderness and the South Lake Tahoe Basin*
  • *Hiking the Big Sur Country: The Ventana Wilderness*
  • *The Geomorphic Evolution of the Yosemite Valley and Sierra Nevada Landscapes*

Ben Schifrin—I was introduced to hiking in the central Sierra by my grandfather, a serious fly-fisherman, amateur naturalist, and professional geologist. He took me on dayhikes as soon as I could walk. I began overnight backpacks, sans parents, into Emigrant Wilderness and Yosemite at age 12. After walking the Pacific Crest Trail in 1973, I wrote a critique of the first edition of Wilderness Press' *The Pacific Crest Trail, Vol. 1: California*. Tom Winnett then asked me to become an author of that book. I completed a High Sierra Hiking Guide for *Pinecrest* (my home turf; the book now out of print) as a college project, to avoid ever having to take a formal English class. My friend and PCT coauthor, Jeff Schaffer, asked me to tackle writing the northern section of his magnum opus, *Yosemite National Park: A Natural-History Guide*. (Ben Schifrin is also author of *Emigrant Wilderness and Northwestern Yosemite* from Wilderness Press.)

Andy Selters—I started backpacking while in high school in 1973, and those late-adolescent experiences in the Sierra seemed so much more meaningful than what I could find in my hometown of Los Angeles. These formative experiences led me to seek a career based around mountains, and so one summer I became the custodian of the Sierra Club hut on Mt. Shasta. At 19 I also took up climbing avidly, and for many years I worked as a climbing guide and instructor for the American Alpine Institute, leading climbs from Alaska to Nepal. Gradually I developed other mountain interests, including photography and the cultures of the Himalaya. Along the way projects for Wilderness Press have stimulated me to see more country and focus my writing and mapping skills.

Wilderness Press books/maps authored or coauthored by Andy Selters are:
* High Sierra Hiking Guides for *Triple Divide Peak* and *Mt. Goddard* (both out of print)
* *The Mt. Shasta Book*
* *The Pacific Crest Trail, Vol. 2: Oregon-Washington*
* 15' maps for *Mt. Whitney, Mt. Pinchot, Mt. Goddard, Mt Abbot,* and *Triple Divide Peak* (out of print)

Jeffrey Van Middlebrook—I got started backpacking in the mid-1960s, when my cousin married into the Curry family, the original owners of Yosemite's concessionaire. He and his new bride encouraged me to visit them in Yosemite, where they managed various High Sierra camps. While still in high school, I took one look at the high country and fell madly in love. Since then I've hiked all of the trails and climbed every major peak in Yosemite National Park. I've logged six end-to-end John Muir Trail and four Tahoe-Yosemite Trail hikes. I've hiked the entire Pacific Crest Trail in California. Farther afield I've done a circumnavigation of the Tetons in Wyoming, and extensive hiking in the European Alps. Closer to home, I've hiked each trail in the Ventana Wilderness many times, including, in 1976, a 1-day, 14-hour solo run of the 65-mile grand loop. For a description of shorter trail runs in the Monterey Peninsula area, see my *Monterey Trail Runner's Guide.*

David Weintraub is a photographer and writer who has been backpacking, climbing, and skiing since the early 1970s. His work has appeared in many books, magazines, and newspapers. *East Bay Trails,* his first Wilderness Press book, appeared in 1998 and was named that year's best-selling title by the Sierra Club bookstore in Oakland. David's second Wilderness Press book, *North Bay Trails,* was published in 1999, and third book, *Adventure Kayaking on Cape Cod,* in 2000. Watch for his future titles, including another in the series of best-selling hiking guides, *Monterey Trails.*

Mike White was born in Portland—in the occasional shadow of Mt. Hood—and eventually fell in love with hiking, backpacking, and climbing in the Oregon Cascades. While gaining a B.A. from Seattle Pacific University, his journeys extended into Washington's North Cascades. When his wife Robin was accepted to medical school, Mike followed her to Reno, where (with better weather) the granite peaks of the Sierra were close at hand. While Mike now calls Reno home, wanderlust has periodically lured him to other areas in the West. In 1992, after 15 years of working with the same engineering firm, he left his last "real" job to write about the outdoors. Mike and his wife have two sons, David and Stephen.

Wilderness Press books authored by Michael White are:
• *Snowshoe Trails of California*
• *Snowshoe Trails of Yosemite*
• *Snowshoe Trails of Tahoe*
• *Nevada Wilderness Areas & Great Basin National Park*
• *The Trinity Alps* (coauthor with Luther Linkhart)

Jason Winnett—In 1960 my father, Thomas Winnett, began taking me into the wild places of California, especially the High Sierra. For this, I will always be grateful. Like John Muir, I keep returning to the Sierra Nevada, this precious "Range of Light." In the mighty Sierra I have loved and learned, healed and grown, and have learned that in the Web of Life all things are connected. And like Muir I have awakened to the urgent need to protect wild places. So, follow in his footsteps and "...go to the mountains and get their good tidings...and nature's peace will flow into you like sunshine into trees."

Wilderness Press books coauthored by Jason Winnett are:
• *Sierra North*
• *Sierra South*

Thomas Winnett has hiked in the Sierra Nevada since 1934 and has written or coauthored 12 hiking guidebooks.

Wilderness Press books in print by Thomas Winnett are:
• *Sierra North*
• *Sierra South*
• High Sierra Hiking Guides for *Tuolumne Meadows* and *Mt. Whitney*
• *Guide to the John Muir Trail*
• *The Pacific Crest Trail, Vol. 1: California*

Dorothy Whitnah—Hampered for years by age and infirmity from her once-active outdoor traipsing, Dorothy died in 2001. Besides being an amateur Bay Area naturalist and historian, she was a longtime Wilderness Press author and personal friend. Her *Point Reyes* book offers perhaps the most comprehensive guide to the National Seashore—for those who want some human and natural history, discussion of ongoing geologic forces with current park facilities, with their hiking trails. An *Outdoor Guide to the San Francisco Bay Area* and *A Guide to the Golden Gate National Recreation Area* are, alas, out of print.

Michael Zanger—From as far back as my memory reaches I've loved the outdoors. After impatiently waiting through a weeklong (interminable) snow-storm to see Mt. Shasta for the first time, it was a stunning, soul-wrenching vision! I started Shasta Mountain Guides in 1972 after deciding I wanted to make every effort to make a living at what I love—the outdoors and climbing. (Michael Zanger is coauthor of *The Mt. Shasta Book* from Wilderness Press.)

Index

Separate Index of Trails on page 509

20 Lakes Basin 367

A

Agnew Meadows 285-286, 289, 291-292, 359, 361, 365-366
Alpine 27
Alta Morris Lake 429
altitude sickness 12
American Lake 242
Anderson Gulch Camp 138, 140
Anderson Peak 64
Angeles Crest 67
Angeles National Forest 68, 71, 75, 78-79, 83
Ansel Adams Wilderness 162, 286, 291, 297, 304, 362
Apache Peak 47
Apache Spring 47
Arch Rock 131
Arndt Lake 391
Arrowhead Lake 283
Ash Creek 474
Ash Creek Falls 472, 474
Avalanche Lake 422

B

Babcock Lake 323, 356
Baboon Lakes 250
backcountry travel classifications 18
Badger Lakes 288
Barney Lake (Hoover Wilderness) 381, 383, 386-389
Barney Lake (John Muir Wilderness) 282
Bayview Campground 431-432
bear box 10, 17
    at campsites 167, 171, 177, 191, 194, 198, 208, 218, 223, 229, 231-233, 308, 311, 308, 345
    at trailhead 16, 167, 191
bear canister 10, 17, 162, 216, 229, 286, 292, 361
Bear Creek 144
Bear Lake 405
Bear Valley Creek 131
Bear Valley Visitor Center 128, 132
Bearpaw Meadow 179
Bearpaw Ranger Station 179
bears, black 10, 16-18, 77, 84, 134, 162, 167, 177,191, 216, 223, 229, 231, 239, 255, 268, 274, 286-287,292, 308, 317, 335, 349, 361, 376, 381, 440

Bell Creek 400, 405
Beville Lake 194
Benson Pass 392
Big Arroyo 175, 177, 181
Big Arroyo Creek 180
Big Basin Redwoods State Park 110-111, 114-115
Big Bird Lake 195-196
Big Falls 59
Big Five Lakes 170-171
Big Oak Flat Information Center 335
Big Pete Meadow 258
Big Pine Creek, North Fork 243-244
Big Pothole Lake 231
Big Santa Anita Canyon 73-74
Big Sur River 89
Bishop 22, 219, 247, 249, 264, 277
Bishop Creek, Middle Fork 249-250
Bishop Creek, North Fork 267-268
Bishop Pass 256
Black Lake (Caribou Wilderness) 465, 467
Black Lake (John Muir Wilderness) 246
Blossom Lakes 209-210
Blue Lake (Hoover Wilderness) 250, 377
Blue Lake (Warner Mountains) 477
Blue Lakes Road 415-416, 418
Bolam Glacier 474
Boothe Lake 324, 357
boots, tips 20
Boulder Creek Lakes 149
Brewer Creek 474
Bridgeport 22, 379, 383, 396-397
Bridgeport Ranger Station 383, 396
Bubbs Creek 231-232
Buck Creek 197-198
Buck Lakes 403
Buckeye Hot Springs 397
Budd Creek 341
Bull Lake 256
Bullfrog Lakes 211, 231
Bunnell Cascade 312
Burro Pass 393
Burst Rock 400
Butano Ridge 110-111

C

Cajon Mountain 53
California Campfire Permit 71
California Falls 333
Canyon Creek 144-145

Canyon Creek Falls 144
Canyon Creek Lakes 143, 145, 147
Caribou Lake 464-465
Caribou Wilderness 452, 463
Carmel River 90-91
Carson Pass 407, 412-413, 419
Carson-Iceberg Wilderness 407-408
Cascade Falls 432-433
Cascade Gulch 473
Cascade Lake 371
Cascade Range 133, 407, 451-453
Cathedral Creek 334
Cathedral Lakes 343
Cathedral Pass 343
Cecile Lake 294
Cedar Spring Camp 46
Cedarville 476
Channel Lake 424
Chantry Flat 74
Charlton Peak 65
Cherry Creek, North Fork 403; West Fork 404
Chewing Gum Lake 401
Chews Ridge 87
Chicken Spring Lake 216, 219, 223
Chilao Visitor Center 79
China Camp 87-88
Chittenden Lake 299, 301-302
Chocolate Lakes 256
Cienaga Mirth 244
Cinder Cone 460
Clear Creek 474
Clear Lake 477
Cleghorn Mountain 53
Cleveland National Forest 23-24, 33, 36-37
Cloud Canyon 195
Cloudburst Summit 67, 70
Clover Meadow Ranger Station 305
Coast Camp 127, 130-132
Coast Creek 131
Coast Ranges 84, 93, 133-134
Coffee Creek Ranger Station 154
Colby Meadow 261
Cold Creek 474
Cold Spring Campground 207, 212
Cone Peak 90
Coolidge Meadow Lake 403
Cooney Lake 377
Cottonwood Creek 216
Cottonwood Lake (South Warner Wilderness) 487
Cottonwood Lakes (John Muir Wilderness) 215-217
Cottonwood Pass 223
cougars (see mountain lions)
Courtright Reservoir 237

Cow Meadow Lake 403
Cowboy Lake 465
Coyote Creek 93, 95-99, 105, 107
Crabtree Meadow 225
Crabtree Ranger Station 182, 225
Crag Lake 441
Crag Peak 441
Crater Pool 458
Crescent Meadow 175, 177, 179
Crown Lake 395-396
Crown Point 395-396
Cryptosporidium 12
Crystal Lake Recreation Area 69
Cypress Lake 468

D

Deadman Canyon 190, 195
Deadman Canyon Creek 195
Deer Lakes 279-283, 399, 403-404
Del Valle Regional Park 117, 125
Desert Divide 46
Desolation Lake (Desolation Wilderness) 424
Desolation Lakes (John Muir Wilderness) 263, 270
Desolation Valley 421
Desolation Wilderness 407-408, 427, 432, 440
Devils Canyon 77-79
Devils Postpile 293-294
Diablo Range 93
Dicks Lake 433-434
Dicks Peak 428-429, 433-434
Diller Canyon 473-474
Dingleberry Lake 250
Dinkey Creek Ranger Station 240
Divide Meadow 131
Donohue Pass 362-363
Double Cone Peak 90
Duck Lake 282
Duck Pass 280, 282
Dusy Basin 257-258
Duty Ershim OHV Route 238

E

Eagle Creek 413-414
Eagle Falls Picnic Area 431-432, 439, 443
Eagle Lake 435-436
Eagle Peak 477
Eagle Scout Peak 180
East Bay Regional Park District 117, 125
East Fork Station 81
East Lake 378
Ebbetts Pass 407, 412-413
Echo Creek 312, 322, 351
Echo Lake 456

Echo Valley 312, 322
Ediza Lake 291, 293
Eel River 133
El Dorado National Forest 425
El Dorado National Forest Information Center 421, 425, 429, 437
Eleanor Lake 465
Elephants Back 413
Elizabeth Lake 349-350
Elizabeth Pass 196
Emerald Bay 431-432, 439
Emerald Lake (Caribou Wilderness) 465, 468
Emerald Lake (John Muir Wilderness) 365
Emerald Pool 308, 310-311
Emeric Lake 323-324, 353
Emerson Lake 268
Emigrant Basin 399
Emigrant Lake 403
Emigrant Wilderness 297, 400, 405
Evelyn Lake 208
Evolution Creek 260-261
Evolution Lake 260-261
Evolution Meadow 261

F

Fantastic Lava Beds 458, 460
Farewell Gap 210-211
Feather River Canyon, North Fork 407
Fifth Lake 245
Fish Fork Canyon 82
Fishermans Camp 36
fishing 147, 153, 239, 246, 351, 353, 399, 403
Flat Lake 299, 303-304
Fleming Lake 239
Fletcher Creek 323-324, 353, 355-357
Fletcher Lake, Upper 354
Florence Creek 356
Flower Lake 231
Fontanillis Lake 434
Forestdale Divide 413, 416-418
Forester Lake 169
Forester Pass 232
Forsaken Lake 270
Fourth Lake 245
Fowler Creek 207
Franklin Lakes 166, 168
Franklin Pass 167, 169
Frata Lake 424
Frog Lake (Mokelumne Wilderness) 418
Frog Lakes (Hoover Wilderness) 377
Fuller Ridge Camp 49
Funston Creek 181

G

Gallison Lake 355
Garnet Lake 285, 361, 365-366
Gefo Lake 423-424
Gem Lake (Caribou Wilderness) 468
Gem Lake (Emigrant Wilderness) 404
geology 53, 133, 160, 287, 296, 309, 344-346
George Lake 250
Giardia (Giardiasis) 12, 15
Gilman Lake 378
Gilmore Lake 429
Glen Alpine 427
Glen Alpine Creek 428
Glen Aulin 333
Glen Aulin backpackers' camp 319
Glen Aulin High Sierra Camp 319, 333
Glines Canyon 375
Golden Bear Lake 232
Golden Creek 275
Golden Gate Transit 128
Golden Trout Wilderness 161-162, 210, 216
Graeagle 445, 449
Granite Chief Wilderness 407-408
Granite Dome 403
Granite Lake 432-433
Grass Lake 445-446
Grassy Creek 457-460
Great Basin 476
Green Creek 375, 377-379
Green Lake 375, 378
Greenstone Lake 370, 372
Grouse Lake 442
Grouse Ridge Recreation Area 407, 409
Grover Hot Springs 419
Guitar Lake 183, 225
Guyot Creek 223

H

Half Dome 340-341, 345
Half Moon Lake 427-429
Happy Isles 307-308, 312, 340, 346
Heart Lake 231
Henry W. Coe State Park 93, 95, 100, 103, 107
Hidden Lake (Desolation Wilderness) 441
Hidden Lake (Lassen Volcanic National Park) 459
Hidden Valley 474
Hiding Canyon Camp 90
High Creek 58
High Creek Camp 57-58
High Sierra Camps 316
hiking, rate and time tips 19
Hockett Meadow 206, 208
Hoover Lakes 377-378

Hoover Wilderness 280, 297, 370, 376, 382, 386, 388, 396
Horse Camp 472-473
Horse Creek 208
Horseshoe Lake 455, 458-459
Horseshoe Lake Ranger Station 459
Horseshoe Meadow 216, 219, 222-223
Horsetail Falls 422
Horsethief Canyon 27-29
human impact 14
Humboldt-Toiyabe National Forest 396
Hummingbird Lake 371
Humphreys Basin 263, 267-270
Humphreys Lake 270
Hunting Hollow 103-104, 107
Hutchinson Meadow 263
hypothermia 12

I

Iceberg Lake 294
Idyllwild 40, 51
Independence 22, 235
Inspiration Point 67-68
Inyo National Forest 219, 225, 235, 247, 250, 264, 270, 277, 280, 283, 288, 295, 366, 370, 372
Iron Fork 82
Island Pass 359, 364
Iverson Creek 113

J

Jackass Peak 98
Jacks Peak 428-429
Jamison Lake 445, 448
Jeff Davis Peak 416
Jennie Lake 201-203
Jennie Lakes Wilderness 201-203
Jepson Peak 65
Jewel Lake 464-465
Jewelry Lake 404
JO Pass 203
John Muir Wilderness 161-162, 184, 216, 229, 237, 255, 268, 274, 280-281
Junction Meadow 182
June Lake 22
Junipero Serra Peak 90

K

Kaweah Gap 179-180
Kaweah River 167-168
Kearsarge Lake 231
Kearsarge Pass 229, 231
Kelham Beach 130

Kern Canyon 181
Kern Canyon Fault 182
Kern Hot Spring 181
Kern River 182
Kern Trench 181-182
Kerrick Canyon 386-387, 391
Kerrick Meadow 390
Kings Canyon National Park 161, 192, 201, 255
Klamath Mountains 133, 160
Klamath National Forest 451

L

L Lake 143, 147-149
Lady Lake 299, 301
Laguna Mountains 23, 31
Lake Aloha 421, 423-425
Lake Genevieve 440-441
Lake George 279
Lake Helen 371-372
Lake McDermand 260
Lake of the Woods 423-425
Lake Sabrina 249
Lake Tahoe 407-408
Lake Tahoe Visitor Center 439
Lakes Basin Recreation Area 407, 446
Lane Camp 115
Lassen Peak 451
Lassen Volcanic National Park 452, 455, 461
LeConte Falls 333
Lee Vining 22, 351, 366, 372, 379
Leopold Lake 402
Lewis Creek 323, 353, 355-356
lightening 13, 63-64
Lillian Lake 299-300, 303
Lily Pad Lake 413, 415
Limantour Beach 132
Limber Pine Bench Camp 62, 64
Linderman Lake 486
Little Charlton Peak 65
Little Claire Lake 169
Little Desert Peak 46
Little Five Lakes 166, 171, 180
Little Jackass Canyon 138, 140
Little Jamison Canyon 445, 447
Little Jamison Creek 446-447
Little Jimmy Camp 69
Little Kern River 206, 210
Little Pete Meadow 258
Little Pothole Lake 231
Little Rock Creek 70
Little Tahquitz Camp 48
Little Yosemite Valley 307-308, 311-312, 345
Live Oak Spring 46

Loch Leven 268
Lodgepole Campground 190
Lodgepole Visitor Center 186, 191, 198
logging 134, 137, 481
Lone Pine 21 219, 222, 235
Lone Pine Creek 185, 197
Long Lake 217, 255-256, 403
Long Meadow 343-344
Long Ridge Open Space Preserve 110-111
Long Valley 39
Los Cruzeros 95, 98-99
Los Padres Dam 87-88, 92
Los Padres Reservoir 91
Lost Canyon 170
Lost Coast 133
Lost Lake (Kings Canyon National Park) 194
Lost Lakes (Toiyabe National Forest) 413, 417
Lost Spring 95, 99
Lost Valley 312
Lovers Camp 157
Lower Golden Trout Lake 263
Lundy Canyon 371-372
Lyell Canyon 362

M

Madera Creek 304
Madera Peak 301
Maggies Peaks 433
Mahogany Flat 234
Mammoth Lakes 22, 277, 283, 289, 292, 295, 361, 366
Mammoth Ranger Station 295
Marble Mountain Wilderness 157-160
Marble Valley 158
Marion Mountain 48
Mariposa-Minarets Ranger District Office 305
Mariuolumne Dome 343
Markleville 413, 419
Marmot Lake 270
marmots 10, 185, 255
Matterhorn Canyon 386-387, 393
Matterhorn Creek 393
Matterhorn Peak 386, 394
Maxson Meadows 238
May Lake 320
McClure Meadow 261
McGee Lake 333-334
Medicine Lakes Highlands 451
Medlicott Dome 343
Meeks Bay 439-440
Meeks Creek 440-441
Merced Lake 307-308, 311-312
Merced River 311, 346
Midnight Lake 249-250

Midpeninsula Open Space District 112
mileage 19
Mill Creek (Hoover Wilderness) 370
Mill Creek (San Bernardino National Forest) 58
Mill Creek Ranger Station 57, 59, 63, 65
Miller Field 98
Millers Point 131
Minaret Lake 293-294
Minaret Summit 361
Mineral King Ranger Station 173, 213
Mineral King Road 167
Mineral King Valley 207
mining 32, 82, 375-376, 406, 446
Miter Basin 218
Modoc Plateau 476
Mokelumne Wilderness 407-408, 414
Mono Pass 274
Monterey Peninsula 84
Moraine Dome 311
Moraine Lake 181
Morris Lake 145
Morrison Creek 331
Mosquito Flat 273
mosquitos 10
mountain lions 11, 77, 84, 89, 128
Mt. Barnard 233
Mt. Hoffman 320
Mt. Humphreys 270
Mt. Muir 183
Mt. San Antonio 54
Mt. San Jacinto State Park 48, 51
Mt. San Jacinto State Wilderness 40, 43, 47, 50-51
Mt. Shasta 451-452, 471-475
Mt. Shasta Wilderness 451, 475
Mt. Starr 274
Mt. Tallac 429
Mt. Tyndall 233
Mt. Versteeg 233
Mt. Whitney 59, 183, 222, 225
Mt. Whitney Ranger Station 219
Mt. Wilson Observatory 71
Mt. Zion 73-74
Mud Creek 474-475
Mud Lake 276
Muir Gorge 332
Muir Pass 259-260
Muir Trail Ranch 262
Muir, John 1, 39, 67, 296, 329, 331, 471-472
Murdock Lake 392
Muriel Lake 270
Murrieta 35
Murrieta Falls 123

N

Narrows, the (East Fork Coyote Creek) 98-99
Narrows, the (East Fork San Gabriel River) 81-82
National Forest Adventure Pass 29, 32, 37, 59, 68, 75, 78, 83
Needle Rock Visitor Center 138, 141
Nelson Lake 349, 351
Nevada Fall 307-308, 311, 346
New Army Pass 217
Nine Lake Basin 177
Nipple, The 416-417
Noble Canyon 31, 33
Noble Canyon Creek 31
North Caribou Peak 468
North Divide Lake 468
North Lake 254, 267
North Palisade 247
Nutter Lake 378

O

Odell Lake 372
Ohlone Wilderness 117
Olaine Lake 292, 364
Old Baldy 54
Onion Valley 228-229
Orchard Camp 137-138
Outpost Camp 185

P

packing, tips 20
Paddlesack Lake 270
Palm Springs 39, 52
Palm Springs Aerial Tramway 39-41, 52
Palm View Peak 47
Panther Creek 198
Pate Valley 329, 331
Patterson Lake 479-480, 483, 485, 487-488
Peeler Lake 381-383, 386-387, 389
Peninsular Ranges 23-24
Pennsylvania Creek 413-414
Penny Pines trailhead 31-32
Penrod Canyon 45
Pepperdine Trailhead 480, 485
Pescadero Creek County Park 113
Phipps Lake 442
Phipps Pass 442
photography 19
Pilgrim Creek 474
Pilot Knob 270
Pine Creek 479-482
Pine Creek Wilderness 23, 27-29
Pine Ridge 89

Pine Ridge Ranger District 239-40
Pine Valley 87, 89-90
Pine Valley Camp 89-90
Pine Valley Creek 23, 27-29
Pinto Lake 166, 172, 403
Pioneer Basin 273, 275
Pitt Lake 422
Piute Creek (Emigrant Wilderness) 404
Piute Creek (John Muir Wilderness) 262, 269,
Piute Creek (Yosemite National Park) 391-392, 394,
Piute Lake 268, 404
Piute Pass 268
Plumas-Eureka State Park 407
Point Reyes Hostel 131-132
Point Reyes National Seashore 127
Point Reyes Peninsula 128
poison oak 14, 29, 32, 78, 97, 99, 119, 128, 130
Poop Out Pass 202
Portola Redwoods State Park 110-111, 113, 115
Post Corral Canyon 402
Post Corral Creek 238
Poverty Flat 95, 97-98
Powell Lake 401
Precipice Lake 180
Princes Camp 92
Punchbowl Fault 82
Pyramid Creek 422, 424
Pyramid Lake 424
Pyramid Peak 424

R

Rae Lake 237, 239
Rafferty Creek 325, 362
Rainbow Lake (Ansel Adams Wilderness) 299, 303-304
Rainbow Lake (Lassen Volcanic National Park) 455, 460
Raisin Lake 320
Rancheria Creek 390-391
Ranger Lake 190, 194
rattlesnakes 11, 29, 35, 84, 91, 107, 332
Raymond Lake 414
Redfern Pond 103, 106-107
Rim Lake 468
Roaring River 194-95
Roaring River Ranger Station 190, 194-95
Robinson Creek 381-383, 388-389, 396
Robinson Lakes 394
Rock Creek 181-182, 218, 223, 274
Rock Island Pass 395
Rock Lake 445, 448
Rogers Lake 392
Ropi Lake 422-424

Rose Peak 122
Round Valley Camp 39
Rubicon Lake 441
Ruby Lake 274, 363, 365
Rush Creek 363
Ruwau Lake 256

S

Saddlebag Lake 369-370, 372
Saddlerock Lake 256
San Andreas Fault 53, 82, 133
San Bernardino Mountains 49, 53, 57, 62-65
San Bernardino National Forest 40, 51, 59, 65
San Bernardino Peak 62, 64
San Bernardino Peak trailhead 63-64
San Francisco Bay 93
San Francisco Bay Area 127
San Gabriel Fault
San Gabriel Mountains, 53-54, 73, 82
San Gabriel River, East Fork 81; Fish Fork 82;
    Iron Fork 82
San Gabriel Wilderness 77-78
San Gorgonio Mountain 49-50, 53, 57-59, 62,
    65
San Gorgonio Pass 43
San Gorgonio Wilderness 53, 63, 65
San Jacinto Mountains 23, 24, 40, 43-52
San Jacinto Peak 24, 39-41, 43, 48-50
San Jacinto Ranger District 51
San Jacinto River 48
San Jacinto Wilderness 51
San Joaquin River, Middle Fork 286, 289, 292;
    South Fork 261-262
San Mateo Canyon 24, 35-37
San Mateo Canyon Wilderness 35-36
sanitation 15
Santa Ana Mountains 23-24
Santa Clara County 93
Santa Cruz Mountains 110
Santa Lucia Range 84
Santa Maria Beach 130
Santa Rosa Plateau Ecological Reserve 37
Sapphire Lake 260
Sawtooth Mountain 145-146, 148
Sawtooth Pass/Timber Gap trailhead 167
Scott River Ranger Station 160
Sculptured Beach 130
Seavey Pass 391
Sequoia National Park 161, 167, 177, 197, 201,
    215-217, 219, 223
Sequoia-Kings Canyon National Park 167,
    177, 191, 199, 223, 229
Seventh Lake 246
Seville Lake 194

Shadow Creek 292-293
Shadow Lake (Desolation Wilderness) 441
Shadow Lake (John Muir Wilderness) 292-
    293, 365
Shamrock Lake 371
Shastina 452, 474
Sheep Mountain Wilderness 69, 82-83
Shell Mountain 202
Shepherd Pass 234
Sherrold Lake 413
Shields Peak 65
Siberian Outpost 217-218, 223
Sierra Madre Fault 53
Sierra National Forest 239, 274
Silicon Valley 93
Silliman Pass 192
Sinkyone Wilderness State Park 133-134
Sister Lake 392
Sixth Lake 245-246
Skelton Lake 283
Sky Camp 127, 129, 131
Sky High Lakes Basin 157-160
Sky Parlor Meadow 181
Sky trailhead 131
Slate Creek 110, 112
Slate Creek Camp 112, 115
sleeping bags 21
Slide Canyon 394
Slide Mountain 394-395
Smedburg Lake 392
Smith Lake 145
Snag Lake 455, 457, 460
snow bridges 14
Snow Canyon 51
snow cornices 14
Snow Creek 50
Snow Lake 395
Soda Creek 170
Soldier Lakes 218
Soledad Fault 53
Sonora 405-406
Sonora Pass 407
South Divide Lake 464-465, 468
South Fork Lakes 216-217
South Lake 254
South Lake Tahoe 429
South Warner Wilderness 476, 481, 486
Spitler Peak 47
Spring Creek 402
Spring Meadow 402
Spruce Grove Camp 74
Square Lake 263, 270
Squaw Peak 477, 486-487
Squaw Valley Creek 475
Staniford Lake 303

Stanislaus National Forest 405
Starvation Lake 402
Steelhead Lake 370-371
Stewarts Camp 123
Stony Ridge Lake 441
Strawberry Junction Camp 48
Strawberry Valley 48
stream crossings 14, 90, 167-168, 179, 181
Sturtevant Falls 74
Sugarloaf Creek 194
Summit Lake (Hoover Wilderness) 269, 275, 375, 377
Summit Lake (Lassen Volcanic National Park) 455-456
Summit Lake (Toiyabe National Forest) 415
Summit Lake Ranger Station 456
Sunol Backpack Area 120
Sunol Regional Wilderness 117-118, 125
Sunrise backpackers' camp 321
Sunrise Creek 344-345
Sunrise High Sierra Camp 321, 344
Sunrise Lakes 321
Sunrise Mountain 344
Sunset Lakes 415
Surprise Lake 392
Surprise Valley 476
Susie Lake 429
Swan Lake 458
Sykes Hot Spring 84, 89
Symmes Creek 228-229, 334

T

Tahquitz Peak 48
Tangle Blue Creek 151-154
Tangle Blue Lake 151-154
Tawny Point 233
Temple Crag 244
Ten Lakes 334-335
Tenaja Canyon 35-36
Tenaja Ranger Station 35
Tenaya Lake 317, 320, 326
Third Lake 245
Thousand Island Lake 285-288, 359-361, 364
Thousand Lakes Wilderness 452
Three Rivers 167, 173, 179, 191, 199, 206
ticks 12, 90, 128
Timber Gap 172
Timberline Lake 183, 225
Toejam Lake 402
Toem Lake 423-424
Toiyabe National Forest 379, 383
Tomahawk Lake 263, 270
Trabuco Ranger District 36
Trail Crest 184

Trail Fork Springs Camp 64
Trail Lakes 275
trailhead parking 16
Transverse Ranges 53-54
trekking poles 21
Triangle Lake 464, 467
Trinity Alps 133
Trinity Alps Wilderness 143, 152, 154
Tuolumne Falls 318
Tuolumne Meadows 317, 326, 340-341, 349, 353, 359-360
Tuolumne Meadows Lodge 361, 366, 372
Tuolumne Meadows Ranger Station 325
Tuolumne Pass 324-325, 354, 357
Tuolumne Peak 329, 334
Tuolumne River 318, 325; Dana Fork 362; Lyell Fork 362-363
Turnaround Lake 464-465
Twin Bridges 421
Twin Lakes (Lassen Volcanic National) 455-458, 461, 464, 466
Twin Lakes (Sequoia National Forest) 192
Twin Lakes (Toiyabe National Forest) 381, 387
Tyndall Frog Ponds 233

U

Unicorn Creek 350
Unicorn Peak 350
Upper Ranger Meadow 196
Usal Beach 137-138, 141
Usal Camp 137

V

Vandever Mountain 211
Vasquez Peak 106-107
Velma Lakes 433-435, 443
Ventana Wilderness 84, 87
Vernal Fall 307-309, 346
Vidette Meadow 232
Vincent Gap 81-82
Virginia Lakes 375-376
Virginia Lakes Resort 379
Virginia Pass 375
Vivian Creek 58
Vogelsang High Sierra Camp 323-324, 355
Vogelsang Lake 325, 355

W

Waca Lake 424
Wades Lake 445-447, 449
Wahoo Lakes 270
Wales Lake 233
Walker 22

Wallace Creek 182
Wallace Lake 233
Wanda Lake 260
Warner Mountains 476-477
Warren Peak 479, 483
Wasco Lake 370
water contamination 12, 15, 162
Waterwheel Falls 333
Weaver Lake 201
Weaverville 149, 151
Weaverville Ranger District 149
West Lake 378, 378
Wheeler Camp 138, 140
White Cascade 319
White Mountain Ranger Station 247
White Wolf 330
Whitesides Meadow 402
Whitney Creek 182-183, 225
Whitney Falls 472, 474
Whitney Glacier 474
Whitney Portal 175, 177, 185, 222-223, 225
Willson Camp 106
Wilson Creek 392-393
Wilson Meadow Lake 403
Winnemucca Lake 418
Winter Creek 74
Wire Lakes 402, 403
Wolf Creek Meadows 408
Wood Lake 403
Wright Lakes 233

Y

Y Meadow Lake 402
Yosemite Concession Services 316
Yosemite National Park 296, 329, 351, 362, 367, 390
Yosemite Valley 296, 340-341, 347

Index of Trails

Apache Spring Trail 47
Atwell Hockett Trail 208

Babcock Lake Trail 323
Barney Lake Trail 387
Basin Trail 110, 113-114
Bear Creek Trail 113
Bear Lake Trail 405
Bear Valley Trail 128, 131
Bishop Pass Trail 255-256
Blossom Lakes Trail 210
Blue Lake National Recreation Trail 483
Blue Lake Trail 249
Bull/Chocolate Lakes Trail 255
Bullfrog Lakes Trail 211
Boulder Creek Trail 145, 149
Bowl Trail 105
Buckboard Trail 122
Burst Rock Trail 399-400

Canyon Creek Trail 143-145, 149, 158
Canyon View Trail 119
Carmel River Trail 88
Cedar Spring Trail 46
Center Basin Trail 232
Chagoopa Falls 181
Chewing Gum Lake Trail 401
China Hole Trail 99-100
Chittenden Lake Trail 301-302
Church Creek Trail 89
Coast Trail 128, 130, 132
Corral Trail 96, 100
Cottonwood Pass Trail 219
Crabtree Trail 399, 403-405

Deadman Canyon Trail 195
Deer Lake Trail 402
Devils Canyon Trail 77
Duck Pass Trail 282

East Carson Trail 408
Echo Creek Trail 322
Elizabeth Pass Trail 195-196
Emerald Lake Trail 468
Emeric Lake Trail 324
Espinosa Trail 28-29
Evelyn Lake Trail 208

Falls Creek Road 51
Farewell Gap Trail 210-211
Fernandez Trail 300, 304
Fish Trail 96
Fishermans Camp Trail 36

Fletcher Creek Trail 322-324
Forest Trail 100

Gabrielino National Recreation Trail 74
Glacier Trail 246
Gem Lake Trail 468

Hell-for-Sure Pass Trail 239
Hickory Oaks Trail 111-112
High Sierra Trail 175-186, 197, 222
High Trail 288
Hollow Tree Trail 115

Jennie Lake Trail 201-203
John Muir Trail 162, 182, 225, 233, 254, 258,
    261-262, 285, 287-288, 308, 311, 321, 325, 340-
    347, 353, 359, 362, 363
JO Pass Trail 203

Kearsarge Pass Trail 229, 230
Kern River Trail 181
Kerrick Canyon Trail 389

Lady Lake Trail 301
Lewis Creek Trail 322
Lillian Loop Trail 301, 303-304
Live Oak Spring Trail 46
Lost Coast Trail 137-141
Lost Spring Trail 99
Lower Cathedral Lakes Trail 343
Lyman Willson Ridge Trail 105

Mahoney Meadows Road 98-99
Manzanita Point Road 100
May Lake Trail 333-334
McCorkle Trail 119-120
Meadow Trail 131
Merced Lake Trail 311, 322
Mid Road 121
Middle Ridge Trail 97
Mist Trail 307-309
Mono Creek Trail 275
Mt. Baden-Powell Trail 68
Mt. Whitney Trail 184
Mt. Williamson Trail 70
Mt. Wittenberg Trail 128
Mt. Zion Trail 74

Noble Canyon Trail 31-33
Noble Canyon National Recreation Trail 31
North Fork Trail 243, 245-246

Ohlone Wilderness Regional Trail 117-125

Old Tenaja Road 36
Over the Hill Trail 197
Owl Peak Trail 486

Pacific Crest Trail 23, 43, 45-49, 67-70, 158-159, 162, 182, 218, 223, 286-288, 292, 333, 364, 407, 412-413, 429, 443, 451, 458, 461, 391-393
Peters Creek Loop 113
Pine Creek Trail 477, 479-483
Pine Ridge Trail 88-89
Piute Creek Trail 262
Poverty Flat Road 98
Puerto Suelo Trail 90

Rainbow Lake Trail 303
Raymond Lake Trail 414
Redfern Pond Trail
River Trail 286, 292, 365
Robinson Creek Trail 387, 396
Rock & Jamison Lakes Trail 447
Rock Creek Trail 217-218, 223
Rock Island Pass Trail 395

Sabrina Basin Trail 249
San Jacinto Peak Trail 48-49
San Mateo Canyon Trail 36
Schafer Corral Trail 99
Seville Lake/Rowell Meadow Trail 194
Shadow Creek Trail 365
Siberian Pass Trail 223
Skinners Ridge Trail 90
Sky Trail 129
Skyline-to-the-Sea Trail 115
Slate Creek Trail 113
Snow Canyon Road 51
Soda Creek Trail 169
Springs Trail 100
Squaw Peak Trail 486
Sturtevant Trail 74
Summit Trail 476-477, 479-480, 482-483, 485-488

Tahoe-Yosemite Trail 418, 439, 443
Tar Gap Trail 207-208
Ten Lakes Trail 334
Toejam Lake Trail 402
Tunnel Spring Trail 46

Wagon Road 106-107
Walton Trail 304
Ward Road Trail 112
Weaver Lake Trail 201-203
Wet Meadows Trail 209-210
Winter Creek Trail 74-75
Wire Lakes Trail 402

Woodward Valley Trail 129

Vandeburg Lake 301
Velma Lakes Trail 435
Vivian Creek Trail 58
Vogelsang Pass Trail 355

Y Meadow Lake Trail 402